Sea War

1939–1945

Janusz Piekalkiewicz

Sea War

1939–1945

Translated from the German by Peter Spurgeon
Tek Translation & International Print Ltd.
London–New York

Originally published as *Seekrieg 1939–1945*
© 1980 Südwest Verlag GmbH & Co. KG, München
Historical Times, Inc., Harrisburg, PA 17105
© 1987 by Historical Times, Inc.
All rights reserved. Published 1987
Printed in the United States of America
94 93 92 91 90 89 88 87   8 7 6 5 4 3 2 1

First published in English in the UK 1987 by Blandford Press,
Link House, West Street, Poole, Dorset, BH15 1LL
ISBN 0-7137-1665-7

Distributed in the United States by
Sterling Publishing Co., Inc.
2 Park Avenue, New York, NY 10016

Library of Congress Cataloging in Publication Data
Piekalkiewicz, Janusz.
  Sea war, 1939–1945.

  Translation of: Seekrieg 1939–1945.
  Bibliography: p.
  Includes index.
  1. World War, 1939–1945—Naval operations—chronology.
I. Title.
D770.P5313   1987   940.54′5′0202   86-3092
ISBN 0-918678-17-X

Typeset by Duncanphototype, Camp Hill, PA 17011
Printed by Kingsport Press, Kingsport, TN 37662

Contents

6 Bibliography
and
source of
illustrations

8 Acknowledgments

8 Foreword

9 Prologue

The War Years

19 **1939**

53 **1940**

109 **1941**

185 **1942**

245 **1943**

289 **1944**

321 **1945**

345 The "smaller
fleets":

Organisation
Structure
Strength

351 Index

Bibliography

ANDENAES, J./RISTE, O./SKODVIN, M., *Norway and the Second World War,* Oslo, 1966

BALLENTINE, D. S., *U. S. Naval Logistics in the Second World War,* Princeton, 1949

BELOV, M. I., *Severnyi morskoi Put [Northern Sea Run],* Leningrad, 1957

BENNETT, G., *Battle of the River Plate,* London, 1972

BUCHANAN, A. R., *The Navy's Air War: A Mission Completed by the Aviation History Unit, OP-519 B, DCNO (Air),* New York, 1946

BUCKLEY, CH., *Greece and Crete, 1941,* H.M.S.O., London, 1952

CAMPBELL, J./MACINTYRE, D., *The Kola Run: A Record of Arctic Convoys 1941-1945,* London, 1958

CHURCHILL, W. S., *The Second World War,* Vols. 1-6, London, 1948-53

DENLINGER/SUTHERLAND/GRAY, CH. B., *War in the Pacific: A Study in Navies, Peoples and Battle Problems,* New York, 1936

Documents of the London Naval Conference 1935, Dec. 1935-March 1936, H.M.S.O., London, 1936

DÖNITZ, K., *Zehn Jahre und zwanzig Tage [Ten Years and Twenty Days],* Bonn, 1958

Deutsche Strategie zur See im Zweiten Weltkrieg [German Sea Strategy in WW II]. Die Antworten des Grossadmirals auf 40 Fragen. Frankfurt/M. 1970

EREMEEV, L. M./SERGIN, A. P., *Podvodnye lodki inostrannykh flotov vo Vtoroi Mirovoi Voine [Submarines of Foreign Fleets in the Second World War],* Moscow, 1962

FEIS, H., *The Road to Pearl Harbor: The Coming of the War between the United States and Japan,* Princeton, 1950

FUCHIDA, M./OKUMIJA, M./PINEAU, R., *Midway: The Battle that Doomed Japan,* U.S. Naval Inst., Annapolis, 1955

FUKAYA, H., *Japan's Wartime Carrier Construction.* In: U.S. Nav. Inst. Proceedings, Sept. 1955

FUKUDOME, S., *Hawaii Operation.* In: U.S. Nav. Inst. Proceedings, Dec. 1955

FUKUDOME, S., *Strategic Aspects of the Battle of Formosa.* In: U.S. Nav. Inst. Proceedings, Dec. 1952

GELFOND, G. M., *Sovietskii Flotvo Voine s Yaponei [Soviet Fleet in the War with Japan],* Moscow, 1958

GRECANYUK, N./DMITRIEV, V. I./KRINISYI, F., *Baltiiskii Flot [The Baltic Fleet],* Moscow, 1960

HARDING, LORD J., *Mediterranean Strategy 1939-1945,* Cambridge, 1960

HASHIMOTO, M., *Sunk: The Story of the Japanese Submarine Fleet, 1942-1945,* London, 1954

History of the Second World War, H.M.S.O., London, 1950

History of the U.S. Marine Corps Operations in World War II, Vols. 1-3, U.S. Marine Corps, Hist. Branch G-3 Div., Washington, 1958

Hitler's Weisungen für die Kriegführung 1939-1945. [Hitler's Wartime Directives 1939-1945]. Dokumente d. OKW. Hrsg. v. WALTHER HUBATSCH. Frankfurt/M. 1962

HUBATSCH, W., *"Weserübung": Die deutsche Besetzung von Dänemark u. Norwegen 1940 [Weser Exercise: German Occupation of Denmark and Norway],* Göttingen, 1960

HÜMMELCHEN, G., *Unternehmen "Eisstoss": Der Angriff d. Luftflotte 1 gegen d. russische Ostseeflotte im April 1942 [Luftwaffe Attacks on Baltic Fleet].* In: Marine-Rundschau Jg. 56, 1959, H. 4

INOGUCHI, R./NAKAJIMA, T./PINEAU, R., *The Divine Wind: Japan's Kamikaze Force in World War II,* U.S. Naval Inst., Annapolis, 1958

ISAKOW, I. S., *The Red Fleet in the Second World War,* London, 1944

ISELY, A./CROWL, A., *The U.S. Marines and Amphibious War,* Princeton, 1951

Istoriya Velikoi Otecestvennoi Voiny Sovietskogo Soyuza 1941-1945 [History of the Great Patriotic War of the Soviet Union 1941-1945], Editorial Committee: P. N. POSPELOV chairman, et al., Vol. 1-6, Moscow, 1960-1965

JACHINO, A., *La Sorpresa di Matapan [Surprise at Matapan],* Milan, 1957

JAMES, SIR W. R. (Admiral), *The British Navies in the Second World War,* New York, 1947

KAMMERER, A., *La Tragédie de Mers el-Kébir: L'Angleterre et la flotte française [The Mers el-Kébir Tragedy],* Paris, 1945

KLEE, K., *Das Unternehmen "Seelöwe": Die geplante deutsche Landung in England 1940 [Operation Sea Lion Invasion of England],* Göttingen, 1958

KOSLOV, I. A./SLOMIN, V. S., *Severnyi Flot [Northern Fleet],* Moscow, 1966

Kriegstagebuch des Oberkommandos der Wehrmacht 1940-1945 [War Diaries of the German High Command]. Geführt von Helmuth Greiner u. Percy Ernst Schramm. Im Auftr. d. Arbeitskreises f. Wehrforchung hrsg. v. PERCY ERNST SCHRAMM. Vols. 1-4 plus suppl. to Vol. 4. Frankfurt/ M. 1961-69

KUZNETSOV, N. G., *Na flotakh boevaya Trevoga [Battle Stations with the Fleet],* Moscow, 1971

LANGMAID, R., *The Med: The Royal Navy in the Mediterranean 1939-1945,* London, 1948

La Marina nella Seconda Guerra mondiale [Official Italian naval history], 1-19, Ufficio Storico della Marina Militare, Rome, 1950

LEIGHTON, R. M., *U.S. Merchant Shipping and the British Import Crisis.* In: Command Decisions, Washington, 1960

LE MASSON, H., *La Marine moderne de guerre et son évolution [Development of Modern Navies],* T. 2. 1951. 2. Porteavions, sousmarins, escorteurs. (Coll Visages de la marine. 10.)

LENTON, H. T., *Royal Netherlands Navy,* London, 1968

LOKTIONOV, I., *Dunaiskaya Flotiliya vo Velikoi Otechestvennoi Voine 1951-1945 [The Danube Flotilla in the Great Patriotic War],* Moscow, 1962

LUND, P./LUDLAM, H., *PQ 17—Convoy to Hell: The Survivors' Story (July 1942),* London, 1968

MACARTHUR, D., *Reports of General MacArthur,* Vol. 1, 2, suppl. (to Vol. 1), Gov. Pr. Off., Washington, 1966. Vol. 1.: *The Campaigns of MacArthur in the Pacific.* Vol. 1., suppl.: *MacArthur in Japan: The Occupation Military Phase.* Vol. 2: *Japanese Operations against MacArthur's Forces.*

MAKSIMOV, S. N., *Oborona Sevastopolya 1941-1942 [Defence of Sevastopol],* Moscow, 1959

MATLOFF, M., *The Anvil Decision: Crossroads of Strategy.* In: Command Decisions, Washington, 1960

MEISTER, J., *Der Seekrieg in den osteuropäischen Gewässern 1941-1945 [Sea war in East European Waters],* Munich, 1958

MEYER, L. J., *The Decision to Invade North Africa (Torch).* In: Command Decisions, Washington, 1960

MORISON, S. E., *History of United States Naval Operations in World War II,* Vols. 1-15, Boston, 1947-62

MORTON, L., *Japan's Decision for War.* In: Command Decisions, Washington, 1960

The Decision to Withdraw to Bataan. In: Command Decisions, Washington, 1960

MÜHLEISEN, H. O., *Kreta 1941: Das Unternehmen "Merkur" 20. Mai bis 1. Juni 1941 [Operation "Mercury" Crete 1941],* Freiburg, 1968. (Einzelschriften zur militär. Geschichte des 2. Weltkrieges. 3.)

Naval Staff (Trade Division) Admiralty B. R. 1337: British and Foreign Merchant Vessels Lost or Damaged by Enemy Action during Second World War, From 3 September 1939 to 2 September 1945, Admiralty, London, 1945

Nederlands-Indie contra Japan [Dutch East Indies against Japan], Samengesteld door de Krijgsgeschiedkundige Sectie van het Hoofdkwartier van de Generale Staf, D. 1-7, s'Gravenhage 1949–61

Official History of New Zealand in the Second World War 1939-1945, Vols. 1.3–5.11.20–24, Wellington War History Branch, *Operationsgebiet östliche Ostsee und der finnische-baltische Raum 1944 [East Baltic and Finnish-Baltic Operational Area],* Stuttgart, 1961 (Beitr. zur Militär- und Kriegsgesch. 2.)

PERTEK, J., *Wielkie dni Malej Floty [Great Days of the Small Fleet],* Posnan, 1958

PERTEK, J./SUPINSKI, W., *Wojna morska 1939-1945 [Naval Warfare 1939-1945],* Poznan, 1959

PETER, K., *Schlachtkreuzer "Scharnhorst": Kampf und Untergang [The Scharnhorst Story],* Berlin, 1951

PIEKALKIEWICZ, J., *Luftkrieg 39-45 [Air War 39-45],* Munich, 1978

POPE, D., *Flag 4: The Battle of Coastal Forces in the Mediterranean,* London, 1954

PRATT, F., *The Torpedoes that Failed.* In: *The Atlantic Monthly,* July 1950

RAEDER, E., *Mein Leben [My Life],* Vols. 1 and 2, Tübingen, 1956–57

ROHWER, J./HÜMMELCHEN, G., *Chronik des Seekrieges 1939-1945 [Sea War 1939-1945],* Oldenburg, 1968

ROHWER, J., *Geleitzug-Schlachten [Convoy Battles],* Stuttgart, 1975

ROHWER, J./JÄCKEL, E., *Die Funkaufklärung und ihre Rolle im 2. Weltkrieg [Radio Intelligence in WW2],* Stuttgart, 1979

ROSKILL, S. W., *The White Ensign: The British Navy at War 1939-1945,* U.S. Naval Inst., Annapolis, 1966 – Royal Navy. Oldenburg, Hamburg, 1961

RUGE, F., *Der Seekrieg 1939-45 [Sea War 1939-45],* Stuttgart, 1954

Rommel und die Invasion [Rommel and the Invasion]. Erinnerungen. Stuttgart, 1959

SALEWSKI, M., *Die deutsche Seekriegsleitung 1935-1945 [German Naval Command 1935-1945].* Frankfurt/M. 1970. Vol. 1: *1935-1941 – Das Ende der deutschen Schlachtschiffe im Zweiten Weltkrieg [End of the German Battleships in WW II].* In: Militärgeschichtliche Mitteilungen. 2, 1972

SCHAEFFER, H., *U 977,* Wiesbaden, 1950

SMITH, P. C., *Task Force 57: The British Pacific Fleet 1944-1945,* London, 1969

SOMMER, T., *Deutschland und Japan zwischen den Mächten 1935-40 [Germany and Japan 1935-40],* Tübingen, 1962

STACEY, C. P., *The Victory Campaign: The Operations in Northwest Europe 1944-1945,* The Queen's Printer, Ottawa, 1960 (Official History of the Canadian Army in the Second World War)

STANFORD, A., *Force Mulberry: The Artificial Harbor of U.S. Normandy Beaches in World War II,* New York, 1951

STEEN, E. A., *Norges Sjøkrig 1940-1945 [Norwegian sea war 1940-1945] (Utg. ved. d. Krigshistoriske Avdeling),* Vols. 1–7, Oslo, 1954–69

TANAKA, R., *Japan's Losing Struggle for Guadalcanal.* In: U.S. Nav. Inst. Proceedings 82, 1956

The Japanese Story of the Battle of Midway: A Transl., Office of Naval Intelligence, U.S. Navy. U.S. Gov. Pr. Off., Washington, 1947

TRIBUTS, V. F., *Krasnoznammenyi Baltiiskii Flot na zavershayushcem etape Velikoi Otechestvennoi Voiny [Baltic Red Banner Fleet in the Last Stage of the Great Patriotic War].* In: Voennoistoricheskii Zhurnal 7, 1965, No. 3

TSUJI, M., *Singapore, the Japanese Version,* Sydney, 1960

TUCKER, G. N., *The Naval Service of Canada: Its Official History,* Vols. 1, 2, Ottawa, 1952

U.S. CONGRESS: *79. Congr., 2. Sess. 1945. Investigation of the Pearl Harbor Attack. Report of the Joint Committee on the . . . Hearings of the Joint Committee on the . . . P. 1–39* (of which *p. 1–11 Hearings, P. 12–21 Exhibits, P. 22–39 Earlier Inquiries),* Gov. Pr. Off., Washington, 1946

U.S. JOINT ARMY-NAVY ASSESSMENT COMMITTEE, *Japanese Naval and Merchant Shipping Losses during World War II by All Causes,* Gov. Pr. Off., Washington, 1947

United States Naval Chronology, World War II, prep. in the Hist. Div., Office of the Chief of Naval Operations, Navy Department, U.S. Pr. Off., Washington, 1955

WILLOUGHBY, M. F., *The U.S. Coast Guard in World War II,* U.S. Naval Inst., Annapolis, 1957

VYUNENKO, N. P./MORDVINOV, R. N., *Voennye Flotilii vo Velikoi Otechestvennoi Voine [Naval Flotilla in the Great Patriotic War],* Moscow, 1957

ZINGALI, G., *L'Invasione della Sicilia [Invasion of Sicily]. Avvenimenti militari e responsabilita politiche.* Catania, 1962

Archives

GREAT BRITAIN:
Admiralty, Naval Staff, Operations Division – Admiralty, Naval Staff, Trade Division – Admiralty, Naval Staff, Anti-Submarine Division – Admiralty, Western Approaches Command – Naval Historical Branch, Foreign Documents Section (Germ.) – Public Record Office (PRO)

USA:
US Navy Department, Division of Naval History – US National Archives

ITALY:
Ufficio Storico della Marina Militare

FRANCE:
Service Historique des Marines

Annuals – Reports

Brassey's Naval Annual 1946, 1947 – Jane's Fighting Ships 1944, 1945 – Les Flottes de Combat 1947 – Weyers Taschenbuch der Kriegsflotten 1939, 1940, 1941, 1942

Geheime Berichte des Sicherheitsdienstes der SS zur innenpolitischen Lage: Meldungen aus dem Reich, Berichte zur innenpolitischen Lage, SD-Berichte zu Inlandsfragen; Bundesarchiv, Koblenz: R 58 Reichssicherheitshauptamt (Nr. 160–178); BOBERACH, H.: *Meldungen aus dem Reich, Neuwied,* Berlin, 1965 *[Secret Reports of the SS Security Service]*

Tagesparolen des Reichspressechefs (Reichspropagandaamt Hessen-Nassau, Frankfurt/M.), *Sammlung Oberheitmann:* Bundesarchiv, Koblenz; KRÜMMER, K.: *Aufzeichnungen über Teilnahme an den Ministerkonferenzen,* Bd. 1 und 2; Politisches Archiv des Auswärtigen Amtes, Bonn; BOELKE, W. A.: *Kriegspropaganda 1939-41, Geheime Ministerkonferenzen im Reichspropagandaministerium,* Stuttgart, 1966; BOELCKE, W. A.: *Wollt Ihr den totalen Krieg?* Stuttgart, 1967 *[Reich press secretary's memoranda and other official sources]*

Magazines

London Gazette – Marine Rundschau – Military Review – Morskoy Sbornik – Morze – The Navy – La Revue Maritime – Rivista Maritima – Sveriges Flotta – United States Naval Institute Proceedings – Wehrwissenschaftliche Rundschau – Woyenno-istoriczeskiy zurnal – Wojskowy Przeglad Historyczny

Picture Libraries

Bundesarchiv Koblenz – Etablissement Cinématographique et Photographique des Armées, Fort D'Ivry – Imperial War Museum, London – National Archives, Washington, D.C. – Navy Department (National Archives) – Official US Air Force – Official US Marine Corps – Sikorski-Institut, London – F. Bordoni Archives, Rome—M. R. de Launay Archives, Paris—J. S. Middleton Archives, London—A. Stilles Archives, New York—K. Kirchner Archives—J. K. Piekalkiewicz Archives

Acknowledgements

I would like to express my warm thanks to:
Dr. M. Haupt, M. Nilges, Bundesarchiv Koblenz—Dr. Fricke, Dr. Wieseotte, Militärgeschichtliches Forschungsamt, Freiburg—Dr. M. Lindemann, Mrs. H. Rajkovic, Institut für Zeitungsforschung, Dortmund—Prof. Dr. J. Rohwer, W. Haupt and colleagues, Bibliothek für Zeitgeschichte, Stuttgart—Dr. Sack and colleagues, Zentralbibliothek der Bundeswehr, Düsseldorf—Col. E. Raunio, Finnish Embassy, Bonn—Brigadier Sionta, Greek Embassy, Bonn—Col. (Staff) G. L. Manfredi, Italian Embassy, Bonn—Lt. Col. (Staff) L. Tvilde, Norwegian Embassy, Bonn—Mrs. I. Köpf, Librarian, Mrs. A. Heiming, US Embassy, Bonn—Dr. F. G. Maier and colleagues, Schweizerische Landesbibliothek, Bern—J. S. Lucas, P. H. Reed, Imperial War Museum, London—the entire staff of the Photographic Library, Imperial War Museum, London—Capt. R. Dembinski, Capt. W. Milewski, Capt. St. Zurakowski, K. Barbaski (Engineer), Sikorski Institute London—

R. M. Coppock, Ministry of Defence, Naval Historical Branch, London—Lt. Col. Dousset, P. Roland, Etablissement Cinématographique et Photographique des Armées, Fort D'Ivry—W. H. Leary, National Archives, Washington, D.C.—P. H. Maddocks, Library and Photographic Services, United States Naval Institute, Annapolis, Maryland—Mrs. A. F. Hoover, Photographic Section Naval History Division, Washington, D.C.—Brig. Gen. E. Simmons, Marine Corps History and Museum Division, Navy Yard, Washington, D.C.—W. J. Armstrong, Ph.D., History Office, US Naval Air Systems Command, Washington, D.C.—Mrs. J. Koontz, Operational Archives Branch, Naval History Division, Dept. of the Navy, Washington, D.C.—Rear Admiral R. Fadda, Stato Maggiore della Marina, Rome—Dr. D. Bradley, Münster—F. Hahn, Marineschule, Mürwik—Comdr. J. Heibei, Meckenheim—Dr. C. H. Hermann, Rheinbach—H. König, Bretzenheim—K. Kirchner, Erlangen—Col. W. D. Kasprowicz, London—H. Limmer, Munich—U. Schefold, H. P. Piehl, Südwest Verlag, Munich

My special thanks are due to:
Major R. L. Walton, OBE, London
Capt. B. D. Samuelson, Washington, D.C.

Foreword

Sea War 1939–1945 is the third volume in a trilogy by Janusz Piekalkiewicz on the Second World War, which began with *Air War 1939–1945*. This present volume follows the procedure adopted in the first volume in that here, too, the events are presented in chronological order with the most important events seen from the viewpoint of the opposing sides—this time on the world's seas.

Official reports, internal directives and statements from the participating powers, press and radio reports—including many from neutral countries—convey the atmosphere of those days. The portrayal of the strategical and tactical context rounds off the overall picture. The most important naval engagements are described exactly and objectively. In addition to the very informative text, great importance has been placed on the documentary illustrations.

In view of the wealth of material, it was decided to avoid giving, once again, an exhaustive description of what is already well known from the vast amount of specialist literature. On the other hand, the main developments and events have been brought out with particular care. Thanks to this concentration on important facts and especially dramatic incidents, the author can report in more detail on the largely unknown facts that he has brought to light after years of research.

As the *Air War 1939–1945* has done already, this book will certainly reach a large circle of readers and find an important place in contemporary research as a useful reference work.

As stated in a wise old saying, "Tell me the past and I will tell you the future." It will become known to everyone reading this highly dramatic, yet completely factual documentation.

The Publishers

Prologue

Versailles. 7 May 1919. At a plenary assembly of the peace conference, the German delegation was handed the peace terms. The entire naval fleet, interned since November 1918, was to be surrendered. Germany retained merely a small navy ("provisional" navy) with 1,500 officers and 15,000 other ranks. Aircraft and submarines were banned. At the time, practically everything that remained of the German High Seas fleet at the end of the First World War, including their crews, was interned in the British naval base of Scapa Flow.

On the afternoon of 21 June 1919, the calm bay of Scapa Flow resembled a giant cemetery for ships. Within a few hours, German sailors had sunk eleven battleships, five battlecruisers and eight cruisers as well as fifty torpedo boats to prevent their being manned by the British. After complying with the order to surrender further units to the victorious powers, in accordance with Article 181 of the Treaty of Versailles, the "provisional German Navy" was left with only six obsolete battleships of the "Deutschland" or "Lothringen" class, six old light cruisers and twenty-four scarcely serviceable torpedo boats suitable only for extended coastal-protection service. According to the terms of the Treaty of Versailles, not even this small number of ships could be retained in service. In addition, the peace treaty expressly emphasised, "Germany would only allow itself to be disarmed in order to make it possible for all countries to limit armaments." The British and American fleets now ruled the seven seas, and both powers tried to put a limit on the growth of French and, above all, Japanese sea power.

From 12 November 1921 to 6 February 1922, a conference was held in Washington to discuss questions on naval armament "in connection with the problems of the Pacific Ocean." Five sea powers took part in the conference: Great Britain, USA, France, Italy and Japan. Belgium, China, the Netherlands and Portugal were invited to attend. Although officially there were discussions on the restrictions on armaments, in fact the USA and Great Britain were more concerned to restrict Japanese expansion. The Washington agreement was greeted as a "triumph of diplomacy" leading to a permanent peace. The ratification of the agreements led rather to a certain stagnation in armaments by the sea powers.

Defeated Germany, which was not allowed to take part in the conference, tried to get around the harsh terms of the Versailles Treaty. From 1920 the German Navy had been promoting various projects abroad, with German builders predominantly engaged in their development. In 1922 with the financial assistance of the German Navy, the German shipyards, Deutsche Werften AG, Weser, Germania-Werft, Vulkan-Werft, were running the Ingenieurs Kantoor voor Scheepsbouw in The Hague, who were secretly acting as a U-boat construction point for Germany. The submarines that were designed there and built for the Spanish, Swedish, Finnish and Turkish navies were the forerunners of the later German U-boats. German U-boat crews — disguised as tourists — gathered in Finnish naval bases for their initial submarine training. Likewise, the Soviet Union gladly allowed the testing of important German submarine parts in its naval dockyards, while German engineers helped to correct errors in the Red Fleet's submarines. The shortage of funds in the Weimar Republic's coffers meant that it was scarcely able to finance the building-up of the navy even within the permitted limits, but the many preparations were silently approved by the government. The German Navy encouraged the building of a fleet of fast merchantmen which would be suitable for conversion to auxiliary cruisers. It planned to use small steamers as minesweepers, and chartered sporting aircraft for air defence maneuvers by its warships.

Right: Battleships of the French navy

Left: "The British and US fleets now control the seven seas." Battleships of the Royal Navy.

Transcontinental radio transmissions, breaking opponents' codes as well as ciphering and deciphering were practised energetically.

On 1 October 1928, Admiral Erich Raeder took over command of the navy. The first priority of operational planning by naval command was directed toward unity of thought and action in leadership and the chain of command. The command also considered Poland and her closest ally – France.

The president of the USA, Herbert C. Hoover, worried by worldwide rearmament, called a further conference 22 January 1930 in London on naval disarmament. The result was that Great Britain finally endorsed the ratios laid down in Washington in 1922 on proportionate naval strength relating to battleships and cruisers. In addition, an agreement on submarines was signed in London,

although there was no international unity on this theme. According to protocol, submarines were to restrict their warfare in accordance with the dictates of the prize regulations: They had to operate on the surface, stop enemy or neutral ships by firing warning shots if necessary and establish, by means of a prize crew, whether contraband – essential war goods – was on board. This was a very risky business for a submarine, especially if the merchantman was armed or tried to ram the submarine. If the prize crew found contraband, the ship was liable to be sunk. But first of all, the "safety of the crew had to be secured." As life boats were not considered "sufficient safety" on the high seas, the crews of the boats sunk had to be taken on board the submarine. Unlimited warfare by U-boats was in complete contrast; it meant the sinking without warning of ships found in previously advised prohibited zones.

In February 1935 — two years after Hitler's "seizure of power" — building was commenced on the first twelve U-boats in a screened-off section of the Germania shipyards in Kiel. When news about this activity spread, there was scarcely any reaction to this gross violation of the Versailles Treaty — much to Hitler's astonishment. And when France hoped that the coming German rearmament would be the subject of political discussion, Great Britain suddenly showed itself ready to negotiate a separate naval agreement with Hitler. Great Britain, in accordance with its policy of equilibrium on the Continent, supported Germany financially with long-term loans so that the country could rearm — thereby creating a counterweight to France.

On 16 March 1935, Germany shook itself free of the rearmament restrictions imposed by the Treaty of Versailles. Conscription was once again introduced. On 18 June 1935 in London, an Anglo-German naval agreement was signed. "This is the happiest day of my life!" confessed Hitler to Admiral Raeder. Germany undertook to hold its entire naval strength at 35 percent of that of the British Commonwealth. Subject to certain conditions, parity in numbers for submarines was admitted. The British believed that they could afford to make this compromise, as Germany, at the time of the Disarmament Conference 22 March 1932 and the Anglo-German Submarine Agreement, undertook to conduct economic warfare in accordance with

Right: The British battleship *Ramillies*

Below: La Spezia, the Italian naval base, with battleships in foreground and destroyers beyond

the protocol of 1930. It was Hitler's wish that Germany acknowledge British naval supremacy and thereby "develop a closer relationship with Great Britain." From the political point of view, the armaments restrictions contained in the Versailles Treaty were rescinded by this (in foreign policy as well as domestic policy), and indirectly the German "military sovereignty," arbitrarily announced by Hitler on 16 March 1935, was also acknowledged. Hitler now had freedom of action to release systematically the German Navy from the current restrictions. Anthony Eden stated in the Commons, "At least the sea powers will now know how many ships Germany will build and can act accordingly." But appearances can be deceptive, and it only came to light after the war that, as a rule, Hitler caused incorrect details on the strength of his newly built "big ships" to be given out.

On 29 June 1935, exactly eleven days after the signing of the Anglo-German Naval Agreement, the German Navy put the *U 1* into service — its first submarine since 1918. This ship was a faithful copy of the submarine type II-A, designed in The Hague and supplied to Finland. In naval jargon it was called the "Canoe" because of its size.

On 28 September 1935, the first U-boat flotilla was formed. It was called the "Weddigen" flotilla and consisted of three submarines (*U 7–9*). At the same time, an additional six submarines served as training ships. A day later, Comdr. Karl Dönitz took over the command of this first flotilla. From this moment on, a submarine was launched every two weeks in the Kiel shipyards.

The problems of putting together a modern, powerful navy and the attendant strategy were now being earnestly discussed in all countries. The basic objectives of the Royal Navy had hardly changed from those of the First World War — to

prevent a German breakout from the North Sea and the Baltic. British naval supremacy had to make possible the transport to the British Isles of supplies and reinforcements from all over the world — war material from North America and manpower from the British Empire. The Admiralty was quite convinced that Germany would never again dare to conduct unrestricted submarine warfare, as this policy had once before driven the USA into the enemy camp. In addition, official British opinion considered that the submarine was no longer a dangerous weapon, as it could be traced down by "Asdic," the secret underwater sound-location equipment. Consequently, it would not be worthwhile for other sea powers to expand the submarine arm. In other grave miscalculations, nobody believed that submarines could engage the enemy at night; and the use of aircraft in combatting the submarine was completely disregarded. As far as the British Admiralty was concerned, surface raiders attacking merchantmen were a far greater danger than the U-boat.

Because of international treaties, the US naval forces were able to maintain the same strength as the Royal Navy and both regarded their battle fleets as their main fighting force. Aircraft carriers, cruisers and destroyers were to serve merely in the defence of these fleets. Escort vessels for defence against submarines had been completely left out of consideration as the US Navy — despite

the lessons learned in the First World War — rejected the convoy system. In contrast to the Royal Navy's Fleet Air Arm, the US Naval Air Service was an integral part of the American fleet.

The extremely powerful French Navy was confronted by the uncertain political situation in France in the mid-thirties. Politicians meddling in the ship-building program, coupled with the many strikes, led the French government to place orders for escort vessels with British shipyards.

The Italian Navy, the most important power in the Mediterranean, built a relatively large number of submarines as an alternative to a battle fleet but ignored aircraft carriers. The Italians made enormous progress in the training of frogmen and in the development of small naval combat units such as manned torpedoes.

At this time, the Soviet Navy was falling behind. During the purges 1936–38, many of the most senior officers were eliminated. The Red Fleet only in 1937 became an independent force with its own People's Commissariat. Despite the ideological differences, Stalin sought help in the USA for the construction of battleships and also in fascist Italy for cruisers; and he approached Hitler for help with the building of submarines.

Japan was the strongest sea power after Great Britain and the USA. In 1934, Japan repudiated the Washington Agreement and resolved to build a navy large enough to control the Pacific. The

Japanese endeavored to reach a level of absolute supremacy in every vessel category. In addition, Japanese aircraft-carrier pilots received what was far and away the best training. Nevertheless, the absence of radar equipment was serious, and submarine danger was so underestimated that neither escort vessels nor a convoy system was planned.

In May 1938, during the Sudetenland crisis, Hitler told Adm. Raeder for the first time that he reckoned war would break out, although he did not expect it before 1944. Further, he said that Great Britain would be among Germany's enemies. Hitler ordered steps to be taken to realise a further large-scale expansion of the German Navy; in addition, Naval High Command instituted a planning committee to draw up the basis for sea warfare against Great Britain. Raeder had notions of a mighty fleet which would neutralise Ger-many's unfavorable strategical naval position, vis-à-vis the lack of naval bases, by means of superior speed and a far-reaching radius of action. He recommended Hitler either to build a fleet of large capital ships which would be in a position not only to attack the British Home Fleet successfully, but to cut off British supplies as well; or, as an alternative, to build U-boats and armored ships (i.e. the pocket-battleships). The latter choice would indeed offer a quicker solution but, in his view, would be distinctly one-sided.

Hitler decided on the first solution. On 27 January 1939, he accepted the gigantic Z plan which provisionally scheduled for the end of 1947 a final target of 10 battleships, 3 pocket-battleships, 12 type-P cruisers, 8 aircraft carriers, 5 heavy cruisers, 24 light cruisers, 36 reconnaissance cruisers, 70 destroyers, 78 torpedo boats, 162 long-range

Left: Murmansk, the Red Fleet's naval base, with a Soviet submarine in foreground

Right: 12/8/1938, Kiel: the launching of the German aircraft carrier, the *Graf Zeppelin* (31,367 tons)

U-boats, 27 special-duty U-boats and 60 U-boats for home waters. The crucial strategic error was that the mammoth plan concentrated on large capital ships; and these vessels were very susceptible to air attack. In addition, neither the operational significance of air war nor the navigational problem was taken into account. Worse, when the war came (and because of Hitler's aggressive policy, it came barely nine months later and not "some time during 1944"), the Kriegsmarine had to commence operations with but a fraction of its intended naval units against Great Britain, the mightiest sea power in the world.

Because Adm. Raeder was regarded as the advocate of the "big ships," the planned U-boat construction, called for by Dönitz since 1937 under the Z plan, was neglected. In contrast, Capt. Dönitz, who was by now the officer commanding submarines, held the opinion that three hundred front-line U-boats would be necessary for waging successful economic war against Great Britain. He had developed new tactics for his U-boats: Merchantmen in convoys were to be attacked by U-boats in packs. The high command of the navy maintained its previous stance — U-boats were to be used singly as before.

Moreover, on 27 January 1939, the German Navy lost a weapon essential for the war at sea. The Commander-in-Chief (Luftwaffe), Hermann Göring, whose guiding principle was "if it flies it's mine," compelled Raeder to give up an independent naval air arm. All that was left for the navy was sea reconnaissance.

On 28 April 1939, Hitler, in his speech given before the Reichstag, repudiated the Anglo-German Naval Agreement with Great Britain. In May 1939, Dönitz carried out the first and last peacetime maneuvers of the U-boat arm in the Atlantic. Between Cape Trafalgar and the western approaches to the English Channel, twenty U-boats practised tactics as a pack.

On 15 August 1939, Dönitz was unexpectedly recalled from a stay at a health resort and told he was to implement mobilisation orders for a planned deployment of the U-boats.

On 19 August 1939, the first fourteen German U-boats, types VII and IX, left Kiel and Wilhelmshaven to take up waiting positions for the Battle of the Atlantic.

On 21 August 1939, the pocket-battleship *Admiral Graf Spee* set sail from Wilhelmshaven bound for the South Atlantic.

On 23 August 1939, Royal Air Force Coastal Command put its emergency plan into operation. Its aircraft took off on reconnaissance flights over the North Sea in the hope of tracking down German submarines and ships on their way to the Atlantic. But the German naval units were already out of range of the British aircraft. At this time, Coastal Command had some three hundred fewer aircraft than at the end of World War I. The crews had not been trained for battle against the U-boat, and their machines were completely unsuited for long operations over water. The Royal Navy had too few escort vessels and destroyers to offer the Atlantic convoys even minimum protection against the U-boats.

On the same day, the last French and the last Polish ship passed through the Kiel Canal.

Also on August 23, Hitler's foreign minister, von Ribbentrop, flew to Moscow for the signing of a nonaggression pact. The pact, which was signed with the Soviet Union on the following day, made it possible for the German Naval High Command to relocate their heavy units in the North Sea. As Adm. Raeder said, "The conclusion of the nonaggression pact with the Soviet Union shortly before the outbreak of war in 1939 was of particular importance for the Navy with its weak forces. With this pact they were freed from worries about the Baltic, once the Polish naval forces had been eliminated. The Baltic coast and the supplies of ore coming from Sweden during the summer months were secured without pulling naval units out of the North Sea area. Members of the U-boat command staff took the view that thanks to the Hitler-Stalin pact, freedom from attack in the east meant that if necessary even a long-term economic war with Great Britain could be successfully sustained.

In Memel, two hours before midnight on August 23, naval assault troops under the command of Lt. Hennigsen, an élite unit specially trained for hand-to-hand combat on land, were put on alert. Toward 11:00 P.M., six minesweepers entered the harbor of Memel and under cover of darkness took on board the 225 men of the assault company.

On 24 August 1939, the last British steamer left the port of Hamburg. The following day, German merchant shipping received a preliminary alert. Ships were instructed in coded messages to leave the customary shipping lanes immediately. They were no longer subordinate to their shipping companies but to the German Ministry of Transport. Camouflaged with grey paint, the freighters were to return to their home ports by the route to the north of the British Isles and to take notice of the ice reports of the German sailing vessel *Arthur II*, which was cruising to the north of Iceland.

On the same day the pocket-battleship *Deutschland*, sister ship of the *Admiral Graf Spee*, set sail from Wilhelmshaven. Both ships reached their waiting positions in the vastness of the Atlantic

The battleship *Gneisenau* with destroyer escort and a
Heinkel He 115 floatplane as submarine hunter

without being discovered by the Royal Navy.

During the following night, south of Bornholm, the six minesweepers carrying the Hennigsen marine assault company kept their rendezvous with the old ship-of-the-line, now the training ship *Schleswig-Holstein* (Capt. Kleikamp). Heavy equipment and weapons were stowed below deck on board the battleship and the marine assault company was quartered in the storerooms.

During his talks 25 August 1939 with the British ambassador, Sir Nevile Henderson, Hitler mentioned the pact that had been signed with the Soviet Union and tried to talk Britain out of supporting Poland. "The pact with Russia will give Germany security, even economic security, during an incessant state of war." Now, thanks to the pact with Moscow, Hitler no longer needed to fear a blockade and could risk war with Great Britain.

In the meantime, in London the Operational Intelligence Centre (OIC) had been mobilised. The OIC belonged to the Naval Intelligence Division (NID) and was engaged in decoding enemy radio transmissions. Under the pretext of large-scale coastal defence exercises, the OIC was placed on a war footing.

Shortly after 4:00 P.M. on 25 August 1939, the *Schleswig-Holstein* sailed into Danzig-Neufahrwasser harbor, paying a "friendly visit" to Danzig, a city and area under the protection of the League of Nations but economically joined to Poland. This visit, agreed to by the Polish government, was to honor the memory of the cruiser *Magdeburg* which sank twenty-five years previously to the day and whose crew were buried in Danzig. The ship made fast opposite the Westerplatte, a flat sandy peninsula one and one-quarter miles long and 1,800 feet wide. By resolution dated 14 March 1924, the League of Nations granted Poland the Westerplatte "as a place to unload, store and transport explosives and military equipment." Poland built on the Westerplatte "outpost" a harbor, warehouses, cranes, as well as a barracks for soldiers in company strength. In the event of war, the Polish personnel had orders to resist the enemy for twelve hours.

While thousands of Danzigers waved to the *Schleswig-Holstein* and on deck the cadets lined up in rank and file, below decks the order for arms inspection was given to the Hennigsen assault company. The company had orders to launch an attack against the Westerplatte the next morning, 26 August 1939, at 4:45, backed up by intensive artillery support from the *Schleswig-Holstein*. Shortly before disembarkation, which was planned for 9:30 P.M., the order to attack was rescinded. Having learned of a treaty of assistance concluded between Great Britain and Poland and also of Mussolini's refusal to join in the war, Hitler postponed the opening of hostilities.

On the same day, August 26, the Trade Division of the Admiralty took over control of the entire British merchant fleet. Commanders responsible for individual sea areas prepared the introduction of the convoy system. During the afternoon, the officer commanding the Polish submarine arm, Capt. Mohuczy, moved his staff together with the submarines *Sep, Rys* and *Zbik* to Hela. The headquarters of Rear Adm. Unrug, Commander-in-Chief of the Polish Navy, were also situated there. Józef Unrug had been a senior officer in the German Imperial Navy in command of training in the German U-boat arm during the last years of World War I. One of his ablest pupils was Karl Dönitz.

After the conclusion by Poland and Great Britain early in 1939 of a military cooperation agreement in the event of an attack by Germany against Poland, the Polish naval command drew up three operational plans for the fleet. One plan, codenamed "Worek" (English "sack"), related to submarine operations. Subs were to hamper any German landing operations undertaken on the Hela peninsula or in the Gulf of Danzig. The submarines *Orzel* and *Wilk*, at anchor in Oxhöft, the Polish naval base at Gdynia, were to operate in the Gulf of Danzig, and the submarines *Sep, Rys* and *Zbik* were to operate off the coast of Hela. The Polish Navy comprised four destroyers, five submarines, one minelayer, two old torpedo boats, two gunboats and six small obsolete minesweepers together with a number of auxiliary vessels, many of which dated back to World War I. The Germans already had three light cruisers (*Nürnberg, Leipzig* and *Köln*), one battleship (*Schleswig-Holstein*), ten destroyers, four torpedo boats, six high-speed launches and one escort vessel, forty-nine minesweepers and minelayers with five escort vessels, and one torpedo boat for the officer commanding Minesweepers East; in addition, there were fourteen U-boats of which two were training ships, nine submarine hunters, eight patrol vessels, two gunnery training ships, four supply vessels and also four naval aviation groups (ten operational squadrons). The German High Command placed the Naval Group East under the command of Adm. Albrecht.

On 27 August 1939, six more German U-boats left port. During the morning, the Naval High Command (OKM) broadcast to the German merchant fleet via Radio Norddeich to "implement all possible measures to reach home ports or the ports of friendly or neutral countries within the next four days." This message caused a degree of confusion among the masters of those merchantmen that were already homeward bound. A number of them turned around and tried to reach a neutral port at top speed.

During the afternoon of 28 August 1939, the OKM did indeed revoke its four-day directive, but it had led to the undoing of a number of ships that were now unable to reach their home port before outbreak of war.

On 29 August 1939, six more German U-boats arrived at their waiting positions. There were now thirty-five German U-boats at operational readiness between Gibraltar and the southern tip of Iceland. The smaller coastal U-boats took up station in the North Sea with the order to lay mines at the entrances to British ports and Royal Navy bases.

On 30 August 1939, the Polish destroyers *Burza, Blyskawica* and *Grom* received the order to make for the North Sea immediately at maximum speed to take up contact with the Royal Navy. At 4:00 P.M., they weighed anchor and set out from their naval base at Gdynia.

On 31 August 1939, the pocket-battleship *Deutschland* appeared off the southern tip of Greenland and was provisioned by the tanker *Westerwald*. The ship then set course southwards towards latitude 30 degrees. On the same day at 6:35 P.M., a second order for arms inspection was given to the Hennigsen assault company on board the *Schleswig-Holstein*. On 1 September 1939 at 4:45 A.M., the attack definitely would commence. The battleship would be towed to the immediate vicinity of the Westerplatte for the artillery attack. Hein Denker, a leading-seaman, stated "From 2300 hours we were set ashore and took up our assault positions. We knew that we were to get a two-hour support bombardment from the *Schleswig-Holstein*."

During the night of 31 August/1 September 1939, the Polish gunboat *General Haller* took over patrol duties in the Gulf of Danzig. From twilight onward it slowly cruised between Gdynia and Hela. On the deck of the remaining destroyer *Wicher*, which was lying in the shipyards at Gdynia, the mate Krassowski was on guard duty: "It really was a beautiful evening; a fine haze hung over the harbor, and the wind carried from far away the squeaking of the cranes in the merchant port. A tug made fast alongside the *Wicher*, bringing bread and water. There was peace all around and the first harbor lights were reflected on the waves."

Order of the Day to the Navy

1 September 1939

The Führer's call has gone out to us. In this hour of crisis we are ready to answer for the honor, rights and freedom of the Fatherland. Mindful of our glorious traditions, we shall fight this war with unswerving faith in our Führer, and a firm belief in the greatness of our people and our Reich. Long live the Führer!

The Commander-in-Chief of the Navy,
Raeder, Admiral

Germany Attacks Poland

Friday 1 September 1939, Warsaw
The Polish *PAT* News Agency reported:

The first hostile acts were carried out during the night by German forces. The Luftwaffe bombed the Polish coastal resort of Puck (Putzig) in the area of Gdynia.

1 September 1939
The *German High Command* issued the following communiqué:

German naval units have taken up stations off the Gulf of Danzig and are securing the Baltic Sea. The training ship *Schleswig-Holstein*, lying in Neufahrwasser harbor, opened fire on the Polish-occupied Westerplatte. The Luftwaffe bombed the naval base at Gdynia.

The Navy in the Baltic

Sunday 3 September 1939
The German *DNB* News Agency reported:

German naval units off the Gulf of Danzig this morning fired on the naval base and fortifications on the Hela peninsula. Subsequently, naval air for-mations made repeated bombing attacks on the naval base at Gdynia.

Warning to Neutral Shipping
Monday 4 September 1939, Berlin
The *DNB* Agency reported:

German vessels are carrying out minelaying operations in the western waters of the Baltic in order to exclude the British fleet. Vessels belonging to neutral countries are accordingly given due warning.

4 September 1939, Berlin
The *German High Command* issued the following communiqué:

Yesterday units of the German navy again carried out successful operations. Destroyers effectively bombarded enemy shipping in the Hela naval base. A Polish submarine was sunk off the Gulf of Danzig. Renewed air attacks against Gdynia and Hela resulted in the sinking of the Polish destroyer *Wicher*. The minelayer *Gryf* suffered severe damage.

The Sinking of the Athenia

4 September 1939, London
The *United Press Agency* reported:

With the torpedoing of the British passenger liner *Athenia* early this morning, Germany struck the first heavy blow of the war against Britain. The ship was sunk approximately 200 nautical miles off the northwest coast of Scotland with 1,400 passengers on board. It is not yet known how many have been rescued. The *Athenia* put to sea on Friday from Glasgow, bound for Montreal, and left Liverpool on Saturday at 4:00 P.M. The Donaldson Atlantic Line Ltd. of Glasgow states that a large number of Americans and Canadians were on

board. The sinking of this ship is reminiscent of the *Lusitania* in the First World War.

Mines in the Baltic
4 September 1939, Stockholm
The Swedish newspaper *Svenska Dagbladet* reported:

As already reported, the German Navy has blocked the Store Belt and The Ore Sound outside Danish and Swedish territorial waters. The Ore Sound can be navigated only with the assistance of pilots and the Store Belt is impassable. Germany has cordoned off the Baltic by means of this minefield. Danish naval units are currently mining the Store Belt and the Lille Belt in order to block off the Baltic. The population of the Danish island of Sprogoe in the Store Belt has already been evacuated.

The Commerce War Has Begun

Tuesday 5 September 1939, London
The *Exchange* News Agency reported:

During the afternoon of 4 September, more German merchant vessels were seized on the high seas, and some were sunk after their crews had been taken off. In the Baltic and North seas a number of ships, including a Danish cutter, ran into mines.

9/1/1939, 4:45 A.M.: The former battleship of the Imperial Navy, the training ship *Schleswig-Holstein* (Capt. Kleikamp), opens fire on the Westerplatte fortress.

On the Westerplatte
5 September 1939
the *PAT* Agency reported:

All Poland is watching with admiration and concern the heroic defence put up by the garrison of the Westerplatte, where a Polish infantry detachment continues to repulse attacks launched by immensely superior forces backed up by bombardments from the heavy guns of the battleship *Schleswig-Holstein*.

British List of War Contraband
Thursday 7 September 1939, London
The French *Havas* News Agency reported:

The Royal proclamation dated 4 September relating to the contraband of war distinguishes between absolute contraband — weapons, munitions, explosives, chemical products or products usable in war; combustibles of all kinds; land, air and sea-transport vehicles; all broadcasting and information-relaying equipment, tools, instruments as well as equipment; geographical maps, tables and documents necessary in the conduct of warfare;

and in addition, bullion, foreign currencies or debt instruments – and conditional contraband – all kinds of foodstuffs, clothing, etc.

Friday 8 September 1939
The *German High Command* issued the following communiqué:

The garrison of the Westerplatte in Danzig has surrendered. Resistance was broken by companies of engineers, naval assault troops and the SS-Heimwehr, with the cooperation of the *Schleswig-Holstein*.

Monday 11 September 1939, Berlin
The *German High Command* issued the following communiqué:

The encirclement of the Polish naval base at Gdynia continues. Neustadt and Putzig are in German hands. Naval units are supporting the army's action by effectively bombarding Polish batteries and the port of Gydnia.

German List of War Contraband
Wednesday 13 September 1939, Berlin
The *DNB* Agency reported:

The Reich government has promulgated the following law: As the British government has drawn up a list of conditional contraband and included in this list foodstuffs and other essential goods, the Reich government, for its part, now feels compelled to undertake similar measures. The following proclamation is therefore issued. Under the provisions of Article 24 of the Regulations Governing Prizes dated 28 August 1939, the following substances and objects are to be regarded as contraband (conditional contraband) – foodstuffs (including livestock), luxury items, feedingstuffs and clothing, and objects and materials used in the production thereof. This proclamation comes into force on 14 September 1939.

Friday 15 September 1939
The *German High Command* issued the following communiqué:

The city of Gdynia is in our hands. Naval units joined in the fighting for Gdynia and on the Hela peninsula with telling effect. An entry into the south harbor of Gdynia was effected.

Above right: Declaration of war, London, 9/4/1939

Right: 9/3/1939, the British passenger liner *Athenia* torpedoed by *U 30* (Lt. Comdr. Lemp)

The Sinking of the Courageous

Monday 18 September 1939, London
The *British Ministry of Information* issued the following communiqué:

At the time of its sinking, the aircraft carrier *Courageous* was not carrying its full complement of aircraft. Accordingly, there was a reduced number of crew on board.

Polish Submarine in the Gulf of Finland
Tuesday 19 September 1939, Reval (Tallinn)
The *Reuters* News Agency reported:

The Polish submarine *Orzel*, which was interned here last week, escaped during the night despite artillery fire by Estonian guns. Several army personnel were killed in the attempt to stop the submarine. The vessel was immediately pursued by aircraft. The breechblocks of the *Orzel*'s guns, and fourteen of her twenty torpedoes had been removed the previous day.

19 September 1939, Moscow
The *TASS* News Agency reported:

According to reports from Leningrad, Polish submarines are said to be hiding in Baltic ports

with the connivance and support of the governments of the Baltic states. The C-in-C of the Soviet Black Sea fleet will take the necessary measures against possible action by submarines staying in Baltic waters.

Wednesday 20 September 1939
The *German High Command* issued the following communiqué:

The fighting around Gdynia was concluded yesterday with the capture of the naval base. Here, too, several thousand prisoners were taken. The training ship *Schleswig-Holstein* and units belonging to the commander of the minesweepers successfully engaged in the fighting.

Polish Submarines in Sweden

Friday 22 September 1939, Stockholm
Svenska Dagbladet reported:

The two Polish submarines that took refuge in Swedish waters are the *Rys* and *Sep*. They had crews numbering sixty-six and fifty-six men respectively. The vessels were disarmed upon reaching Swedish territorial waters and brought to the Barholm fortress outside Stockholm. The crews have been interned.

Sinking of a Soviet Steamer
Wednesday 27 September 1939, Moscow
The *TASS* News Agency reported:

Toward 6:00 P.M. today a Polish submarine torpedoed the 400-ton steamer *Metallist*, causing it to sink. A patrol boat was able to save nineteen of the twenty-four man crew.

Monday 2 October 1939
The *German High Command* issued the following communiqué:

The last stronghold of Polish resistance, the fortified Hela peninsula yesterday surrendered unconditionally before the assault, prepared jointly by the army and navy, was carried out. The garrison, comprising fifty-two officers — including the commander of the Polish fleet, Rear Adm. von Unrug — and four hundred other ranks, will lay down their arms this morning.

The Loss of the Royal Oak

Monday 16 October 1939, New York
The *United Press Agency* reported:

The loss of the British battleship *Royal Oak* is described in the US press as a very heavy blow. This latest development raises important strategical problems. The *Royal Oak* was evidently sunk by a torpedo possessing a destructive power that

has not previously been experienced in sea battles. Can this possibly be the new deadly secret weapon that Hitler threatened in his Danzig speech on 9/19/1939?

Tuesday 17 October 1939
The *German High Command* issued the following communiqué:

According to the report made by the German U-boat commander, the torpedoeing of the battleship *Royal Oak* and the battlecruiser *Repulse* took place in Scapa Flow.

No Further Official Denials
17 October 1939, London
The *Reuters* News Agency reported:

If the Germans claim to have sunk the most important units of the Royal Navy, it is because they hope, among other things, to learn more about the actual position of these naval vessels through British official denials. They know that if the Home Fleet has set sail, it must observe radio silence. The immediate denial of a claimed sinking would prove to the Germans that the fleet is in contact with the Admiralty and has not left port. For this reason, the Admiralty will issue no further official denials. The false reports issued by the Germans serve the purpose of influencing neutral countries.

Above: October 1939, a stranded British mine on the North Sea coast

Above right: 9/17/1939, North Atlantic, the British aircraft carrier *Courageous* (Capt. Makeig-Jones) torpedoed by *U 29* (Lt. Comdr. Schuhart)

Right: September 1939, Southampton, a British passenger liner is converted into an armed merchant cruiser.

W. Churchill to the Admiralty
Thursday 19 November 1939

As a measure of retaliation, it may become necessary to feed large numbers of floating mines into the Rhine. . . . The type of mine required is therefore a small one, perhaps no bigger than a football. The current of the river is at most about seven miles an hour and three or four at ordinary times, but it is quite easy to verify this. . . . The clockwork apparatus in the mine should ensure that the mine should automatically sink, or preferably explode, before reaching Dutch territory. . . . It would be a convenience if the mine was so constructed that it could go off if stranded after a certain amount of time. By these means one could spread alarm and confusion on the German banks. It would be necessary in addition that the mine should float a convenient distance beneath the surface so as to be invisible. . . . An alternative would be to throw very large numbers of camouflage globes — tin shells — into the river, which would spread confusion and exhaust remedial activities . . . .

British Auxiliary Cruiser Sunk
Sunday 26 November 1939, London
The *Reuters* News Agency reported:

The armed merchant cruiser *Rawalpindi* (16,000

tons) has been sunk. According to Admiralty reports, it is feared that all but one officer and fourteen crew have been lost.

Another Victim Claimed by Magnetic Mines
Monday 27 November 1939, London
The *Reuters* News Agency reported:
Up until now, 171 survivors from the former Polish passenger liner *Pilsudski* have been brought safely ashore at English ports. It seems that the vessel was not torpedoed, but struck two mines in succession. According to the latest information received, the number of victims on the *Pilsudski* is said to amount to no more than seven.

Tuesday 28 November 1939
The *German High Command* issued the following communiqué:
German naval units commanded by Vice-Adm. Marschall have carried out a reconnaissance in the area between the Faroes and Greenland by passing through North Atlantic waters. During these activities they intercepted the British armed merchant cruiser *Rawalpindi*, which was destroyed after a short engagement. Despite immediate rescue operations, only twenty-six of the crew of the' armed merchant cruiser were saved.

British Blockade

Tuesday 28 November 1939, London
The *Reuters* News Agency reported:
The Order in Council relating to the capture of German export goods has been published this evening and will come into force on 4 December. Among other things, the order provides that all merchant ships leaving an enemy port or a port in territory occupied or controlled by the enemy can be seized in a British or Allied port. All merchant ships leaving a non-enemy port which nevertheless have goods of enemy origin on board can likewise be seized. Goods unloaded in a British or Allied port shall be supervised by the Prize Court. If they are not seized, they shall be retained or sold, whereupon the proceeds shall accrue to the Prize Court.

Directive No. 8

The Chief of the German   Berlin, 12/11/1939
High Command
Most secret document
Ref: Supplement to Directive No. 8 on the conduct of the war

The Führer has ordered that the following amendments be made to No. 4 para. 1 of the Directive No. 8:
In addition to the U-boats, surface units will also be released for engagement in the measures for blocking Belgian and Dutch ports during the night before the attack. In so doing, the principle must be observed that any advance warning of these two countries, thereby jeopardising the element of surprise in the landing operations, must be avoided. For this reason, the time gap, as with the U-boats, between the commencement of blocking activities and the commencement of the assault on land should be kept to a minimum. If, however, it can be seen that because of unfavorable circumstances, such as bright moonlight, the attack cannot be carried out unobserved, surface vessels shall under such circumstances not be employed.

(signed) Keitel

Sea Battle Off the East Coast of South America

Thursday 14 December 1939, London
The *Associated Press* reported:
A battle has been taking place since 6:00 this morning between three British cruisers and the pocket-battleship *Admiral Scheer*. The *Admiral Scheer* is said to have received a number of hits and broken off the action. The British cruiser *Exeter* was damaged and ceased pursuit operations while the two other cruisers, *Achilles* and *Ajax*, pursued the German ship into the coastal waters of Uruguay.

14 December 1939
The *German High Command* issued the following communiqué:
The battleship *Admiral Graf Spee*, one of the battleships operating in Atlantic waters since the

Right: 12/14/1939, British press reports, "British Warships Attack the *Admiral Scheer.*" The German deception was successful, as in reality the ship concerned was the *Admiral Graf Spee.*

Left: November 1939, Atlantic, on board a German merchantman seized by the Royal Navy, the captain undergoes interrogation.

outbreak of war, pushed forward to the convoy route La Plata (Argentina)–European waters and sank the British steamer *Tairoa* (7,983 gross tons) and *Streonshalla* (3,895 gross tons). In so doing, the battleship exchanged fire with the heavy British cruiser *Exeter* and the light cruisers *Ajax* and *Achilles.* During the battle, the German battleship caused heavy damage to the numerically superior enemy forces. Because of heavy damage, the *Exeter* had to disengage from the action. One of the light cruisers was also heavily damaged. The *Admiral Graf Spee* also received several hits and is currently in the port of Montevideo (Uruguay).

It Was Not the Admiral Scheer . . .
14 December 1939, London
The *Reuters* News Agency reported:

The Uruguayan authorities have confirmed that the German naval vessel concerned was not the *Admiral Scheer* but the *Admiral Graf Spee.*

Prisoners and Casualties
Friday 15 December 1939
The *United Press Agency* reported:

British seamen, who had been taken prisoner by the *Admiral Graf Spee* after the sinking of their ships, stated upon being set free in Montevideo that they had been well treated by their German captors . . . . On Friday morning, the thirty-five German seamen who had lost their lives were buried in a communal grave under a cross in the Cementerio del Norte.

Decision by the Government of Uruguay
Saturday 16 December 1939, London
The *Reuters* News Agency reported:

The pocket-battleship *Admiral Graf Spee* has been instructed by the government of Uruguay to quit the port of Montevideo by Sunday, 5:00 P.M.

The ship is said to be ready to put to sea at any moment.

Note by the First Lord of the Admiralty
16 December 1939, London

The effectual stoppage of Swedish iron ore shipments to Germany via Norway ranks as a major offensive operation of war . . . . Swedish iron ore shipments from Lulea have already been cut off by the winter ice. Any attempts by the Soviet icebreaker to open up access to the port must not be allowed. The transport of ore from Narvik must be stopped by laying successively a series of small minefields in Norwegian territorial waters at the two or three suitable points on the coast that will force the ore ships to quit territorial waters and come to the high seas where, if German, they will be taken as prize or, if neutral, be subjected to our contraband control.

Monday 18 December 1939
The *German High Command* issued the following communiqué:

The battleship *Admiral Graf Spee* has not been given enough time by the government of Uruguay to undertake the repairs necessary for putting the vessel in a seaworthy condition. The Führer and Commander-in-Chief of the Armed Forces has therefore given the captain orders to sail his ship outside territorial waters and scuttle it by blowing it up. This order was carried out on 17 December toward 8:00 P.M.

Scuttling of the Admiral Graf Spee

18 December 1939, Montevideo
The *United Press Agency* reported:

A crowd of some 20,000 watched with bated breath as the *Admiral Graf Spee* weighed anchor

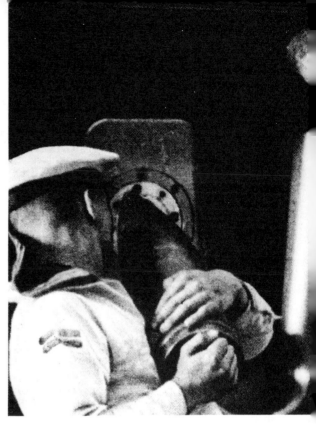

Above: 12/17/1939, at the mouth of the Plate River: An explosion looking like the mushroom cloud of an atomic bomb rises over the *Admiral Graf Spee*.

Above right: Gunners loading on the *Admiral Graf Spee*

Below: Advertising must go on—even in wartime.

and at 6:20 P.M. steamed out of the port accompanied by six dinghies and the cruiser *Uruguay*. The German ship, moving slowly, hove to at a distance of some four nautical miles. Two Argentine tugs with a lighter came up close to the *Admiral Graf Spee*, as did the dinghies. After a few minutes, these vessels drew back from the pocket-battleship. Shortly afterward, a tremendous explosion shook Montevideo and covered the area in an orange-yellow light. The *Graf Spee* settled back with only the superstructure remaining above water.

The Scuttling of German Ships
20 December 1939, London
The *Havas* Agency reported:

With the sinking of the German liner *Columbus* (32,565 gross tons)—one of the most beautiful ships in the world—by its own crew, the number of German ships scuttled has risen to 23. The total tonnage amounts to 139,423. In addition, 19 ships with a total tonnage of 88,128 have been captured by the Allies.

Finnish-Soviet War

Friday 22 December 1939, Paris
The *Havas* Agency reported:

Apparently the Soviet Union has requested from Germany the immediate supply of four warships to reinforce their offensive against Finland. The

German Naval High Command has declined to comply with this request.

Soviet Fleet in Action
22 December 1939, Helsinki
UPI reported:

A cruiser and a destroyer of the Red Fleet yesterday went into action off Mokta. Finnish coastal batteries drove the Soviet ships off.

Trotski Against the Soviet Attack
Thursday 28 December 1939, Mexico
The *Reuters* News Agency reported:

Leon Trotski, living in Mexico in exile, has spoken out during a radio address against the Soviet action in Finland.

The Soviet Union on the Battle of the River Plate
Sunday 31 December 1939, Leningrad
The Soviet newspaper *Red Fleet* reported:

Nobody would dare say that the loss of a German battleship is a brilliant victory for the British Fleet. This is rather a demonstration, unprecedented in history, of the impotence of the British. Upon the morning of December 13, the battleship started an artillery duel with the *Exeter*, and within a few minutes obliged the cruiser to withdraw from the action. According to the latest information, the *Exeter* sank near the Argentine coast, en route for the Falkland Islands.

Strategy and Tactics

SEPTEMBER TO DECEMBER 1939

Friday 1 September 1939. Platoon leader Edward Luszynski, one of the soldiers stationed in the Westerplatte fortress, reported: "In the early morning, at around 4:45, I was awakened by a massive clap of thunder, followed shortly by another. Convinced there was a storm gathering, I sprang out of bed to close the window. Suddenly I heard a bang and at the same time a burst of machine-gun fire crashed through the window above my head, showering glass splinters on me." The old German battleship *Schleswig-Holstein* (14,900 tons), now a training ship lying at anchor in Danzig's Neufahrwasser harbor only 400 yards distant, had opened fire with her nineteen guns on the Westerplatte which was shrouded by the thick morning mist. The Second World War had begun.

When the bombardment by the *Schleswig-Holstein* ceased, an attack was mounted by the SS assault company Danziger Heimwehr together with the assault company Hennigsen. Despite their poor defensive armament—consisting of a 7.5-cm field gun of 1897 vintage; two 3.7-cm antitank guns; four 8.1-cm mortars; 16 heavy and 25 light machine guns; 160 rifles and 1,000 hand grenades—the small Polish force of some 180 men repulsed the first attack.

Toward 6:00 A.M., a heavy air raid by the Luftwaffe wiped out the base of the naval aviation division at Putzig, killing the commanding officer, Lt. Comdr. E. Szystowski, who became the first naval officer to lose his life in the Second World War. As soon as the Fleet Command in Hela received the distress signal from the Westerplatte—"We are being attacked"—it issued orders to the Polish submarine force to carry out plan Vorek—proceed submerged to prearranged battle stations.

Toward 2:00 P.M., Oxhöft, the naval base at Gdynia, was attacked by Stukas of the 1st Air Division. They sank the small repair vessel *Nurek*, and shortly after that the torpedo boat *Mazur*; these two ships were the first to be sunk by aircraft bombs in this war. Through their periscopes the Polish submarines *Orzel* and *Wilk* were able to observe the German air attacks on Hela harbor and on the largest Polish naval vessels, the destroyer *Wicher* and the minelayer *Gryf*. Despite heavy antiaircraft fire from Polish naval vessels and shore installations, these ships, the only ones strong enough to do battle, were extensively damaged. In this, the first major sea-air battle of World War II, the antiaircraft guns of the sinking torpedo boat *Mazur* continued firing when the waves were already washing over the decks.

On Saturday 2 September 1939, strong German patrols near the Westerplatte were already active by first light. At around 9:35 A.M., the first attack by German seaplanes against the Polish submarine *Rys* took place. Although the submarine did not suffer a direct hit, there was a leak in the stern causing a loss of oil. At 11:50 A.M. the *Schleswig-Holstein* turned her guns on the Westerplatte, and at the same time 15-cm howitzers as well as 8.8-cm guns fired from the mouth of the Vistula, and heavy machine guns opened up from storehouse roofs in Neufahrwasser. Shortly afterward, a German reconnaissance aircraft appeared and at about 6:00 P.M., sixty dive bombers attacked the Westerplatte. After this inferno, the defence was disorganized, communications interrupted and all the mortars put out of action. As a salvo from the *Schleswig-Holstein* had already destroyed on the first day the only 7.5-cm field gun available, nothing was left to the defenders but machine guns and two light antitank guns.

At 12:38 P.M., the Polish submarine *Sep* attacked the German destroyer *Friedrich Ihn*. Although the destroyer was travelling at a speed of only 7 knots at a distance of 450 yards, the torpedoes missed their target. The destroyer immediately attacked the Polish submarine with depth charges and, after seeing a lifebuoy from the submarine on the water, reported it as having been sunk.

On the same day in the harbor at Hela, the Polish destroyer *Wicher* and the minelayer *Gryf* were converted into floating batteries. Without any chance of moving, the anchored ships became a primary target for German artillery and bombers.

Also on 2 September 1939, the British coastal patrol vessel *Lorna* intercepted the former steamer *Zeinikos*, now named the *Tiger Hill*, several nautical miles off Tel Aviv. The rusty freighter, with another vessel in tow, had on board 1,400 illegal immigrants, Jewish refugees from Poland, Rumania and Bulgaria. The captain and crew of the *Tiger Hill* climbed into the lifeboats and rowed to shore in order to escape arrest by the British mandate authority in Palestine. The passengers took control of the ship and continued their journey, running the steamer aground in shallow water near Sukria. The crew of the British patrol boat attempted to board the immigrants' ship and opened fire. Two of the refugees were killed and a number wounded. And so the Royal Navy in its first action in World War II opened fire not on a German naval vessel, but against those people who had managed to escape the clutches of the National Socialist state.

On the evening of 2 September 1939, the *Bremen* was plowing through the waves at 27 knots on course for Greenland. A considerable part of the Royal Navy was out hunting this luxury liner. British submarines were lurking at the exits of German ports. Two cruisers accompanied by eight destroyers were patrolling off the coast of Norway, and the greater part of the Home Fleet was out scouring the North Atlantic. But nobody expected this fast vessel to be in the dangerous icefields of the Denmark Strait where *Titanic* met its end in 1912. The *Bremen* hurried past the pocket-battleship *Deutschland*, only forty nautical miles away, without anybody knowing.

The *Wicher* and *Gryf*, lying in the harbor at Hela, together with the H. Laskowski 15-cm coastal battery, repulsed an attack launched by German destroyers from a distance of twelve nautical miles in the early hours of 3 September 1939. The destroyers withdrew under cover of a smoke screen. One of their number, hit by the coastal battery, was rendered unmaneuverable and had to be towed away.

On 3 September 1939, Great Britain and France declared war on Germany. At 1:30 P.M., the German High Command gave the order that hostilities were to be opened against Great Britain immediately. At that time, Germany had only eighteen

Above: A U-boat's lookout constantly scans the horizon for signs of smoke trails.

Left: 9/1/1939, Westerplatte: Dense clouds of smoke cover the Polish bastion. To the right of the picture is the training ship *Schleswig-Holstein*.

1 Knot = 1 nautical mile (1,852 m)

operational front-line submarines, which had to conduct the merchant war according to the regulations governing prizes. In this first phase of the Battle of the Atlantic, which lasted until June 1940, German U-boats operated in the eastern area of the North Atlantic between the Hebrides and Gibraltar with a focal point west of the English Channel. Great Britain commenced the blockade of Germany. While the pocket-battleship *Deutschland* managed to pass through the Denmark Strait and reach its waiting area off Greenland, the pocket-battleship *Admiral Graf Spee* had crossed unnoticed over the North Atlantic trade route and had already reached the South Atlantic. Each vessel was accompanied by a supply ship.

Major German surface vessels were equipped with radar. This fire control equipment (code name "Seetakt," literally "sea-beat") supplied the ships' guns with target data; it was also called the "mattress" because of its latticed antennae on the foremast. At this time, the equipment still operated on a 2.40-meter wavelength and had a radius of up to 30 kilometers (16 nautical miles).

The use of Seetakt and the absence of radar equipment in the Royal Navy made it possible for the German Navy to break through to the west and east of Iceland and also elude the Royal Navy into the Denmark Strait. Seetakt was frequently responsible for detecting Allied convoys in the vast stretches of the Atlantic, and also for keeping rendezvous with German supply ships.

Around midday September 3, a Blenheim reconnaissance aircraft of 139 Squadron took off from the airfield at Wyton, Huntingdonshire. The first operational mission of the RAF during the war took place against the German Navy. After two hours the pilot, Flying Officer A. McPherson, sighted units of the German Navy lying in the Schillig roads near Wilhelmshaven and immediately started to take aerial photographs. As the aircraft was flying at an altitude of over 19,000 feet, the radio equipment froze up, and this vital report from the pilot regarding the position of the German fleet did not arrive. However, he returned with seventy-five photographs and was able to record in his logbook, "Operation carried out – the first aircraft of the RAF to fly over German territory."

Toward 3:00 P.M. the same day, the Polish minelayer *Gryf* was destroyed in Hela harbor. The crew was successful in saving three 12-cm caliber guns from the wreck, which were then used in defence of the peninsula. Shortly afterward the destroyer *Wicher,* hit by four bombs, capsized. At 4:00, the gunboat *General Haller* sank. With the sinking of the *Wicher* and the *Gryf*, the two most dangerous units of the Polish navy were removed, which al-

lowed the German Navy to carry out minesweeping operations in the Gulf of Danzig practically undisturbed.

On the evening of 3 September 1939, the English passenger liner *Carinthia* left New York, bound for Great Britain. On board the ship in the detention cell was a 27-year-old German woman, Helene Mutterer, a stewardess on the Cunard liner *Georgic*, who became the first British "prisoner of war." She was put aboard the *Carinthia* in New York and bundled off to England.

Immediately after the declaration of war, both the Allies and the Germans published lists of war contraband showing those goods which, upon conveyance by neutral shipping, were liable to be seized at sea. In Great Britain, the convoy system was immediately instituted for ships putting to sea from British ports. Individual sailings from Great Britain were no longer permitted, and in overseas ports preparations were being made for making up convoys to Great Britain.

At the start of the war, Great Britain had 2,000 fewer merchant vessels than at the end of World War I. As the total population had grown in the intervening period by some four million and oil consumption had increased tenfold, problems of supply were to have a dramatic effect.

During the night of 3/4 September 1939, Lt. Comdr. Lemp, commander of the *U 30*, sighted a blacked-out ship following a zig-zag course. Lemp, believing the ship to be an armed merchant cruiser, sank the vessel with three torpedoes. The vessel

was, however, the passenger liner *Athenia* (13,000 tons), 250 nautical miles west of Ireland en route for the US. The survivors were picked up by the Norwegian tanker *Knut Nelson*, the Swedish yacht *Southern Cross*, the US freighter *City of Flint* as well as the British torpedo boats *Electra* and *Escort*. One hundred twelve passengers lost their lives, including twenty-eight Americans.

The Minister of Propaganda, Dr. Goebbels, at first denied responsibility for the torpedoeing, saying that the British themselves sank the ship on Churchill's orders so as to bring about America's entry into the war. Upon his return, Lemp received orders from the commander of the submarine arm, Capt. Karl Dönitz, to maintain complete silence regarding the sinking. The entry in the U-boat's log for 3 September 1939 was removed.

On Monday 4 September 1939, Winston Churchill was made First Lord of the Admiralty; he stated, "The first hours of a war can be a vital consequence for a navy. I therefore informed the Admiralty that I would immediately take up my duties and be in my office at 6 A.M."

In the early hours of September 4, the *Schleswig-Holstein*, together with smaller units of the German Navy and a battery of heavy 21-cm howitzers brought in from East Prussia, attempted to break Polish resistance in the Westerplatte. The position of the defenders was extremely difficult. They were exhausted by the continuous fighting; in addition, their casualties, who already numbered one-third of the entire garrison, were not being

Right: Dr. Goebbels, Minister of Propaganda, tries to substantiate his claim that the *Athenia* was definitely not sunk by a German U-boat.

Left: September 1939 in the naval base of Hela: the Polish minelayer *Gryf* sunk by the Luftwaffe

Below: September 1939, the Hela peninsula with naval base

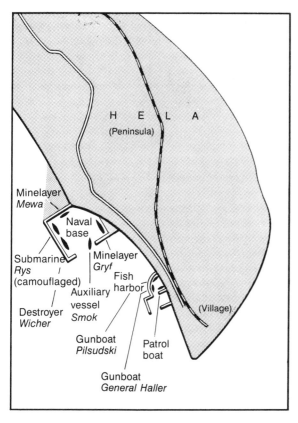

provided for. Moreover, radio reports coming in from the rest of Poland did nothing to raise the soldiers' morale. Nonetheless, all German attacks launched this day were thrown back.

At the same time, RAF Bomber Command attacked German naval units lying in the Schillig roads near Wilhelmshaven and off Brunsbüttel at the western exit of the Kiel Canal. The pocket-battleship *Admiral Scheer* received a few direct hits, but none of the bombs exploded. Five out of the twenty-nine British aircraft were shot down.

At 8:15 A.M. on Tuesday 5 September 1939, *U 47* (Lt. Comdr. Prien) sank the first British freighter of the war, a small steamer named the *Bosnia*. At 2:00 P.M., *U 48* (Lt. Comdr. Schultze) sighted an armed merchant ship showing no national flag.

Schultze signaled the suspicious vessel to stop by firing shots across its bow. The vessel immediately hoisted the British ensign and at the same time radioed, "Chased by a U-boat and am being fired at." Thereupon the *U 48* fired a torpedo. The *Royal Sceptre* became the first armed merchant vessel to be sunk by a German U-boat in World War II.

When Hitler learned about the SOS transmitted by the *Royal Sceptre*, the U-boats were ordered to sink or take prize all ships which, when stopped, continued to make use of their radio equipment.

One of the devices used by Britain against the U-boat was "Asdic," a submarine-locating device which transmitted sound waves horizontally and worked on the echo principle. Two or three ships in the convoy were needed to locate the position of the submarine. One of these vessels then had to place itself over the submarine's position and drop depth charges. Subsequently, Asdic contact was immediately taken up again once the turbulence caused by the exploding depth charges had subsided.

On September 5, an Avro Anson of 233 Squadron (Coastal Command) attacked a surfaced submarine off the east coast of Scotland. The aircraft dropped two 50-kg bombs on the submarine, which was already diving. Both bombs struck the surface of the water and rebounded. After the aerial explosion, fragments of the bombs penetrated the fuel tanks of the aircraft, and the crew had to ditch in St. Andrew's Bay. The submarine, which happened to belong to the Royal Navy, suffered no damage.

On Wednesday 6 September 1939, the Westerplatte was relatively quiet. The defenders were disturbed only by the fire from the training ship and the 15-cm and 8.8-cm batteries. In the meantime, a Northern Patrol was being made up from elderly cruisers in Great Britain to maintain continual patrols of the area between Great Britain and Iceland. By this time, Hitler was already seeking to enlist the aid of the Soviet Union, as he was determined to break the blockade. The German ambassador in Moscow, Graf von der Schulenburg, informed the Soviet government of intentions to divert blockade-runners to Murmansk and that Soviet assistance would be expected, even to unload and forward merchandise by rail to Leningrad, where it would be taken on board by German cargo vessels. The German Foreign Office asked for immediate advice by telegraph regarding Moscow's reaction to this communiqué.

The largest German passenger liner, the *Bremen* (51,731 gross tons), was at this time still on course to the safe harbor of Murmansk. Commodore Adolf Ahrens stated, "At about 2:15 P.M., the heavy anchor chain rattled through the hawse; the *Bremen* had reached the port of Murmansk, having covered 4,045 nautical miles since leaving New York. To cover this distance, the ship had been on the move for six days, thirteen hours and thirty-six minutes."

On Thursday 7 September 1939, the *Schleswig-Holstein* commenced firing on the Westerplatte at 4:15 A.M., as did the field artillery at the mouth of the Vistula. In addition, there were mortars taking part which had been brought forward right up to the Westerplatte together with a large number of machine guns. Once again, the defenders threw back an infantry attack in the last resistance shown by the Polish garrison. At 10:15, the Westerplatte capitulated.

Also on this date, Hitler gave orders that no French merchant vessels were to be attacked and French waters were not to be mined.

During the night of 7/8 September 1939, the Polish submarine *Zbik* laid the twenty mines it had carried and then proceeded to a new operational area. The German *U 22* (Lt. Comdr. Winter) sighted the *Zbik*, which had hove to and was lying 650 yards away. At 11:09 P.M., the *U 22* approached to within 200 yards and fired a torpedo which, according to the report, "struck the submarine directly behind the tower and destroyed it." It was in fact destroyed by the faulty detonation of the magnetic firing pistol in the torpedo, something that would give U-boat commanders a great deal of trouble during the subsequent course of the

war.

On Friday 8 September 1939, the commander of the Polish submarine *Orzel* fell sick. As this officer, Comdr. Kloczkowski, was a suspected typhus case, his hospitalization became a matter of absolute urgency. On the same day, the pocket-battleship *Admiral Graf Spee* (Capt. Langsdorff) and its supply ship *Altmark* (Capt. Dau) reached the equator.

In the meantime, the German ambassador in Moscow reported that he had just received an advice from the Soviet government that German merchant ships might regularly put into Murmansk and that the transport of their cargoes to Leningrad would be assured.

The German Navy now planned to use for their operations the well-developed Soviet Arctic Ocean base at Murmansk, which was outside the British blockade and ice free year round. But as Stalin was aware that Murmansk was not isolated from foreign access by sea, he instructed Foreign Minister Molotov to recommend that the Germans use the remote Teribierka Bay, some thirty miles east of Kolski Bay. This suggestion was turned down by the German Naval High Command, as Teribierka was not suitable for their purposes. Subsequently, the German naval attaché in Moscow, Norbert von Baumbach, had further discussions with Molotov. The Soviet foreign minister then offered the German Navy the Zapadnaya-Litsa Bay in a cordoned

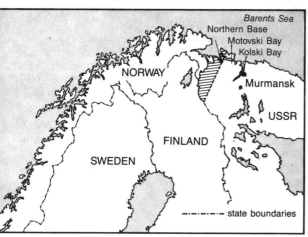

Above left: Section from the secret map "Basis Nord" (Northern Base), northwest of Murmansk

Above: Mala-Zapadnaya-Litsa Bay: The Northern Base was established here with Stalin's permission as a base for the German Navy.

Below: Murmansk and the surrounding territory (shaded section = territory ceded by Finland to the USSR in February 1940)

off frontier area, as "this bay possesses considerably better anchorage than Teribierka."

During the night of Sunday 10 September 1939, the British destroyers *Express* and *Esk* laid the first minefield off the German North Sea coast. Several hours later, the steamer *Magdepur* sank off Aldeburgh, the first vessel to fall victim to a German magnetic mine.

In the meantime, the *Graf Spee* and the *Altmark* had reached the waters between Trinidad and St. Helena. The name on the stern of the *Admiral Graf Spee* was now *Admiral Scheer*.

Also on September 10, the British submarine *Triton* sighted a nonidentifiable submarine. The commander of the *Triton* gave the order to attack, made toward the unknown boat and rammed it. The submarine sank immediately. Only afterward did it become apparent that it was the British submarine *Oxley* with a crew of fifty-four. It was the first submarine to be sunk by another submarine in World War II.

As complete mastery of the air by the Luftwaffe made it impossible for Polish submarines to exploit their aptitude for operations on the high sea, the order went out on Monday 11 September 1939 — "Try to break through to England."

During the night of 11/12 September 1939, a German U-boat succeeded in getting through the English Channel before Franco-British minefields made the passage almost impossible.

On Tuesday 12 September 1939, the Polish submarine *Wilk* reported its intention to break out of the Baltic immediately and set course for the British Isles.

Left: September 1939, North Sea coast: Defusing a stranded British mine

Right: The Polish submarine *Orzel* built in Vlissingen in the Netherlands. Maiden voyage: 1/15/1939. Displacement: 1,110/1,473.5 t. Armament: 1 Bofors gun, 10.5 cm; 1 twin antiaircraft cannon, 4 cm; 12 torpedo tubes. Speed: 10 knots surface speed, 5 knots submerged. Complement: 60.

On Wednesday 13 September 1939, the French Navy recorded its first loss. When the minelayer *Platon* was about to defuse its mines in Casablanca before delivery, one of them exploded. The *Platon* was completely destroyed, and 215 of the crew lost their lives.

During the night of 13/14 September 1939, three Polish minesweepers of the Bird class laid a minefield of sixty mines some five nautical miles south of the Hela lighthouse.

On Thursday 14 September 1939, the *U 39* (Lt. Comdr. Glattes) torpedoed the aircraft carrier *Ark Royal* (21,652 gross tons) off the Hebrides. The carrier was escorted by a number of destroyers belonging to Northern Patrol. Equipped with Asdic, they were to seek out the U-boats. Three torpedoes with magnetic firing pistols were fired. Two of these exploded prematurely: Instead of exploding under the keel, they exploded close to the ship's side, causing slight damage to the paintwork. Three escort destroyers immediately took up pursuit and attacked the *U 39* with depth charges. The badly damaged U-boat was suddenly flung up to the surface and sank shortly afterward. A number of the crew were saved.

The *U 39* was the first German submarine to be sunk by the Royal Navy. The carrier-borne aircraft taking part in the pursuit used a type of bomb specially developed for antisubmarine warfare. Two of the attackers were hit by fragments of their own bombs and crashed. Lt. Comdr. Lemp's *U 30*, which was in the vicinity, took the aircrew pris-

oner. Not only was the *U 39* the first German submarine to be sunk, it was also the first to fall victim to the unreliability of the magnetic detonator and steering device with which German torpedoes were equipped.

During the evening twilight on 14 September 1939, the Polish submarine *Wilk*, while making its attempt to break through to England, trailed behind a Swedish convoy that had been made up to pass through the minefields off the Swedish coast. The submarine followed behind the rearmost lights of the convoy. Suddenly the lookout sighted through the gun aperture two warships heading toward them from the opposite direction. On board the *Wilk* was established with some consternation that the two warships were, in fact, German destroyers. But the narrow shipping channel made any change in course impossible; and the Polish submarine had to pass within fifty yards of the German destroyers. One of them briefly switched on its searchlight and trained it on the submarine — apparently the destroyer assumed the sub was escorting the Swedish convoy.

On the same evening, the Polish submarine *Orzel* dropped anchor off the Reval roads and radioed, "We have to put a sick man ashore, and we have an engine defect. May we put into port? Orzel." At 1:03 A.M., a motorboat with Estonian officers and several sailors on board came alongside. The *Orzel* was taken by a pilot into the naval harbor of Reval and was allocated a berth behind the gunboat *Laine*.

On Friday 15 September 1939, the Polish submarine *Sep* attempted to break out through The Ore Sound in the direction of Great Britain. The attempt had to be given up, as it was uncertain if the submarine was in a position to dive.

In Reval at the same time, whether the submarine *Orzel* could continue its voyage within twenty-four hours was no longer certain because German tanker *Thalatta* (which was lying in port) also wished to set sail. According to international legal provisions, a warship may not leave a neutral harbor until twenty-four hours after the departure of any enemy merchantman. So the *Orzel* had to remain at least one day longer. Under pressure from Berlin and Moscow, the Estonian authorities suddenly declared that they were obliged to intern the *Orzel*.

Under the command of Estonian officers, a guard went aboard, who took ashore all navigational documents, sea charts, the entire stock of munitions, the gun breechblocks and almost all the torpedoes. Secret documents were destroyed in good time. The crew was informed of imminent internment, but the 28-year-old Lt. Piasecki, who was now acting first officer, resolved to get the submarine prepared for a breakout with the agreement of the new captain, Lt. Comdr. Grudzinski. Left in the stern tubes on board the submarine, there were still six torpedoes that could only be removed by crane. For the removal, the submarine had to turn about. Now the *Orzel* was again lying in the direction of travel. Unloading the six remaining torpedoes was put back by the Estonian Navy until Monday because of the upcoming weekend.

On September 15 also, the Belgian merchantman *Alex van Opstal* (5,965 gross tons) ran against a mine laid by *U 26* (Lt. Comdr. Ewerth). It was the first ship belonging to a neutral country to be sunk during the war.

On Saturday 16 September 1939, the first convoy left Halifax in Canada for England.

On Sunday 17 September 1939, the Polish submarine *Sep* reached Swedish territorial waters at 4:45 A.M. near Landsort where she was interned. During the evening twilight, the *U 29* (Lt. Comdr. Schuhart) sighted the aircraft carrier *Courageous* off the Irish coast just as it was turning into the wind to enable its aircraft to land. *U 29* fired three torpedoes at 7:00 P.M. The following explosions were so powerful that the submarine captain assumed that his own vessel had been hit by depth charges. The *Courageous* (22,500 gross tons) with forty-eight aircraft on board had received two direct hits amidships from a distance of 3,500 yards. The carrier broke up and sank within fifteen minutes.

Astonishingly, the five destroyers belonging to the carrier's escort group, although equipped with Asdic, did not warn of the presence of a German U-boat. More than 500 of the complement of 1,260 were lost, including the captain of the ship. The *Courageous* was the first aircraft carrier to be sunk in World War II. After this loss, the British Admiralty no longer used their carriers as submarine hunters.

At approximately 3:00 A.M. during the night of 17/18 September 1939, the two Estonian guards on board the *Orzel* were overpowered and taken prisoner. A Polish sailor, Chojecki, used a hatchet to cut through the cable of the nearby searchlight; after that, the telephone wires were severed. Thereupon, the vessel silently cast off. The diesel engines were started up and the submarine left the pier, making off for the harbor exit. Suddenly the *Orzel* stuck fast. It had run onto one of the many sandbanks in the harbor basin and rammed the mole. At once, sirens started to howl, searchlights lit up the entire harbor basin, and the Estonians opened up with machine-gun fire. The submarine's two motors were set to hard astern. This time, the slight breeze coming from the direction of land gave the Poles some assistance.

Lt. Piasecki stated, "Thick exhaust fumes from the diesel motors turning hard astern clouded our ship in thick smoke. The *Orzel*, with its final endeavors, slowly worked free. After we had finally left the harbor, the Estonian heavy 15-cm coastal batteries in the area of Naissaar Island opened fire. But the water here was already some sixty-five feet deep, and the *Orzel* was able to dive slowly."

On 18 September 1939, while the Soviet TASS News Agency blamed Estonia for assisting the escape of the Polish submarine, the *Orzel* remained on the sea bed for the entire day. From time to time, heavy explosions shook the vessel's hull. Estonian and Soviet destroyers were hunting the escaped Polish submarine.

But the escape gave the Soviet authorities a welcome excuse to increase pressure on Estonia. Molotov claimed that the Estonians had helped the Poles escape and that the *Orzel* now represented a threat to Soviet shipping.

During the evening of September 18, the *Orzel* left Estonian territorial waters and set a course in the direction of the island of Gotland. At this time, the commander, Lt. Comdr. Grudzinski, decided that despite the missing navigational equipment and sea charts, he would remain in the Baltic as long as his supplies of fuel and fresh water permitted. Grudzinski hoped that a suitable opportunity would arise to attack German units.

On the same date, the Polish submarine *Rys*, with two badly damaged periscopes, reached Swedish coastal waters. The vessel had only 16.5 tons of fuel left, which was insufficient for the voyage to England. *Rys* was taken by pilot into Stavnäs harbor and interned.

On Tuesday 19 September 1939, Churchill drew up plans to lay a minefield in Norwegian territorial waters to stop the transport of Swedish iron ore from Narvik to Germany. Churchill said to the First Sea Lord and others, "I brought to the notice of the cabinet this morning the importance of stopping the Norwegian transportation of Swedish iron ore from Narvik, which will begin as soon as the ice forms in the Gulf of Bothnia."

Nevertheless, Churchill was unsuccessful in putting his plan through, as the Foreign Office shrank from violating Norwegian neutrality.

On Wednesday 20 September 1939, the Royal Navy succeeded in taking prisoner the commander of the U-boat *U 27*, Lt. Comdr. Franz, together with his crew. The *U 27* was attacked by the destroyers *Fortune* and *Forrester* and, in a hopeless position, the German commander gave the order to abandon the sinking submarine.

During the night of 20/21 September 1939, the

Great Britain introduced the convoy system immediately upon the outbreak of the war.

Polish submarine *Orzel* surfaced to the east of Gotland near the Östergarn lighthouse. The only dinghy was given to the two Estonian guards who had been taken prisoner and about whom the Soviet propaganda machine spread news of their murder. Before they were set loose, they were given some provisions and 50 dollars each for their return from Sweden to Estonia. They were also given a letter in English for the commander of the Estonian fleet, stating that they had been overpowered by the Poles so they could not raise the alarm.

The most serious problem for the Polish submarine was not the question of navigation. The Estonians had confiscated all their sea charts except for two of the Polish coast, which were now worthless. In this almost hopeless situation, the 25-year-old navigation officer, Lt. Mokrski, discovered in a cupboard overlooked by the Estonians and up-to-date handbook with a list in German of beacons and signal positions. From these documents, with their precise geographic details of the sectors and characteristics of each individual lighthouse and buoy, Lt. Mokrski was able to draw up navigational charts for the Baltic and the channels.

On Thursday 21 September 1939, the Polish submarine *Wilk* reached the British naval base of Scapa Flow.

On Sunday 24 September 1939, Hitler rescinded the order not to attack French ships.

In the early hours of 25 September 1939, the *Schleswig-Holstein* together with her sister ship *Schlesien*, under the protection of two minesweeper flotillas, left the port of Danzig to attack the Polish Laskowski battery on the Hela peninsula. The batteries immediately returned fire and with their third salvo hit the first of the ships, the *Schlesien*. After the *Schlesien* withdrew under cover of an artificial smoke screen, the Laskowski battery commenced firing on the *Schleswig-Holstein* and scored a hit on the side of the training ship.

On the same day, the Polish submarine *Zbik*, escorted by a Swedish pilot boat, sailed into Sandhamn harbor where it was interned.

On Tuesday 26 September 1939, TASS News Agency reported that a Polish submarine had carried out a torpedo attack on the Soviet steamer *Pionier*, although without success, while the freighter *Metallist* (968 gross tons) had been torpedoed and sunk in the Gulf of Narva by the same submarine. A number of the crew lost their lives during the incident. Two years later, in the autumn of 1941, it became known that Capt. R. Osipov sailed the *Metallist* into the Gulf of Narva to sink

it there on the orders of the Leningrad party secretary, A. R. Zdanov and the C-in-C of the Soviet Navy, Adm. N. G. Kuznecov. He was to report that the vessel had been torpedoed by a Polish submarine. The Soviet submarine *S.C. 303* and the torpedo boat *Tuca* were already waiting at the

place arranged for the sinking. After the crew of the *Metallist* had been taken off the ship, the *S.C. 303* fired three torpedoes and failed to score a hit. Finally, the torpedo boat *Tuca* sank the steamer by gunfire. To make subsequent salvage operations easier, a shallow spot had been chosen as a precautionary measure so that the *Metallist* sank only as far as deck level, with the superstructure remaining above water.

At this time, the Estonian foreign minister, Karl Selter, was in Moscow at the invitation of the Soviet government. When the TASS Agency and Radio Moscow reported that a Polish submarine had sunk the Soviet steamer *Metallist* in Estonian territorial waters, Foreign Minister Molotov and Commissar Mikoyan summoned the Estonian foreign minister and declared that Estonia's weak military position was intolerable for the Soviet Union and her security. A mutual-assistance treaty would need to be concluded in which Estonia would cede air and naval bases to the USSR. After Selter's protests, Molotov resorted to open threats: Should Estonia resist these demands, the Soviet government "would see itself compelled to carry out its wishes by force."

While Selter held discussions with his government, the Kremlin repeated its point of view in the form of an ultimatum without a time limit. In the meantime, the Soviet fleet had entered Estonian territorial waters; Soviet bombers flew over Reval, and Estonian frontier guards reported that strong Soviet troop movements were taking place on the other side of the border. After Estonian appeals for assistance to Germany and the Western Allies and Finland remained unanswered, this small country had to bend to the will of her powerful neighbor. Estonia was occupied and later became a Soviet republic "at the wish of the Estonian people."

Also on 26 September 1939, the British Admiralty issued a communiqué that shortly all British merchantmen would be armed. This decision, even though it related in the main to obsolete guns dating from World War I, was seized upon by Hitler as a justification to attack all armed ships without warning.

On Saturday 30 September 1939, Hitler gave instructions that the prize regulations were no longer to be applied to the sea area west of Great Britain and Ireland as far as latitude 15 degrees.

On the same day, the *Admiral Graf Spee*, disguised as the *Admiral Scheer*, sank the British freighter *Clement* (5,051 gross tons). In accordance with naval traditions, the captain of the *Graf Spee*, Capt. Langsdorff, radioed a message to a Brasilian station to keep a watch out for the lifeboats of the *Clement*.

By the end of September 1939, almost 300,000 tons of goods destined for Germany had been seized by the Royal Navy as prize. The hunt for German blockade-runners by British warships had practically crippled German shipping. On the other hand, German submarines succeeded in sinking forty-eight merchant vessels amounting to a total of 178,644 gross tons, in the North Atlantic and North Sea in the first month of the war.

Their own losses amounted to two U-boats.

In the meantime, the French Navy watched over a large area of the Mediterranean. In coastal waters as well as in the Bay of Biscay, French naval units took part in the hunt for German submarines; and in the mid-Atlantic, a powerful French squadron, based in Dakar, supported the Royal Navy in the battle against German surface units.

In September, German cruisers, destroyers and minelayers laid the extended system of minefields known as the "Western Wall," which stretched northward from Dutch territorial waters for about 150 nautical miles. These minefields, made known by the German naval H. Q., represented a flank protection against British attacks. The Western Wall also protected the German bight from the North Sea as far as Skagerrak.

On Sunday 1 October 1939, the III Battalion 374 Infantry Regiment again attacked the Polish positions on the Hela peninsula. At the same time, the German minesweepers *M 4*, *M 111*, *M 132* and *Nettelbek* opened fire jointly with the army batteries and a naval railway battery. At 2:00 P.M., the commander of the Polish naval units on Hela requested a ceasefire and offered to negotiate a surrender, bringing to an end all Polish resistance on the Baltic coast.

At 2:30, the German minesweeper *M 85* sank within one minute of being hit below the water line. Twenty-three of the crew went down with the ship; the captain and forty-seven sailors were saved. In the only success attributable to Polish submarines, *M 85* ran into a mine laid by the submarine *Zbik*. The employment of Polish submarines had more psychological success than any obvious effect. Their mere presence in the Baltic was a nuisance to the Germans as, until the middle of October, they were compelled to employ minesweepers on antisubmarine duties. Despite repeated German reports to the contrary, none of the Polish submarines were lost. On 1 October 1939, the Admiralty advised their merchantmen to ram enemy submarines. Fron then on, all British merchantmen sailed nights with their lights dimmed, while German naval H. Q. gradually allowed their ships to attack without warning in the waters around Great Britain.

On Tuesday 3 October 1939, the delegates of twenty-one republics meeting in Panama resolved to declare an "American Security Zone" that was to consist of a broad stretch of 300–600 nautical miles around their coasts in which no war activities might take place. These waters were to be closed

In Remembrance of your stay on board the „Deutschland". Good luck!

Wennerker
Captain

One of the most striking souvenirs of the war at sea. This photo was given to Capt. Randall by the captain of the *Deutschland*, which sank Capt. Randall's ship, the *Stonegate*, on 10/5/1939 and took him on board. On 10/9/1939, Capt. Randall was transferred to the captured *City of Flint*. Several weeks later he succeeded in escaping via Norway back to England.

to warships of the combatant powers. A newly formed Atlantic Squadron of the US Navy would be charged with guarding this neutrality zone.

On Thursday 5 October 1939, eight strong British and French battle groups were formed to hunt the pocket-battleship *Admiral Graf Spee*. Any one of these groups was quite capable of defeating the *Graf Spee* on its own. Churchill stated that the disproportionate relationship between the enemy forces and the countermeasures to which he was forced was annoying. By way of security measures, the British authorities sent several South Atlantic convoys back to their ports.

On Friday 6 October 1939, the pocket-battleship *Deutschland* reached the Pan American Military Zone and sank the British steamer *Stonegate* (5,044 gross tons).

On this Friday, the last Polish troops, commanded by Gen. Kleeberg in the Lublin region, capitulated. All that remained was the Polish submarine *Orzel* cruising without navigational charts and hardly any weapons, seeking in vain for a target for its remaining torpedoes. In the meantime,

the crew had run out of fresh water, as the distilling apparatus had been damaged. Additionally, the rudder was no longer functioning correctly, and the fuel supply was gradually coming to an end.

By Saturday 7 October 1939, 161,000 soldiers, 24,000 vehicles and 140,000 tons of equipment belonging to the British Expeditionary Force were transported across the English Channel without loss. The German Navy made scarcely any attempt to stop the transport of the British forces to France. On this day, the captain of the Polish submarine *Orzel* decided to break through from the Baltic to the British Isles.

On 7 October 1939, a three-day thrust by strong German surface units—the battleship *Gneisenau* and the cruiser *Köln*, accompanied by nine destroyers—set out toward the Norwegian coast in order to tempt the British Home Fleet into the operational radius of the Luftwaffe. But as Germany did not possess a fleet air arm specially trained and equipped for sea warfare, the attacks by German bombers were ineffective.

On Sunday 8 October 1939, Lt. Comdr. Prien commanding *U 47* left Kiel and set course for Scapa Flow, the main base of the Royal Navy. The submarine, which had been commissioned nine months previously, had a complement of forty. It passed through the Kiel Canal into the North Sea. A wind force of strength 7 was registered at the time.

On the same evening, toward 7:00, the Polish submarine *Orzel* surfaced again. The Swedish flag, a bed sheet painted with oil color, was hoisted and the name was removed from the turret. The sub now passed through The Ore Sound close to Trelleborg. Out to sea the silhouettes of darkened ships, including several German torpedo boats, could be recognized. Unexpectedly, a land-based searchlight switched on and remained just in front of the submarine; it had no choice but to carry on, as the water at this point was too shallow for diving. Suddenly a strong shuddering went through the submarine; it had struck a reef. All hands were ordered on deck and the crew, with the exception of three artificers, assembled on deck wearing their life jackets. The diesel engines were run at maximum revs, and the steel plating of the hull screeched over the stone. The submarine pushed forward powerfully, moving over the underwater obstacle; it passed through the narrowest point in The Sound in ninety minutes. Toward midnight, the lights of Copenhagen came into view. The *Orzel* now had to submerge again and spend the entire day on the sea bottom at a depth of approximately one hundred feet. The voyage was not resumed until about 8:30 P.M. on October 9.

On Tuesday 10 October 1939 at 6:00 P.M., Capt. A. H. Brown of the British steamer *Huntsman* (8,300 gross tons) sighted a warship in the South Atlantic making toward him at full speed. Seeing the French tricolor at the masthead, Capt. Brown was convinced that the ship was the French battleship *Dunkerque*. But suddenly the tricolor was replaced. Shortly after that, the prize crew put aboard by the *Admiral Graf Spee* (the ship's true identity) discovered documents relating to the secret code which Capt. Brown had not thrown overboard and which gave precise details of the routes taken by merchant shipping. A radio operator from the *Graf Spee* transmitted an interrupted mayday call from the British vessel, giving a false name and position and stating, "This ship has been torpedoed by a German U-boat."

On the same day, Adm. Raeder agreed with Hitler at a conference in Berlin that the commerce war against England would have to be stepped up. At the same time, Hitler declined, from political reasons, to construct U-boats in the Soviet Union or to purchase Soviet-made U-boats. Despite this, the German Navy demanded that their cruisers, submarines and auxiliary units be provided with fuel and provisions in Soviet ports. Ammunition was to be transported from Germany direct by road to the Soviet ports. In addition, Raeder hoped that Soviet vessels would undertake the provisioning of German cruisers and U-boats at sea in order to extend their operational period. At the conference also, the admiral gave a dissertation before Hitler on the strategic importance of Norway.

On Friday 13 October 1939, Dönitz gave a pack of nine German U-boats orders to carry out the first experiments with the new wolf-pack tactics. Nevertheless, only three out of the nine submarines were available to attack convoy HG 3 southwest of Ireland. This operation, which lasted until October 19, was led by Comdr. Hartmann of *U 37*. But the difficulties encountered in these wolf-pack tactics were considerable, as the convoy immediately scattered, and, additionally, there were a number of faulty torpedoes. The U-boats did finally manage to sink a few ships.

During the early hours of 13 October 1939, Lt. Comdr. Prien, commanding *U 47*, was within sight of the Orkneys. A fresh northeasterly breeze was blowing; the sky was bright and clear with only light clouds. Scapa Flow itself lay behind a number of small islands, and the passages between these islands had been blocked by nets and sunken ships; only the main channel remained clear. This operation was not without danger, as *U 47* was not fitted with DF-equipment; and there was the additional danger that they could surface close to an enemy warship or be rammed by a ship's bow.

During the night of 13/14 October 1939, while Prien was navigating the northern entrance into the bay, the Northern Lights glowed, which should have made it very easy for the defence to have picked out the U-boat, travelling as it was on the surface and picking its way through the many obstacles and blockships. On land, all was in total darkness and the blockships in the sound had the effect of a stage backdrop. As Prien stated, "Then suddenly it was light; the whole bay opened out, right up to the horizon. The burning sky was reflected in the calm sea. It looked as though the sea had been lit up from the ocean bed. I said to those below, 'We've made it!'"

Prien turned into the bay toward the southwest. At last he found two major units lying close together. *U 47* fired off a salvo of torpedoes. The first hits exploded either on the bows of the battleship *Royal Oak* (Capt. Benn) or against its anchor cables. To quote Prien, "It sounded like an explosion far away in the mountains."

At 12:59 A.M., a tremendous shudder went through the hull of the *Royal Oak*. Capt. Benn suspected an explosion and went down to the lower decks to make certain. Rear Adm. H. E. C. Blagrove (Rear Admiral Second Battle Squadron), who was on board, also refused to believe that the well-hidden ship lying at anchor could have been hit by a torpedo. He assumed that it was an internal explosion or a German air attack. Still on the surface, *U 47* withdrew from the target in order to

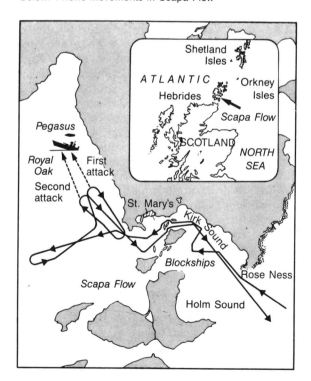

Above: Battleship *Royal Oak* (Capt. Benn), which was sunk by *U 47* (Lt. Comdr. Prien)

Below: Prien's movements in Scapa Flow

reload two torpedo tubes. Despite the explosion, all was still peaceful in the harbor. *U 47* stopped in the middle of the bay; when the tubes were reported ready, she took a wide detour back to Kirk Sound.

At 1:23 A.M., Prien reported, "Three torpedoes fired at the target from the forward tubes and course resumed toward the outlet from the bay. Three minutes later there was a tremendous explosion from the battleship. Water columns spouted up, signs of fire were visible and bits of wreckage were flung through the air. Now the harbor began to liven up! Destroyers turned on their lights and morse-code messages were transmitted from all quarters." In just two minutes, the *Royal Oak* (29,000 tons) sank. The greater part of the crew were at their battle stations, but the ship rapidly capsized. A total of 833 enlisted and officers, including Capt. Benn and Rear Adm. Blagrove, lost their lives.

The *U 47* moved southward toward the turn-off points of the Kirk Sound and Skerry Sound, hugging the coast to avoid being spotted by the searching destroyers. In Prien's words, "The ship crept quietly back through the gap. It was dark around us. Only from the distance could we hear the sound of exploding depth charges, becoming ever quieter. Then the open sea lay before us."

On Sunday 14 October 1939, the Admiralty is-

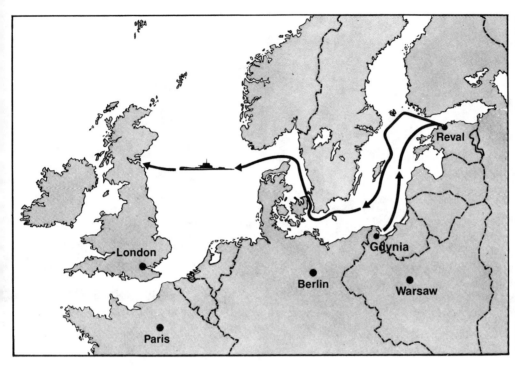

Left: The odyssey of the Polish submarine *Orzel*

Right: 10/18/1939, Berlin: Lt. Comdr. Prien, "the bull of Scapa Flow," before the Brandenburger Tor

sued a communiqué on the loss of the *Royal Oak*. Dönitz said, "I first heard of the success of the operation from the British."

The same morning, the Polish submarine *Orzel*, making toward the Firth of Forth, radioed, "Supposed position 06.30 on appointed place for Polish Navy. Beg permission entrance and pilot, have no chart. *Orzel*"

Toward 11:00, the British destroyer *Valorous* found the *Orzel* some thirty nautical miles to the west of the Isle of May. The odyssey that had lasted forty-four days was over. Churchill said, "The escape of the submarine *Orzel* is an epic."

Toward the middle of October 1939, a new U-boat offensive was commenced against Allied shipping. As a first step, the approaches to British ports were mined.

At the same time in Moscow, Commissar Mikoyan was proposing an accelerated supplying of German repair ships, transport ships and tugs through the Arctic Canal into the Zapadnaya-Litsa Bay. The military attaché, von Baumbach, reported to Berlin, "In this matter we remain dependent only upon the capacity of the floating repair units despatched by us. We may repair all types and sizes of warship in the Zapadnaya-Litsa Bay." At the suggestion of von Baumbach, Adm. Raeder gave the name "North Base" to this enclave of the German Kriegsmarine on the Arctic Ocean.

And so, thanks to the Soviet Union, Hitler obtained his only naval base beyond the reach of the British blockade. After the Naval High command

asked Dönitz if he considered it worthwhile having facilities for provisioning U-boats in the North Base, he immediately suggested a timetable for provisioning the first U-boats from 18 to 23 November 1939. Basically, Moscow agreed with these proposals. But it gave authorization for the provisioning of only one U-boat in the North Base, which disappointed Dönitz to the extent that his first reaction was to terminate the entire procedure. Despite that, Raeder observed, "The significance of economic help by the Soviets is decisive. Russia's offer is so extensive that the commercial blockade will with all certainty lead to nothing."

On Monday 16 October 1939, Hitler agreed that in future all enemy merchant ships could be torpedoed without warning; and, after previous warning, passenger ships in convoy could be sunk. On the same day, German bombers attacked the Firth of Forth in the first attempt to make an air strike at the British fleet at its moorings. The cruisers *Southampton* and *Edinburgh* and also the destroyer *Mohawk* suffered slight damage. Twenty-five officers and enlisted were killed or wounded. Four German bombers failed to return, three being shot down by fighters and one by flak.

On Tuesday 17 October 1939, the OKM gave U-boat commanders a free hand to attack without warning any ship known to belong to the enemy.

Toward midday, Lt. Comdr. Prien with his *U 47* put into Wilhelmshaven. Adm. Raeder was on the quay to welcome the submarine and Capt. Dönitz was promoted to rear admiral on the deck of the

U 47. The crew of *U 47* flew in Hitler's private aircraft to Berlin where Prien was decorated by Hitler with the Knight's Cross of the Iron Cross. The National Socialist propaganda machine made Prien a national hero. Churchill wrote, "This episode, which must be regarded as a feat of arms on the part of the German U-boat commander, gave a shock to public opinion."

On Thursday 19 October 1939, Hitler announced that any ship with dimmed lights sailing on a route up to latitude twenty degrees was to be attacked and sunk.

By 20 October 1939, nineteen merchantmen totalling 59,027 gross tons had fallen victim to magnetic mines, and a much larger number had been damaged. Adm. Raeder now wished to exploit the chances of success present and also laid mines by aircraft at the approaches to each British harbor, something that would be impossible to achieve by surface or underwater minelayers.

In the first twelve weeks of the war, British destroyers and minelayers laid a minefield with a total of 3,636 mines between Cape Gris-Nez and Folkestone.

In October 1939, three German submarines — *U 12*, *U 40* and *U 60* — sank and a fourth submarine was damaged trying to get through the Anglo-French minefield laid in the Channel. After these losses, the German naval command issued strict orders to U-boat commanders to go around Great Britain via the North Atlantic.

At the end of October 1939, the Luftwaffe bombed British convoys along the east coast, at first sporadically and without success. At that time, merchant ships were armed only with weak and obsolete antiaircraft guns.

Magnetic mines, laid by German submarines on the sea bed in shallow coastal waters, were a secret weapon that had a devastating effect. They were electromagnetically detonated by the changes in the earth's magnetic field brought about by the steel hull of a ship. In most cases, the shock wave broke off the keel of the ship. The hope was that the British would not be able to develop a countermeasure. And in fact along the coasts, in the bays and estuaries, British ships inexplicably went down. The success of the magnetic mines was attributed to torpedo hits or orthodox mines which, by some unknown mechanism, made the work of the minesweepers more difficult.

In October 1939, German submarines in the Atlantic and the North Sea sank thirty-four merchantmen totalling 168,140 gross tons. German losses amounted to five U-boats.

On Wednesday 1 November 1939, the German embassy in Moscow reported that talks had commenced on the subject of raw material transports through the Soviet Union. Graf von der Schulenburg emphasized that the Soviet Union was prepared to import the raw materials that Germany had purchased before the war now warehoused abroad. He added, "The Soviet Union places the highest value on the utmost discretion and complete secrecy with regard to these transactions." Mikoyan described the effort as a German-Soviet conspiracy which should be known only by a very few persons. He certainly had reason for saying that, for the conspiracy represented the grossest violation of the rules of neutrality.

The pocket-battleship *Deutschland* was at that time patrolling to the south of Greenland. The ship was in no danger of being discovered, but it also had little chance of sinking enemy shipping in this area. On 1 November 1939, Naval High Command ordered its return. Its score of ships sunk was indeed modest: two Allied freighters totalling 7,000 gross tons. Churchill wrote, "The mere presence of this powerful ship upon our main trade routes had however imposed, as was intended, a serious strain upon our escorts and hunting groups in the North Atlantic."

On Tuesday 7 November 1939, the USA declared the sea areas off the British and French coasts to be war zones, which US merchant vessels were forbidden to enter.

On the same day, the two Polish destroyers *Blyskawica* and *Grom* received orders to patrol in the southern area of the North Sea in the waters between England and Holland. The two ships were east of Lowestoft with their visibility limited by fog when toward 8:00 A.M. two floatplanes were reported. At first, the aircraft circled some distance away and then, around 8:45, they flew directly toward the Polish destroyers. The crews believed that the aircraft were British, but when the planes got closer, they saw the crosses on the aircraft and immediately opened fire. When a long black object fell from the fuselage of the floatplane, one of the crews believed that the aircraft had lost a float. But when a white trail was seen on the water and the "float" — sometimes diving, sometimes springing out of the water — ran toward one of the destroyers, the surprised crew recognised a torpedo, which narrowly missed the destroyer. This torpedo attack was the first launched by a German aircraft against an Allied ship.

On Wednesday 15 November 1939, the pocket-battleship *Deutschland* reached Kiel without incident.

In the middle of November 1939, the German naval attaché in Moscow, von Baumbach, visited the North Base in the Zapadnaya-Litsa Bay. Von Baumbach reported, "The North Base resembles the Bay of Cattaro. It is seven nautical miles long and very winding. The surrounding cliffs and rocky islands which rise to about 250 to 300 feet obstruct any and every view into the inner regions of the bay, both from the sea as well as from the Finnish border which is some fifteen miles away. The base also offers considerable protection against storms. There are a limited number of potential berths available for warships up to the size of the pocket-battleships. The bay is considerably more suitable than the Teribierka Bay and is far and away the most suitable right up to the area of Cape Svatov Noss at the approaches to the White Sea."

On Friday 17 November 1939, the escalation in the U-boat war was intensified by orders that merchant shipping, if clearly identifiable as enemy shipping, could be immediately attacked. From this day, unrestricted U-boat warfare commenced against British and French commercial shipping. Eleven weeks had passed since the outbreak of war, and already a situation had arisen similar to that in World War I, which at that time only arose after two and a half years of fighting.

On the same day, the *Deutschland*, lying at anchor in Kiel harbor, was given the classification "heavy cruiser" and renamed the *Lützow* so that — according to Hitler — the possible loss of a ship with the name *"Deutschland"* would not have any psychological effect. In addition, there was the desire to cover up the sale to the Soviet Union, arranged for April 1940, of the cruiser L *(Lützow)*, still under construction.

On Sunday 19 November 1939, the *Admiral Graf Spee* returned once again to Atlantic waters after a foray into the Indian Ocean between Durban and South Madagascar.

On Monday 20 November 1939, the first mine-laying operations by seaplane were carried out. During this operation, a total of seven magnetic mines were dropped without incident off the harbor approaches at Harwich, King's Channel and the Thames estuary. During the following night, an additional ten mines were to be dropped and twenty-four on 22 November. These new German mining operations were directed against shipping lanes on the east coast of England where an annual total of some fifty million tons of goods were transported; and they were accorded the highest priority.

On Tuesday 21 November 1939, the battleships *Gneisenau* (Capt. Netzbandt) and *Scharnhorst* (Capt. Hoffmann) put to sea under the command of Adm. Marschall in the direction of the area between Iceland and the Faroes, from which position they would attack units of the Northern Patrol. At the same time, there was to be a foray into the Atlantic in order to relieve the *Admiral Graf Spee*, which was operating in those waters.

On the same day, the newest British light cruiser *Belfast* hit a mine in the Firth of Forth and was heavily damaged.

On Wednesday 22 November 1939 between 9:00 and 10:00 P.M., an He 115 belonging to 3 Squadron of 106 Coastal Wing was sighted in the area around Shoeburyness. It dropped by parachute an object, which resembled a sailor's kitbag, into the Thames estuary where a number of merchant ships

were at anchor. In this area at low tide, large areas of mud flats are revealed, so that during the early afternoon of 23 November 1939, two mines were found in the mud flats. A special unit of the Royal Navy (HMS *Vernon*) was immediately informed. Lt. Comdr. Ouvry, together with Chief Petty Officer Baldwin, examined one of the mines while Lt. Comdr. Lewis and Able Seaman Vearncombe waited at a safe distance. By prearrangement, Ouvry advised Lewis by means of signals of each operation undertaken so that if anything happened to him, the knowledge gained would be available when it came to dismantling the second mine. That same evening Ouvry and his team were able to report to the Admiralty that the mine had been recovered intact and was on its way to Portsmouth for detailed examination.

Toward evening on Thursday 23 November 1939, the British armed merchant cruiser *Rawalpindi* (Capt. Kennedy), patrolling between Iceland and the Faroes, sighted an enemy warship bearing down upon them at high speed. The merchant cruiser suspected that it was the pocket-battleship *Deutschland* returning from an Atlantic patrol and issued an appropriate report. Shortly afterwards in the evening twilight, the battlecruiser *Scharnhorst* met up with the *Rawalpindi*. This merchant cruiser, which formed a part of the Northern Patrol, was a converted passenger ship armed with four old six-inch (15.2 cm) guns; but Capt. Kennedy nevertheless accepted the hopeless challenge. The *Scharnhorst* sustained one hit and then, with her 28-cm guns, swiftly put its opponent out of action. The *Rawalpindi* was already ablaze when the *Gneisenau*'s guns opened fire on the merchant

cruiser. Shortly after dark, the *Rawalpindi* went down with the captain and 270 of the crew. For almost two hours the *Scharnhorst* and *Gneisenau* searched for survivors, the only time that German capital ships took such a risk during World War II. Out of the thirty-eight survivors, twenty-seven were taken prisoner by the Germans. A further eleven survivors were picked up by a British ship after thirty-six hours.

Even while the German battlecruisers were picking up survivors, the British cruiser *Newcastle* came into the vicinity. Because of the darkness and heavy rain squalls, the cruiser could not maintain contact with the German battlecruisers, which set off eastward at full steam. The German vessels were certainly sighted by a number of British patrol vessels but were not identified, and they reached Wilhelmshaven without incident. The British were unaware that the foray of the two battlecruisers took place thanks to the German radio interception service that had been successful in the most important task of all—breaking the British naval code.

On Friday 24 November 1939, a team of scientists began examining the mines that had been recovered two days earlier. A curved aluminum disk in a rubber partition was first removed from the body of the mine. Upon finding this, the scientists thought they were dealing with an acoustic device that would have been activated by sound. But a scale bearing the word "GAUSS" had been fitted into the aluminum dome. "GAUSS" is the unit in the electromagnetic measuring system. The mine, therefore, was magnetic. Now that this secret had been discovered, a new system of minesweeping had to be developed.

On Saturday 25 November 1939, Hitler ordered that a concentrated attempt be undertaken to cut off England from the outside world by means of the U-boat arm.

On Monday 27 November 1939, a number of experiments were conducted with the cruiser *Manchester* to counteract German magnetic mines. The experiments showed that ships could be demagnetised by girdling them with an electric cable that had a powerful current passed through it.

On Tuesday 28 November 1939, the *Admiral Graf Spee* had its outline changed. A gun turret with two 28-cm tubes made of wood and sail canvas was surmounted on the fo'c's'le. A second funnel, also made of wood and sail canvas, had already been fitted. Some of the ship's crew were put to work painting the entire ship dark green. This camouflage color and the additional construction gave the "new" German cruiser the appearance of the battlecruiser *Renown*. The ship's stern now bore the name *Admiral Scheer* on one side and *Deutschland* on the other.

On Thursday 30 November 1939, the Soviet Union attacked Finland without any prior declaration of war. The Soviet Baltic fleet attacked the capital Helsinki.

Above all, Stalin's intentions were to block off the Gulf of Finland from both coasts to prevent enemy warships and supply vessels penetrating the Gulf. This would also have the effect of better protecting road access to Leningrad. The Finnish border was to be pushed far enough back to put Leningrad beyond the range of heavy artillery. The border in the far north near Petsamo (now "Pechenga" in the USSR) was to be redrawn because, from the Soviet point of view, "it runs unfavorably and unnaturally at that point."

Several hours later, Soviet warships and supply vessels, supported by the Soviet air force and coastal batteries, set land forces ashore on the Finnish islands. The largest Finnish units, the warships *Väinämäinen* and *Ilmarinen*, lying in the ice under white camouflage, were used successfully as flak batteries. They shot down a number of Soviet bombers.

On the same day, the British Admiralty undertook the first preparatory measures for the implementation of a giant minefield between Scotland and Ireland to cause German submarines difficulty in going around the British Isles from the north.

At the end of November 1939, the British blockade was intensified. All merchandise of German origin carried on neutral ships was regarded by Great Britain and France as contraband and confiscated without any regard to ownership.

The Soviet attack on Finland gave Churchill, using supplies for Finland as a pretext, a welcome chance to threaten the port of Narvik, so important for Germany, Churchill stated, "I sympathised ardently with the Finns and supported all proposals for their aid; and I welcome this new and favorable breeze as a means of achieving the major strategic advantage of cutting off the vital iron ore supplies of Germany."

If Narvik were to become an Allied base for supplying Finland, there would then be a possibility of stopping German ships loading Swedish ore and transporting it without risk along the coast of Norway to Germany.

In November 1939 in the Atlantic and North Sea, German U-boats sank twenty-eight merchantmen totalling 74,623 gross tons. German losses amounted to one U-boat. Although the amount in fact was equal only to one-half of the tonnage sunk in October, there was also the loss through mines of twenty-seven ships totalling 120,958 gross tons.

On Friday 1 December 1939, Great Britain introduced the Navicert [navigation certificate] System by which a transit certificate for goods was issued to neutral ships by an Allied representative in the port of shipment after the representative had assured himself that no contraband was loaded on board.

On the same day, the Germans declared the shallow waters off the coasts of Great Britain "an area of first warning of mines." In this area, German U-boats were to torpedo without warning all ships with the exception of neutral vessels.

On 1 December 1939, the meteorological observation ship *Sachsenwald* and the *Cordillera*, used for accommodation and crews' quarters, had anchored at the North Base in Zapadnaya-Litsa Bay. They were then joined by the tanker *Jan Wellem*, giving the base a significant provisioning capacity.

Upon the outbreak of the Soviet-Finnish Winter War, the Soviet Union requested a concession on the part of the German Navy. The German embassy in Moscow was informed that the Red Fleet was planning a submarine blockade of Finland in the Gulf of Bothnia. Ambassador von der Schulenburg directed an enquiry to the C-in-C of the Naval High Command as to whether German shipping proceeding toward north Sweden could carry fuel and provisions for Soviet submarines and discreetly hand these over at sea. The ambassador personally recommended that the Soviet request be fulfilled.

As Molotov promised that any supplies made available to Soviet submarines by Germany would be repaid in kind, "where the Germans might wish it," the possibility of opening a second base in the Far East arose. The German naval attaché von

Daily Mail

FOR KING AND EMPIRE

NO. 13,602   TUESDAY, NOVEMBER 28, 1939   ONE PENNY

RAWALPINDI WAS SUNK BY THE DEUTSCHLAND

40-Minute Battle, Down with Colours Flying

THE Rawalpindi, it was revealed by the Admiralty last night, was sunk by the German "pocket battleship" Deutschland and another warship, believed to be the cruiser Emden, in the first sea battle of the war. She went down, ablaze from end to end but with Colours flying, after every gun had been put out of action.

On the British side the action was fought by a crew of reservists and pensioners. Not a man on board was drawn from the active list of the Royal Navy.

Here is the story related by the handful of survivors as told in the statement issued by the Admiralty:

"The armed merchant-cruiser Rawalpindi, which was manned by merchant seamen, reservists, and pensioners of the Royal Navy, and men of the Royal Naval Reserve and Royal Naval Volunteer Reserve, was forming part of the Northern Patrol by which the contraband control of German trade is enforced.

"This duty is particularly arduous on account of the long dark nights in severe cold, and required for its

Navy Code Will Start Blockade

Neutrals Told To-day

By Daily Mail Reporter

THE British Navy awaits the code signal from the

Guns that Sank Rawalpindi

THREE 11in. guns in the "pocket" battleship's forward turret go into action during manoeuvres. Inset : Deutschland's crew line her deck—a peacetime picture. The "Pocket Raider" special diagram in BACK Page.

NAZI TO R.A.F.: 'I SALUTE YOU'

Finland Makes Offer

From RALPH HEWINS, "Daily Mail" Special Correspondent

HELSINKI, Tuesday Morning.

FINLAND is ready to withdraw her troops from the Leningrad frontier if the Soviet forces are also moved back.

This is Helsinki's reply to Russia's demand for the Finnish withdrawal following Sunday's frontier incident.

The Soviet alleges that Finnish guns fired seven shells, killing four Russian soldiers.

The reply was handed to M. Molotov, Soviet Premier and Foreign Commissar, early this morning.

It suggests that a joint border commission should hold an inquiry into the incident.

The Finnish Government say that no shot was fired from the Finnish side of the frontier : but seven cannon shots were heard from the Soviet side.

Soviet Anger Mounts.—Page TWO.

LATEST NEWS

Here, too, the British press was groping in the dark: The armed merchant cruiser *Rawalpindi* had, in fact, been sunk by the battlecruiser *Scharnhorst*.

Baumbach was promised a base on the Bering Sea. German diplomatic circles in Japan objected for political reasons.

The degree to which Stalin was prepared to co-operate with Germany, despite his own difficulties brought about by war, was evidenced by Moscow when permission was given to provision the heavy cruiser *Admiral Hipper* in the North Base. German Naval High Command considered the risk to be too great and so waived the Soviet offer.

On Saturday 2 December 1939, the *Admiral Graf Spee* stopped the freighter *Doric Star* (10,000 gross tons) off the coast of Africa. On this occasion, a radio operator was successful in transmitting a mayday call giving his exact position. The last mayday from the *Doric Star*, transmitted at 12:45 P.M., was picked up by the small freighter *Port Chalmers* in the area of St. Helena. The British Admiralty thereby learned that the *Admiral Graf Spee* had returned to South Atlantic waters and immediately advised Allied naval units in this area.

The report also reached Com. Harwood at his Port Stanley base on the Falklands. Harwood was in command of the South American Division with two heavy cruisers, the *Exeter* and *Cumberland*. Of the two other cruisers under Harwood's command, the *Achilles* at this time was off Rio de Janeiro, and the *Ajax* was heading toward the River Plate.

On Sunday 3 December 1939, the Soviet Union commenced its blockade against Finland with two submarine squadrons patrolling off the south coast of Finland in the Gulf of Bothnia.

Also on 3 December 1939, the pocket-battleship *Admiral Graf Spee*, disguised as the *Admiral Scheer*, sank the British freighter *Tairoa* (7,983 gross tons). The radio operator was successful in sending off a mayday call reporting that the ship had been attacked by the German heavy cruiser *Admiral Scheer*.

During the afternoon, Com. Harwood became certain, once he had fixed the *Admiral Scheer*'s position with the help of the distress call and calculated her average speed, that the ship would very likely reach the Plate estuary by dawn on 13 December. Once there, it would commence operations against British merchant shipping. Com. Harwood thereupon issued the necessary orders to the units under his command and gave instructions for strict radio silence.

On Monday 4 December 1939, the most important battleship in the Royal Navy, the *Nelson*, flagship of Adm. Forbes, ran against a German mine near Loch Ewe and was so badly damaged that it had to spend several months in dock.

On Wednesday 6 December 1939, the last meeting took place between the *Admiral Graf Spee* and the supply ship *Altmark* for the purposes of taking on provisions and fuel. The 180 British seamen from the sunken merchantmen, held prisoner on board the *Admiral Graf Spee*, were then divided

47

The *Admiral Graf Spee*'s radio section

into two groups. Captains and chief engineers were to remain on board the pocket-battleship, while British petty officers and ratings were to be taken on board the *Altmark* with the other prisoners and transported to Germany. The *Altmark* then steamed off in a northerly direction.

On Thursday 7 December 1939, the *Admiral Graf Spee* stopped the freighter *Streonshalh* (3,895 gross tons). The radio operator did not manage to send a distress call. As the prize crew approached the steamer, the captain threw two sacks overboard. The German party was successful in fishing out one of the sacks, which contained a detailed plan showing Allied merchant shipping routes from the River Plate to Great Britain. The *Admiral Graf Spee* sank the freighter and Capt. Langsdorff immediately set course for the River Plate.

At the same time, the German destroyers *Hans Lody* and *Erich Giese* were carrying out mining operations off the east coast of England. On their return voyage they sighted two English J-class destroyers. The German destroyer each fired off a torpedo. The destroyer *Jersey* was hit and burst into flames, and the second destroyer laid a smoke screen around itself and the *Jersey*. This was the first exchange of fire between German and English destroyers.

On Sunday 10 December 1939, the British Admiralty issued orders that all warships were to be girdled with copper cable as a protective measure against magnetic mines. Cable was also provided for merchantmen. This process, known as "degaussing," required no structural alterations or complicated mechanisms. A number of ships additionally required supplementary electrical installations. As a provisional protection, copper cable could be wrapped around the ship's hull in a few days. The delay to shipping was reduced to an absolute minimum, although the weekly requirements of valuable copper cable amounted to approximately 2,500,000 yards, the entire British capacity. In addition, a technically trained staff was required to supervise the installation according to the exact requirements of each ship in each port. To reduce the enormous consumption of copper cable, a new simplified process of demagnetisation was developed, known as "wiping." This method required only a few hours. A heavy copper cable was laid alongside the ship and given a powerful electric charge from harbor installations. The process had to be repeated after a few months, however. "Wiping" was not suitable for larger ships, but it was a blessing for small coastal vessels navigating in the danger zones and meant a considerable easing of the pressure on the organisation dealing with "degaussing" by coiling.

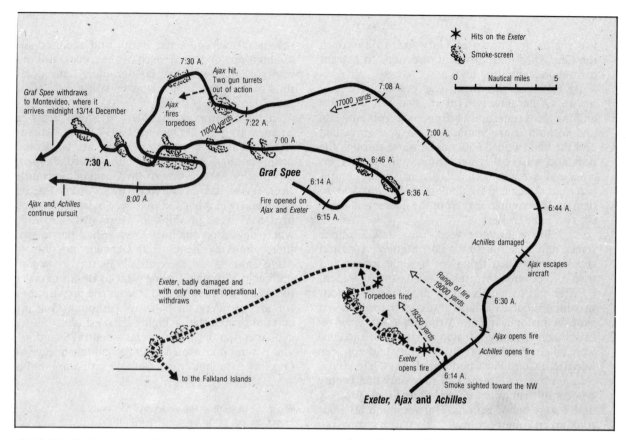

Hits on the *Exeter*

Smoke-screen

0   Nautical miles   5

7:30 A.

Ajax hit.
Two gun turrets
out of action

7:08 A.

17000 yards

Graf Spee withdraws
to Montevideo, where it
arrives midnight 13/14 December

Ajax
fires
torpedoes

7:22 A.

7:00 A.

11000 yards

7:00 A.

7:30 A.

6:46 A.

Graf Spee

6:14 A.

6:36 A.

8:00 A.

Fire opened on
Ajax and *Exeter*

6:44 A.

Ajax and *Achilles*
continue pursuit

6:15 A.

Achilles damaged

Ajax escapes
aircraft

Exeter, badly damaged and
with only one turret operational,
withdraws

Range of fire
19000 yards

6:30 A.

Torpedoes fired

19350 yards

Ajax opens fire

Achilles opens fire

Exeter
opens fire

6:14 A.
Smoke sighted toward the NW

to the Falkland Islands

Exeter, Ajax and Achilles

12/13/1939: The battle of the River Plate between the
Admiral Graf Spee and numerically stronger British forces

On Tuesday 12 December 1939 at 7:00 A.M., the British light cruisers *Ajax* and *Achilles* met up with the heavy cruiser *Exeter* at the approaches to the Plate shipping roads. Toward 12:00, Com. Harwood gave orders to his units to attack the German pocket-battleship as soon as it came into sight. At this moment, the *Admiral Graf Spee* was approaching the British squadron at a speed of approximately 15 knots.

On Wednesday 13 December 1939 at 5:52 A.M., the lookout on the *Admiral Graf Spee* reported two masts and then three on the port bow at a distance of approximately seventeen nautical miles. The *Graf Spee* steamed full ahead toward the unidentified ships. It was presumed that the long-awaited convoy was ahead of them. At about 6:00, the order was given, "Action stations!" The no. 1 gunnery officer, F. Rasenack, reported, "By the time we realised that our opponents were three warships, it was too late to change course." At 6:08, precisely twenty-four hours after Com. Harwood had gathered together his forces, the light cruiser *Ajax* reported smoke trails from the east; eight minutes later *Exeter* gave the signal, "I believe this is a pocket-battleship."

At 6:25, the *Graf Spee* altered course to 115 de-

grees in order to attack from the starboard. Convinced that his radar-directed armament would give him a decisive advantage, Capt. Langsdorff gave the command to make course toward the British cruisers. The pocket-battleship opened fire from a distance of eleven nautical miles, one turret being directed toward the *Exeter*, the other toward *Ajax*. Instead of keeping the assailants as long as possible at a safe distance under fire, the *Graf Spee* gave up its main advantage: the greater range of her guns. Harwood, who was on board the *Ajax*, used his three ships to attack the *Graf Spee* from three different directions in order to confuse the pocket-battleship's gunfire. Nevertheless, Langsdorff concentrated his fire exclusively on the *Exeter*. A hail of 28-cm shells put the B turret on the *Exeter* out of action. Shell splinters killed practically everybody on the bridge and destroyed communication with the ship's interior. But the *Exeter* had already damaged the *Admiral Graf Spee*, and *Ajax* and *Achilles* had scored hits with their six-inch guns (15.2 cm).

The *Admiral Graf Spee* was superior to each one of its assailants individually, and the ship's best chance of success was to destroy the British cruisers one after the other without risking serious damage to itself. The 28-cm (11 in.) guns had a range some 8,000 yards greater than the guns on the British cruisers, and none of these could have withstood the fire for very long. Their sole chance was the tactics chosen by Harwood: to approach the *Graf Spee* from different directions to prevent it from concentrating its fire.

By 6:50 A.M. the *Exeter* was practically out of action. Of her three gun turrets, two were unusable and the third (astern) was firing only from one gun and without instruments. The fire was spreading and she had shipped 650 tons of water through the bow and was now lying almost nine feet deeper. *Ajax* and *Achilles*, with only six-inch guns, continued their attack and finally forced the *Graf Spee* to turn its 28-cm guns away from the *Exeter* and on to the two light cruisers.

At 7:30 the *Exeter* ceased firing, laid a smoke screen and set a course for Port Stanley. *Ajax* and *Achilles* continued firing for a while longer and then also covered themselves with a smoke screen.

After approximately ninety minutes, the action, in which radar calculation was used for the first time in history, ended. Although *Graf Spee* received some twenty hits and thirty-six of the crew were killed, the ship's fighting ability had not been impaired. Com. Harwood stated, "At 07.38 hours, *Achilles* reported to me that they only had twenty percent of their ammunition left and that turrets X and Y were out of action." Harwood and his ships took up an easterly course: "I therefore resolved to break off the engagement and take it up again under the cover of darkness." From now on the *Graf Spee*, which had set course for the River Plate and was steaming at twenty-four knots, was shadowed by the cruisers *Achilles* and *Ajax* at a distance of approximately 14 nautical miles. Capt. Langsdorff decided to make course for the nearest neutral port—Montevideo, where the damage to his ship could be repaired and the wounded taken ashore. In the meantime, the cruiser *Cumberland* and other British warships had set course for the Plate estuary to reduce the chances of the *Graf Spee* breaking through.

At midnight, the *Graf Spee* put into the port of Montevideo. The damaged warship had ammunition sufficient to supply its six heavy guns only for another eighty minutes action. The *Graf Spee*'s balance sheet amounted to nine ships sunk with a total tonnage of 50,089.

The British now intended to keep the *Graf Spee* in Montevideo until such time as the aircraft carrier *Ark Royal* and the battlecruiser *Renown* could arrive from the north. Ingeniously, radio reports from the BBC in London spoke of strong British forces off the Plate estuary, causing Langsdorff to suspect that in addition to the *Achilles* and *Ajax*, the aircraft carrier *Ark Royal* and the battlecruiser *Renown* were waiting for him. In reality, the *Renown* and *Ark Royal* were still a thousand nautical miles from Montevideo. Capt. Langsdorff had in the meantime contacted Berlin and reported his assumptions on the strength of the forces, still out of sight, that were waiting for him. Langsdorff thus became the first victim in World War II of radio deception.

In the meantime, the *Bremen* finally reached Bremerhaven on 13 December 1939. Com. Ahrens stated, "The joy at having won the race twice, and having brought safely home our beloved *Bremen*, this precious possession of the German mercantile fleet, can be seen in everyone's eyes." Adm. Raeder particularly emphasised that the Soviet Union had held back foreign ships in Murmansk for three whole days after the liner *Bremen* had put to sea, thereby making the return to Germany possible.

On Thursday 14 December 1939, the Norwegian politician Vidkun Quisling went to Berlin in order to discuss with Hitler and Raeder the preparations for a coup d'état in Norway. Although Quisling certainly submitted a highly detailed plan, Hitler explained that he would prefer a neutral Scandinavia. Several hours later, after he had taken leave of Quisling (who had warned of a British amphibious

Right: 12/19/1939 in the Atlantic: The luxury liner *Columbus*, the largest ship ever to be scuttled

Below: 12/17/1939, the Plate estuary: After the explosion, the *Admiral Graf Spee* settles on the bottom in shallow water.

operation), Hitler gave the high command orders to prepare a study as a first step for an invasion of Norway. Coincidence claims that Churchill gave similar instructions to the British General Staff on the same day.

Around dawn on 17 December 1939, the demolition party on board the *Admiral Graf Spee*, moored in Montevideo harbor, was at work. The crew of the pocket-battleship was taken on board by the German freighter *Takoma* during the late afternoon. Only the commander and forty men remained on the *Admiral Graf Spee*. At 5:30 P.M., the pocket-battleship raised anchor and left the harbor for the River Plate. One boat after the other cast off, and finally the motor launch with the commander. Shortly afterward, a massive explosion shook the city. Rasenack stated, "I saw clearly how two 28-cm gun barrels from the rear turret were flung into the air like matchsticks. A column of smoke rose three hundred meters over the vessel and more explosions followed, one after the other." The ship sank only half-way in the shallow, nine-foot water. The crew was interned. The scuttling of the *Admiral Graf Spee* was to disrupt German commerce-raiding operations for several months. Churchill stated, "At any rate, the outcome of the action off the River Plate had an exhilarating effect and lightened the dreary and oppressive winter through which we were passing."

The British fleet now took up the hunt for the *Altmark*, the supply ship of the *Graf Spee*.

On Monday 18 December 1939, the Soviet battleship *Oktyabrskaya Revolyuciya* (Capt. Vdovicenko), which belonged to the Baltic Squadron, joined with five destroyers in the bombardment of the Finnish coastal batteries on Koivisto Island.

Newspaper reporters took innumerable photographs of the wrecked *Admiral Graf Spee* lying at the mouth of the Plate. Specialists in the Secret Service discovered on one of these photos a mysterious structure fitted over the bridge of the pocket-battleship. A radar expert was immediately despatched to Montevideo. After he had examined the antennae, he reported back to London that in his opinion the structure was radio direction-finding equipment for gunnery control. Similar equipment was not to be brought into service in the Royal Navy until sometime during the next two years.

On Tuesday 19 December 1939 at 3:30 P.M., the British destroyer *Hyperion* sighted a large passenger liner some two hundred nautical miles east of Norfolk, Virginia (USA). This was the German luxury liner *Columbus* (32,581 gross tons), one of the finest and fastest ships in the world. The crew of the *Columbus* was prepared for this moment: On the command of Capt. W. Dähne, "Sink the ship," they opened up the sea-cocks and poured petrol into the air shafts. The *Columbus*, the pride of the German passenger fleet, was set alight. And so ended the four months and five days of her wanderings on her voyage from New York back to her home country. The crew took to the lifeboats and scarcely ten minutes later the liner, wreathed in thick clouds of smoke, sank to the bottom of the sea. The US destroyer *Tuscaloosa* picked up the German seamen. The *Columbus* was the largest ship in maritime history to be scuttled by her own crew.

On the morning of 20 December 1939, the commander of the *Admiral Graf Spee*, Capt. Langsdorff, was found dead in his hotel room in Buenos Aires. In full uniform, stretched out on the German naval ensign, he had shot himself in the head.

On Thursday 28 December 1939, *U 30* (Lt. Comdr. Lemp) torpedoed the British battleship *Barham* off the Clyde estuary. The *Barham* had to spend some time in dock for repairs.

At the insistence of Adm. Raeder, Hitler decided on Saturday 30 December 1939 that the ships of those countries chartering or selling vessels to Great Britain would be attacked or even sunk by U-boats without warning.

On Sunday 31 December 1939, a German-Soviet economic conference lasting three hours took place in the Kremlin with Stalin in attendance. This was the first of three such conferences. In his report, Hitler's special envoy, Ambassador Ritter, commented subsequently, "The most significant item was the fact that Stalin used here for the first time the expression 'mutual assistance': He said that the Soviet government did not regard the trade agreement as an ordinary agreement, but as a contract for 'mutual assistance'. The Soviet Union was ready to support Germany by supplying raw materials and foodstuffs which could be sold in other quarters in exchange for valuable foreign currencies."

During the conference, the provisions for supplies of iron to Germany were discussed. With regard to warships, Stalin was particularly pleased that Hitler was prepared to sell him the modern heavy cruiser L (*Lützow*). Stalin also expressed his willingness to supply a part of Soviet stocks of metals and also to purchase metals from third-party countries on Germany's behalf.

In December 1939, fifty percent of all successful U-boat attacks were carried out at night on the surface, confirming the effectiveness of the new operational assault tactics dictated by Dönitz, which in addition rendered the Asdic apparatus ineffective, as it could only detect submerged submarines. With this new form of tactics, there was no longer any need to give each U-boat pack an operational commander and therefore, at the moment of attack, each U-boat commander had total operational freedom. The success of each undertaking now depended upon the skill and capability of the individual commander.

At the end of 1939, the commanders of German submarines operating in the vicinity of British naval and air bases received orders not to jeopardise the safety of their ships by stopping to pick up survivors.

In the first four months of the war, aircraft of Coastal Command reported fifty-seven sightings of German U-boats; and forty U-boats were attacked and eight damaged. The aircraft did not, however, succeed in sinking a single U-boat.

In December 1939, German U-boats operating in the Atlantic and North Sea sank 37 merchantmen totalling 100,413 gross tons. German losses amounted to one submarine. Losses caused by mines were almost as high as losses by U-boats. In December alone, 33 Allied ships totalling 82,712 tons were sunk by German mines. In comparison to the 470 magnetic mines employed, the Allied shipping losses were comparatively high. By the end of 1939, they had amounted to a total of 79 ships with a total tonnage of 162,697 gross tons.

1940

January–June

Thursday 11 January 1940
The *German High Command* issued the following communiqué:

The Luftwaffe continued reconnaissance operations over the English and Scottish east coasts and the Shetlands. Three British patrol boats were attacked off the Scottish coast, and an armed merchant cruiser, which opened fire on the German reconnaissance aircraft, was attacked and sunk.

The Altmark

Saturday 17 February 1940, Oslo
The *Associated Press* reported:

During the night, a British destroyer in Norwegian territorial waters forceably took possession of the German steamer *Altmark* and, according to British reports, freed three hundred to four hundred English seamen held prisoner on board.

Norwegian Statement
17 February 1940, Oslo
The *Foreign Ministry* stated:

Yesterday afternoon the German steamer *Altmark* entered Norwegian territorial waters escorted by a Norwegian torpedo boat. At 4:30 P.M., two British destroyers attempted to stop the *Altmark* by firing warning shots. The Norwegian torpedo boat protested, and the *Altmark* turned into the Jösingfjord. After a fresh protest by the Norwegian torpedo boat, the British units, now a cruiser and five destroyers, withdrew beyond the three-mile limit. Later on, a destroyer again entered Norwegian territorial waters close to the coast and turned on its searchlights. At 11:00 P.M., the British destroyer entered the fjord and boarded the *Altmark*. British prisoners held on board the *Altmark* were taken on board the British naval units. The Norwegian escort, which consisted only of two small torpedo boats, could do nothing but protest energetically.

Freed Seamen
17 February 1940, London
The *Reuters* News Agency reported:

Among the freed prisoners there were fifty-five officers and twenty seamen, including the captains of the British steamers *Huntsman* and *Tairoa*, both of which had been sunk by the *Graf Spee*.

German Report
17 February 1940, Berlin
The German *DNB* News Agency reported:

British naval units have been guilty of an unprecedented violation of Norwegian neutrality. They attempted, at two hundred yards from the shore, in Norwegian territorial waters, to go alongside the completely unarmed German merchantman *Altmark* and board it. After this unbelievable act of force that scorned the most elementary facets of international law, reports were received of another outrageous assault on the *Altmark*, which in its details represents an unparallelled act of piracy by the British and a further permanent stain on the British Navy's honor.

Rostock *Taken Prize by the French Navy*
Monday 19 February 1940, London
The *Reuters* News Agency reported:

The German freighter *Rostock* (2,542 gross tons), which was en route from Vigo, Spain, to Germany, was taken prize by the French Navy.

Soviet Fleet in Black Sea Maneuvers
Thursday 22 February 1940, Moscow
The *DNB* Agency reported:

We have heard that recently the Soviet fleet has been carrying out extensive maneuvers in the Black

Above: 2/17/1940, Jösingfjord, South Norway, the *Altmark* (Capt. Dau) shortly after liberation by the British destroyer *Cossack* (Capt. Vian)

Sea. All classes of vessel, of which almost two-thirds were new warships recently built in Soviet shipyards, have taken part in the maneuvers. In addition, the maneuvers included exercises by coastal artillery and naval aviation units.

British Blockade of Murmansk?

Friday 23 February 1940, Copenhagen
Berlinske Tidende reported:

The British fleet has commenced a blockade of Murmansk, as we hear, with an entire squadron of warships, including units that previously had been keeping Norwegian territorial waters and the area up to the Kolafjord under surveillance. This blockade is said not to be an intervention on behalf of Finland but is intended to be a means of watching out for German ships that fled to the northernmost ports of the USSR upon the outbreak of war and are now gradually attempting to return to Germany via Norwegian territorial waters. Additionally, the blockade will watch out for German ships apparently carrying war material to the Soviets via Murmansk.

The "Weser Exercise"

The Führer and Supreme Commander of the Armed Forces   Berlin, 3/1/1940

Most secret document

Directive for the "Weser Exercise"

1. The development of the situation in Scandinavia requires that all preparations be undertaken to occupy Denmark and Norway (Plan Weserübung) with units of the armed forces. By these means, British inroads into Scandinavia and the Baltic should be obviated, our iron ore supplies in Sweden secured, and the base for operations by the navy and Luftwaffe against Great Britain extended.

It is incumbent upon the navy and Luftwaffe to secure the undertaking, insofar as possible, against attacks by British naval and air units. The forces to be used for the Weser Exercise shall be kept as numerically weak as possible, having regard to our military and political strength vis-à-vis the Nordic states. The weakness in numbers of our forces must be compensated by resolute action and the element of surprise. Basically, we must try insofar as possible to give the undertaking the aspect of a peaceful occupation, the objective of which is the armed protection of the neutrality of the Nordic states. The corresponding demands will be made to the individual governments upon the commencement of the occupation. Should it be necessary, demonstration of naval and air power will give the required emphasis.

2. The naval units and units engaged by the Luftwaffe shall remain under the command of the respective naval or Luftwaffe commander. They are to be employed in close cooperation with the officer commanding Group XXI. This ruling shall not be applicable to the Luftwaffe 1 Reconnaissance Squadron (F) and 2 battalion motorised flak units which, until the successful occupation of Denmark, are to be placed under the direct control of Group XXI.

(signed) Adolf Hitler

Below: 4/3/1940, Operation Weserübung, German merchantmen of the "export squadron" bound for Norway

W. Churchill to the First Sea Lord
Thursday 14 March 1940

Now that we are not allowed to interfere with the Norwegian Corridor, would it not be possible to have one or two merchant ships of sufficient speed specially strengthened in the bow and, if possible, equipped with a ram? These vessels would carry merchandise and travel up the leads looking for German ore ships or any other German merchant vessels, and then ram them by accident.

Sunday 17 March 1940
The *German High Command* issued the following communiqué:

Because of the results of recent reconnaissance operations by the Luftwaffe, large bomber formations attacked units of the British Navy lying in Scapa Flow during the evening of 16 March.

During the attack, three battleships and a cruiser received direct hits by bombs and were heavily damaged. Three more warships were probably damaged.

W. Churchill to the First Sea Lord
Monday 25 March 1940

I see charges of looting preferred against our men in the German press. I should not think it necessary to mention this but for the fact that it has come to my notice that the *Altmark* captain's watch, chronometer, and Iron Cross were stolen and are now in the hands of some of the sailors as souvenirs. Anything of this kind must be stopped with the utmost strictness. No souvenir of any value can be preserved without being reported and obtaining permission. Personal property of enemies may be confiscated by the State but never by individuals.

Cessation of Coastal Shipping
Monday 8 April 1940, Bergen
The *United Press Agency* reported:
  The entire Norwegian coastal shipping has been terminated because of the mining of Norwegian waters. Ships en route to Bergen were detained in Aalesund, Molde and Kristiansand.

Attempted Landing in Norway?

8 April 1940, Oslo
The *Norwegian Telegram Office* reported:
  The German troopship *Rio de Janeiro* (9,000 tons) carrying infantrymen was today torpedoed by a British submarine off Lillesand in south Norway. Norwegian vessels saved 130 men; ten bodies were washed ashore; and several hundred men are still floating in the water. The survivors said that Stettin was the port of embarkation, although they had no idea where they were being taken. It is feared in Norway that the *Rio de Janeiro* belongs to a larger German unit that will attempt a landing during the next few hours in south Norway, in association with the advance of the German fleet through Danish waters.

Violation of Neutrality
8 April 1940, Oslo
The *Norwegian Telegram Office* reported:
  Sea traffic between Trondheim and Bodö has been terminated. The fast steamer travelling northward has had to remain in Bodö pending further orders, and another fast steamer coming from the north was stopped. Three large freighters coming from the south were stopped by British warships and had to drop anchor in the outer harbor of Bodö. British naval patrols are passing so close to the coast that they can be seen from the landing stage in Bodö. A British cruiser in the Vestfjord has stopped three steamers and prohibited them from continuing their voyage to Bodö and in one case even fired off a warning shot.

British Sabotage Attempt on the Danube?
8 April 1940, Berlin
The *DNB* Agency reported:
  The Foreign Office is in possession of documents relating to a large-scale sabotage attempt on the Danube by the British Secret Service . . . . Orders and directives found show the intention to undertake landing operations and carry out sabotage operations on this basis if dynamiting is disrupted by border patrols or regular army patrols of one of the Southeast European countries. Certain points on the banks of the Danube and the Iron Gate are to be blown up and barges sunk in the waterways.

Anglo-French Minefields
8 April 1940, London
The *Reuters* News Agency reported:
  Minelaying operations on the Norwegian coast were successfully carried out early today. French and British warships took part in the operation.

Tuesday 9 April 1940
The *German High Command* issued the following communiqué:
  (Special report) In order to counteract current British attacks on the neutrality of Denmark and Norway, the German armed forces have taken over armed protection of these countries.

Germans March into Denmark

9 April 1940, London
The *Reuters* News Agency reported:
  According to reports emanating from Copenhagen, German troops in Schleswig have today crossed the Danish frontier.

Surprise German Operations
9 April 1940, Stockholm
The *United Press Agency* reported:
  We have now heard that the occupation by German troops of Narvik, Bergen and Stavanger was made possible by German naval personnel, disguised as ordinary sailors, entering these ports on German iron ore freighters and suddenly landing on the quaysides. It is reported that in many places they then threw hand grenades at the port officials and personnel while clambering down onto the piers from the German ships.

Naval Engagement near Narvik

Wednesday 10 April 1940
The *British Admiralty* issued the following communiqué:
  At dawn today, the destroyer *Hunter* was sunk during the fighting around Narvik. The destroyer *Hardy* ran aground.

W. Churchill to Admiral Pound
10 April 1940, London
  The Germans have succeeded in occupying all

the ports on the Norwegian coast, including Narvik, and large-scale operations will be required to turn them out of any of them. Norwegian neutrality and our respect for it have made it impossible to prevent this ruthless coup . . . . We must seal up Bergen with a watchful minefield and concentrate on Narvik, for which long and severe fighting will be required. . . . We must also take our advantages in the Faroes.

Sea Battle Off the Coast of Norway

Thursday 11 April 1940, London
Radio Stockholm reported:

Since last night the largest sea battle of all time has been taking place in a sector of approximately 1,100 nautical miles in a north-south direction in which, on the Allied side, 150 warships and 800

4/10/1940, Narvik, German destroyers land mountain troops in the blazing harbor.

airplanes are taking part, and on the German side, 100 warships and 1,000 airplanes are taking part.

German Crews on Norwegian Warships
Saturday 13 April 1940, Berlin
The *DNB* Agency reported:

The German Navy has taken over units of the Norwegian Navy found in the occupied Norwegian ports and put them in commission with German crews.

Seven German Destroyers Sunk
Sunday 14 April 1940
The *Admiralty* issued the following communiqué:

Since the attack that the Second Destroyer Flotilla undertook on Wednesday against the German destroyers in Narvik, the enemy has been blocked up in the Fjord of Narvik by reinforcements. Yesterday at midday, the battleship *Warspite* and a strong destroyer squadron accompanied by minesweepers and other units entered the fjord in order

to attack the German destroyers, some of which had sought refuge in the harbor and were already damaged. The operation also served as a means of attacking the coastal batteries on the banks of the fjord.

Landing of British Troops in Norway
Monday 15 April 1940
The *Admiralty* and *War Office* issued the following joint communiqué:
British forces have landed at various points in Norway.

A Week Without Losses

Tuesday 16 April 1940
The *Admiralty* issued the following communiqué:
The British merchant fleet has, for the first time since the outbreak of war, sustained no losses during the week ending midnight on Sunday last.

British Occupation of the Faroes
16 April 1940, London
The *Reuters* News Agency reported:
Undersecretary Butler at the Foreign Office informed Parliament that British troops had landed on the Faroes. On 10 April, the governor of the Faroes replied to a British government note, stating that he was prepared to grant advantages to the British government, under present conditions, to prevent German troops gaining a foothold on the Faroe Islands. With regard to Greenland, no one was yet in a position to make a statement.

Thursday 18 April 1940
The *German High Command* issued the following communiqué:
In the Narvik area, weak British forces attempted on 17 April for the first time to land in Herjangsfjord in the vicinity of Elvegaardsmoen. German troops thwarted the attempt.

Surveillance on Danube Shipping
18 April 1940, Belgrade
The French *Havas* News Agency reported:
The permanent International Danube Commission that met in Belgrade yesterday accepted a resolution relating to the security of shipping and covering the following four points:
1. Ships that have been converted into armed vessels may not use the Danube.
2. The crews of all ships in all harbors shall be subjected to passport control.
3. Ships carrying weapons, cement, explosives or other material with a destructive effect may not pass the Iron Gate unless they have special permission from the bordering countries.

Above: 4/17/1940, Narvik area, Allied Expeditionary Corps before landing in Norway; in the background a covering aircraft

Right: April 1940, German destroyers off the Norwegian coast

4. The present customs control shall be replaced by a much stronger control.

Losses by the British Merchant Fleet
18 April 1940, London
The *Minister of Shipping* announced:
Since the outbreak of war until 10 April 1940, a total of eighty-one British merchant vessels, including seventeen tankers, have been sunk by German U-boats.

The British in Namsos

Friday 19 April 1940, Stockholm
The *Reuters* News Agency reported:
In the area of Trondheim, the Germans have been making feverish preparations to counter the expected attack by British and Norwegian forces, after British units landed at Namsos, eighty miles north of Trondheim. In the vicinity of Steinkjer, some twenty miles south of Namsos, there is a concentration of Norwegian troops. German reinforcements have been flown in by large transport aircraft. All the bridges around Trondheim are reportedly mined.

Naval Policy of the USA
19 April 1940, Washington
The *United Press Agency* reported:
The Senate has approved expenditure for the

construction of two 45,000-ton battleships, an aircraft carrier, two cruisers, eight destroyers and six submarines.

French Troops Landed
Saturday 20 April 1940, London
The *Havas* Agency reported:

British and French units of the Expeditionary Corps have landed in Norway without loss.

W. Churchill to Sir James Lithgow and Controller
Tuesday 30 April 1940, London

These figures of our shipping gains from the German aggression against Norway and Denmark amount roughly to 750 ships, aggregating 3,000,000 tons. The effect of this upon our shipping and shipbuilding position requires to be considered.

Swiss Radio Beromünster

30 April 1940

It is three weeks ago today since German troops marched into Denmark and German warships sailed into Norway's principal ports to occupy those Scandinavian kingdoms. This sudden expansion of the war, which broke out eight months ago between the leading powers and which has claimed these two happy, neutral countries as victims, now dominates everything and, unless we are mistaken, will dominate everything for a long time. This expedition developed from a Blitzkrieg into a bitter mountain war fought over harsh terrain and under harsh weather conditions. The Norwegian resistance, at first tentative and then resolute, suffered from the fact that above all mobilisation came too late, that the army was insufficient in numbers and fought in groups spread over the entire country. In addition, the training of the Norwegian Army was not always sufficient to meet the demands of modern warfare; their armament was not equal to an enemy equipped with automatic weapons, Panzer formations and bombers. In this connection, we remember a passage from the Pope's Christmas message, spoken as it was from the heart to every citizen of a small country: "The will to live of one people," said Pious XII, "may never by synonymous with the death sentence of another people."

War in the West!

Friday 10 May 1940
The *German High Command* issued the following communiqué:

At 5:30 this morning, German troops crossed the Dutch, Luxembourg and Belgian frontiers. Enemy resistance on the frontiers is everywhere being overcome by sharp action, frequently in the closest cooperation with the Luftwaffe.

British Troops Land in Iceland
10 May 1940, London
The *British Foreign Office* stated:

Since the German occupation of Denmark, we have had to reckon with an attack upon Iceland. It is clear that the Icelandic government with its small armed forces is not in a position to resist a German attack. The British government has therefore resolved to forestall a possible German coup and has today landed British troops on Iceland.

Evacuation of Dunkirk

Thursday 30 May 1940
The *British Ministry of Information* made the following announcement:

British army units not directly involved in the fighting in northern France have been evacuated with the support of the Royal Navy. These operations are being continued successfully, and a number of troopships have already arrived in England. At present, fighting is raging in the coastal areas.

Sunday 2 June 1940, London
The *Reuters* News Agency reported:
An eyewitness report on the evacuation of British and French troops from Dunkirk states:

"I spent Thursday in a naval base on the south coast of England where the ships entrusted with the evacuation were entering port and putting out to sea again. For several days and nights there was intense activity. Transports, destroyers and fishing smacks were overloaded with soldiers, almost to the point of sinking. Most of the ships had been the targets of attacks by enemy aircraft. In order to get on board, thousands of men had had to wade through the water, often shoulder-deep. Even while they were clambering aboard, they were attacked by German bombers with machine-gun fire. A Scottish regiment, whose men were utterly exhausted, nevertheless continued firing at enemy aircraft with their rifles. I got on board a destroyer that had just arrived. The ship had been hit twelve times by bombs, and its captain had been killed. Despite all that, it managed to get the troops back to England safely."

Evacuation across the Channel Completed

4 June 1940, Paris
The *Havas* Agency reported:
The French Adm. Abrial was the last person to leave Dunkirk this morning at 7:00.

Sunday 9 June 1940
The *German High Command* issued the following communiqué:
German naval units, including the battlecruisers *Gneisenau* and *Scharnhorst*, under the command of Adm. Marschall have gone to the support of the German forces fighting around Narvik.

Monday 10 June 1940
The *German High Command* issued the following communiqué:
(Special report) The German ensign is at last flying over Narvik itself. Norwegian forces ceased hostilities in the night of 9/10 June. Surrender terms are currently being negotiated.

Sinking of a British Cruiser

Saturday 15 June 1940
The *Admiralty* issued the following communiqué:
The cruiser *Calypso* (4,180 tons) has been sunk by an Italian submarine in the Mediterranean. One officer and thirty-eight seamen are missing and are feared to have lost their lives. The cruiser *Calypso*, with a complement of over four hundred, was the first British warship to be sunk by the Italians.

Sunday 23 June 1940
The *German High Command* issued the following communiqué:
(Special report) On 22 June at 6:50 P.M., German summer time, the Franco-German armistice was signed in the forest of Compiègne . . . . For the time being, details of the armistice cannot be revealed.

Dismissal of General de Gaulle

23 June 1940, Bordeaux
The *Havas* Agency reported:
General de Gaulle, because of a speech that he made yesterday via the BBC in London, has been dismissed by the Cabinet upon the proposal of Gen. Weygand. Further measures against de Gaulle are not hereby excluded.

Strategy and Tactics

JANUARY TO JUNE 1940

At the beginning of 1940, the whole of central and western Europe lay under a thick blanket of snow; even major rivers were frozen over and ports in the Gulf of Bothnia such as Malmö and Göteborg were iced up. Swedish iron ore, which was of considerable strategic importance for Germany, now had to be shipped via the ice-free Norwegian port of Narvik. From this point southward, the ore was shipped on German vessels under the protection of Norwegian territorial waters as far as the Skagerrak. From there until its final destination in German ports, the ore was under the protection of German naval units. Already by the autumn of 1939, the Allies were seriously considering mining the sea route along the Norwegian coast in order to prevent these supplies getting through.

5/28/1940, Dunkirk, thick smoke clouds, visible for miles, mark the retreat of British troops from the continent of Europe.

On Saturday 27 January 1940, Hitler gave orders to make preparations for the invasion of Norway in case of emergency. He had conceived the plan to occupy Norway primarily on the basis of military considerations, but the opportunity of securing iron ore shipments by establishing naval bases also played an important role.

Coincidence has it that at the same time, the Allied Supreme War Council met in Paris. The conference resolved to make up an expeditionary corps as aid for Finland. To avoid any confrontation with the Soviet Union, the members of this corps were to be declared volunteers. At the same time, this would serve as a pretext for the occupation of Narvik. Accordingly, only a part of the corps would be sent on to Finland.

On Monday 29 January 1940, a second German-Soviet conference took place in the Kremlin in the presence of Stalin, Molotov and Mikoyan. Discussions were held on the gunnery and equipment in the turrets to be fitted to those warships which Germany was to supply the Soviet Union. Stalin, who showed great expertise and interest, urged that a larger caliber gun be fitted. At this meeting, negotiations were also conducted on the sale of the cruiser L (*Lützow*). As it was hardly likely that the USSR would be buying warships from Germany in order to use them against Germany, Moscow was assumed to be preparing for a war against Great Britain.

During the winter of 1939/40, on the convoy route across the North Atlantic alone there was an unprotected area of almost 1,700 nautical miles through which merchantmen had to sail without a protective escort. Even larger gaps existed on other important sea routes.

In January 1940, Great Britain speeded up the demagnetisation, or "degaussing," of ships as a protection against the new German magnetic mines. Despite these measures, twenty-one ships aggregating 77,116 gross tons were lost during this month to German mines.

During the same month, the commander of the German submarine arm prepared a book of shortened signals with a view to diminishing as far as possible the submarines' risk of being located. This system allowed U-boat commanders to send messages to the C-in-C submarines from their operating areas, using reduced signals with few digits that, in the light of previous experience, would scarcely give the enemy any chance of locating the U-boats.

Also, in January 1940, the Soviet minelayers *Murman* and *Puskin* laid a minefield comprising two hundred mines between Vardö and the Rybachi peninsula to secure the occupied Finnish territory around Petsamo and to ward off anticipated Allied operations.

In January 1940, German U-boats operating in the Atlantic and the North Sea sank fifty-eight merchantmen totalling 178,884 gross tons. Ger-

Above: Lt. Gen. Eduard Dietl, the defender of Narvik, after the successful conclusion of hostilities in Norway

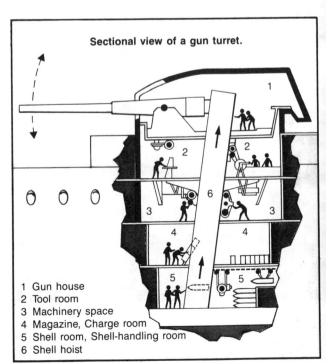

Sectional view of a gun turret.

1 Gun house
2 Tool room
3 Machinery space
4 Magazine, Charge room
5 Shell room, Shell-handling room
6 Shell hoist

mans lost one submarine.

On Tuesday 6 February 1940, the German naval attaché in Moscow, von Baumbach, reported that the Soviet Union had granted the German auxiliary cruiser, ship no. 45 *Komet*, free passage through the planned north-east passage in the Arctic Ocean. This sea route — not accessible to the Royal Navy — represented the shortest route to the Pacific.

On Saturday 10 February 1940, Germany and the USSR signed an economic agreement in the Kremlin. Stalin undertook to supply in the first twelve months, among other things, 1,000,000 tons of feedingstuffs as well as 900,000 tons of oil including the full production from the Polish oil-producing area of Drohobycz. To make it easier for the German armaments industry to import strategically important raw materials from the Near and Far East and to circumvent the Allied blockade, the Soviets reduced by half their freight costs of the Trans-Siberian Railway.

On Sunday 11 February 1940, ten days after the first offensive, a renewed offensive on the Karelian Isthmus was launched by the Soviet 7th and 13th armies. Owing to icing up in the Gulf of Finland, the Red fleet was unable to offer any support. After the breakthrough in the Summa area, the Finnish army was forced to pull its southern flank back to a position east of Vyborg.

On the same day in Moscow, the purchase contract for the German heavy cruiser L (for which the name *Lützow* had been provided) was concluded.

Armoring of a heavy cruiser

On Monday 12 February 1940, the British minesweeper *Cleaner* sank the German submarine *U 33* (Lt. Comdr. von Dresky) in the Clyde estuary while the U-boat was trying to lay mines. During rescue of the crew, three wheels of the top-secret Enigma (navy) message decoding machine were also salvaged.

On Thursday 15 February 1940, Germany declared that all British merchant ships would be treated exactly the same as warships.

On Friday 16 February 1940, the British destroyer *Cossack* (Capt. Vian) sighted the tanker *Altmark* (Capt. Dau) off the Norwegian coast south of Bergen. This former supply ship to the pocket-battleship *Admiral Graf Spee*, en route to Germany with a number of British prisoners on board, had been hunted for some time. The *Altmark* succeeded with the assistance of two Norwegian torpedo boats in running into the Jösingfjord, where it dropped anchor. The British destroyer *Cossack* followed, only to be informed by the Norwegians that the tanker had already been searched, was unarmed, and therefore entitled to proceed in neutral waters.

The *Cossack* thereupon withdrew and requested further instructions from the Admiralty. Churchill gave orders to Capt. Vian to enter Norwegian waters again, board the *Altmark* and free the prisoners.

During the night, the *Cossack* again appeared in Jösingfjord, and Vian demanded that the Norwegians return the *Altmark* to Bergen where it would be subjected to a further, joint examination. The Norwegians refused. Suddenly the *Cossack* made toward the *Altmark*. The tanker attempted to force the *Cossack* aground with its stern and in so doing

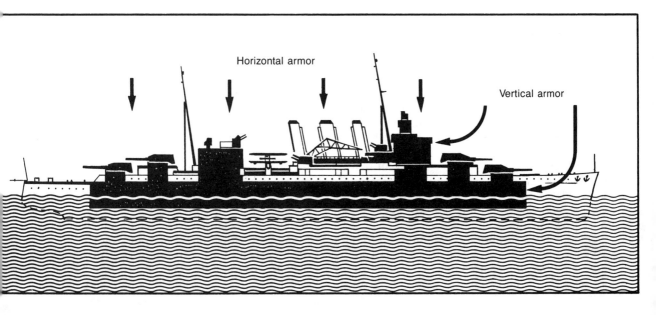

Horizontal armor

Vertical armor

ran itself aground. The *Cossack* went alongside, and a British boarding party went aboard the *Altmark*. After a short struggle, in which seven German seamen were killed and five wounded, 303 prisoners held on board were freed with the cry, "The Navy's here." According to British sources, two automatic antiaircraft guns and four machine guns were also found on board the *Altmark*. The Norwegians had, in fact, not searched the *Altmark* at all.

Toward midnight, the *Cossack* steamed out of the fjord with the freed seamen on board. This operation was received in Great Britain with the same enthusiasm as the destruction of the *Admiral Graf Spee* in December 1939. Churchill wrote, "Both these events strengthened my hand and the prestige of the Admiralty." In Germany, Italy and the Soviet Union, on the other hand, the incident was described as an act of British piracy. Adm. Raeder stated, "Through this event, the entire Norwegian problem takes on an entirely different aspect, as it is now unequivocally clear that the Norwegian government was not in a position to maintain its own neutrality."

On Sunday 18 February 1940, the Nordmark Operation commenced. The battlecruisers *Gneisenau* and *Scharnhorst* accompanied by the heavy cruiser *Hipper* and two destroyers went out to at-

tack convoy traffic between Britain and Scandinavia. After a successful operation, the undertaking was broken off in the Shetland-Norway area.

On Tuesday 20 February 1940, Hitler ordered Gen. von Falkenhorst, commander of the XXI Army Corps (Koblenz), who had taken part in the fighting in Finland in World War I, to proceed to Berlin. Falkenhorst stated, "Hitler referred to my experiences in Finland, told me to take a seat and tell him what I had done there. I had scarcely begun when he interrupted me and led me to a map-covered table. Hitler then said to me, 'I have a similar action in mind, the occupation of Norway. I am in possession of reports, according to which the British intend landing there, and I want to be there before them . . . . The occupation of Norway by Britain would be a strategic turning movement which would lead to the Baltic where we have neither troops nor coastal defences . . . . The enemy would then be in a position to march on Berlin and break the backbone of our two fronts.' Finally he said to me, 'I appoint you commander of this expedition.'" Falkenhorst was therewith put in charge of the staff preparing the Weser Exercise, which was to become the code name for the invasion of Norway. After he left the Reichskanzlei, Falkenhorst first bought himself a guidebook by way of a crash course on Norway.

During the first weeks of February 1940, German reconnaissance aircraft reported increasingly strong concentrations of British fishing vessels off the Dogger Bank. The German Navy recognised a chance to seize a few of these ships, thereby acquiring maps on British minefields. The operation was given the code name "Vikings" and was to be carried out by the 1 Destroyer Flotilla (Com. Bonte). Naval Group Command West was not informed that the Luftwaffe was planning an operation for the same day. For their part, X Air Corps knew nothing about a destroyer operation in the North Sea.

On the morning of 22 February 1940, six German destroyers made their way between the thick ice floes around Wilhelmshaven and set course for the Dogger Bank. Toward 6:00 P.M., eight Heinkel He 111s belonging to II Wing of 26 Bomber Group took off from Neumünster to carry out commerce raiding between the Thames estuary and the Firth of Forth. In the meantime, since the onset of darkness the destroyers were steering between the gaps in the German minefield. At around 7:30, the destroyers sighted an unidentified aircraft approaching from astern. The air raid alarm was given and the destroyer *Leberecht Maass*, leading the formation, fired off the recognition signal. The aircraft, however, made no answer and the destroyer's antiaircraft guns commenced firing. The airplane circled so low over one of the destroyers that despite the darkness the German crosses on the wings were clearly visible. The antiaircraft fire was discontinued. Suddenly, a number of bomb explosions were heard and the *Leberecht Maass* sent off the Morse signal, "I have been hit, need assistance." The ship had received a direct hit in the superstructure. Shortly after that, a mighty explosion tore the 2,232-ton ship apart, and it sank immediately. The other destroyers started to pick up survivors. During this, a second explosion lit up the darkness. The destroyer *Max Schulz* (2,232 tons) went down within minutes with its entire crew. As a torpedo had been sighted, the rescue operation had to be terminated. The crew of the destroyer *Erich Koellner* managed to save approximately sixty seamen from the *Leberecht Maass*.

Some members of the naval and air force investigation committee appointed by Hitler established, "The loss of the two destroyers was possibly caused by 50-kg bombs dropped by our own aircraft." After the war, it was discovered that the Royal Navy in January 1940 had laid mines in the lanes left in the German minefield, and it was highly probable that the destroyers fell victims to

mines as well as German bombs. This incident was an example of insufficient cooperation between naval and air force commands.

At the end of February 1940, the British Admiralty realised that its offensive against German U-boats was a failure. The convoy system remained the best defence against U-boats. During this month, only six ships sailing in convoy were lost to U-boats; in comparison, forty-three ships sailing alone were lost. But at this time, sufficient escort vessels were not available to allow each convoy at least two escorts. In total, two dozen destroyers dating from World War I, several dozen gunboats and a few rusty fishing vessels were free for escort duty with convoys. In February 1940, Allied shipping losses amounted to almost a quarter million tons. The ten operational German submarines in the Atlantic and North Sea alone sank forty-nine merchantmen, representing a total of 185,950 gross tons. Fifteen ships with a total of 54,740 gross tons were lost through mines. German losses amounted to five U-boats.

On Friday 1 March 1940, Hitler issued his instructions on carrying out the Weser Exercise. Denmark, too, was to be occupied as a strategically important jumping-off point, also for the protection of the German supply lines. A great deal of care went into the planning of the coup against the iron ore port of Narvik, the strategic key point in Norway. But Narvik was over 1,500 miles from the nearest German naval base. The ten destroyers that were to transport the landing forces to Narvik represented almost half of the German Navy's total destroyer force. They could, however, attempt the return voyage from Narvik only if they had been supplied with the necessary fuel. The decision was made to use the tanker and U-boat supply ship *Jan Wellem* (12,000 gross tons), which at that time was lying in the North Base placed at the disposal of the German Navy by Stalin as a secret naval base. And so the North Base achieved an unusual operational significance vis-à-vis the Weser Exercise. The *Jan Wellem* was to drop anchor in Narvik on the day before the assault. It was later shown that the *Jan Wellem* was, in fact, the only supply ship that appeared in Narvik at this critical moment and thereby made a very considerable contribution to Germany's success. Adm. Raeder stated, "The sole tanker to arrive punctually in Narvik during the Norwegian occupation came from Polarskoye."

On Saturday 2 March 1940, German aircraft for the first time attacked shipping in the English Channel. German bombers from the 26 Bomber Group sank the British passenger ship *Domala* (8,441 gross tons) off the Isle of Wight.

On Monday 4 March 1940, Dönitz was ordered

by the Naval High Command to cancel further departures of U-boats. U-boats already at sea were ordered not to engage off the Norwegian coast. Operational readiness of all naval units was to be speeded up. Operation Weser Exercise was about to begin.

On the following day, 5 March 1940, Dönitz had to order several U-boats off the Norwegian coast to investigate the defence installations there.

At the beginning of March 1940, the British Admiralty together with the Secret Service prepared an action on the strategically important Iron Gate. A considerable proportion of German oil requirements were transported through this narrow area of the Danube. The Greek steamer *Dionysia* (1,542 gross tons) was to play a significant role in this action. The British Secret Service which, among other things, was used to resist illegal Jewish emigration to Palestine, now negotiated a deal with the Jewish underground organisation Haganah. In return for the appropriate charter fees and the promise to maintain silence on the illegal refugee transports from Sulina, at the mouth of the Danube, to Haifa, the Haganah would lend their British opposite numbers the steamer *Dionysia* for the assault on the Iron Gate.

On Thursday 7 March 1940, the largest passenger ship in the world, the British luxury liner *Queen Elizabeth* (83,673 gross tons) made its maiden voyage to New York. The pictures of the arrival of the giant steamer were published in the press. German naval command thereby discovered the copper cable girdling the hull and learned of the British countermeasures against magnetic mines.

During the night of 11 March 1940, the first German auxiliary cruiser, or "commerce raider," ship no. 16 *Atlantis* (Capt. Rogge) — the former freighter *Goldenfels* (7,862 gross tons) — left Kiel. Disguised as a Norwegian motor vessel, it was on the way to its operational area. It was armed with six 15-cm guns; a 7.5-cm gun; two 3.7-cm antiaircraft guns; two 2-cm antiaircraft guns; six torpedo tubes; two floatplanes of the Arado type; a high-speed launch; and it had 420 mines on board. The auxiliary cruiser had to slip unnoticed into the Atlantic and there attack Allied merchant shipping. The *Atlantis* was the first of twelve German commerce raiders that the German Navy converted from merchant ships during the course of the war. The primary objective of these auxiliary cruisers was to fill gaps that were left, as a result of the Norwegian operations, in the surface raiders previously engaged in the commerce war. As a rule, the cruisers were captained by former training ship commanders. They were attended at widely dispersed, secret rendezvous points by supply ships that provided oil and provisions as and when the

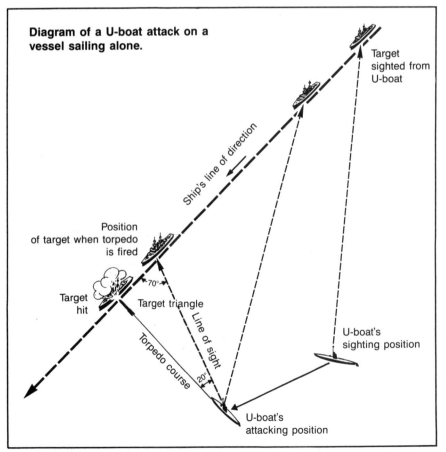

Diagram of a U-boat attack on a vessel sailing alone.

Target sighted from U-boat

Ship's line of direction

Position of target when torpedo is fired

Target hit

Target triangle

70°

Line of sight

Torpedo course

20°

U-boat's sighting position

U-boat's attacking position

Above right: The former whaling supply ship *Jan Wellem* converted into a tanker and transport, played a significant role in Hitler's plans to occupy Narvik.

Below right: The *Jan Wellem* in Narvik with the destroyed iron ore harbor in the background

Left: U-boat's method of attack

need arose.

The tactics employed by the auxiliary cruiser were, pretending friendly intentions, to attack only those merchant vessels sailing alone and, if possible, to fall upon them at night. These ghost ships had an operational radius of some 60,000 nautical miles, which in theory meant that they could sail two and a half times around the world at an average speed of eighteen knots. If an area became too dangerous for them, they would change their disguise and proceed to other, distant hunting grounds. This caused a number of problems for Allied shipping, as the auxiliary cruiser was always difficult to find and, thanks to its armament, could in practice be defeated only by a cruiser. The raiders were ordered to avoid any confrontation with warships, not to attack convoys, and to main-

tain strict radio silence. Their duty was to operate in areas where there were currently no German U-boats. Their preferred disguise for these operations was that of a neutral merchant ship. Their presence was intended to force the British to employ a considerable number of surface units. Some interruption of enemy sea communications was also anticipated.

The employment of commerce raiders was based on experience gained in World War I with the German auxiliary cruiser *Möwe* and *Wolf*. By means of simple alteration to the superstructure and the paint scheme, they could be made to resemble specific types of merchant vessels known to be in their operational area.

Also, care was taken to make provision for the frequently severe boredom of the crews during the

long months of continuous cruising. Commerce raiders showed films on board; they carried extensive libraries, as well as music facilities and parlor games; even a system of on-board leave was introduced. Those on leave were exempt from all duties unless, of course, the alarm was sounded. The commerce raider *Kormoran* even had a swimming pool.

The necessary underwater repairs were carried out by divers, which was frequently of decisive importance because the commerce raider had to operate for months at a stretch without being able to put into a base. One of the problems encountered in longer cruises in tropical waters was the increasing concentration of seaweed, which in time reduced the ship's speed to such an extent that it could no longer overtake modern merchant ships.

On Tuesday 12 March 1940, a cease-fire was signed in Moscow, ending the Soviet-Finnish Winter War. The peace treaty required Finland to cede the Karelian Isthmus including Vyborg, together with additional Karelian territory and the Finnish part of the Rybachi peninsula, to the Soviet Union. The Hangö peninsula, situated at the approach to the Gulf of Finland, was "leased" to the Soviet Union for the establishment of a base.

On Wednesday 13 March 1940, Berlin received a report that British submarines were patrolling off

Above: 3/7/1940, New York: This photo of the luxury liner *Queen Elizabeth* shows the British countermeasures against magnetic mines.

Right: The operational areas of German commerce raiders

the south coast of Norway. Two days later, on Friday 15 March 1940, a number of English officers landed in the Norwegian port of Bergen as "semi-official visitors."

On Thursday 28 March 1940, the Allied Supreme War Council—meeting in London to discuss Operation Wilfred—resolved to undertake the mining of Norwegian waters on 5 April 1940. At the same time, Allied troops were to be landed near Narvik, Trondheim, Stavanger and Bergen. The first contingent for Narvik was to leave Scottish ports 8 April 1940. Likewise, Operation Royal Marines was to commence on 5 April, an operation that Churchill had been planning for months. The First Lord of the Admiralty wanted to drop floating mines in the Rhine from aircraft to destroy bridges and hamper shipping on that river. As no agreement could be achieved (the French government feared reprisals from the German side) Chamberlain saw a welcome excuse to further de-

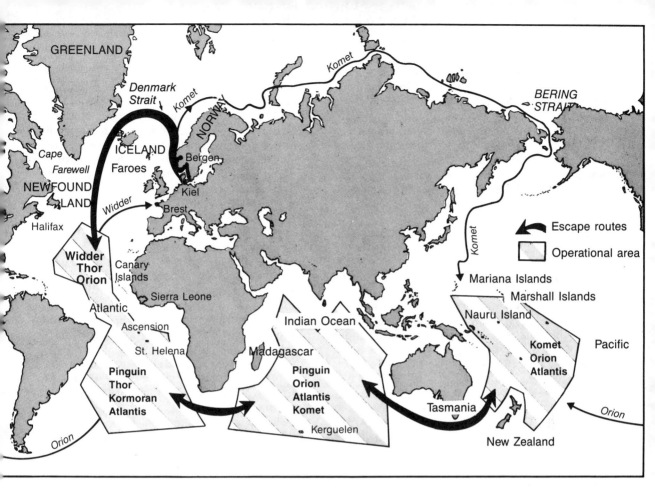

lay British intervention in Norway. He adjourned Operation Wilfred.

During March 1940, the Admiralty again transferred the Home Fleet to Scapa Flow, which had been evacuated after the spectacular U-boat attack under Lt. Comdr. Prien. At the same time, the Royal Navy sealed off the approaches from the North Sea to the Atlantic in the Shetlands area by means of a large-scale minefield. Official circles in London believed that all possible measures had now been taken to protect British supply lines across the Atlantic against German naval operations.

In March 1940, German U-boats operating in the Atlantic and North Sea sank twenty-three merchant vessels totalling 66,246 gross tons, while fourteen ships totalling 35,501 gross tons were lost to mines. German losses amounted to two submarines.

On Wednesday 3 April 1940, the German Navy commenced Operation Weser Exercise. The first steamers — the "export squadron" — put to sea with heavy equipment, artillery, flak, ammunition and provisions to take up their positions promptly for the planned operation. Their destination was, as decided in Moscow, the Soviet port of Murmansk. The steamers *Bärenfels* (7,600 gross tons) and *Alster* (8,500 gross tons) with ammunition and

Rauenfels (8,500 gross tons) with 15-cm batteries, 8.8-cm antiaircraft gun, heavy infantry guns and antitank weapons put to sea from Hamburg. At the same time, the tanker *Kattegatt* (6,000 gross tons) left Wilhelmshaven. Not one of these supply ships, disguised as ordinary merchantmen, reached its destination. All were either sunk en route by RAF aircraft, captured by British naval surface units or torpedoed by British submarines.

For the first amphibious operation of World War II, the German Navy engaged two battlecruisers, one pocket-battleship, two heavy cruisers, four light cruisers, fourteen destroyers, seven torpedo boats, thirty U-boats and also minesweepers and auxiliary vessels, freighters and tankers.

Also on 3 April 1940, the British Secret Service informed the War Office and Foreign Office that a large number of German ships with troops on board were gathering in those German ports nearest to Norway. During a Cabinet meeting, the British Secretary of State for War stated that he had knowledge of strong forces of troops concentrating at Rostock, and it seemed that an invasion of Scandinavia was imminent. This report was, however, interpreted as meaning that German troops were merely at a state of operational readiness in case any anticipated Allied assault on Norway took place. And once again the commencement of the Norwegian operation was put back until 8 April – and it was precisely this decision that made it possible for Hitler to land in Norway before the Allies.

On Thursday 4 April 1940, the German ambassador in Helsinki, von Blücher, said that he had heard from reliable sources that an Allied operation against Narvik and Bergen was imminent.

On the same day Col. Oster, head of section in the Foreign/Intelligence branch of the OKW, informed the Dutch military attaché in Berlin, Maj. Sass, of Operation Weser Exercise, also Operation Case Yellow, the code-name for the attack on France. Maj. Sass immediately informed his Swedish colleagues and the Danish ambassador Zahle. They despatched this information by special courier the same day to their respective governments. But the authorities competent in London and Paris were of the opinion that this was all a hoax put out by the German high command as a provocation.

Saturday 6 April 1940, the weather became increasingly cloudy with medium visibility and rain showers. The forces destined for transport on warships were embarked in Wilhelmshaven, Wesermünde, Kiel, Cuxhaven, Travemünde and Swinemünde. Some hours later, Vice-Adm. Lütjens put to sea with his fleet, bound for Norway. The battlecruisers *Scharnhorst* (Capt. Hoffmann) and *Gneisenau* (Capt. Netzbandt) were also a part of his command.

During the afternoon, the seasoned 139 Mountain Rifle Regiment (Col. Windisch) accompanied by the staff of 3 Mountain Division (Maj. Gen. Dietl) arrived at Bremen railway station. Their embarkation at Wesermünde began immediately. The objective of the Austrian Mountain Rifle Regiment was, according to the operational plan Weser Exercise North, to occupy Narvik. Only the combatant units and their equipment and arms were embarked on the destroyers. Their heavy weapons, flak, the greater part of their ammunition and provisions had already been on the way for the last three days aboard the "export squadron." Each destroyer had on board 200–250 men who were grouped in self-contained units at a state of operational readiness. Despite all the signs of an imminent German operation, the British Admiralty issued no particular orders on this day to bring the Home Fleet to immediate readiness.

On 6 April 1940, the second German commerce raider, the ship no. 36 *Orion* (Comdr. Weyher), put to sea from the Elbe. The *Orion*'s operational area was the South Atlantic. Its complement comprised 377 men; its armament, six 15-cm guns, a 7.5-cm gun, one 3.7-cm antiaircraft gun, four 2-cm antiaircraft guns, six torpedo tubes, two floatplanes of the Arado type and 228 mines. It was the former

Kurmark (7,021 gross tons), built in 1936.

Also on 6 April 1940, the tanker *Jan Wellem* left the secret German North Base in the Soviet Union at 10:00 P.M., carrying fuel and large quantities of supplies to provision the mountain troops landing in the iron ore port and also the destroyers for their return voyage. Three hours later, No. I Group left Wesermünde, their objective to take Narvik. The destroyers sailed with dimmed lights downstream into the North Sea. It was only then that the mountain troops were given their orders and learned of their destination. For practically all the troops, this trip to sea was their first.

At 3:00 A.M. on Sunday 7 April 1940, the battlecruisers *Scharnhorst* and *Gneisenau* put to sea to secure the approaches to Narvik against heavy enemy surface units. The 1,100 nautical miles to be covered were not without danger, as the route would take the battlecruisers through an area in which Great Britain had supremacy. And so in contrast to the Luftwaffe and the army, the navy had to employ practically their entire resources for Operation Weser Exercise. But there was no doubt that only the element of total surprise could lead to success, as this operational plan, drawn up by Hitler, broke all the known rules of strategical planning. Accordingly, the C-in-C of the Naval Group Command East, Adm. Carls, reckoned with a loss of approximately fifty percent of all forces engaged.

During the morning of 7 April 1940, RAF reconnaissance aircraft brought back aerial photos of Kiel harbor in which could be seen an unusually large number of warships and merchant ships. At midday, the British Admiralty was informed that reports relating to specific German intentions were available. This radio message was, however, reduced in value by the commentary, "All these reports are of dubious value and could very well be nothing more than a further move in the war of nerves."

Some hours later, an RAF reconnaissance aircraft reported that it had spotted a German fleet at the mouth of the Skagerrak on a northerly course. At this report, the Home Fleet under Adm. Forbes left Scapa Flow at 8:30 P.M. with the battleships *Valiant* and *Rodney*, the battlecruiser *Repulse*, as well as two cruisers and ten destroyers. At 10:00, the cruisers *Galatea* and *Arethusa*, together with four more destroyers under the command of Vice-Adm. Edward-Collins, put to sea from Rosyth. Vice-Adm. Cunningham's First Cruiser Squadron, which had been embarking troops at Rosyth for the occupation of strategically important Norwegian ports, received Admiralty orders to disembark the soldiers immediately and join the Fleet at sea. When the units put to sea from Rosyth and Scapa

4/6/1940, Weser Exercise, the fleet commanded by Vice-Adm. Lütjens en route for Norway with the battlecruiser *Scharnhorst* in the background

Flow, they were convinced that they were out to stop a German squadron attempting to make a breakthrough into the Atlantic.

Throughout the entire night, the British fleet pushed northward through heavy seas but then turned southward again. And so the Royal Navy missed the decisive moment at sea. This fateful command made it impossible for the fleet to repulse German landing forces before they established themselves in the Norwegian ports.

It was as black as pitch during the night of 7/8 April 1940 when the two German groups bound for Narvik and Trondheim, in a force-9 gale, passed the danger point between the Shetlands and the Norwegian coast, an area that was normally strongly guarded by the Royal Navy. There was an unusually rough sea at the time, and heavy damage was sustained by all the destroyers. Ammunition boxes and heavy weapons, lashed down firmly on deck, were swept overboard by giant waves. The mountain troops were seasick, ten men were swept overboard, and there were numerous injuries.

During the same night between 4:30 and 5:00 A.M. off Narvik, four British destroyers continued minelaying activities under the code-name "Wilfred," covered by the battlecruiser *Renown*, a cruiser and eight destroyers. Even at this time, the Admiralty did not believe that a German operation against Norway was taking place.

On the morning of 8 April 1940 at 8:30, the British destroyer *Glowworm* (Lt. Comdr. Roope) reported that it was in action against a German destroyer approximately 150 nautical miles southwest of the Vestfjord. Shortly afterward, a second German destroyer appeared and then the heavy

cruiser *Admiral Hipper*. The British ship came in contact with the German fleet only by chance: The destroyer *Glowworm* had remained behind to look for a seaman who had been swept overboard during the heavy storm and, in so doing, met the *Admiral Hipper* and four escort destroyers. The German units had the German II Group on board with 1,700 infantrymen.

When the heavy cruiser opened fire, the *Glowworm* retired behind a smoke screen and fired from a distance of approximately 3,000 yards a salvo of three torpedoes, which only just missed their target. Thereupon, the *Admiral Hipper* pressed on through the smoke screen and saw the British destroyer coming straight on at full speed. With no possible chance for the 14,000-ton cruiser to avoid a collision, the *Glowworm* rammed the powerful cruiser and tore a hole forty yards wide in its side. Badly damaged, the *Glowworm* went up in flames several minutes later. The *Admiral Hipper* rescued forty survivors including the British commander, who shortly before reaching the cruiser's deck fell back exhausted and was lost.

On 8 April 1940, the German *DNB* News Agency reported, "On 5 April we learned that the following vessels were proceeding up the Danube: the tugs *Britannia*, *Danubia Shell*, *King George*, *Scotland* and *Lord Byron*, accompanied by British motor launches; a chartered Greek freighter *Dionysia* with four barges; and the tug *Albion* with five barges. Owing to loose talk by members of the British crews, the following details have become known: The British vessels were carrying large quantities of revolvers; signal pistols; hand grenades; machine guns; ships' guns; depth charges;

mines; and five British officers, a number of RAF officers, over 100 specially trained British soldiers disguised as seamen and carrying special passes, as well as technical personnel belonging to engineer battalions. The objective of this military expedition, organised down to the last details, was to make the Danube unusable at various points for trade with Germany, and by these methods to interrupt trade between the Southeast European countries and Germany."

During the morning of the same day, the Polish submarine *Orzel*, a part of the Royal Navy since its adventurous escape from Reval in September 1939, sighted a freighter off Lillesand steaming in a northerly direction, carrying neither nationality markings nor the identifying marks of a shipping company. When the submarine came closer, it was established that the ship's name, *Rio de Janeiro*, and her home port, Hamburg, had been painted over. The submarine surfaced and ordered the freighter to heave to. The ship tried to escape but was caught by the submarine. After heaving to, and after an interval of several minutes, a boat was lowered, which slowly approached the *Orzel*. The submarine then intercepted radio messages coming from the ship and sighted two patrol boats approaching from the Norwegian coast. At 12:05 P.M. the commander, Lt. Comdr. Grudzinski, gave orders to fire a torpedo. The second torpedo struck the *Rio de Janeiro* in the first successful torpedo attack by a Polish vessel during this war.

The Norwegian patrol boats picked up from the sinking freighter 120 German soldiers, who stated that they were on their way to Bergen in answer to appeals for help from the Oslo government. This unequivocal proof of German intentions to invade Norway was nevertheless ignored. The police chief in Lillesand reported to the nearby Norwegian naval staff that the ship was carrying German troops with cannons and horses, but no interest was shown, and he was referred to the General Staff. But here, too, he could find nobody to listen to him. When he pointed out that the men were in uniform, the admiral at the other end of the telephone said, "Oh yes, everyone's doing that in Germany these days," and hung up. Finally when the police chief telephoned the Ministry of the Interior, he was given orders to disarm the German troops. The Norwegian Cabinet now gave orders to offer resistance to all approaching warships.

That evening, the news reached the British Admiralty that German mountain troops were on board the *Rio de Janeiro*. This message, marked urgent, nevertheless landed in an in-tray for "routine matters" so that it was not found by the officer competent until the following morning. Paris and London now decided to send a British brigade and

Top: April 1940, Operation Weser Exercise: The capture of Narvik, one of the most important objectives

Above: 4/8/1940, the British destroyer *Glowworm* capsizes after ramming the heavy cruiser *Admiral Hipper*.

Right: The German freighter *Rio de Janeiro*, sunk by the Polish submarine *Orzel* (Lt. Comdr. Grudzinski)

a French contingent to Narvik to occupy the iron ore harbor and to press on as far as the Swedish border. Allied troops were also due to be landed in Bergen, Namsos and Trondheim to prevent the Germans from occupying these bases.

During the night of 8/9 April 1940, the weather became even worse than the previous night, and the storm increased. The German destroyers pitched and tossed in the strong northwesterly storm. On board, nobody had any idea that the bad weather had made the British destroyer flotilla stay close to the Vestfjord, sheltered by the off-lying Lofoten Islands. And so the German I Group was able to go through the Vestfjord and on to Narvik undetected.

During the night, the *Admiral Hipper*, lying off Trondheim, radioed in English to the Norwegian coastal battery, "At the command of the Norwegian government, we wish to anchor in Trondheim. We have no hostile intentions." This deception allowed the German forces to pass through the most dangerous part of the approaches. The Norwegian gunners were blinded with searchlights. Only the battery in Hysnes opened fire, but it was silenced by the *Admiral Hipper*'s guns.

At dawn on Tuesday 9 April 1940, the British battlecruiser *Renown* sighted in the snowstorm and heavy seas two darkened ships off the Vestfjord: The battlecruisers *Scharnhorst* and *Gneisenau* were returning from Narvik where they had been employed on escort duties. The *Renown* opened fire from a distance of 18,000 yards. A direct hit destroyed the main gun control on the *Gneisenau*, causing the ship to cease firing. The *Scharnhorst* received two hits but suffered little damage. The two German battlecruisers screened themselves with smoke and disappeared.

At the same time, two German minesweepers entered the Oslofjord to land troops near the coastal batteries. In the meantime, a Norwegian minelayer opened fire and damaged the cruiser *Emden*. The V Group passed through the Dröbak Straits when suddenly from a distance of five hundred yards, the 28-cm guns of fortress Oscarsborg opened fire on the cruiser *Blücher* (14,000 tons). The camouflaged torpedo battery Koholm likewise scored two hits and the *Blücher* sank immediately, taking with it several senior officers of the German administrative staff and almost the entire crew.

The remaining German ships including the cruiser *Lützow*, the former pocket-battleship *Deutschland*, withdrew. The attempt to force a passage through the Oslofjord was discontinued until the fortress Oscarsborg surrendered during the afternoon after a massive air attack. The capture of the Norwegian capital was undertaken by paratroops who landed at the Oslo-Fornebu airport.

The German forces that took Oslo and the most important Norwegian ports were relatively small.

At no point was the first landing carried out by more than three thousand men.

At the port of Bergen, the light cruiser *Köln* radioed in perfect English, "British cruiser 'Cairo' I am proceeding to Bergen for a short visit." The Norwegians were reassured, as the cruiser did not hold its guns in a ready-to-fire position. Suspicions were first aroused when a cutter carrying a German landing party approached the bank. The coastal batteries were, however, unable to aim through their blind spot at the rapidly approaching cutter. Egersund was occupied without a struggle and Stavanger subdued after a powerful air attack. In Bergen, Norwegian coastal batteries succeeded in damaging the gunnery training ship *Bremse* and the light cruiser *Königsberg*.

When, during the morning of 9 April 1940, Adm. Forbes wanted to open fire on the Germans who were disembarking their troops, the Admiralty refused such an operation: "We do not know whether the coastal defences are still in Norwegian hands, and we do not wish to subject our irreplaceable ships to unnecessary hazards." Off the port of Narvik, two Norwegian coastal warships opposed the German destroyers; they were sunk after a brief exchange of fire. In the ore harbor, twenty-nine merchantmen lying at anchor were surprised by the German destroyer flotilla. The crews could not do much more than either wave in a friendly manner or make their ships ready to put to sea as soon as possible. Thanks to the twilight and thick, driving snow, the element of surprise was successful: Five enemy steamers were sunk and nine were beached partially in flames.

During the early dawn, the German 5 Mountain Rifle Division commenced disembarkation. The Norwegian 13th Infantry Regiment stationed here offered only weak resistance. After disembarking the troops, the ten German destroyers attempted to top up their fuel supplies and repair storm damage to make themselves ready for sea. It then became apparent that the tanker *Jan Wellem* was unable to pump the fuel quickly enough, and so the destroyers were unable, as planned, to put to sea again in the shortest possible time.

When the Admiralty received the radio message that the Germans had already landed in Narvik, they refused to believe the report and assumed that it referred to Larvik, a small whaling harbor near Oslo. When the message was once again confirmed, it was presumed that possibly a single German freighter had succeeded, under cover of the appalling weather, to land a handful of soldiers.

The German ambassador, Graf von der Schulenburg, reported from Moscow to the German foreign minister, "The eagerly awaited reply by the Soviet Union to the German action in Scandinavia was overwhelmingly favorable." Molotov stated to the German ambassador, "We wish Germany complete success with her defence measures."

During the afternoon, the Luftwaffe mounted heavy attacks against British ships off the Narvik coast. At the same time, eighty-eight bombers of the X Air Corps (Gen. Geisler) carried out attacks against the British fleet to the west of Bergen: The destroyer *Gurkha* was sunk, the cruisers *Glasgow* and *Southampton* damaged, and the battleship *Rodney* hit. The British surface units then gave up their attempt to land troops in Bergen. The British submarine *Truant* (Lt. Comdr. Hutchinson) sighted that same day the light cruiser *Karlsruhe* shortly after it put to sea from Kristiansand. The submarine damaged the 6,650-ton cruiser with its three torpedoes so badly that it had to be sunk by its own escort vessels.

During the afternoon of 9 April 1940, a press report on an enemy ship in the port of Narvik caused the Admiralty to order Capt. Warburton-Lee, the officer commanding the destroyer flotilla, "Proceed to Narvik and sink or capture enemy ship." Capt. Warburton-Lee entered Vestfjord in the twilight with the five destroyers of his flotilla and learned from the pilots that the approach to the harbor was mined. He was also told that Narvik was already in German hands and that twice as many destroyers would be lying there. He radioed this information off to the Admiralty, who refused to send reinforcements. Churchill stated, "In fact, we in the Admiralty were not prepared to risk the *Renown* — one of our only three battlecruisers — in such an enterprise." The Admiralty's reply was, "Capt. Warburton-Lee alone can judge what action he should take."

By the evening of 9 April 1940, the most important Norwegian ports had fallen into German hands. This had been accomplished within forty-eight hours. In Denmark, practically no resistance was encountered. Approximately one thousand soldiers were landed in Copenhagen. The Allies reacted hesitantly to the German invasion of Norway. Neither reconnaissance aircraft nor reports from agents had given the Allies a clear picture of what was happening, and the German landings came as a complete surprise.

The British surface units were unsuccessful in stopping the much weaker German units carrying the troops. And the British Admiralty missed its chance to cut off the German formations in Norway. If the Skagerrak had been blocked between Denmark and Norway (and there were sufficient submarines available to do just that), the German landing forces would have been in a very critical position.

In the early hours of 10 April 1940 while the

destroyers in Narvik were being slowly refuelled from the *Jan Wellem*, the five destroyers of Second Destroyer Flotilla commanded by Capt. Warburton-Lee steamed unnoticed under cover of mists into the Vestfjord. In a surprise attack, a number of merchant ships, as well as the German destroyers *Wilhelm Heidkamp* and *Anton Schmitt* (2,232 tons), were sunk, two more damaged by gunfire, and two made unseaworthy. When the British destroyers withdrew after the attack, they came into contact with the remaining destroyers of I Group. In this action, Capt. Warburton-Lee was fatally wounded, the destroyers *Hardy* and *Hunter* sunk, and two more British destroyers badly damaged. Upon putting out to sea, the remaining British destroyers encountered and sank the German freighter *Rauenfels* (9,460 gross tons), which was carrying reserve ammunition.

Around midday, the clouds opened up and the clear sky made possible the use of aircraft. Fifteen Skua dive bombers from 800 and 803 Squadrons of the Fleet Air Arm took off from their base at Hatston (Orkney). At the extreme limits of their operational range, they sighted the light cruiser *Königsberg*, which had been damaged by Norwegian coastal batteries, and immediately attacked. After three direct hits by 500-lb. bombs, the cruiser sank. The Fleet Air Arm lost one aircraft. Never before in the history of the war at sea had a ship of this size been sunk by aircraft.

In the afternoon, the heavy cruiser *Lützow* (formerly the pocket-battleship *Deutschland*) left the Oslofjord to return to Kiel.

On the same evening, the German destroyers attempted to leave Narvik and head out into the Atlantic for the return journey. British cruisers and destroyers at the mouth of the Vestfjord barred the way. At this, the German destroyers went back and moored in Narvik harbor.

On Thursday 11 April 1940, the heavy cruiser *Lützow* was torpedoed by the submarine *Spearfish* (Lt. Comdr. Forbes) just off the Kattegat and so badly damaged that it had to be towed back to Kiel where it remained in dock for an entire year.

On Saturday 13 April 1940, under conditions of poor visibility and driving snow, nine British destroyers, on this occasion supported by the battleship *Warspite*, made a surprise foray into the Vestfjord up to the ore port. In the following action, eight German destroyers were lost. By evening, not one of the ten destroyers that four days earlier had brought the mountain infantry to Narvik still survived. Some 2,100 survivors of the crews were saved and were able to reinforce the troops under the command of Maj. Gen. Dietl, whose mountain infantry were now in the surrounding mountains.

On Sunday 14 April 1940, the first Allied troops, the British 24th Brigade (Brig. Fraser) landed in Norway to come to the assistance of the Norwegian 6th Division (Maj. Gen. Fleischer). The choice of Harstad, the remote port to the north of Narvik, for this first landing caused the Admiralty to have doubts. From Harstad the brigade could neither disrupt the German supply route to Narvik, nor attack the port itself without amphibious back-up operations. Brig. Fraser had while still at sea refused a direct assault on Narvik. He kept to instructions that prohibited him from firing upon areas in which civilians were present. After the landing in Harstad, Brig. Fraser reported that he was not in a position to advance to Narvik "before the snow has melted." And the snow would last some three to four weeks.

On Monday 15 April 1940, units of the British 49th Division (Maj. Gen. Carton de Wiart) disembarked. The operation was conducted with the intention of cutting off the Germans in Trondheim, but the snow hindered troop movements and the British advance was suddenly thwarted south of Namsos.

Also on this day, the British destroyers *Fearless* and *Brazen* located the *U-49* (Lt. Comdr. von Gossler) off the Vaagöfjord and sank it with depth charges. Among the debris that was thrown up, various secret documents were found, including a map giving the U-boat positions in Norwegian waters.

On the same day, the Bugsier shipping company in Bremen took over the heavy cruiser L (*Lützow*), which was still under construction, in order to tow it from the Deschimag shipyards to Leningrad where it was to be completed in the Ordzhonikidze shipyards under the guidance of German technicians.

During the night of 15/16 April 1940, *U 47* (Lt. Comdr. Prien) reached the Vaagöfjord where a large number of Allied transports and cruisers were lying at anchor. Prien fired off eight torpedoes without scoring a single hit. The attack failed because of torpedo faults like those reported on numerous occasions in 1939 and 1940.

On Tuesday 16 April 1940, British forces occupied the Faroes with the agreement of the governor.

On Wednesday 17 April 1940, the position of the hard-pressed German mountain troops in Narvik had become so critical that Hitler was considering giving the Dietl group permission to cross into neutral Sweden. It was not until evening that Col.-Gen. Jodl persuaded Hitler to give the order to the defenders of Narvik, "Hold on for as long as possible."

On Thursday 18 April 1940, troops belonging to a French mountain rifle brigade, the 5th Chasseurs

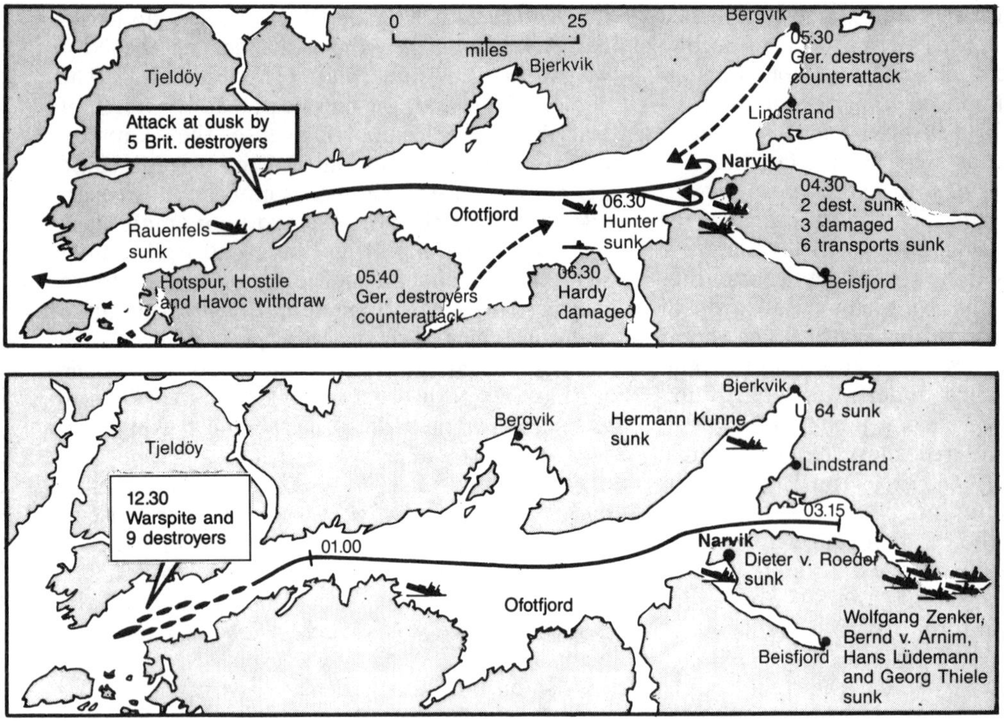

0 25
miles
Bergvik
05.30
Ger. destroyers
counterattack
Bjerkvik
Tjeldöy
Attack at dusk by
5 Brit. destroyers
Lindstrand
Narvik
04.30
2 dest. sunk
3 damaged
6 transports sunk
Ofotfjord
06.30
Hunter
sunk
Rauenfels
sunk
Hotspur, Hostile
and Havoc withdraw
05.40
Ger. destroyers
counterattack
06.30
Hardy
damaged
Beisfjord
Bjerkvik
U 64 sunk
Bergvik
Hermann Kunne
sunk
Tjeldöy
Lindstrand
12.30
Warspite and
9 destroyers
03.15
01.00
Narvik
Dieter v. Roeder
sunk
Ofotfjord
Wolfgang Zenker,
Bernd v. Arnim,
Hans Lüdemann
and Georg Thiele
sunk
Beisfjord

Left: Narvik, attacks by British destroyers on 4/11/1940 and 4/13/1940

Right: 4/15/1940, Bremen, the Hipper class "L" *(Lützow)* heavy cruiser after launching en route for Leningrad

Below: 4//15/1940, British troopships off Namsos

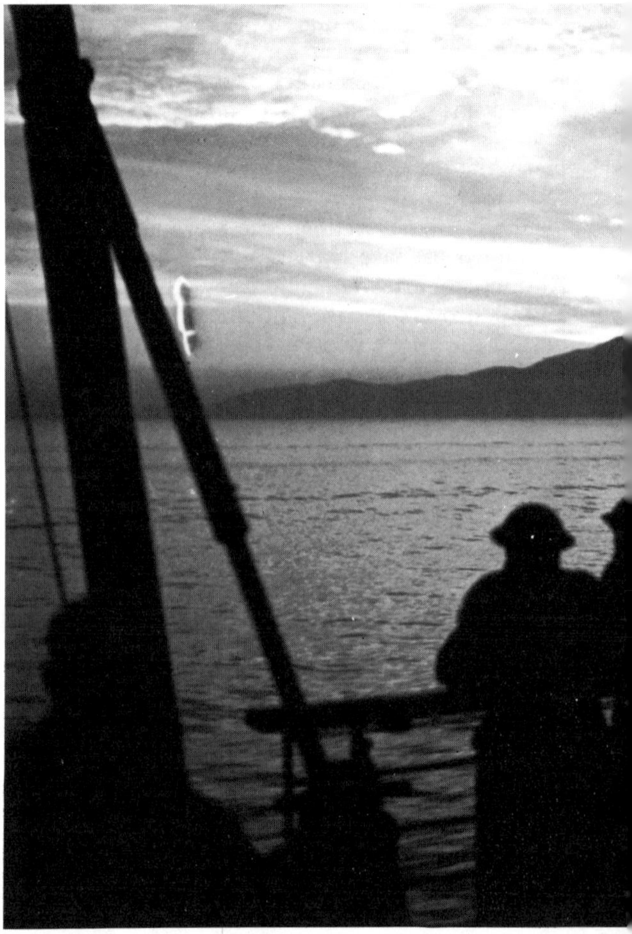

Alpins Demi-Brigade (Gen. Béthouart), landed in Namsos.

On Monday 22 April 1940, the French auxiliary cruiser *Ville d'Alger* brought 1,100 men as reinforcements to Namsos. Heavy snowstorms and the damaged harbor installations prevented the vessel from tying up at the quay. Consequently everything had to be landed laboriously by tender. When it became light, the *Ville d'Alger* had to put to sea because of the risk of German bombing attacks. On board, were still 350 soldiers, the entire complement of antiaircraft guns and all the mules.

On Saturday 27 April 1940, three French freighters succeeded in landing reserve supplies—including fuel, small-caliber guns and ammunition—in Namsos. A little later German bombers attacked, and everything went up in flames. Before the last freighter could leave the harbor, the order was given to evacuate Namsos.

By early 1940, the Admiralty was already able to employ effective equipment in sufficient quantities to counteract the German magnetic mine. Of approximately four hundred minesweepers available, the majority of which were converted fishing smacks, about half were fitted with a device for sweeping magnetic mines. Losses due to mines fell accordingly: In April 1940 only eleven ships totalling 19,799 gross tons were lost.

During April, German U-boats sank only six merchant vessels totalling 30,927 gross tons; and Germany lost six submarines. This fiasco was

brought about by providing U-boats for the Operation "Weser Exercise and, above all, by the increasing incidence of torpedo failure. Adm. Raeder stated, "The knowledge of the failure of our torpedo weapon on the U-boat was devastating. It gave rise to a grave crisis of confidence . . . . It robbed the U-boats of many certain successes, which could have had a decisive effect on the further course of the war at sea."

On Wednesday 1 May 1940, Lt. Comdr. Kretschmer, the most successful U-boat commander of all, took over command of the *U 99*, a type VII C submarine. This particular type now became one of the most frequently built German warships.

On Thursday 2 May 1940, the evacuation of Allied troops from Namsos was completed. The city, together with its harbor installations, was in flames. The Luftwaffe attacked the evacuation transports without respite. After a direct hit on the French destroyer *Bison* (Capt. Bouan), the ship's ammunition chamber blew up, and the survivors were rescued by the British destroyer *Afridi* (Capt. Vian), which was itself sunk by Stukas two hours later. Shortly after that, the last survivors of the destroyer *Bison* only just escaped another catastrophe.

On the morning of 3 May 1940, the German commerce raider *Atlantis* sighted a steamer between Cape Town and Freetown. The commerce raider, disguised as the freighter *Kasii Maru*, was sailing under the Japanese flag. The *Atlantis* then hoist the German war ensign and radioed the warning, "Do not use your radio." At the same time, a warning shot was fired across the bows of the other ship. The British freighter *Scientist* (6,200 gross tons) nevertheless radioed a call for assistance. The *Scientist* did not stop until a number of shots had been fired. The prize commando went on board in order to examine the ship's documents and the load carried. After putting explosive charges in place, the freighter was sunk. The *Scientist* became the first ship to be sunk by a German commerce raider.

On Sunday 5 May 1940, two German Arado floatplanes belonging to 706 Coastal Wing took off from their base near Aalborg. They sighted a surfaced British submarine close to Swedish territorial waters and forced it to stop. One of the aircraft landed near the submarine and ordered the commander to come to the airplane. The vessel was the large minelaying submarine *Shark*, which had struck a mine the previous evening and had been badly damaged. German naval vessels, summoned by the floatplanes, towed the *Shark* back to Wilhelmshaven. The *Shark* was the first submarine to be captured by aircraft. On the same day, troops of the 13th Demi-Brigade of the French Foreign Legion (Col. Magrin-Verneret) disembarked in Tromsö. The Polish 1st Independent Mountain Brigade (Gen. Szyszko-Bochusz) was not permitted to land here because, as it was reported, "The population fears German air raids."

During the night of 5/6 May 1940, the third German auxiliary cruiser, ship no. 21 *Widder* (Comdr. von Ruckteschell), left Hamburg. Previously this vessel was the *Neumark* (7,851 gross tons). It carried a complement of 363. Her armament consisted of six 15-cm guns; four 3.7-cm antiaircraft guns; two 2-cm antiaircraft guns; two torpedo tubes; two floatplanes; and sixty mines.

By Tuesday 7 May 1940, the convoy carrying the 4,873 men of the Polish Mountain Brigade had spent two days cruising off the Norwegian coast before the men were disembarked at Harstad—two weeks after they had embarked on 23 April 1940.

At the time Narvik was defended by a German force amounting to some 5,400, comprising two thousand riflemen reinforced by the crews of the sunken destroyers, and some six hundred troops who had been flown in. The Allied forces in the Narvik area amounted to 24,000.

During the night of 9/10 May 1940, German aircraft laid mines off the Dutch and Belgian coasts. At 5:35 A.M., the German western offensive began on a front ranging from the North Sea to Luxembourg. After its losses in Operation Weser Exercise, the Kriegsmarine played practically no part in the operations against Holland, Belgium and France. During the occupation of Norway, Hitler had demanded the reckless engagement of the fleet in order to cover the operations on land. And now, with the Weser Exercise coming to an end, the only capital ship remaining operational was the battlecruiser *Gneisenau*. During the first weeks of the western offensive, only two U-boats were operating at the northern approaches to the English Channel. Securing units of the Kriegsmarine that were operating in the Deutsche Bucht first heard of the new situation on the radio.

On Friday 10 May 1940, British troops occupied Iceland. Cruisers of the Home Fleet transported an advance detachment of the Royal Marines to Reykjavik. Also on 10 May 1940, Chamberlain resigned. Winston Churchill now became prime minister, and his former position as First Lord of the Admiralty was taken up by A. V. Alexander. The resignation of the British government was a consequence of the defeat of Allied troops in Norway. The new prime minister immediately constituted a national War Cabinet that represented a coalition of all the political parties.

On Sunday 12 May 1940 toward 8:00 P.M., a concentration of British naval units in the Vestfjord near Narvik began in snow and rain showers. At midnight, a red flare was sent up and the ships of the Royal Navy opened fire on the coast with all guns. After an artillery bombardment lasting two hours, the French alpine troops (Gen. Béthouart) landed and made a rapid thrust in the direction of the ore port.

On Monday 13 May 1940, Queen Wilhelmina of the Netherlands, Crown Princess Juliana and the Prince Consort Bernhard arrived in England on a destroyer. Units of the Dutch Fleet also succeeded in reaching England. Later they were to join with the Royal Navy in fighting the Kriegsmarine. A number of powerful naval units remained in the Dutch colonies in Southeast Asia.

On Tuesday 14 May 1940, the heavy cruiser *Lützow* reached Leningrad. Rear Adm. Feige of the Engineering Branch and seventy German technicians had travelled aboard the cruiser. According to German plans, the cruiser was to be commissioned in 1942. The armament consisted of eight German 20.3-cm guns and twelve 10.5-cm antiaircraft guns and twelve 3.7-cm antiaircraft cannons and twelve torpedo tubes.

On Wednesday 15 May 1940, *U 37* (Lt. Comdr. Oehrn) entered the Atlantic area. This was a new type IX A submarine. Lt. Comdr. Oehrn was among the finest of the U-boat commanders, and his ship was carrying torpedoes with an improved magnetic firing pistol. After an interval of almost six weeks, *U 37* was the first submarine to operate

5/6/1940, Wilhelmshaven, the British submarine *Shark* captured by two German Ar 196 A-3 floatplanes

northwest of Cape Finisterre.

On the same day, Churchill sent to President Roosevelt his first message as prime minister, a request for forty or fifty old US destroyers. In his reply, which Churchill received on 18 May, Roosevelt wrote that the US Navy had to be deployed over the Atlantic and Pacific and ". . . the ships could not be spared, not even on a temporary basis."

Within a few days, in France advance units of the German Panzers had carried out a long, sweeping movement through the reputably impassable Ardennes country and had reached Abbéville at the mouth of the Somme. The British Expeditionary Force (Gen. Lord Gort) was cut off from the main body of the French Army.

On Sunday 19 May 1940 at 4:30 P.M., the British War Cabinet was informed that the C-in-C of the British Expeditionary Force, Lord Gort, ". . . was examining a possible withdrawal towards Dunkirk if that were forced upon him." Only ten days had elapsed since the beginning of the German offensive. Some hours later the responsibility for a possible evacuation from the mainland, Operation Dynamo, was given to Adm. Ramsay, the flag officer at Dover.

On Tuesday 21 May 1940, after German armored formations had reached the Channel coast, Adm. Raeder informed Hitler that no preparations had been made for a potential invasion of England. Raeder wished to avoid if at all possible involving the German Navy, after its heavy losses during the Weser Exercise, in any difficult short-term tasks. Four weeks were to elapse before Raeder had another chance of discussing with the Führer the possibility of a landing in England.

During the afternoon of 23 May 1940, Göring informed Hitler by telephone that the destruction of the British Army units withdrawing to Dunkirk should be the grand task of the National-Socialist Luftwaffe.

On Friday 24 May 1940, the Admiralty broke off operations in Norway. Churchill stated, "The conquest of Narvik must be continued so that the harbor can be destroyed and our evacuation covered."

The same day, the armored forces commanded by Gen. von Kleist stopped short just in front of Dunkirk. A twenty-mile-long sector along the Aa River was covered by only one British battalion; only a few of the bridges had been blown up or mined ready for blowing up. But Hitler's intention was to save his Panzers for the second phase of the French campaign. In addition, he relied upon Göring's promise that the British and French troops, cut off in the Dunkirk sector, would be destroyed by his Luftwaffe. But the bombers' bases were too far from Dunkirk, and in any event the area was covered by mist for three decisive days.

On Monday 27 May 1940, the Admiralty gave orders to commence Operation Dynamo. During the evening, lighters, yachts, barges, fishing craft, pleasure boats, tugs from the Thames and lifeboats from passenger ships, which had been assembled in the ports and harbors along the Channel, set course for the beaches of Dunkirk.

At the same time, strong Allied naval units entered the Vestfjord and at 11:40 P.M. opened fire on the German coastal front around Narvik. After this artillery preparation and two weeks of fighting, Allied forces entered Narvik. The Norwegians were given the honor of being the first to enter the city. Dietl's group was still holding the ore railway east of Narvik. Allied commanders had been under orders for the previous twenty-four hours to blow up the harbor installations and evacuation Narvik.

On Tuesday 28 May 1940, the first day of Operation Dynamo, only 17,804 soldiers crossed the Channel to England. The steamer *Monas Isle* was the first ship to arrive in Dunkirk and was fired at by German batteries in Gravelines when it put to sea again. It had one hundred dead on board.

On the same day, the king of the Belgians, Leopold III, capitulated and went into German captivity. The Belgian Cabinet had flown to London where it formed a government in exile.

On Wednesday 29 May 1940, the Admiralty engaged one cruiser, eight destroyers and twenty-six assorted vessels for Operation Dynamo. This day saw the evacuation of 47,310 men.

On Thursday 30 May 1940, the third day of Operation Dynamo, a total of 860 ships of all kinds was deployed. A total of 300 German bombers were ready to take off but were unable to carry out any attacks at Dunkirk because of low cloud. This day saw the evacuation of 53,823 men to English ports.

On Friday 31 May 1940, the fourth day of Operation Dynamo, 68,014 Allied troops were evacuated. The sea remained calm, and despite the presence of German bombers, an uninterrupted shuttle of small craft picked up men from the beaches or out of the water and ferried them from the shore to the larger ships. The small craft making up the evacuation fleet were unaccustomed targets for the Stukas, whose bombs buried themselves deep in the sand dunes so that they had little effect upon exploding. The decisive factor was, however, the local air superiority gained over Dunkirk by the deployment of Spitfire squadrons operating from base in England. Nothing was to be seen of the German Navy, neither surface units nor U-boats.

During May 1940, the Allies lost through mines twenty ships totalling 47,716 gross tons; German U-boats operating in the North Sea and Atlantic sank fifteen merchant vessels totalling 63,407 gross tons. German losses amounted to one U-boat.

During this month, the so-called permanent German War Directive No. 154 came into force. This directive prohibited the rescue of survivors from enemy ships sunk in the waters immediately surrounding the British Isles.

On Saturday 1 June 1940, the evacuation of Dunkirk reached its zenith. By midnight 64,429 troops had landed in England, of which almost one-third had been picked up from the beaches in small craft under heavy air attacks and artillery fire. RAF fighters successfully covered the evacuation of the British Expeditionary Force, the Germans having lost for the first time air superiority over the general Dunkirk area.

On the same day, Norwegian naval bases were used for the first time by German U-boats.

During the morning of 2 June 1940, some four thousand British troops in Dunkirk with seven antiaircraft guns and twelve antitank weapons still held the reducing bridgehead backed up by a large number of French forces. By now evacuation was possible only at night.

During the night of 2/3 June 1940, thirteen packet boats, eleven torpedo boats, five paddle steamers and an armada of small craft and tugs towing long columns of boats behind them appeared off Dunkirk. They were reinforced by a number of warships and one hundred French fishing smacks. The last of the British rearguard had been embarked by midnight. While 34,000 French troops, some still engaging German forces, were left behind on the beaches, many of the ships were still empty when the rearguard was forced to pull out at dawn. At 3:30 A.M. the last ship, the destroyer *Shikari*, left Dunkirk harbor with 338 men on board. During the night 26,256 men had been evacuated. At 9:40, the German 4th Army (Col.-Gen. von Kluge) occupied the town and harbor.

There is no parallel in modern warfare to Operation Dynamo. Altogether 225,000 British and 112,000 French troops were evacuated, even though the majority had lost all their equipment. Of the British Expeditionary Force, eighty-five percent reached England. Of the 848 ships of all types, seventy-two, including seven destroyers, were lost. Of the smaller craft, 163 were lost, most of them sunk by the Luftwaffe.

On Tuesday 4 June 1940, Operation Juno began. The battlecruisers *Scharnhorst* and *Gneisenau*, together with the heavy cruiser *Admiral Hipper*, were ordered northward to intercept the Allied evacuation transports. On this occasion too, both battlecruisers were successful in putting to sea from Kiel without the British Admiralty knowing. While the Royal Navy was busy securing the evacuation transports from Narvik, the German ships reached Trondheim.

During the night of 4/5 June 1940, Hitler gave

Norway, an attack by the Luftwaffe on British troopships gathered off the coast

orders after the occupation of Dunkirk that church bells in the Reich should be rung for three days to celebrate the ending of the "greatest battle in the history of the world."

On Thursday 6 June 1940, the auxiliary cruiser, ship no. 10 *Thor* (Capt. Kähler), set sail from Kiel. The cruiser was formerly the *Santa Cruz* (3,862 gross tons) with a complement of 345. The armament comprised six 15-cm guns, two 3.7-cm anti-aircraft guns, two 2-cm antiaircraft guns, two double torpedo tubes, two floatplanes and three hundred moored mines.

On Friday 7 June 1940, the German Naval High Command heard that the Allied were evacuating Narvik. Upon hearing this news, Adm. Marschall resolved to attack the British convoy at sea.

On Saturday 8 June 1940, the Germans successfully interfered with radio transmissions sent by a troopship attempting to warn Allied ships of an enemy squadron lurking in the vicinity. At 4:00 P.M., *Scharnhorst* and *Gneisenau* sighted the smoke trails from the aircraft carrier *Glorious*, escorted by the destroyers *Ardent* and *Acasta*.

The aircraft carrier, whose escort consisted merely of the two destroyers, had no chance of survival once it had been sighted by the German battlecruisers. The *Glorious* certainly had a number of Swordfish torpedo bombers on board, but these were not, for some inexplicable reason, flying patrols to secure their own ship. The crew of the aircraft carrier, completely surprised, made desperate attempts to get the torpedo bombers armed and into the air. At 4:30, the *Scharnhorst* opened fire from a distance of fifteen nautical miles. Several hits were scored on the forward hangar and a fire broke out. At 5:40, the aircraft carrier *Glorious* sank, wreathed in smoke. The two escort destroyers attacked the German battlecruisers with torpedoes but were themselves sunk. In all, 1,474 officers and enlisted men of the Royal Navy and 41 of the RAF were killed. The *Glorious* was the first aircraft carrier to be sunk by surface units. During the action, the *Scharnhorst* was hit by a torpedo, and the battlecruiser, heavily damaged, went back to Trondheim. By their action, the *Glorious* and her escorts saved from certain catastrophe the weakly protected evacuation convoy, sailing 100 nautical miles to the north.

On Sunday 9 June 1940, *U 37* (Lt. Comdr. Oehrn) arrived in Wilhelmshaven. During an operational sortie, lasting some three weeks, it had sunk 47,000 gross tons. The captain's report showed that out of five torpedoes with magnetic firing pistols, two detonated prematurely and two presumably did not detonate at all. After this Dönitz finally banned the use of these torpedoes, and from then on only torpedoes with impact detonation were to be employed.

On Monday 10 June 1940, Italy declared war on France and Great Britain. Italian troops crossed the French border. At that time, the Italian Navy consisted of six capital ships of which the four most modern were being re-equipped and only the two oldest ships were in a state of operational readiness. In addition, there were 19 cruisers, 59 destroyers, 67 torpedo boats and 116 submarines. Numerically the fleet was strong, but there was a large number of obsolete units, and the service suffered as a result of the insufficient training of its crews. The shortage of oil precluded extensive operations being undertaken. And just like the Kriegsmarine, the Italian Navy had no naval aviation division of its own. Even its torpedo-strike aircraft were subordinate to the Regia Aeronautica, the Italian air force. The Italian High Command entered the war without any overall strategy. The objective of the Italian fleet was to secure lines of communication between Italy, Libya and the East African colonies and to launch attacks against British convoys. The high command nevertheless did not approve the navy's plan to occupy Malta which at that time was weakly defended. This decision proved later to be a very serious mistake.

Also on 10 June, Norwegian troops under Maj. Gen. Ruge capitulated. Operation Weser Exercise was over. Adm. Raeder stated, "It was the first time that the three separate arms of the Wehrmacht carried out such a large-scale operation in close tactical cooperation."

The Weser Exercise, which at that time was the largest land operation in German military history, cost the German Navy one heavy cruiser, two light cruisers, ten modern destroyers, four submarines and a number of smaller units. Damage was sustained by two battlecruisers, two heavy cruisers and a number of smaller units.

During the operation, the Allies lost one aircraft carrier, two cruisers, nine destroyers, six submarines and various smaller units. In addition, four cruisers, eight destroyers and a number of smaller units were badly damaged.

German Naval High Command called the use of major naval units against Norway "a serious strategical error." As a result of these losses, the German Navy was no longer in a position to support a potential invasion of England. The delays in restoring damaged units to operational readiness also had a detrimental effect. Despite Great Britain's defeat in Norway, one considerable advantage accrued: The country acquired almost ninety percent of the enormous Norwegian Merchant Navy, a total of 1,024 ships including two hundred modern tankers that were capable of transporting to Britain some forty percent of the Allied forces' fuel requirements. The Norwegian Merchant Navy was administered in London by Nortraship, an organisation that worked closely with the exiled Norwegian government to whom charter fees for freight-carrying operations accrued.

One of the most astounding facts to emerge from the Weser Exercise was that in contrast to the German radio intelligence service (B-Dienst), which managed to keep the German Naval High Command fully informed on the movements of all Allied naval units, the Allies gained practically no intelligence from their Secret Service sources.

On Wednesday 12 June 1940, the Italian submarine *Bagnolini* (Comdr. Tosoni-Pittoni) sank with one torpedo the British light cruiser *Calypso* south of Crete. This was the first success achieved by the Italian Navy.

At dawn on 14 June 1940, the French Third Squadron (Vice-Adm. Duplat) based in Toulon carried out an operation in Italian waters. Four heavy cruisers and eleven destroyers opened fire on the oil storage tanks and military installations on the Lugerian coast and in the port of Genoa. No Italian aircraft appeared, and the coastal artillery scored only one hit: The destroyer *Albatros* received a 15.2-cm shell in the boiler room.

On Sunday 16 June 1940, the French sloop *La Curieuse* forced the Italian submarine *Provana* (Comdr. Botta) to surface and then sank it by ramming. This was the first Italian submarine to be sunk by the French Navy. During the night 16/17 June 1940, Marshal Pétain proposed an armistice to Germany.

On Monday 17 June 1940 during Operation Aerial, the evacuation of Allied troops from the Bay of Biscay, the troopship *Lancastria* was sunk by Luftwaffe bombers while in the St. Nazaire harbor roads. Although the former passenger ship did not go down at once, approximately 3,000 of the 5,300 troops on board drowned, as not enough life jackets were available. Press reports on this disaster were not released. Churchill stated, "The newspapers have got enough disaster for today at least." The prime minister later refused to lift the ban on publication, and so the misfortune remained unpublished until some years later.

Evacuation operations code-named "Aerial" and "Cycle" nonetheless made it possible to evacuate 192,000 troops from the Bay if Biscay and the northern coast of France, saving them from the threat of being taken prisoners of war.

On Wednesday 19 June 1940, German S-boats, high-speed motor torpedo boats known also as E-boats, operating form Dutch, Belgian and French ports launched attacks against targets

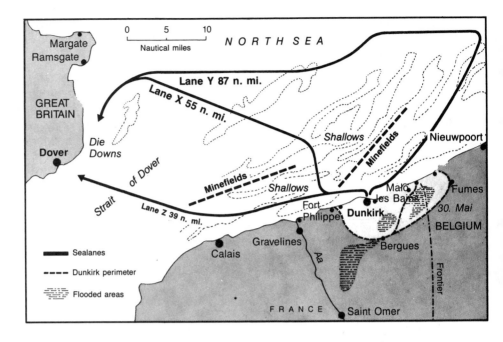

Operation Dynamo, the three sealanes for the evacuation of Dunkirk

along the south coast of England. S-boats *S 19* and *S 26* sank the freighter *Roseburn* off Dungeness.

On the same day, after an artillery duel in the Red Sea the small British trawler *Moonstone* captured the undamaged Italian submarine *Galilei* (Comdr. Nardi) and towed it to Aden. After evaluation of various secret documents and other intelligence found on board, two more Italian submarines were sunk in the Persian Gulf.

On Thursday 20 June 1940, the French government asked the Italian government for an armistice. At the same time, the German radio intelligence service pulled off the biggest coup of the French campaign. To prevent units of the French Navy escaping to England after the collapse of France, the radio intelligence service, thanks to their knowledge of the French naval code, issued to all French ships bearing the signature of "Admiral Darlan" a coded message forbidding them to leave port. The radio message had the effect of spreading even more confusion among the units of the French Navy than there was before. One of the French naval radio operators answered this radio order with a curt "Blast it!" The bogus radio message helped to ensure that when the cease-fire was observed at the front, the majority of French vessels remained in their home port.

On this day, the battlecruiser *Gneisenau*, together with the heavy cruiser *Admiral Hipper*, made a dummy foray in the direction of Iceland as a cover for the return of the damaged *Scharnhorst* lying in Trondheim. The British submarine *Clyde* (Lt. Comdr. Ingham) lying off Trondheim attacked the *Gneisenau* and scored a hit on its bows with a torpedo.

While the French armistice commission in Rome was sitting at the table with the Italian delegates on Friday 21 June 1940, the French battleship *Lorraine* opened fire on the Italian port of Bardia in North Africa. French naval aircraft attacked Taranto and Livorno in the last operation undertaken by the French Navy against the Italian fleet.

Even before the armistice had been signed, the German 2 Minesweeper Flotilla (Comdr. von Kamptz) entered Brest. The minesweepers immediately commenced securing the approaches to harbors in West Brittany, Brest, Lorient and St. Nazaire for German submarines and cleared the areas of French mines.

On Saturday 22 June 1940, after the conclusion of the Franco-German armistice, German troops occupied the French coast from Dunkirk to the Spanish frontier. One of the most important clauses of the armistice affecting the French Navy read, "The fleet must be gathered together in ports yet to be specified and there disarmed. The German government formally declares that it has no intentions of deploying French warships for its own purpose." At Hitler's command the French Fleet was made subordinate to the Vichy government.

At the beginning of the war, the French Merchant Navy aggregated three million tons. Of this figure, 271,000 gross tons were lost by enemy action; a further 450,000 were seized by Great Britain; 196,000 were interned in American ports; 25,000 were detained in foreign ports; and 275,000 were requisitioned by Germany after the occupation of France.

The occupation of the French coastline made a profound change in Germany's maritime strategy for the first time in its history: The Germans were now in a position to operate with direct access to Atlantic waters. And while the armistice was being signed by the French and German delegates in Compiègne on 22 June 1940, long convoys of motor transports were leaving Wilhelmshaven, loaded with torpedoes and equipment destined for the new U-boat bases on the west coast of France.

On the same day, the auxiliary cruiser, ship no. 33 *Pinguin* (Capt. Krüder), the former *Kandelfels* (7,766 gross tons), put to sea from the Sörgulenfjord to make for its operational area in the Antarctic and Indian Ocean. The crew numbered 420 men. The armament comprised six 15-cm guns; a 7.5-cm gun; two 3.7-cm antiaircraft guns; two 2-cm antiaircraft guns; four torpedo tubes; two floatplanes; and 420 mines.

On Tuesday 25 June 1940, hostilities in France ceased as from 1:35 A.M. In Gibraltar on this day, the British Force H was being formed under Vice-Adm. Somerville. The duty of this unit was to fill the gap left in the western Mediterranean after the French capitulation. The evacuation of Allied troops from the north coast of France and in the Bay of Biscay ended. The Royal Navy was successful in evacuating 144,171 British; 24,325 Polish; 18,246 French; 4,938 Czech; 136 Belgian troops; and some 50,000 civilians. All were brought safely to Great Britain.

On Thursday 27 June 1940, orders were given to the port authorities in Portsmouth and Plymouth to intern French ships in these ports. During the morning, Churchill declared a blockade on all Europe from the North Cape down to the Spanish border.

On Friday 28 June 1940, the Free French Navy, or Forces Navales Françaises Libres (FNFL), was created. Four French merchantmen and an auxiliary naval vessel comprised the first squadron of the new navy. The commanding officer and organiser was Vice-Adm. Muselier, whose idea it was to replace the French tricolor flown by the ships with a blue flag bearing a white cross of Lorraine.

Right: The French Navy's capital ships took part in the war at sea right up until the capitulation.

Below: 6/17/1940, Loire estuary, the troopship *Lancastria* goes down with the loss of 3,000 lives.

Later the cross of Lorraine became the symbol of the Free French of Gen. de Gaulle. The first French naval units to resume hostilities against the Axis powers included the submarine-minelayer *Rubis* (Lt. Comdr. Cabanier).

On Sunday 30 June 1940, Vice-Adm. Dönitz landed in Vannes (Brittany) in a Junkers Ju 52. He wished to supervise the new U-boat bases and their installations in person. With the Atlantic ports on the French coast, U-boats would now be spared travelling the extra 450 nautical miles to the Atlantic around the north of Britain. The economic efficiency ratio for military operations regarding each individual submarine at sea was thereby increased by twenty-two percent. Even the smaller type II submarine (250 tons) could now be deployed against convoys. More importantly, there was now a possibility of closer cooperation with the Luftwaffe, which could now deploy its reconnaissance aircraft far over the Atlantic and attack convoys. Including the Norwegian ports, the German Reich now controlled the entire North Sea up to the polar regions. This enabled U-boats, blockade-runners and commerce raiders (auxiliary cruisers) to break out into the Atlantic. The commerce raiders and blockade-runners could proceed to distant waters without crossing areas where they would be likely to meet the Royal Navy. In June, German U-boats were once again operating in the main shipping lanes across the Atlantic. Although an

average of only six U-boats could be deployed at any one time, they established a new record: They managed to sink one ship every twenty-four hours. June 1940 was the most successful month to date. A total of 36 Allied ships totalling 355,431 gross tons were sunk by U-boats, because the defence measures undertaken against an expected German invasion meant that practically no escort vessels were employed. German losses amounted to one U-boat. This month saw the end of the first phase of the Battle of the Atlantic, which had commenced on 3 September 1939. During the second phase, which lasted until March 1941, German U-boats operated in wolf packs against convoys in the North Atlantic. On average, there were twelve U-boats at sea.

Immediately after the French campaign, operating from its new French bases, the Luftwaffe was able to commence attacks against shipping along the south and southeast coasts of England using Stukas, bombers and the Luftwaffe's own torpedo-strike aircraft.

The German merchant marine had suffered heavy losses. By June 1940, they had lost an aggregate of almost 600,000 tons in the first ten months of the war, mainly during attempts to get back home. The Operation Weser Exercise cost approximately 250,000 gross tons.

In the middle of 1940, a better and more effective cooperation was developed between the sur-

Vice-Adm. Emile Muselier, C-in-C of the Free French Navy

face units of Western Command and the aircraft of RAF Coastal Command, one of the most important requirements for the subsequent outcome of the Battle of the Atlantic. In the meantime, British minesweepers were increased to a total of seven hundred vessels. Minesweeping flotillas were now stationed in every important trading port to keep the approaches clear. Half of the minesweepers were now in a position to clear magnetic as well as moored mines.

At that time, under conditions of utmost secrecy, a strike force was created in Britain which would occupy the Spanish and Portuguese islands in the Atlantic and, above all, the Azores if the Iberian peninsula were to be annexed.

The events of the first half of the year gave the German Navy an extended operational base stretching from Kirkenes to Biarritz. From the point of view of strategy overall, an opportunity was presented to make the Mediterranean area the main point of operations so that Britain could be attacked where it was weakest—Suez, the Near East and North Africa. The withdrawal from the European mainland forced Britain to alter its strategy from a Continental to a predominantly maritime strategy.

Illustrierter Beobachter

HUMOR

Öl für Deutschland aus Rußland —

Zeichnung: Stroda / Delke.

Öl für England aus Moſſul

A cartoon from a German periodical. On left, massive oil supplies from Russia to Germany. On right, oil for Britain being sent to the bottom by a U-boat.

86

1940

July–December

Statement Made to Parliament

4 July 1940, London
The *Reuters* News Agency reported:

Prime Minister Churchill this afternoon made a statement on the war situation before a packed House of Commons. Churchill first stated with regret that measures had had to be undertaken to prevent the French fleet from falling into German hands. The resolution of the British government to take action against the French fleet had been adopted unanimously. Yesterday morning Britain took the greater part of the French fleet under its control or compelled the fleet by use of appropriate force to accept the British terms. Two battleships, two light cruisers, a number of submarines including the large submarine *Surcouf*, eight destroyers and two hundred small minelayers and submarine hunters have been taken over in Portsmouth, Plymouth and Sheerness after a short notification to their commanders – insofar as this was possible. The operation was carried out without bloodshed, except in the case of the submarine *Surcouf* in which two British officers and one rating and a French seaman were killed and several sailors wounded.

British Attack

Thursday 4 July 1940, Clermont-Ferrand
The French *Havas* News Agency reported:

In view of this irresponsible attack, the French government has issued orders to French naval units lying in the Alexandria roads next to the British fleet to weigh anchor and put to sea, using force if necessary. After yesterday's abhorrent assault by our Allies, the French Admiralty has given immediate instructions to all warships at sea to stop all British merchantmen and reciprocate further attacks. French ships lying in British harbors have been ordered to force an exit and, pursuant to the terms of the armistice, make for Brest.

French Warnings

Saturday 6 July 1940, Vichy
The *French War Ministry* issued the following communiqué:

The C-in-C of the French Navy and Minister of Naval Affairs have warned seamen of all ranks and all good Frenchmen about the more than dubious character of Adm. Muselier, who has emigrated to England and entered the service of that country against his own fatherland . . . . Adm. (retired) Muselier will be brought to justice before the courts of his homeland.

Sunday 7 July 1940, Toulouse
The *French War Ministry* issued the following communiqué:

The court competent for the 17th Military Area assembled in Toulouse to consider the case of the French general, de Gaulle, currently in England. In his absence he has been sentenced to four years imprisonment and a fine of one hundred francs for insubordination and the incitement of military personnel to insubordination.

Confiscation of British Merchantmen

Monday 8 July 1940, Shanghai
The *Domei* Agency reported:

The authorities in French Indochina on Saturday seized all British merchantmen in the port of Haiphong.

The War in the Mediterranean

8 July 1940, Rome
The *Italian High Command* issued the following communiqué:

Yesterday the naval bases at Malta and Alexandria were again successfully attacked. Two Italian aircraft failed to return.

Directive No. 16.

The Führer and Supreme Commander of the Armed Forces   Führer H.Q.
7/16/1940

Most secret document!

Directive No. 16 relating to preparations for the invasion of Great Britain.

As Great Britain, despite the hopelessness of her military situation, still shows no signs of being ready to reach an agreement, I have decided to prepare landing operations against Britain and, if necessary, carry them out.

The purpose of these operations is to eliminate Britain as a base for the continuation of the war against Germany and, if it should prove necessary, to occupy the country completely. In this regard I herewith order the following:

1. The landings must be in the nature of a surprise attack on a broad front stretching from around Ramsgate to the area west of the Isle of Wight. Units of the Luftwaffe will be assigned the role of artillery and units of the Kriegsmarine the role of assault engineers. The question whether it is expedient to mount limited operations to occupy the Isle of Wight, for instance, or Cornwall before the main assault is to be examined from the point of view of each branch of the armed forces. The results are to be reported to me. I reserve the right to make any decision.

Preparations for the overall operation are to be completed by the middle of August.

Friday 19 July 1940, Berlin

The *German High Command* issued the following communiqué:

The German submarine arm has achieved further success. A U-boat has sunk 31,300 gross tons of enemy shipping capacity. Another U-boat knocked out a large armed merchantman in a strongly escorted convoy.

. . . *denn wir fahren gegen Engeland*

"We're Marching Against England"
Today, let's sing a song
and drink a glass of cool wine,
let the glasses ring their accord, the hour has come.
Give me your dear hand
and so farewell my love
as we are marching against England . . . .

Our flag flies from the masthead,
and it proclaims Germany's might,
and we won't put up with the English
laughing at us much longer.
Give me your hand . . . .

If you should get news that I am no more,
and that I sleep in the bosom of the sea,
don't weep for me, just think
that I shed my blood
for the Fatherland.
Give me your hand . . . .

Action off Crete

Saturday 20 July 1940, Rome
The *Italian High Command* issued the following communiqué:

A naval battle took place yesterday at sunrise in the area around Crete. The action lasted three hours. Our light cruisers *Giovanni delle Bande Nere* and *Bartolomeo Colleoni* opposed a formation of two 7,000-ton cruisers of the "Sydney" class, as well as four torpedo boats. Despite the clear superiority of the enemy forces, our cruisers engaged the enemy, causing him to suffer severe damage. The cruiser *Bartolomeo Colleoni* was badly damaged and sank. A large number of the crew were saved. Italian bomber formations scored hits on the enemy units, causing an enemy ship to burst into flames and sink. All our aircraft returned safely.

Wednesday 14 August 1940
The *German High Command* issued the following communiqué:

On 13 August, German bomber formations attacked harbor and quay installations in Wallsend, Hartlepool, Bournemouth and Plymouth, armament factories in Exeter and Bristol, as well as oil installations in North Killingham.

Italian Navy Successes

Sunday 8 September 1940, Rome
The *Italian High Command* issued the following communiqué:

One of our submarines has sunk an enemy warship patrolling in the area off Gibraltar. Bomber squadrons accompanied by fighter formations have attacked the naval base on Malta. Damage was caused and fires started, and a submarine lying in dock was hit. Enemy fighters attempted to attack our bombers and their fighter escort. One enemy fighter was shot down over the coast, another over the sea, and a third probably crashed. All our aircraft returned to base, although some aircrew were wounded. In the Red Sea, our aircraft attacked an enemy convoy. A heavily damaged steamer had to be abandoned by its crew.

Attempted Invasion Likely?

Saturday 14 September 1940, London
The *Reuters* News Agency reported:

The general opinion here, that an invasion will be attempted in the immediate future, has gained ground. The general public reacts to such rumors as calmly and cautiously as the authorities and military circles. A report issued by United Press that a German operational order relating to all services was issued 16 September has certainly been noticed but has had no alarming effect. It is assumed that the German fleet, to the extent that it has survived in Norwegian campaign, will be employed on a large scale for the first time.

Deployment of French Warships
14 September 1940, Vichy
The *Havas* Agency reported:

Accompanied by three destroyers, the light cruisers *Montcalm*, *Georges Leygues* and *Gloire* have set sail from Toulon and arrived in Dakar in the first large-scale naval movement since the armistice. An official reason for the deployment has not been given. The reason has, however, been assumed to be that France must secure its vital lines of communication vis-à-vis food supplies awaiting transport to France.

W. Churchill to General Ismay
Wednesday 18 September 1940

Pray find out if there is any possibility of spreading a sheet of burning oil over one or more of the invasion ports. This is nothing more than the old story of the fire ship with modern improvements which was tried at the time of the Armada near Dunkirk. The Admiralty can certainly find out something about it.

Sunday 22 September 1940
The *German High Command* issued the following communiqué:

A submarine commanded by Lt. Comdr. Schepke has sunk eight enemy merchant ships totalling 61,300 gross tons. At the same time, other submarines have reported the sinking of eight more enemy merchant ships totalling 35,700 gross tons. Including the enemy merchant ships reported sunk yesterday, 176,000 gross tons of enemy shipping capacity has been sunk by our U-boats in two days, representing a peak figure in the war. Moreover, the success was achieved in areas where the enemy deploys strong antisubmarine forces.

W. Churchill to General Smuts
22 September 1940

You will have seen my message about Dakar . . . . If Dakar fell under German control and became a U-boat base, the consequences to the Cape route would be deadly. We have therefore set out upon the business of putting de Gaulle into Dakar, peaceably if we can, forceably if we must, and the expedition now about to strike seems to have the necessary force.

De Gaulle in Dakar

Monday 23 September 1940, Vichy
The *French Foreign Ministry* reported:

The former general, de Gaulle, has entered Dakar with a British squadron and given the French authorities an ultimatum demanding that Dakar be surrendered. The ultimatum was rejected. The British ships then opened fire on Dakar. We were of the opinion that the former general, de Gaulle, had fled to England in order to continue hostilities against our former enemies. These events contradict this. De Gaulle is, in fact, directing foreign forces against his own countrymen. Those Frenchmen who have previously hesitated to call him a traitor have now had their eyes opened.

French Air Attack on Gibraltar

Tuesday 24 September 1940, Rome
The Italian *Stefani* News Agency reported:

As a reprisal for the bombardment of Dakar yesterday morning, 120 French aircraft based in Morocco attacked Gibraltar.

No Attack on Gibraltar?
24 September 1940, Vichy
The *United Press Agency* reported:

The French government has issued an official denial of reports, according to which French aircraft were said to have attacked Gibraltar. Up until now, no reprisals have been undertaken, but "French reprisals are imminent."

Loss of a French Submarine
Wednesday 25 September 1940, Vichy
The *French Ministry for Naval Affairs* issued the following communiqué:

The French submarine *Persée* sank in the area around Dakar after it had been successfully attacked by a British cruiser. The greater part of the crew were rescued.

Air Attack against British Shipping
25 September 1940, Vichy
The *United Press Agency* reported:

A French bomber squadron has attacked British ships lying off Dakar. During the attack, an air battle took place in which one French and three British aircraft were shot down.

Just Like Napoleon's Old Guard
Friday 27 September 1940, Vichy
The *United Press Agency* reported:

The British cruiser *Adelaide* advised the commander of the French gunboat *Dumont d'Urville*, which was in the area of New Caledonia, of Adm. Muselier's invitation to join Gen. de Gaulle's forces. The commander, Capt. de Quivrecourt, by way of reply to the invitation signalled one word, "merde."

7/19/1940, off Crete, the Italian light cruiser *Bartolomeo Colleoni* seen from the deck of the cruiser *Sydney*

Withdrawal of the Royal Navy

27 September 1940, Buenos Aires
The *United Press Agency* reported:

The British withdrawal from Dakar has caused great astonishment throughout South America. The view was held here that the British would spare no efforts to occupy this strategically important point that is of great interest to the South American states.

Swiss Radio Beromunster

Thursday 31 October 1940

The degree to which the Mediterranean has become important in the present war has been shown recently by the events in Greece. Italy accused the Greek government of actions violating Greek neutrality and demanded that strategically important points in Greece be occupied by Italian forces. The rejection of this ultimatum by the Greek government caused hostilities to open between Italian and Greek troops on the Greco-Albanian frontier. Great Britain gave Greece a guarantee more than a year ago, and the British have declared that they are prepared to offer immediate assistance. These events took place so recently that it is quite impossible to say anything upon either the development of military operations or the political consequences of the Greco-Italian conflict.

Expansion of the Swedish Navy

Wednesday 13 November 1940, Stockholm
The Swedish Newspaper *Svenska Dagbladet* reported:

To strengthen further the Swedish Navy, already increased by sixty new units—destroyers, motor torpedo boats, submarines and minesweepers—last year, the government has today approved the building of two light cruisers at a cost of 100 million kroner and a number of destroyers and submarines for 41.4 million kroner.

British Attack on Taranto

Thursday 14 November 1940, Rome
The *Stefani* Agency reported:

The Italian Armed Forces report no. 138 brought news of an enemy air attack on Taranto the night of 12 November. Yesterday in the House of Commons, Churchill gave a completely fabricated version of this event. The Italian authorities do not consider it necessary to make any reply to the tendentious distortion of facts contained in statements made by Churchill and the First Lord of the Admiralty. During the next few days, precise details relating to the attack on Taranto as well as the overall situation of the naval war in the Mediterranean will be released.

Swiss Radio Beromünster

14 November 1940

The merchant ships that link Great Britain with the rest of the world can now travel only in convoys escorted and protected by British warships. The blockade of Great Britain—in other words, the dislocation of her exports and imports by means of U-boats and air attacks—is one of the most important tactics employed by the German High Command against Britain. Every day merchantmen forming a part of the convoys are torpedoed, attacked and sunk. During recent weeks, losses by the British Merchant Navy of shipping capacity have reached the highest figures recorded since the outbreak of the war. In the last speech given by the prime minister, Winston Churchill, the worries caused by this serious endangering of lines of communication became apparent . . . . Without doubt, the war at sea is one of the most important aspects of the current conflict. No one should be under any illusion about that, even though it is in the very nature of sea warfare that these events are less obvious than campaigns fought by armies on land. For it has never been the duty of a fleet to engage prematurely in naval battles. For every power that has one at its disposal, a high seas fleet represents a valuable reserve that is only rarely risked at an inopportune moment. From time to time, its mere presence and the organising of an efficient system of patrols by smaller units is enough to maintain the maritime supremacy of the strongest fleet.

A Second "Western Wall"

Saturday 7 December 1940, Berlin
The *United Press Agency* reported:
    The "second German Western Wall," a chain of fortifications and heavy batteries along the coast of the Continental mainland facing England and the Atlantic, is after four months nearly completed. The excavators have been transported elsewhere, and a specialist workforce, just sufficient for the completion of the last works outstanding on the massive gun emplacements, remains. The new Atlantic Wall differs fundamentally from the Western Wall (known to the Allies as the Siegfried Line) in that it has not only a defensive but also an offensive role. In addition to coastal batteries in the sand dunes, a strong belt of antiaircraft defences is available. Construction works on the second Western Wall were commenced before the ink of the signatures to the Armistice Treaty was dry. Tens of thousands of members of the Todt Organisation immediately commenced work on the concrete constructions and continued working day and night up until last week.

Criticisms of the Naval High Command
7 December 1940, London
The *United Press Agency* reported:
    In the House of Commons and in the press, demands have been made for energetic measures to

be taken to secure shipping. A number of newspapers have prophesied a change of personnel in naval staff, whereby Sir Dudley Pound is to be replaced by a younger officer. A. J. Cummings in the *News Chronicle* wrote, "A number of very competent naval officers have voiced criticisms of the measures adopted by the Admiralty in combatting the menace to our shipping. These methods have been described as obsolete and ineffective. Many are of the opinion that Sir Dudley Pound should retire honorably and make it possible for Lord Alexander, the First Lord of the Admiralty, to appoint a suitable successor."

Clashes on the Mekong
Monday 9 December 1940, Hanoi
The *United Press Agency* reported:
    Yesterday morning Siamese troops without provocation opened fire with a machine gun on the French bank of the Mekong near Vientiane. Fire was returned without casualties. During the afternoon, firing was again resumed. At 5:00 P.M., Siamese bombers dropped ten bombs on Vientiane, injuring one civilian and setting a house on fire. In addition, two huts were destroyed. During the last three months, the French authorities have remained calm and shown willingness to negotiate; nevertheless, they cannot continue to suffer these provocations. This morning French aircraft dropped twenty-two bombs on the Siamese town of Lacon to the southeast of Vientiane.

W. Churchill to the First Lord of the Admiralty
Saturday 14 December 1940
    Pray let me have a complete report on the condition of the American destroyers in which numerous defects are visible and the limited use that we have been able to put them to.

Tuesday 17 December 1940
The *German High Command* issued the following communiqué:
    Lt. Comdr. Kretschmer, who has just returned with his U-boat, sank 34,935 gross tons of enemy shipping capacity during this operational patrol. This officer has now sunk a total of 252,100 gross tons and is the first U-boat commander whose score of tonnage sunk exceeds the 250,000-ton mark.

Royal Navy Bombards Bardia

Friday 20 December 1940
The *British Admiralty* issued the following communiqué:
    From the evening of 13 December until midday on 18 December, heavy and light units of the Brit-

ish Mediterranean Fleet bombarded the area of Bardia at short range. On the afternoon of 17 December, a capital ship of the British fleet was unsuccessfully attacked by Italian torpedo bombers during the bombardment. Enemy coastal batteries directed fire on our warships without scoring a hit. Fires that had been burning slowly in Bardia since Sunday had become very severe by Tuesday. Early Tuesday morning, a British naval vessel successfully made a close-range attack on the harbor in Bardia. Despite heavy machine-gun fire, the warship pressed into the inner harbor and sank three transport vessels. The fleet was able in the meantime to carry off prisoners. British naval aircraft participated in the action with the Royal Air Force. The maritime operations are continuing.

20 December 1940
The *German High Command* issued the following communiqué:

A submarine has reported sinking its fortieth enemy merchant ship. The commander of this vessel, Lt. Comdr. Schepke, has reached a total tonnage sunk of 208,975 gross tons and has become the third U-boat commander whose score of tonnage sunk exceeds 200,000 tons.

Strategy and Tactics

JULY TO DECEMBER 1940

In the summer of 1940, Hitler controlled Europe from the Vistula to the Atlantic and from the North Cape to the Pyrenees. The Italian empire reached as far as North Africa and Somaliland. After the defeat of France, Great Britain was on her own. Immediately after the signing of the Franco-German Armistice, Hitler decided that attention should be directed toward planning landing operations on the British mainland.

In order to avoid all risks—the Germans could still possibly seize control of the French fleet in defiance of the Franco-German Armistice terms—Churchill ordered the fleet to be put out of action. He wanted to prove at the same time that Britain was firmly resolved to continue the struggle with all the means at her disposal.

In the early hours of 3 July 1940, British sailors armed with rubber truncheons overpowered five thousand French seamen on board ships lying in Channel ports in England. The battleships *Paris* and *Courbet*, the destroyers *Leopard*, *Mistral* and *Ouragan*, six torpedo boats, five submarines, the submarine-cruiser *Surcouf* and over one hundred smaller vessels were confiscated by the British and incorporated into the Royal Navy. The officers of the destroyer *Mistral* opened the sea-cocks. The scuttling of the ship was, however, frustrated, as the commander was threatened that his crew, locked in below, would go down with the ship. There were a number of fatalities and injuries on the largest submarine in the world, the *Surcouf*. The French crews were taken to a camp near Liverpool, and the officers were interned on the Isle of Man.

During the afternoon of 3 July 1940, the newly constituted Force H (Vice-Adm. Somerville), comprising one battlecruiser, two battleships, one aircraft carrier, two cruisers and eleven destroyers, carried out Operation Catapult, an attack on the French fleet in the naval base of Mers el–Kébir near Oran. Vice-Adm. Somerville delivered an ultimatum to Vice-Adm. Gensoul either to join Force H or scuttle his ships. Somerville negotiated for almost nine hours and from time to time requested the Admiralty for different orders.

7/3/1940, Oran/Mers el–Kébir, the heavily damaged battleship *Bretagne* shortly before capsizing

Left: 7/3/1940, Oran/ Mers el–Kébir, on the deck of a French warship after a torpedo attack

Below: 7/9/1940, off Punta Stilo, the battle-cruiser *Hood* exchanging fire with the Italian battlegroup (Adm. Campioni)

Churchill, however, remained resolute.

At 5:40 P.M., after the ultimatum had expired, the Royal Navy opened fire on the overfull anchorage of the French fleet. The anchored ships were not ready for action and presented an easy target. The battleship *Bretagne* sank after a number of direct hits (977 dead); the battleship *Dunkerque* was heavily damaged (210 dead); the heavy destroyer *Mogador* received a direct hit in the stern (42 dead); and the battleship *Provence* was heavily damaged. The battleship *Strasbourg*, together with the destroyers *Le Terrible*, *Tigre*, *Volta*, *Lynx* and *Kersaint*, managed to weigh anchor and steam full ahead through a minefield laid by the British. Despite continuing attacks by carrier-borne aircraft and fire from the ships' guns, these vessels managed to reach Toulon without damage. The total losses of the French Navy on this day amounted to 1,147 dead.

Operation Catapult was at this time the largest and most successful undertaking by the Royal Navy. British and French forces fired at each other for the first time since the Battle of Waterloo 125 years previous. Churchill stated, "The elimination of the French Navy as an important factor almost at a single stroke by violent action produced a profound impression in every country." When the Admiralty urged Adm. Cunningham, the officer commanding the eastern Mediterranean area, to attack the French fleet lying in Alexandria, he radioed back to London, "I am totally against this proposal. Due to the critical situation with regard to ammunition, I have no wish to engage my ships unless it's against the enemy."

On the same day, the German auxiliary cruiser, ship no. 45 *Komet* (Capt. Eyssen), put to sea from Gdynia. Formerly it was the banana boat *Ems* (3,287 gross tons). With a complement of 269, it was the smallest of the German commerce raiders. Its armament comprised six 15-cm guns; one 6-cm cannon; two 3.7-cm antiaircraft guns; four 2-cm antiaircraft guns; six torpedo boats; a motor launch; two Ar 196 floatplanes; and thirty magnetic mines. Ship no. 45, with ten metric tons of paint on board for its various camouflage patterns, made for the Norwegian port of Bergen. From there it reemerged as the Soviet freighter *Deniev* ("home port" Leningrad) and in this disguise made for Novaya Zemlya, islands in the Barents Sea. Soviet ice-breakers accompanied it through the shipping route north of Siberia into its East Asian operating area.

On Thursday 4 July 1940, operating from bases in France, the German Luftwaffe commenced attacks against British shipping. The Stukas, Ju 87s belonging to 2 Dive Bomber Group, attacked a

convoy off the British coast and sank five ships. Nine more were damaged, and S-boats destroyed the freighter *Elmcrest* (4,343 gross tons) with the same convoy and torpedoed two other ships.

On Friday 5 July 1940, the Vichy government broke off diplomatic relations with Great Britain but did not declare war. Naval forces in the Mediterranean, which were now under the control of the Vichy government, comprised one battleship; one aircraft carrier; four heavy and eight light cruisers; thirty destroyers; and seventy submarines. Practically all these units were in the naval base at Toulon.

During the early dawn of 6 July 1940, the Royal Navy again appeared off Mers el-Kébir (Oran). Three waves of torpedo bombers from the aircraft carrier *Ark Royal* attacked the French battleship *Dunkerque*. One torpedo hit a vessel lying alongside the battleship, causing its depth charges to explode and damage the *Dunkerque* extensively. The carrier-borne aircraft opened fire on the rescued French sailors. Altogether, 150 men lost their lives.

On the same day, the officer commanding Brest declared the base ready to accept U-boats.

On Sunday 7 July 1940, Adm. Cunningham reached an agreement with French Vice-Adm. Godfroy regarding the fate of the French squadron Force X, stationed in Alexandria. When the squadron surrendered its supply of fuel and deposited the breechblocks of its guns as well as stocks of torpedo detonators with the French consulate, Cunningham agreed not to make any attempt to take the ships by force. On the same day, the first German U-boat *U 30* (Lt. Comdr. Lemp) entered the base at Brest to take torpedoes on board.

On Monday 8 July 1940, a motor torpedo boat of the Royal Navy attacked the French battleship *Richelieu* lying in Dakar and attempted to destroy the rudders and propellers with depth charges. Torpedo-strike aircraft from the British carrier *Hermes* again attacked the battleship, scoring a direct hit. The *Richelieu*, however, remained operational.

On Tuesday 9 July 1940, a naval engagement took place near Punta Stilo (Calabria) between the Alexandria-based squadron Force B (Adm. Cunningham) and considerably stronger Italian naval forces backed up by aircraft. After the battleship *Warspite* scored a direct hit on the Italian battleship *Giulio Cesare* from a distance of sixteen nautical miles and severely damaged it, the Italian battle group (Adm. Campioni) broke off the engagement despite the fact that they had a superior situation, owing to the nearness of their home ports. This battle was the first important encounter between the Italian Navy and the Royal Navy.

Italian land-based aircraft managed to score only a few hits.

On Wednesday 10 July 1940, Adm. Darlan informed the Vichy cabinet that he had called upon the Italian Ministry for Naval Affairs to mount a joint naval action with him against Alexandria in order to liberate Vice-Adm. Godfroy's French squadron that was cut off there. Darlan proposed at the same time an attack by the French on the British colony of Sierra Leone and a bombing attack on Gibraltar.

On Friday 12 July 1940, I Wing 40 Bomber Group was posted to Bordeaux-Mérignac. This wing was equipped with the Focke-Wulf Fw 200 "Kondor," a long-range bomber and reconnaissance aircraft that was intended for operations over the North Atlantic for the time being.

On the same day, an Fw 200 attacked the small 255-ton trawler *Volante* some five nautical miles off the south coast of Ireland. Five of the trawler's crew were killed by machine-gun fire. It was the first ship to be sunk by an Fw 200 during the Battle of the Atlantic.

From Monday 15 July 1940, Britain finally gave up the southern approach around Ireland. At this time, the Royal Navy laid extensive minefields in the northwesterly and southwesterly approaches to the English Channel in one of the first measures undertaken as a defence against the expected German invasion.

The same day, Hitler demanded the Vichy government's authorisation to occupy ports and bases in French North Africa by way of a counter-consideration for the agreed maintenance of the French fleet at operational readiness. Marshal Pétain, however, refused outright and immediately ordered Adm. Darlan to undertake all preparations for a resumption of the war in North Africa if the Germans should violate the terms of the armistice agreement.

On Thursday 16 July 1940, Hitler issued Directive No. 16, relating to Operation Sea Lion, the invasion of Britain.

At this time, Germany had some 1.2 million tons of shipping capacity available, which had to suffice for all purposes. More than half of this total would be required for transporting the invasion forces. Transport capacity available amounted to 155 steamships aggregating 700,000 gross tons; 1,722 ferries; 471 tugs; and 1,160 motorboats. Small pleasure steamers, yachts and rivercraft were requisitioned. The Siebel aircraft factory manufactured "Siebel ferries" which, driven by old aero-engines, were scheduled as armored landing craft. Barges, requisitioned from all over Europe, were provided with a concrete layer on the bottom and a ramp in the bow. They were to be towed in pairs

by tugs across the Channel, loaded with troops, armored vehicles, equipment and mules. Many of these vessels could only be employed in cross-Channel operations when there was a force 1–2 wind, which was seldom. This armada would have crossed the Channel at a speed below that of the sailing ships that brought Caesar to England two thousand years earlier—and in the face of the world's most powerful fleet lying in wait along the coast of Britain. At this time, Germany had for all practical purposes not one single operational capital ship available to secure the invasion. The whole venture was a risky improvisation that did not fulfill the demands of a carefully planned amphibious operation.

On Thursday 18 July 1940, the British Admiralty seized all French merchant ships in the Suez Canal area.

During a naval battle that took place on 19 July 1940 between British and Italian naval units near Cape Spada, the Italian light cruiser *Bartolomeo Colleoni* (Capt. Novara) was sunk by the Australian light cruiser *Sydney* (Capt. Collins) and the destroyers *Havoc* and *Ilex*. It was the first larger Italian vessel to be lost.

On Sunday 21 July 1940, five days after his orders to prepare Operation Sea Lion, Hitler gave orders to "consider an eastern offensive against the Soviet Union that is to be carried out in 1941." There can be no better example than this of the defectiveness of Hitler's strategical thinking.

On Sunday 28 July 1940, British submarines (B patrol) commenced watching activities on the German naval bases along the Bay of Biscay.

On the same day, the first engagement between a German and a British auxiliary cruiser took place. The British armed merchant cruiser *Alcantara* (22,209 gross tons) met up with the German commerce raider *Thor* (3,862 gross tons), disguised as the Yugoslavian steamer *Vis* out of Split. The *Alcantara* was badly damaged and just managed to reach Rio de Janeiro. The German auxiliary cruiser, which had a few cables and tubes damaged by one shell, repaired the damage in two hours and continued its operations.

At the end of July 1940, the British Admiralty created a new department charged with matters relating to German commerce raiders. Each commerce raider confirmed was given an initial by way of identification, as the German name of the ship was unknown. The *Atlantis*, for example, was identified as Raider C.

July 1940, near Ostend, Operation Sea Lion, the invasion of England, is tried out.

On Wednesday 31 July 1940, Great Britain declared a blockade of the entire French coastline. The British were convinced that everything coming into unoccupied France would directly benefit Germany. The Vichy government, which had declared itself strictly neutral, had, in fact, introduced the death penalty for any French national found guilty of participating in the war against Hitler.

On the same day, Churchill again asked President Roosevelt for the transfer of US destroyers. The Royal Navy had concentrated its destroyer force in southern English waters and had lost eleven destroyers in ten days through air raids. Churchill wrote, "Mr. President, with great respect I must tell you . . . this is a thing to do *now*."

In July 1940, German bombers, dive bombers and torpedo-strike aircraft destroyed thirty-three merchantmen aggregating approximately 70,000 gross tons. Four other freighters aggregating 35,000 gross tons ran against mines that had been dropped from German aircraft. During this month, German U-boats sank thirty-eight ships totalling 194,922 gross tons. German losses amounted to one U-boat.

In Britain preparations for the mass production of armored landing craft were commenced despite the German air raids, the U-boat successes and the invasion threat. Plans were made to use the landing craft for future commando raids.

On Thursday 1 August 1940, a German heavy battery, the "Grosser Kurfürst," comprising four 28-cm guns, was installed at Cape Gris-Nez. On the same day, Hitler issued Directive No. 17, containing orders for "escalated sea and air warfare" against Britain. The operating area for U-boats was considerably extended westward, and within the established zones attack without warning, including against passenger vessels, was permitted.

On Thursday 15 August 1940, the Italian submarine *Delfino* sank off the port of Tenos in the Aegean Sea, the Greek cruiser *Helli*, the first Greek vessel lost since the beginning of the war.

On Saturday 17 August 1940, the German High Command announced a total blockade of the British Isles. Hitler announced that even neutral ships would be sunk without warning.

On Tuesday 20 August 1940, U-boat *U A* (Lt. Comdr. Cohausz) returned to its operational port. During patrols in its operational area off Freetown in West Africa and during the return voyage, the boat sank a total of seven ships, aggregating 40,706 gross tons, in the first operation by a German submarine in southern waters.

On Sunday 24 August 1940, the battleship *Bismarck* was declared ready for operations.

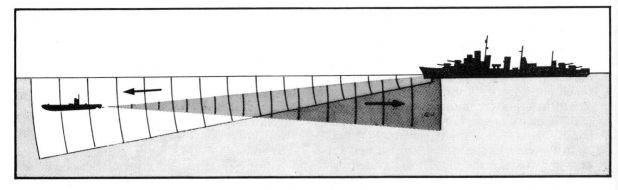

On Thursday 29 August 1940, the operational department of the C-in-C of submarines, Vice-Adm. Dönitz, was transferred from Sengwarden near Wilhelmshaven to offices in the Boulevard Suchet in the Bois de Boulogne area of Paris.

On Friday 30 August 1940, the German radio intelligence service succeeded in deciphering the navigation instructions for Convoy SC-2, made up of twenty-three ships. This marked the beginning of the first successful group attack launched by U-boats, an operation using wolf-pack tactics typical of the second phase of the Battle of the Atlantic. On the same day, Italian Vice-Adm. Perona, C-in-C of submarines Atlantic, occupied the newly completed base at La Pallice. The Italian submarines were placed under the unified command of Rear Adm. Dönitz. The Italian submarine base in Bordeaux was given the code-name Betasom ("beta" for base, "som" for sommergibile, Italian for submarine).

In August 1940, the 9 Air Division commenced intensive mining of harbors on the Thames estuary, as well as harbors along the eastern, southern and southwestern coasts of England. Extensive air raids on convoys and harbors caused British shipping heavy losses. During these operations, a new type of acoustic mine was deployed for the first time. The mine was detonated by the sound of a ship's propellers.

Here are some significant events in the Battle of the Atlantic that were not regarded as being especially important at the time. The German Naval High Command noticed in August 1940 that the Allies were attempting to divert their convoys around known U-boat positions. Accordingly, some convoys were diverted at the last moment and the rendezvous moved by approximately fifty nautical miles. In addition, in August 1940 the British Admiralty suddenly changed their cipher procedures. For the time being, the activities of the German radio intelligence service were made impossible.

U-boats employing the new wolf-pack tactics that Dönitz had conceived before the war gave the escort ships a nasty surprise. Escorts could locate submerged U-boats by the use of Asdic, but surface attacks made Asdic ineffective; also, such attacks usually took place at night when the escort ships were practically blind. The methods in these tactics involved an attack by several U-boats simultaneously against the convoy and its escorts in accordance with a precise plan, rather like a pincer movement. A further advantage of wolf-pack tactics was that U-boats when conducting a search, maintaining a distance from each other of 10–15 nautical miles, could cover a relatively large area with small forces.

If a convoy was discovered by a patrolling U-boat athwart its would-be course, the C-in-C of U-boats would in each instance detail a U-boat to maintain contact with the convoy during the day. This U-boat would have the task of attracting other U-boats to the convoy by radio. Once the entire pack had found the convoy, they would attempt to take up a favorable position before nightfall. Once dark, the U-boats would penetrate the convoy's ranks. Their surface attacks resembled those of an S-boat, 45 degrees ahead, giving a relatively short torpedo run, which allowed the attacked ship scarcely enough time to attempt any evading maneuver. Escort vessels were not provided with radar at that time, and they had to seek out the attacking submarine. This was made all the more difficult because of the submarine's low-lying profile and the fact that the U-boat travelling on the surface was faster than most of the escorts. The most difficult task of the wolf packs was locating convoys in the vast stretches of the East Atlantic. The U-boat's bridge was only about fif-

teen feet above the waterline, so a convoy sailing twenty nautical miles away was below the horizon and invisible to the U-boat.

One important disadvantage with wolf-pack tactics was that the U-boat maintaining contact with the convoy had to send to the C-in-C of U-boats numerous radio messages on the convoy's course, changes in the course, speed and position. These messages were almost always picked up by British direction-finding stations, enabling the Admiralty to gain some indication of the formation and position of the U-boats, although in the autumn of 1940 the British were not yet able to decipher the messages. The Germans experimented with short-form signals thereby reducing the transmission time, which prevented enemy direction-finding stations from gaining an accurate fix on the submarine transmitting.

To counter the U-boat menace, all intelligence relating to U-boats was gathered at the Admiralty's operations center. Urgent messages from British escorts, the merchantmen actually under attack, air and radio reconnaissance and the results of the locating stations' activities were all gathered by the center. After entry on a general map of the U-boat position area, these reports gave a really accurate fix, in minutes, of the U-boat that was transmitting. On another map, position, course and speed of all convoys at sea and ships travelling alone were constantly updated. Thanks to this combination of "U-boat position" and "merchant shipping position," evasion tactics and defence measures could be worked out. The first priority was to radio orders to the convoy to change course in order to evade assembled U-boats.

In August 1940, there were on average eight or nine U-boats in the operational areas, and among them they sank fifty-six ships totalling 267,618 gross tons, some 700–900 gross tons per U-boat per day. German losses amounted to three U-boats. Dönitz said, "This figure shows how very much more favorable the position would have been if we could have had more U-boats operating at that time."

During the same month, the British Admiralty gradually released French naval units that had been seized on 3 July 1940 in British ports. The vessels were handed over to the Free French Navy under the command of Adm. Muselier.

In August 1940, the Italian fleet reached maximum strength with give operational battleships, two of which were among the most modern in the world. Also in August 1940, the technical director of the Signal Corps Service of the US Army, W. F. Friedman, succeeded with his team in breaking the code of a Japanese "Purple" enciphering machine developed from the German Engima machine. This machine was used to encode messages of the Japanese diplomatic service.

On Monday 2 September 1940, the Lend-Lease agreement drawn up between the USA and Great Britain was made public. In return for fifty old US destroyers acquired by Great Britain, the USA was granted bases in the Bahamas, Jamaica, Antigua, Santa Lucia, the Bermudas, Argentia (Newfoundland) and in British Guiana for a term of ninety-nine years.

At the same time, the first three US destroyers arrived in Halifax in Canada. After a short ceremony, they put to sea for the Battle of the Atlantic. The British named most of the destroyers after cities in both Great Britain and the USA. As the destroyers had been in mothballs for almost twenty-two years, a fundamental overhaul in the dockyards was more than necessary. In the opinion of the British seamen, the worst shortcomings were apparent during the first night: The crews' quarters were fitted with bunks, and many a British sailor spent a sleepless night asking why the US Navy had done away with hammocks. The handing over of the fifty rusty destroyers meant — so far as the war in Europe was concerned — a U-turn in the policies of the US government, which legally was bound to neutrality.

On Wednesday 4 September 1940, the first Italian submarine to leave La Spezia arrived in Bordeaux. The submarine *Alessandro Malaspina* (Lt. Comdr. Leoni) had sunk an 8,406-ton English freighter on the way to Bordeaux, the first success achieved by an Italian submarine in the Atlantic. Seven more Italian submarines were already on the

way to their new base in the Bay of Biscay. It very soon became apparent that the Italian submarines were hardly suitable for operations in the rough Atlantic waters. On the same day, four German S-boats belonging to the I S-boat Flotilla (Lt. Comdr. Birnbacher) sank five ships and damaged another in a convoy to the northeast of Great Yarmouth.

The destroyers, torpedo boats and S-boats of the Kriegsmarine now laid an extended minefield with several thousand mines reaching from the eastern approaches to the Channel up to the Irish Sea. This field was to protect German lines of communication close to the coast and, above all, the naval bases on the west coast of France.

On Thursday 5 September 1940 at 5:00 A.M., the German commerce raider *Komet* had put the Bering Strait behind it. The *Komet* was the only German ship that took the northeast passage without overwintering under shelter. The *Komet* took only eighteen days actual travelling time to cover the Siberian sea passage of some 3,000 nautical miles, 720 of which were through ice. Once again the *Komet* adopted the disguise of the Soviet freighter *Deniev* and took course toward its operational area.

The appearance of the German commerce raider *Komet* in the Pacific occurred simultaneously with a very critical phase in Great Britain when every ship sunk represented a considerable loss.

On Monday 9 September 1940, it was officially announced that the US Navy had awarded contracts for the construction of 210 warships including seven battleships and twelve aircraft carriers.

During the night of 12/13 September 1940, the Royal Air Force carried out bombing attacks on

Left: Old US destroyers exchanged for a number of British bases

Above center: September 1940, Bordeaux, Italian submarine in its base

Above right: German S-boat's method of attack

Right: September 1940, near Ostend, landing exercises for Operation Sea Lion. It was postponed for an indefinite period.

the ports of Flushing, Ostend, Dunkirk, Calais and Boulogne where the invasion barges for Operation Sea Lion were gathered.

On Friday 13 September 1940, the Italian Army under Marshal Graziani commenced its offensive across the Libyan-Egyptian border.

During the night of 14/15 September 1940, British bombers again successfully attacked the invasion barges in ports between Antwerp and Boulogne.

On Monday 16 September 1940, Italian troops occupied the Egyptian port of Sidi Barrani. They were, however, held up when the Royal Navy launched massive attacks against supplies and reinforcements coming in by sea.

On Tuesday 17 September 1940, Hitler decided

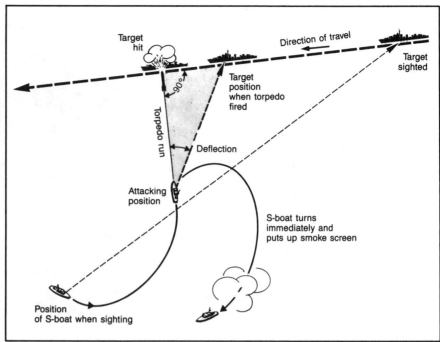

Target
hit

Direction of travel

Target
sighted

90°

Target
position
when torpedo
fired

Torpedo run

Deflection

Attacking
position

S-boat turns
immediately and
puts up smoke screen

Position
of S-boat when sighting

after the heavy losses sustained by the Luftwaffe on 15 September to postpone Operation Sea Lion indefinitely.

Although he had practically given up the idea of a landing in England, Hitler nonetheless continued to make unlimited preparations. The entire German shipyard capacity was fully employed with barges, tugs and trawlers for Operation Sea Lion. At Hitler's express instructions, everything else had to be put back. Not only was the completion of the battleship *Tirpitz* delayed, but also the construction of U-boats and essential repairs to U-boats.

In the middle of September 1940, the eight intact destroyers that the Kriegsmarine still had at its disposal were moved to Brest.

On Friday 20 September 1940, *U 47* (Lt. Comdr. Prien) successfully gathered together five U-boats and, with this wolf pack, attacked Convoy HX-72. During two nights, the pack sank twelve out of a total of forty-one ships, aggregating 77,863 gross tons, and succeeded in heavily damaging another ship.

On the same day, the Italian Expeditionary Corps was transported without loss from Brindisi to Albania to take part in the Greek campaign. A total of 40,310 men, 701 vehicles and 33,535 tons of material were carried across the Adriatic Sea.

On Monday 23 September 1940, Operation Menace began. The British Force H (Vice-Adm. Somerville) with the battleships *Barham* and *Resolution*, the aircraft carrier *Ark Royal*, three heavy cruisers, six destroyers, a squadron from the Free French Navy, as well as the troopships *Pennland* (16,381 gross tons) and *Westernland* (16,479 gross tons) appeared off Dakar. The task force was to land 4,000 British soldiers together with 2,400 troops of the French Foreign Legion. It was Gen. de Gaulle's intention to occupy this important base and harbor, which had the only large-scale dock (over six hundred yards long) between Gibraltar and Cape Town. But the forces in Dakar remained loyal to Vichy and rejected Gen. de Gaulle's ultimatum. The coastal batteries opened fire on the task force and damaged three British ships. The landing of de Gaulle's troops east of the town was delayed by the fog, which became increasingly thick.

During the morning of 24 September 1940, British battleships and heavy cruisers opened fire on the coastal batteries and the harbor of Dakar in which the French ships, the battleship *Richelieu*, two light cruisers and three destroyers, were lying. The French submarine *Ajax* was sunk by a British destroyer.

On Tuesday 24 September 1940, the *Admiral Hipper* tried to reach the open waters of the Atlantic. Engine room faults caused it to break off the planned operation and head for home.

On the same day, the Vichy government issued orders for the naval base and city of Gibraltar to be bombarded. Six bomber squadrons of the former French Armée de l'Air and four squadrons of the French Navy were deployed in the operation. The sixty-four bombers were based at Oran, Tafaroui (Algeria), Meknès, Mediouna, Port Lyautey (Morocco). This action was accepted both by the German and Italian armistice commissions. The order was given to Brig. Gen. Tarnier, commander of the air forces in Morocco.

The most modern aircraft available to the French took part in the attack, which consisted of several waves of bombers. Shortly after 12:20 P.M. the first squadrons, GB I/23 and GB II/23, both flying Léo 45s, took off from their Meknès base and set course for Gibraltar. The area south of the fortress, the south mole and a large ship in harbor were heavily damaged. Fires broke out in the northern part of Gibraltar.

On the next day, 25 September 1940, the French bomber formation was reinforced by additional squadrons, making a total of eighty-three bombers carrying out the raid, under good weather conditions, between 3:00 and 4:40 P.M. On this occasion, there was no fighter escort. The crews reported heavy antiaircraft fire, as on the previous day. And again, on this day no British fighter opposition was encountered. The formation dropped fifty-six tons of bombs. One Léo bomber (GB II/23), based at Meknès and flown by Lt. Court, was shot down by British antiaircraft guns and crashed into the sea. Thirteen aircraft were lightly damaged. Reconnaissance aircraft confirmed hits on the naval base and harbor installations. This attack was the largest action carried out by French bomber forces since the outbreak of the war.

Also on 25 September 1940, British battleships again bombarded the town and harbor of Dakar. The French submarine *Bévéziers* (Lt. Comdr. Lancelot), just out of the dockyards and still freshly painted with red lead, torpedoed the *Resolution*. The badly damaged battleship was listing heavily but, with sixty dead and one hundred wounded on board, was towed toward Cape Town. Churchill gave orders to break off the operation, which was damaging British prestige. In London, furious generals urged Churchill to replace de Gaulle with a new head of the Free French forces. French losses in Dakar amounted to 100 dead and 182 wounded.

9/24/1940, Dakar, the freighter *Tacoma* in flames after an attack by a British warship

On Thursday 26 September 1940, Grand Adm. Raeder attempted to talk Hitler into moving the main thrust of the German war effort to the Mediterranean area — but without success. Inexcusably, Hitler continued to regard the Mediterranean as a troublesome side show.

On Sunday 29 September 1940, toward 10:30 P.M. an Italian submarine that had left port, accompanied by a manned torpedo, on an enemy attack was sunk approximately twenty-two nautical miles west of Alexandria by the Australian destroyer *Stuart* and a Short Sunderland flying boat. Some of the crew, including one of the two builders of the manned torpedo *Maiali*, were taken prison by the British.

In September 1940, German U-boats destroyed a total of fifty-two merchant vessels totalling 256,737 gross tons. One German U-boat was lost. By September 1940, in the first twelve months of the war, twelve German U-boats had been sunk, but during the same period twenty eight more had been built. Ten of these were the small type II (250 tons), which were not suitable for Atlantic operations.

In autumn there was a short breathing space for Allied shipping. Fierce storms raging in the Atlantic hindered the U-boats to such an extent that spotting convoys from the low-lying towers, constantly swept over by high seas, was made considerably more difficult. Although the four-motored Fw 200 could always track shipping, there were too few of them and not all were made available for sea reconnaissance. In addition, the German Navy had no authority to give orders to 40 Bomber

Group stationed in Bordeaux. Nevertheless, the employment of Fw 200s as reconnaissance aircraft also had its disadvantages; for example, the aircraft frequently gave inexact reports of convoy positions, which prevented success by the U-boats.

During September the secret German naval base in the Soviet Union, North Base, was wound up. The Russian base was by now hardly ever used, as, in the meantime, a number of Norwegian and French naval bases had been occupied. Raeder stated, "After the occupation of Norway, this base was no longer required by us. I sent the Russian naval staff a telegram of thanks for the services they had rendered us."

As the British Admiralty had been forced to deploy a large part of their destroyer fleet in the defence of Britain against the threatened invasion, U-boats July through September 1940 sank 217 merchantmen in the weakly escorted convoys. These successes were achieved by élite U-boat captains such as Prien, Kretschmer, Schepke, Schultze, Endrass and Wolfarth, most of whom operated individually. These months were known by U-boat commanders as the "golden age."

From the outbreak of war to the end of September 1940, the German Navy and Air Force together sank 1,102 merchantmen aggregating 4 million gross tons.

On Thursday 10 October 1940, the Soviet submarine *SC 423* (Capt. 3rd Grade Zaydulin) entered the harbor of Vladivostok, becoming the first submarine to use the Siberian sea route from Murmansk.

On Saturday 12 October 1940, Hitler gave orders to postpone Operation Sea Lion until spring 1941.

On Monday 21 October 1940, the Italian Navy repeated its attempt to attack the harbor in Gibraltar with manned torpedoes. The submarine *Scirè*
(Lt. Comdr. Borghese) set out from La Spezia with three manned torpedoes in a special container.

On Wednesday 23 October 1940, the former pocket-battleship *Admiral Scheer* (Capt. Krancke), converted into a heavy cruiser, put to sea from Gdynia to take part in the Atlantic commerce war. Unnoticed by British air reconnaissance, the cruiser slipped along the Norwegian coast northward and from there crossed through the Denmark Strait into the Atlantic.

On Friday 25 October 1940, during a conference Vice-Adm. Dönitz discussed with Hitler the construction of bombproof U-boat shelters on the French coast. Dönitz intended that all U-boats sheltering at their bases along the French west coast would be under bombproof concrete protection during periods allotted for rest, arming and dockyard repairs.

On Saturday 26 October 1940, the British passenger liner *Empress of Britain* (42,348 gross tons) was attacked by an Fw 200 (Lt. Jope) seventy nautical miles northwest of Ireland. Hits in the engine room caused a fire. Two destroyers that came to the rescue helped to extinguish the fire and took the ship in tow.

On Monday 28 October 1940, the *U 32* (Lt. Jenisch), directed by radio, sighted the damaged *Empress of Britain* and the two destroyers. The U-boat sank the liner with two torpedoes. The *Empress of Britain* was the largest Allied passenger liner to be sunk by the Germans in World War II.

On the same day at 5:30 A.M., Italian troops marched into Greece from Albania.

On Tuesday 29 October 1940, one day after Mussolini's attack on Greece, the British occupied Crete, thereby creating a key base in the Mediterranean.

On Thursday 31 October 1940, the commerce raider ship no. 21 *Widder* (Comdr. von Ruckteschell) entered Brest with engine trouble. *Widder* was the first German commerce raider to return from an operational patrol. Its operational area was the Atlantic, primarily the Trinidad-Azores route, where its successes included nine ships totalling 49,321 gross tons and a tanker (9,323 gross tons) taken as prize and later used in Norway as a repair ship. In 1945 the tanker was returned to Great Britain.

On 31 October 1940 toward 1:30 A.M., the Italian submarine *Scirè* approached the Bay of Algeciras opposite Gibraltar. The Submarine lay on the bottom at a depth of forty-five feet. The crew commenced removing the manned torpedoes from their containers.

Technical faults were immediately apparent. The compass on the first torpedo malfunctioned. De-

Left: British reports on the success at Taranto

Above right: 11/12 November 1940, British air raid on Taranto

Right: 11/11/1940, on board the *Illustrious*, bombs for the carrier's aircraft

spite repeated attempts, the torpedo remained nonoperational and had to be left on the bottom. The torpedo crewmen both swam to the Spanish coast two miles away, where waiting Italian agents gave further help. The water pump on the second torpedo failed, and shortly afterward the oxygen equipment failed. The crew dropped the warhead and sailed the machine to the Spanish coast. At 7:10, they were picked up by Italian agents. It was this time that one of the torpedo's crewmen made a fatal mistake: He pushed the machine with its motor running back into the water, presuming it would sink. But the British detected the torpedo, salvaged it and copied the design. It became the prototype for the British small-vessels war. The crew of the third torpedo also had bad luck. One man lost his life during the action—his body was later fished out of the harbor by the British—while the completely exhausted steersman of the torpedo, unable to reach the Spanish coast, climbed aboard one of the neutral ships lying at the mole. He was discovered by British auxiliary police searching the vessel and taken prisoner.

In October 1940, German U-boats sank sixty-one merchantmen totalling 344,684 gross tons. Germans lost one U-boat.

During the evening of 5 November 1940, the heavy cruiser *Admiral Scheer* sighted Convoy HX-84 in the North Atlantic. The British armed merchant cruiser *Jervis Bay* (Capt. Fegen), which was escorting this convoy, engaged the *Admiral Scheer* to give the convoy a chance of escaping. The heavy cruiser, however, was not hit, as the range of the merchant cruiser's guns were some nine thousand yards shorter than the German guns. When the *Jervis Bay*, burning extensively, went down with its entire crew, the convoy was so widely scattered that the *Admiral Scheer* succeeded in sinking only five ships. Among these was the British tanker *San Demetrio*, which was set on fire and abandoned by the crew.

On Wednesday 6 November 1940, one of the lifeboats from the *San Demetrio* sighted that ship, covered with dense smoke but still afloat. The lifeboat went alongside the tanker and several men reboarded the ship. The deck was red hot. The fire was successfully extinguished and the engines restarted. The *San Demetrio* now began its adventurous journey back to Great Britain. Without navigational equipment and only a school atlas that had been found on board, the crew brought the tanker back to Britain with a large part of its valuable cargo of oil.

The operations conducted by the *Admiral Scheer* led to a hunt for this cruiser by the Royal Navy in mid-Atlantic waters.

When Adm. Cunningham discovered that the Italian Navy was avoiding a decisive confrontation at sea, he resolved to seek out the Italian fleet in its main bases.

During the night of 11/12 November 1940, British torpedo bombers and other bombers attacked the Italian naval base at Taranto (Operational Judgment). At that time, the Italian fleet was ready to set sail from Taranto the following day to bombard Suda (Crete), where units of the British Mediterranean Fleet were stationed. Shortly after dusk, the aircraft carrier *Illustrious*, some 140 nautical miles southeast of Taranto, released the first wave, twelve biplane Swordfish torpedo bombers fitted with supplementary fuel tanks, led by Lt. Comdr. K. Williamson. The second wave, commanded by Lt. Comdr. J. W. Hall, consisting of only eight aircraft because of a number of technical faults, followed one hour later. One aircraft after another flew between the barrage balloons, dropping their torpedoes accurately over the gap in the torpedo net some 600–700 yards from their targets. During the operation, some of the aircraft flew so low that their wheels skimmed along the water. Had the torpedoes been dropped from a greater height, they would have been smashed to pieces upon contact with the water.

Antiaircraft guns put up a massive barrage. Lit by the moon and flares, the Italian warships stood out in clear relief against the western sky. The *Conte di Cavour* received one torpedo hit and the *Littorio* two. Then the second wave appeared, which despite its reduced strength scored one hit on the *Caio Duilio* and two further hits on the *Littorio*. Only one aircraft was lost from each of

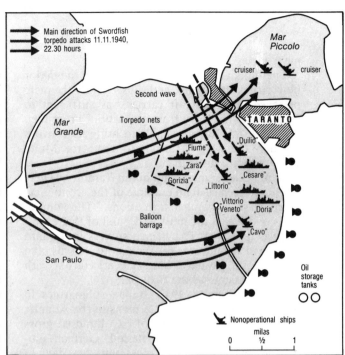

the two formations attacking. The three bombed battleships sank at anchor. Although the *Littorio* and *Caio Duilio* were later raised and repaired, they were put out of action for five or six months. The *Conte di Cavour* was never again put into service. The bombing attacks on the cruisers and destroyers in the inner harbor were less successful; the only bombs that struck their target failed to explode.

"I have good news for you," said Churchill in the House of Commons, waving the victory telegram, "the balance of naval power in the Mediterranean has changed." The remaining Italian warships were withdrawn to Naples. As a consequence, the east-

ern part of the Mediterranean was free of major units of the Italian Navy. This tactical and strategical success was achieved at a cost of just two British aircraft. One airman was killed and three were taken prisoner.

The attack by the carrier-borne torpedo bombers on the naval base of Taranto put half of the Italian battleships out of action and confirmed the importance of aircraft carriers during this new age of sea warfare.

The aircraft carrier had replaced the large-caliber ship's guns as a principal weapon in sea warfare. For the first time, a battle fleet had been eliminated in its own harbor without the opposing navy having fired a shot.

The Italian fleet never recovered from the major blow struck in Taranto, and subsequently the mere presence of an aircraft carrier was sufficient to keep the Italian Navy from any action. From then on, the Royal Navy was able to bring its convoys through the Mediterranean to reinforce Malta without major difficulty.

Adm. Cunningham said about Taranto, "There has never been such an example of the economical deployment of bomber formations." The admiral had no idea that the most avid pupil of that example was in Tokyo. The British success in Taranto convinced Japanese Adm. Yamamoto that his plan to attack the US naval base at Pearl Harbor with aircraft carriers was the right one.

By 30 November 1940, Italian submarines in joint operations with the Germans in the Atlantic had each sunk an average of two hundred gross tons per day. In the same period, German submarines each sank 1,115 gross tons per day. In November 1940, long-range Fw 200 bombers sank eighteen ships totalling 66,000 gross tons, and thirty-four merchantmen totalling 173,995 gross tons were lost in the Atlantic to U-boats. German losses amounted to three U-boats.

On Tuesday December 1940, the commerce raider ship no. 41 *Kormoran* (Capt. Detmers) put to sea from Gdynia. It was formerly the *Steiermark* (8,736 gross tons) and had a complement of four hundred. The *Kormoran* was the biggest of all the German merchant raiders, with armament comprising six 15-cm guns; two 3.7-cm antiaircraft guns; five 2-cm antiaircraft guns; six torpedo tubes; a high-speed launch; two Ar 196 floatplanes; and 390 mines.

On Thursday 5 December 1940, the German commerce raider *Thor* encountered the British armed merchant cruiser *Carnavon Castle* (20,122 gross tons) in the early morning mist southeast of Rio de Janeiro. The British commander, Capt. Hardy, opened fire on the *Thor*. At 8:02, after having failed to score a single hit, the *Carnavon Castle*, badly damaged itself and with thirty-seven dead and eighty-seven wounded on board, took a northerly course and withdrew. The Royal Navy ordered an immediate large-scale hunt for the German commerce raider, in which the British cruisers *Cumberland*, *Enterprise* and *Newcastle* took part. They were, however, unsuccessful.

The two engagements with the commerce raider *Thor* by the British armed merchant cruisers — *Alcantara* on 28 July 1940 and now the *Carnavon Castle* — represented the only chance the Admiralty was to have in 1940 of destroying even one of the elusive German commerce raiders.

On Sunday 7 December 1940, the cruiser *Admiral Hipper* (Capt. Meisel) steamed unobserved through the Denmark Strait into the North Atlantic.

On Monday 9 December 1940, the successful British offensive in Cyrenaica commenced, led by Gen. Wavell.

On Tuesday 10 December 1940, the Italian Navy was reorganised because of its repeated failures. Adm. Riccardi replaced Chief of Naval Staff Adm. Cavagnari, and Adm. Campioni became the Deputy Chief of Naval Staff. Fleet command was taken over by Adm. Iachino, the former commander of 2 Cruiser Squadron.

In December 1940, the German Naval High Command fitted magnetic and acoustic mines with a new type of delayed action fuse. In the second week of December, the German IX Air Corps (Lt. Gen. Coeler) carried out a large-scale minelaying operation. Between 12 and 19 December 1940, 299 mines were laid at the mouth of the Thames during night operations.

In the middle of December 1940, almost six months after the occupation of the Atlantic coast naval bases, the U-boat arm was still without a reliable long-range reconnaissance service. Dönitz stated, "Without long-range reconnaissance and the guidance of U-boats to their targets, either by reconnaissance or by radio intelligence, the U-boats remain underemployed at sea. If they should lose a convoy, aircraft can more easily find it again and guide the U-boats back into contact." Dönitz energetically demanded better support and cooperation by the Luftwaffe in matters of reconnaissance. Only because of personal contact between him and the future officer commanding the Atlantic air units, Lt. Col. Harlinghausen, a former naval officer, at least two Fw 200s would in future undertake daily long-range reconnaissance flights on behalf of the U-boat arm.

On Wednesday 18 December 1940, the British battleships *Valiant* and *Warspite* bombarded the supplies and reinforcements harbor at Valona (Albania), an important base for the Italian armed forces.

On the same day, Hitler signed Directive No. 21 (Operation Barbarossa) for the offensive against the Soviet Union. After months of vacillating, Hitler therewith decided to give up any maritime strategy against Great Britain. The German armed forces would now "beat Britain in the expanses of the Soviet Union." This decision for a Continental strategy meant that the main emphasis of German armaments would now be dictated by the requirements of the army. Raeder stated, "I said to Hitler that he could not possibly start a war on two fronts after he had so frequently emphasised that he would never repeat the stupid mistakes of the 1914

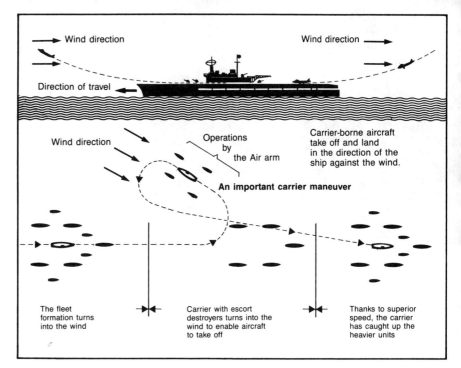

Right: An important maneuver by aircraft carriers—turning into the wind for aircraft taking off and landing

Wind direction

Wind direction

Direction of travel

Wind direction

Operations by the Air arm

Carrier-borne aircraft take off and land in the direction of the ship against the wind.

An important carrier maneuver

The fleet formation turns into the wind

Carrier with escort destroyers turns into the wind to enable aircraft to take off

Thanks to superior speed, the carrier has caught up the heavier units

Below: Sectional view of the carrier. Hangars and boiler rooms determine the shape of the vessel.

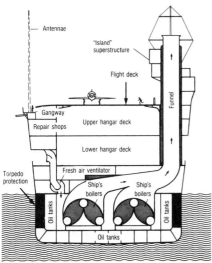

Antennae

"Island" superstructure

Flight deck

Funnel

Gangway

Repair shops

Upper hangar deck

Lower hangar deck

Torpedo protection

Fresh air ventilator

Ship's boilers

Ship's boilers

Oil tanks

Oil tanks

Oil tanks

government. I tried to convince Hitler that a thrust in the Mediterranean should be carried out simultaneously with a thrust against Russia."

On Friday 20 December 1940, the British Admiralty decided to route the convoys through the North Atlantic closer to the ice regions. Additionally, a number of aircraft, and more vessels than previously, were assigned for escort duties.

On Tuesday 24 December 1940, the Greek submarine *Papanicolis* (Lt. Iatrides) operating in the Adriatic attacked an Italian supply convoy bound for Albania and sank a transport vessel of 3,952 tons.

Also on Christmas Eve, the Norwegian fishing boat *Vita* (Capt. Larsen) put to sea from a secret base near Flemington House to the north of Lerwick in the Shetlands. These voyages from the Shetlands to Norway became known as the "Shet-land bus service." The undertaking, run jointly by the Norwegian section of the Special Operations Executive (SOE) and the British Secret Service, was led by Major L. H. Mitchell and Comdr. Horvard together with Norwegian fishing boat owners. Later the fishing smacks were replaced by whalers, British high-speed motor launches and American submarine hunters. They laid mines off the Norwegian coast; transported arms, ammunition and explosives for the Norwegian underground organisation Milorg; recruited SOE agents; and transported Norwegian volunteers back to Scotland on each voyage. Subsequently, the base for the Shetland bus flotilla was transferred to Lunna Voe on Yell Sound and expanded. Approximately one hundred sailors comprised the crews of which four were on the move at any given time.

Also on 24 December 1940, the heavy cruiser *Admiral Hipper* sighted a convoy comprising twenty ships on the shipping lane to Sierra Leone and shadowed it throughout the night. The convoy was made up of heavy naval units and troopships destined for the Middle East.

During the morning of 25 December 1940, the cruiser exchanged fire briefly with the convoy vessels. The unusually strong convoy escorts, together with engine-room failure, caused the *Admiral Hipper* to break off the engagement.

Only one U-boat served on operational patrol over Christmas 1940, the remainder either serving as training ships or lying in the dockyards.

On Friday 27 December 1940, the arrival of the cruiser *Admiral Hipper*, the first heavy unit to reach Brest, signalled the commencement of a new phase in the commerce war: German surface war-

Above: Vice-Adm. Dönitz awarding decorations to U-boat crews

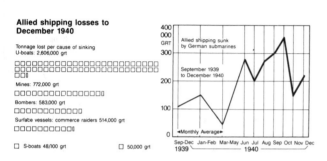

Allied shipping losses to December 1940

Tonnage lost per cause of sinking
U-boats: 2,606,000 grt

□□□
□□□

Mines: 772,000 grt
□□□□□□□□□□□□□□□

Bombers: 583,000 grt
□□□□□□□□□□□□

Surface vessels: commerce raiders 514,000 grt
□□□□□□□□□□□

□ S-boats 48,000 grt   □ 50,000 grt

Allied shipping sunk by German submarines
September 1939 to December 1940

◄Monthly Average►

Sep-Dec 1939 | Jan-Feb | Mar-May | Jun | Jul | Aug | Sep | Oct | Nov | Dec 1940

ships would try to exploit the advantages of the naval base at Brest, which was situated close to the British flank.

On Saturday 28 December 1940, the first German blockade-runner, the motor vessel *Ermland* (later the *Weserland*), put to sea from the Japanese port of Kobe, bound for Europe.

On the initiative of the German naval attaché in Tokyo, Vice-Adm. Wennecker, an organisation was built up in Japan that was to provide the German armaments industry with desperately needed raw materials. German merchantmen lying in Japanese ports since the outbreak of war were now to be employed as blockade-runners bringing these goods, essential for the war effort, back to Germany.

At the end of December 1940, upon their return to their base at Bordeaux, the Italian submarines had to go into dock. Air intake and exhaust tubes for diesel motors had to be fitted; electrical installations damaged by sea water were replaced; and, above all, their high conning towers were replaced by lower towers.

By the end of 1940, British ships and aircraft had sunk twenty-eight ships, totalling 190,000 gross tons, transporting supplies to North Africa, thereby bringing about in December the catastrophic collapse of the Italian Army in Cyrenaica. This defeat came as a total surprise for Hitler. Only a month previously, he was of the opinion that the situation was so favorable that he could count on an early Italian offensive.

In the second half of 1940, U-boats sank 343 merchantmen totalling 1,700,000 gross tons, an average of some 240,000 destroyed per month. These losses forced the British Admiralty to route the convoys away from the southernmost tip of Ireland and instead route them via the longer voyage around the northern tip of Iceland; nevertheless, thirty-nine more merchantmen, totalling 229,501 gross tons, were sunk by U-boats in the Atlantic. No U-boats were lost during this period.

Hitler had accorded U-boat building such low priority that after fifteen months of war, the thirty-one U-boats lost in the period could not be replaced. The German Navy had been allocated a total of only five percent of total steel output. So, at the end of 1940, the operational strength of the U-boat arm had fallen to the record low of twenty-one submarines. Dönitz said, "It was a decisive error on the part of our political leadership that they failed to recognise the significance of the total change to our advantage in our geographical and strategical situation . . . . We had gained harbors giving direct access to the Atlantic and failed to exploit these to the utmost for the U-boat war at sea, because we had failed to build a sufficient number of submarines." Without doubt, this mistaken decision helped to save Great Britain.

In 1940, the commerce raiders caused heavy losses in the Pacific, Atlantic and Indian Ocean. The six German auxiliary cruisers sank a total of fifty-four ships totalling 367,000 gross tons. In addition, they caused considerable confusion in British shipping circles. Mines laid by the German commerce raiders also caused further losses. In the short term, Great Britain was partially able to offset these enormous losses by organisational measures applied to the peacetime merchant shipping fleet.

At this time, the obligatory escort for a convoy was increased to two ships. Churchill wrote, "As the end of the year approached, both its light and its shadows stood out harshly on the picture. We were alive. We had beaten the German Air Force. There had been no invasion of the Island."

On the last day of 1940, in the vastness of the South Atlantic and in oppressive heat, the heavy cruiser *Admiral Scheer* met up with the commerce raider *Thor*, two German supply ships, the tanker *Eurofeld* (5,863 gross tons) and the *Nordmark* (22,850 gross tons), as well as the prize *Duguesa* (8,652 gross tons), a British refrigerated cargo ship with 3,500 tons of beef and 15 million eggs on board—certainly the largest gathering of German ships in the southern hemisphere during the entire war.

1941

January–June

Swiss Radio Beromünster

Thursday 2 January 1941

It sounds almost like a declaration of war when Roosevelt tells his people that there can be no peace with National Socialism; as such a peace could be nothing more than an armistice leading to a massive arms race and the greatest commerce war in history. In other words, Roosevelt has linked America's fate with England's in that he has stated that the future security of the United States depends upon the outcome of this war. . . . The fateful decision by Roosevelt can mean danger for Britain's enemies in the relatively near future but not yet in the immediate weeks or months to come. For Great Britain, it means that she will be dependent on a larger and less immediately endangered ally to continue her desperate war of existence.

Italian Torpedo Bombers in Action

Saturday 11 January 1941, Rome

The *Italian High Command* issued the following communiqué:

In the Strait of Messina, enemy fleet formations were repeatedly attacked by our torpedo bombers and motor torpedo boats. Two torpedo bombers — Capt. Bernardini, commander, 1st Lt. Bassigo, observer, and 1st Lt. Caponetti, pilot — scored a hit on an aircraft carrier with a torpedo.

Air Attack on the Illustrious

Thursday 16 January 1941, Cairo

The *Exchange* News Agency reported:

We have just heard that the aircraft carrier *Illustrious*, damaged last week by a bomb, has man-aged to reach a British naval base under its own steam.

Loss of the Cruiser Southampton

16 January 1941, London

The *British Admiralty* issued the following communiqué:

The cruiser *Southampton* (9,100 tons), damaged by bombs in the Mediterranean last Friday, has had to be abandoned. The attempt to tow the cruiser into port could not be continued because of an explosion in its boilers.

Further Attack on the Illustrious

Friday 17 January 1941, Berlin

The German *DNB* News Agency reported:

The British aircraft carrier *Illustrious* was yesterday repeatedly attacked by German dive bombers. Heavy-caliber bombs and medium-caliber bombs hit the vessel. Competent German authorities believe that the British Admiralty will not succeed before the end of the war in restoring the *Illustrious* to an operational condition.

A U-boat Hears the Führer

From Herbert Kühn, war correspondent
Völkischer Beobachter, 1/31/1941

U-boat *U* . . . is slowly beating a path through the rough green seas. On its bridge stand the men who week after week make war on England with this small ship. . . . Suddenly a shot comes up from below through the hatch, "The Führer's speaking!" As if electrified, everybody that can be spared from the deck rushes below to the control room. The petty officer radio operator, our Karlheinz, fiddles with the receiver and suddenly we hear the sound of the Badenweiler march. The announcer describes the enthusiasm that we can hear coming over the air! No one stays in his bunk, there's no one who was on the last watch who has not squeezed into a small space in the tight throng around the radio! . . .

The captain has also jumped down from the bridge and now sits surrounded by his brave men. They all look oily and dirty, not at all the "smart lads in blue" as they have so often been imagined. But the eyes, the eyes! Their eyes gleam bright like burning coals in the bearded, weather-beaten faces. In spirit they are back in Berlin, back in the sports arena in the Potsdamer Strasse!

And now the Führer speaks! Here on the edge of the Atlantic we hear his voice clearly and distinctly. We listen to his opinions, direct and to the point. We too applaud and cry bravo and Heil, just as they are in Berlin! We nod to each other, we grin contentedly and we're happy. We know that the Führer speaks to us; the first soldier of Greater Germany is speaking to his comrades!

"Every ship, whether it's escorted or whether it isn't, that crosses our torpedo tubes will be torpedoed!"

The tremendous enthusiasm that accompanies these words calls for the highest enthusiasm from us as well. The Führer has spoken to us personally. These words were addressed to us, to us in the navy and, above all, his men in the U-boats! And we'll present him with a good round number of ships destroyed in loyal fulfillment of his words. Deep within us, from the captain to the youngest sailor, is the happiness of this moment. Can there be anything finer, anything more proudly received in the Fatherland than the Führer's words? . . .

Those up above on the bridge heard parts of the speech through the speaking tube. And these men too, these men up here on watch, they too stand spellbound by the Führer's words. Deep inside us, our oath of allegiance is reaffirmed, "Führer command, we obey!"

Fire Number 3!

Lt. Comdr. Schepke tells the youth of Berlin about the U-boat war
Völkischer Beobachter, 2/5/1941

It was a small U-boat that put out into the North Sea at the beginning of the war. It certainly had torpedo tubes, but there was no gun on the deck as there would be with a larger U-boat, only a machine gun. The operational radius was limited. But the crew, who have to spend a long time living together in a limited amount of space, build up a very special form of comradeship: On board a submarine with its relatively small crew, each man is dependent on the other.

It is this comradeship that makes us proud and certain of victory. Which U-boat man would want to miss that moment when the lookout reports, "Smoke trails sighted. Two masts on the horizon." That is our British enemy who must be trapped and hit. It's then necessary to know the speed of the enemy, to calculate his course in a few seconds and bring the U-boat into the correct firing position. When the commander gives the order "Fire number 3," one of the crew stands in the control room with a stop watch and counts the seconds. The entire crew waits anxiously, perhaps they are already disappointed, and then a shock goes through the boat and cheers break out, "We've got him, we've hit the British ship!"

Directive No. 23

The Supreme Commander of the Armed Forces
Berlin, 2/6/1941

Secret!
Officers only
Guidelines for the conduct of war against the British military economy

1.) The effect of our warfare against Britain to date:

In contrast to our earlier estimations, the most devastating effect in the fight against the British military economy has been caused by the high losses of merchantmen through marine and air force activities. This effect has been further increased by the destruction of harbor installations and the destruction of large quantities of supplies as well as through the reduced employment of ships when they are forced to travel in convoys.

A further considerable increase may be expected through the additional deployment of submarines this year, which can within a foreseeable period lead to the collapse of the British power to resist.

2.) The consequences for our conduct of the war:

During the next few months, the effect of sea warfare on the enemy merchant fleet will be increased by the extended deployment of submarines and surface warships. In contrast, the extent of our air attacks will not be maintained, as employment in other theaters of war will cause an increasing number of Luftwaffe units to be withdrawn from operations against the British Isles.

Consequently it will be necessary in future to concentrate air attacks primarily against such targets whose destruction will have the same effect as the war at sea. Only by these methods can we expect a decisive outcome to the war within the foreseeable future.

(signed) Adolf Hitler

Official Denial by Greece
Saturday 8 February 1941, Athens
The *Greek Admiralty* issued the following communiqué:

Since the outbreak of the war, despite reports to the contrary, no Greek warship has been sunk by the Italian Navy, but during the same period it can be said with certainty that three Italian submarines in the Adriatic and three freighters totalling 35,000 tons have been sunk.

Naval Attack on Genoa

Monday 10 February 1941
The *British Admiralty* issued the following communiqué:

Detailed information on our operations against the Italian naval base in the Bay of Genoa shows that the bombardment by our fleet and aircraft was more successful than had at first been assumed. Our naval force under the command of Vice-Adm. Sir James Somerville comprised the battleships *Renown* and *Malaya*, the aircraft carrier *Ark Royal* and the cruiser *Sheffield*, as well as

a number of smaller units. Military objectives in the port of Genoa and the surrounding area were effectively bombarded. During the attacks, more than three hundred tons of shells were fired.

On Board HMS Malaya
10 February 1941
The naval correspondent of the *Exchange* News Agency reported:

The attack took the Italians completely by surprise. When we left the harbor, only a few of those on board the *Malaya* knew the action that awaited us. . . . The voyage along the Italian coast took place without incident. On Sunday at 7:00 A.M., the command "action stations" was given, and the target, which had been kept secret up until then, was revealed. On the approaches to the Gulf of Genoa, we met neither patrol boats nor aircraft. A little later, we sighted Genoa. The aircraft from the *Malaya* and from the cruiser *Sheffield* were launched by catapult. They were to serve as artillery spotters together with the carrier-borne aircraft from the *Ark Royal*. Suddenly the customary red-green lights from the Italian coast signalled the question, "Who are you?" A few seconds later, the first salvo was fired from the *Renown*'s guns into the harbor installations of Genoa. At the same time, the *Malaya* fired a broadside at the inner harbor. To the right of us, the cruiser *Sheffield* fired at the Ansaldo works. It lasted a full fifteen minutes before the Italian coastal batteries went

In a home base: The U-boat crew goes ashore.

into action. Their fire was weak and unaimed. Out of twenty or twenty-one shells, the nearest was five hundred yards away.

Radio for Small Merchant Ships
Saturday 15 February 1941, London
The *Reuters* News Agency reported:

British merchant ships under 1,600 tons, which up until now have not been obliged to have radio equipment on board, must in future be fitted with a radio receiver that will enable them to hear the BBC's broadcasts. This directive has been issued by the Ministry of Shipping, who have further ordered that these ships must listen in at the broadcasting times for the BBC news programs.

Practical Report
Luftwaffe frontline news sheet, February 1941

Deception measures on ships: According to intelligence received from neutral sources, measures employed by ships under attack to mislead aircrews include faking direct hits. Apparent fires (caused by using burning tar barrels?) are produced on deck and the crew takes to the boats.

British Surprise Assault against the Lofoten Isles
Wednesday 5 March 1941, Berlin
The *DNB* Agency reported:

During the morning of 4 March, British light naval forces attempted a surprise assault against an unfortified island off north Norway. After a short bombardment claiming as victims some of the fishing vessels lying there, soldiers were landed who took some Germans and some Norwegian fishermen as prisoners. After a short stay, the enemy ships left Norwegian waters at full speed to escape German countermeasures. German experts believe that these were British propaganda operations without any military significance.

Thursday 6 March 1941, London
The *Reuters* News Agency reported:

The Norwegian forces deployed in the attack on the Lofoten Islands were soldiers trained in England. Since the cessation of hostilities in Norway, they have been employed as a special unit for Allied operations. We understand that British ships carrying out the attack on the Lofotens did not just take off Germans and supporters of Quisling, but also more than three hundred Norwegians remaining loyal to the former government, who volunteered to take ship for England.

Swiss Radio Beromünster

Thursday 13 March 1941
The most important event of the week has been

the passing and enactment of the Lend-Lease law in the United States of America. Through this law, the aid plan in favor of Britain and Greece, proposed by Pres. Roosevelt for the first time last December, will now have legal effect. At the same time, the president will receive extraordinary powers to implement this aid plan. . . . The view is expressed in Berlin and Rome that it is now too late for aid to Britain. In any event, Axis strategy will aim to put an end to the war by such forceful and decisive action that American aid will become pointless.

Secret report of the *SS Security Service* on the internal political situation:
No. 174, 27 March 1941 (Extract)

I. General: The increasing successes of German sea and air forces in the Atlantic Ocean have been received with grateful joy and much enthusiasm. The news on the successful operation by a German naval formation in the North Atlantic has caused particular jubilation.

New Operation by Italian Assault Boats
Friday 28 March 1941, Rome
The *Italian High Command* issued the following communiqué:

The night of 26 March, assault boats of the Italian Navy entered the Suda Bay (Crete) and attacked British warships and transports lying at anchor, thereby causing the enemy heavy losses. An enemy warship was sunk.

Serious Anglo-French Incident
Sunday 30 March 1941, Vichy
The *French Ministry for Naval Affairs* issued the following communiqué:

Today at 9:00 A.M., a strong British formation attacked a convoy consisting of French merchant ships in French waters between Nemours and Oran. The convoy was under the protection of only one torpedo boat and was en route from Casablanca to Oran. Under the protective fire of the escort ship, the French convoy successfully reached the harbor at Nemours.

German and Italian Seamen in Custody
Monday 31 March 1941, Berlin
The *United Press Agency* reported:

With regard to the seizure of Italian, Danish and German ships in the USA, an authoritative German source has stated, "This is quite possibly an event of historical significance." An official German statement will be made at a later date.

The British battleship *Malaya* (31,465 tons). It took part in the bombardment of Genoa on 2/10/1941.

Swiss Radio Beromünster

Thursday 3 April 1941

The military events in Abyssinia possibly have a closer connection with events in the Near East than may at first be apparent. Two factors determined the great energy and speed with which troops of the British Empire and their Allies launched the concentrated offensive against the Abyssinian interior: The first is the coming rainy season that will commence in the middle of April; the second is the necessity to release forces tied down in Abyssinia so as to deploy them elsewhere. As soon as the port of Mesewa in Eritrea is in British hands, the troops previously stationed in the Red Sea area can be engaged in either Singapore or the Mediterranean, as Italy will have lost her last port on the Red Sea. In East Abyssinia, with the fall of Harer and Dire Dawa, the most important points on the road to Addis Ababa are in British hands.

New Raid on Brest
Friday 4 April 1941, London
The *British Air Ministry* issued the following communiqué:

Reconnaissance flights have shown that the German battlecruisers *Scharnhorst* and *Gneisenau* are at present in the docks at Brest. Despite the bad weather, a concentrated raid was carried out last night by heavy bombers from RAF Bomber Command and Coastal Command against harbor installations in Brest.

Joint Convoy System
4 April 1941, New York
The Washington correspondent of *The New York Times* reported:

Official sources have stated that discussions have taken place between representatives of the British and American navies on plans for a joint convoy system.

US Officers as Observers
Sunday 6 April 1941, Washington
The *Reuters* News Agency reported:

The task of these observers is to draw up a report based on the accumulated experiences of US bombers in the war. American naval officers have, in the same capacity, taken part in operations in the Atlantic and Mediterranean on board British warships.

Schepke
Kretschmer
Prien

Was ist aus diesen drei Offizieren geworden, den berühmtesten deutschen U-Bootkommandanten, den einzigen, welchen Hitler das Eichenlaub zum Ritterkreuz verliehen hat?

Schepke ist tot. Das deutsche OKW musste es zugeben. Kretschmer ist kriegsgefangen. Das deutsche OKW musste es zugeben.

UND PRIEN? Wer hat neuerdings etwas von Prien gehört? Was hat das OKW über Prien zu sagen?

WO IST
PRIEN ?

Leaflet dropped by the RAF over Germany in May 1941.

The British Blockade
Monday 7 April 1941, Marseilles
The *United Press Agency* reported:

The British have reinforced their blockade patrols in the Strait of Gibraltar after four French merchant steamers recently succeeded in reaching Oran from Casablanca, escorted by one destroyer. Five British destroyers now patrol the Strait of Gibraltar to ensure that no ship passes through the straits without being subjected to British inspection. Currently there are said to be thirty merchantmen and five tankers in the harbor at Gibraltar, waiting for clearance by British inspectors. The majority of these ships are sailing under the French ensign.

British Warships Repaired in the USA
Tuesday 8 April 1941, Washington
The *Exchange* News Agency reported:

The naval minister Knox requested journalists not to release precise details on the recent arrival in the USA of certain British warships that are being repaired and overhauled under the Lend-Lease agreement. The minister declared, "Such publication could only serve the interests of the Axis powers, and I appeal for your cooperation when I ask you to be discreet."

War in the Balkans

8 April 1941, Sydney
The *Australian Minister for Naval Affairs* issued the following communiqué:

British troopships bound for Greece as well as supplies of material and ammunition have arrived without loss, although the Italian fleet and the Axis air forces tried everything to disrupt the undertaking.

Explosion in Piraeus
8 April 1941, Athens
The *Greece Ministry of Security* announced:

A merchant ship carrying ammunition and explosives blew up in the port of Piraeus, causing considerable damage.

W. Churchill to the Minister of Information
Monday 14 April 1941

The publication of the weekly sinkings is to be discontinued henceforth – i.e. no more, no publication next Tuesday. When the press ask why have the week's figures not come out, the answer will be they are to be published monthly instead of weekly. . . . We shall have a lot of worse things than that to put up with in the near future.

W. Churchill to the Chief of Air Staff (RAF)
Thursday 17 April 1941

It must be recognised that the inability of Bomber Command to hit the enemy cruisers in Brest constitutes a very definite failure of this arm. No serious low-level daylight attack has been attempted.

W. Churchill to President Roosevelt
Thursday 24 April 1941

Another area in which we are having considerable trouble is that from Freetown up through the Cape Verdes to the Azores . . . (for yourself alone). . . . Of course, the moment Spain gives way or is attacked we shall despatch two expeditions which we have long been holding in readiness, one from Britain to one of the islands in the Azores, and subsequently to a second island in the Cape Verdes.

Turning Point in the Battle of the Atlantic?

Friday 25 April 1941
The *German High Command* issued the following communiqué:

The submarines commanded by Comdr. Kretschmer and Lt. Comdr. Schepke have not returned from their operational patrols. Both ships recently participated under difficult conditions in the destruction of enemy convoys and, in so doing, considerably increased their total of successes.

In addition to the destruction of three enemy destroyers – two of which were sunk during his last patrol—Comdr. Kretschmer has now sunk a total of 313,611 gross tons, including the armed merchant cruisers *Laurentic* and *Forfar*. Lt. Comdr. Schepke has sunk 233,971 gross tons of enemy shipping capacity.

These two commanders, in recognition of their magnificent services in the German people's war for freedom, have been awarded the Oak Leaves to the Knight's Cross of the Iron Cross and, together with their brave crews, have won everlasting glory. Some of the crews, including Comdr. Kretschmer, were taken prisoner.

The Strongest Battleship in the World
25 April 1941, London
The *Reuters* News Agency reported:

The new battleship *Prince of Wales* is so constructed that it cannot be sunk. If damages are sustained, the effect will be reduced by an elaborate system of watertight subdivisions below decks. The constructional plans are being kept even more secret than those for the *King George V.* The *Prince of Wales* is the strongest battleship in the world.

Evacuation of Greece

Monday 28 April 1941, Cairo
The *C-in-C Middle East* issued the following communiqué:

Evacuation of the British Expeditionary Corps from Greece has commenced and has so far been carried out successfully.

W. Churchill to General Wavell
28 April 1941

It seems clear from our information that a heavy airborne attack by German troops and bombers will soon be made on Crete. Let me know what forces you have on the island and what your plans are. The island must be stubbornly defended.

Catalina Flying Boat in the Battle of the Atlantic
28 April 1941, London
The *Exchange* News Agency reported:

Because of the arrival of numerous aircrews from Canada, Coastal Command has been able to form a number of new squadrons that will be used immediately in the Battle of the Atlantic. The formation of these new squadrons is above all attributable to the arrival in this country of the Consolidated Catalina flying boats which have a range of some three thousand miles. These flying boats are equipped with the most modern weapons and carry a new type of depth charge for use against U-boats. A Catalina's crew normally numbers seven.

One of the last photos of Comdr. Günter Prien

Secret report of the *SS Security Service* on the internal political situation:
No. 181, 28 April 1941 (Extract)

The report of the loss of the U-boat heroes Schepke and Kretschmer, whose fate is spoken of by the population with the deepest sympathy, has brought to the fore the discussions that have been taking place among the people regarding the U-boat arm. This was particularly so after the current reports, as for some time before the loss of these U-boats, the high command reports had not contained any news of large-scale sinkings.

The question of the escalated U-boat war in the spring is now being discussed with increasing concern. From one high command report to the next, the figures of tonnage sunk by U-boats are being increasingly questioned. The recently reported loss is now being seen as confirmation of the rumors and suppositions that have been circulating for some time: that the British have discovered a new, certain method, perhaps special bombs or "U-boat traps," for the destruction of U-boats (Dresden, Kiel, Halle, Leipzig, Stuttgart, Stettin, Weimar, Würzburg, Koblenz and others).

The concern repeatedly expressed by the population regarding Prien's fate (he has not been mentioned in the high command's reports for some time) has been renewed and intensified, as no one has heard of him in a long time. In the attempts of the population to explain the reduced success of the U-boats, the suspicion has been expressed by some individuals that the U-boats are surely preparing for the invasion of Britain and are held in readiness to block the Channel. The short tour of inspection by Grand Adm. Raeder is seen as possible proof of this.

W. Churchill to General Ismay
Tuesday 29 April 1941

Is it not rather strange that, when we announced that the port of Benghazi while in our occupation was of no use, and, secondly, that on our evacuation we had completely blocked it, the enemy are using it freely?

Yugoslav Warships in British Bases
Thursday 1 May 1941
The *British Admiralty* issued the following communiqué:

The Yugoslav submarine *Nebojša* as well as two Yugoslav torpedo boats have entered a British naval base and joined the British fleet.

Secret report of the *SS Security Service* on the internal political situation:
No. 183, Monday 5 May 1941 (Extract)

The Battle of the Atlantic is being followed with the deepest interest. The tributes paid on the loss of the U-boats commanded by Kretschmer and Schepke and the mention of the dangers to which U-boats are subjected have been brought to the fore. Numerous rumors are being circulated that the British have been successful in developing an absolutely certain countermeasure against the U-boat. Questions are being asked with the greatest concern about the fate of Prien's ship.

Swiss Radio Beromünster

Friday 9 May 1941

The war in the Balkans—the fourth this century—has come to an end. . . . The conclusion of the war in the Balkans means the occupation of the Aegean Isles by German troops and the occupation of the Ionic Isles by Italian forces, fully blocking the Dardanelles and the west coast of Turkey. The cautious policy maintained by Turkey was shown when she did nothing to prevent the passage of transport vessels carrying German troops from the Black Sea through the Dardanelles to the Greek Isles in the Aegean. In fact, the well-known Montreux agreement on sea channels and straits obliges Turkey to allow free passage to merchant shipping; only warships can be denied entry.

Shipping Losses in April
Saturday 10 May 1941, London
The *Exchange* News Agency reported:

Because of the contradictory reports in the foreign press regarding the overall losses of Allied

shipping in April 1941, the official return for tonnage lost for the previous month was released yesterday: 106 ships totalling 488,124 gross tons.

Requisitioning of European Ships
Friday 16 May 1941, Washington
The *United Press Agency* reported:

The bill submitted to the Senate, which would enable Pres. Roosevelt to requisition foreign ships lying in US ports, was passed fifty-nine votes to twenty.

Ship Building to be Increased
16 May 1941, Washington
The *Exchange* News Agency reported:

The mass production of merchant ships is in full swing. The first of the two hundred freighters planned was laid down a few days ago, the second last Thursday and the third will follow on Monday. The construction, now two weeks ahead of schedule, has encouraged estimates that a medium-sized merchant ship will be launched at the latest five months after being laid down.

Guards Placed on French Ships
16 May 1941, Washington
The *US Coast Guard* reported:

Armed guards have been placed on all French ships in US ports. Ten ships including the *Normandie* have been affected by this measure. No reason was given. Official sources simply said, "You may draw your own conclusions."

Above: 5/28/1941, British report on the sinking of the *Bismarck*

Left: 5/26/1941, German report on the sinking of the *Hood*

Deployment of Iraqi Bombers
Sunday 18 May 1941, Baghdad
Iraqi Headquarters issued the following communiqué:

On Friday Iraqi Air Force bombers successfully attacked British ships lying off the port of Basra.

Promotions in the Red Fleet
Friday 23 May 1941, Moscow
The *Exchange* News Agency reported:

Stalin has carried out a considerable number of promotions and appointments in the Red fleet. The appointments comprise two vice-admirals, seven rear admirals and, in addition, eight major generals and four generals for coastal protection as well as two major generals for the fleet command.

Friday 23 May 1941
The *German High Command* issued the following communiqué:

The submarine commanded by Comdr. Günter Prien has not returned from its last operational patrol. The ship must now be considered lost. Comdr. Prien, the hero of the Scapa Flow, decorated by the Führer with the Oak Leaves to the Knight's Cross of the Iron Cross in recognition of his outstanding services, lives on with his brave crew in the hearts of all Germans.

Battlecruiser Hood Sunk!
Saturday 24 May 1941
The *British Admiralty* issued the following communiqué:

Early this morning, the Royal Navy attacked units of the German Kriegsmarine, including the 35,000-ton battleship *Bismarck*, off the coast of Greenland. During the engagement, the British battlecruiser *Hood* received a direct hit in the ammunition chamber and blew up. It is feared that very few of the crew have survived. The *Bismarck* was damaged, and the pursuit of the German formation continues.

24 May 1941
The *German High Command* issued the following communiqué:

A German battle formation led by Adm. Lütjens, operating in the Atlantic, encountered strong British naval forces in the area around Iceland. The battleship *Bismarck* destroyed a British battlecruiser, presumably the *Hood*, during the engagement. Another British warship was forced to withdraw. The German naval force continued its operation, having suffered only slight damage.

Order of the Day from the C-in-C U-boats
"Günter Prien will always be with us."
Völkischer Beobachter Berlin, 5/24/1941
The Commander-in-Chief of the U-boat arm, Vice-Adm. Dönitz, issued the following Order of the Day to the U-boat arm:

Günter Prien, the hero of Scapa Flow, has made his last patrol. We of the U-boat service bow our heads in proud mourning and salute him and his men. Even though he is covered by the mighty ocean, Günter Prien will always be among us. No U-boat will ever head westward without his presence, his spirit going with it. No blow will be struck against England by us without his help, pressing forward the attack. Brimming over with youthful vigor and a dare-devil spirit, he will be an eternal example for the submarine service. We have lost him and yet we have him with us again—he has become for us a symbol of our firm resolve to carry on the fight against England. In his spirit, the battle continues.

Sunday 25 May 1941
The *German High Command* issued the following communiqué:

A special communiqué has already stated that a German naval formation led by Adm. Lütjens encountered a powerful British naval formation in the area around Iceland. After a short but intense engagement, the battleship *Bismarck* sank the British battlecruiser *Hood*, the largest ship in the

British Navy. Another battleship of the latest type, the "King George V" class, was damaged and forced to withdraw. The German formation continued its operations without loss.

Torpedo Bombers Attack the Bismarck
Monday 26 May 1941
The *British Admiralty* issued the following communiqué:

Torpedo bombers of the Royal Navy continued to pursue the German naval formation led by the *Bismarck*. British naval units also took part in the pursuit.

Daily Memorandum of the Reich Press Secretary
26 May 1941

The Minister first refers to some very useful American voices on the sinking of the *Hood*, which we must, of course, build up. The British claim that they pursued the *Bismarck* should be disputed but certainly without mentioning the British claim that their aircraft fired a torpedo at a German ship.

Daily Memorandum of the Reich Press Secretary
Tuesday 27 May 1941

With regard to the as yet uncertain outcome of the *Bismarck*'s action with superior enemy forces, the Minister deems to expedient not to go into the matter of the *Bismarck* and the *Hood* for the mo-

Above: The pride of the Royal Navy, the battlecruiser *Hood* (42,100 tons)

Right: The most powerful battleship in the world at that time, the *Bismarck* (41,700 tons)

ment. Both German radio and press should rather divert the entire naval debate once more to the Mediterranean area.

The Bismarck *Sunk*

Wednesday 28 May 1941
The *German High Command* issued the following communiqué:

As announced yesterday, the battleship *Bismarck*, after its successful engagement off Iceland on 26 May, was crippled by a torpedo launched by enemy torpedo aircraft. True to the last message broadcast by the fleet commander, Adm. Lütjens, the battleship, defeated by the overwhelmingly superior enemy force, sank on the morning of 27 May with its commander Capt. Lindemann and his brave crew, her colors still flying.

Lord Mountbatten Rescued
28 May 1941, Alexandria
The *Exchange* News Agency reported:

The captain of a cruiser just arrived in Alexan-

dria has described the extent of the German air attacks on the Royal Navy in the waters around Crete. Frequently no fewer than five hundred German bombers simultaneously attacked British units. Within two hours on Thursday morning, more than 186 bombs were dropped on a single British warship. Lord Louis Mountbatten — who is related to the British Royal Family — was rescued after the ship he captained, the destroyer *Kelly*, was sunk in the attack.

Italian Flyers' Successes
28 May 1941, Rome
The *Italian High Command* issued the following communiqué:

During Wednesday night, our air formations bombed the base at Malta. . . . On 26 May, Italian and German units attacked a number of British naval vessels some one hundred miles east of Derna, scoring hits on an aircraft carrier, a cruiser, a destroyer and four steamers. Heavy bombs caused an explosion on another cruiser. Military installations and ships in the harbor of Tobruk were also bombed.

Syria and Lebanon Are Blockaded Areas

28 May 1941, London
The *Exchange* News Agency reported:

With immediate effect, Syria and Lebanon are to be regarded as enemy-occupied areas and thereby included in the British blockade regulations.

Italian Troops Land on Crete
Thursday 29 May 1941, Rome
The Italian *Stefani* News Agency reported:

Italian marine and land forces have landed in eastern Crete and have established a new front against the British. These landings have made a decisive contribution to the large-scale attack against the British stronghold there.

Heavy Cruiser York *Sunk*
29 May 1941
The *British Admiralty* issued the following communiqué:

When the fighting for Crete broke out, the cruiser *York*, damaged some time ago and lying in Suda Bay for repairs, was repeatedly bombed and must be considered lost. Two of the crew were killed and five wounded.

Survivors from the Battlecruiser Hood
29 May 1941, London
The *Reuters* News Agency reported:

It is feared that only one officer and three other ranks have survived from the *Hood*. The ship was destroyed so suddenly that those crew who were not immediately killed had practically no chance of escape. The *Hood*'s normal complement amounted to 1,341.

The Sinking of the Bismarck
Saturday 31 May 1941, London
The *Reuters* News Agency reported:

Officers and men who took part in the pursuit of the *Bismarck* state that it was hit by eight to nine torpedoes. The Germans fought very bravely. While rescue operations were going on, the word went out that enemy submarines were in the area, and the British ships had to withdraw. The *Bismarck* is said to have continued firing until its guns were silenced, and to have given no indication of surrender. The battleship went down with its colors flying.

A German Gift
Saturday 7 June 1941, Santiago de Chile
The *DNB* Agency reported:

During a ceremony yesterday, the German ambassador, the Freiherr von Schoen, presented a sailing ship, the *Privall*, to the Chilean Navy as a gift from the German government.

The Defence of Malta
Sunday 8 June 1941, Valetta
The *Reuters* News Agency reported:

The governor of Malta declared in a radio broadcast that the people must prepare for an invasion.

British Landing Foiled

Monday 9 June 1941, Vichy
The *French War Ministry* issued the following communiqué:

British naval forces consisting of a heavy cruiser, two cruisers and five torpedo boats landed a small number of troops on the coast of Lebanon south of Beirut. The British troops, armed with machine guns, were immediately taken prisoner.

Fighting in Syria
9 June 1941
From *General Wilson's Headquarters*:

A British squadron of cruisers and destroyers is supporting troop operations and maintaining contact with them.

Secret report of the *SS Security Service* on the internal political situation:
No. 194, 16 June 1941 (Extract)

In a large number of individual reports it has recently been pointed out that bulletins in the press and on the radio are primarily examined by the population to see whether they might indicate a

On board a German warship, radio operator with an Enigma-M enciphering machine

shortening or lengthening of the war. . . . Whereas one certainly acknowledges the consistency of successes achieved in the sea war, opinion is constantly encountered among the population that despite the heaviest blows, Britain simply cannot be beaten and that US aid could, in fact, gradually become effective. . . . Referring to the reporting on the *Bismarck*, many people took exception to the controversial statements in the German press that Britain only partially revealed her losses at sea, or not at all. The losses shown in the comprehensive report of the German High Command were read with great interest by the population, who expressed disbelief that only the three U-boats of our most experienced commanders were lost.

War in the East

Sunday 22 June 1941
The *German High Command* issued the following communiqué:

Hostilities on the Soviet border have been in progress since early this morning. An attempt by the enemy to penetrate into East Prussia was beaten back with heavy losses. German fighters shot down a large number of Soviet bombers.

Strategy and Tactics

JANUARY TO JUNE 1941

At the beginning of 1941, political developments had far more influence on the Battle of the Atlantic than the raw winter weather, the fogs and the storms. Germany, busy with preparations for Operation Barbarossa, the attack on the Soviet Union, had to cut back the U-boat offensive. Equipping the army and producing aircraft now took priority. Likewise, the transport system, which was burdened to the utmost, could no longer keep pace with the requirements of the U-boat war.

At the beginning of 1941, six German commerce raiders made their way to the southern half of the hemisphere.

In the first days of January, captains in the Royal Navy received instructions to be on the lookout for any possibility of capturing a German enciphering machine or any relevant documentation and equipment. The British Admiralty's intelligence division, NID, made up a team of specialists who put to sea on the destroyer *Somali* (Capt. Caslon), their task to seize enciphering machines or equipment during the planned commando operations or when capturing German weather-reporting ships or supply ships.

The most important source of intelligence for both the British Army and the RAF was — thanks to a copy of Enigma — the German radio transmissions themselves. The secret of this enciphering machine, which was used by both the German Army and Luftwaffe, had already been laid bare by British experts in spring 1940. But the naval Enigma-M had its own peculiar construction, and the NID cryptanalysts, despite the most intensive efforts, did not manage to crack it until early 1941 during Operation Ultra.

This operation had a long prehistory. In 1932, three young Polish mathematicians in Warsaw, J. Rózÿcki, M. Rejewski and H. Zygalski, unravelled the secret of the German Enigma machine through intensive studies of the cyclical theory. And a few months before the German invasion of Poland in summer 1939, the three scientists accomplished a real masterstroke: They copied the Enigma machine. Maj. G. Bertrand, head of DY section of the French intelligence service, went to Warsaw on 24 July 1939. The British specialists, Comdr. Denniston and the mathematician D. Knox, were also present. And two days later they received the most valuable gift that Poland could give its allies before war broke out: two copies of the German enciphering machine. One of these machines went to Paris and the other went to London, where at first it was regarded with a great deal of skepticism.

In autumn 1939, cryptanalysts in the Secret Intelligence Service (SIS) established their headquarters at Bletchley Park, a country seat north of London. Here an ancestor of the computer could be found, which was to help in decoding Enigma messages of the Germany Army or Luftwaffe. A special security classification, "Top Secret Ultra," was introduced for all intelligence gleaned from or relating to the German cipher procedures. Churchill stated that it was better to lose a battle than reveal this essential source of intelligence.

On Sunday 5 January 1941, British troops under Gen. Wavell occupied the port of Bardia on the Libyan-Egyptian border.

On Tuesday 7 January 1941, at Hitler's orders, I Wing of 40 Bomber Group, flying Fw 200 Kondors from Bordeaux-Mérignac, was placed under the tactical control of the C-in-C U-boats for sea reconnaissance patrols. Reichsmarschall Göring, who was on a hunting trip when this order was given, tried on his return from leave to persuade Dönitz not to implement the order.

On Friday 10 January 1941, Ju 87 dive bombers of the X Air Corps (Gen. Geisler) carried out attacks on Force A (Adm. Cunningham). The *Illustrious*, the first carrier to be fitted with a four-inch armored deck, was hit six times by 1,000-lb. bombs. On fire and with heavily damaged steering gear, the carrier nonetheless reached Malta. The entry of German Luftwaffe units in the Mediterranean had a considerable effect on the strategic situation.

On Saturday 11 January 1941, the Ju 87s of X Air Corps took off for an attack on the Royal Navy in the Mediterranean. The cruiser *Southampton*, which was in the Malta area, received a number of hits and had to be abandoned that evening.

On Tuesday 14 January 1941, the radio operator on the commerce raider, ship no. 33 *Pinguin* (Capt. Krüger), which at that time was operating in the Arctic, picked up radio messages from a whaling fleet. The following day the commerce raider succeeded in surprising the fleet and taking as prize two whale-processing ships; an oil transporter aggregating 36,530 gross tons with 22,200 tons of whale oil on board; and eleven whalers aggregating 3,417 gross tons. With the exception of three whalers, the prizes all reached West France by March 1941. The whale oil fulfilled Germany's requirements for margarine production for a whole week.

On Wednesday 22 January 1941, the British XIIIth Corps (Lt. Gen. O'Connor), backed up by artillery fire from the *Terror* and the gunboats *Aphis* and *Ladybird*, occupied the important Libyan port of Tobruk. The Italian gunnery training ship *San Giorgio* was blown up by its crew. On the same day, the battlecruisers *Scharnhorst* and *Gneisenau* left Kiel to try once again to break out into the Atlantic to conduct commerce warfare (Operation Berlin).

On Thursday 23 January 1941, the British Admiralty's intelligence division commenced Operation Rubble. This enterprise was led by George Binney, later Comdr. Sir George Binney RNVR, the representative of the British government's iron and steel organisation in Sweden and a collaborator of the Naval Intelligence Division. Under his command, five Norwegian freighters—the *Lizabeth Bakke* (5,450 gross tons), *John Bakke* (4,718 gross tons), *Tai Shan* (6,962 gross tons), *Taurus* (4,767 gross tons) and *Dicto* (5,263 gross tons)—set sail for Great Britain. They were fully laden with goods of the utmost strategical importance, which the British government had officially purchased in neutral Sweden and which included 25,000 tons of Swedish high-quality steel and ball bearings. The operation took place under a good omen, the five blockade-runners only just missed the battlecruisers *Scharnhorst* and *Gneisenau*, which had just passed through the Kattegat on their way to Operation Berlin. After the freighters had passed through the heavily mined Skagerrak, which was constantly patrolled by the Kriegsmarine, they were met by units of the Home Fleet, the cruisers *Naiad*, *Aurora*, *Edinburgh* and *Birmingham* as well as the destroyers *Escapade*, *Echo* and *Electra*. This operation was the largest blockade-running effort of the war.

In the second half of January 1941, the C-in-C of the Combined Japanese Fleet, Adm. Yamamoto, a former student at Harvard and later the naval attaché in Washington, sent his friend Adm. Onischi a confidential letter in which he outlined his plan for a surprise attack on Pearl Harbor. He asked if he considered that such an attack would be feasible. It was Yamamoto's intention to concentrate the attack on the US battleships and aircraft carriers and to sink as many of them as possible. His aim was to cripple the Americans' fighting spirit. In addition, Yamamoto was one of the first to recognise the supreme importance of a combined fleet and air operation for the future conduct of the war. Using the modern aircraft carriers he had had built, Yamamoto intended neutralising the power of the USA in the South Pacific for a long period during which the Japanese Army would be in a position to conquer Southeast Asia, the Philippines and the Dutch East Indies. His decision was made easier by the fact that the power relationship between the navies of Japan and the USA was in the ratio of approximately four to five, had never been so favorable, and could only get worse in the near future.

Adm. Onischi summoned Comdr. Genda, a 36-year-old officer in the naval air arm. Genda, who was serving on the aircraft carrier *Kaga*, had the reputation of being the most brilliant officer in his particular branch of the service. His verdict on

the plan of attack on Pearl Harbor was, "Difficult, but not impossible." Comdr. Genda was now given the task of working out the tactical details of the air attack.

Two days later, Genda submitted his detailed plan to Adm. Onischi. In his opinion, every available aircraft carrier should be deployed for this operation. The attack would need to take place at daybreak so that the approach of the bombers and torpedo bombers would be protected by the dark. To a remark made by Onischi that the waters of Pearl Harbor would be too shallow for dropping torpedoes, Genda replied that one would just have to solve this problem.

On Friday 24 January 1941, US Secretary of the Navy Frank Knox wrote to his colleague, Secretary of War H. L. Stimson, "It is quite possible that the Japanese will open hostilities with a sudden attack on the fleet or the naval base at Pearl Harbor."

On Saturday 25 January 1941, the heavily damaged aircraft carrier *Illustrious* arrived in Alexandria from Malta. After provisional repairs, the carrier went through the Suez Canal, and then across the Indian Ocean to the USA, where it had to remain in the dockyards at Norfolk for a year.

On Monday 27 January 1941, the US ambassador in Tokyo sent a coded telegram to Washington, "My Peruvian colleague has heard from a number of sources, including a Japanese source, that Japan is planning a surprise attack on Pearl Harbor in the event of a conflict with America. . . .

Although he considers the idea to be quite fantastic, he will nonetheless not withhold this information from us." Adm. Kimmel, C-in-C of the Pacific Fleet, said, "The Navy's intelligence service did not, however, believe this rumor."

In January 1941, losses sustained by the British Merchant Navy exceeded by far the building capacity of British shipyards. In addition, the number of damaged vessels was so high that the dockyards were able to accept no more. To speed up repairs, the building of new freighters had to be put back.

On Wednesday 29 January 1941, a secret conference commenced in Washington between the Imperial General Staff of Great Britain and the General Staff of the USA to discuss measures to be taken if America should enter the war. The theme was the establishment of a coordinated command.

In January 1941, German U-boats in the Atlantic sank seventeen merchant vessels totalling 98,702 gross tons, without loss to themselves; and 40 Bomber Group, flying four-engined Fw 200s, sank fifteen ships totalling 63,175 gross tons. At this time there were twenty two U-boats operational.

On Saturday 1 February 1941, the US Navy created the Atlantic Fleet under the command of Adm. King, who immediately prepared a convoy protection service and U-boat hunters.

On the same day, the heavy cruiser *Admiral Hipper* (Capt. Meisel) put to sea from Brest for a second Atlantic operation. It took a southerly course to commence operations on the Gibraltar convoy lanes.

On Tuesday 4 February 1941, unnoticed by the Royal Navy, the battlecruisers *Scharnhorst* (Capt. Hoffmann) and *Gneisenau* (Capt. Fein) passed through the Denmark Strait.

On Thursday 6 February 1941, Hitler issued his "Directive No. 23, setting out the guidelines for the war against the British economy." In this directive, Hitler confirmed that the most effective method of conquering Britain was to destroy her shipping capacity; in addition, British ships, shipyards and harbor installations should become increasingly a target for the Luftwaffe.

On Friday 7 February 1941, Western Approaches Command (Adm. Noble) was moved from Plymouth to Liverpool. This command center for western sea communications with Great Britain was responsible for the planned and secured arrival of the convoys and worked closely with RAF Coastal Command. Accordingly, the deployment of surface units and aircraft formations could be coordinated in the battle against the German U-boats.

On the same day, Göring demanded that Dönitz return I Wing 40 Bomber Group (I/KG 40); otherwise, he threatened, the wing would be deprived of supplies of spare parts.

On Saturday 8 February 1941, the first convoy left Naples with German units, later known as the Afrika Korps, bound for Tripoli. Three German steamers, with an Italian destroyer and three torpedo boats as escort, reached their destination in North Africa without encountering the enemy.

In early morning, Sunday 9 February 1941, units of the British Gibraltar-based squadron Force H (Vice-Adm. Somerville) appeared off Genoa. The battlecruiser *Renown*, the battleship *Malaya* and the light cruiser *Sheffield* opened fire on the docks, harbor installations and the industrial area. Four freighters and a training ship were sunk, and eighteen ships were damaged. The aircraft from the carrier *Ark Royal* laid mines on the approaches to La Spezia and bombed the oil refineries at Livorno. The heavy mist prevented the Italian coastal batteries from firing accurately. Although the Italian fleet had put out to sea from Naples, they did not succeed in catching Force H on its return voyage. And so the British squadron reached Gibraltar without further incident.

Also on 9 February 1941, the only combined operation mounted by the U-boat arm and the

Luftwaffe took place in the Atlantic off Cape St. Vincent. The *U 37* (Lt. Comdr. Clausen), while en route toward West Africa, sighted Convoy HG-53 making for England. By means of DF signals, the submarine directed 2 Squadron 40 Bomber Group (Capt. Fliegel) and the heavy cruiser *Admiral Hipper* to the convoy. At midday, five Fw 200s attacked the convoy and sank five ships aggregating 9,200 gross tons.

On Monday 10 February 1941, the British cruisers *Capetown*, *Ceres* and *Shropshire* belonging to the East Indies Fleet Force T (Vice-Adm. Leatham) appeared off the coast of Somalia in Italian East Africa and opened fire on Italian troop concentrations. Swordfish from the carrier *Hermes* successfully attacked the capital Magadiscio (Mogadishu) and the port of Chisimaio (Kismayu).

On Tuesday 11 February 1941, the heavy cruiser *Admiral Hipper* again attacked Convoy HG-53 and sank one of the ships. Out of the sixteen freighters in this convoy, nine ships totalling 15,218 gross tons were destroyed. Late that evening, the *Admiral Hipper* also sighted Convoy SLS-64 sailing without any escort vessel.

The morning of 12 February 1941, the *Admiral Hipper* attacked Convoy SLS-64 and, according to British statements, seven out of nineteen ships were sunk (32,800 gross tons), and two more were

heavily damaged.

On Friday 14 February 1941, the *Admiral Hipper* returned to Brest after an operational tour lasting twelve days.

On the same day, South African troops (Gen. Cunningham) occupied Kismayu on the Somalian coast. This operation was backed up by the aircraft carrier *Hermes* (Capt. Onslow), four cruisers and a number of destroyers belonging to Force T (Vice-Adm. Leatham).

Also on 14 February 1941, guarded by Italian destroyers and torpedo boats, the second convoy carrying German troops and equipment entered harbor in Tripoli.

On Monday 17 February 1941, Commandos 50 and 52, which had been made up in Egypt, undertook their first operation in the conquest of the strategically important Dodecanes Isles in the Aegean, the occupation of Kos. The landing, however, went wrong from the start, as the boats could not find a suitable landing place.

On Tuesday 18 February 1941, aircraft from 2 Squadron 4 Bomber Group (Capt. Kühl) carried out mining operations in the Suez Canal for the first time.

On the same day, German troops in North Africa were titled German Afrika Korps (DAK).

On Wednesday 19 February 1941, an Fw 200

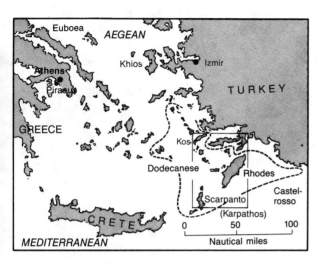

Above and below: The Mediterranean war theater: Aegean—Dodecanes—Rhodes

Left: 2/14/1941, the coast of Somalia, South African troops landing (Gen. Cunningham)

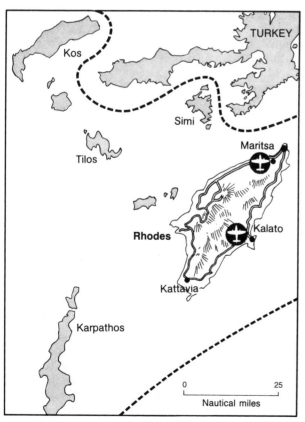

belonging to I Wing 40 Bomber Group (Maj. Petersen) sighted Convoy OB-287 from Liverpool. The aircraft crew reported the position of the convoy to the C-in-C U-boats as being northwest of Cape Wrath, which was, however, inexact. The Fw 200 sank the freighter *Gracia* (5,642 gross tons) and the tanker *Housatonic* (5,559 gross tons). Five German and three Italian submarines could not, however, find the reported convoy.

And again on the following day, 20 February 1941, the German and Italian U-boats sought Convoy OB-287 in vain. Two Fw 200s sighted the convoy once again. They badly damaged the tanker *D. L. Harper* (12,223 gross tons) as well as the freighters *St. Rosario* (4,312 gross tons) and *Rosenborg* (1,997 gross tons).

On Friday 21 February 1941, an Fw 200 again attacked a tanker that was sunk by *U 96* (Lt. Comdr. Lehmann-Willenbrock) a few hours later. After other U-boats had sought the convoy in vain, Dönitz called the operation off.

On Saturday 22 February 1941, the battlecruisers *Scharnhorst* and *Gneisenau* sighted a convoy on a westerly course some five hundred nautical miles east of Newfoundland. They sank five merchantmen aggregating 25,784 gross tons. They then took a southeasterly course, refuelled in mid-Atlantic from a supply ship and transferred their operational area to the region off Sierra Leone.

On the same day, the heavy cruiser *Admiral Scheer* (Capt. Krancke) was discovered by an aircraft from the British light cruiser *Glasgow*. Thereupon, Force T (Vice-Adm. Leatham), comprising six cruisers and the carrier *Hermes*, tried to catch the *Admiral Scheer*. Capt. Krancke was lucky. The weather worsened so rapidly that the *Glasgow*'s aircraft was unable to find the German cruiser. The *Admiral Scheer* then set course for the Atlantic, and Force T had to give up the pursuit.

On Tuesday 25 February 1941, toward 4:00 P.M., *U 47* (Lt. Comdr. Prien) sighted a number of freighters belonging to Convoy OB-290. Shortly afterward, an enemy aircraft was reported and *U 47* had to break off pursuit. However, a radio message on the position of the convoy was transmitted to U-boat command, which deployed three German and two Italian submarines against the convoy. During the night, *U 47* succeeded in again approaching Convoy OB-290 and sinking three ships and damaging a tanker.

On the same day, two British destroyers and a gunboat put two hundred men from Commando 50 together with a small detachment of Royal Marines ashore on the island of Castelrosso (now Kastellorizon) east of Rhodes. The small Italian garrison was taken by surprise and put up no serious resistance.

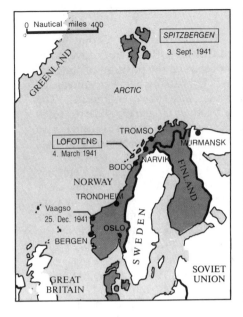

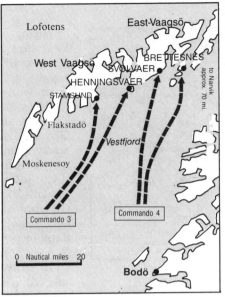

Above: On 3/4/1941, British Commandos 3 and 4 carry out the highly successful raid on the Lofotens (Norway).

Right: Early 1941, Britain, the first Commando exercises in a landing craft.

The next day, 26 February 1941, the Italian destroyers *Crispi* and *Sella*, together with the torpedo boats *Lince* and *Lupo*, brought up reinforcements from Rhodes to Castelrosso. Supported by the guns of the warships, the Italian garrison now went over to the offensive. The Commandos radioed for reinforcements. A number of British destroyers put to sea from Cyprus with further troops but were sent southward instead of northward in error and arrived in Alexandria. Castelrosso had to be abandoned the night of 27 February 1941 after powerful Italian counterattacks that caused considerable losses.

At midday on the same day, an Fw 200 from I/KG 40 (Bomber Group 40), which had been summoned by *U 47* (Lt. Comdr. Prien), attacked Convoy OB-290. Toward 3:00 P.M., five more Fw 200s appeared. The six Kondors destroyed the merchantmen *Llanwern* (4,966 gross tons), *Leeds City* (4,758 gross tons), the Dutch freighter *Amstelland* (8,156 gross tons), the *Mahanada* (7,181 gross tons), the *Swinburne* (4,659 gross tons), *Beursplein* (4,368 gross tons), and *Solferino* (2,162 gross tons), a total of 36,250 gross tons, and damaged four more freighters totalling 20,755 gross tons in the most successful operation launched by the bomber group against Allied shipping.

On Thursday 27 February 1941, the New Zealand light cruiser *Leander* (Capt. Bevan) sighted in the Indian Ocean southwest of the Maldives the only Italian commerce raider in operation, *Ramb I* (Lt. Comdr. Bonezzi), 3,667 gross tons, and sank it.

At this time, the British Commando forces were gaining ever-increasing significance for future amphibious operations.

The Commandos were to carry out their operations along the coasts of North and West Europe as well as the Mediterranean. They were trained and armed for small-scale shock troop operations. Churchill expected much from their activities; in addition to maintaining British morale, there would be a weakening of German morale, as practically no section of the coast of occupied Europe would be safe from their operations.

In February 1941, U-boats operating in the Atlantic sank, without loss to themselves, forty-two merchantmen totalling 207,649 gross tons, the Fw 200s of 40 Bomber Group sank a total of twenty-two ships (84,515 gross tons).

From November 1940 until February 1941, only ten out of twenty-four U-boats were in operational use.

In February 1941, eighteen months after the outbreak of war, the British cabinet ordered that submarines would also sink enemy merchant shipping without prior warning.

On Saturday 1 March 1941, the US Navy formed a Support Force Atlantic Fleet (Rear Adm. Bristol), made up of three destroyer flotillas and four flying boat reconnaissance squadrons. The fleet's task was to secure the supply convoys to Iceland, to which neutral merchantmen would attach themselves in addition to American transports. On 1 March 1941 the British Admiralty stated that 3,434 Allied merchantmen had already been

equipped with guns.

At the beginning of March 1941, seven Type IX U-boats operated in loosely organised groups along the African coast around Freetown. They could be meaningfully deployed in this area only if they could be fuelled en route. At this time, Capt. Rothe, who had been in the harbor of Las Palmas in the Spanish Canaries since the beginning of September 1939 with his tanker *Charlotte Schliemann* (7,747 gross tons), received radio orders to put to sea the following night. The Spanish police cordonned off a large area around the harbor so that no unauthorised person could witness the ship's departure. Officials explained that a Spanish vessel carrying ammunition had put into the harbor where its dangerous cargo was to be unloaded. During darkness, the *Charlotte Schliemann*'s diesel engines, which had been silent for nineteen months, were started up. The tanker left port with dimmed lights and under its own power.

Not until they had reached the open sea did the crew find out that their tanker was to be used as a supply ship for U-boats and must not fall into enemy hands under any circumstances. The ship, fully laden with 10,800 tons of fuel, pitched heavily through the Atlantic swell toward its operational area.

During the night of 3/4 March 1941, *U 124* (Lt. Comdr. Schulz) approached the *Charlotte Schliemann* from out of the darkness and took on fuel and provisions. During the two following nights, *U 105* (Lt. Comdr. Schewe) and *U 106* (Lt. Comdr. Oesten) also received fuel and supplies.

On Tuesday 4 March 1941, the first Commando raid of the year in North Europe, Operation Claymore under the command of Brig. Haydon, targeted several harbors on the Lofoten Islands. The plan was to destroy there the cod-liver oil works responsible for forty percent of Norway's entire capacity and also to destroy any ships in the harbor. Composed of the two former Channel ferries *Queen Emma* and *Princess Beatrix* — tenders for the landing craft — escorted by five destroyers including the *Somali* (Capt. Caslon) with the NID contingent from the British Admiralty on board, the landing fleet succeeded in entering port intact. A German patrol boat, NN 04 *Krebs*, a former trawler, defended itself vigorously but was destroyed. The captain, before dying, managed to throw the Enigma enciphering machine overboard with the cipher documents. He was, however, unable to destroy various secret documents. After the survivors had left the burning patrol boat, the British prize crew from the destroyer *Somali* boarded the vessel and found boxes with the reserve cipher wheels of Enigma-M, which were not in use this particular day.

Five hundred men of Commandos 3 and 4, including fifty-two engineers and a dozen Norwegian exiles, took part in the operation. In addition to eleven cod-liver oil factories in Brettesnes, Henningsvaer, Stamsund and Svolvaer, the power station and a number of tanks containing 3.5 million liters of oil were blown up. The telegraph office was still intact and Lt. Richard Wills from Commando 4 sent Adolf Hitler in Berlin a telegram with the message, "You said in your last speech German troops would meet the English wherever they landed. Where are your troops? Signed Wills 2nd Lieutenant."

The Luftwaffe on the Norwegian mainland was certainly alerted, but the airfields were made non-operational by weather conditions. Ten ships at anchor in the port, aggregating more than 20,000 gross tons, were sunk, including the merchant ship *Hamburg* (5,470 gross tons). Two hundred and fifteen soldiers belonging to the German occupation forces and ten Quislings, Norwegian collaborators, were taken prisoner; three hundred Norwegian volunteers returned to Britain with the force. The return voyage, under the protection of light cruisers *Edinburgh* and *Nigeria* of the Home Fleet, passed without incident. This operation was the biggest and most successful Commando raid primarily because of the captured Enigma wheels and the destruction of large quantities of raw materials required in the production of nitroglycerine and of vitamins A and B. British casualties amounted to one officer who accidentally shot himself in the foot.

The Enigma wheels made it possible for British cryptanalysts to make the final breakthrough in the German Navy coding called "Home Waters," and they could now decipher transmissions from the weather ships in the Arctic.

On Wednesday 5 March 1941, Operation Lustre began, requiring the transport of British troops, including Australians and New Zealanders, from Alexandria to Greece mainly on merchant vessels. The Royal Navy had to escort these transports through the Aegean, a further burden for Force A (Adm. Cunningham).

On Thursday 6 March 1941, Churchill proclaimed "the Battle of the Atlantic." He formed "the Battle of the Atlantic Committee," whose meetings took place on a weekly basis. The Committee envisaged discharging 40,000 men from the forces to help in the dockyards with repairs to 100,000 tons of shipping capacity.

Also on Thursday 6 March 1941, U 70 (Lt. Comdr. Matz) and U 99 (Lt. Comdr. Kretschmer) received orders from the C-in-C U-boats at nightfall to join U 47 (Comdr. Prien). Prien was maintaining contact with a large convoy, OB-293, and was waiting to attack until a pack could be gathered. U 70 torpedoed two ships totalling 13,916 gross tons. Suddenly, at only one thousand yards distance, the British corvettes Arbutus and Camelia appeared and forced U 70 to dive. They dropped depth charges and destroyed the submarine. Lt. Comdr. Kretschmer with U 99 sank a tanker and severely damaged the whaler Terje Viken (20,638 gross tons).

On Friday 7 March 1941 under Operation Lustre, the first British troops disembarked in the harbors of Piraeus and Volos.

Late in the evening of 7 March 1941, U 47 (Comdr. Prien) again tried to attack Convoy OB-293. During rain squalls, the U 47 was forced by the destroyer Wolverine (Comdr. Rowland) to dive and was finally sunk with depth charges.

On Tuesday 11 March 1941, the Lend-Lease agreement came into force in the USA, allowing Great Britain to acquire in the USA without payment — and therefore it was virtually given away — everything necessary for the continuation of the war. The condition that matériel had to be carried in ships belonging to the combatant nations remained in force for the time being.

On Saturday 15 March 1941, the battlecruisers Scharnhorst and Gneisenau sank thirteen ships totalling 617,773 gross tons, which had left a convoy breaking up off the coast of Newfoundland. In addition, the Gneisenau took three tankers prize. Shortly afterward the Gneisenau was sighted by the battleship Rodney, but succeeded in escaping.

On the same day, the Italian small vessels were formed into an independent unit. They were withdrawn from 1 Flotilla of the Italian Navy, and 10 Flotilla was created as a camouflage measure. These units were now fully independent of the remainder of the fleet.

During the evening of 15 March 1941, U 110 (Lt. Comdr. Lemp) sighted Convoy HX-112 made up of forty-one ships and escorted by five destroyers and two corvettes. Upon receiving the "maintaining contact" message from U 110, the C-in-C U-boats deployed U 37, U 74, U 99 and U 100, which were in the area.

During the night of 15/16 March 1941, U 110 torpedoed a tanker.

On Sunday 16 March 1941, two Heinkel He 111s (X Air Corps) attacked units of the British Mediterranean Fleet during an armed reconnaissance west of Crete. Upon their return, the aircrews reported torpedo hits on two heavy units which they incorrectly described as battleships. As this success would have meant a considerable weakening of the Royal Navy's forces in the Mediterranean, German High Command, as a result of this false report, pressed the Italian Navy into making an attack in the eastern Mediterranean north and south of Crete in support of the German offensive against Greece planned for 6 April.

During 16 March 1941, U 37 (Lt. Comdr. Clausen), U 100 (Lt. Comdr. Schepke) and U 110 (Lt. Comdr. Lemp) attempted to attack Convoy HX-112 jointly, but without success. First of all, U 99 (Lt. Comdr. Kretschmer) had managed to slip between the escort vessels, approach the convoy, and get into a favorable firing position. It sank two steamers and three tankers aggregating 34,505 gross tons, damaged another tanker and withdrew, having fired its last torpedo. U 100, which thirty minutes earlier had been forced by depth charges to surface, was sighted at a distance of a thousand yards by the destroyer Vanoc, who rammed it before it could dive again. Lt. Comdr. Schepke was crushed on the bridge of his ship and lost both his legs. As the destroyer made full astern to disengage from the submarine, Schepke was thrown overboard. Five of the U 100's crews were saved. Comdr. Power stated, "This was a happy moment for us, a successful climax in a long arduous struggle. We had taken revenge for the losses in the convoy."

In the first successful use of radar equipment by surface units against U-boats, Kretschmer's U 99 was detected by Asdic shortly after Vanoc picked up survivors from the U 100. The destroyer Walker (Capt. MacIntyre) damaged U 99 with depth charges and forced it to surface. Walker opened fire, and the crew left the sinking submarine. Lt.

3/16/1941, Bremerhaven, a mischievous prank. Because of a clip over the ear, the luxury liner *Bremen* was set ablaze.

Comdr. Kretschmer, the most successful U-boat commander during World War II with 313,611 tons to his credit, was taken prisoner with thirty-nine of his crew.

The death of the submarine commanders Prien and Schepke and the capture of Kretschmer marked the turning point in the Battle of the Atlantic. Never again would such significant results be achieved by U-boats operating individually. The "golden age" — the second and, for all German naval units, the most successful phase in the Battle of the Atlantic, with monthly figures of eight ships for each U-boat at sea — terminated with the loss of the three leading U-boat aces. Now the third phase of the Battle of the Atlantic, which lasted until December 1941, took place with laborious, bitter duels between U-boat packs and escort vessels, and onerous operations to hunt the U-boat packs in the North Atlantic.

On 16 March 1941 in Bremerhaven, the fire alarm was raised. In flames was the flagship of the Norddeutsche Lloyd, the luxury liner *Bremen*, camouflaged and made ready as troopship *No. 802* for the invasion of England. The fire spread over the entire ship, and attempts to put it out were unsuccessful. The *Bremen* was flooded and run

aground to save at least the valuable machinery installations. Even the secret police, the Gestapo, were unsuccessful in establishing the precise cause of the fire that destroyed this giant vessel. The only certainty was that the fire broke out in the expensively furnished, wood-panelled dining room, which now served as a mattress store. The Gestapo, who at first had suspected a plot of British Secret Service, pounced all the more feverishly on the tale related by a fifteen-year-old boy, Walter Schmidt. He claimed to have set Germany's largest passenger liner on fire as revenge for a clip over the ear given him by a superior. The boy was executed, and the *Bremen* went to the breaker's yard.

On Thursday 20 March 1941, a part of Force H (Vice-Adm. Somerville) left Gibraltar with the battlecruiser *Renown*, the light cruiser *Sheffield* and the aircraft carrier *Ark Royal* to intercept the battlecruisers *Scharnhorst* and *Gneisenau* on their homeward voyage. The Home Fleet also deployed all available units. The battlecruisers were, however, given prior warning by the German radio intelligence service, and they managed to evade their pursuers.

On Saturday 22 March 1941, the *Scharnhorst* and *Gneisenau* put into Brest, having completed their commerce war, Operation Berlin. They had sunk twenty-two ships totalling 115,622 gross tons. By order of the Naval High Command, eight hundred German dockyard workers, specialists in U-boat repairs, were immediately directed to Brest

THE DAILY MAIL, Monday, March 31, 1941.

WHO KNOWS?

Who knows that awful stuffed-up feeling, unable to smell, unable to taste, unable to Hear? - THE CHRONIC CATARRH SUFFERER. "Mentholatum" STOPS catarrh where it starts. This antiseptic breaks it a fresh - when applied to the nostrils—deprives mucus, into nasal tissues, calms inflammation, stops infection and opens up stuffed breathing passages. "Mentholatum" Never hurts from reliable chemists, 50, and 1/3, including purchase tax.

Daily Mail

FOR KING AND EMPIRE

NO. 14,018   ★   MONDAY, MARCH 31, 1941   ONE PENNY

LATE WAR NEWS SPECIAL

THE BEST CYCLE PUMP IN THE WORLD
Bluemel's

GREATEST NAVAL VICTORY OF WAR

3 Cruisers and 3 Destroyers Sunk by Cunningham

THE greatest naval victory of the war has been won by the British Mediterranean Fleet. Six Italian warships—three 10,000-tons cruisers and three destroyers—have been sunk in the Eastern Mediterranean during a long and sustained action which began last Friday.

More Aid in Atlantic War Now

By CAPTAIN BERNARD ACWORTH, D.S.O., R.N.

THE great victory of Admiral Sir Andrew Cunningham cannot fail to have important repercussions in the Atlantic, where reinforcements from the Mediterranean would be welcome.

Little at present can be said about the tactics of this remarkable sea action pending further reports, but the most extraordinary feature at present known is the absence of damage to our own ships.

The 8in. guns of the Zara class, to which the sunk cruisers belong, could engage our ships at any practicable range, and the Italians have had the reputation of being good gunners.

Two destroyers are claimed in the official communiqué, but last night it was reported from Athens that survivors from a sunken Italian destroyer not named by the Admiralty had been landed at the Piraeus.

An earlier official communiqué stated that at least one battleship of the 35,000-tons Littorio class—most powerful ships in the Italian Navy—had been damaged, and two cruisers severely damaged.

It is not yet clear whether these are two of the three cruisers now stated to have been sunk.

In addition, three other warships, two cruisers, and a destroyer have been damaged by British planes, which caught them, limping for home, in the Ionian Sea.

In this long action none of our ships was damaged or had any casualties. Two British planes have not yet returned.

THE Navy sank this trio of heavy cruisers — Pola, Zara, and Fiume. They are three of the four in the Zara class, and their loss halves Italy's remaining heavy cruiser strength. Each displaced 10,000 tons and carried eight 8in. guns. Zara and Fiume were completed in 1931, Pola in 1932. They were designed to carry two seaplanes, had an official speed of 32 knots, and a crew of 726. When this picture was taken the ship were lined up at Naples for inspection by Hitler.

Nazis Rush for Home

SLAVS READY

From TERENCE ATHERTON, Daily Mail Correspondent

BELGRADE, Sunday.

CLOSURE of the frontier between Yugoslavia and Styria (Austria) by the Yugoslavia authorities was announced over the German radio to-night.

Only passenger traffic on the Marberg-Graz line is being allowed to continue, according to this German report, which has not yet been confirmed here.

FRENCH BOMB OUR DESTROYERS

Intercepting a Convoy

FRENCH shore batteries and bomber formations yesterday attacked British warships after they had challenged a convoy believed to be carrying war materials for Germany.

Our warships, which were undamaged, scored hits on the French batteries, but refrained from shelling the merchant ships "in the

French Coast Pounded

BIG RAF RAID

THE R.A.F. made another heavy attack on the German invasion ports along the French coast last night, and fires were seen blazing within a few minutes of the raid starting.

Watchers on the English side of the Channel saw unmistakable bomb flashes from Calais to Boulogne and the thud of big explosions was heard and even felt.

Ace RAF Men Reach Singapore

SINGAPORE, Sunday.

CRACK pilots of the Battle of Britain—one a D.F.C with 20 victories—are among strong R.A.F. and Army reinforcements which arrived in British Malaya.

Most of the Army reinforcements consist of Indian regiments, but there are also mechanised units.

Air Chief Marshal Sir Robert Brooke - Popham, Commander-in-Chief, Far East, said to-day that British troops and R.A.F. units were the first to reach the Far East from the United Kingdom since the war.

Many of the British soldiers have seen war service, and are equipped with some of the latest British material, designed as a result of the lessons learned in the first year of the war.—Reuter.

SLEET IN STRAITS

Weather in the Straits of Dover last night was cold and cloudy with the wind in the north-east, following showers of sleet during the day. The sea was fairly calm and visibility was good.

SPY EXECUTED

Rome, Sunday.—A foreign named Giovanni Sparrow been executed somewhere in Southern Italy for espionage is officially announced in Rome.—B.U.P.

---

to maintain and repair the *Scharnhorst* and *Gneisenau*, bringing about a considerable delay in essential U-boat repairs. As a consequence, the sinkings in the Atlantic were reduced.

On Monday 24 March 1941, Lt. Gen. Rommel began his offensive in North Africa with the capture of El Agheila. Up to this time, the Italo-German troopships had suffered no losses. They either took the route hugging the Tunisian coast or went around Malta, staying outside the range of the torpedo bombers stationed there.

On Tuesday 25 March 1941 at 11:30 P.M., the Italian destroyers *Crispi* and *Sella*, ten nautical miles from Suda Bay (Crete), put off, under the command of Lt. Comdr. Faggioni, six assault boats, each a fast fifteen-foot-long motor launch with a one-man crew and six hundred pounds of explosive in the bow. At a distance of a hundred yards from the target, the crewman would throw himself overboard while the boat steered itself on toward the target. Despite three protective barriers, the boats succeeded in penetrating into the bay. The boats were not discovered by the British until after the last barrier was reached, whereupon fire was opened. The British heavy cruiser *York* went down, and another assault boat sank the tanker *Pericles* (8,324 gross tons). Because of the strong defences, a number of boats were unable to reach their targets; others were destroyed by gunfire. The crewmen of the assault boats were all taken prisoner.

By 25 March 1941, the cryptanalysts working on Ultra already had details of the Italian naval

Above: The first British report on the greatest naval victory of the war in European waters

Above right: The course of the Battle of Matapan

Below right: 3/28/1941, near Cape Matapan, British carrier-borne aircraft during the torpedo attack

operation planned for 6 April 1941. Wing commander F. W. Winterbotham, who was responsible for passing a number of Enigma decrypts to Churchill, said, "It was lucky for us that the details of the operational plan were radioed to the Luftwaffe, which was to be responsible for the air security of the Italian battle fleet. We intercepted the radio transmissions and passed them on to Adm. Cunningham in good time."

On Wednesday 26 March 1941, the heavy cruiser *Admiral Scheer* passed unnoticed on its return voyage through the Denmark Strait while the greater part of the Home Fleet was out searching for the battlecruisers *Scharnhorst* and *Gneisenau*.

As a consequence of the Luftwaffe report dated 16 March 1941, the chief of the Italian Naval Staff, Adm. Riccardi, in the first initiative undertaken by the Italian Navy, planned a surprise armed reconnaissance in the waters west of Crete to attack the British convoys to Greece.

On 26 March 1941, the Italian fleet put to sea with the modern battleship *Vittorio Veneto* (fleet commander Adm. Iachino), five heavy cruisers, two light cruisers, thirteen destroyers and air cover provided by the X Air Corps. Their objective was

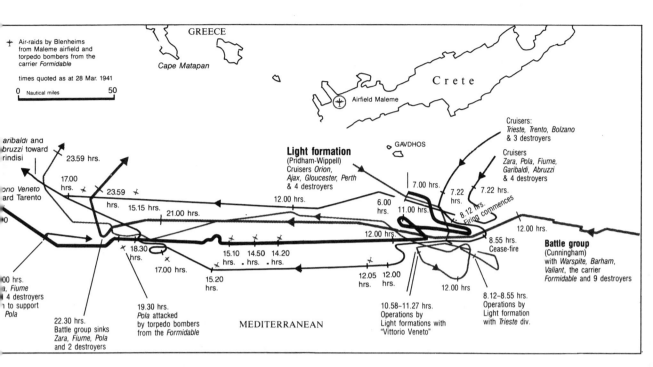

GREECE

Cape Matapan

Crete

+ Air-raids by Blenheims
from Maleme airfield and
torpedo bombers from the
carrier *Formidable*

times quoted as at 28 Mar. 1941

0 ————————— 50
Nautical miles

Airfield Maleme

GAVDHOS

Light formation
(Pridham-Wippell)
Cruisers *Orion,
Ajax, Gloucester, Perth*
& 4 destroyers

Cruisers:
Trieste, Trento, Bolzano
& 3 destroyers

Cruisers
*Zara, Pola, Fiume,
Garibaldi, Abruzzi*
& 4 destroyers

aribaldi and
bruzzi toward
rindisi

23.59 hrs.

17.00
hrs.

*rio Veneto
ard Tarento*

23.59
hrs.

15.15 hrs.

21.00 hrs.

12.00 hrs.

7.00 hrs.

6.00
hrs.

11.00 hrs.

7.22
hrs.

7.22 hrs.

8.12 hrs.
Firing commences

12.00 hrs.

12.00 hrs.

8.55 hrs.
Cease-fire

Battle group
(Cunningham)
with *Warspite, Barham,
Valiant*, the carrier
Formidable and 9 destroyers

18.30
hrs.

15.10
hrs.

14.50
hrs.

14.20
hrs.

17.00 hrs.

15.20
hrs.

12.05
hrs.

12.00
hrs.

12.00 hrs

8.12–8.55 hrs.
Operations by
Light formation
with *Trieste* div.

00 hrs.
a, *Fiume*
4 destroyers
n to support
Pola

22.30 hrs.
Battle group sinks
Zara, Fiume, Pola
and 2 destroyers

19.30 hrs.
Pola attacked
by torpedo bombers
from the *Formidable*

MEDITERRANEAN

10.58–11.27 hrs.
Operations by
Light formations with
"*Vittorio Veneto*"

to cripple supplies to Greece from Crete and Egypt by attacks targeted against British convoys and the Mediterranean Fleet. But the hunters became the hunted. Adm. Cunningham pulled his fleet out of the battle area and attempted to give the impression that he was unprepared. Despite the threat presented by the German Luftwaffe, the admiral sent off a flying boat in order to give the impression that information on the presence of the Italian fleet in the Aegean came from a reconnaissance aircraft.

On Thursday 27 March 1941, the *Vittorio Veneto* intercepted a report from a British reconnaissance flying boat that three Italian cruisers had been sighted eighty nautical miles east of Sicily heading towards Crete. Riccardi and Iachino were now aware that it would be impossible to surprise the enemy, and as a consequence any chance of intercepting a British convoy would diminish. But in order not to annoy the Germans, at whose insistence this operation had taken place, Riccardi

took a decision with serious consequences and gave orders to carry on with the mission. In fact, as Ultra reported, the flying boat sighted on 27 March 1941 three Italian cruisers some 320 nautical miles west of Crete on a southeasterly course. Thereupon, Cunningham ordered the three battleships in Alexandria to make ready to put to sea, while he ostentatiously left the harbor area carrying his golf clubs in order to mislead enemy agents. Later on, he went back secretly and during the twilight put to sea with his three battleships, the *Warspite, Barham* and *Valiant*, the aircraft carrier *Formidable* and nine destroyers.

At dawn on 28 March 1941, an aircraft from the carrier *Formidable* reported an Italian formation of four cruisers and six destroyers on a southeasterly course making for the Aegean. This was the vanguard of the much stronger formation of Adm. Iachino. At 7:45 A.M., the British cruiser squadron sighted the enemy, attacked and then shortly afterward withdrew at maximum speed to draw the italians into the range of the three battleships, in Cunningham's formation, still seventy nautical miles to the east. And toward 11:00 A.M. on 28 March 1941, not far from Cape Matapan, the battle commenced. That afternoon aircraft from the *Formidable* joined with aircraft from Greece and Crete in an attack on the *Vittorio Veneto*. Damaged by torpedoes and bombs, it withdrew after fifteen minutes and made toward the northwest at a speed of nineteen knots. The crew, with the greatest effort, succeeded in preventing the ship from taking water and brought it to Taranto. After the attack by the carrier aircraft, Iachino was convinced that, although a British carrier with a cruiser and destroyer escort was at sea, the three British battleships had not yet left Alexandria. On the basis of his air reconnaissance reports, the Italian admiral calculated that the nearest British ship would be at least 170 nautical miles away.

The Italian cruisers now took positions around the *Vittorio Veneto* to protect it from further air attacks, and the British carrier-borne aircraft bombed the heavy cruiser *Pola*. During the twilight, the lookouts on the battleships *Warspite*, *Barham* and *Valiant* saw a number of Italian ships crossing athwart their course at a distance of two nautical miles. Completely unaware, the cruisers *Zara* and *Fiume* (Rear Adm. Cattaneos) passed by the British battleships. Cunningham stated, "Never in the whole of my life have I experienced such a tense moment. The enemy was within reach, scarcely two nautical miles away, at the shortest firing range."

At 10:27 P.M., British destroyers turned their searchlights on the heavy cruiser *Fiume*, which then received a broadside from the fifteen-inch guns of the *Warspite* and *Valiant* from a distance of 1.5 nautical miles. Five shells from the first salvo from the *Warspite* hit beneath the upper deck; the sixth shell took the rear turret overboard. Cunningham said, "We could see entire turrets and masses of wreckage flying through the air and falling into the water. . . . Within the shortest possible time, the ships were nothing more than glowing torches."

While the Italians during this night engagement were quite literally groping in the dark, the British fire was directed by radar. Without firing a single shot, the Italian cruisers *Fiume* and *Zara*, as well as the heavy destroyers *Alfieri* and *Carducci*, sank. At daybreak, the badly damaged *Pola* went down. The sinking of the *Pola* marked the end of the Battle of Matapan. The Italians had lost five precious warships, as well as approximately three thousand officers and men. The sole British loss amounted to one Swordfish biplane.

This battle ended with the undisputed British mastery of the eastern Mediterranean waters. The battle was at the same time the first large-scale battle of World War II in European waters and marked the transition from naval battles that, as in World War I, were fought with heavy guns and torpedoes to the later carrier operations in the Pacific that ushered in the age of the aircraft carrier.

The Italians had not been trained in night operations, as they believed that these would not be practical for larger ships. Further, the Italian Navy lacked a flashless cordite propellant charge that

obviated dazzling the gunners. The navy was not provided with radar and could therefore neither employ its main weapons nor direct them during the hours of darkness. But the decisive factor was that there were no Italian aircraft carriers.

The night of 30/31 March 1941, the Royal Air Force mounted a bombing attack against the *Scharnhorst* and *Gneisenau*, which had only the day before reentered port. A total of 109 aircraft attacked the two battlecruisers in Brest without success in the first of a long series of attempts mounted by RAF Bomber Command to destroy the two dangerous warships.

After three months during which not a single U-boat was lost, five were lost in March 1941.

Although March 1941 was the first black month for the German submarine arm, they nevertheless sank forty-three merchantmen totalling 236,113 gross tons.

More and more Allied ships were now included in the strict convoy system, and when the US-built Catalina flying boats were deployed in the early part of 1941, convoy protection was extended to some six hundred nautical miles around the British Isles. This again forced the U-boats to avoid the northwesterly route. At this time the Admiralty put into service the first of the fast motor torpedo boats, the equivalent of the German S-boats.

On Tuesday 1 April 1941, the Admiralty acquired operational control of RAF Coastal Command. In so doing, deployment of these aircraft could be coordinated with the convoys. At this time Coastal Command had at its disposal more than 110 aircraft fitted with ASV radar (Air to Surface Vessel radar), radio direction-finding equipment for use against surface vessels. This DF equipment, although liable to malfunction in those days, helped to ensure that the U-boats could no longer surface freely at night.

On the same day, the *Admiral Scheer* (Capt. Krancke) reached Kiel. During its operational patrol, which had lasted 147 days, the heavy cruiser had sunk seventeen ships totalling 113,233 gross tons and was thus the most successful surface vessel in World War II.

On Wednesday 2 April 1941, Operation Lustre was concluded. Some 58,000 men were transported from Alexandria to Greece. During the operation, twenty-five ships totalling 115,026 gross tons were sunk by Italian naval units and the Luftwaffe. At

The British Short Sunderland flying boat, nicknamed by the Luftwaffe "Flying Porcupine" because of its numerous machine gun defence positions, played a major role as a U-boat hunter.

the same time, the Afrika Korps pushed forward toward Benghazi, and the Royal Navy attempted to prevent the transport of further German forces and their equipment to Tripoli.

On Thursday 3 April 1941, a coupe d'état took place in Iraq. Gen. Ali el Ghailani toppled the pro-British regent Emir Abdul Illah. The German Luftwaffe planned an air bridge to Iraq, and the Soviet Union was the first country to recognise the new government.

The German High Command Foreign/Intelligence section supported the Iraqi nationalists. Half of the Arabic Brigade of the Brandenburgers—the troops of the German intelligence arm—were deployed in Iraq.

On Friday 4 April 1941 toward 6:00 A.M., the commerce raider ship no. 10 *Thor* (Capt. Kähler) sighted the British auxiliary cruiser *Voltaire* (13,245 gross tons), making toward ship no. 10. Almost immediately an exchange of fire commenced, and the *Voltaire* was set on fire shortly after the first salvos; nevertheless, the port and stern guns continued firing, served by the commander and his first officer in person.

After some fifty-five minutes, the *Voltaire* sank. The *Thor* picked up 197 survivors. The radio installation of the *Voltaire* was destroyed at the very beginning of the engagement, and so the British Admiralty knew nothing of the fate of the ship

until the end of the war. The sinking of the British auxiliary cruiser, whose tonnage was five times that of the *Thor*, proved the value in battle of the German commerce raider. The *Thor* suffered only the destruction of its main antennae by a shell that, moreover, was the only hit scored by the *Voltaire*.

On the same day, 4 April 1941, the *Ermland*, which had left Kobe on 28 December 1940, put into Bordeaux as the first of the blockade-runners that succeeded in bringing cargo from Japan to one of the German-occupied European ports.

Also on 4 April 1941, the British Admiralty received permission for warships to have essential repairs carried out in the US dockyards.

On Monday evening, 7 April 1941, eleven He 111s of 2 Squadron/4 Bomber Group (Capt. Kühl), belonging to X Air Corps, attacked the port of Piraeus. One of the bombs hit the British ammunition ship *Clan Frazer*, causing the cargo of 250 tons of explosives to blow up. The explosion wrecked the harbor from one end to the other and sank twelve ships totalling 51,569 gross tons, including sixty lighters and twenty-five motor yachts. The C-in-C of the Mediterranean Fleet, Adm. Cunningham, said, "A devastating blow."

This direct hit deprived British forces of the only well-equipped supply harbor available to them. The effects of the bombing attack meant that the

weak British Expeditionary Corps and the Greek armed forces could conduct only small-scale operations.

On Tuesday 8 April 1941, British troops occupied Mesewa (Eritrea), the most important Italian war harbor in East Africa, effecting the final blow for Italian troops stationed on the Red Sea. Five destroyers attempted a desperate operation against Port Sudan but were attacked some ten nautical miles from their objective by aircraft from the carrier *Eagle*. Those that were not put out of action and sunk by the aircraft scuttled themselves. A number of Italian S-boats and eighteen larger merchantmen totalling 94,324 gross tons were scuttled by their crews. Four Italian submarines were able to escape and finally reached the base in Bordeaux after a voyage around the Cape of Good Hope that lasted several weeks. The small coastal submarine *Perla* was included in the escape, an astonishing feat for so small a vessel.

On Thursday 10 April 1941, the US destroyer *Niblack* (Lt. Comdr. Durgin), while picking up survivors from a merchant ship off Iceland, dropped depth charges on a German U-boat, which was not identified. This was the first action by an American warship against German naval units.

The night of 10/11 April 1941, British bombers again attacked the harbor in Brest. Three bombers scored hits on the forward gun turrets of the *Gneisenau*. Eighty of the crew were killed in this action.

On Tuesday 15 April 1941, ten Yugoslav floatplanes escaped from their base in Boka-Kotorska and reached Suda Bay in Crete. In addition, two Yugoslav torpedo boats, the *Kajmakcalan* and *Durmitor*, and the submarine *Nebosya* escaped to Alexandria where, together with the floatplanes, they created the Royal Yugoslav Navy in exile.

In the middle of April 1941, the Naval Intelligence Division was able to establish an approximate position of the German weather ships in the area between Iceland and the Shetlands. Thereupon, the NID drew up a plan to take the ships prize and acquire any cipher material. With the radio experts Lt. Bacon and Capt. Haines in transport, three cruisers set sail, accompanied by four escort destroyers, to track down the weather ships *München* and *Lauenburg*.

During the evening of 16 April 1941, the destroyers *Janus*, *Jervis*, *Mohawk* and *Nubian* belonging to the 14th Destroyer Flotilla (Capt. Mack), Force K, intercepted and completely destroyed off Kerkenna Islands a convoy made up of four steamers from the German 20 Transport Squadron and the Italian freighter *Sabaudia* (1,590 gross tons) bringing in supplies and equipment for the Afrika Korps. The Italian escort destroyer *Tarigo* (Comdr. Cristofaro) hit the *Mohawk* with a torpedo; but during the further course of the action, the *Tarigo* and two other Italian escort destroyers were either sunk or severely damaged. Of the three thousand soldiers being transported, only 1,248 survived in this first destroyer battle in the Mediterranean.

On Thursday 17 April 1941, Yugoslav warships, taken by surprise in their harbors when the ceasefire was declared, were seized by the Italian Navy. Previously, a number had been plundered by the local population. Toward 6:00 P.M., Lieutenants Masera and Sasic blew themselves up together with their destroyer, the *Zagreb*.

On Friday 18 April 1941, British and Indian troops landed in Basra on the Persian Gulf to secure Britain's interests in Iraq and protect the important oil refineries in Mosul, thereby preventing a takeover by the Axis powers. Naval aircraft from the carrier *Hermes* joined RAF aircraft from the air base at Shaibah in attacking military targets along the Euphrates.

During the night of 19/20 April 1941, the British Commando 7 comprising some 450 men undertook a landing near Bardia in order to disrupt the supply line of the Afrika Korps. The Commando was transported by the *Glengyle* and went ashore in assault boats protected by the cruiser *Coventry* and three destroyers. Not a shot was fired. The heavily armed shock troops, however, found no German troops that they could surprise. The Commandos, who had to carry explosives ashore in crates, found no worthwhile target apart from an unprotected dump with old motor tires. Shortly before sunrise, they had to withdraw in order to embark under cover of darkness. In the hurry, a number of Commandos who had lost their way were left behind. The next day, they were found wandering around in the desert and taken prisoner by the Germans.

On Monday 21 April 1941, Greece capitulated.

On Thursday 24 April 1941, the British Chief of the Imperial General Staff recommended an invasion of the Canary Islands in the fear that Hitler could get there first as he had done in Norway. The prime minister agreed and called the undertaking Operation Puma, as he envisaged using a big cat to seize the Canaries. In the harbor at Inveraray (Scotland) ships and troops were assembled for this operation. The soldiers were to be transported in four Channel ferries and seven transporters. Lt. Gen. Alexander was to lead the expedition from the battleship *Nelson*. The escort duties were to be undertaken by three aircraft carriers, two cruisers and five destroyers.

Also on the 24 April 1941, the US Navy ex-

4/18/1941, Basra (Iraq), the "Tiger Regatta," an armada made up from old gunboats, was meant to protect British interests.

tended the area of its neutrality patrols in the Atlantic as far as longitude 26° west and latitude 20° south. This line between the eastern and western hemispheres was henceforth the effective border of the USA in the Atlantic. It was soon pushed even further toward the east and included Iceland. Churchill stated that the American warships now controlled the waters in the western hemisphere and reported enemy movements to the British within this region.

The British Operation Demon, the evacuation of Greece, began on 24 April 1941. On the same day, the last British fighter in Greece was shot down, and the complete air supremacy achieved by the Germans in the eastern Mediterranean became a heavy burden for the British fleet, which was carrying out the evacuation of troops. As the harbor installations had been heavily damaged by German air attacks, embarkation had to take place in small fishing ports and along the open coast. The soldiers had to force march to the assembly points before destroying their heavy weapons. As the Luftwaffe did not undertake night operations and there were no attacks by Italian warships, the British succeeded in embarking more than 50,000 men over five nights.

The Alexandria Squadron Force H (Vice-Adm. Somerville) deployed all its smaller units as well as six cruisers and nineteen destroyers for Operation Demon. German aircraft sank two destroyers and four troopships totalling 40,480 gross tons. Some twelve thousand British troops were killed or taken

prisoner in Greece. German losses during the entire Greek campaign amounted to one hundred dead and thirty-five hundred wounded or missing. After the evacuation of Greece, Lt. Gen. Freyberg took over the defence of Crete with New Zealand troops.

On Tuesday 29 April 1941, two British cruisers and six destroyers attempted to take off eight thousand men and fourteen hundred Yugoslav refugees from the beach near Spakia. When the ships arrived, the area had already been occupied by German troops, and only 450 men on the beaches to the east could be embarked.

During the evening of 30 April 1941, the commerce raider ship no. 10 *Thor* tied up in Hamburg after a patrol that lasted 329 days. The ship had covered 57,532 nautical miles and during its ten months in the Atlantic, Antarctic and Pacific had sunk some twelve ships totalling 96,602 gross tons.

By the end of the month, the remainder of the Greek fleet had reached Alexandria: the old cruiser *Georgius*, six destroyers, three torpedo boats, some auxiliary vessels, freighters and passenger ships. The majority of these were ordered off to the dockyards of Calcutta and Bombay for repairs before being deployed in the Indian Ocean as escort vessels. Some of the ships returned to Alexandria and remained in the eastern Mediterranean on escort duties.

In April 1941, there were thirty-two U-boats operational, seven fewer than at the beginning of the war. In this month, in the Atlantic, they sank forty-six merchant ships totalling 260,414 gross tons. German losses amounted to two U-boats. The Luftwaffe sank 116 ships (323,000 gross tons), the greatest success of the entire war.

In April 1941, the C-in-C boats established that the British Admiralty must have at its disposal unknown methods with which to locate the U-boat packs. The German radio intelligence service had proof that the convoys often received orders to make unexpected changes in course to circumnavigate the U-boat packs. Additionally, location of convoys became increasingly difficult. Feverish research was conducted into possible causes, one of which was attributed to a new kind of radar equipment. Since April 1941, Allied air reconnaissance operating from Scotland, Newfoundland, Greenland, Canada and Iceland had a perfect overview of the sea route from Canada to Scotland. German surface units now found it practically impossible to pass unobserved through the waters south or north of Iceland.

In April the escort vessels were equipped with a new type of flare suspended from a parachute in place of the old rocket flares. The new flares lit up a radius of a thousand yards for forty to fifty seconds. They cast upon the water a reflection visible for up to three nautical miles, which immediately lit up any U-boat on the surface.

On Friday 2 May 1941, radio messages from the German weather ship *München* — already in the North Atlantic for the planned Atlantic raid Operation Rheinübung ("Rhine exercise") by the battleship *Bismarck* and the heavy cruiser *Prinz Eugen* — were repeatedly intercepted by British direction-finding stations. The cruisers *Manchester*, *Edinburgh* and *Birmingham* with four destroyers including the *Somali* put to sea to capture the *München*.

On Saturday 3 May 1941, ships in the harbor of Inveraray commenced loading for the intended occupation of the Canaries. The action was set for 17 May but was postponed several times; and then Operation Puma became Operation Pilgrim, and was finally postponed indefinitely.

In the first week of May 1941, the Luftwaffe mounted heavy air attacks on the harbor at Liverpool for five consecutive nights. A total of 625 bombers dropped 905 tons of bombs and incendiaries. They destroyed eighteen merchant ships (35,605 gross tons), and 25 ships more, aggregating 92,964 gross tons, were heavily damaged. Almost half of the docks were put out of action and the turnaround capacity of the port was reduced by some seventy-five percent.

On Wednesday 7 May 1941, the cruiser *Edinburgh* sighted the *München* off the Faroes. The British cruiser opened fire, and flames could be

seen on the *München*. The destroyer *Somali*, with its team of specialists, immediately went alongside to prevent scuttling. The crew of the weather ship succeeded in destroying their Enigma-M and the secret documents before getting into the lifeboats. The prize crew from the *Somali* nevertheless found on board important cipher documents, including the short-signal weather reports book, signal and code books, and current Enigma settings. The destroyer *Nestor* rushed the captured material back to Scapa Flow.

On Thursday 8 May 1941, the commerce raider ship no. 33 *Pinguin* (Capt. Krüger) was sighted in the Indian Ocean near the Seychelles by the aircraft from the heavy cruiser *Cornwall* (Capt. Mainwaring). Although practically deceived by the perfect camouflage, the *Cornwall* found it strange that no one came on deck to wave to them. Shortly afterward the cruiser opened fire. A hit in the mines chamber on the *Pinguin* caused a heavy explosion, and the ship went down. The *Pinguin* was the first German commerce raider to be sunk,

Left: Lt. Comdr. Fritz Julius Lemp (right) leaving Lorient on his last patrol

Below: 5/9/1941, off Greenland, the *U 110* forced to the surface; on the right the British corvette *Aubrietia*.

and, with thirty-two ships destroyed or taken prize (154,619 gross tons), it was the most successful commerce raider in World War II.

In the evening that same day, close to Greenland the *U 110* (Lt. Comdr. Lemp), which sank the British passenger ship *Athenia* on 3 September 1939, discovered Convoy HX-123 and the following day toward midday sank two ships in the convoy, totalling 7,585 gross tons. What then happened was one of the best-kept secrets of World War II and the years following.

The British corvette *Aubrietia* dropped one depth charge after the other. Suddenly *U 110* came to the surface and the crew abandoned the damaged submarine under a hail of fire. The destroyer *Bulldog* was picking up German survivors when Capt. Baker-Cresswell, the commander, noticed that the enemy U-boat was still afloat. When the U-boat's commander, Lemp, noticed to his horror that the U-boat was still afloat, he swam back in order to scuttle it. Before he could climb aboard, however, he was shot by the prize crew. The crew of the U-boat, who had been rescued, were locked below decks, convinced that their ship had gone down.

The prize crew, lead by Lt. Balme, went aboard the *U 110*. The lieutenant said, "The lamps were still burning and total silence reigned. It was a fine, new ship, scrupulously clean and equipped with a splendid galley. We were impressed by the quality of the U-boat's provisions. We removed all secret equipment, maps and documents up through the conning tower and into our cutter. Our engineer officer came across to see if he could get the U-boat's engines going again, but was unsuccessful. When we had removed everything that was of any value and interest to us onto the *Bulldog*, we made the U-boat ready for towing." The boarding party captured an Enigma-M enciphering machine, the current signal and code books, the U-boat short-signals book, the important special Enigma settings (printed on water-soluble paper), the entire cipher wheels, transmission documents and the intelligence log.

The news of the capture of a U-boat with its entire Enigma-M enciphering machine and the secret documentation—the only case of this happening in World War II—caused great excitement at the Admiralty and was classified under Ultra (secret). To what extent the *U 110* operation (code-named Primrose in the Intelligence Service archives) affected the outcome of the war can only be judged by historians when the British Intelligence Service opens its archives. (Some secret papers dating to the time of the Service's founder, Sir Francis Walsingham (1536–90), are still on the confidential list.)

A flying boat with specialists on board approached the *Bulldog*. But shortly before reaching Iceland, the *U 110* suddenly raised its bows and sank. "The petals of your flower have a rare beauty," radioed the First Sea Lord to Capt. Baker-Cresswell when he saw the captured equipment. King George VI said that it was the most important individual success of the war.

The cipher material and settings found on board *U 110* were valid to the end of 1941 and gave NID a chance to finally decrypt the Hydra cipher used by the U-boats and the C-in-C U-boats. Another important secret document related to the scheduled change in Enigma-M settings, a procedure that was carried out twice daily in accordance with regulations. This document made deciphering of U-boat radio traffic even easier. For the first time the British Admiralty was able to gain a clear-cut overview of German U-boat operations, a fact that was decisive in the course of the U-boat war.

On Sunday 11 May 1941, the Arabic Brigade of the German Brandenburgers captured two gunboats and some fifty supply ships on the Tigris.

On Monday 12 May 1941, the British carried out Operation Tiger, whereby a convoy transported 238 tanks and 43 fighters to Alexandria for the British army in Egypt. The convoy was escorted by battleships, aircraft carriers, cruisers and destroyers with the loss of only one freighter.

On the same day, Hitler, accompanied by his staff, visited the battleship *Bismarck* lying in Gdynia.

From Thursday 15 May 1941 the British Mediterranean Fleet stayed in the waters around Crete.

On Saturday 17 May 1941, the Greco-British troops on Crete (42,646 men including 10,258 Greeks) were on stand-by alert, awaiting a German attack at any time.

On Sunday 18 May 1941, under the command of Adm. Lütjens the fleet commander, the battleship *Bismarck* (Capt. Lindemann) and the heavy cruiser *Prinz Eugen* (Capt. Brinkmann) put to sea to carry out Operation Rhine Exercise, to date the biggest operation involving German surface units. Two supply ships and five tankers were waiting at various points in Norwegian waters and the North Atlantic. Two reconnaissance ships set sail in advance of the main party to seek out favorable operational areas. The route taken by the battle group for their breakout from the Baltic was cleared of all shipping.

On Tuesday 20 May 1941, Operation Mercury, the German airborne landing on Crete, commenced. Bombers belonging to the VIII Air Corps (Gen. von Richthofen) bombed British troop concentrations on Crete. The first wave of paratroops landed without incident. Subsequently, resistance

intensified.

Also on 20 May 1941, the *Bismarck* and *Prinz Eugen* were sighted in the Skagerrak.

The same evening, the British military attaché in Stockholm, Capt. Denham, radioed to London, "Utmost urgency, Kattegat 20 May today 15.00 hours two large warships plus three destroyers, five escort vessels, ten or twelve aircraft have passed through course northwest."

On Wednesday 21 May 1941, the battle group was discovered refuelling in the Korsfjord near Bergen by a British reconnaissance aircraft.

On this day also, the *U 69* (Lt. Comdr. Metzler) sank the first US merchantman, *Robin Moore*, on the sea route between New York and Cape Town.

That evening, the battle group left the Korsfjord. At the same time, the battlecruiser *Hood*, battleship *Prince of Wales* and six destroyers left Scapa Flow for the sea area south of Iceland.

At 5:30 A.M. on Thursday 22 May 1941, the Ju 88s of 2 Dive Bomber Group Immelmann (Lt. Col. Dinort) took off to attack Royal Navy vessels off Crete and scored a number of hits on the battleship *Warspite* (Capt. Crutchley). At this time, in addition to the vessels of Force D, the cruisers *Gloucester* (Capt. Rowley) and *Fiji* (Capt. Williams-Powlett) and the destroyers *Greyhound* and *Griffin* were twenty-five nautical miles off the north coast of Crete. Several hits put two gun turrets on the cruiser *Naiad* out of action. Shortly before midday, the second formation, Force C

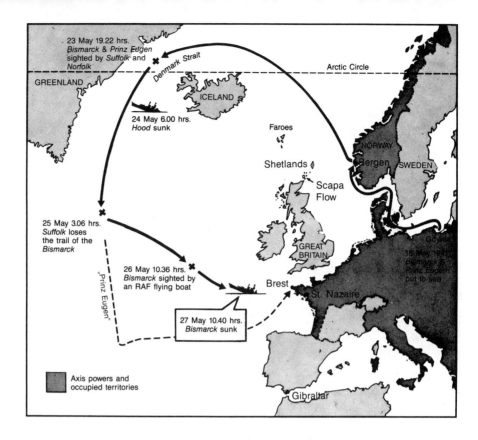

Right: The voyage of the *Bismarck*

- 23 May 19.22 hrs.
  Bismarck & Prinz Eugen
  sighted by *Suffolk* and
  Norfolk

Denmark Strait

Arctic Circle

GREENLAND

ICELAND

24 May 6.00 hrs.
Hood sunk

Faroes

NORWAY

Bergen

SWEDEN

Shetlands

Scapa
Flow

25 May 3.06 hrs.
Suffolk loses
the trail of the
Bismarck

GREAT
BRITAIN

Gdynia

18 May 1941
*Bismarck &
Prinz Eugen*
put to sea

"Prinz Eugen"

26 May 10.36 hrs.
Bismarck sighted by
an RAF flying boat

Brest

St. Nazaire

27 May 10.40 hrs.
Bismarck sunk

Left: 5/24/1941, the Denmark Strait, the last photo of the *Hood* before it was lost—taken from the deck of the *Prince of Wales*

Axis powers and
occupied territories

Gibraltar

(Rear Adm. King), was sighted and ten minutes later the battleship *Warspite* (flagship of Adm. Rawlings) was badly damaged. Toward 1:00 P.M. the destroyer *Greyhound* sank after two direct hits. Several formations of Ju 87 Stukas and Me 109 fighter bombers dived on lone cruisers. The *Gloucester* was hit immediately. Wreathed in clouds of black smoke, the cruiser went round slowly in circles and, after an internal explosion, sank at about 4:00, losing 45 officers and 648 crew. The first sea-air battle in history, after lasting several days, was decided conclusively in favor of the German Luftwaffe.

Without having achieved air supremacy, German troops brought by sea to Crete would have been completely lost. And so German bombers were able to cause the British Mediterranean Fleet such considerable losses that it was forced to withdraw from the waters north of Crete.

Also on 22 May 1941, the Home Fleet (Adm. Tovey) put to sea after British reconnaissance aircraft established that the Korsfjord was empty.

On the same day after returning from a flight over Scapa Flow, a German pilot incorrectly reported that the had seen four large ships lying there. This information was relayed to Adm. Lütjens on the assumption that he had successfully broken through without being observed.

Around midnight of 22 May 1941, a squadron commanded by Lt. Oesterlin sailing out of Piraeus with twenty motor yachts and some 2,300 mountain troops on board was caught by the British Force D (Rear Adm. Glennie) off the coast of Crete and almost entirely destroyed. The second convoy, carrying some four thousand mountain troops, was rescued at the last moment by bombers of the VIII Air Corps.

On Friday 23 May 1941, after having been kept secret for almost two months, the loss of *U 47* was confirmed. On this day, the German High Command communiqué reported that the U-boat commanded by Comdr. Prien had failed to return from its last patrol.

The evening of 23 May 1941, the German battle group in the Denmark Strait was discovered by the British cruisers *Norfolk* and *Suffolk*, after which the *Bismarck* and *Prinz Eugen* sailed close to the Arctic Circle so that the two cruisers could shadow them only from astern. In so doing, the *Prinz Eugen* went so heavily into the ice that its starboard screw was damaged.

On the same day, Roosevelt gave orders to make up a force of 25,000 men that was to be ready to undertake an invasion of the Azores within four weeks. The Portuguese government immediately raised a strong protest, as they wished to have neither the Americans nor the British on their islands until such time as the Axis powers infringed Portuguese neutrality.

Early Saturday 24 May 1941, the German battle

themselves around his legs. Then, just as he was beginning to lose consciousness, he suddenly remembered the jackknife that all sailors carry with them. He desperately felt for and found the knife and with a couple of strokes freed himself from his boots and the antennae. Then he reached the surface, his lungs almost bursting. Tilburn, who was himself a gunner, has categorically denied the version of the *Hood*'s sinking that was originally given out by the National Socialist propaganda service and is even today still current: that the *Hood* went down as a result of one salvo. In fact, he has confirmed that the German fire was accurate from start to finish, "Throughout the action, *Bismarck*'s gunnery was deadly accurate."

The *Prinz Eugen* survived the action fully unscathed. The *Bismarck*, however, was damaged several times, including a hit in an oil tank. The precious fuel ran out leaving a clear, telltale oil trail. Adm. Lütjens now decided to break off the operation. He chose, however, not to return to Norway but to disappear into the vast expanses of the Atlantic and then make for Brest. And now two more battleships, a battlecruiser, a cruiser and Force H (Vice-Adm. Somerville) with the carrier *Ark Royal* were ordered northward to hunt the German battle group.

During the night of 24/25 May 1941, Adm. Lütjens released the heavy cruiser *Prinz Eugen* to take independent action. The cruisers pursuing the battleship *Bismarck* lost radar contact with it.

The same night, a convoy of Italian troop transports comprising four former passenger ships were attacked en route to Tripoli by British warships. East of Sicily, the British submarine *Upholder* (Lt. Comdr. Wanklyn) sank the steamer *Conte Rosso* (17,879 gross tons). Of the 2,500 soldiers on board, 1,680 were rescued.

On Sunday 25 May 1941, the *Bismarck* took a southeasterly course without knowing that the British fleet had lost contact for the last thirty hours. Lütjens, who continued to believe he was being shadowed, put through to Hitler a personal message reporting the success, and described in a radio transmission, lasting almost half an hour, the action with the battlecruiser *Hood*. By the time the high command ordered radio traffic to be broken off, it was already too late: Before the transmission had terminated, the British Admiralty was in receipt of location reports. The information transmitted to the commander of the Home Fleet, Adm. Tovey, was incorrectly evaluated on his flagship, and he assumed that the *Bismarck* was on a northerly course. Tovey ordered the Home Fleet to take up this course and for seven hours pursued his opponent in the wrong direction.

group met up with the British battlecruiser *Hood* (Capt. Kerr) and the battleship *Prince of Wales* (Capt. Leech). Both ships opened fire at a range of seventeen nautical miles. The *Prinz Eugen* scored the first hit close to the *Hood*'s mainmast, causing a rapidly spreading fire to break out. The *Bismarck* had also hit the *Hood*. Suddenly a huge flame shot up, the *Hood* exploded amidships and disappeared in a vast pall of smoke.

Four hours later the destroyer *Electra* reached the spot where the *Hood* had gone down. Three exhausted seamen were found clinging to pieces of wreckage, trying with their last reserves of strength to keep above water despite the thick coating of oil on the surface. Not a sound could be heard; no bodies were seen; not a trace of Great Britain's proudest warship remained.

William Dundas, Robert Tilburn and Edward Briggs were the names of the three men, the only survivors out of 1,418 officers, crew and dockyard workers. Dundas was on the closed upper bridge with the officer of the watch. Tilburn, an antiaircraft gunner, was at his battle station with a four-inch antiaircraft gun on the port side of the deck. Briggs, a runner for the adjutant of Vice-Adm. Holland, was standing on the compass platform at the time of the explosion. Dundas managed to get free from the bridge before the *Hood* sank. Briggs could only remember the massive explosion, a giant sheet of flame and how the battlecruiser fell apart. Then he was swimming through a lake of burning oil. Tilburn was dragged into the water just before the *Hood* was fully submerged. Hampered by his oilskins, a thick fur coat and heavy boots, he went down like a stone. At a depth of thirty feet, the wires from the radio mast wrapped

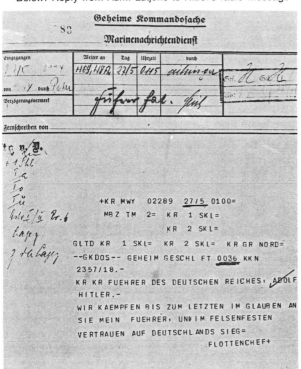

Left: 5/26/1941, a Swordfish returns to the carrier *Ark Royal* after a mission.

Above: The battleship *Bismarck* during the action—taken from the deck of the *Prinz Eugen*

Below: Reply from Adm. Lütjens to Hitler's radio message

Finally, on Monday 26 May 1941 at 10:36 A.M., a Catalina flying boat (Flying Officer Briggs) from 209 Squadron (Coastal Command) sighted the *Bismarck* some seven hundred nautical miles from its port of destination, Brest, and reported its position.

That afternoon, fifteen Swordfish aircraft took off from the *Ark Royal* in bad weather to attack the *Bismarck*. A torpedo hit the port rudder installations, jamming the rudder at an angle of fifteen degrees and making the ship unmaneuverable.

For the first time in the history of sea warfare, a carrier aircraft had attacked a battleship on the high sea. The crews of the Swordfish reported that immediately after the torpedoing, the *Bismarck* completed two full circles and then came to a standstill with its bows facing the north.

Adm. Lütjens is said to have offered an immediate award of the Iron Cross to anybody who succeeded in releasing the jammed rudder, but to no avail.

At 9:52 P.M., the destroyer *Cossack* (Capt. Vian), together with the five destroyers under his command, received orders to take up contact with the *Bismarck*. The Polish destroyer *Piorun* (Comdr. Plawski), which was attached to the formation, sighted the *Bismarck* in the twilight some nine nautical miles away and exchanged fire with the battleship for fifty-nine minutes.

On Tuesday 27 May 1941, Adm. Lütjens—two days after his fifty-second birthday—received at 1:53 A.M. the last radioed message from the Führer, "For Fleet Commander, I thank you in the name of the entire German people—Adolf Hitler. To the crew of the battleship *Bismarck*, the whole of Germany is with you. What is possible will be done.

Your devotion to duty will strengthen our people in their struggle for their existence." Shortly afterward, at 8:47, the battleship *Rodney* (Capt. Dalrymple-Hamilton) and one minute later the *King George V* (Adm. Tovey) opened fire on the *Bismarck*, which returned fire at 8:50 and continued to defend itself until its guns were silenced.

The last signal sent by the *Bismarck*: "U-boat transmit for the intelligence log. Fleet Commander."

At 10:15 A.M., Adm. Tovey ordered the engagement to be broken off, as *King George V* and *Rodney* had to retire because of fuel shortage. At 10:10, the cruiser *Norfolk* (Capt. Phillips) fired four torpedoes at the *Bismarck*, which was on fire. Ten minutes later, the heavy cruiser *Dorsetshire* (Capt. Martin) attacked with two torpedoes and fired the third and last torpedo at the stationary battleship at 10:36. Comdr. (Eng.) G. Junack stated, "Toward 10.15 hours I received orders from the Chief Engineer to prepare the ship for scuttling. That was the last command I received on board the *Bismarck*. Shortly afterward the entire communications system failed. Finally, after carrying out the orders of the Chief Engineer, I left the engine room with the engines turning slowly. . . .

"The flag was still flying from the mast and the guns in the two turrets aft were still pointing towards the sky. . . . After a threefold 'Sieg Heil' I gave the order to abandon ship."

Shortly afterward, the ship turned over on its side and went down within four minutes.

Adm. Tovey said, "The *Bismarck* had put up a most gallant fight against impossible odds, worthy of the old days of the Imperial German Navy, and she went down her colors flying."

The heavy cruiser *Dorsetshire* (Capt. Martin) and the destroyer *Maori* (Comdr. Armstrong) picked up 110 men including two officers.

Some hours later, the destroyer *Cossack* (Capt. Vian) crossed these waters on its homeward voyage. One of the seamen spotted amid wreckage and bodies a black cat floating on a board. The destroyer stopped and picked up the soaking-wet animal, which was shivering with cold. The cat was given the name Oscar, and so the *Bismarck*'s mascot joined the Royal Navy.

Later, the *U 75* (Lt. Comdr. Ringelmann) reached the spot where the battleship went down and managed to pick up five survivors. The following night, the weather ship *Sachsenwald* picked up three more men. Out of a total of 2,400 officers and crew, 118 were saved.

Eight battleships and battlecruisers, two aircraft carriers, for heavy and seven light cruisers, twenty-one destroyers, six submarines and several land-based aircraft were deployed by the Royal Navy for the pursuit of the *Bismarck*.

The torpedo strike by a carrier-borne aircraft that helped to sink the *Bismarck* marked a new tactic in sea warfare and demonstrated that the role of the battleship was reducing.

The sinking of the *Bismarck* ended the German Navy's plans to decide the Battle of the Atlantic with surface craft. The main thrust of this battle was now transferred to the U-boats. Grand Adm. Raeder stated, "The consequences of the loss of the *Bismarck* were far-reaching for the Naval High Command. Indeed, even Hitler's attitude toward the proposals I put forward for the war at sea was very different. . . . First of all, he forbade further surface units to be sent out into the Atlantic."

The Naval High Command now saw that the only chance of deploying large ships with any chance of success was by forays from Norwegian bases out into the direction of the Arctic Sea.

From Halifax, on 27 May 1941, Convoy HX-129 put to sea the first convoy that had protection against U-boats for the entire voyage across the North Atlantic.

On the same day that the *Bismarck* went down, hostilities in Crete ended. On the evening of 27 May 1941, Lt. Gen. Freyberg received orders to evacuate Crete. The British fleet had to pay a heavy bill in the fighting for this island: Two battleships, *Barham* and *Warspite*, as well as the aircraft carrier *Formidable*, six cruisers and seven destroyers were heavily damaged, and six destroyers were lost.

If, however, Force H stationed in Gibraltar had taken part in the fighting for Crete with its battle-cruisers *Renown*, carrier *Ark Royal*, the cruiser *Sheffield* and six destroyers, Operation Mercury would presumably have had to be abandoned. Instead, this formation put to sea on 24 May 1941 to hunt the *Bismarck* in the Atlantic.

In May 1941, the air and sea forces of the Axis powers sank fifty-eight merchant vessels totalling 325,400 gross tons. One German U-boat, *U 110* (Lt. Comdr. Lemp), was lost.

From May 1941, approximately thirty U-boats were engaged in operations, but a number had to be deployed from time to time between Bordeaux and the Azores to protect blockade-runners entering port and leaving again.

During the same month, British submarines sank German and Italian shipping capacity amounting to more than 100,000 gross tons.

Dönitz now transferred the operational area of the U-boat packs some two hundred nautical miles further west, beyond the range of the Coastal Command aircraft stationed in Northern Ireland. This decision rationalised economic warfare —

6/9/1941, Eastern Mediterranean area, the French destroyer *Valmy* under fire from the British destroyer *Janus*

transfer the main thrust of U-boat deployment to where the greatest number of merchantmen could be sunk for minimum U-boat losses.

The documents captured on the weather ship *München* (7 May 1941) and location of German U-boat radio transmissions by British land-based stations made it possible for the Admiralty to seize or sink weather ships, supply ships and reconnaissance vessels stationed in the Atlantic for Operation Rhine Exercise.

By the end of May 1941, with the exception of the *Altmark* captured in February 1941, not a single supply ship had been captured. But now the British Admiralty set to work.

On Tuesday 3 June 1941, the supply tanker *Belchen* (6,367 gross tons) was sunk by the British cruisers *Aurora* (Capt. Agnew) and *Kenya* (Capt. Denny) in the waters between Greenland and Labrador.

On the next day, 4 June 1941, the reconnaissance ship *Gonzenheim* (4,000 gross tons) was set alight by its crew seven hundred nautical miles west of Brest after it had sighted the approaching battleship *Nelson* and then suddenly the cruiser *Neptune* (Capt. O'Connor).

At the same time, the British armed merchant cruiser *Marsdale* (4,890 gross tons) captured the supply tanker *Gedania* (8,923 gross tons) in the same area. Capt. Paradeis was unable to destroy secret documents. The British Admiralty gained precise details about meeting points for the provisioning of U-boats, warships and commerce raiders, as well as a list of weather ships, routes taken by the blockade-runners and radio documents with ciphers. And not quite twenty-four hours later, the crew of the supply tanker *Esso Hamburg* (9,849 gross tons) prepared to scuttle their ship between Freetown and Natal off the South African coast to avoid being taken prize.

The following day, 5 June 1941, the captain of the supply tanker *Egerland* (9,798 gross tons), also in the area between the Canaries and Freetown, ordered the ship to be scuttled when the heavy cruiser *London* (Capt. Servaes) and the destroyer *Brilliant* attempted a capture.

This sudden loss of the German supply ships changed the strategical position at sea and at the same time brought about a change in German operational command. The Kriegsmarine, which had no bases outside Europe, had at least been offered a chance of supplementing essential fuel and provisions by means of the supply ships. In future, only short-term operations were feasible.

On Sunday 8 June 1941, British troops (Gen. Wilson) and the 1st Division of the Free French (Gen. Le Gentilhomme) attacked mandate territories in Syria and Lebanon defended by Vichy French units (Gen. Dentz). The Vichy French naval commander, Rear Adm. Gouton, had at his disposal on the Syrian coast the destroyers *Valmy* (Comdr. Guiot) and *Guépard* with the flotilla commander Capt. de Lafond, as well as the submarines *Caimon*, *Morse*, *Souffleur*, the sloop *Elan* and several weakly armed sweepers. On the British side, this operation was led by Vice-Adm. King with the cruisers *Ajax* (Capt. McCarthy), *Coventry*, *Phoebe* and eight destroyers and a number of submarines.

The British attack was caused by the fear that German Luftwaffe formations, with the assent of the Vichy government, could be transferred to

Syria after the conquest of Crete. This confrontation between the Royal Navy and the French Navy brought about bitter sea battles.

The night of 8/9 June 1941, under protection of two destroyers and the antiaircraft cruiser *Coventry*, the men of Commando 11 (Lt. Col. Pedder) were set ashore on the Syrian coast from the parent ship *Glengyle*. Their task was to secure the bridge over the Litani River some twenty miles north of the Palestinian border and hold it, undamaged, until the vanguard of the attack force could get there. The Commandos found that the bridge had already been blown up by the French. The decision was then made to establish a bridgehead on the north bank of the Litani to make it easier for the army to cross the river. Two companies of Commandos landed on the south bank. All three groups encountered stiff resistance and also fire from their own vanguard, which had arrived in the meantime. This Commando raid was also dogged by bad luck; a third of the men were lost.

On Monday 9 June 1941, the French destroyers *Valmy* and *Guépard* exchanged fire with the British destroyer *Janus*. The British cruiser *Leander* and six destroyers arrived off the coast of Syria as reinforcements.

On the same day in Basra, Indian troops and their equipment were embarked on improvised transport vessels making up the Tigris Regatta. This motley collection of old paddle-steamers and Arabian feluccas, escorted by the Australian sloop *Yarra*, proceeded up the Tigris towards Kut, a strategically important location.

On Wednesday 11 June 1941, British troops carried out a surprise landing near Assab, which they duly took, the last Italian base on the Red Sea.

On Thursday 12 June 1941, a British Expeditionary Corps landed near Sidon and forced the French to withdraw.

German bombers stationed on Crete participated in the naval engagements off the coast of Syria, making it more difficult for the British to fight the modern French destroyers.

Also on 12 June 1941, the British cruiser *Sheffield* (Capt. Maund) sighted the German supply tanker *Friedrich Breme* (10,397 gross tons) in the North Atlantic. Before the crew managed to scuttle their ship, the British prize crew discovered various secret documents on board.

Three days later, on Sunday 15 June 1941, the British light cruiser *Dunedin* captured the U-boat supply ship *Lothringen* (10,746 gross tons) in mid-Atlantic. Although the crew managed to throw the Enigma-M overboard in good time, the prize crew nevertheless took possession of a number of secret documents.

On the same day, the Luftwaffe attempted to

come to the aid of the hard-pressed French naval forces. Junkers Ju 88s of II Wing, 1 Training Group (Capt. Kollewe) attacked British warships off the Syrian coast, scoring hits on the destroyers *Illex* and *Isis*. (Although the German group was called a "Lehrgeschwader," literally a training group, it was in fact an élite unit. — Trans.)

That evening, French aircraft belonging to the 4th Naval Air Group bombed the British naval units off the Syrian coast.

On Monday 16 June 1941, a British torpedo aircraft sank the destroyer *Chevalier Paul*, which had left Toulon for Syria carrying ammunition supplies.

On Tuesday 17 June 1941, British bombers attacked the second French destroyer in Beirut carrying ammunition supplies from France.

By Wednesday 18 June 1941, German minelayers had laid three minefields in the Baltic between Memel and Oland.

The following day, 19 June 1941, Adm. Kusnezov, People's Commissar for the Red Fleet, declared a state of emergency.

In drawing up his plans for Operation Barbarossa, Hitler counted on a rapid victory by Blitzkrieg, without having to engage the Kriegsmarine. In June 1941 the Kriegsmarine was, in fact, in a very critical situation. The *Bismarck* had been sunk; the new battleship *Tirpitz* was not yet operational; the battlecruisers *Scharnhorst* and *Gneisenau*, together with the heavy cruiser *Prinz Eugen*,

Above: 12/6/1941, North Atlantic, the *Friedrich Breme*, a supply tanker forming part of the Operation Rhine Exercise, coming under fire shortly before being taken by the cruiser *Sheffield*

Below: Adm. Nikolai Kusnezov: naval attaché and naval adviser in Spain 1936–37; People's Commissar for the Red fleet from 1939

were confined to Brest by constant British air raids. The heavy cruisers *Admiral Scheer* and *Admiral Hipper* were in the dockyards for repairs; the heavy cruiser *Lützow* was put out of action by a torpedo strike; and of the four light cruisers, only the *Köln* and the *Nürnberg* were completely operational. Of the torpedo boats and destroyers recently laid down, only a few were as yet ready for front-line service.

In the morning of Saturday 21 June 1941, the remaining German specialists working on the cruiser *Lützow* — sold by Germany to the Soviet Union — left Leningrad under the pretext of returning home for leave. Rear Adm. (Eng.) Feige, who had been supervising the works from the German side, had returned home at the end of April 1941 because of ill health. The construction of the cruiser initially started under the description "Project 53" and from the middle of February 1941 bore the name *Petropavlovsk*. The commander was Capt. 1st Grade A. G. Vanifatev. According to Soviet data of 21 June 1941, the German 20.3-cm guns for turrets A, B and D were fitted and ready to fire. The guns for turret C were still in Germany.

The evening of 21 June 1941, the minelaying operations were concluded after three days of activity (code-name Wartburg I-III). Shortly before sunset German merchant vessels in the Baltic received radio orders to make for the nearest German, Finnish or Swedish ports.

Kusnezov stated, "At 11:15 P.M. the C-in-C of the Baltic Fleet received oral orders from me to proceed to full emergency and to make use of his weapons if threatened." At 11:30, the minelayers belonging to Group North (Comdr. von Schönermarkt) commenced laying mines between the Fanöfjord and Dagö in the Gulf of Finland. Another group laid a minefield some thirty nautical miles east. The two groups were observed by a Soviet battleship and several destroyers. Two aircraft from the Red air fleet attempted to disrupt the operations. The minelayers picked up Morse code messages by searchlight from the Soviet coastal batteries.

On Sunday 22 June 1941, the day of the Red fleet, the German attack on the Soviet Union, Operation Barbarossa, began. Kusnezov stated, "At 3:15 A.M. the C-in-C of the Black Sea Fleet telephoned me from Sevastapol and reported an attack by German aircraft. Well, so it's war. . . . Although I had been following the course of events with great attention and was, to a certain extent, prepared for a possible attack by Hitler Germany on our Fatherland, I was shocked when I first received the news."

The deployment of German forces in the Baltic was restricted to securing the German coastline as

Above and right: Summer 1941, the same picture on both sides of the North Sea: above, a German flotilla and to the right, a British flotilla. Light units commence their daily operations in coastal waters.

well as merchant shipping and, at the same time, was meant to prevent the Soviets breaking out into the Baltic. The German Navy wished to wait until the German Army occupied Leningrad and neutralised the Red fleet lying there. At the beginning of Operation Barbarossa the German Navy, apart from a few S-boats and U-boats, had only auxiliary warships and smaller units at its disposal.

The Soviet fleet consisted of the North fleet (Vice-Adm. Golovko), the Baltic fleet (Vice-Adm. Tribuz), the Black Sea fleet with the Danube flotilla (Vice-Adm. Oktyabrski) and the Pacific fleet (Adm. Yumasev). The most important task for the Soviet fleet was direct cooperation with the army groups in the coastal areas. From autumn 1939 until summer 1941, the Red fleet was almost completely re-armed and considerably strengthened. The organisation of the fleet was uncomplicated and practical. The unlimited power of command over strong naval formations proved particularly useful. Well-equipped naval coastal batteries and a number of marine brigades meant the navy could

defend its harbors and landing operations with its own resources. Against this, however, there was the distinct disadvantage of the limited number of special purpose vessels; there was, for example, a lack of ships for landing operations. Also, little attention had been paid to the development of radar up to this date. On the other hand, the Soviet submarine arm numbered 254 submarines and was the largest in the world by a considerable margin. Despite the recognisable deployment of the German forces, no Soviet U-boats were at action stations in the Baltic.

On 22 June 1941 *U 48* (Lt. Comdr. Schultze) returned to Kiel from its last operational patrol. During twelve enemy patrols under three different commanders, *U 48* had sunk fifty-four Allied merchant ships totalling 322,292 gross tons, and had damaged a sloop and two ships totalling 11,024 gross tons. It was the most successful U-boat in World War II.

The night of 22/23 June, the *Guëpard* fought an action with two British cruisers and six destroyers off the coast of Syria. The French destroyer managed to withdraw under cover of darkness.

On Monday 23 June 1941, the first large-scale convoy battle took place between a German U-boat pack and an escort group. That morning the Admiralty received advance warning through a

deciphered Enigma-M message – showing incidentally how important Ultra reports were in the war against the U-boat – that ten enemy submarines were grouping south of Greenland to attack Convoy HX-133, bound for England from Halifax. The convoy was immediately ordered to change course. Additional ships were sent to support the escort group. For five days and five nights, ten U-boats fought thirteen escort vessels. The *U 556* (Lt. Comdr. Wolfarth) and *U 651* (Lt. Comdr. Lohmeyer) were sunk by the escort vessels, and five Allied merchantmen were lost. In this incident the tactic of reinforcing threatened escort groups was first put into practice. After the experiences gleaned from this encounter, the Admiralty created a year later the "support group," a weapon which proved its worth – especially in Atlantic waters.

On Wednesday 25 June 1941, the British submarine *Parthian* (Comdr. Rimington) torpedoed and sank the French submarine *Souffleur* off the Syrian coast.

Shortly afterward the French tanker *Adour*, carrying the entire fuel supplies for the French forces in the Middle East, was attacked and badly damaged by a British torpedo aircraft.

On the same day, in the Atlantic the weather-reporting ship *Lauenburg* was located by the British destroyer *Bedouin*, which was equipped with

short-wave DF equipment. The cruiser *Nigeria* and the three remaining escort destroyers captured the *Lauenburg*. An NID specialist, Lt. Bacon, secured valuable maps and cipher documents found on board. The NID could now decipher further codes used by the German Navy as, for example, those used by the U-boats in the Mediterranean under the names "Medusa" and "Neptune" and operating codes for surface warships taking part in special operations. The Germans undertook various investigations – which, however, led to no positive result – with the sinking or taking prize of almost all the German supply ships reserved for Operation Rhine Exercise together with the weather-reporting ships. The belief was still held that any enemy deciphering could be countered by scheduled changes in the code settings. The British, for their part, carried out all operations, which were in fact attributable to their having mastered German ciphers, to give the impression that the information had come from other sources such as agents, DF location or aerial photographic reconnaissance.

Late 26 June 1941, the Soviet submarine base at Libau (Liepaja) in Latvia was evacuated before the submarines lying there were ready for operations. As the Red army was not in a position to hold the Baltic, the Soviet fleet lost its most important bases and had to use almost all its ships for the

Summer 1941, Eastern Mediterranean area, aboard a French naval vessel. Light antiaircraft gun awaiting a fresh attack by British aircraft. Hostilities between the former Allies were conducted with the utmost severity.

evacuation of troops or provisioning armies cut off in this area.

In June 1941, the total number of aircraft in Coastal Command had increased only by a third over the September 1939 total. Although seventy-five percent of the aircraft had already been fitted with radar of the type ASV Mark II, which was theoretically capable of detecting any U-boat on the surface in any weather and even at night, the overwhelming majority of U-boats were directly sighted by members of the aircrews.

From June 1941 the commerce raiders that had put to sea in 1940 were the sole German surface warships operating against enemy merchant shipping on the high seas, except the Arctic Ocean. From January to June 1941 they sank thirty-eight merchant ships totalling 191,000 gross tons.

Stepping up the U-boat construction program

had its first effects in June 1941. The planned number of fifteen boats was achieved, and this exceeded losses. And so in June 1941 thirty-nine U-boats were operational, which meant that the total operational in September and October 1939 had now again been reached. But there was now an almost insoluble problem for the C-in-C U-boats, how to crew the newly built ships with trained submariners and commanders. Quite simply, the new crews lacked experience.

1941

July–December

W. Churchill to J. V. Stalin
Tuesday 8 July 1941

We are all very glad here that the Russian armies are making such strong and spirited resistance to the utterly unprovoked and merciless invasion of the Nazis. There is a general admiration of the bravery and tenacity of the soldiers and people. We shall do everything to help you that time, geography and our growing resources allow. . . . On Saturday night over two hundred heavy bombers attacked German towns, some carrying three tons apiece, and last night nearly 250 heavy bombers were operating. . . . Besides this, the Admiralty have at my desire prepared a serious operation to come off in the near future in the Arctic, after which I hope contact will be established between the British and Russian navies.

How Long Does a German Submariner Live?
Thursday 10 July 1941
RAF leaflet "Luftpost" N-8/1941

On 5 July naval officers spoke on the German broadcasting station Deutschlandsender. They admitted that German U-boats to make good losses must continually be manned by fresh crews. One of the officers, who has been lucky enough to survive twelve operational patrols, described himself as "an old U-boat man." Another added that now the nights were shorter, things could get very much worse. . . .

A few months ago, life-assurance companies in neutral countries calculated that the average life expectancy of a German U-boat man after his taking up front-line duties amounted to sixty-two days. According to the observations made by this German naval officer, that particular calculation is no longer valid. The life of a German U-boat man today certainly wouldn't last sixty-two days!

Swiss Radio Beromünster

Friday 11 July 1941

For almost three weeks the Soviet Army has borne the brunt of the war conducted by Germany and her allies for the New Order. . . . Pres. Roosevelt has chosen this moment when the German armies are engaged in Russia to take the first step toward a military intervention in Europe. There is no other description for the occupation of Iceland by an American force. In any event, this despatch of American troops to Iceland, which took place on 7 July, is at the same time a military and political demonstration by the Washington government. Germany's particularly strong reaction to Roosevelt's step is therefore quite understandable. Berlin has judged the step a very significant act of war policy, and the German press has described it as a "warlike provocation." The landing of American troops is therefore important as a military demonstration, because this island – situated between Scotland and Greenland – is in the middle of the German blockade area. In any event, American policy has passed from the stage of developing naval bases for the protection of the western hemisphere to a new stage in which it actually undertakes protection of ocean lines of communication.

Air Attacks against the Scharnhorst and Gneisenau
Friday 25 July 1941, London
The *Exchange* News Agency reported:

British reconnaissance aircraft established on Wednesday that the German battlecruiser *Scharnhorst* has left Brest and has entered the harbor of La Pallice 240 nautical miles south. On Thursday afternoon in broad daylight a further attack, lasting almost an hour, was mounted against the *Scharnhorst* in La Pallice and at the same time against the battlecruiser *Gneisenau* in Brest. . . . During the raid on Brest, Americans used Flying Fortress bombers for the first time.

Italian Assault Boats Off Valetta
Sunday 27 July 1941
The *British Admiralty* issued the following communiqué:

Yesterday at daybreak an attack by S-boats was mounted against the port of Valetta on Malta. The attack was thrown back, causing the enemy heavy losses. Precise details are not yet known, but we do know that approximately one dozen enemy S-boats were sunk by coastal defences and the RAF. Some prisoners were taken and bodies recovered.

Attack on British Convoy

Saturday 2 August 1941, Rome
The Italian *Stefani* News Agency reported:

During the attacks by Italian air and sea forces 23–25 July against a strongly protected British convoy trying to break through from Gibraltar to the eastern Mediterranean area, the enemy suffered the following losses: six steamers totalling between ten thousand and fifteen thousand gross tons, including a tanker. The losses can be determined from communiqués issued by the Admiralty, as well as accurate and irrefutable reports. The destroyer *Fearless* was hit by an aerial torpedo and finally had to be sunk by British units.

Iron Cross for Italian U-Boat Commanders
Monday 2 August 1941, Rome
The German *DNB* News Agency reported:

Lt. Comdr. Mario Pollina, the Italian commander of the submarine *Marconi*, was awarded the Iron Cross by the Führer. Lt. Comdr. Pollina attacked an escorted enemy convoy in the Atlantic and sank thirty thousand tons of armed shipping capacity.

Swiss Radio Beromünster
Friday 15 August 1941

This summer the sea and air war has increased in intensity. . . . News on the Battle of the Atlantic is somewhat sparse from both sides. For some time now the British have not released details on the losses suffered by their merchant fleet and the number of German submarines sunk. According to German information, during July the U-boats sank fewer British and Allied merchant ships than in previous months. According to statements made by the British deputy prime minister, Attlee, German U-boats have come into operation in increasing numbers since early this year, and although British shipping has suffered heavy losses, the British are content with the outcome in the last couple of months.

W. Churchill to the First Sea Lord
Monday 25 August 1941

It should be possible in the near future to place a deterrent squadron in the Indian Ocean. This squadron should consist of the smallest number of the best ships (e.g. *Prince of Wales* and *Repulse*). If we consider the burden placed upon us by the *Tirpitz*—the only large battleship remaining to Germany—despite our fifteen to sixteen battleships and battlecruisers, then we can judge what effect the presence of a small but very battleworthy and fast fleet in Far Eastern waters would have on the Japanese Admiralty.

Anglo-Soviet Intervention in Iran

25 August 1941, London
The *United Press Agency* reported:

Moscow radio has announced that Soviet troops have marched into Iran. We have also just heard that this morning British troops crossed the border into Iran.

Fighting against the Iranian Navy
25 August 1941, General Wavell's Headquarters
The *Exchange* News Agency reported:

Naval units in the Persian Gulf, to whom marine landing troops have been allocated, are under the command of Gen. Wavell whose headquarters reported that after overcoming some opposition and smashing the Iranian coastal batteries, marines have landed near Bondar and Shahpur some seventy miles east of the Iraqi-Iranian border. They will secure the landing of further troops.

The Iranian Army in Action
25 August 1941, Teheran
The *Headquarters of the Iranian Army* issued the following communiqué:

Greenland, US troops landing: US tanker with patrol boats

In Kuzistan British forces have attacked the harbors of Bondar, Shahpur and Khorramshahr and have taken possession of some ships. British aircraft have attacked Ahwaz and motorised columns have pushed forward in the direction of Kermanshah from Khanaqin. The Iranian Army has opposed the British troops pushing forward, and hostilities have broken out. The Iranian government has instituted immediate discussions to ascertain the reason for crossing the border.

Swift British Advance
Wednesday 27 August 1941, General Wavell's Headquarters
The *Exchange* News Agency reported:
Fly   In the Persian Gulf, an Iranian flotilla of gunboats attempted to mount an attack against British naval units. In a short engagement, the enemy units were either sunk or put out of action.

Tenacious Resistance by the Iranian Navy
27 August 1941, Simla
The *Exchange* News Agency reported:
During the naval engagements in the Persian Gulf, the Iranian Rear Adm. Bayendor has been killed. Two Iranian units were sunk. The British naval forces brought in the following units: four gunboats, two tugs, a supply ship and a floating dock (6,000 tons). No British losses were suffered.

Iranian Oil-producing Area in British Hands
Saturday 30 August 1941
General Wavell's Headquarters issued the following communiqué:
The advance of British and Soviet troops in Iran has proceeded swiftly. The entire oilfields are now in British hands. According to the latest reports from Iran, Soviet troops are some forty miles from Teheran. In Teheran itself, a state of siege has been announced and a curfew imposed during the hours of darkness.

U-boat Attacks on US Destroyers
Friday 5 September 1941, Washington
The *US Naval Ministry* reported:
The US destroyer *Greer* has been attacked by a

U-boat off Iceland. The torpedoes, however, missed their target. The *Greer* immediately went on the offensive and dropped depth charges. No positive result was detected. The *Greer* was on its way to Iceland with mail for the troops. The incident took place yesterday morning.

The Battle of the Atlantic

Saturday 6 September 1941, London
The *British Admiralty* issued the following communiqué:

The number of U-boats deployed by the Germans in August was not less but more than in May, as Italian submarines have also been deployed in increasing numbers in the Battle of the Atlantic. Nevertheless, Allied shipping losses have been successfully reduced from almost 600,000 tons in May by about a third to a quarter within the last three months. In contrast, the number of German and Italian submarines sunk has increased considerably. Corvettes and reconnaissance aircraft have been particularly successful in antisubmarine activities.

The Greer *Incident*
Sunday 7 September 1941, Washington
The *Exchange* News Agency reported:

The naval minister, Knox, has stated that the German version of the incident, that the US destroyer *Greer* was the first to attack, is untrue. It must be expressly emphasised that the German U-boat fired off its torpedoes and only then did the *Greer* return the fire.

"Roosevelt is being provocative"
7 September 1941, Berlin
The *DNB* Agency reported:

On 4 September on a position of 62°31″ north and 27°06″ west, a German U-boat was attacked with depth charges at 12:30 P.M. in the German blockade area and then continuously harried. The German U-boat was not in a position to establish the nationality of the destroyer attacking. In justifiable self-defence, the U-boat at 2:39 fired off two torpedoes which missed the target. The destroyer continued to attack with depth charges until midnight, but without success. If an American official source, for instance the Department of the Navy, claims that the attack was committed by a German U-boat, it can only be giving some semblance of legitimacy to an aggressive act perpetrated by an

American destroyer against a U-boat in contravention of American neutrality. The act of aggression itself is proof that Roosevelt, in contrast with his statements, has issued general orders to American destroyers not just to report the position of German ships and U-boats, in complete contravention of American neutrality, but actually to attack these ships. In addition, Roosevelt is attempting with all the means at his disposal to provoke incidents that would drag the American people into a war against Germany.

The secret report of the *SS Security Service* on the internal political situation:
No. 218, 8 September 1941 (Extract)

There is a mixed reaction to the reports relating to the war at sea. The statements made by Lt. Comdr. Kell—"What are our U-boats doing?"— have had a favorable effect as precise information, where these reports have appeared in the press. The fact has been well received that this question, which is of intense interest for the majority of the population, has been publicly taken up. A part of the population continues to believe that the seas have become emptier. The opinion is held that Britain in cooperation with the USA has so secured shipping on the northern route that defence against the U-boats has become particularly effective.

Left: 8/24/1941, the Gulf, British troops under Gen. Wavell land near the Iranian border.

British Action on Spitzbergen

Tuesday 9 September 1941, London
The *Reuters* News Agency reported:

The occupation of Spitzbergen was the first operation undertaken by Canadian troops outside Great Britain for a year. The landing operations took place speedily and unexpectedly at a point 650 nautical miles from the North Pole. The Norwegian troops.

Sinking of a US Steamer
Saturday 13 September 1941, Washington
The *US Foreign Office* issued the following report:

The American merchantman *Montana* has been torpedoed in Icelandic waters. . . . This torpedo attack was observed from an aircraft. The crew of the merchantman were rescued.

Roosevelt's "Order to Shoot"
13 September 1941, Berlin
the *DNB* Agency reported:

In addition to Roosevelt's speech this evening, the press has been occupied above all with the remarks made by American Secretary of State Cordell Hull, according to which Roosevelt's "orders to shoot" are being carried out on all the seven seas. The press regards this as a high-water mark of an openly admitted provocation by the United States.

Right: 8/25/1941, Korramshahr on the Gulf, the flagship of the Iranian fleet, *Babr* (950 tons), a gunboat built in 1932 in Italy, falls victim to the British attack.

Reinforcing the US Atlantic Fleet

Wednesday 17 September 1941, Washington
The *Reuters* News Agency reported:

The US Atlantic Fleet has now undertaken to protect ships that ply the Atlantic between the USA and Iceland. In practical terms, this protection means the introduction of the convoy system. To carry out its task, the Atlantic Fleet has been increased by more than 125 warships.

The Losses of the Italian Navy

Saturday 20 September 1941, Rome
The *Italian High Command* issued the following communiqué:

Two of our motor vessels with troops on board, sailing in convoy, were torpedoed off Tripoli. Nearly all the troops and the ships' crews were saved by the escorting warships and other units.

Monday 22 September 1941
The *German High Command* issued the following communiqué:

Yesterday the Luftwaffe carried out numerous attacks on Soviet shipping with particular success. It sank one cruiser, two destroyers, one antiaircraft ship, as well as nine merchant ships totalling some 25,000 tons in the Black Sea. Two warships more and two large merchantmen were set alight. In the sea area west of Kronstadt, the battleship *October Revolution* and the heavy cruiser *Kirov* were both hit twice by bombs; another heavy cruiser was hit four times; and, in addition, three destroyers, one minesweeper and one gunboat were damaged by hits. As already announced in a special communiqué, U-boats operating in the Atlantic attacked two enemy convoys and a merchantman sailing alone. In tenacious fighting they sank thirteen merchant ships, including four tankers totalling 82,500 tons. Another ship was damaged by torpedoes.

Surprise Attack on Gibraltar by the Italians

Tuesday 23 September 1941
The *British Admiralty* issued the following communiqué:

During an attack by Italian units on the harbor at Gibraltar last Saturday, an old ship's hull was sunk. Any further claims made by the Italians must be regarded as incorrect.

A Symbolic Act

23 September 1941
RAF leaflet "Luftpost" N-19/1941

The night of 16 September, Lt. Comdr. Lyndon Spencer of the American naval cutter *Ingham* received orders from Washington to have the ship painted grey. The *Ingham* was lying in Thao near Lisbon. At that time, it was the only American warship in European coastal waters. Previously, the *Ingham* had been painted yellow and white to distinguish it from ships of the combatant powers. Repainting the ship was commenced the morning of 17 September and was finished around 4:00 P.M. The cutter then put to sea with dimmed lights, ready for action. A symbolic operation. The American fleet is no longer "non-combatant" from this moment on. The fleet has already pursued ships belonging to the Axis powers. In reply to the question whether American ships may give armed escort for vessels carrying freight destined for Great Britain, the American naval minister, Col. Knox, replied, "Since World War I numerous new methods have been added to the convoy system for the protection of merchant shipping. We are using them all!"

Soviet Official Denial

Thursday 25 September 1941, Moscow
The *TASS* News Agency reported:

On 22 September, the German High Command communiqué claimed that the German Luftwaffe had attacked the Red fleet and sunk several ships. In fact, no ships were hit. In contrast, Soviet units recently sank fourteen German transport vessels and a Finnish ship. Two German transporters and several torpedo boats were damaged.

Once Again 24 Ships Sunk

Sunday 28 September 1941, Berlin
The *DNB* Agency reported:

The German Navy has shown in the past week from 20 to 27 September that it is continuing the Battle of the Atlantic with success. During one week the navy attacked three convoys, including one to the west of Africa, sinking twenty-four ships totalling 160,500 tons. The vessels sunk included four tankers.

Battleship Nelson Slightly Damaged

Tuesday 30 September 1941, London
The *Reuters* News Agency reported:

During an attack by Italian aircraft on a large British convoy in the Mediterranean, thirteen Italian aircraft, including ten dive bombers, were shot down. The slightly damaged warship was the battleship *Nelson*, which was hit by a torpedo, reducing her speed. No losses were suffered among the crew. British losses amounted to three naval aircraft.

9/3/1941, Spitsbergen, British engineers blowing up the Barentsberg radio station.

German Official Denial
Wednesday 1 October 1941, Berlin
The *DNB* Agency reported:

The Soviet report, according to which the cruiser *Köln* has been sunk in the Baltic by Soviet naval units and coastal batteries, is, completely fictitious.

Secret report of the *SS Security Service* on the internal political situation:
No. 229, 16 October 1941 (Extract)

The shots of an operational U-boat with Lt. Comdr. Endrass were described as the highlight of the newsreel. They were generally described as the best shots of a U-boat in action that have ever been shown. In watching the sequence, one had the feeling of being there on the spot, experiencing the torpedoing of the steamer amid the convoy, fully involved with the enemy destroyer's attack and breathing with relief when the damage to the U-boat was repaired and the danger had passed.

Friday 17 October 1941
The *German High Command* issued the following communiqué:

In the sea area off Odessa, the German Luftwaffe has attacked with great success enemy transporters fleeing from the city. During bombing attacks the Luftwaffe sank six merchantmen totalling approximately thirty thousand tons. Eight other large ships were badly damaged and a Soviet S-boat destroyed.

Orders to US Ships in East Asia
17 October 1941, Washington
The *Reuters* News Agency reported:

All US merchant ships have been ordered to leave Japanese and Chinese waters because of, as the US Fleet Command has expressed it, "the situation in the Pacific." The captains have been ordered to proceed to the nearest Allied port.

Odessa Evacuated

Saturday 18 October 1941, Moscow
The *Reuters* News Agency reported:

According to the Soviet Army communiqué issued at midnight, the evacuation of Soviet troops from Odessa, planned by the Army High Command during the last eight days, has been carried out according to plan. The troops, who had fulfilled their task in the Odessa area, were transported without loss by the Red fleet to other fronts. The German radio put out reports, without any foundation, stating that Soviet troops were forced to evacuate the city because of German and Rumanian attacks. In fact, the evacuation of Odessa was a result of a directive from the Soviet High Command that was given for strategic reasons without any pressure by the German and Rumanian troops.

W. Churchill to the First Lord of the Admiralty
Wednesday 5 November 1941

I much regret that the number of U-boat prisoners taken by us should have been published. I commented unfavorably upon this publication six months ago. The figure is so small that it advertises to the world the failure of all our efforts against them. There was absolutely no need to make such a disclosure, gratuitously encouraging the enemy and discouraging our friends.

Were you aware beforehand that this was going to be done?

Navy Action in the Mediterranean
Monday 10 November 1941, Rome
The *Italian High Command* issued the following communiqué:

One of our convoys in the mid-Mediterranean was attacked by a British naval formation the night of 9 November. The merchant ships involved were sunk. Some of our destroyers escorting the convoy undertook torpedo attacks, and two were sunk. Another destroyer was hit and returned to port without serious damage.

British Destroyer Cossack *Sunk*
10 November 1941
The *British Admiralty* issued the following communiqué:

The destroyer *Cossack*, which undertook the surprise attack in Norwegian waters on the German steamer *Altmark* releasing a large number of British prisoners of war, has been sunk.

Revision of the US Neutrality Act
Friday 14 November 1941, Washington
The *United Press* Agency reported:

The House of Representatives has approved a revision of the Neutrality Act 212 votes to 194. Therefore, in future US merchantmen can be armed and may enter the war zone. The new act, which had already been approved last Friday by the Senate, has been submitted to Pres. Roosevelt for signing. The act is likely to come into force next Monday. It is anticipated that the US Navy will immediately start to mount guns on US merchantmen.

Ark Royal *Sunk*
14 November 1941, London
The *United Press Agency* reported:

The aircraft carrier *Ark Royal* was attacked late yesterday afternoon by a U-boat in the Mediterranean east of Gibraltar. The carrier suffered heavy damage in the engine room after having been struck by a torpedo. An attempt was made to tow the carrier into Gabraltar but it began to list badly and finally sank early this morning.

W. Churchill to the First Lord of the Admiralty
14 November 1941

I am much disquieted by these facts. We are sinking less than two U-boats a month. They are increasing by nearly twenty. The failure of our methods, about which so much was proclaimed by the Admiralty before the war, is painfully apparent.

Deployment of US Ships in the War Zones
Wednesday 19 November 1941, Washington
The *US Naval Ministry* issued the following communiqué:

The first armed US merchantmen have been deployed for traffic with Great Britain as well as the sea lanes to Murmansk and Archangel.

W. Churchill to the Prime Ministers of Australia, New Zealand and South Africa
Thursday 20 November 1941

In order to warn off Japan, we are sending our latest battleship, the *Prince of Wales*, to support

Left: 12/2/1941, the battleship *Prince of Wales* entering Singapore

Right: 11/14/1941, in the Mediterranean, the aircraft carrier *Ark Royal* goes down within sight of Gibraltar after a torpedo strike by *U 81*.

the *Repulse* in the Indian Ocean. In so doing, we have rejected the protests of the C-in-C Home Fleet who has pointed out the serious risk involved.

W. Churchill to Admiral Cunningham C-in-C Mediterranean
Sunday 23 November 1941

I asked the First Sea Lord to wireless you today about the vital importance of intercepting surface ships bringing reinforcements, supplies and, above all, fuel to Benghazi. Our information here shows a number of vessels now approaching or starting. Request has been made by enemy for air protection, but this cannot be given owing to absorption in battle of his African air force. . . . The stopping of these ships may save thousands of lives, apart from aiding a victory of cardinal importance.

The Prince of Wales *in Singapore*
Tuesday 2 December 1941, Singapore
The *Reuters* News Agency reported:

The new British battleship *Prince of Wales* (35,000 tons) has arrived in Singapore.

Crisis in the Far East

Wednesday 3 December 1941, London
The *United Press Agency* reported:

The course of events in the Far East has been followed with greater calm in Britain after the British Admiralty reported the creation of a completely new Eastern Fleet. . . . Certainly the Admiralty did not unintentionally state that the *Prince of Wales* will belong to this new fleet. It is otherwise unusual for details on the composition of

British fleet formations to be given, certainly not during a war.

Roosevelt's Question in Tokyo
3 December 1941, Washington
The *United Press Agency* reported:

Pres. Roosevelt stated to the press that he had requested Undersecretary of State Sumner Wells to ask via Japanese mediators why Japan has sent far more land, sea and air forces to Indochina than was provided for in the agreement between Japan and Vichy. The president pointed out that his inquiry was made in a very polite form, and he hoped he would receive a prompt reply from the Japanese government.

All Leave Cancelled in Singapore
Saturday 6 December 1941, Singapore
The *Reuters* News Agency reported:

All leave for officers and ratings in the fleet has been cancelled. Shortly afterward, RAF personnel on leave were also recalled to their units.

Crisis in the Pacific
Sunday 7 December 1941, Washington
The *Reuters* News Agency reported:

Two large convoys with strong protective escorts were sighted yesterday morning southwest of Cape Camau, the southernmost tip of Indochina, making toward the Gulf of Siam.

December 1941, Pacific, Japanese aircraft carrier advancing

War in the Pacific

Monday 8 December 1941, Honolulu
The *United Press Agency* reported:

The US fleet put to sea from Pearl Harbor last night. Later, flashes were observed at sea off Oahu; gunfire could be heard clearly on the mainland.

200 Allied Ships Seized
Tuesday 9 December 1941, Tokyo
The *Headquarters of the Imperial Japanese Navy* issued the following communiqué:

Yesterday, two hundred enemy merchantmen totalling 800,000 gross tons were seized, including the steamer *President Harrison* (15,000 gross tons).

Red Fleet in Action
9 December 1941, Moscow
The *TASS* News Agency reported:

Led by the battleship *Parishskaya Kommuna*, the Soviet fleet succeeded in bringing off a particularly audacious undertaking. Accompanied by three cruisers and several destroyers, the battleship steamed through the Kerch Strait and took up position along the coast of the Sea of Azov between Mariupol and Taganrog. Supported by air force units, they bombarded for several hours the German lines of retreat along the coast, and gun emplacements and fortified positions near Mariupol.

The Blocking of New York Harbor
Thursday 11 December 1941, Washington
The *US Navy Department* issued the following communiqué:

The approaches to New York harbor have been blocked by mines. In future all shipping entering the harbor will be escorted by patrol vessels from the entrance to the Ambrose channel.

US Aircraft Carrier Lexington *Sunk*
11 December 1941, Tokyo
The *Headquarters of the Imperial Navy* issued the following communiqué:

The American aircraft carrier sunk by Japanese submarines off Honolulu on the first day of the war was, in fact, the 33,000-ton *Lexington*.

The Two Most Modern Battleships Sunk

11 December 1941, Tokyo
The *Naval Division of the Imperial Headquarters* issued the following communiqué:

The Japanese Navy lost only three aircraft during yesterday's engagement in Malaysian waters when the *Repulse* and *Prince of Wales* were sunk.

11 December 1941, London
A war correspondent of the *Daily Express*, who was on board the *Repulse*, reported:

After the ship was hit and started to list, we had only one thought — to get on deck as quickly as possible. At that moment, the *Repulse* had already listed to such an extent that we were scarcely six feet from the surface of the water. Together with hundreds of officers and crew, I jumped into the lukewarm sea and practically choked in the thick oil slick covering the water. After a short space of time — it seemed like hours to me — I was pulled into a lifeboat.

11 December 1941, Singapore
The *Reuters* News Agency reported:

More than two thousand officers and crew are officially reported to have been rescued from the HMS *Prince of Wales* and HMS *Repulse*. The survivors have been disembarked in Singapore.

Daily Memorandum of the Reich Press Secretary
11 December 1941

The Minister states that a general mood of deep despondency is prevalent in Britain as a result of the heavy shipping losses. The German Propaganda Ministry should not, however, fall into the error of making too much of this despondency. As shown after Dunkirk, an exaggerated presentation could cause the German public to get a totally wrong idea. The ministry should also take into account that British propaganda, in a most ingenious manner, deliberately allows public morale to fall sharply after such setbacks to change the mood back into a well-founded optimism, after a short interval, with the slogan "Now it really isn't as bad as all that."

Swiss Radio Beromünster

Friday 12 December 1941
During a few days, the war has been extended to new countries and continents that give contemporary events a new visage if not a new direction. . . . Europe is only a relatively small area and possibly no longer the most important theater in the further development of the war. But events in Europe will nevertheless exert some influence on developments in America, China, the Pacific, the Orient and in Africa as, by the same token, the fate of Europe will be decided to an unimagined extent by events in America, in the Near and Far East and Africa. In the light of the most recent events, the smallness, poverty and dependence of Europe have for the first time become remarkably clear.

W. Churchill to Foreign Secretary Eden (at sea)
12 December 1941

The loss of the *Prince of Wales* and *Repulse*, together with United States losses at Pearl Harbor, gives Japan full battle-fleet command of the Pacific. They can attack with any force overseas at any point. Happily, the area is so vast that the use of their power can only be partial and limited. . . . On the other hand, accession of United States makes amends for all, and with time and patience will give certain victory.

Only Three Had Experience of Submarines
12 December 1941
RAF leaflet "Luftpost" N-26/1941

U 570 had to surrender to an RAF flying boat. *U 570* was a brand new ship. It had been at sea only four days. On the voyage along the Norwegian coast, it sighted a British flying boat and made an overly hasty move to dive. In so doing, it ran against a reef and its bow as well as its sound detector were damaged. But as there were insufficient skilled workers in Trondheim, only the bow could be repaired, and it had to put to sea with a malfunctioning sound detector. The captain had never before been on an operational patrol, and only three of his crew had submarine service experience. The only real U-boat officer on board was the engineer officer Lt. (Eng) E. Menzel. The engines weren't working properly, and the crew suffered badly from seasickness.

Surprise Attack on the Lofotens
Friday 19 December 1941, London
The *Reuters* News Agency reported:
British troops have landed on the small island of Maalöy and on the southwest tip of the island of Vaagsö. The entire German garrison on Maalöy were killed or taken prisoner and military installations and ammunition dumps blown up. A battery was destroyed. In the south of Vaagsö, the Germans put up an energetic resistance, and we suffered some losses in street fighting before we were able to occupy the city completely.

Sinking of a Soviet Submarine
19 December 1941, Bucharest
The *DNB* Agency reported:
The Rumanian destroyer *King Ferdinand* yesterday sank a Soviet submarine in the Black Sea. The submarine had attempted to attack the destroyer. Two torpedoes were fired, and one hit the submarine, which sank immediately.

Engagement by the Dutch East Indies Fleet
Saturday 20 December 1941, Batavia
The *Dutch Admiralty* issued the following communiqué:
During continued attacks against the Japanese Navy, a third cruiser has been put out of action and a large troopship has been set on fire. The battle is continuing. Another ship, which had float planes on board, exploded and was last seen in flames.

Japanese Submarines Off the US Coast?

Sunday 21 December 1941, Seattle
The *Reuters* News Agency reported:
A large enemy submarine has fired at and torpedoed the US tanker *Emideo* (6,900 gross tons) off the California coast. Five members of the ship's crew are missing.

Hong Kong Completely Cut Off
Monday 22 December 1941, Tokyo
The *Domei* Agency reported:
The entire area surrounding Hong Kong is under the control of the Japanese Navy. British warships anchored off Hong Kong have been completely encircled and are awaiting their destruction.

22 December 1941
The *German High Command* issued the following communiqué:
A U-boat commanded by Lt. Comdr. Bigalk, operating in the Atlantic, has torpedoed and sunk a British aircraft carrier.

Surprise Attack on Saint Pierre and Miquelon
Friday 26 December 1941, London
The *Headquarters of the Free French* issued the following communiqué:
In accordance with the wish of the population, the flag officer commanding the Free French, Adm. Muselier, has occupied the islands of Saint Pierre and Miquelon in the name of the Free French Committee. . . . Saint Pierre and Miquelon are the largest islands of two groups of smaller islands close to the south coast of Newfoundland. There are 4,200 inhabitants. . . . The population sang the Marseillaise and gave Adm. Muselier an ovation when he placed a wreath on the war memorial.

Surprise in Britain
26 December 1941, London
The *Exchange* News Agency reported:
The news that Adm. Muselier has occupied the islands of Saint Pierre and Miquelon came as a complete surprise. As far as is known at this point, Adm. Muselier acted without the knowledge or the agreement of Great Britain and the USA. Muselier's ships should not have put to sea from a British port for Newfoundland. Due note has been taken here of the negative reaction in the USA.

Strategy and Tactics

JULY TO DECEMBER 1941

In summer 1941, the ever-increasing participation of the US Navy in the Battle of the Atlantic brought about a further escalation in the war at sea. Churchill stated that the delivery of fifty destroyers to Great Britain was a positively non-neutral act by the United States. According to all the rules of history, the act would have justified a declaration of war by Germany against the USA.

The delivery of the fifty US destroyers at the express wish of the prime minister also covered another danger, very much hoped for by Churchill, a direct confrontation between the USA and Germany.

The destroyers were, in fact, all of the same type, the USA still possessing eighty more of the same kind that, now that they were gradually being used more and more as convoy escort vessels, were scarcely distinguishable from those sailing under the British flag. This similarity put a lot of pressure on the German U-boat commanders, as they were fully aware of their responsibility — a torpedo sinking the wrong target could very well lead their country into conflict with another powerful adversary.

From Tuesday 1 July 1941, the US Navy deployed its aircraft on patrols against German U-boats for the first time. One patrol, Wing 7, left their base at Argentia (Newfoundland) for a reconnaissance over the Northwest Atlantic. The night of 1/2 July 1941, the RAF again attacked the harbor at Brest. The German cruiser *Prinz Eugen* (Capt. Brinkmann) was hit by a heavy bomb, which crashed through a number of decks to the gunnery control center. Sixty of the crew were killed. The ship was out of action for the next six months.

On Monday 7 July 1941, the 1st Brigade/US Marine Corps (Brig. Gen. Marston) landed in Iceland and relieved the British occupation force. These men were the first American troops on European soil.

On Wednesday 9 July 1941, the French destroyers *Guépard*, *Valmy* and *Vauquelin* put to sea from Banias (Syria) for Salonika. They were to transport the Vichy French units, who had arrived there by rail with the assistance of the Germans, to Syria as reinforcements. Supplies and equipment as well as antiaircraft guns and ammunition were loaded onto two freighters. When the formation was sighted 206 nautical miles off the Syrian coast, it was ordered back to Toulon.

On Monday 14 July 1941, an armistice was signed in Syria. The French submarines *Caiman* and *Morse* succeeded in reaching Bizerta, and the other ships made for neutral ports.

On the same day, Hitler, who considered the Eastern campaign to be as good as settled, transferred the industrial emphasis to U-boat construction and aircraft production, as specified in his Directive No. 32.

On Sunday 20 July 1941, Dönitz transferred the operational area of the U-boats closer to the British Isles. He hoped to be able to attack with greater success, protected by the longer nights and sup-

12/10/1941, 1:30 P.M., off the Malaysian coast, a British escort destroyer picks up crew survivors from the *Prince of Wales*

ported by Luftwaffe air reconnaissance patrols.

On Thursday 24 July 1941, 149 bombers of the RAF attacked the naval base at La Pallice. The battlecruiser *Scharnhorst* was hit several times, suffering severe damage.

On Friday 25 July 1941, during an almost moonless night and in calm seas, the Italian X Flotilla carried out attacks on Malta harbor. The frigate *Diana*, a former yacht, had eight assault boats as well as two fast assault craft, each with a manned-torpedo crew, on board. The formation was detected by a British radar station. The first torpedo crewman, Maj. Tessei, who was also commander of X Flotilla and inventor of the two-man "Maiali" torpedo ("maiali" means "pigs"), forced the protective nets on the first girder of the San Elmo bridge; but the torpedo crewmen lost their lives in so doing. The first assault boat was hit by the British defence and crashed out of control against a bridge pier. The assault boat explosion caused the girder to collapse, blocking the entrance to the harbor for the boats following, which were sunk by the coastal batteries. The next torpedo crewmen, who were to press into the harbor, were driven onto the coast by damaged motors. In addition to the loss of all the assault boats and fast assault craft deployed, fifteen men lost their lives and eighteen were taken prisoner.

On Monday 28 July 1941, Pres. Roosevelt's adviser, Harry Hopkins, flew to Moscow. He offered the Soviet Union a program of immediate assistance as well as support should the war prove to be of a long duration. Stalin's immediate needs were above all tanks, steel, aircraft, heavy machine guns and antiaircraft guns and ammunition.

On Wednesday 30 July 1941, Adm. Nagumo, head of the Japanese Admiralty, informed Emperor Hirohito of his operational plan for the navy.

In July 1941, the C-in-C U-boats again attempted to introduce combined operations between Fw 200s and U-boats on the convoy route between Britain and Gibraltar.

At the end of the month, the Japanese occupied the military bases in South Indochina (Vietnam) after an agreement concluded with the Vichy French government. From this point, the entire Philippines, Singapore and Borneo were within range of their bombers.

In July 1941, German submarines operating in the Atlantic sank seventeen merchant ships totalling 61,471 gross tons, without loss to themselves. Two months previously the figure had been 305,734 gross tons. The cause of this reverse was that the Admiralty was now in a position to decrypt U-boat radio transmissions—thanks to operations connected with Ultra. The convoys

were diverted around the known U-boat positions. German U-boats were now becoming more and more reliant upon accidental sightings of convoys. The C-in-C U-boats was still uncertain as to the reason for the sudden changes in course undertaken by convoys, but he still made intensive endeavors to provide the U-boats with information on convoy movements. One of their methods was for U-boats positioned near the Britain-Gibraltar route to operate on messages received from German agents' observation posts in the city of Algeciras, opposite Gibraltar, which were now equipped with the latest infrared equipment and were tracking the convoys. From July 1941, all convoys leaving Great Britain for North America were escorted for the entire voyage.

During the same month, US shipyards commenced building escort destroyers for the Royal Navy (a monthly figure of ten ships).

At this time, after strong protests were lodged by Great Britain, the Spanish authorities no longer dared to allow German submarines to be provisioned in harbor on the Canary Islands.

On Friday 1 August 1941, the USA banned the export of aviation fuel and oil to countries outside the western hemisphere, as a reply to the Japanese occupation of South Indochina. This ban hit Japan particularly hard and made it impossible for the Japanese to purchase oil in the Dutch East Indies and Malaya in their own name. Pres. Roosevelt also prohibited the loading and unloading of Japanese vessels in American ports. Iron and steel likewise could not be supplied to Japan. In addition, Great Britain and the USA blocked Japanese credit balances held in their countries. Tokyo now had two options: either give way to Roosevelt's demands and evacuate Indochina, which was to have served as a jumping-off point southward, or war with the USA.

On Saturday 2 August 1941, the American aid program (Lend-Lease) commenced supplies to the Soviet Union.

At this time, the Fw 200s adopted new tactics. Instead of attacking convoys themselves, they transmitted location signals to the U-boats. So despite Enigma messages, the Admiralty was no longer in a position to divert convoys on the Britain-Gibraltar route.

As a measure in the war against the Fw 200 long-range reconnaissance aircraft, catapults were mounted, similar to those on the old seaplane carrier *Pegasus* and other such units. These ships were equipped with naval fighters, and they protected convoys from German reconnaissance aircraft. One idea, which is said to have emanated from Churchill, was the installation of catapults on merchants ships as well. These ships, known as CAM-

August 1941, North Atlantic, a Sea Hurricane launched by catapult from a CAM-ship

ships (Catapult Armed Merchantmen), carried a Sea Hurricane fighter, which was catapulted off when an Fw 200 appeared; a few CAMs carried two Sea Hurricanes. The first CAM-ship was the *Michael E.*, which was, however, torpedoed and sunk together with its Hurricane. A total of fifty merchantmen were equipped with catapults.

On Sunday 3 August 1941, Lt. Everett catapulted off the *Maplin* and succeeded in shooting down an Fw 200 belonging to I/KG 40. No matter how the air battle between Sea Hurricane and Kondor was resolved, the fighter pilot was faced with a difficult decision. Should he try to make it to the coast (often a great distance away), or should he ditch close to the convoy (not without its own particular dangers.) As the Hurricane often sank in seconds, pilots generally preferred parachuting out. But landing near the convoy was no guarantee of being picked up. Ships had difficulty sighting the pilot and his raft, and no ship dared stop if U-boats were thought to be in the vicinity.

On Monday 11 August 1941, British Beaufighters attacked the port of Syracuse and torpedoed the Italian hospital ship *California* (13,060 gross tons).

On Tuesday 12 August 1941, on board the US cruiser *Augusta* in the Bay of Argentia Pres. Roosevelt and Prime Minister Churchill proclaimed the Atlantic Charter, the basis of a new world order after the end of the war.

On Saturday 16 August 1941, the German 11th Army (Col. Gen. Ritter von Schobert) occupied Nikolayev, one of the most important Soviet naval bases. In addition, in the Marti shipyards and the naval arsenal the *Sovietskaya Ukraina* (45,000 tons), partially destroyed by its own crew, the heavy cruiser *Ordzhonikidze*, four destroyers, three submarines and two gunboats were captured.

Early 19 August 1941, the Royal Navy carried out the highly secret Operation Cutting off South America. This operation was the cutting and salvaging of parts of the undersea cable between Africa and South America.

On Wednesday 20 August 1941, Col. Farthing, chief of the air force units stationed on Hawaii, submitted a memorandum to the War Department. He wrote that in the event of an attack on Pearl Harbor, the Japanese would probably deploy six aircraft carriers and would attack at dawn from a northerly direction. Col. Farthing then requested a permanent patrol of the air space around Hawaii by means of some 180 long-range reconnaissance aircraft. At that time, there were only twelve such aircraft on Hawaii.

On Thursday 21 August 1941, the first British experimental convoy, Dervish, left Hvalfjord (Iceland) for the Soviet Union. The convoy consisted of seven merchantmen and was escorted by two cruisers and the carrier *Victorious*. One of the ships, the old carrier *Argus*, had aboard twenty-four Hurricane fighters that were to be handed over to the Soviet Union within the terms of the Lend-Lease agreement. Fifteen fighters more were carried in crates on the decks of other ships.

On Saturday 23 August 1941, after 510 days in the Atlantic, Pacific and Indian Oceans, the commerce raider ship no. 36 *Orion* (Capt. Weyher) entered Bordeaux. Its total success achieved was ten merchantmen totalling 62,915 gross tons, and two more freighters totalling 21,125 gross tons, which were sunk in conjunction with ship no. 45 *Komet* (Rear Adm. Eyssen). After that, the *Orion* was used as a repair ship and gunnery ship (*Hektor*) until 4 May 1945 when it was destroyed by a bomb off Swinemünde in the last days of the war.

On Sunday 24 August 1941, the Soviet Baltic Fleet (Vice-Adm. Tribuz), together with units of X Security Corps, was transferred from the naval base at Reval in Estonia to Kronstadt (Leningrad). Some 170 warships and merchantmen tried to break through the German Juminda minefield. By 29 August 1941, one staff ship, five destroyers, three patrol boats, three minesweepers, three submarines, three gunboats, two auxiliary vessels (net-laying duties), one torpedo boat, one U-boat hunter, seven evacuation vessels, thirteen steamers totalling 23,550 gross tons and two ferries were lost. The Battle of the Mines of Reval was the most successful mining operation of the war at sea.

On the same day, under the pretext of preventing "an attempt by the Axis powers to seize control of Iran," British and Soviet troops entered this neutral country from the south and west, in reality for purposes of securing supplies of war material, using this route to the Soviet Union. The mixed formation of British, Australian and Indian warships under the operational control of the East India Station carried out a number of landings with troops of the British Iraq Force (Lt. Gen. Quinan) to occupy the Iranian oil refineries in Abadan and the oilfields in Ahwaz on the Persian Gulf (Operation Countenance). At 9:00 P.M., units of the Indian 18th Infantry Brigade (Brig. Lochner) embarked on motor boats in Basra (Iraq) and made toward the oil refineries at the northern end of the Persian Gulf on the other side of Shatt-al-Arab, fifty miles away. The planned landing at dawn went wrong. Some of the overladen boats ran onto sandbanks, and there were two tankers at the precise point where the troops were to be disembarked. When the alarm sirens were sounded in the refineries, the local defence units opened fire. The British ship *Shoreham* sank an Iranian gunboat. While the Iranian troops went over to a resolute defence, threatening to blow up the refineries at any moment, the installations continued to operate.

On the other side of the river Karun, which separates Abadan from the mainland, British colonial troops attacked the naval base at Khorramshahr. British field artillery opened fire on the fort and the radio station. During the action, the C-in-C of the Iranian Navy, Rear Adm. Bayendor, was killed together with eight officers and over one hundred enlisted. The British now attacked the weak Iranian fleet. The Australian sloop *Yarra* took the gunboats *Chahbaaz* and *Karkass* and sank the gunboat *Babr*. The Australian auxiliary cruiser *Kanimbla* (Capt. Adams), with colonial troops on board, together with two sloops, a gunboat, a corvette and several auxiliary vessels, captured four German merchantmen (27,949 gross tons) and an Italian tanker and three freighters (17,960 gross tons) in the harbor of Bandar–e Shahpur some fifty nautical miles from Khorramshahr. The German merchantmen *Weissenfels* (7,861 gross tons) was set alight by its own crew and destroyed. In the harbor area, British soldiers took prisoner 340 Germans who claimed to be tourists. The strategically important oil refineries of Abadan were not captured until 8:00 P.M.

In the meantime, Soviet troops with vessels from the Red Caspian Flotilla landed at various points along the Iranian coast on the Caspian Sea. They met hardly any resistance. All Iranian vessels, including the luxury yacht belonging to the shah, the patrol boats *Charokh*, *Simorgh* and several smaller steamers were taken over by the Soviets.

Early Monday 25 August 1941, British Force K (Rear Adm. Vian) with the cruisers *Aurora* (Capt. Agnew) and *Nigeria* as well as a troopship, the former luxury liner *Empress of Canada*, appeared off West Spitsbergen (Operation Gauntlet). As no landing boats were available, lifeboats had to be used to land British troops under the command of Brig. Potts. Despite expectations, everything remained quiet on shore, and the soldiers disembarked without a shot being fired. Their task was to destroy the colliery installations. The surprised inhabitants of the island were informed that they were to be evacuated within nine hours, the Russians to Archangel and the Norwegians to Scotland. No German troops were encountered, and so the operation went off according to plan.

The demolition party remained on the island for two days. Although thick black clouds of smoke from the burning oil tanks and coal dumps rose over Spitsbergen, no German aircraft appeared. The radio station was left intact, and the Norwegian radio operators sent off the weather reports to Norway every day. As they reported low cloud over the Spitsbergen area, German reconnaissance aircraft stayed away. Three colliers coming from Norway were taken prize and their German crews made prisoner. After the British formation left the Icefjord, the engineers blew up the power station, the radio station and, most important of all, the meteorological station. Then they embarked on one of the destroyers. Only on Saturday 6 September 1941 did the Germans learn of the landing of British troops on Spitsbergen.

On Wednesday 27 August 1941 at 8:30 A.M., a Hudson aircraft flown by Squadron Leader Thompson of 269 Squadron (Coastal Command) sighted a German U-boat some eighty nautical miles south of Iceland. After the U-boat, *U 570* (Lt. Rahmlow), had been damaged by four depth charges, its commander hoisted the white flag and surrendered to the Hudson circling above.

Thompson radioed for assistance and a Catalina flying boat from 209 Squadron was sent out. That evening, two destroyers and the arm trawler *Northern Chief* appeared. The signal was made, "If you make any attempt to scuttle your U-boat, I shall save nobody and fire on your life rafts." After the crew was taken off, *U 570* was towed to Iceland. Although all the secret documents and the enciphering machine had been thrown overboard, the capture of *U 570* was a grievous blow for the German submarine arm. British U-boat specialists were able to gather important data: gauging handling depth of dive, qualities and the sounds of the individual motors. They established, among other things, that the hull of the submarine had been made from 2.5-cm steel carefully welded and riveted and able to withstand the water pressure at a depth of over 450 feet. Detonators on the depth charges were now changed to be effective to a depth of nearly 600 feet. Three weeks later, on 19 September 1941, *U 570* was commissioned into the Royal Navy as *HMS Graph* (Lt. Colvin).

At the end of August 1941, German U-boats were again withdrawn from the Baltic, as no worthwhile targets were to be found there.

On Thursday 28 August 1941, the British submarine *Unique* (Lt. Comdr. Hezlet) torpedoed the Italian troopship *Esperia* (11,398 gross tons), part of a large convoy bound for Tripoli. It went down only eleven nautical miles from its port of destination; 1,139 of the 1,170 troops on board were saved.

On the same day, the resistance of the Iranian troops was broken, and the shah abdicated in favor of his 22-year-old son Reza Pahlevi. From this moment until the end of the war, five million tons of war material from the USA and Great Britain reached the Soviet Union via Iran.

On Sunday 31 August 1941, the first British experimental convoy, Dervish, arrived in Archangel. The convoy had not encountered the enemy during the voyage from Iceland.

In August 1941, German U-boats in the Atlantic sank twenty-two merchantmen totalling 67,638 gross tons. The German losses amounted to four U-boats.

During the same month, Great Britain was able — for the first time since January 1941 — to import almost one million tons of various goods per week, thereby reaching a minimum existence level.

At this time, attacks by the German S-boats against convoys in the coastal waters south of England continued to present difficulties. The S-boats

At the end of 1941, British and Soviet troops entered Iran. Their objective was to secure the route for supplies to Russia and the oil wells.

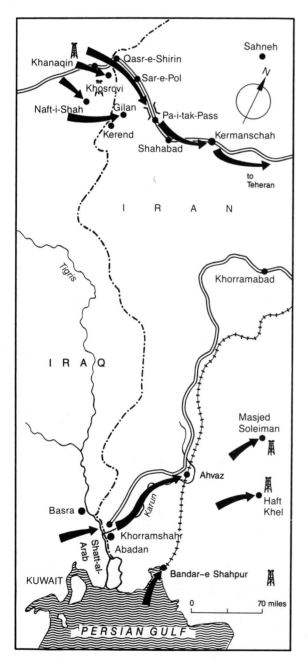

waited at night on the convoy routes and were seldom seen by the escort vessels because of their very low profile. The attacks were usually not noticed until the first torpedoes exploded and the S-boats, making use of the cover of darkness, made off at their top speed (up to forty-two knots).

On Monday 1 September 1941, the US Atlantic Fleet undertook to secure the fast convoys in the North Atlantic, and the Denmark Strait Patrol (Rear Adm. Giffen), with a force amounting to two battleships, two heavy cruisers and thirteen destroyers, patrolled the Denmark Strait. Their base was situated at Hvalfjord (Iceland).

On Tuesday 2 September 1941, the first section of the U-boat pens in Lorient, on the Atlantic coast of Brittany, was put into operation. The building of U-boat bunkers was the responsibility of the head of Naval Building, ministerial director Eckhardt, who built the first harbor in Helgoland. The special commissioner charged with major constructions for the navy on the Atlantic coast was a naval consultant surveyor named Triebel. He formed the planning body Kriegsmarine — Werft Lorient, the naval dockyard in Lorient whose field

of activity covered the area from Brest to Bordeaux. The actual constructions were carried out by the Todt Organisation directed by the government architect Dorsch.

At this time, U-boat bunkers were being built in Brest, Lorient, St. Nazaire, La Pallice and Bordeaux. Approximately fifteen thousand workers participated in the naval construction program. The costs for the U-boat pens in Lorient amounted to some 400 million Reichsmarks. Each bunker had an average of twelve pens and each pen contained three U-boats. A total of 500,000 cubic yards of concrete was required in the building of a U-boat bunker. The reinforced-concrete roof was up to twenty feet thick and was later increased even to thirty feet; an antibomb netting was fitted over the roof. Only once did a Grand Slam bomb (a six-ton bomb) succeed in making a hole in the concrete roof. U-boat bunker construction went on around the clock. The AOC-in-C (Air Officer Commanding in Chief) of Coastal Command requested permission from the Battle of the Atlantic Committee to bomb the building sites for the U-boat bunkers; his request was refused.

On Thursday 4 September 1941, the commander of the US destroyer *Greer*, Lt. Comdr. Frost, was informed by an RAF Hudson from 269 Squadron (Coastal Command) that a German submarine was not far off his position. The American destroyer

8/28/1941, Iceland, *U 570* (Lt. Rahmlow) forced to surrender to an RAF Hudson (Sqn. Ldr. Thompson)

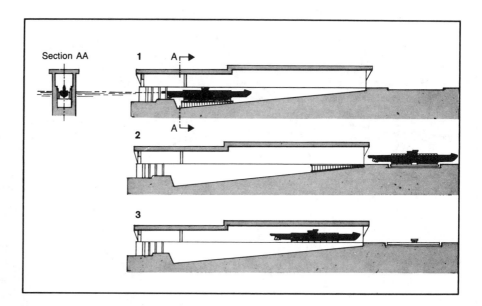

A world first: Lorient, a submarine entering the pen

1. The U-boat is brought in by towing gear and placed on the dock transporter and keyway transporter.

2. The U-boat is towed with the dock transporter with a side-mounted winch. A locomotive moves the boat and dock transporter onto the moving platform.

3. Boat and dock transporter are moved into the pen by means of the loco.

Section AA

also located the submerged U-boat. In the meantime, the Hudson dropped depth charges. The U-boat that was being attacked, *U 652* (Lt. Fraatz), attempted to torpedo the *Greer*, believing it had dropped the depth charges. The *Greer* avoided the torpedoes and then started to drop depth charges on the *U 652*, although unsuccessfully. This event, known as the "*Greer* Incident," was blown up by the US war propaganda service into a serious affair.

On Monday 7 September 1941, the Soviet cruiser *Maxim Gorki*, lying in the Leningrad commercial harbor, and the battleship *Marat*, lying in the Kronstadt shipping canal, opened fire on the vanguard of the German 18th Army (Col. Gen. von Küchler), which at the time was south of Leningrad.

On Thursday 11 September 1941, Pres. Roosevelt — motivated by the "*Greer* Incident" — gave orders to attack all German and Italian shipping in those waters, the protection of which was deemed necessary for American defence. With this "shoot on sight" order, the US Navy took an active part in the Battle of the Atlantic.

Despite the pressure applied by the German Naval High Command, Hitler refused to countermand his orders, according to which German U-boats were not allowed to torpedo American ships. Except for a specified zone in the North Atlantic, they were allowed to attack only warships of a cruiser size and upward, and only then if they were completely satisfied that the vessels were identifiable as enemy units.

On Saturday 13 September 1941 during fighting for Ösel Island, German and Finnish warships were giving artillery support when the Finnish coastal warship *Ilmarinen* (Comdr. Goransson)

struck a floating mine and went down with 271 of the crew, only 132 being rescued.

On Tuesday 16 September 1941, the first group of German U-boats (Goeben Group), comprising six submarines, was transferred to the Mediterranean. The group was now under the operational control of the Naval Group Command South in Sofia. Despite the objections raised by the C-in-C U-boats, Hitler ordered that the group be sent to the Mediterranean to secure lines of communication and supplies to North Africa. In fact, the British were at this time sinking up to seventy percent of all convoys. The U-boats suffered heavy losses and could do nothing to prevent the British advance in North Africa. They certainly achieved great tactical success, but because of their transfer to the Mediterranean, the U-boat war in the Atlantic was brought practically to a standstill. Adm. Dönitz said, "The fact that sinking enemy shipping capacity was the principal objective of German naval strategy, and therefore the principal objective of the U-boats, was not taken into consideration."

The Mediterranean was anything but suitable for the U-boats. Most of the operational areas were within range of land-based aircraft, which, in the fine weather conditions prevalent in these waters, could actually spot the U-boats at a depth of forty-five feet — in contrast to the Atlantic where visibility was restricted to a depth of twenty-seven feet.

From 16 September 1941, German Army coastal batteries fired from positions on the Bay of Kronstadt at warships lying off Leningrad. During these actions, the battleships *Marat*, *Maxim Gorki* and the cruiser *Petropavlovsk* (the former *Lützow*) suffered a number of hits. Midday, the cruiser *Petropavlovsk*, which was still unfinished, was hit fifty-

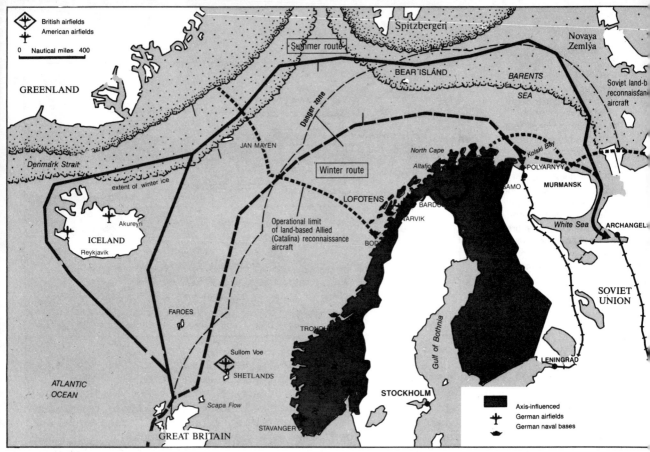

three times by 21-cm and 17-cm caliber shells. After a fire had broken out on deck, the ship turned onto its port side on the harbor bottom and only the quay-wall prevented it from capsizing completely. Ten of the crew were killed and twenty soldiers injured.

The inland waters of the Soviet Union with their many ramifications made it possible at times to deploy whole flotillas in key sectors. And so, for example, in the autumn of 1941, gunboats belonging to the Volga Flotilla lying on the Moskva river participated in the defence of the Soviet capital. In contrast, German operations on inland waters were insignificant, owing to the shortage of suitable vessels. Close to the coast, the Soviet motor torpedo boats proved themselves, once again, to be dangerous opponents.

In September 1941, the first Liberator squadron of Coastal Command became operational. Patrols between Iceland and Great Britain were carried out with this long-range aircraft.

From the middle of September 1941, increased German U-boat production made itself felt. From these new ships a northern group was made up that was to operate between Iceland, Greenland and Newfoundland.

On Wednesday 17 September 1941, US destroyers undertook for the first time the securing of a British convoy in the North Atlantic between Newfoundland and Iceland.

On Thursday 18 September 1941, the British submarine *Upholder* (Lt. Comdr. Wanklyn) destroyed two large troopships, the *Oceania* and the *Neptunia*, both approximately 19,500 gross tons, which were part of an Italian convoy bound for Tripoli. The escort destroyers rescued 6,500 soldiers; 384 perished.

On Saturday 20 September 1941, the German Naval High Command created the Baltic Fleet (Vice-Adm. Ciliax) — comprising the battleship *Tirpitz*, the heavy cruiser *Admiral Scheer*, two light cruisers, three destroyers, a torpedo boat flotilla, minelayers and minesweepers — whose task it was to prevent a possible breakout by the Soviet naval units lying in Kronstadt.

The night of 20/21 September 1941, the Italian submarine *Sciré* (Commander, the Count Borghese) penetrated the Bay of Gibraltar. At 1:00 A.M., the crews of the new, improved two-man torpedoes (type SSB) were set off with their equipment. In the roads and in the naval harbor, they sank the British tanker *Fiona* (2,444 gross tons), as well as the *Denbydale* (8,145 gross tons), and caused considerable damage to the motor ship *Durham* (10,893 gross tons). The three torpedo crews succeeded in reaching Spanish territory.

On Tuesday 23 September 1941, German bomber squadrons of Air Fleet 1 (Col. Gen. Keller) carried out attacks from advance bases in the Minsk area against heavy units of the Soviet fleet

Right: September 1941. This is the only remaining photo of the model on which the Japanese airmen practised the attack on Pearl Harbor. The models represent the battleships *Nevada, Arizona, Tennessee, West Virginia, Maryland* and *Oklahoma.*

Left: The Murmansk convoy routes

lying in Kronstadt harbor and roads. Squadrons 1 and 3 of 2 Dive Bomber Group took off from Tyrkovo at 8:45 A.M. for their objective, the battleships *Marat* and *October Revolution.* The 23,600-ton battleship *Marat,* with its twelve 30.5-cm and sixteen 12-cm guns, had already been badly damaged when, after a direct hit, it broke in two and sank. This was the first time a battleship was sunk by a dive bomber.

In the middle of September 1941, Japan opened negotiations with the USA with a view to mitigating the trade blockade. After tough talks, it was agreed that Japan could send two passenger liners, but without commercial goods, to the USA and Hawaii. These passenger liners, *Tatuta Maru* and *Taijo Maru,* were Japan's chance of completing the final preparations for a surprise attack on Pearl Harbor.

On Monday 29 September 1941—after the German Naval High Command realised that the Soviet warships did not intend any breakout into the Baltic, and the attempted occupation of Leningrad had failed—the Baltic Fleet, created on 20 September 1941, was dissolved.

In the meantime, the first convoy, PQ-1, made its way from Reykjavik (Iceland) to Archangel. The convoy, which consisted of ten merchantmen with armaments escorted by a cruiser and two destroyers, reached its Soviet port of destination without loss. The shortest route, even if the most

dangerous, led from the North Cape close to the limit of the ice. This route was within range of German Luftwaffe aircraft stationed in Norwegian bases. Astonishingly, the convoys were not attacked by the Germans during the early months. The British Admiralty entrusted the organisation of this convoy to Com. P. Q. Roberts, whose initials identified the convoy returning from the USSR—QP.

On the same day in Moscow, Stalin agreed with Great Britain's representative, Lord Beaverbrook, and the representative of the USA, Harry Hopkins, the full extent of the Lend-Lease agreement. Stalin answered the reading out of the long list of supplies with the words, "I am enthusiastic!" His interpreter jumped up and cried, "Now we shall win the war."

At the end of September 1941, Fleet 1 commenced training for the attack on Pearl Harbor under Comdr. Genda. Several hundred airplanes took part in the exercise. Bombers, dive bombers, torpedo bombers and fighters made up one task force whose leader, Comdr. Fuchida, was a former acquaintance of Genda at the Naval Academy. The Bay of Kagoshima on the Japanese island of Kyushu was chosen as the training area for the torpedo attacks because of its similarity with the bay of Pearl Harbor. The tactics of torpedo attacks in shallow waters were tried out. Peasants in the neighborhood protested because the constant noise of engines put their hens off laying.

In the meantime, a torpedo with fins and a stabilising system for use in shallow waters was being further developed in the Imperial Navy's research institute. It resembled the torpedo used by the British in their attack on Taranto (11 November 1940).

During the second half of September 1941, aircraft from the escort carrier *Audacity* (Comdr. Mackendrick) were used for the first time to protect a convoy against Fw 200s and German U-boats. The small auxiliary carrier *Audacity* was the former freighter *Hannover*, captured in February 1940 off Santo Domingo. The superstructure had been removed and American aircraft — Grumman Wildcat fighters, known in the Royal Navy as Martlets — were stored on the wooden deck. In the absence of a proper hangar, all maintenance had to be carried out in the open.

In August 1941, war material and strategically important provisions destined for Great Britain were for the main part carried in American ships with American escorts.

In September 1941 German U-boats operating in the Atlantic sank fifty-four merchant vessels totalling 208,822 gross tons. German losses amounted to two U-boats.

On Wednesday 1 October 1941, the map maneuvers of the Japanese General Staff took place in the military academy in Tokyo when the operational problems of a southern operation were examined. The Japanese air and naval forces were completely superior to their opponents in the Pacific and Southeast Asia. At that point, the Imperial Navy comprised 10 battleships, 6 aircraft carriers, 5 aircraft tenders, 6 auxiliary aircraft carriers, 12 heavy cruisers, 5 coastal warships, 28 light cruisers, 2 cruisers for mine operations, 127 destroyers and 69 submarines.

By 6 October 1941, the Soviet 175 Rifle Division had been successfully evacuated from Odessa to Sevastopol by sea.

On Thursday 16 October 1941, Stalin ordered the final evacuation of Odessa, and at 3:00 A.M. the last units of the Black Sea Fleet left this port. A total of five divisions comprising eighty thousand soldiers and fifteen thousand party members, specialist workers and civilians were brought to Sevastopol on fifteen warships including two cruisers and four destroyers, twenty-one transporters and a number of smaller vessels. The evacuation was not troubled by the Germans until the afternoon when aircraft attacked the transports.

On Friday 17 October 1941, 350 nautical miles southwest of Iceland, *U 568* (Lt. Comdr. Preuss) sighted the US destroyer *Kearny* (Lt. Comdr. Davis). Preuss believed the *Kearny* to be a British destroyer and attacked with torpedoes. One of them struck the destroyer on the starboard side and exploded in the forward boiler room. Eleven men were killed and nineteen wounded. The *Kearny* reached the Hvalfjord with the assistance of the American destroyers *Greer* and *Monssen*.

On Monday 20 October 1941, the Imperial Navy made its last preparations for a surprise attack on Pearl Harbor in the event negotiations with the USA broke down. The carrier-borne dive bombers and torpedo bombers, to be used to cripple the American Navy, carried out their last practice runs using live ammunition. They were able to look back over a long tradition — a Japanese airman, as early as 26 September 1914, sank a ship for the first time in the history of air warfare. The ship was, incidentally, a German minelayer. This success was achieved by the pilot of a Farman seaplane dropping artillery shells by hand in the Bay of Kiaochow in the German-leased territory of Tsingtao in China.

On Wednesday 22 October 1941, one of the two Japanese passenger liners that the US government had allowed to visit Hawaii or San Francisco set sail from Yokohama. The *Taijo Maru* took the northern route, scheduled for the planned attack by the Japanese fleet on Pearl Harbor.

The Japanese liner had two special envoys on board, Comdr. Suzuki, a specialist on the American air forces in the Pacific, and Comdr. Maichima, a specialist on the American submarine arm.

During the entire voyage of some two thousand nautical miles, the two officers searched the sea day and night. The results of their investigation exceeded all expectations. The *Taijo Maru* did not encounter a single ship until Hawaii.

On Thursday 23 October 1941, the first of the two Japanese ships, *Tatuta Maru*, reached Honolulu. When the Japanese consul general, Kita, came aboard the ship, the captain handed him a sealed envelope from the General Staff containing a request that he immediately draw up a detailed map showing all military installations on Pearl Harbor.

The night of 24 October 1941, *U 563* (Lt. Bargsten) torpedoed the destroyer *Cossack* (Capt. Berthen) in the North Atlantic. The destroyer went down on 26 October 1941. The cat, Oscar, who after the sinking of the battleship *Bismarck* had been rescued by the *Cossack*, was once again one of those to be saved. One of the British destroyers took Oscar to Gibraltar where he was taken over by the crew of the *Ark Royal*.

In October 1941, German S-boats and minesweepers were to be transferred from the North Sea to the Mediterranean. The German Naval Command charged Capt. von Conradi with transfer-

10/19/1941, Hvalfjord, Iceland, the destroyer *Kearny*, the first US warship to be torpedoed by a U-boat

ring these units via inland waterways across Europe. The ships were to go via the Rhine, and the Rhône through unoccupied France. The Vichy government requested that the transfer be given as little publicity as possible and placed a French escort officer at the Germans' disposal. In Rotterdam the craft were disguised with false smokestacks as ordinary river tugs. Their crews were dressed in civilian clothes, and all visible weapons were removed from the deck. And so, in a few weeks, the vessels traveled from Rotterdam to Chalon-sur-Saône. There they had to wait until the level of the river Rhône was sufficiently high. Supported by the French authorities and unnoticed by the British Intelligence Service, the ships were able to reach at speed the mouth of the Rhône. There was then a stretch of open water as far as La Spezia, the Italian naval base, where the craft were once again armed. The S-boats were deployed off Malta, the minesweepers off the African coast and Tobruk.

In Great Britain in the autumn of 1941, plans were drawn up untiringly for an invasion of the Continent. The officer who had built up the Commandos, Admiral of the Fleet Sir Roger Keyes, had now reached the age of seventy. Through his in-

dustry in pressing forward the design and construction of landing craft, the admiral had performed an invaluable service – nevertheless Churchill replaced him with a younger man to head the amphibian operations. The choice fell on the energetic 41-year-old Capt. Lord Louis Mountbatten, a cousin of King George VI.

On Monday 27 October 1941, the appointment of Lord Mountbatten as head of the Directorate of Combined Operations brought a change in policy with it. In contrast with Adm. Keyes – who planned large-scale operations for up to ten thousand Commandos that Great Britain was not in a position to implement – Lord Mountbatten preferred to implement a number of smaller but more frequent raids, and he sold this idea to Churchill. The staff, which had been renamed the Combined Operations Headquarters (COHQ), now used the experience gained in commando operations in the preparation of large-scale landings.

In the early hours of 31 October 1941, *U 552* (Lt. Comdr. Topp) sighted Convoy HX-156, accompanied by five destroyers of an American escort group (Comdr. Webb), proceeding from Halifax to Great Britain. The U-boat torpedoed the US destroyer *Reuben James* – which went down with 115 men, 46 being saved—the first US warship to be sunk by a German U-boat.

In October 1941, German U-boats operating in the Atlantic sank thirty-two merchant vessels totalling 156,500 gross tons. Of the eighty operational German U-boats, two were lost.

At 8:30 A.M. on Saturday 1 November 1941, the second Japanese liner, *Taijo Maru*, arrived at Honolulu. The actual time was no coincidence, as the attack on Pearl Harbor was planned for a weekend and at the same time. The US Navy was known to put in on a Friday to Pearl Harbor, where it remained at precisely delineated points at anchor over Sunday while a part of the crews went on shore leave in Honlulu. Both Japanese specialists on board the *Taijo Maru* were there to gain an impression of the life and activity that took place on a weekend in the naval base at Pearl Harbor. The Japanese master spy in Honolulu, Yoshikawa (Morimura), succeeded—despite American checkpoints—in smuggling a whole file of various reports aboard the *Taijo Maru*.

On Sunday 2 November 1941, four British cruisers off Cape Town captured a French convoy, consisting of five freighters and a number of liners totalling almost forty thousand tons, sailing from Madagascar to France. The French Vichy naval authorities immediately ordered the submarines *Le Glorieux* and *Le Héros* to attack the British ships.

On Wednesday 5 November 1941, four more German U-boats were transferred to the Mediterranean, where they were to form the Arnauld Group.

On Thursday 6 November 1941, there was a further escalation of incidents between Germany and the USA. The US cruiser *Omaha* (Capt. Chandler) took prize the German blockade-runner *Odenwald* (5,095 gross tons) off the Brazilian coast.

On the same day, six Japanese aircraft carriers, whose aircraft were to attack Pearl Harbor, carried out practice maneuvers corresponding to the planned operation. Over 350 aircraft attacked target vessels some two hundred nautical miles away, the same distance as between the subsequent taking-off point and Pearl Harbor.

The night of 8/9 November 1941, two British cruisers and two destroyers of Force K (Rear Adm. Vian) attacked an Italian convoy that had been sighted the previous day by an RAF reconnaissance aircraft. The entire convoy, consisting of seven transports (39,055 gross tons) carrying valuable supplies for North Africa, was sunk together with two escort destroyers. Two more vessels were heavily damaged.

As the Italian escort vessels were not equipped with radar, they had been totally helpless in the face of the weaker British formation. Conse-

quently, the stronger Italian escort units, comprising two heavy cruisers and ten destroyers, had been unable to prevent the sinking of their freighters and tankers. Only 704 survivors were picked up.

On Monday 10 November 1941, the ships scheduled to take part in the attack on Pearl Harbor put to sea from Tokyo individually with orders to maintain complete radio silence. Vice-Adm. Nagumo, C-in-C of 1 Naval Air Fleet, led the attack squadron. The aircraft carriers *Akagi*, *Hiryu*, *Shokaku*, *Soryu*, *Zuikaku* with a total of 423 aircraft—the largest air force that had ever put to sea—were placed under his command. In addition, the supporting formation (Vice-Adm. Mikawa) comprising two battleships and two heavy cruisers were subordinate to Nagumo. Three submarines as well as eight supply ships and tankers were also attached to the formation.

The assembly point selected for the ships was the remote Hittokappu Bay off of the Kurile Islands of Japan. Nearly one thousand nautical miles north of Tokyo, this remote bay is notorious for waters barely navigable because of the continual fog banks. Crews and pilots from the carriers were issued with tropical kit in addition to winter kit to disguise the northerly course.

Telegraphists from the carriers remained ashore and continued their duties to give the impression that their units would remain around the Japanese mainland. Soldiers from the Imperial Army were dressed in naval uniform and allowed to walk around Tokyo, a measure designed to cover the absence of the greater part of the Japanese fleet. Crews belonging to Japanese warships still in port were given shore leave to keep up the customary sight of sailors ashore. To conceal the absence of so many carrier-borne aircraft, other air units were posted into the Tokyo area.

Also on 10 November 1941, a 59-man Commando troop (Col. Laycock) embarked on the submarines *Talisman* and *Torbay* with orders to attack Gen. Rommel's headquarters.

Plans had been drawn up to eliminate the command of the German Afrika Korps the same night the British counteroffensive in North Africa (Operation Crusader) was to begin.

On Thursday 13 November 1941, the largest British aircraft carrier in the Mediterranean, *Ark Royal* (Capt. Maund), was torpedoed by the *U 81* (Lt. Comdr. Guggenberger) east of Gibraltar. The escort vessels undertook immediate rescue operations and tried to tow the carrier, which was listing badly, back to Gibraltar.

The next morning, 14 November 1941, the *Ark Royal* sank within sight of harbor. A report issued by an investigating committee showed that the *Ark Royal* had been lost because of insufficient internal protection against leaking and an overhasty abandoning of the ship.

Only one sailor lost his life. The crew of the carrier (including Oscar of the *Bismarck*, who was taken over by the *Ark Royal* when his previous ship, the *Cossack*, was sunk) remained for some time in Gibraltar. Oscar was said to bring bad luck; in the space of only five months, the battleship *Bismarck*, the destroyer *Cossack* and the aircraft carrier *Ark Royal* — and he was on all of these ships — went down. Oscar now remained in the office of the harbor master in Gibraltar. The entry in the archives of the Royal Navy states, "Oscar, the *Bismarck*'s cat, finished his days at the Home for Sailors in Belfast," around 1955.

The night of 17/18 November 1941, the Commando formation (Lt. Col. Keyes) that had landed from the two submarines attacked the prefect's building in Beda Littoria to liquidate Rommel and his staff. According to information received from the British Intelligence Service, this building housed the headquarters of the German Afrika Korps. In pouring rain, at half-past midnight, some thirty men of the Commando forced their

way into the building. After a short but heavy exchange of fire, the Commando had to withdraw. The storm, however, prevented the submarines waiting offshore from taking the men aboard again. At daybreak, the Commandos were surrounded by Germans, and the survivors were taken prisoner. Only two of the Commando force escaped. After weeks of marching through the desert, they succeeded in reaching the British lines.

By means of this Commando raid Rommel — who was held in high esteem by the British troops — was to have been eliminated, thereby improving British morale. However, the headquarters of Rommel were never situated in the building attacked and, in any event, Rommel was in Rome the day of the attack. When Rommel heard about the attack, he gave orders that the Commandos were to be treated as ordinary prisoners of war, although they wore no uniforms, merely overalls, and their status as combatant troops was in some doubt.

Because of the destruction of the supply convoys to the Afrika Korps, a shortage of fuel and ammunition existed. Consequently, cruisers, destroyers and U-boats now had to be used as freighters for the supply of fuel and ammunition. Warships, which were not provided with the necessary stowage space, carried barrels and crates stacked in the gangways and on deck, introducing enormous risks in the event of enemy action. In addition, the amount of fuel that could be transported by a light cruiser (approximately two hundred cubic yards) was not enough even for one day's fighting.

On Tuesday 18 November 1941 in pouring rain, the British 8th Army under Gen. Cunningham began its offensive in North Africa in an attempt to relieve Tobruk. The Afrika Korps supply crisis again reached a high point — no convoy had gotten through for five weeks.

The night of 18/19 November 1941, the midget-submarine transporters *J-16*, *J-18*, *J-22* and *J-24* put to sea from a Japanese naval base, carrying five type A midget submarines on board, destination Pearl Harbor, some 3,800 nautical miles away. The midget submarines were made fast to the afterdecks of these transporters, which were submarine-cruisers. These midget submarines, whose crew consisted of the commander and an electro-engineer, each carried two torpedoes that were fired from tubes, one superimposed above the other and situated in the bow. The two-man crew was carried aboard the submarine until the operational target area was reached.

On Wednesday 19 November 1941 in the Indian Ocean some 170 nautical miles off the west Australian coast, an event unique in the history of sea

Below: "Oscar, the Bismarck's Cat," a pastel portrait by Mrs. Georgina Shaw-Baker, National Maritime Museum, Greenwich, 1980

warfare occurred. An armed merchant ship sank a modern cruiser — and in daylight, too.

The German commerce raider ship no. 41 *Kormoran* (Capt. Detmers) was sighted by the Australian light cruiser *Sydney* (Capt. Burnett). While exchanging signals, the *Sydney* approached to within half a nautical mile of the *Kormoran*, when suddenly the commerce raider dropped its disguise and opened fire. Capt. Detmers said, "At such short range, all our shells found their target. Our antiaircraft pom-poms opened fire on the enemy torpedo-tube installations and the entire upper deck. The army 3.7-cm Pak held the enemy's bridge in check. We fired off two torpedoes." The *Sydney* was hit in the fo'c'sle, and both forward turrets were put out of action. Nevertheless, shells from the third turret hit the *Kormoran* in the engine room a number of times. The *Sydney*, on fire, disappeared and was never seen again. Burning oil on board the *Kormoran* could not be extinguished, and the ship had to be abandoned. The greater part of the çrew reached the coast of Australia in lifeboats. The successes achieved by the *Kormoran* amounted to eleven merchant ships, totalling 68,274 gross tons, taken prize or sunk, in addition to the light cruiser *Sydney*.

On Saturday 22 November 1941 the German commerce raider ship no. 16 *Atlantis* met the *U 126* (Lt. Comdr. Bauer) in the South Atlantic to refuel it. Thanks to Enigma, the British Admiralty had decrypted the instructions transmitted by the C-in-C U-boats to *U 126* and ordered the heavy cruiser *Devonshire* (Capt. Oliver) into the relevant sea area south of the equator. The German commerce raider, hunted down, had to scuttle itself, which put an end to the longest voyage made by a commerce raider: The *Atlantis* had covered 102,000 nautical miles in 622 days and had sunk twenty-two merchant vessels totalling 145,697 gross tons.

After the *Devonshire* had made off, the *U 126* surfaced and took in tow the six lifeboats from the *Atlantis* with their 350 survivors. Twice a day, a dinghy from the *U 126* took a hot meal to the rescued sailors. After two days, on 24 November 1941, the *U 126* met the supply ship *Python* (Comdr. Lueders), directed to the spot to take the crew of the *Atlantis* on board.

On Monday 24 November 1941, some one hundred nautical miles west of Crete, Force K (Rear Adm. Vian) attacked a German convoy carrying supplies for the Afrika Korps and sank the transporters *Procida* (1,842 gross tons) and *Maritza* (2,910 gross tons). The battleships *Queen Elizabeth*, *Valiant* and *Barham* put to sea in support of Force K, their task being to block Italian supply routes.

On the afternoon of 25 November 1941, a massive explosion north of Bardia shook the British battleship formation. *U 331* (Lt. the Freiherr von Tiesenhausen) had broken through the British escort vessels. Three torpedoes, one after the other, hit the *Barham* (Capt. Cooke), and the heavily damaged battleship immediately took a list to port. A massive cloud of smoke rose, and the battleship went down with 861 men. The *Barham* was the sole Allied battleship to be sunk by a U-boat on the high seas. The British now had only two battleships in the entire Mediterranean to counter five Italian heavy units, some of which were the most modern battleships available.

On the same day, Pres. Roosevelt held discussions with Secretary of State Hull, Secretary of War Stimson, Secretary of the Navy Knox, Gen. Marshall and Adm. Stark. The president had decided to break off negotiations with Japan and wished to discuss how to counter a Japanese attack that, according to secret information, was liable to take place at any moment. Stimson said, "It is debatable how one can make Japan fire the first shot." Pres. Roosevelt knew that he could only avoid war in the Pacific if he gave way to Japanese demands. Thanks to having cracked the secret code of the Japanese in summer 1940, American counterespionage was able to decrypt the entire exchange of telegrams between Tokyo and the Japanese embassy in Washington. Through fear that the Japanese might realise their code had been broken, the decisive news was withheld from precisely those points that most needed it. Adm. Kimmel, who was responsible for the defence of Hawaii and was also the C-in-C of the Pacific Fleet, asserted at a later date that none of this information was known to him.

The Japanese Intelligence Service in Hawaii had, in the meantime, provided an entire series of intelligence reports covering the anchorage of each individual warship or details of air patrols. The former naval lieutenant, Yoshikawa, who at that time was in the office of the Japanese Consulate in Honolulu under the assumed name Morimura, was the best of the Japanese intelligence agents. He understood so well how to disguise his espionage activities that he was the only member of the consulate who was not on the "black list" of the American counterespionage service.

On 25 November 1941, the US Navy introduced compulsory convoys for merchantmen in the Pacific.

On Wednesday 26 November 1941 at 6:00 A.M., the Japanese task force under the command of Adm. Yamamoto put to sea from Hittokappu on an easterly course. This course was to be held until 4 December and was to allay suspicions about the

Above: The Australian light cruiser *Sydney* (Capt. Burns), sunk by the German commerce raider ship no. 41 *Kormoran*

Below: 11/22/1941, South Atlantic, the crew of the German commerce raider ship no. 16 *Atlantis* in lifeboats. The *Atlantis*, in flames, can be seen on the horizon.

real target. Under complete radio silence, speed was set at twelve to thirteen knots to suit the slower tankers.

On Sunday 30 November 1941, the commerce raider ship no. 45 *Komet* (Rear. Adm. Eyssen) put into Hamburg. In the 516 days of its operation, it had sailed over the northern Siberian sea routes to Asia, operated in East Asian and Australian waters and covered 87,000 nautical miles. In so doing it had sunk six ships totalling 31,005 gross tons, as well as destroyed phosphate works on Nauro (western Pacific) by gunfire. It had destroyed two other ships (21,125 gross tons) in conjunction with the German commerce raider *Orion*. This was the end of the operations of the first wave of German commerce raiders, the *Thor*, *Atlantis*, *Widder*, *Pinguin*, *Orion* and *Komet*. On the same day in the Bay of Biscay, a Whitley bomber of RAF 502 Squadron located *U 206* (Lt. Comdr. Opitz) on the surface from a distance of five nautical miles by ASV radar. The bomber attacked *U 206* and sank it, the only U-boat to be sunk in 1941 by air patrols over the Biscay area by RAF Coastal Command.

In November 1941, U-boats operating in the Atlantic and Mediterranean sank only nineteen merchant vessels totalling 91,628 gross tons. German losses amounted to five U-boats.

On Monday 1 December 1941, the German supply ship *Python* met the *U 68* (Comdr. Merten) and *U A* (Comdr. Eckermann) in mid–South Atlantic waters. Here, too, the Admiralty knew about the secret meeting, and the heavy cruiser *Dorsetshire* (Capt. Agar) was to intercept the German units. After the *Dorsetshire* sighted the supply vessel and immediately fired off a warning salvo, the *Python* crew, together with the survivors from the *Atlantis*, a total of 415 men, took to the lifeboats and scuttled their ship. When the cruiser was out of sight, *U 68* and *U A* took the lifeboats in tow and started their 2,500 nautical mile voyage home.

On Tuesday 2 December 1941, a coded radio message was received by the commander of the Japanese task force, stating that the date of the attack was to be 7 December 1941. The formation met such appalling storms and fog that several ships lost men overboard. But at least the bad weather prevented the Japanese ships from being discovered. Further reports — disguised as advertising slogans from a radio station — from the Japanese Intelligence Service in Hong Kong advised that the torpedo nets and barrage balloons had arrived but had not yet been put into position.

On Wednesday 3 December 1941, *U 129* (Lt. Comdr. Clausen) took the entire crew of the commerce raider *Python* on board. Between 5 and 18 December 1941, another German and four Italian submarines took the rescued seamen on board. They were all disembarked in St. Nazaire by 29 December 1941.

On Thursday 4 December 1941, the Japanese task force changed course toward the southeast and made for the Hawaiian islands. The ships were fuelled to the limit of their capacity. Only during early afternoon was the Emperor's declaration of war read out to the crews.

That evening, the Japanese midget submarines reached their operational positions ten nautical miles south of Pearl Harbor. At midnight the midget submarines commenced their operation. Their orders were to penetrate into the harbor channel and destroy any torpedo nets they found, as well as to prevent the US fleet putting to sea. The midge submarines were unable to fulfill their mission and also failed to return.

On Friday 5 December 1941, Hitler ordered Air Fleet 2 (Field Marshal Kesselring) from the Eastern

Right: Meeting in mid-Atlantic, a German U-boat takes on fuel from a supply ship.

Far right: 12/7/1941, the Japanese attack on Pearl Harbor

Front to Libya and Sicily, as the catastrophic losses suffered by the Italo-German supply convoys to North Africa were continuing.

On Saturday 6 December 1941, the first German blockade-runner, *Rio Grande* (6,062 gross tons), commanded by Capt. von Allwörden, reached the port of Kobe.

On the same say, the Soviet Western Front (Gen. Zhukov) went on the offensive. For the first time, German troops on the approaches to Moscow were thrown back from their advance positions by the Soviet divisions.

Right: Sunday, 12/7/1941, inferno of Pearl Harbor, ". . . despite this, still intact as a naval base."

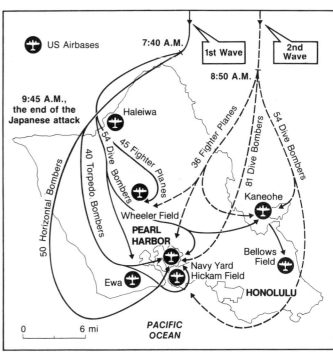

On Sunday 7 December 1941 at around 5:30 A.M. long-range reconnaissance aircraft were catapulted from the *Chikuma* and *Tone*. Their mission was to carry out the final reconnaissance of the US naval base at Pearl Harbor. At the same time, the carriers turned full east into the wind and increased their speed up to twenty-four knots. At 7:30, the carriers reached that position from which the aircraft were to start, some seventy nautical miles north of Oahu Island. Twenty minutes later 353 aircraft, the strongest formation that had ever left a carrier squadron, was underway to Pearl Harbor.

The attack was such a complete surprise that practically no antiaircraft action occurred. The light Flak on board warships was certainly manned, but the ammunition was locked in the ammunition chambers. Nearly all the aircraft on the US airfields on Hawaii were put out of action by the attack. Gen. Marshall stated, "Pearl Harbor was the only reasonably equipped US base with sufficient means to resist a Japanese attack. There were 1,017 antiaircraft guns on land and aboard the ships, and 222 aircraft, of which 152 were fighters."

The Japanese airmen sank the battleships *Arizona*, *California*, *Nevada*, *Oklahoma*, *West Virginia*, the minelayer *Oglada* and the target ship *Utah*; severely damaged in part the battleships *Maryland*, *Pennsylvania*, *Tennessee* (sixty percent of the US Navy's total stock of battleships were sunk or damaged), the light cruisers *Helena*, *Honolulu* and *Raleigh*, three destroyers, one aircraft tender and one repair ship. The Americans suffered 2,403 fatalities and 1,178 wounded; in addition, 188 aircraft were destroyed. The Japanese losses amounted to five torpedo bombers, fifteen dive bombers and nine fighters with a total of fifty-five men, as well as five midget submarines and their crews. The torpedoes and bombs dropped weighed 138.5 tons overall. The torpedo was the same type used by the British during their attack on the naval base at Taranto (11/12 November 1940); its success was the result of its wooden side fins, which could be regulated and which made it possible to predetermine the draught.

The purpose of this operation (securing the sea flank of the Japanese advance into the regions of

South Asia that produced raw materials) was certainly achieved by eliminating the US fleet. But as the attack concentrated on the battleships and airfields, the efficient dockyards and the gigantic oil storage tanks with approximately 120 million gallons of fuel remained undamaged — and Pearl Harbor survived intact as a naval base. In addition, only the obsolete American battleships were hit. The most important targets, the four aircraft carriers, had been ordered to proceed to Pearl Harbor but had been held up by a storm. These carriers were of prime importance for the further conduct of the war by the American staff. At the beginning, Adm. Yamamoto was in a distinct minority when he voiced his view, "This war will cause us a lot of problems in the future. The fact that we achieved a minor success at Pearl Harbor means nothing."

The attack wasn't only a surprise for the Americans; Grand Adm. Raeder stated, "The news of the attack by the Japanese on 7 December 1941 came as a complete surprise for us."

"We are all in the same boat now," said Roosevelt to Churchill when he telephoned him.

On the same day, Japanese troops landed in Siam and Malaya. The base at Luzon in the Philippines was destroyed, and Midway was bombarded by the destroyers *Akebon* and *Ushio*, Hong Kong was bombarded, Waku and Mindanao were attacked.

Immediately after the attack on Pearl Harbor, the captains of American submarines were ordered to conduct unlimited warfare against Japan. Neither the name of the commander nor the details of ships sunk were released, as the Japanese might then have treated any American submarine crews taken prisoner as war criminals. Although the Germans' success in conducting surface attacks at night was known, the American submarines attacked almost exclusively during daylight from the submerged position. In contrast to the Japanese submarine arm, which was never deployed for a planned economic war, the Americans sank considerable numbers of ships during their operations against Japanese shipping.

At the beginning of the war, there were fifty American submarines in the Pacific.

The afternoon of 8 December 1941, the British battleships *Prince of Wales* (Capt. Leach) and *Repulse* (Capt. Tennant) left Singapore with four escort destroyers to cut supplies and reinforcements from the Japanese troops who had landed on the Malaysian coast. As this operation was to be a surprise attack, a protective air cover was refused because the squadron might have been sighted by Japanese reconnaissance aircraft or submarines. Antiaircraft guns on the *Prince of Wales* were so strong that the battleship was considered invincible. It was the first British battleship equipped with the new antiaircraft pom-pom guns popularly known as "Chicago Pianos." Four batteries, each containing twenty-five barrels, could fire sixty-thousand rounds per minute. The *Repulse*, likewise, possessed antiaircraft defensive fire that was among the most powerful in the Royal Navy.

On Tuesday 9 December 1941, Hitler rescinded all restrictions on U-boat operations against US warships in the American security zones. The C-in-C U-boats wanted to make full use of this moment, long anticipated, and deliver a surprise offensive by the U-boats against US merchant shipping close to the eastern seaboard of North America. Dönitz stated, "My request dated 9 December 1941 to proceed as soon as possible with twelve U-boats to the American coast was not approved by the German Naval High Command."

On the morning of 10 December 1941, the first Japanese landed on the Philippine coast. The defence of the archipelago was the responsibility of one of the most striking personalities of the war, Gen. Douglas MacArthur. He was also the C-in-C of American troops in the Far East (USAFFE).

At the same time on 10 December 1941, the Japanese 22nd Naval Air Group (Rear Adm. Matsunaga), carrying out an armed reconnaissance with its thirty bombers and torpedo-strike aircraft, sighted the British battleships *Prince of Wales* and *Repulse*.

In less than ninety minutes, the battleships were sunk in a textbook case of bombing and torpedo attack, for a loss of just four Japanese aircraft. The Japanese sent a signal to the British destroyers, "You may pick up survivors."

This disaster for the British Far East Fleet (Force C) marked the end of the age of the battleship. Up to this time, the conviction was generally held that a modern battleship could successfully defend itself at sea against aircraft attacks. The loss of the most modern battleships decided the fate of Malaya. Moreover, the news of the landing of the Japanese force that the two ships were supposed to attack was shown to be false. Two buffaloes had wandered into a minefield, and the subsequent explosion was thought to be Japanese artillery fire.

The sinking of these powerful fighting ships showed also that operations by battleships without their own air cover were no longer possible if the enemy possessed strong air forces.

On Thursday 11 December 1941, a few minutes after Germany and Italy declared war on the USA, an American Lightning fighter stationed on Iceland shot down over the Atlantic a long-range reconnaissance Fw 200, the first German aircraft to be shot down by a US pilot.

On Friday 12 December 1941, Churchill crossed the Atlantic on the battleship *Duke of York*, despite the stormy seas, to the US for the Arcadia Conference with Pres. Roosevelt. While still on board ship, Churchill drew up his memorandum on the necessity of a large-scale landing operation in occupied Europe.

Also on 12 December 1941, the second wave of Japanese landed on the northern tip of Luzon (Philippines) near the small town of Aparri, and also on the south coast of the Bicol peninsula near Legaspi.

On Saturday 13 December 1941 in the Chancellery, Hitler discussed German and Japanese war plans with the Japanese ambassador, Oshima. Hitler stated that his principal aims were the destruction of Russia, the advance through the Caucasus southward, and the torpedoing of the Anglo-Saxon Royal Navy and Merchant Navy. "Even now, the tonnage available to the Anglo-Saxon countries is insufficient to transport an expeditionary army to the Continent." Gen. Ashima informed the Führer, "It would be a distinct advantage when Japan attacks India from the east, if German troops could threaten India from the west. Let's meet in India!" Hitler mentioned briefly the necessity of preventing American supplies coming in through Vladivostock. In answer to this point, Oshima said that cutting off American traffic to Vladivostock would be very easy, especially as American ships would have to pass through the Straits to get there, and these could be covered by artillery fire. In addition, he was convinced that America would not ship any more supplies to the USSR:

On Wednesday 17 December 1941, a Martlet fighter from the *Audacity* attacked *U 131* (Lt. Comdr. Baumann) with depth charges while the U-boat pack Seeräuber (Buccaneer) was attacking Convoy HG-76 en route from Gibraltar to Britain. The light Flak guns on the U-boat shot down the fighter, the first aircraft to be shot down by a submarine.

During the second half of December, Swordfish torpedo bombers equipped with ASV radar, which had managed to get off the sinking carrier *Ark Royal* 12 November 1941, flew night patrols against German submarines continuing to negotiate successfully the Strait of Gibraltar into the Mediterranean. In one of these operations the night of 18/19 December 1941, they destroyed *U 451* (Lt. Comdr. Hoffman), the first time a sub-

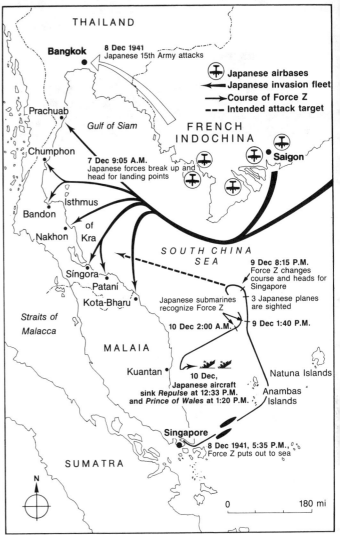

10 December 1941, the sinking of the British battleships *Repulse* and *Prince of Wales*

marine was sunk by an aircraft at night.

The night of 18/19 December 1941, the Italian Navy carried out its most spectacular operation of World War II. Three two-man torpedoes—manned by Lt. Comdr. Durand de la Penne with Petty Officer Bianchi; Capt. Marceglia with Leading Seaman Schergat; and Capt. Martellotta with Petty Officer Marino—left the submarine *Sciré* (Lt. Comdr. the Count Borghese) and penetrated into the strongly guarded harbor of Alexandria through the gap in the defences left for the battle group commanded by Rear Adm. Vian. The three torpedo crews were now in the vicinity of their objectives; two were to attack the battleships *Queen Elizabeth* (Capt. Barry) and *Valiant* (Capt. Morgan); and the third was to attack an aircraft carrier. If the carrier was no longer there, it was to attack a large tanker.

The first torpedo reached the battleship *Valiant* at 2:19 A.M. Its motor suddenly stopped running and the vessel sank to the bottom, fifty feet below. The steersman, Lt. Comdr. de la Penne, dived

Above: Italian two-man torpedo, torpedo crew fixing the explosive charges into position

Right: 12/27/1941, raid on the Lofotens, Commandos helping a badly wounded comrade back to a landing craft

which was below the waterline. At that moment, the lights went out and the mess decks were completely flooded."

The *Queen Elizabeth* and the *Valiant* settled on the bottom. A third explosion tore the stern off the fleet tanker *Sagona* (7,554 gross tons). The destroyer *Jervis*, which was alongside the tanker taking on fuel, was damaged.

". . . an unusual example of courage and ability," said Churchill when he heard that these two mighty warships together with almost two thousand crewmen had been put out of action by only

down after the torpedo and found that an old hawser had wrapped itself around the vessel's screw. The second man, the frogman, P/O Bianchi, had disappeared without trace.

De la Penne said, "I then tried to move the torpedo along the bottom. It was almost twenty-five feet long and correspondingly heavy. I had sunk into the mud up to my chest, and now I had to drag the thing. It was a terrible effort, but I succeeded in pulling the torpedo until it was under the battleship. I then set the detonator and shortly after lost consciousness. I found myself back on the surface of the water. At first, somebody started firing at me, and then I climbed onto one of the buoys to which the battleship was made fast. It was here that I found my frogman again. I waited until the British took us on board. . . . As there were only another ten or twenty minutes before the thing went off, I demanded to speak to the captain. I told him that the ship would blow up and that he, if he wished, could evacuate his crew safely. The captain asked me once again where the explosive was situated. I did not tell him. And so the captain locked me once again in the ammunition chamber. I sensed the explosion; when I came round again I was in the water. A part of the ship had burst open. I climbed back on the deck where there were still a few seamen. When I went past, they stood up and saluted. Even today, I can still see the captain staring at me while his ship went down. . . . The sun was rising over the stern of the *Queen Elizabeth* lying alongside, and while I was looking at this ship, the explosive under the *Queen Elizabeth* went up."

Gunner Wilkins of the *Queen Elizabeth* stated, "At 06.00 hours, the mines exploded with a terrible detonation. I had just gone down to my mess deck four Italian torpedo crewmen. This Italian operation had cancelled out the victory at sea that had been won. The strategically favorable position — there was not a single British battleship in the Mediterranean — was, however, not exploited by the Italian Navy.

On Sunday 21 December 1941, the Luftwaffe units of Air Fleet 2, transferred from the Eastern Front to Sicily, commenced continuous air raids on Malta. The attacks were directed mainly against the airfields on the island and the flying-boat base at Kalafrana.

On the same day, the escort carrier *Audacity* was sunk off the coast of Portugal by *U 751* (Lt. Comdr. Bigalk). In the few weeks it had been operational, this small auxiliary carrier had proved itself so well — particularly against the Fw 200 Kondors — that the Admiralty placed orders in the USA for a number of these small escort carriers. A hangar, as well as a flight deck, was built on the hulls of the Liberty ships.

On Monday 22 December 1941, Operation Anklet, the British raid on the Lofoten Islands, commenced. Rear Adm. L. K. H. Hamilton put to sea

from Scapa Flow with the cruiser *Arethusa*, eight destroyers and several landing craft, as well as auxiliary ships. Four days later the formation put into the Vestfjord, and at 6:00 A.M. the 260 men of Commando 12 (Lt. Col. Harrison) went ashore, while the German garrison was still in a Christmas mood. The Commandos occupied the fish-oil factories on the western side of Moskenesöy Island as well as the radio station Tind and destroyed them. Two Norwegian steamers were taken prize, and the German patrol boat *Geier* was sunk. The second radio station, Napp, was also blown up. After German bombers had damaged the cruiser *Arethusa*, the operation was suddenly terminated.

Gen. de Gaulle also used the Christmas holidays for a landing operation. He ordered Vice-Adm. Muselier to occupy the islands of Saint Pierre and Miquelon off Newfoundland, deploying the submarine cruiser *Surcouf* belonging to the Free French together with the corvettes *Aconit*, *Alysse* and *Mimosa*. Great Britain, and above all the USA, protested against this action and demanded that de Gaulle relinquish the two islands, which remained true to Vichy France.

On Wednesday 24 December 1941, two days after the formation commanded by Rear Adm. Hamilton had left Scapa Flow, Rear Adm. Burrough left Scapa Flow with the cruiser *Kenya*, four destroyers and two landing craft on Operation Archery, a Commando raid against the South Norwegian harbor of Vaagsö.

On Thursday 25 December 1941, the Japanese occupied Hong Kong.

The Japanese now successfully employed the air tactics of concentrated bomber operations and deployed a number of carrier formations in a limited tactical war theater. The Japanese fleet could maneuver freely and unhampered under the protection of carrier-borne aircraft and maintain its strategic initiative. The Japanese air force was powerful and efficient at the beginning of the war, and its torpedo bombers in particular were a feared opponent.

Early 26 December 1941, the Soviets carried out surprise landings on the north coast of the Kerch peninsula. Formations of the Asov flotilla (Rear Adm. Gorskov) disembarked units of the 51st Army (Lt. Gen. Lvov) under cover of a smoke screen off the coast. As there were no landing craft, the soldiers and their tanks together with their heavy equipment had to be transported on ordinary boats and barges to the land, where they encountered determined resistance by the Germans.

On Saturday 27 December 1941 after a prior bombardment by warships supported by the RAF, Commandos 2 and 3 (Col. J. Durnford-Slater),

reinforced by a Norwegian company, went ashore at 9:00 A.M. in the area of Vaagsö and Maalöy in five groups totalling 485 men. In South Vaagsö, German troops put up a tenacious resistance that was only broken after street fighting resulting in a number of casualties. The fish processing factory and signals installations were destroyed. Two German patrol boats and five freighters totalling 13,778 gross tons were sunk or beached, including the merchantman *Anhalt* (5,870 gross tons). The Commandos were joined on the return voyage by 343 young Norwegians. The most valuable booty was the codebook of the German Navy, found in the wireless room on the patrol boat V 5108/*Föhn*. This raid was the first undertaken by Commandos against a strongly defended harbor.

In December 1941, the third phase of the Battle of the Atlantic, which had commenced in April 1941, came to an end. On average there were thirty U-boats at sea.

By 28 December 1941, only five out of twelve U-boats demanded by Vice-Adm. Dönitz for the submarine operation—Operation Paukenschlag (drumbeat)—against shipping on the American coast had been made available by the base at Lorient: the U 66 (Comdr. Zapp), which made for Cape Hatteras; U 109 (Lt. Comdr. Bleichrodt),

The successes of the German U-boat packs from March to December 1941

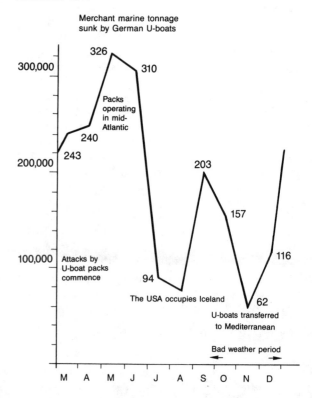

Merchant marine tonnage sunk by German U-boats

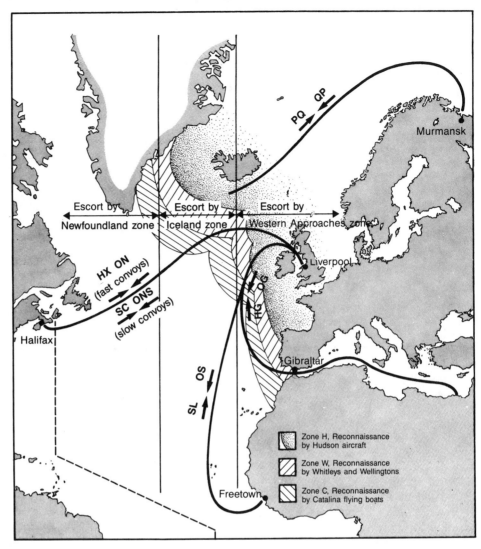

The most important convoy routes in 1941

which made for Halifax, *U 123* (Lt. Comdr. Hardegen) to the coast south of New York; *U 125* (Lt. Comdr. Folkers) to the approaches to New York harbor; and *U 130* (Comdr. Kals), which made for the mouth of the St. Lawrence river.

On Monday 29 December 1941, the main landing by the Soviets with units of the 44th Army (Maj. Gen. Pervuchin) took place in Feodosiya (Crimea). Their objective was to cut off the German forces on the Kerch peninsula, the 46th Infantry Division commanded by Lt. Gen. Count Sponeck, and then advance across the Crimea to relieve Sevastopol. This put the German 11th Army (Gen. von Manstein) in a serious position. The Soviet landing troops tied up such strong German forces that the assault on Sevastopol had to be put back by six months.

Despite everything, 1941 was a decisive year for the Red fleet. They suffered the most severe losses between June and December 1941, and these losses proved to be the heaviest in the entire war. The Soviets were at least successful in pulling back their remaining units to Leningrad.

By the end of December 1941, the P. Q. and Q. P. convoys with Lend-Lease supplies for the Soviet Union entered Murmansk and Archangel without loss — against all expectations. Hitler only attributed slight importance to these convoys, as he regarded the USSR as already defeated. And so during the first four months, among other things, fourteen hundred lorries, eight hundred aircraft and six hundred tanks were transported by this route. Of the six P. Q. convoys — a total of forty-five ships — only one ship, damaged by ice, had to turn back. Of the Q. P. convoys returning in the opposite direction, four ships were lost through ice damage. Not one of the ten convoys had to fight German forces.

In December 1941, German U-boats operating in the Atlantic and Mediterranean sank twenty-three merchant ships totalling 106,687 gross tons. German losses amounted to ten U-boats.

During the second half of the year, every seventh U-boat attacked by surface craft was sunk and every third heavily damaged.

During 1941, the Allied and neutral countries

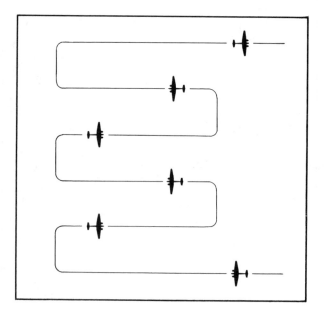

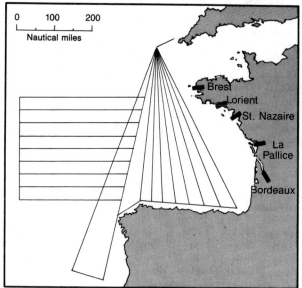

Above: Diagram showing method of Coastal Command patrol over the Bay of Biscay

Right: December 1941, air surveillance over the Bay of Biscay; routes prescribed by Coastal Command

lost 1,299 ships aggregating 4,328,558 gross tons, of which 875 ships totalling 3,295,900 gross tons were lost in the Battle of the Atlantic. The German U-boat arm in 1941 lost thirty-five submarines, twenty-five of which were lost in the Atlantic. The losses sustained by the Italian fleet amounted to five hundred merchantmen totalling more than 1,626,000 gross tons, almost thirty percent of their entire shipping capacity.

In 1941, the German merchant marine lost a total of 335,000 gross tons, which included losses sustained in the Mediterranean and blockade-runners sunk. U-boat successes achieved since March 1941 had, nevertheless, fallen back by half. In December 1941 the German U-boat arm had ninety-one units at its disposal, twenty-three of which were in the Mediterranean; three more were to proceed to that area at the orders of the German Naval High Command; six were operational to the west of Gibraltar; and four were deployed off Norway. Of the remaining fifty-five submarines, some thirty-three were under repair in the dockyards. There were only twenty-two submarines in the Atlantic, of which half were en route either to or from their operational areas at any one time. In fact, there were only ten to twelve U-boats simultaneously on operational patrol; in other words, only twelve percent of the front-line U-boats available. The construction of new U-boats had by now equalled out losses sustained. At this time, only a few British cruisers and destroyers were left in the East Mediterranean. And so once again the Italo-German convoys could put to sea for North Africa.

From December 1941, the British introduced a new antisubmarine weapon, the Hedgehog, that consisted of multibarrelled mountings, similar to mine throwers, to automatically stabilise the rolling motion of a ship. The Hedgehog fired off at a distance of 180 yards a ripple salvo of twenty-four missiles, each weighing approximately sixty pounds. The U-boat, when hit, was destroyed by the cluster of explosive charges. One serious disadvantage was that the Hedgehog, in contrast to the depth charge, exploded only on impact: There was no explosion if the salvo missed its target.

Like seabirds that could approach prey unseen because of their white-colored feathers, white-painted aircraft were concluded to have a thirty-five percent better chance than black-painted aircraft of escaping detection even at night, by a surfaced U-boat. Consequently, all RAF Coastal Command aircraft used in antisubmarine activities were camouflaged white on their under surfaces.

Despite all the measures undertaken, shipping losses sustained by the Allies were very high and exceeded by a considerable margin the new-building capacity of the shipyards.

On average there were three sinkings by German U-boats for each new ship built. But a turn in the Battle of the Atlantic was already discernible in the second half of the year. The British Admiralty estimated that between July and December 1941, thanks to the evaluation of Enigma reports, losses fell back by at least one million tons.

1942

January–June

Success Achieved by Italian Torpedo-men

Friday 9 January 1942, Rome
The *Italian High Command* issued the following communiqué:

During the action reported in yesterday's army communiqué, carried out against Alexandria harbor by assault units of the fleet, a second battleship of the "Barham" type was damaged in addition to a battleship of the "Valiant" type.

W. Churchill to the First Sea Lord

9 January 1942
The incident at Alexandria, which was so unpleasant, has raised in my mind the question of the security of Scapa Flow against this form of attack. Are we in fact patrolling the entrances with depth charges every twenty minutes? No doubt the strong currents would give far greater protection than the calm water of Alexandria. How does the matter stand?

Danger on the American Coast?

Thursday 15 January 1942, Washington
The *United Press Agency* reported:

As stated by a spokesman for the US Navy yesterday, the U-boat threat along the American coast is continually increasing so that it is now necessary to warn the entire merchant marine accordingly.

U-boats off New York

Friday 16 January 1942, Washington
The *Exchange* News Agency reported:

It seems certain that the submarines cruising off the port of New York are German.

W. Churchill to General Ismay

Sunday 18 January 1942
Please report what is being done to emulate the exploits of the Italians in Alexandria harbor and similar methods of this kind. At the beginning of the war Col. Jefferis had a number of bright ideas on this subject, which received very little encouragement. Is there any reason why we should be incapable of the same kind of scientific aggressive action that the Italians have shown? One would have thought we should have been in the lead.

Please state the exact position.

Saturday 24 January 1942
The *German High Command* issued the following communiqué:

As already reported by a special communiqué, in their first appearance in North American and Canadian waters, German U-boats have already caused considerable damage to enemy supply shipping. They have sunk immediately off the enemy coast eighteen merchantmen totalling 125,000 gross tons. Another ship and an escort vessel were torpedoed.

During these engagements, the U-boat commanded by Lt. Comdr. Hardegen particularly distinguished itself, this submarine alone having sunk off New York eight ships, including three tankers, totalling 53,000 gross tons.

U-boats in American Waters

Monday 26 January 1942, Washington
The *US Navy Department* issued the following communiqué:

The Norwegian steamer *Varanger* (9,000 gross tons) was sunk off the east coast of the USA on Saturday by an enemy submarine. The crew of the ship were saved. Since 14 January, five ships have been sunk along the Atlantic coast of the USA.

US Troops in Northern Ireland
Tuesday 27 January 1942, Washington
The *Exchange* News Agency reported:
The safe arrival in Northern Ireland of US forces, which did not lose a single man on the crossing, has been judged in all America as a success for the Allied navies.

Secret report of the SS Security Service on the internal political situation:
No. 256, 2 February 1942 (Extract)
The Führer's explanation—that U-boat successes in recent months have only fallen back so strongly because the USA has arbitrarily declared more and more of the Atlantic to be their own territorial waters—has caused widespread astonishment. Now that there is no further danger of violating neutrality, one is counting on the large-scale deployment of German U-boats, as announced by the Führer in one of his earlier speeches. The latest successes achieved by the German U-boat arm in American coastal waters are already seen as the start of further, even greater successes in the war against enemy shipping capacity.

Every Day One U-boat

Friday 6 February 1942, Washington
The *Reuters* News Agency reported:
Adm. Land, who is responsible for the building of merchant shipping, stated, "According to various sources of information, Germany is now building a submarine every day, the building time for which is shorter than the time previously required to destroy an enemy U-boat. The threat to our essential lines of communication is constantly increasing. We shall combat this danger with all the means at our disposal."

Air and Sea Battle in the Channel

Friday 13 February 1942, London
The *British Admiralty* and *Air Ministry* issued the following joint communiqué:
Yesterday British aircraft reported toward 11:00 A.M. that an enemy fleet formation—consisting of the battlecruisers *Scharnhorst* and *Gneisenau* as well as the heavy cruiser *Prinz Eugen* and a number of destroyers, torpedo boats and minesweepers—was approaching the Pas de Calais from the

A German U-boat leaving its base for an operational patrol. Some five to seven weeks were required in travelling time to and from distant operational areas.

west. The enemy units were accompanied by a large number of aircraft. At this time visibility was between three and five nautical miles. Cloud formation was so low that the enemy ships could not be seen from the English coast.

General Percival to General Wavell
13 February 1942, Singapore
Enemy now within five thousand yards of sea front, which brings whole of Singapore town within field artillery range. We are also in danger of being driven off water and food supplies. In opinion of commanders, troops already committed are too exhausted either to withstand strong attack or to launch counterattack. . . . There must come a stage when in the interests of the troops and civil population further bloodshed will serve no useful purpose. Your instructions of 10 February are being carried out, but in above circumstances would you consider giving me wider discretionary powers?

General Wavell to General Percival
Saturday 14 February 1942, Calcutta
You must continue to inflict maximum damage on enemy for as long as possible by house-to-house fighting if necessary. Your action in tying

down enemy and inflicting casualties may have vital influence in other theaters. Fully appreciate your situation, but continued action essential.

General Percival to General Wavell
Sunday 15 February 1942, Singapore

Owing to the losses from enemy action, water, petrol, food and ammunition practically finished. Unable therefore to continue the fight any longer. All ranks have done their best and are grateful for your help.

Strong Criticism in London

15 February 1942, London
The *Associated Press* reported:

The breakthrough of the German battlecruisers through the Channel has led to considerable disputes in British naval circles. Above all, the question has been asked what was the point in bombing the naval base in Brest at a cost of one hundred British aircraft without having achieved anything positive. . . . Another question asked how it was anticipated that German battlecruisers would attempt an early breakout from Brest harbor into the Channel, yet when the German formation actually made the attempt, they were discovered not as soon as they put into the Channel, but only toward 11:00 A.M. — and even then, only by accident. Why had no preparations been made to attack the German units immediately by torpedo bombers and small, fast assault craft?

The RAF's Failure
15 February 1942, New York
The *Baltimore Sun* reported:

One can only assume that for nearly one year the Royal Air Force has been bombing the wrong targets in Brest harbor, as the breakout of the German unit poses a riddle. This operation by the German Navy was carried out in such a manner that one can only wish that American commanders would act in such a fashion in a similar situation.

Daily Memorandum of the Reich Press Secretary
Thursday 19 February 1942

The German press continues to publish the career, pictures and stories of Churchill, which are too positive and could lead to popularising Churchill in the eyes of the German people. The minister therefore places with immediate effect all pictures of Churchill under censorship. Churchill must also be described in the German press as a liar, his neglected family circumstances highlighted and his amateurish manner of conducting war emphasised.

A Neutral Seaman Experiences the War

Karl Schöttli from Regensdorf, the only radio operator of the SS *St. Gotthard,* sailing under the Swiss flag
Private papers, Zürich, February 1942

When a neutral ship puts into a harbor of one of the combatant powers, each member of the crew is

Above: 12/2/1942, the Channel, breakout by the German formation

Right: Daily occurrence in the Battle of the Atlantic, an Allied ship goes down.

examined very thoroughly. The ship is scarcely tied up alongside the quay when, at the same moment as the doctor, officials from the harbor secret police and the coastguards secret service come aboard, and one crewman after the other is called into the mess or the captain's cabin. And then the questioning begins. . . . The official compares the answers carefully with the details on the passport. Then there are more questions—questions are really fired at you when you are being investigated by four, six and more officials. . . .

New York. I am sitting in the captain's cabin facing five US officials. I have already gone over the details in my passport. And also questions on my previous trips abroad, my profession, my previous employment and several other matters I have answered to the satisfaction of the officials, and none of my former employers appears on the "black list." "Do you also do military service?" I answer, and when they know that I am an officer, one of them who has been looking through a book poses some interim questions: "What is Colonel X doing?"—"I don't know."—"Has Major Y pub-

lished a new book recently?"—"I've never heard of a major of that name."—"How are things going with Captain Z? . . ."

This really is going too far. "Gentlemen, you have heard that I am an officer. You will get no answers from me on military matters even if, as you claim, the officers you have mentioned are friends of yours."

Another official suddenly fires off the question, "Do you belong to a club?" I answer yes, and the officials exchange meaningful glances. And now once again I am caught up in a crossfire of questions. "Where is this club? What does it do? Do you shoot? Does it carry out military exercises?" These people want to know all this and much more besides. I give the information freely and give five Americans a basic run-down on Swiss gymnastic traditions, the results of the last gymnastic display in the Canton of Zürich, the Regensdorf athletic club's latest open evening and a number of specialised gynmastic expressions! . . .

Anybody who, after putting into a port, can answer all the questions of the examining officials to their satisfaction will receive permission to go ashore. But anybody who thinks that this cross-questioning is then ended will be badly disappointed. What he has experienced up to now related to high officialdom. But now, once he is on terra firma, something else starts. In more than one port, after a certain interval the same people

always turned up wherever I wanted to go with my shipmates, whichever pub we wanted to visit. Sometimes one, sometimes several would sit close to us but seem to take no notice of us; just like us, order one or several drinks; stay sitting in the bar when we left; and several minutes later join us in the next bar. How these people always managed to ferret us out remains a mystery to me — but I am nonetheless convinced that what is called spying on somebody functions perfectly in Italy, America and Portugal. Our shadows only occasionally attempted to get into conversation with us. Mostly they just sat within earshot. I have no idea if they ever managed to make head or tail of our Zürich and Berne dialects. . . .

As a radio operator at sea, one often takes part — one could almost certainly say a direct part — in the war at sea. . . . I was the sole radio operator on the *Gotthard*. The duty watch amounted to eight hours, as a rule. In the meantime, the so-called "auto alarm" took over the SOS watch. When a ship sent out the well-known May-day call, it didn't begin at once with the three letters but first gave twelve signals, each four seconds long with a one-second interval between. The auto alarm was so regulated that it reacted upon receiving the third or fourth signal; a red lamp lit up on the bridge and alarm bells rang at various points in the ship. One such alarm was situated in the radio operator's cabin. . . .

Suddenly the auto alarm bell rings over my head. Barefoot and in my pajamas, I scurry over to the radio cabin. Quick as lightning, the apparatus is switched on, the antennae are switched over, but it takes some twenty seconds before the valves are warm and I can receive. . . . The ship is rolling heavily, and a wave throws cold water through the half-open door over my bare legs. There is a whistling noise in the apparatus, and I fiddle with the controls. Ah, yes — now I've got him! He seems to be working with an emergency set that has only a limited range; his main radio installation must be out of action. "SOS — SOS — de O'Shela — O'Shela . . ." I try to wedge myself with my knees under the table, as I need to keep both hands free and we are rolling badly. "Torpedoed, help immediately — position 3530 north 7345 west . . . SOS — SOS — SOS — de O'Shela — O'Shela — PSN 3530 N 7345 W fire around — help. . ." Poor devil, it's a tanker — torpedoed and its load of aviation spirit has flowed out, on fire, and is turning the sea around them into a flaming hell from which there can be no escape — and the radio operator sending out his call for help knows this as well as I do. His "SOS — SOS — SOS" keeps on coming. I put my oilskins over my pajamas and put on my slippers. Swiftly up to the bridge. It's as black as pitch, but I know the way. We bend over the charts. "There's nothing we can do — it's too far away," says the first mate who has this watch.

Swiss Radio Beromünster

Friday 20 February 1942

The most important events are 1) the break-through of the large German warships through the Channel 12 February; and 2) the surrender of the city and fortress of Singapore 15 February. Both events signify defeats for Britain, and in particular British sea power, and have thus awakened in Britain itself a corresponding uneasiness that has the appearance of an internal political crisis. . . . Singapore was equipped as a naval base with powerful coastal batteries and harbor installations, but was not equipped for defence against land and air forces. And so this mighty sea fortress was able to withstand an enemy attack from the land (from the Malaysian coast) for a mere seven days. This base was not attacked by the Japanese from the open sea, against which Singapore was secured. The massive guns of Singapore might well have had a destructive effect against large warships — but they were helpless against the barges and launches carrying from the Malaysian mainland Japanese infantry with their automatic weapons. The fall of Singapore has dramatically changed the position in East Asia. The shortest route to India has thereby fallen into Japanese hands.

Queen Wilhelmina to the Dutch Navy

Wednesday 4 March 1942, London
The *Reuters* News Agency reported:

The Dutch naval minister yesterday read over the BBC a message from Queen Wilhelmina that gave full recognition of the courageous behavior of the Dutch Navy in Pacific waters. "This battle corresponds to the heroic spirit that once motivated the admirals and seamen of Holland and is fully worthy of our great past. I am certain that I speak for all Dutch people when I say that our navy will arise again stronger than ever. . . . We have not been beaten, and for the Dutch people the war continues. History will know how to speak of the courage of our navy and its great bravery. The manner in which our sailors conduct themselves is for us a guarantee of victory."

American Reinforcements in Northern Ireland

4 March 1942, in a Northern Irish port
The *United Press Agency* reported:

Thousands of soldiers of the American Army have landed in Northern Ireland to reinforce the first US Expeditionary Corps that arrived here some time ago.

Secret Japanese Transmitter

Thursday 5 March, Santiago de Chile
The *Exchange* News Agency reported:

The police authorities have discovered a secret Japanese transmitter in Puerto Montt that was continually transmitting to Japan weather reports and shipping movements.

The German C-in-C Navy to the German High Command

Thursday 12 March 1942

The Japanese have recognised the great strategic importance of Madagascar for the war at sea. According to reports submitted to us, they plan to establish naval bases on Madagascar as well as Ceylon to cut off shipping to the Indian Ocean and the Persian Gulf. From these points they will be able to attack successfully shipping proceeding around the Cape.

W. Churchill to General Smuts

Tuesday 24 March 1942

As arrival of Japanese in Madagascar would not be effectively resisted by the Vichy French and would be disastrous to the safety of our Middle East convoys and most menacing to South Africa, we have decided to storm and occupy Diégo-Suarez. Assaulting force leaves tonight, intermingled with a convoy of fifty thousand men for the East. Operation is, we believe, on a sufficiently large scale to be successful.

Saturday 28 March 1942
The *German High Command* issued the following communiqué:

On 28 March shortly before midnight, enemy aircraft in several waves flew over St. Nazaire and dropped a number of bombs, which caused no damage. These intrusions were apparently to divert the attention of the coastal defences. While the Flak was firing at the aircraft, British light naval units attempted to penetrate the Loire estuary but were discovered by naval batteries, which opened fire. . . .

While fast assault boats made for various points along the coast, a destroyer made for the flood-gates. The naval batteries spread their fire. After a short interval, the destroyer went up with a mighty explosion before it could reach the floodgates. At various points in the bay, motor torpedo boats and fast assault boats were sunk almost simultaneously by the coastal batteries. In this mass attack, several enemy vessels succeeded in putting troops ashore. These troops were dispersed by immediate attacks in which units from all three branches of the armed forces took part. Cut off from their retreat,

Close to the US Atlantic coast a German U-boat lies in wait: view through the periscope.

they fled in small groups to surrounding houses where, to a man, they surrendered.

Attack on a Convoy in the Arctic

Tuesday 31 March 1942
The *British Admiralty* issued the following communiqué:

British and Soviet naval forces have repulsed attacks by enemy surface and submarine forces that attempted to prevent the arrival in the Soviet Union of a convoy carrying American and British supplies.

Directive No. 41

Directive No. 41 of the German High Command
Sunday 5 April 1942

The winter campaign is coming to an end. A defensive success of the greatest importance for German arms has been achieved by the bravery and self-sacrifice of the soldiers on the Eastern Front. . . .

The objective is to destroy irrevocably what fighting spirit still remains in the Soviets and to neutralise the most important sources of strength for the war insofar as possible. . . .

IV. German Navy: In the Black Sea, the main task of the navy — to the extent that their resources of attack and securing units as well as shipping capacity allows it — is the provisioning of the army and the Luftwaffe by sea transports.

With regard to the as yet unbroken powers of resistance of the Russian Black Sea Fleet, it is of special importance that light naval units to be transferred to the Black Sea are made ready for operations there as soon as possible.

The Baltic is to be secured by confining Russian naval units in the inner Gulf of Finland.

Police Raid on the Panama Canal

Monday 6 April 1942, Panama
The *Exchange* News Agency reported:

Approximately seven hundred nationals of the Axis powers have been held in Panama and then taken to the USA where they are being detained in internment camps. This figure includes 184 Japanese citizens liable for military service who have, in part, had military training.

Night on the Bottom of the Ocean

From Dr. Harald Busch, war correspondent
With the *German Navy,* April 1942

We are more than forty men, crowded up together in the slender hull of the steel fish. Every scrap of room is occupied on the decks, in the compartments and in the gangways, where by chance there are no sacks or boxes. There are even two men lying covered in their blankets, dozing, sleeping and snoring with a vengeance on the table in the rates' mess. There is a remarkable peace in the ship, a leaden peace with only the trapping and knocking of the engineers from the diesel-engine room echoing through the next few hours. And then that too dies away. The engineers have finished their repair work. Apart from the watch-keepers, everybody is now asleep.

Moisture such as you find on winter window-panes covers the sides of the ship, all flat surfaces, fixtures, the thousands of tubes and pipes, valves, hand-wheels and everything else. Drops of moisture run everywhere. Everything is wet.

The cold comes down from the conning tower into the control room and gradually spreads through all the compartments. One person rummages through his locker looking for a magazine; he wants to read. In the gangways between the diesel and the electric motors, crewmen—those men whose bunks are occupied—are lying close together. (Two men must share a bunk, but under normal conditions when the ship is on the move, only half the crew—relieved from watch by the other half—sleeps at a time.) Oh Lord, how narrow such a ship is, a ship that goes on such long voyages! Every now and again an airlock, or something similar, gurgles in one of the tanks. Such a noise makes the uncanny silence even more noticeable. We are lying on the bottom. No sound penetrates from the outside to us in here. We can no longer hear the splashing and rasping of the sea against the outer deck and outer casing of the ship above our heads as we can when we're travelling on the surface. Nothing can be heard. We can no longer hear the strong purring sound of the diesels, nor the gentle humming when we are travelling underwater, nor can we hear the sound of the radio that, as long as we are on the surface, reverberates incessantly through all the compartments of our narrow ship; no conversation among the crew can be heard. It is silent, magically, almost oppressively silent here on the bed of the ocean. Everybody is now asleep.

The few watchkeepers sit silently, dozing and reading. Every now and again they turn a page. One of them is eating, mechanically, an apple from those which are kept, as long as the stores last, in baskets in the bow compartment not far from the electric engines. Around midnight, coffee is produced for the watchkeepers; it was brewed up in the deserted galley by one of the engine room crewmen. The new watch gets ready; quietly, wake them up gently, a tap on the arm; up they come and relieve the watch, after they too have had a cup of hot coffee. And now the previous watch settle down on the spaces that have become vacant: The watch is changed. Five minutes later there is exactly the same picture as there was before—but with new faces. And just at this moment, the senior rate on watch in the control center bends down to the cupboard near the chart desk and reads the graduated measuring dials to check the chemical composition of the air on board the ship. Then he

switches on the ventilation system for a while, and, buzzing, it sucks in the air from all the compartments, passing it through the purifiers to absorb the increased carbon dioxide content. Additional oxygen is not yet necessary. We haven't been lying long underwater, so completely shut off from the outside world.

Two Thousandth Air Raid on Malta
Wednesday 8 April 1942, Valetta
The *Reuters* News Agency reported:
Yesterday Malta experienced its two thousandth air raid since the beginning of the war, and it was the heaviest raid to date. Antiaircraft guns put up a heavy barrage. There are, as yet, no complete reports available, but four enemy aircraft are known to have been shot down.

Bataan in Japanese Hands
Thursday 9 April 1942, Washington
As already reported by the War Department, the defenders of Bataan have probably been overcome by the Japanese.

The Japanese in the Bismarck Archipelago
9 April 1942, Melbourne
The *Reuters* News Agency reported:
Reconnaissance flights undertaken by air force units over the Bismarck Archipelago have shown that Lorengau has, according to all appearances, been occupied by the Japanese for some time.

US Aircraft Carriers off Tokyo?

Monday 20 April 1942, London
The *Reuters* News Agency reported:
According to radio messages with Radio Tokyo's call sign that were presumably meant for Japan's German Axis partners, approximately one hundred American B-25 bombers are said to have taken part in attacks on Tokyo and other Japanese cities. On the assumption that this report is based on factual evidence, the raid must have been carried out by American Navy airmen from aircraft carriers, as the B-25 has a maximum range of 1,700 miles. Significantly, an attack by aircraft carriers would show that the US Navy has regained complete freedom of movement, as it seems most unlikely that the American Department of the Navy would allow its aircraft carriers to operate off the Japanese coast without strong protective escort.

Secret report of the *SS Security Service* on the internal political situation:
No. 279, 27 April 1942 (Extract)
The people have received with great jubilation

All night on the bottom of the sea, ". . . more than forty men, crowded up together in the slender hull of the steel fish."

statements made by the Führer on the German U-boat arm and, above all, the information that the number of German U-boats would grow from month to month and that the highest number of U-boats deployed in World War I has already been exceeded with a good margin. Widespread hope has been awakened that the German U-boats will, in future, be used to a greater extent against enemy shipping than has been the case so far.

British Forces off Madagascar
Tuesday 5 May 1942
The *British Admiralty* issued the following communiqué:

As the Allies have resolved to forestall any Japanese attack against the French naval base of Diégo-Suarez on Madagascar, British naval and land forces appeared today off Madagascar.

J. W. Stalin to W. Churchill
Wednesday 6 May 1942

I have a request for you. Some ninety steamers loaded with various important war materials for the USSR are bottled up at present in Iceland or in the approaches from America to Iceland. I understand that the sailing of the ships may be delayed

for a considerable period because of the difficulties in the organisation of British escorts for these convoys. I am fully aware of the difficulties involved and of the sacrifices that Great Britain has already made in this matter. Nevertheless I feel obliged to approach you with the request to take all possible measures to ensure the arrival of the above-mentioned materials in the USSR during May, as this is of the utmost importance for our front. Please accept my sincere greetings and the best wishes for all success.

Severe Fighting on Madagascar
6 May 1942, London
The *United Press Agency* reported:

The British Admiralty and the War Office have reported today that British units on Madagascar have met determined resistance during their advance. Military circles have expressed great caution on the prospects of the campaign on Madagascar. Some observers reckon the fighting will continue for some time, especially if the French defenders should take up positions in the mountains.

Sea Battles in Arctic
Friday 8 May 1942
The *British Admiralty* issued the following communiqué:

A few details may now be made known relating to the operations that recently took place in the Arctic. These actions relate to two convoys. One convoy was transporting important war material to the Soviet Union, and the other was on the return journey. For several days the enemy undertook measures with maximum effort to prevent the passage of both convoys by deploying light surface units and U-boats together with aircraft. Although we suffered several losses, practically the entire convoy destined for the USSR reached its objective.

W. Churchill to J. W. Stalin
Saturday 9 May 1942

I have received your telegram of 6 May, and thank you for your message and greetings. We are resolved to fight our way through to you with the maximum amount of war materials. On account of *Tirpitz* and other enemy surface ships at Trondheim, the passage of every convoy has become a serious fleet operation. We shall continue to do our utmost.

Naval Battle in the Coral Sea

9 May 1942, Washington
The *United Press Agency* reported:

The American public are following the outcome

of the naval battle of the Coral Sea with extraordinary excitement. Radio stations, cinemas and theaters have informed us that they interrupt their programs when further communiqués are received on the course of the fighting. . . . According to official communiqués, the naval battle in the Coral Sea seems to have ended for the time being. The Japanese fleet, which has been divided into three formations, is currently carrying out maneuvers upon which no report, as yet, may be issued.

9 May 1942, Tokyo
The *Imperial Headquarters,* at 3:40 A.M. local time, announced the following further results of the fighting in the Coral Sea:

The overwhelming Japanese victory in the Coral Sea has hit the Allies particularly hard. The Americans, who lost the greater part of their battleships in the first days of the war in Pearl Harbor, can ill afford the loss of any of their remaining major units. Above all, there is the loss of two precious aircraft carriers that will have irrevocably crippled America's fighting capacity.

Japanese Warships in Manila
Sunday 10 May 1942, Tokyo
The German *DNB* News Agency reported:

After the fall of Corregidor and the sweeping of all mines from Manila Bay, the first units of the Japanese Navy yesterday entered the harbor in Manila.

Monday 1 June 1942
The *German High Command* issued the following communiqué:

The battle against the supply and merchant shipping of Great Britain and the United States was particularly successful in May. Naval and Luftwaffe units sank 170 enemy ships totalling 924,400 gross tons. In addition, sixty-six ships were damaged, some heavily, by bombs or torpedoes.

Japanese Submarines off Sydney
1 June 1942, Melbourne
The *Headquarters of the Allied Forces in Australia* issued the following communiqué:

During an enemy attack in Sydney waters, three Japanese midget-submarines were destroyed. The attempted enemy attack failed, and only a small harbor-steamer of no military importance was damaged.

Japanese Submarines off Madagascar
Friday 5 June 1942, Tokyo
The *Imperial Headquarters* issued the following communiqué:

Right: 5/5/1941, Diégo-Suarez, Madagascar, Operation Ironclad—the British invasion of French Madagascar

Below: Necessary camouflage on a U-boat in a French port on the Atlantic

Special units of the Japanese submarine arm carried out a surprise attack at dawn on 31 May against Diégo-Suarez (Madagascar), during which a battleship of the Queen Elizabeth class (36,600 tons) and a light cruiser of the Arethusa class (5,280 tons) were torpedoed and badly damaged.

Air Battles over Midway
5 June 1942, New York
A communiqué issued by *Admiral Nimitz* on the Japanese attack on Midway:

This morning at 6:35, Midway was attacked by Japanese carrier-borne aircraft. A large number of enemy aircraft were shot down.

Japanese Submarine Attack on Sydney
Monday 8 June 1942, Melbourne
The *United Press Agency* reported:

The outer districts of Sydney and Newcastle were fired upon, presumably by an enemy submarine. Damage was not considerable and casualties are said to be light.

British Advance on Madagascar
8 June 1942, Cape Town
The *Exchange* News Agency reported:

British forces on Madagascar have further extended their control over the island. A motorised unit has pushed forward to the East Coast some two hundred miles away and has occupied Antalaha, four hundred miles northeast of the capital.

Warning to the French Population
8 June 1942, London
The *Reuters* News Agency reported:

The British Broadcasting Corporation early

Convoy Battle in the Mediterranean

Wednesday 17 June 1942
The *German High Command* issued the following communiqué:

As already announced by special communiqué, units of the German Luftwaffe and Navy in cooperation with Italian naval and air force units dealt a series of heavy blows against enemy supply shipping in the Mediterranean. From 13 to 15 June, strongly escorted British convoys were attacked by German air force and naval units, which sank four cruisers and destroyers, two patrol vessels and six merchantmen totalling 56,000 gross tons. In addition, a destroyer and eight merchantmen were hit by torpedoes and destroyed by fire or so badly damaged that one must reckon with their complete loss. Another six warships and six merchantmen were hit by bombs or torpedoes. In air battles with the fighter aircraft deployed to secure the convoys, the German Luftwaffe shot down thirty-three enemy aircraft. Ten German aircraft were lost.

today issued the following warning to the population of the French coastal areas: "After the Commando raid on St. Nazaire, we issued a warning to all French people, above all those in the coastal areas. Today we are issuing the second warning to the French population. We again turn to all French people living in the blockaded zones from the Belgian frontier down to the Pyrenees. The coastal areas of occupied France are in increasing danger of becoming the scene of military operations. . . ."

Reorganisation of the Dutch Navy

Thursday 18 June 1942, Colombo
The *Exchange* News Agency reported:

Adm. Helfrich, C-in-C of Dutch naval forces in the Far East, has today stated that a large number of Dutch seamen and marines involved in the fighting on the Dutch East Indies are presently

being reequipped on Ceylon and formed into new battle units.

Losses Sustained by the Swedish Merchant Marine
Friday 19 June 1942, Stockholm
The Swedish newspaper *Svenska Dagbladet* reported:

Since the beginning of the war, the Swedish mercantile marine has lost a total of 165 ships aggregating 400,000 tons; in other words, more than a quarter of the entire shipping capacity has been lost. A total of 854 people have lost their lives in these actions.

The Fall of Tobruk

Wednesday 24 June 1942, Alexandria
The *Reuters* News Agency reported:

British warships left the harbor of Tobruk at the very last moment and, in fact, were fired upon by German artillery that had taken up positions along the quayside. Several hundred sailors were successfully taken off. A number of transporters, tankers and other vessels that escaped the enemy fire undamaged were also among the units putting to sea.

The seamen did not learn of the fall of Tobruk until the very last minute; in fact, not until they saw German tanks advance up the main streets firing on ships that were still in the harbor.

Secret U-boat Base
Thursday 25 June 1942, Rio de Janeiro
The *Reuters* News Agency reported:

The Brazilian Coastguard Service has discovered a provisioning station for Axis submarines situated on the Gurupi estuary in the mangrove swamps of the equatorial coast on the border between the states of Para and Maranho. The entire store of supplies was confiscated and the station destroyed. The Brazilian authorities took charge of a quantity of incriminating material, which has already led to numerous arrests.

German U-boats Put Saboteurs Ashore

Monday 29 June 1942, Washington
The *Associated Press* reported:

The head of the FBI, Edgar Hoover, announced yesterday that the service had been successful in arresting all saboteurs who had recently been put

ashore in the USA from German U-boats. Some of them were disguised as mineworkers and were to carry out sabotage activities in mines, naval depots and stores. A second group was meant to plant time bombs and explosives on board ships, similar to an activity that was carried out in World War I. One of the saboteurs who landed placed himself at the disposal of the criminal investigation department immediately on landing.

Provisioning in the South Atlantic

From Dr. Hanskarl Kanigs, war correspondent
With the German Navy, June 1942

The dark dot rapidly gets bigger. Soon the turret of a U-boat can be made out and then the grey broad hull of the supply ship gets closer to us through the azure sea. Its antiaircraft guns point up threateningly toward the skies, and the feeling of a certain safety here in the middle of the Atlantic finds its expression in the enthusiastic waving by our men. Two German U-boats exchange greetings in the middle of the vast expanses of the Atlantic. . . . Their two captains lean over the bridge railings holding their megaphones, the "whisper-

Secret meeting point somewhere in the Atlantic, provisioning at sea—additional provisions and fuel extend the U-boat's operational deployment by several weeks.

ing tubes," to their mouths and make a short speech. The dinghies are released swiftly. . . . But fuelling activities begin immediately. Pipes are laid across the outer deck, steel hawsers are paid out, inlet valves are screwed into position and our ship takes on new strength for a few more thousand miles of voyaging. As the sea is calm, the pipe connection between the two ships moves only slightly in the weak swell and requires no special supervision. Despite all this, full security measures are, of course, taken and a number of lookouts take up position to counter any surprise by the enemy. A type of shuttle service is set up for taking on provisions. Across each tackle on the tanker's port side, a heavy cable is run, and onto the end of the cable a dinghy is fixed. When the end of the cable is pulled, at the double, over to our side by a few men, the dinghy comes across to us; when the tanker's men carry out the same maneuver, back the dinghy goes to them. And so many good things find their way across to us which are picked up in careful haste by our men on the outer deck and then taken through the tower hatch and stored away inside the submarine. In the meantime, a number of young sailors appear on the bridge with their mail. They don't want to miss this opportunity of sending home a letter where in place of the usual details relating to "billet" they can write the words "South Atlantic."

Fuelling takes several hours. The crew make full use of this special day to get away from the daily grind. Those who are not on duty swim around the ship in the clear blue water and then stretch themselves out on the fo'c's'le and roast themselves in the sun. . . . Finally the fuelling is finished, and, in the words of the chief engineer, the ship has drunk its fill like a child at its mother's breast. . . . Then the hawsers are cast off, the pipe connections are dismantled, and with a humming from the diesels both submarines get under way. "Have a good journey and see you ashore!" Caps and arms are waved, our ship's siren sounds while the supply ship becomes smaller and smaller until it has finally disappeared.

Strategy and Tactics

January to June 1942

On the morning of 1 January 1942, most of the troops to be deployed in the operations on the Kerch peninsula were in their assault positions. They were units of the 386th Rifle Division, transported from Novorossisk to Sevastopol by the heavy cruiser *Molotov,* the destroyer *Tashkent* and two transporters. Despite the strong troop reinforcements in the Feodosiya region together with the units stationed in Sevastopol, the Germans were unsuccessful in stemming the Soviet advance towards Ak-Manay. The Kerch peninsula was now completely cut off.

On Friday 2 January 1942, an Allied Murmansk-bound convoy, PQ-7, suffered the loss of a ship for the first time. The *U 134* (Lt. Comdr. Schendel) torpedoed and sank the British freighter *Waziristan* (5,135 gross tons) in the Arctic Ocean.

On the same day, the Japanese 48th Division occupied Manila, which had been declared an open city. US and Philippine units pulled back from Luzon to the impassable Bataan peninsula and the strongly fortified rocky island of Corregidor situated off the entrance to Manila Bay. The defence of the Philippines was in the hands of Gen. MacArthur, one of the greatest and most controversial of American war heroes. Since 1935 the former chief of staff of the US Army had been "on loan" to the Philippines to organise the defence of the archipelago until he was appointed 26 July 1941 Commander-in-Chief in the South Pacific (US Army Forces in the Far East, USAFFAE).

After Manila had been taken by the Japanese, the president of the Philippines, Manuel L. Quezon, together with his family and several members of his government also withdrew to Corregidor. When Pres. Quezon enquired about the possibility of evacuation for himself, his family and some loyal politicians, MacArthur stated that this would be "too dangerous," as even the provisioning of the US troops surrounded on Corregidor could only be maintained by submarines and seaplanes.

The next day, Saturday 3 January 1942, Pres. Quezon radioed the National Bank of the Philippines in New York and requested that US $500,000 be transferred to the private account of Gen. MacArthur; US $75,000 to his chief of staff, Maj. Gen. Sutherland; US $45,000 to his deputy, Brig. Gen. Marshall; and US $20,000 to his personal adjutant, Lt. Col. Huff.

Also on 3 January 1942, the American, British, Dutch, and Australasian Command (ABDA) was formed in the Dutch East Indies under the command of Gen. Wavell.

By this date also, the entire Kerch peninsula was again in Soviet hands. The landing operations on Kerch were carried out by the Soviets with great determination. Above all, the Soviets lacked air support and, as a consequence, Red fleet transports that had penetrated into Feodosiya harbor suffered heavy losses. Owing to the shortage of landing craft, under artillery fire warships disembarked the troops straight onto the pier.

January 1942, Corregidor,
Gen. MacArthur in conversation with Pres. Manuel L. Quezon

The night of 4/5 January 1942, eight hundred men from a Soviet marine battalion landed in Yevpatoriya, north of Sevastopol. The following night, more units of this battalion landed and made contact with the partisans. After a German counterattack, some of the Soviet units had to be reembarked.

On Sunday 11 January 1942, the Japanese Central Group (Adm. Hirose) carried out landings on the isle of Tarakan (Dutch East Indies); the rich oil resources fell into Japanese hands.

During their advance from island to island, the Japanese developed well-defined tactics. The landing areas were almost always within such convenient range that Japanese land-based aircraft were able to destroy in advance enemy aircraft on the ground. Carrier-borne aircraft were deployed only in special cases; normally they were reserved for the actual war at sea. The landings were achieved under cover of fire from ships' guns and with the cooperation of bombers. Once the troops were on land, airstrips were immediately set up and preparations made for the next move.

On Monday 12 January 1942, the *U 123* (Lt. Comdr. Hardegen) attacked and sank the British steamer *Cyclops* (9,076 gross tons) off New York. Operation Paukenschlag (drum beat), attacks on American shipping off the east coast of America, had begun. Ships in these waters were seldom escorted and had practically no air cover; in addition, few people had any experience of fighting submarines. The U-boats surfaced only at night when they torpedoed or fired on merchantmen clearly silhouetted against the brightly lighted coast.

Operation Paukenschlag heralded the fourth

phase of the Battle of the Atlantic, which lasted until July 1942.

Dönitz stated, "The U-boats found what amounted to almost peacetime conditions on the American coast. The coast was not blacked out; the towns were brightly lighted, as were beacons for shipping, lighthouses and lightships, even though they seemed to be at reduced strength. Shipping used peacetime routes with lights in position. Although five weeks had passed since the declaration of war, few measures seemed to have been adopted against attack by U-boat."

The Arcadia Conference, which had commenced on 20 December 1941, terminated on Wednesday 14 January 1942 in Washington. During this conference Great Britain and the USA agreed upon their war plans and took their basic strategic decisions. "Germany first," the overthrow of Hitler's Germany, was to be the primary objective. Britain's task was to increase the bombing offensive against Germany to bring about Stalin's demand for a "second front." The USA wanted to set up its own air bases in England as soon as possible and take part in the bombing offensive in the second half of the year.

On Saturday 17 January 1942, U 454 (Lt. Comdr. Hackländer) sank the destroyer Matabele and torpedoed the steamer Harmatris (5,395 gross tons), vessels that were a part of Convoy PQ-8. The U 454 belonged to U-boat Ulan Group, the first pack to be deployed against an Arctic convoy.

On Sunday 18 January 1942, 105 Infantry Regiment (Col. Müller), which formed part of the German 11th Army (Gen. von Manstein), reoccupied Feodosiya in the Crimea.

On Thursday 22 January 1942 after discussions in his headquarters, the Wolfsschanze (Wolf's Lair), Hitler told Adm. Fricke, Chief of Staff of the German Naval High Command, that Norway represented the vital zone in the war. Reinforcements, should the need arise, must be put through with absolute ruthlessness. All U-boats would have to proceed to Norway to carry out a proper surveillance of the approaching enemy and provide effective defence.

On Hitler's orders, twelve U-boats of the latest Type VII, the entire Schlei Group, had already been stationed since 15 January 1942 in the area west of the Hebrides and Faroes to repel the supposed invasion of Norway. In contrast, Dönitz had planned to deploy these U-boats off the American east coast.

On Friday 23 January 1942, British air reconnaissance detected the battleship Tirpitz in the Aasfjord, fifteen nautical miles east of Trondheim. At this, the British Admiralty resolved to allow only one convoy on the Iceland-Murmansk-Iceland route at any one time, to avoid unnecessary risks.

On Saturday 24 January 1942, Hitler finally allowed the U-boat Schlei Group to leave the area around the Hebrides and make for its base in the Bay of Biscay.

But only two days later, on 26 January 1942, Hitler changed his mind and again ordered six U-boats to proceed to the area around the Hebrides.

On Wednesday 28 January 1942, Grand Adm. Raeder met the C-in-C of the French Navy, Adm. Darlan, in Paris. During this tete-à-tete the French admiral gave the head of the German Navy important advice that was, however, ignored. Darlan, who presumably had knowledge of the new Allied location systems, warned Raeder against "excessive radio traffic by German U-boats." Raeder stated, "There were circles in France who were inclined to cooperate with us and were prepared to assist us in our fight against Britain. These circles included, as one of the strongest personalities, the C-in-C of the French Navy, Adm. Darlan. . . . I had lengthy and detailed discussions with him in Paris on 28 January 1942, without any other party being present." Because, in the opinion of the Ger-

1/28/1942, Paris, secret meeting of the admirals: The C-in-C of the French Navy, Darlan (left), the C-in-C of the German Navy, Raeder (right)

man Naval High Command, this warning given by the French admiral related simply to the harmless location of actual U-boat radio transmissions, this crucial information was disregarded.

To detect surfaced U-boats at night or in conditions of poor visibility, Allied aircraft and ships deployed as submarine hunters were equipped with a Mark II 50-cm wavelength radar. For U-boat crews, on the other hand, in conditions of poor visibility it was scarcely possible to detect attacking aircraft, and it was scarcely possible to hear them above the noise of the U-boat's diesel motors. To eliminate this danger, the Germans fitted their U-boats with a search receiver, Metox R 600. Because of this heterodyne receiver (wavelength 1.84 m) and its — initially — makeshift antennae (nicknamed the Biscay Cross), radar signals emitted by Allied aircraft, noticeable through their continual bleep and whistling tone, were picked up before the U-boat could be located by the aircraft; the U-boat could dive in good time. In addition, Metox enabled U-boats to detect emissions from the radar on board Allied ships, locate the ships and attack them.

By the end of summer 1942, it was already becoming much more difficult for Allied aircraft to detect German U-boats because of the use of Metox. It was soon shown, however, that the area covered by the Metox frequency was too small, as, above all, the British had developed the new, improved radar equipment that operated on the 10-cm wavelength.

In January 1942, German U-boats operating in the North Sea and Atlantic sank forty-nine merchantmen totalling 276,173 gross tons. German losses amounted to three U-boats.

On Sunday 1 February 1942, the last British and Australian forces withdrew to Singapore island and blew up the causeway to the mainland. On the same day, the Hydra cipher key — used by U-boats in their coded transmissions — was replaced by the Triton key, and front-line U-boats were equipped with a new enciphering machine, Enigma-M 4 (fitted with a supplementary fourth wheel, Alpha). British cryptanalysts succeeded in decrypting parts of the Triton key only at the end of 1942.

On Tuesday 3 February 1942, the American submarine *Trout* (Lt. Comdr. Fenno) carried 3,500

Below: 2/12/1942, the battlecruisers *Scharnhorst* and *Gneisenau* during Operation Cerberus

Right: Operation Cerberus, the up-Channel breakthrough by the German formation

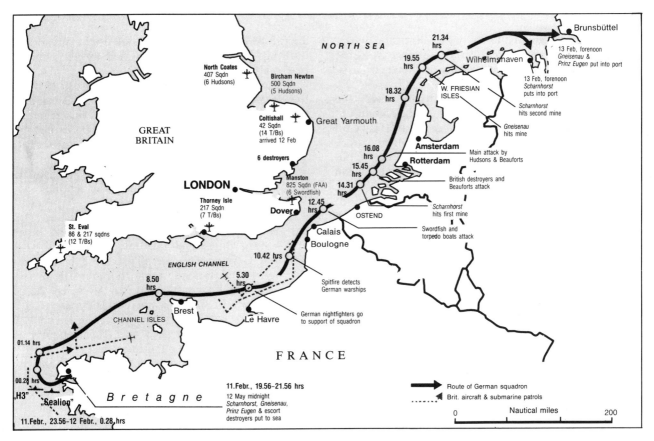

Map labels:

NORTH SEA

Brunsbüttel

21.34 hrs
19.55 hrs
18.32 hrs
16.08 hrs
15.45 hrs
14.31 hrs
12.45 hrs

13 Feb, forenoon
Gneisenau &
Prinz Eugen put into port

Wilhelmshaven

13 Feb, forenoon
Scharnhorst puts into port

W. FRIESIAN ISLES

Scharnhorst hits second mine

Gneisenau hits mine

North Coates
407 Sqdn
(6 Hudsons)

Bircham Newton
500 Sqdn
(5 Hudsons)

Coltishall
42 Sqdn
(14 T/Bs)
arrived 12 Feb

Great Yarmouth

6 destroyers

GREAT BRITAIN

Amsterdam

Rotterdam

Main attack by
Hudsons & Beauforts

British destroyers and
Beauforts attack

Manston
825 Sqdn (FAA)
(6 Swordfish)

LONDON

Thorney Isle
217 Sqdn
(7 T/Bs)

Dover

St. Eval
86 & 217 sqdns
(12 T/Bs)

OSTEND

Scharnhorst
hits first mine

Calais

Swordfish and
torpedo boats attack

Boulogne

10.42 hrs

ENGLISH CHANNEL

5.30 hrs

8.50 hrs

Spitfire detects
German warships

Brest

CHANNEL ISLES

German nightfighters go
to support of squadron

Le Havre

01.14 hrs

FRANCE

00.28 hrs

"H3"

"Sealion"

Bretagne

11.Febr., 23.56–12 Febr., 0.28 hrs

11.Febr., 19.56–21.56 hrs
12 May midnight
*Scharnhorst, Gneisenau,
Prinz Eugen* & escort
destroyers put to sea

→ Route of German squadron
···· Brit. aircraft & submarine patrols

0   Nautical miles   200

---

rounds of ammunition for light antiaircraft guns to Corregidor, where it took twenty tons of gold and silver on board.

On Sunday 8 February 1942, artillery units of the Japanese 25th Army (Lt. Gen. Yamashita), which had landed the previous night on Ubin Island in the eastern part of the Johore Strait, opened fire on Singapore. Japanese bombers attacked the British fortress on Singapore at the same time.

On Monday 9 February 1942, the French luxury liner *Normandie* (83,423 gross tons) was on fire in New York harbor. France's largest passenger liner—taken over by the American Maritime Commission—had been renamed the USS *Lafayette*. During its conversion to a troopship, a fire was caused by carelessness in welding operations. The fire spread so rapidly that the ship could not be saved, and it capsized. The *Lafayette* had to be scrapped.

Since their raiding activities in the Atlantic, the German battlecruisers *Scharnhorst* and *Gneisenau* and the heavy cruiser *Prinz Eugen* had been blocked in the French port of Brest and had become priority targets for RAF bombers. They had been attacked more than three hundred times and had been damaged.

Hitler was convinced that an Allied invasion of Norway was imminent, and the Kriegsmarine would therefore have to prepare the Norwegian coast for possible attacks by Allied forces. With this purpose in mind, the *Scharnhorst, Gneisenau* and *Prinz Eugen* were to be transferred north from Brest. Hitler informed Grand Adm. Raeder, "If your surprise breakthrough up-Channel should prove to be impossible, the most practical thing to do would be to break up the ships and use their guns and crews for the reinforcement of the Norwegian defences."

Raeder replied, "The decision to make a Channel breakthrough was absolutely against my advice. I could not imagine a successful outcome to the operation if the enemy showed sufficient vigilance and readiness. Hitler was, however, quite firm on this point and stated quite unequivocally that he would make the ships nonoperational in Brest and remove their guns if I refused the Channel breakthrough."

Faced with either seeing these valuable units completely destroyed in Brest or accepting the risk of moving them, the Naval High Command decided to risk an escape through the Channel. To deceive the British, the news was spread that the formation was proceeding to the South Atlantic. Tropical helmets, as well as barrels of lubricating oil marked "suitable for tropical conditions," were brought on board. A carnival ashore was announced for Monday 16 February, the Monday preceding Ash Wednesday when carnivals are traditionally held. A number of officers from the three ships received invitations to dinner in Paris, or invitations for a hunting trip.

Late the evening of 11 February 1942, the *Scharnhorst* (Capt. Hoffmann), as the flagship of Vice-Adm. Ciliax, and the *Gneisenau* (Capt. Fein), the heavy cruiser *Prinz Eugen* (Capt. Brinkmann), as well as a number of destroyers and S-boats, put to sea from Brest under the code-name Operation Cerberus, the most audacious operation of the Kriegsmarine in World War II. On this occasion, luck was on the side of the Germans: A French agent in Brest, whose duty was to keep an eye on the German fleet, failed in his task; the British submarine *Sealion* (Lt. Colvin), which patrolled the approaches to the harbor, was forced by bombers to dive; the Hudson reconnaissance aircraft deployed by Coastal Command to carry out surveillance returned to England with a malfunctioning radar set, as did the aircraft patrolling farther to the east.

And so Vice-Adm. Ciliax was successful in slipping out to sea with his heavy units completely unobserved, escorted by six destroyers and fourteen torpedo boats, three S-boat flotillas, twenty-one minesweepers, twenty-two evacuation craft, twenty-one submarine hunters and thirty-seven other auxiliary vessels. The flotilla was further protected by 176 fighters and fighter bombers of Fighter Groups 2 and 26. Subsequently, these groups were supplemented by units from Fighter Group 1 under Col. Galland. At least sixteen German aircraft maintained a continual patrol over the battlecruisers. Despite the network of British coastal radar stations, the formation in the English Channel remained undetected.

On Thursday 12 February 1942 at 10:35 A.M., Sgt. Beaumont, a Spitfire pilot, sighted the German ships after they had already passed Le Touquet. Almost one hour later, the staff of Group 11, RAF, still hesitated to advise Air Marshal Leigh-Mallory, as he was in the process of taking a parade. When an officer expressed his suspicion that it could possibly be the *Scharnhorst* and *Gneisenau* in the Channel, he was advised to go and take an aspirin!

It was not until 1:16 P.M. that British coastal batteries opened fire, and Adm. Sir Bertram Ramsey ordered off MTBs, torpedo bombers and destroyers to stop the German fleet—but without success. A Swordfish formation from 825 Squadron (Lt. Comdr. Esmonde) fearlessly attacked without fighter protection the German ships off Gravelines; all six of the torpedo-strike aircraft were shot down. The German fleet formation now made full steam into the North Sea. More than 240 aircraft of Bomber Command took up the pursuit, but only forty aircraft located their target in the bad weather.

In the only success achieved in the pursuit, first the *Scharnhorst* ran into a mine off the Schelde estuary; the following night both battlecruisers ran into magnetic mines, previously dropped near Terschelling by obsolescent Hampden bombers of 49 and 455 Squadrons. The ghostly armada finally succeeded in reaching its destination. In all, forty-two British aircraft were lost during the action.

The successful outcome to Operation Cerberus was not only attributable to lucky coincidences, but also—and the British did not know it at the time—to the largest jamming operation in history. A dozen German destroyers, operating between Cherbourg and Ostend, jammed radar stations along the English coast at 10:00 A.M. when the formation was between Fécamp and Dieppe.

Churchill stated that to allay complaints a special commission would hold an official enquiry which would report the publishable facts. The appointed commission would punish those guilty for the errors and omissions that had caused so much ill feeling but without their having any idea of the real causes of this failure. Churchill said, "We have learnt since the war that Gen. Martini, the chief of the German radar, had made a careful plan. . . . Our operators therefore did not complain unduly, and nobody suspected anything unusual. By February, however, the jamming had grown so strong that our sea-watching radar was in fact useless."

The success of the breakthrough up-Channel, celebrated with much National Socialist propaganda, was deceptive. The German Navy could certainly chalk up a tactical success, but in reality Operation Cerebus was a strategical withdrawal that meant the renunciation of further oceanic operations. At any rate, Vice-Adm. Ciliax had more luck than his Spanish colleague, Adm. the Duke of Medina Sidonia, whose armada was defeated during a similar attempt in 1588. And the German fleet was the first to dare a Channel breakthrough once again after 354 years.

On Sunday 15 February 1942, Singapore capitulated. This fortress, said to be impregnable, was taken by the Japanese within one week.

The night of 16/17 February 1942, German U-boats opened fire on a number of oil installations in Caribbean ports. The *U 502* (Lt. Comdr. von Rosenstiel) attacked Maracaibo (Venezuela). *U 156* (Comdr. Hartenstein) attacked the port on the island of Aruba; and *U 67* (Lt. Comdr. Müller-Stöckheim) attacked Curaçao—both Dutch possessions. These attacks opened Operation Neuland, which lasted for four weeks, conducted

The submarine-cruiser *Surcouf*, pride of the French Navy, was rammed during the night by a US merchantman.

against shipping in the Caribbean. The C-in-C U-boats had deployed his submarines in this area as their operations off the east coast of America has been made more difficult by the increased protection given to convoys. Churchill stated, "In the Caribbean Sea, amid a wealth of targets, the U-boats chose to prey chiefly on the tankers. . . . Week by week the scale of this massacer grew."

The same night, the battlecruiser *Gneisenau* (Capt. Fein) was so badly damaged during an RAF bombing raid on Kiel that it was no longer operational. After stripping off parts for reutilisation, the ship's hull was sunk 28 March 1945 off the Gdynia harbor roads.

On Tuesday 17 February 1942, the Japanese submarine *I-25* (Lt. Comdr. Tagami) surfaced off Sydney. Taking off in the submarine's floatplane, the pilot, Sgt. Fujita, made the first reconnaissance flight over Sydney, which started a five-week reconnaissance of Australia and a number of islands in the South Pacific.

The night of 17/18 February 1942, the French submarine-cruiser *Surcouf* (Lt. Comdr. Blaison) sank. It had been, at the outbreak of war, the largest submarine in the world (4,218 tons submerged). It had two 20.3-cm guns, two 3.7-cm antiaircraft guns, four machine guns, ten torpedo tubes, and it carried a Besson MB.411 floatplane. The complement numbered 118. While the submarine was on its way to the Panama Canal, it was rammed by the American freighter *Thomson Lykes* in the Caribbean and went down with all hands.

On Thursday 19 February 1942, cable confirmation from the Chase National Bank in New York was received in Fort Mills, Gen. MacArthur's headquarters on Corregidor, stating that the US $500,000 for Gen. MacArthur as well as US $140,000 for his three staff officers had been credited to their private accounts.

The funds represented certainly the largest "present" that had ever been received by a US officer on active service; and acceptance was in gross contravention of US Army regulations. But only a small circle of insiders knew about it. These included Pres. Roosevelt, the US secretary of war, the US minister of the interior, the heads of Chase National Bank, as well as the subsequent president of the Philippines, Manuel Roxas, who was appointed by Gen. MacArthur when the Philippines were liberated. At the time, however, America needed her national hero, MacArthur, and Roosevelt quietly allowed the files on this matter to disappear into the secret archives of the US government.

The following day, 20 February 1942, the American submarine *Swordfish* (Comdr. Smith) slipped into the Bay of Manila, lay on the bottom and surfaced at twilight. It took the Philippine president and his family and a few friends off Corregidor to Mindanao.

And five weeks later, after the situation had become more critical, Gen. MacArthur left Corregidor 24 March 1942 upon the orders of Roosevelt. The general left in a motor torpedo boat with his wife, his young son, the Chinese nursemaid, as well as a number of staff officers. From Mindanao, he asserted that he would return. He then flew to Australia to undertake the defence of that continent.

On 21 February 1942, in the North Atlantic six hundred nautical miles north of Cape Race, the *Toward* of Convoy ONS-67 located for the first time by means of High Frequency Direction Finding (HF/DF) the maintaining-contact short signals transmitted by the *U 155* (Lt. Comdr. Piening). The high-frequency technique now became one of the most important weapons deployed by the Allies in the war against the U-boat. Radar, already used with success, had considerable back-up from shortwave direction-finding equipment HF/DF, known by Allied seamen as "Huff-Duff." This compact automatic device now enabled the first maintaining-contact short signals between U-boats and the C-in-C U-boats, as well as radio traffic between the U-boats themselves, to be located to the area of the ground wave (up to twenty-five nautical miles). These locations gave the precise position of the U-boat (to within some 450/500 yards) and were the decisive reference for radar location by aircraft and ships. HF/DF was employed on escort vessels in the summer of 1942 and subsequently on convoy steamers. The escort vessel made along the HF/DF direction for the U-boat, located it with Asdic once the U-boat was submerged, and then dropped depth charges. Most U-boats were damaged during such attacks and were forced to the surface. They were then sunk either by gunfire or by ramming. By these means, numerous convoys sighted by the U-boat maintaining contact were able to evade the U-boat pack without heavy losses.

On Friday 27 February 1942, Allied naval forces in the Pacific (ABDA) attempted to intercept the Japanese invasion fleet off Java. At 4:12 P.M., the British destroyer *Electra* sighted the Japanese formation. Four minutes later, the sound of gunfire ushered in the first maritime engagement in the Pacific, known as the Battle of the Java Sea.

At 5:07 P.M., Japanese destroyers attacked with torpedoes. The Dutch destroyer *Kortenaer* was hit and sank immediately. The cruiser *Exeter* was hit in the engine room by an artillery salvo; the *Electra* was torpedoed and sunk. After nightfall set in, both sides lost contact with each other.

At 11:30, the Allied cruisers were again found by the Japanese. Shortly afterward, the Japanese formation opened fire. The ammunition chamber on the cruiser *Java* exploded. After being hit by a torpedo, the cruiser *De Ruyter* sank; the cruiser *Java* also went down. Some sixty survivors were floating on wreckage and rafts in the sea. A patrol-

ling Dutch submarine took two badly wounded survivors on board. When a hospital ship from Surabaja reached the scene of the sinking, none of the survivors was to be found. The Battle of the Java Sea finished as a defeat for the Allies. Two cruisers and three destroyers were lost, and the C-in-C of the ABDA Strike Force, Rear Adm. Doorman, was killed: This was the price paid for merely delaying the Japanese landing on Java by twenty-four hours.

The cruiser *De Ruyter* and other ships had been sunk by Japanese Type 93 torpedoes, known as Long Lance because of their unusually long range. This torpedo was the finest produced during World War II. It had a speed of thirty-six knots and could hit a target twenty-two nautical miles away. With a target at half this range, it could reach the unbelievable speed of forty-nine knots. This device was a fraction under thirty feet long, weighed nearly six thousand pounds and had a warhead carrying an explosive charge weighing half a ton—twice as much as American torpedoes at that time. The Long Lance was powered by oxygen, and its development took place years before the war under conditions of utmost secrecy.

Churchill wrote, "In February the U-boat losses in the Atlantic rose to seventy-one ships, of 384,000 tons, all but two of which were sunk in the American zone. This was the highest rate of loss which we had so far suffered throughout the war. It was soon to be surpassed."

In February 1942, German U-boats sank seventy merchantmen totalling 411,560 gross tons. German losses amounted to two U-boats.

On Friday 6 March 1942, the battleship *Tirpitz*

Right: Shortwave direction-finding equipment HF/DF—a dangerous enemy of the German U-boats

Left: 2/23/1942, California, one of the fifteen shells fired by a Japanese submarine hit the jetty at Ellwood oilfield. Damage amounted to US $250.

Below: Using HF/DF equipment, two escort vessels locate a U-boat transmitting and alert the escort group.

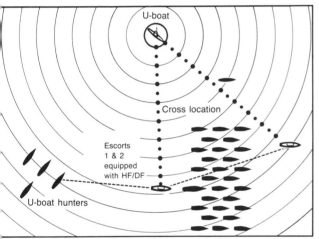

U-boat

Cross location

Escorts 1 & 2 equipped with HF/DF

U-boat hunters

(with Vice-Adm. Ciliax) left Trondheim and, accompanied by three destroyers, set out to make its first foray against merchant shipping. Convoys PQ-12 and QP-8 were accompanied by a support group (Vice-Adm. Curteis) which comprised three battleships, an aircraft carrier, a cruiser and six destroyers. Because of the bad weather, no contact between the opposing forces was made.

By the beginning of March 1942, three months after the attack on Pearl Harbor, the Japanese had already conquered Malaysia and the adjacent islands in the south. A good two months ahead of their planned objectives, they had sustained far lower losses than had been thought possible. The occupation of Burma was also completed without great difficulty. In March, Japanese troops pushed forward from Rangoon north, and the numerically inferior and exhausted defenders were driven back from Burma into India and China.

From Saturday 14 March 1942, eleven U-boats, types VII A, B and C, making up the fourth wave of Operation Paukenschlag commenced individual operations off the coast of North America. These U-boats, with a displacement of 626 to 769 tons, were not intended for long-range operations. But the crews waived personal comfort to make way for provisions and spares. Dönitz stated, "In their endeavors to be able to fight in American waters, the crews were driven to self-help. They filled a number of their fresh water tanks and washing water tanks with fuel."

On Friday 20 March 1942, the first German commerce raider of the second wave, ship no. 28 *Michel* (Capt. von Ruckteschell), put to sea from Lorient. This ship was the former Polish motor vessel *Bielsko* (4,740 gross tons), which had been taken in Danzig in 1939. Its armament consisted of six 15-cm guns, a 10.5-cm gun, four 3.7-cm antiaircraft guns, four 2-cm antiaircraft guns, six torpedo tubes; in addition, it carried a small motorboat, two Ar 196 A3 float planes and a complement of three hundred. Its operational area was to be the Atlantic, Indian and Pacific oceans.

After the successes achieved by the Japanese and their advance toward the Indian Ocean, Churchill now feared that the Axis powers would establish a base on the Vichy French island of Madagascar.

On Monday 23 March 1942, a number of transports put to sea from their base on the Clyde in Scotland to take part in Operation Ironclad, the occupation of Madagascar.

On Tuesday 24 March 1942, the U-boat tanker *UA* (Comdr. Cohausz) carried out the first fuelling operation of World War II some five hundred nautical miles northeast of the Bermudas. These U-boats, dubbed "milch cow" by front-line crews, could carry an additional 432 tons of diesel oil in tanks in their broadened pressure-hulls, together with four torpedoes packed in pressurised containers stowed forward of the tower. A total of ten of these submarine-tankers was built.

The submarine-tanker (type XIV) was a ponderous, large vessel of almost 1,700 tons, not equipped with offensive weapons, and therefore no torpedoes were carried, simply two 3.7-cm antiaircraft guns, and one 2-cm antiaircraft gun. Their complement amounted to fifty-three men. An overall total of seven hundred tons of fuel was carried on these "milch cows," and, according to the distance they had themselves to travel, four hundred to six hundred tons of their load could be supplied to the fighting U-boats. This quantity was sufficient, for example, to allow twelve medium-sixed U-boats to take on fifty tons of fuel each in the Caribbean or ninety tons for the larger Atlantic U-boats to deploy to an operation off the Cape of Good Hope. The submarine-tankers were particularly hunted out by Allied air and naval units. Dönitz stated, "The operational use of the submarine-tankers was considerable after their first deployment in April 1942. In many cases, they had the effect of advancing our bases along the Bay of Biscay practically one thousand to two thousand nautical miles westward. Obviously, the enemy soon found out about this new provisioning potential for our fighting U-boats at sea and took pains to catch the tankers during fuelling operations and destroy them." In the waters of the West Atlantic off the American east coast, U-boats were able to operate during the first three months of 1942 without loss. The number of targets was so large that U-boat commanders carried out attacks only against fully laden freighters.

On Thursday 26 March 1942, the Japanese carrier fleet (Vice-Adm. Nagumo), comprising five aircraft-carriers, four battleships, three heavy cruisers, one light cruiser and eight destroyers, put to sea from Kendari (Celebes). At the same time, the Japanese Malaya Group (Vice-Adm. Ozawa) left its base at Mergui (Burma). This force consisted of one aircraft-carrier, five heavy cruisers, one light cruiser and four destroyers. After the conquest of the Malaysian peninsula, the Japanese General Staff decided to make a breakthrough into the Indian Ocean.

The British Eastern Fleet (Vice-Adm. Somerville), which did not have sufficient aircraft at its disposal, was sent southwestward at this news. Its main forces were five obsolete battleships, three carriers, two heavy and five light cruisers, sixteen destroyers and seven submarines. They set out for a provisional base, Addu-Atoll (Maldives), some six hundred nautical miles from Colombo.

The night of 27/28 March 1942, the French port of St. Nazaire became the scene of a new British raid, Operation Chariot. The objective of the raid was to render the dry docks there inoperable. The special dock in which the French luxury liner *Normandie* had been built could, in an emergency, take the battleship *Tirpitz* should it undertake Atlantic operations, as had the *Bismarck*. The destroyer *Campbeltown* (Lt. Comdr. Beattie) was successful in ramming the floodgates. One Commando force numbering 268, led by Col. Newman, landed with the intention of attacking the U-boat base. But they were wiped out during the resistance by ships' crews trained in hand-to-hand fighting.

Practically all the Commandos were killed or taken prisoner. Only four of their boats succeeded in returning to England. Eight hours later, the *Campbeltown,* loaded with explosives, blew up and destroyed the floodgates. This success was of strategic importance, as there was no other dock on the Atlantic coast capable of taking the *Tirpitz*.

A number of important staff changes were made among the upper echelons of the US Navy. Adm. Kimmel, C-in-C US Fleet and Pacific Fleet at the time of Pearl Harbor, was relieved of his command. Pres. Roosevelt separated the positions of C-in-C US Fleet from the individual C-in-C positions of the various fleets; Adm. King became the C-in-C US Fleet (based in Washington) and Adm. Nimitz became C-in-C Pacific Fleet (based in Pearl Harbor). In March 1942, Adm. King was nominated as chief of staff to the president. Adm. Stark was posted to London as C-in-C US Naval Forces in Europe.

In March 1942, German U-boats sank eighty-four merchantmen totalling 446,044 gross tons. German losses amounted to six U-boats.

From January to March 1942, German U-boat building achieved record figures — an average each month of twenty-six U-boats totalling 28,635 tons.

At the end of the great convoy battles in the North Atlantic, almost all the U-boats, practically out of fuel and torpedoes, had to return to base, leaving hardly any German submarines in the North Atlantic at the end of March and the beginning of April 1942.

On Wednesday 1 April 1942 at 7:00 A.M., Operation Performance began in the Swedish port of Göteborg. Along with several tankers, eleven Norwegian merchantmen laden with strategically important goods — mainly Swedish steel, ball bearings and machines for the production of ball bearings — were to attempt to break through the Kattegat and Skagerrak to Great Britain. This

3/28/1942, St. Nazaire, the British destroyer *Campbeltown* (former US destroyer *Buchanan*) against the floodgates. Shortly after this photo was taken, 4½ tons of explosives hidden in the hull went up, killing several hundred Germans.

operation took place on the initiative of Sir George Binney, an agent of the British Intelligence Service. He had already carried out a similar operation (Operation Rubble) on 23/24 January 1941.

Sir George Binney planned this risky venture with the cooperation of the British military attaché in Stockholm, Capt. Denholm, and with the support of the Admiralty and Churchill, as well as the silent approval of the neutral Swedish government. The German military intelligence deployed their agent in Göteborg, H. G. Wagner, to ascertain details of the British operation. German torpedo boats and S-boats, destroyers and U-boats as well as a number of bombers and flying boats were to be used to seize the eleven Norwegian blockade-runners, which were scheduled to leave Göteborg individually. Sir George Binney led the operation from ashore with the aid of a telegraphist placed at his disposal by the destroyer *Hunter*. Three decrepit destroyers—veterans from the First World War, the *Wallace, Valorous* and *Vanity*—put to sea from the Firth of Forth, and the destroyers *Faulknor, Eskimo* and *Escapade* put to sea from Rosyth to give the blockade-runners some protection. The Norwegian freighters were awaited in the

Skagerrak by German units and bombers; only two merchantmen succeeded in reaching Britain. The lack of air cover by the RAF together with the favorable weather enabled the Luftwaffe to attack the blockade-runners. The bombers sank the tanker *Rigmor* (6,305 gross tons) and scored a number of hits on the tanker *Newton* (10,324 gross tons). Six ships totalling 26,675 gross tons were either sunk by German naval units or scuttled by their own crews. Three freighters managed to put back into Göteborg in good time. This affair caused the German government to raise furious protests in Stockholm, and even the Norwegian government in exile in London sent a sharp note to the British Admiralty, expressing their concern about the fate of the Norwegian seamen taken prisoner by the Germans. In Sweden, Sir George Binney was declared persona non grata. In answer to all this, Anthony Eden, the foreign secretary, said that it was "not as bad as I feared."

On Saturday 4 April 1942, I Air Corps (Gen. Förster) commenced Operation Eisstoss (ice attack). Aircraft from 1 Dive Bomber Group and 1 and 4 Bomber Groups carried out operations against units of the Soviet Baltic Fleet (Vice-Adm. Tribuz) in Leningrad. During the heaviest of the attacks, 4 April 1942 against Kronstadt, 132 German bombers, accompanied by 59 Me 109 fighters, took part. The Naval High Command hoped that Operation Eisstoss would bring about the destruction of the Soviet fleet before the ice melted in the

207

Gulf of Finland.

The following night, during a bombing raid by more than thirty German bombers, the cruisers *Maxim Gorki* and *Petropavlovsk* (the former *Lützow*) were badly damaged, in addition to the battleship *October Revolution*. Also on 4 April 1942, ships lying in the harbors of Trincomalee and Colombo were evacuated when a British reconnaissance flying boat reported sighting southwest of Ceylon the Japanese task force commanded by Vice-Adm. Nagumo. The next day, the two British naval bases on Ceylon were attacked by 180 Japanese carrier-borne aircraft from Nagumo's force. Japanese dive bombers sank the heavy cruisers *Cornwall* (Capt. Mainwaring) and *Dorsetshire* (Capt. Agar) off Ceylon. At the same time, the Malaya group commanded by Vice-Adm. Ozawa made a foray into the Bay of Bengal and in four days sank twenty-three British merchantmen totalling 112,312 gross tons. Five other ships were sunk by Japanese submarines.

For one week, until Wednesday 8 April 1942, heavy air raids against Malta were carried out by the German II Air Corps (Gen. Loerzer) and Italian bomber forces. The objective was to make the island fortress ripe for invasion. Two destroyers and four submarines were sunk in the harbor, and the remainder of the British 10th Submarine Flotilla had to evacuate Malta in mid-April. Thereupon, the situation of the Italo-German convoys immediately improved, and the more often Malta was attacked, the more supplies and reinforcements could reach North Africa. Nevertheless, the favorable moment to subdue Malta by air and sea landings in direct conjunction with the heavy bombardments was missed. On the other hand, Rommel, who was now planning an offensive from El Gazala to the Nile, demanded back-up from all available aircraft in the Mediterranean. His objective, the Suez Canal, was not achieved, but Rommel's decision saved Malta. His supply lines were once again subjected to increasing losses, inevitably contributing to his defeat.

On 8 April 1942, the Bataan peninsula capitulated. Only the US Marines and an élite unit, the Philippine Scouts, succeeded in evacuating Corregidor.

On Thursday 9 April 1942, eighty Japanese dive bombers from Vice-Adm. Nagumo's force sank not far from Ceylon the aircraft carrier *Hermes* (Capt. Onslow), the destroyer *Vampire,* the corvette *Hollyhock* and two tankers. This fleet operation off Ceylon was the high point of Japan's success. After the raid, the two Japanese task forces withdrew toward the Strait of Malacca. This was

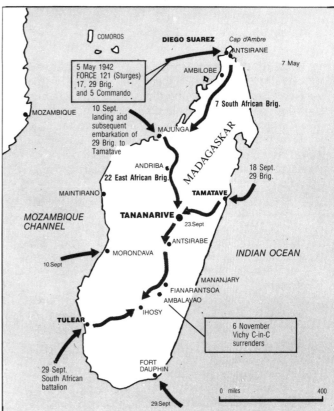

the only foray carried out by the Japanese fleet in the Indian Ocean, and subsequently only Japanese submarines and individual commerce raiders operated in these waters.

The night of 13/14 April 1942, *U 252* (Lt. Comdr. Lerchen) was sunk by the British corvette *Vetch* and the sloop *Stork*. *U 252* was the first loss effected with the new 10-cm type 271 radar equipment.

On Tuesday 14 April 1942, the Italian torpedo boat *Pegaso* sank the British submarine *Upholder* in the Mediterranean off Tripoli. The most successful British submarine had been on its twenty-fourth operational patrol. The commander, Lt. Comdr. Wanklyn, had sunk shipping totalling 140,000 gross tons.

The same day, off the east coast of North America, *U 58* (Lt. Greger) was sunk by the US destroyer *Roper,* the first success achieved by an American surface vessel in these waters.

On Saturday 18 April 1942, sixteen twin-engined B-25 Mitchell bombers under the command of Lt. Col. Doolittle (USAAF) took off from the aircraft carrier *Hornet* to carry out an air raid on Tokyo, 662 nautical miles away. This was an unprecedented achievement by the air arm, as never before had a B-25 taken off from the deck of an aircraft carrier. Heavily armed, these aircraft were scarcely able to reach the necessary take-off speed from the short deck of a carrier. Because the range of these aircraft would not permit a return flight, the sixteen B-25s were to fly to China after the attack.

Thirteen Mitchells dropped their bombs on Tokyo, the other three attacked Osaka, Nagoya and Kobe. Sixteen tons of bombs were dropped. Tokyo had just finished a large-scale air raid exercise, and Doolittle's planes were thought to be stragglers from the bogus attack force.

Bad weather over China forced most of the crews to parachute from their bombers. Eight American flyers were taken prisoners by the Japanese and sentenced to death as war criminals. Three of them were beheaded, and one died in a POW camp.

The most important effect of the Doolittle operation was that a part of the Japanese air arm had to be withdrawn from front-line service to defend the homeland. Adm. Yamamoto, presuming that the American bombers had taken off from a base on Midway, resolved to occupy this island as soon as possible.

In April 1942, German U-boats operating in the Atlantic, North Sea and Mediterranean sank seventy-two merchantmen totalling 394,760 gross tons. German losses amounted to three U-boats.

On Monday 4 May 1942, after six weeks at sea the troopships that had set sail from the Clyde were lying off the northern coast of Madagascar along with a powerful formation comprising one cruiser, four destroyers, six corvettes, six minesweepers, nine transporters, a tanker and seven landing craft. The battleship *Ramillies* (Rear Adm. Syfret), the aircraft carriers *Illustrious* and *Indomitable,* the cruiser *Hermione* and seven destroyers made up the escort group. Rear Adm. Syfret had overall command of Operation Ironclad, while Gen. Sturges, his subordinate, led the landing troops. Most of the soldiers had had no training in amphibious operations. They were to take the French naval base of Diégo-Suarez, a natural harbor in an idyllic setting in a bay reached only by a narrow channel. They were also to take the stronghold of Antsirane.

On Tuesday 5 May 1942 at 4:30 A.M., the British troops made a surprise landing in Courrier Bay to attack Diégo-Suarez from land. The first person they met on the beach was a negro wearing only a sunhat. He greeted them in perfect English, without trace of accent, saying, "Good morning, gentlemen."

The Royal Welch Fusiliers, with a small armored vehicle surrounded by motorcycles, started off toward the city, some twenty miles away. On the way, they stopped the car of a French naval officer who was accompanied by three petty officers. Carrying out their orders, they handed the officer a paper to be given to his headquarters, requiring them to surrender unconditionally. Gen. Sturges said, "I fear that handing over this paper was a great mistake. . . . When the French officer returned, taking with him precise information on the direction of our main advance, orders were given for a counterattack." Col. Claerebout, the French commander, replied over the radio, "Diégo-Suarez will be defended to the last in accordance with the traditions of the French armed forces." At 5:10 A.M., British carrier-borne aircraft attacked the harbor at Diégo-Suarez and the airfields. Apart from torpedoes and bombs, thousands of leaflets were dropped on the city, calling for unconditional surrender. The commerce raider *Bougainville* (former *Victor Schoelcher*) and the submarine *Béveziers* sank in the harbor. The French aircraft were fully destroyed before they could take off. The gunboat *D'Entrecasteaux* just managed to escape the British torpedoes.

Landings in Courrier Bay met no resistance, but there were more mines in the bay than were expected. Toward midday the British corvette *Auricula* ran against a mine and sank. Minesweeping operations caused the schedule for landings to be thoroughly mixed up.

Not until 2:00 A.M. on 6 May 1942 could the British break through the French lines of defence and approach Antsirane fortress.

British marines from the destroyer *Anthony* also landed on this day near Antsirane. After an engagement lasting several hours, in which the crews of the *Bougainville* and *Béveziers* took part, four thousand men including eight hundred Europeans surrendered. The landing troops took prisoner the commandant of the naval depot in addition to a number of other senior officials and freed approximately fifty British prisoners including British secret agent Myers, who was to be executed the following morning. Churchill said, "This was a brilliant action."

The gunboat *D'Entrecasteaux,* whose gunfire made the British advance more difficult, was attacked by the carrier aircraft and sunk.

Also on 6 May 1942, Japanese paratroopers commanded by Gen. Homma forced the last American troops on Corregidor to surrender. The Philippines were now totally in Japanese hands. A total of 11,574 men plagued with hunger and malaria—including Gen. MacArthur's successor Gen. Wainwright—went into captivity along the murderous "death march of Bataan"; only a few survived.

At 1:00 A.M. on 7 May 1942, fighting on Madagascar ceased. The coastal batteries of Antsirane at the entrance to the harbor, however, continued to fire. Lt. Col. Stockwell drove to the fortress in a jeep with a white flag, a trumpeter and two bottles of gin. After a while, he returned with the battery commander. When Rear Adm. Syfret heard of the success of the attack, he put into the Bay of Diégo-Suarez with his fleet. The French submarine *Héros* used this opportunity to try to torpedo the British ships. The submarine was, however, sunk by a Swordfish from the carrier *Illustrious*.

On the morning of 7 May Japanese aerial reconnaissance wrongly reported having seen an aircraft carrier and a cruiser in the waters north of Australia; Vice-Adm. Takagi ordered a large-scale attack. Two ships were sunk, but in reality they were only a tanker and an escorting destroyer, so the operation was scarcely worthwhile.

That evening, Takagi led a second, weaker attack—with devastating consequences for the Japanese: Out of the twenty-seven aircraft deployed, twenty-one were lost. Again, a reconnaissance patrol mistakenly believed it had located Japanese major units, and US carrier-borne aircraft consequently attacked escort units of the Port Moresby invasion fleet. During the action, a small aircraft carrier, the *Shoho*, received a direct hit. It went down within ten minutes, the first Japanese carrier to be sunk by US aircraft. The presence of these American ships in Australian waters led the Japanese admiral to recall the Port Moresby, invasion force first to destroy the Allies' fleet.

At the beginning of May 1942, the Japanese were advancing on all fronts. By the middle of April, the Americans had already received news of an imminent landing operation by the Japanese. Weeks earlier, the new Japanese naval code had been decrypted, and intercepted radio transmis-

5/27/1942, the Arctic, German bombers attack Murmansk-bound Convoy PQ-16 late into the night.

sions stated that an attack on Port Moresby (New Guinea) was planned. At this, Adm. Nimitz ordered all available units southward. Task Force 17 (Rear Adm. Fletcher) with the carriers *Yorktown* and *Lexington* set out from Pearl Harbor with 141 aircraft (42 fighters and 99 bombers), as well as two cruiser groups as an escort. Two other US carriers, *Enterprise* and *Hornet,* were also directed into the South Pacific but arrived too late for the coming battle that history knows as the Battle of the Coral Sea.

On Friday 8 May 1942, reconnaissance aircraft from each side discovered the other's task forces, more or less equal in strength. The Japanese had 121 aircraft, four heavy cruisers and six destroyers; the Americans had 122 aircraft, five heavy cruisers and seven destroyers. The Japanese possssed one advantage in that they had more battle experience and better torpedoes; the American force, however, had more bombers. The Japanese were able to remain under the cover of a band of mist, whereas the Americans had to fight under clear skies. Because of the mist, the small carrier *Zuikaku* was not sighted by the American aircraft. The carrier *Shokaku* received three direct hits by bombs and had to withdraw. After hits by two torpedoes and by a number of bombs that resulted in several explosions, the *Lexington* had to be abandoned and scuttled with torpedoes fired by an American destroyer. The *Yorktown,* a smaller and more maneuverable carrier, was hit only once by a bomb.

The afternoon of 8 May 1942, Adm. Nimitz pulled his carrier formation from the Coral Sea, as the danger to Port Moresby had been staved off in the meantime. The Japanese, convinced that the *Yorktown* had been sunk, also withdrew. Badly damaged, the large Japanese carrier *Shokaku* was nonoperational for the next two months. The carrier *Zuikaku* had lost so many aircraft that it too was temporarily out of commission.

Tactically, the Battle of the Coral Sea was a victory for the Japanese: American losses were considerably higher than the Japanese. The loss of the large aircraft carrier *Lexington* was a bitter blow for the US Navy. But the Americans could certainly chalk up a strategical victory: Adm. Yamamoto's plan to occupy Port Moresby had been thwarted. For the first time in this war, a Japanese invasion attempt had been foiled. And, as this victory happened two days after the surrender of Cor-

regidor, it was of special significance for morale in general.

The Battle of the Coral Sea was the first engagement in history in which surface units did not exchange fire, and the first to be decided by the carrier-borne aircraft of the combatants.

Also on 8 May 1942, the German 11th Army (Col.-Gen. von Manstein) opened its offensive on the Kerch peninsula. Soviet troops of the Crimean Front (Lt. Gen. Koslov) suffered a defeat and had to withdraw across the Strait of Kerch to the Taman peninsula.

On 8 May 1942 the French submarine *Monge* made a daring torpedo attack on the British aircraft carrier *Indomitable* off Diégo-Suarez. The submarine missed its target, however, and was destroyed by depth charges from the destroyer *Active*. The only ships to escape to Dakar and later Toulon were the French submarine *Le Glorieux* and the gunboat *D'Iberville*.

British losses in the capture of Diégo-Suarez amounted to 109 dead and 284 wounded. The French lost some two hundred dead and five hundred wounded. Operation Ironclad was the most successful military operation carried out by the British since the beginning of the war. Churchill said, "The news arrived at a time when we sorely needed success. It was in fact for long months the only sign of good and efficient war direction of which the British public were conscious." But another six months of sporadic fighting were to elapse before French troops on Madagascar finally capitulated.

On Thursday 14 May 1942, permanent convoy traffic was introduced along the North American east coast.

The night of 20/21 May 1942, the second German commerce raider of the second wave, ship no. 23 *Stier* (Comdr. Gerlach) broke out unobserved from the mouth of the Gironde, north of Bordeaux, into the Atlantic. The ship was the former *Cairo* (4,778 gross tons) with a complement of 324. Its armament comprised six 15-cm guns, two 3.7-cm antiaircraft guns, four 2-cm antiaircraft guns, two torpedo tubes, and two type Ar 231 submarine-spotter aircraft. Its operational area was the Atlantic.

On Thursday 21 May 1942, a German agent operating in Reykjavik reported that Convoy PQ-16 had put to sea from Iceland. Four days later, the convoy was located by German aerial reconnaissance. Arctic convoys, which carried supplies and equipment to the Soviet Union, were generally subjected to attacks by the Luftwaffe for two-thirds of their entire route. The operational range of Allied aircraft reached only as far as Jan Mayen Island and left a large region between the island and the area north of Murmansk without air cover. The Royal Navy had to accept, however, the political considerations. And so the convoys at the time they were most at risk were not stopped but were, as shown by Convoy PQ-16 (with 35 merchantmen, the biggest so far), continued at full pressure.

On Wednesday 27 May 1942, 101 Ju 88s from KG 30 (30 Bomber Group) and 7 He 111s from I/KG 26 attacked Convoy PQ-16 until evening, sinking seven freighters totalling 36,987 gross tons. A number of ships were damaged. For close to five days, the convoy's escort units had to endure almost uninterrupted attacks by German torpedo bombers and dive bombers. The convoy, however, remained together.

On Friday 29 May 1942 at 10:30 P.M., an aircraft from the Japanese submarine *I-16* (Comdr. K. Yamada) appeared over the harbor of Diégo-Suarez to carry out a reconnaissance of the Bay of Diégo-Suarez. The Japanese transport submarines *I-16* and *I-20* set off their midget-submarines.

On Saturday 30 May 1942, Convoy PQ-16 entered Kolski Bay near Murmansk, "smaller in number, beaten and exhausted but still in perfect formation." On the same day, German bombers attacked Convoy PQ-16 for the last time but were driven off by Soviet fighters and antiaircraft fire. During this air battle, the most successful flyer of the Soviet North Fleet, Lt. Col. Safanov, was shot down. A total of 32,400 tons of war material, including 147 tanks, 77 aircraft and 770 lorries, were lost together with their transporters.

The night of 30/31 May 1942, the battleship *Ramillies* and the tanker *British Royalty* (6,993 gross tons) were torpedoed by Japanese midget-

submarines in Diégo-Suarez. Showing the high degree to which they were trained, the submarine crews penetrated into the enclosed bay through a tiny approach some one thousand yards across and then carried out the torpedo attacks.

On Sunday 31 May 1942, Japanese transport submarines *I-22*, *I-24* (Comdr. Hanabusa) and *I-27* (Comdr. Yoshimura) set off their midget-submarines close to the Australian coast. Their objective was Sydney harbor. Some of the midget-submarines did, in fact, succeed in reaching Sydney waters. They just missed the cruiser *Chicago* and succeeded only in sinking the *Kuttabul*, used as a residential ship. None of these midget-submarines returned from their operation.

Until the last week in May, German U-boats were deployed in the Atlantic and Mediterranean and North seas, but mainly in the eastern Mediterranean to prevent convoys from carrying supplies along the coast from Alexandria to the 8th Army (Lt. Gen. Cunningham).

In May 1942, German U-boats sank 125 merchantmen totalling 584,788 gross tons. German losses amounted to four U-boats.

Adm. Yamamoto was planning an attack on Midway Island similar in style to the attack on Pearl Harbor. His objective was to challenge the US fleet to a decisive battle in order to achieve absolute supremacy at sea, after further operations against Hawaii.

Midway is a tiny atoll in the Pacific Ocean meas-

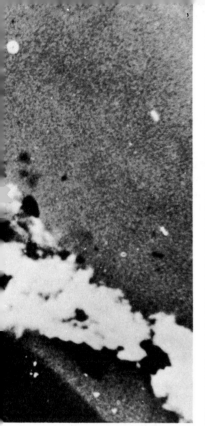

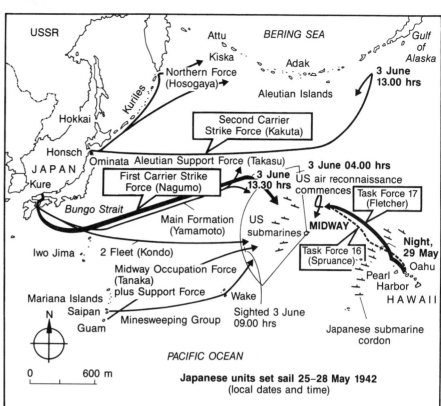

Left: A Japanese carrier plane crashes in flames.

Right: The Battle of Midway saw a turning point—the greatest defeat suffered by Japan for 350 years.

uring only five miles across. Lying midway between Hawaii and Japan, it consists of two tiny islands that are scarcely big enough to take an airfield. The two treeless islands had a radio station, large fuel stores, ammunition depots, a seaplane base, an airport and other important military installations. At the beginning of June 1942, Midway was still the only strong base in American hands in the mid-Pacific west of Hawaii.

By 20 May 1942, Yamamoto had already radioed a detailed operational plan to his fleet. Owing to a technical breakdown, he was forced to use an outdated code that had long since been decrypted by the Americans. The head of radio intelligence on Hawaii, Capt. J. J. Rochefort, was thus able to learn of the intentions of the C-in-C of the Japanese Combined Fleet. During radio messages, the target was only referred to as "the objective," and so Rochefort tried to make his opponent reveal his secret. All Pacific bases were ordered to report possible difficulties, using a code he knew that the Japanese had already cracked. Shortly after Midway reported the nonfunctioning of its distillation plant, Rochefort intercepted the coded report from a Japanese station: "The objective" is suffering from a water shortage. He thus knew Japan's main target, and the following day he learned of its diversionary attack against Dutch Harbor in the Aleutians.

Yamamoto was convinced that the Americans had lost their carriers *Yorktown* and *Lexington* in the Battle of the Coral Sea (3–8 May 1942) and that the carriers *Hornet* and *Enterprise* were still in the South Pacific. After the loss of the US battleships in Pearl Harbor, he was not expecting a lot of resistance on Midway. Yamamoto presumed that Adm. Nimitz would despatch a considerable part of his forces northward to defend the Aleutians against the Japanese diversionary attack, and before Nimitz could recall this force, Yamamoto hoped to have occupied Midway. But the Japanese admiral had no idea that his opponent had his three remaining carriers, *Yorktown, Enterprise* and *Hornet,* in Pearl Harbor and that repairs to the *Yorktown,* which were to have taken three weeks, had been carried out in a record time of three days.

After hurried preparations, six aircraft carriers, seven battleships and ten heavy cruisers with escort units put to sea under Yamamoto's command. A landing fleet was to follow. Another force was to undertake the diversionary attack against the Aleutians. The scene of action between the Aleutians and Midway covered a distance of over 1,800 nautical miles from the north to the mid-Pacific.

The Japanese threw into this battle the largest concentration of ships and aircraft ever seen.

The Americans, who knew the Japanese plan of attack, positioned their three carriers at a specific distance from Midway and waited, together with the aircraft stationed on the island, for the Japanese fleet which was certainly concentrated, but was now to be used wastefully. Meanwhile, on 3 June 1942 as planned, the diversionary attack under Rear Adm. Kakuta set off for the Aleutians, albeit with scant success.

The morning of 4 June 1942, Vice-Adm. Nagumo sent off 108 of his carrier aircraft against Midway while a second, equally strong formation stood ready to take off and attack any enemy warships sighted. The first wave of aircraft from the carriers *Akagi, Kaga, Soryu* and *Hiryu* caused only slight damage on the island, as the Americans, warned by radar, got their aircraft off Midway in good time. Rear Adm. Fletcher, who commanded the task force and had concentrated his carriers far to the northeast of Midway, hoped that the aircraft from the air base on Midway would sight the enemy force before the Japanese had ascertained the position of his ships. And while the four carriers commanded by Nagumo carried out their first attack against Midway, the aircraft on the three American carriers commanded by Fletcher prepared to attack the Japanese.

Lt. Comdr. Tomonaga, leading the Japanese battle group, reported after the first bombing attack on Midway that a second would be necessary to eliminate the defences before a landing could be attempted. The counterattack against Nagumo's carrier force by aircraft stationed on Midway caused only slight damage (and the Americans themselves sustained some aircraft losses) but may well have been the reason for the disastrous decision made by Nagumo. He now decided that the ninety-three torpedo-loaded aircraft in reserve on the carrier decks, in case American warships appeared, should be bomb-loaded and deployed to deliver the final blow against Midway. Therefore, during the next sixty minutes while the weaponry was being changed and the formation that had attacked Midway landed for refuelling and re-arming, the four carriers were absolutely helpless against a surprise attack—all their fighters were airborne, warding off attacks launched by the American Midway-based aircraft.

Shortly after that, Vice-Adm. Nagumo received news that a formation of American ships had been sighted at a distance of some 280 nautical miles. At first the Japanese believed the formation was of only cruisers and destroyers, but at 8:20 A.M., a radio message stated that an aircraft carrier was also in this formation. This piece of news was extremely unpleasant for Nagumo, as most of his aircraft were now bomb-loaded, and his fighters were all in action. He had to wait until the last aircraft returned from the attack on Midway (Lt. Comdr. Tomonaga). In the meantime, American carrier aircraft without fighter protection approached in three waves, a total of forty-one slow torpedo bombers that attacked the Japanese carriers. Without scoring a single hit, thirty-five American machines were shot down by fighters or Flak.

In this moment, while the Japanese carriers were still warding off the torpedo bombers, dive bombers from the carriers *Enterprise* and *Yorktown* appeared. When the first Japanese aircraft, now re-armed with torpedoes instead of bombs, came up in the lifts to the flight deck—the fuel lines were full, there was oil, grease, torpedoes and bombs or ammunition all over the place—thirty-seven US dive bombers dived from 18,000 feet, and no defence was possible against them.

The carrier *Akagi,* Nagumo's flagship, was hit by bombs, which triggered a series of explosions between the aircraft lined up on deck ready to take off. The ship had to be abandoned. The carrier *Kaga,* on fire, sank several hours later, and the carrier *Soryu* went down within twenty minutes of sustaining three direct hits. The aircraft from the sole carrier remaining intact, the *Hiryu,* succeeded in damaging the *Yorktown* so badly that it too had to be abandoned. And then, twenty-four US dive bombers carried out a counterattack against the *Hiryu,* which was badly damaged and sank early 5 June 1942. The loss of their four aircraft carriers forced the Japanese to break off the engagement during the course of that day.

Those twelve minutes at midday on 4 June 1942 had a decisive effect on the outcome of the war in the Pacific: This had been the most rapid change in the fortunes of war that had ever been seen in the history of naval warfare. The occupation of Attu and Kiska in the Aleutian Islands could not compensate for this failure. In addition to the carrier *Yorktown,* the USA lost only one destroyer, 397 men and 150 aircraft. The Japanese lost 3,500 dead, of which 2,155 had been lost on the carriers alone, and approximately 330 aircraft. Naval supremacy in the Pacific now passed to the Americans and made it possible for them to go over to the offensive two months later in the southwest Pacific area on Guadalcanal. The failure at Midway was Japan's greatest defeat since 1598. The extent of this debacle was kept from the Japanese public and was not even made known to the Japanese government.

On Monday 7 June 1942, the German 11th Army (Col.-Gen. von Manstein) opened a large-scale at-

6/6/1942, naval battle near Midway, the Japanese cruiser *Mikuma* after an attack by carrier aircraft from the *Enterprise* and the *Hornet*. Capt. Fleming crashed his damaged aircraft on the *Mikuma* — the wrecked aircraft is on the after turret.

tack against the fortified position of Sevastopol. Units of the Soviet Black Sea Fleet (Vice-Adm. Oktyabrski) disembarked fresh troops and provisions at Sevastopol and took off wounded and civilians.

On Thursday 11 June 1942, German U-boats commenced mine-laying operations off the North American east coast.

On Friday 12 June 1942, a double-convoy operation for the provisioning of Malta commenced in the Mediterranean. A westbound convoy (Operation Harpoon) put to sea from Gibraltar, and an eastbound convoy (Operation Vigorous) put to sea from Alexandria. These two large convoys were protected by strong escort groups. The British Admiralty hoped that by means of these simultaneous operations, the air and naval forces of the Axis powers would be forced to divide their strength. It

was hoped that by these means at least a part of the supplies would reach Malta. Both convoys, however, suffered severe losses. German bombers sank one tanker, four freighters and two destroyers. The *U 205* (Lt. Comdr. Reschke) sank the cruiser *Hermione,* and the German S-boat *S 55* (Lt. Weber) sank the destroyer *Hasty.* Italian aircraft sank the *Tanimbar* (8,168 gross tons). Two British destroyers were lost through attacks by Italian warships and mines. Only two out of seventeen freighters and tankers reached Malta. The Italian Navy during this operation cooperated well with the air forces and achieved its operational objective: disrupting supplies to Malta. The Italians lost the cruiser *Trento,* and their battleship *Littorio* was damaged by a torpedo. After this defeat, the British Admiralty sent no more convoys from Egypt to Malta until the German forces retreated from Libya.

The night of 12/13 June 1942, Soviet submarines attempted to break through the German minefield "Seeigel" (sea urchin), which blocked the entrance from the Gulf of Finland to the Baltic. Out of thirty-three Soviet submarines, only five ships broke through by 19 June 1942. In summer 1942, a total of nine Soviet submarines operated in the Baltic.

At dawn on 13 June 1942, the first group of saboteurs, four men from the German foreign intelligence section, were put ashore from *U 202* (Lt. Comdr. Poser) in the US at Amagansett, Long Island, New York. Led by an agent named Dasch, they were beginning Operation Pastorius.

The night of 16/17 June 1942, the second group of saboteurs, four men led by agent Kerling, were put ashore by *U 584* (Lt. Comdr. Deecke) near Jacksonville at Ponte Vedra, Florida. All eight agents comprising the first and second groups of Operation Pastorius were betrayed by one of their number, a former resident in the USA, George J. Dasch. They were arrested 20 June 1942 by the FBI, brought before the courts and sentenced to death or long-term imprisonment.

On Friday 26 June 1942, Convoy PQ-17 (Comdr. Dowding) put to sea from Reykjavik bound for Archangel. Larger than any previous convoy, it was made up of thirty-six merchantmen. An agent in Reykjavik reported its departure to the Kriegsmarine in good time.

The night of 26/27 June 1942, the Soviet destroyer *Tashkent* succeeded for the last time in entering the beseiged port of Sevastopol. The destroyer landed 944 soldiers, ammunition, medical supplies and provisions, and evacuated 2,300 wounded and civilians. The destroyer also took with it the famous painting of the defence of Sevastopol in 1854/55 during the Crimean War. The *Tashkent* had made a total of forty voyages between Sevastopol and Novorossisk. Soviet submarines and aircraft now provided the only means of contact with the fortress. During their seventy-seven voyages, the submarines landed 3,300 tons of armaments and medical supplies as well as six hundred tons of fuel. They also took off 1,300 wounded and women and children.

The evening of 28 June 1942, 1/KF1G 406 (Coastal Wing) attempted torpedo strikes against Convoy PQ-17 using Heinkel He 115 floatplanes. The attacks were unsuccessful.

On Tuesday 30 June 1942, Stalin gave orders to evacuate Sevastopol.

In June 1942, German U-boats operating in the Atlantic and Mediterranean sank 131 merchant ships totalling 616,904 gross tons. German losses amounted to three U-boats.

During the first half of 1942, the USA extended their logistics and reinforced the security provided for lines of communication and supply. A new amphibious operations group was created for island warfare. The first phase of the American counter-offensive was designed above all to regain the initiative and penetrate the outermost defensive ring of the Japanese home islands.

In the West Atlantic, the introduction of the convoy system in American waters marked the end of the U-boat's golden age.

More and more bombing attacks were launched against German U-boat bases on the French Atlantic coast with US bombers operating during the day and RAF Bomber Command operating at night. Although scarcely any damage was suffered by the massive U-boat bunkers, the French ports were reduced to ruins. Dönitz stated that the British had made a serious mistake in that they did not bomb the bunkers on the Biscay coast while they were being built and still behind waterproof caissons and, as a consequence, in a particularly precarious condition.

The C-in-C U-boats gave orders that the highest possible figures for tonnage sunk were to be reached as quickly as possible and that the Battle of the Atlantic was to be conducted on the principles of economic deployment. In this way, the problem of the long voyages to and from the operational areas would partly be solved by the deployment of U-boat tankers. The German "heavies" were still lying inactive in the Norwegian fjords at this time. Churchill stated that British losses would have been far greater if the Germans had sent their large surface units out into the Atlantic. But Hitler was obsessed with the idea that an immediate invasion of northern Norway was planned.

1942

July–December

Wednesday 1 July 1942
The *German High Command* issued the following communiqué:

The war against enemy supply shipping was again successful in June. A total of 156 enemy ships aggregating 886,000 gross tons was sunk. In addition, fifty-eight enemy merchantmen were damaged by torpedoes or bombs.

Execution of Two Spies

Tuesday 7 July 1942, London
The *Reuters* News Agency reported:

Two agents of the German Secret Service were executed today in an English prison. One of them, George J. Armstrong, a British subject, was active in Gibraltar and radioed reports on shipping movements to the enemy by means of a secret transmitter.

7 July 1942
The *German High Command* issued the following communiqué:

(Special report) Since 2 July a large-scale operation by air and naval forces against enemy convoys to the Soviet Union has taken place in the waters between the North Cape and Spitzbergen, three hundred to four hundred nautical miles from the coast of northern Norway.

Bomber formations and German U-boats have attacked an Anglo-American convoy in the Arctic and largely destroyed it.

Soviet Attack on the Tirpitz

Thursday 9 July 1942, Moscow
The *High Command of the Red Fleet* issued the following communiqué:

After the *Tirpitz* had left its fjord and reached the open sea, its escort destroyers detected the periscope of one of our submarines that was attempting to break through the ring of escorts. The destroyers immediately attacked the submarine which, however, successfully fired its torpedoes. The battleship *Tirpitz* continued its voyage to escape a further attack. The destroyers could not take up pursuit of the submarine, as the battleship, having sustained some damage, urgently needed their protection. The morning of 7 July, Soviet reconnaissance units sighted German ships, including the *Tirpitz*, travelling southward along the Norwegian coast some distance from the point of attack. Whereas it cannot be assumed that the *Tirpitz* will sink as a result of the two torpedo hits scored by our submarine, the repairs may well take several months.

J. W. Stalin to W. Churchill
Thursday 23 July 1942

I have received your communication of 17 July.
. . . Our naval experts consider to be completely unconvincing the reasons put forward by the British to justify the cessation of convoys to the northern ports of the USSR. They are of the opinion that with good will and readiness to fulfill the contracted obligations, these convoys could be undertaken on a regular basis and cause the enemy heavy losses.

Naval Battle off the Solomon Isles

Sunday 9 August 1942, Tokyo
The *Imperial Headquarters* issued the following communiqué:

Since 7 August, Japanese naval units have been launching powerful attacks against Anglo-American naval units in the waters around the Solomon Isles and have dealt destructive blows to enemy warships, as well as transporters.

Italian Submarines Report Successes
9 August 1942, Rome
The *Italian High Command* issued the following communiqué:

Our submarines, under Comdr. Carlo Fecia di Cossato and Lt. Comdr. Francesco d'Alessandro, sank in the Atlantic two steamers and a tanker totalling 24,875 gross tons. Italian submarines operating in the Atlantic and the Mediterranean, Red and Black Seas have, according to closely scrutinised figures, sunk enemy warships and merchantmen totalling 1,018,971 tons.

Fighting on the Solomons
Monday 10 August 1942, Washington
The *US Navy Department* reported:

Our attacks against Japanese forces on the Solomons are continuing. We have, however, met determined resistance. It is as yet too early to state the results or give any estimates on losses sustained by the enemy or ourselves.

Aircraft Carrier Eagle *Sunk*

Wednesday 12 August 1942, London
The *Reuters* News Agency reported:

The aircraft carrier *Eagle* has been sunk by an enemy submarine in the Mediterranean. Most of the crew were saved. One of the submarines operating in the area was destroyed.

German Agents!
Friday 14 August 1942, Ottawa
The *Reuters* News Agency reported:

In Canada, wanted posters have been put up with photos of three agents said to have been landed by German U-boats.

A Ruse Saved a British Convoy
Monday 17 August 1942, Cairo
The *Associated Press* reported:

It can now be told that a ruse of war carried out by the C-in-C Mediterranean, Adm. Sir Henry Harwood, made it possible for the British convoy to Malta to break through. Shortly after the convoy put to sea from Gibraltar, the Axis powers had learned via their intelligence service the time the convoy left Gibraltar but assumed that the convoy was bound for Alexandria. . . . This ruse enabled the major part of the important convoy to reach Malta.

Secret report of the *SS Security Service* on the internal political situation:
No. 309, 17 August 1942 (Extract)

I. General: The special report on the successful attack against a strongly defended enemy convoy in the Mediterranean has brought forth great jubi-

lation. It was noted with particular satisfaction that all the tankers were sunk, and not one of the transporters reached its destination in Egypt. Conclusions have been drawn on the value and importance of the convoy because of the strong escort and because of the dangerous route the British chose to take through the Mediterranean rather than the longer but safer route around the Cape of Good Hope.

U-boat off the Coast of Brazil
Wednesday 19 August 1942, Rio de Janeiro
The *Exchange* News Agency reported:

Last night, a formation of Brazilian and American bombers sank off the coast of Sergipe province an Axis U-boat. This is presumed to be the same submarine that has already torpedoed five Brazilian steamers.

Dieppe Landing

Thursday 21 August 1942
The *German High Command* issued the following communiqué:

As previously announced in a special report, British, American and Canadian troops, together with French troops commanded by de Gaulle, landed yesterday on the French coast near Dieppe on a fifteen-mile front. The force, covered by strong air and naval units, was led by armored detachments. German coastal defence units repelled the attack, causing the enemy to suffer bloody losses.

No Invasion Attempt
20 August 1942, London
Combined Operations Headquarters issued the following communiqué:

Despite our declaration about the Dieppe raid broadcast by the BBC Wednesday at 6:15 A.M. via its French service, German propaganda has claimed that the raid was an attempted invasion thwarted by the Germans. In reality, reembarkation of most of the force commenced six minutes ahead of schedule and was completed according to plan nine hours after the first landing.

The Norwegian Tanker Fleet
20 August 1942, London
Shipping Minister Sunde, of the Norwegian government in exile in London, stated:

The Norwegian tanker fleet has a tonnage

amounting to two million tons, of which eighty percent is made up of fast motor vessels. During the first two years of war, forty percent of fuel imported by Great Britain was carried in Norwegian tankers.

Return from Dieppe
20 August 1942, in a port on the south coast of England
The *United Press Agency* reported:
   The last landing craft to return from Dieppe arrived here this morning. The Commandos brought with them German prisoners, including a number of officers. Several of the prisoners were wounded.

A Lull over Malta
Friday 21 August 1942, Valetta
The *Reuters* News Agency reported:
   The last seventy-two hours have seen a complete lull in the fighting around Malta. A few enemy aircraft have tried to approach the island, but no bombs were dropped. These have been the first three consecutive, undisturbed nights for many months.

Congratulations from Marshal Pétain
Sunday 23 August 1942, Paris
The German *DNB* News Agency reported:
   The German C-in-C West, Field Marshal Rundstedt, has received the following telegram from the military commander in France, Marshal Pétain. He and Pierre Laval, head of the government, have requested Ambassador de Brinon to pass on to the German High Command in France their congratulations for the defensive success by German troops and the rapid mopping-up operations on French soil.

Norwegian Fishing Fleet Seized

Tuesday 25 August 1942, Stockholm
The Swedish newspaper *Svenska Dagbladet* reported:

The greater part of the Norwegian fishing fleet has been requisitioned by the German authorities during the last few days. A number of the ship owners are said to have been pressed into German service.

Largest Naval Battle of the War

Thursday 27 August 1942
From *General MacArthur's Headquarters*:

The largest naval battle of the war has been raging since Sunday. Two more Japanese carriers, a battleship, several cruisers and transporters have joined the Japanese formation operating off the Solomons. It is assumed that the Japanese have brought up at least fifteen thousand men to win back the Solomons.

Japanese Release French Ship

27 August 1942, Vichy
The French *Havas* News Agency reported:

The French steamer *Maréchal Joffre* (11,732 gross tons) and the French freighter *Sikiang* (1,880 gross tons) have put into Saigon from Manila. These two ships — seized by the US authorities on the Philippines — have now been returned by the Japanese to the French.

A Submarine with Guerrillas

Monday 31 August 1942, Tokyo
The *Domei* Agency reported:

The Anglo-Australian attempt to land in darkness a small guerrilla group on New Britain Island from a submarine has — as reported from Rabaul — misfired. The submarine was sunk, and the group was taken prisoner by Japanese naval units. The enemy guerrillas were carrying a powerful short-wave transmitter to stay in contact with their headquarters.

Fierce Fighting on Madagascar

Friday 11 September 1942, London
The *Reuters* News Agency reported:

British marines, land troops, airmen and light fleet units yesterday commenced a new operation, primarily directed against the three important harbors on the island's western coast.

No Japanese Base

11 September 1942
The *Havas Agency* reported:

A statement issued by the governor of Madagascar states, among other things, ". . . at no time have we offered, or would we offer, any support or assistance for Japanese submarines or permitted Japanese aircraft to overfly the island. I make this declaration publicly and the American consul on this island can confirm that."

Surprise Attack Against Tobruk

Tuesday 15 September 1942, London
The *British Admiralty* issued the following communiqué:

Monday night, light naval units, in cooperation with commando troops, carried out a surprise attack against Torbruk. At the same time, RAF bomber formations were deployed. Despite bitter resistance, our troops went ashore and, before they were again embarked, caused the enemy severe losses. The withdrawal was not made without losses to ourselves, but they were to be expected in view of the determined resistance.

Wednesday 16 September 1942
The *German High Command* issued the following communiqué:

As already announced by special report, the British troops that landed near Tobruk the night of 14 September were, after heavy fighting, annihilated or taken prisoner by German and Italian troops acting in close collaboration.

Talks Break Down

Friday 18 September 1942, Vichy
The *Havas Agency* reported:

The state secretary for the colonies has stated that if the governor of Madagascar has attempted to enter into negotiations with the British commander in order to put an end to any bloodshed, British demands were such that no agreement could be reached. The governor-general is therefore determined to defend the island to the last.

Fighting on Madagascar Not Yet Over

Thursday 24 September 1942, Vichy
The report of the *Governor of Madagascar* to the state secretary for the colonies:

After they had defended each foot of the way to the gates of Tananarive, our troops were overwhelmed by the numerically superior enemy and were unable to prevent enemy forces entering the city. I have been in constant contact with Tananarive and was able to follow each phase of the heroic resistance. I must particularly emphasise the resolution shown by all our soldiers. The population remained calm and orderly; in so doing, they showed their belief in the French future of Madagascar.

9/14/1942, Madagascar, fighting between the British and French continued in the rough country. A British assault group in the French-held mountains.

Japanese Submarines in the Atlantic
Friday 25 September 1942, Berlin
The *DNB* Agency reported:

As already reported by the German High Command, Japanese warships have taken up contact with German and Italian units operating in the Atlantic. While German naval units in the Indian Ocean have been cooperating with Japanese units, from now on Japanese submarines will be deployed against enemy supply shipping in the Atlantic.

Swiss Radio Beromünster

25 September 1942
During the week under review, Berlin reported that a major naval battle has taken place on the Arctic route against an Allied convoy, whereby thirty-eight merchantmen carrying war material to Russia are said to have been sunk. Although the British have not denied this battle, conducted against the convoy by German aircraft and U-boats, they have described as a "gross exaggeration" the figure of ships sunk reported by Berlin. In the meantime, the convoy, which consisted of Russian, American and British ships, has entered its Russian port of destination. The number of ships that arrived safely, as well as the quantity of material delivered, is, of course, a military secret, and the Allies have not released any details in this regard.

Secret report of the *SS Security Service* on the internal political situation:
No. 321, 28 September 1942 (Extract)

The entry of Japan into the U-boat war in the Atlantic has been discussed at length. Although only one submarine has put into a German base, one must await results. For many of the population, the report is a further sign of Japanese activity.

Successes Achieved by Italian Submarines
Tuesday 6 October 1942, Rome
The Italian *Stefani* News Agency reported:

We have heard from Naval Headquarters that the Italian submarine *Barbarigo* has sunk in the Atlantic an American cruiser of the "Mississippi" class.

Thursday 8 October 1942
The *German High Command* issued the following communiqué:

During the night of 7 October, S-boats advanced toward the coast of Britain and attacked enemy convoy shipping at various points, sinking four merchantmen totalling 11,500 gross tons, as well as a patrol boat. They also scored torpedo hits on two other steamers but were unable, because of heavy defensive fire, to see if they sank.

W. Churchill to the First Lord of the Admiralty
8 October 1942

I am disquieted to learn that the German E-boats [i.e. S-boats] are getting the upper hand again and that they, by laying mines, are becoming a serious danger to east coast shipping. I had the impression that you had overtaken the mosquito fleet menace. Pray let me have a statement showing the position and also what measures you will take. We cannot possibly allow ourselves to be outmatched in mosquito warfare.

German U-boats off Cape Town

Saturday 10 October 1942, Berlin
The *German High Command* issued the following communiqué:

German U-boats have dealt Anglo-American shipping off South Africa a heavy blow. In a surprise attack, they sank twelve merchantmen totalling 74,000 gross tons in the Cape Town harbor approaches. Other U-boats—operating along the west coast of Africa off the Anglo-American naval base of Freetown; off the South American coast; in the Gulf of St. Lawrence; and during a heavy storm in the North Atlantic—sank ten ships totalling 67,000 gross tons. This number included the 15,000-ton refrigerator ship *Andalusia Star*, which was carrying a cargo of valuable foodstuffs, mainly frozen meat, to Britain. And so our U-boats sank twenty-two ships totalling 141,000 gross tons over a number of war theaters.

Brazil's Part in the U-boat War
Wednesday 14 October 1942, Washington
The *Exchange* News Agency reported:

Naval secretary Knox made known in a press interview that a number of Brazilian warships were already in action on the side of the Allies in the war against the U-boat. The ships were under the command of US Rear Adm. Ingram. A large number of warships are under construction in Brazilian shipyards.

British Commando Operations
Saturday 17 October 1942, Vichy
The *United Press Agency* reported:

The German authorities in Paris announced a short while ago that the British had recently mounted a number of Commando raids on the French coast in the area around Dieppe. All these raids had failed. According to these reports, a British motorboat attempted to put ashore Commandos on the Normandy coast near Anneville, ten miles northwest of Coutances, the night of 7 October toward midnight. They were repelled by German coastal batteries. At the beginning of September the British made a surprise attack on an outpost of the German coastal patrol service on Les Casquets, west of Aurigny Isle. The night of 18 September, a Commando group of six British officers attempted to land near Cherbourg. The boat was sunk by gunfire whereby three officers were drowned, and the remainder swam ashore and were taken prisoner. The German reports list more commando-style raids undertaken by the British, which were directed against weakly defended points; all the raids failed. No further details on these incidents are available.

Heavy Fighting between the British and French

Wednesday 21 October 1942, Nairobi
The *British GOC-in-C East Africa* has issued the following communiqué:

Early Monday morning our troops advanced on Madagascar south of Ambositra. They carried out a flanking movement and attacked strong French forces occupying strongly fortified positions. The enemy was overcome, and fifty prisoners were brought in, including Col. Metras. Our side suffered no losses. The total number of prisoners taken during the operations around Ambositra now exceeds eight hundred. In addition, two guns and a large number of mortars and heavy machine guns were captured.

Right: U-boat base at St. Nazaire, back from an operational patrol! ". . . a beaming jumble of U-boat men . . ."

Left: British leaflet dated autumn 1942 gives advice to U-boat crews.

Where Will the Allies Land?

Friday 6 November 1942
The *Chief of the Italian General Staff, Marshal Cavallero*, recorded in his diary a telephone conversation overheard between Göring and Kesselring:

Göring: According to our calculations, the convoy must be within the operational range of the Luftwaffe in the next forty to fifty hours; everything must be made ready.

Kesselring: Herr Reichsmarschall, if this should relate to an attempted landing in North Africa?

Göring: In my opinion, they will land in Corsica, Sardinia, Derna or Tripoli.

Kesselring: A North African harbor would seem more likely.

Göring: Possible. But not a French one.

Kesselring: If the convoy should pass through the Strait of Sicily, I shall have time enough.

Göring: If they don't want to go to Sardinia, they will certainly go through the Strait of Sicily, which has not been mined at all by the Italians. You should make them aware of that.

French Forces on Madagascar Capitulate

6 November 1942, Vichy
The *Havas Agency* reported:

With the complete agreement of the French government, and in view of the impossibility of further resistance, the governor on Madagascar de-

cided on 5 November to hold cease-fire negotiations with the enemy.

Daily Memorandum of the Reich Press Secretary
6 November 1942

The minister spoke on the events in North Africa and placed all his colleagues under an obligation to allow no pessimism to make itself felt in public during these critical days. He explained the military situation in brief outlines and expressed the hope that Field Marshal Rommel would, as he has so often done before, master the situation.

US Landing in French North Africa

Sunday 8 November 1942, Washington
The *US War Department* issued the following communiqué:

During the hours of darkness, our army, navy and air force units commenced landing operations at numerous points along the French North African coast, which were necessary to protect this area against the increasing threat by the Axis powers. Measures have been taken to inform the French population by radio and leaflets of our activities. These combined operations, undertaken by US forces with units of the Royal Navy and Royal Air Force, are under the command of Gen. Eisenhower, the Allied C-in-C, North African theater of operations.

Above: The British press reports heavy fighting against the French in North Africa.

Right: 11/5/1942, Madagascar, French troops surrender to the British.

Allied Landings Repelled
8 November 1942, Vichy
The *Ministry of Information* issued the following communiqué:

This morning at 3:30, after a heavy bombardment, an Allied landing was attempted in the area of Algiers. At 4:00, enemy motor torpedo boats were repelled. Further attempts to land troops at various points along the North African coast, above all in the area around Oran, were thrown back with heavy losses. Adm. Darlan and Gen. Juin, who lead our operations, have taken all necessary measures at the command of Marshal Pétain.

French Coastal Batteries against US Destroyers
8 November 1942, Algiers
The *Havas Agency* reported:

At 10:30 A.M. a bitter struggle took place in Algiers harbor between French coastal batteries and a French sloop, and an American destroyer that had put into the harbor. The destroyer put ashore troops, who attacked the seaplane base and a power station. A coastal battery finally succeeded in taking the destroyer under fire.

Monday 9 November 1942
The *German High Command* issued the following communiqué:

The Anglo-American fleet units and troopships in the waters north of Algiers have, since 6 November, been under attack day and night by German and Italian bomber formations. According to reports received so far, six warships and four merchantmen have been hit by heavy-caliber bombs.

Heavy French Losses
Wednesday 11 November 1942
From *General Eisenhower's Headquarters*:

A major naval battle has taken place along the Moroccan coast between American and French naval units, as French destroyers intervened in the fighting and attempted to prevent troops from landing. The resistance offered by the French fleet is mainly concentrated around the area of Casablanca, where Adm. Hewitt immediately deployed powerful forces that completely destroyed the French units. Following the example of the naval battles in the Pacific, the US Navy air force used here too its dive bombers with success. Lying in the harbor of Casablanca, the French battleship *Jean Bart* directed heavy gunfire against units of the US Navy, until the battleship was set on fire by

bombers or artillery fire. The land battles along the Atlantic coast increased in intensity, particularly in the areas of Rabat and Casablanca. US armored units and motorised infantry pushed forward close to Casablanca and attacked the city from the south and north.

The Germans March into Unoccupied France
11 November 1942, Vichy
The *Havas Agency* reported:
  As announced over Radio Paris this morning, German troops have received orders to march into the nonoccupied zone. The radio station also broadcast a message from Hitler to Marshal Pétain.

German Forces in Tunisia?
11 November 1942, London
The *Reuters* News Agency reported:
  German fighters and troop-transport aircraft have landed in Tunisia.

Casablanca Capitulates

11 November 1942, Casablanca
The *Exchange* News Agency reported:
  Late yesterday evening, French naval forces and coastal batteries in the area around Casablanca ceased firing. The garrison has offered to surrender.

Operational Again
Thursday 12 November 1942, New York
Admiral Nimitz, C-in-C US Pacific Fleet, issued the following communiqué:
  A number of US warships damaged during the attack on Pearl Harbor are again ready for action. They have been repaired much more swiftly than originally estimated.

Darlan to the French Fleet in Toulon
Friday 13 November 1942
From *General Eisenhower's Headquarters:*
  Adm. Darlan, during a radio message, has ordered the French fleet lying in Toulon to leave port and join the Allies, or at least take the ships where the Germans cannot seize them.

French Resistance Broken

13 November 1942
From *General Eisenhower's Headquarters:*
  With the exception of a few remote bases, the resistance of French forces in French North Africa has ceased.

Fictitious Orders from Admiral Darlan?
13 November 1942, Berlin
The *DNB* Agency reported:
  The DNB Agency has described as false the orders of Adm. Darlan put out by the Anglo-American authorities. Adm. Darlan has not even seen, leave alone approved, these orders.

In Four Days and Fifteen Hours
13 November 1942, San Francisco
The *Associated Press* reported:
  The shipyards of Henry Kaiser and Co. in San Francisco have established a record for shipbuilding that borders on the unbelievable. A merchant ship of 10,500 gross tons was built within four days and fifteen hours from the time it was laid down. Less than forty-eight hours later, the ship was fully equipped and ready for service. The previous record in this yard was ten days.

Swiss Radio Beromünster

13 November 1942
  While attention has been directed completely toward the events in Egypt, where Rommel's army has been on the retreat westward since the British 8th Army broke through at El Alamein, the news came last Sunday that American troops had landed in French North Africa. . . . Seen in the context of the overall war situation, the next objective must be both the 8th Army's offensive in Egypt and then Cyrenaica, as well as the landings in Morocco and Algeria in order to bring lines of

communication in the Mediterranean again under Allied control. It would be of the utmost importance for the Allied supreme command again to control the shortest sea route to India and China after having had to use for so long the enormously extended route around the Cape of Good Hope.

New Naval Battle in the Solomons
Saturday 14 November 1942, Washington
The *US Naval Department* issued the following communiqué:

A number of naval battles that commenced the night of 13 November in the waters around the Solomons are continuing. Both sides have suffered losses. No details will be released before the battle has finished.

Norwegian Seamen
Sunday 15 November 1942, Stockholm
Svenska Dagbladet reported:

Regarding the growing number of Norwegian seamen who flee as soon as their ship approaches the Swedish coast en route from Norway to Germany, the government shipping office in Norway has, at the request of the German occupation authorities, announced that seamen who leave their ship without permission will be punished with imprisonment or death.

State of Emergency in Toulon
Monday 16 November 1942, Toulon
The *Havas Agency* reported:

By order of the naval prefect of Toulon, Adm. Marquis, access to Place Toulon will in future be forbidden to everyone who does not actually live there. Exemptions from this rule will be given only in urgent circumstances.

Goebbel's Speech
Tuesday 17 November 1942, Wuppertal, City Hall
German party comrades!

. . . Churchill had already declared in 1938, 1939 and 1940 that the U-boat danger had been eliminated. But the U-boat danger has become for England more and more of a problem; in fact, in October — the worst weather month — the figure of tonnage sunk rose to 750,000 tons and, in the first half of November, the figure has exceeded that for the entire month of October. But these are figures which cannot be denied. The Americans say that's no problem, we'll build — we'll build these freighters again — no problem. The Americans build a hundred thousand airplanes and eighty thousand tanks; and now an American shipping company with the name of Kaiser has even found a recipe to build a ten thousand tonner in ten days. Now I'm just waiting for the day when an American can manage to deliver a tonner, a ten thousand tonner immediately to order "ready to take away upon ordering."

US Naval Victory in the Solomons
17 November 1942, Washington
The *Reuters* News Agency reported:

In the opinion of some observers, the US Pacific Fleet has achieved the greatest naval victory of the entire war in the waters around the Solomons where twenty-three Japanese ships have been sunk.

Secret report of the *SS Security Service* on the internal political situation:
No. 336, 19 November 1942 (Extract)

The reporting on French North Africa was seen as insufficiently clear by a large part of the population. It could not be deduced whether the French

Challenge to Hitler:
"Admiral Darlan orders the French fleet in Toulon to join the Allies," reports the British press, falsely, on 11/13/1942.

in North Africa were putting up a resistance or not. This omission led to a criticism of the way in which the news from North Africa was reported. This impression was only softened by the reports on the successes achieved by our bombers and U-boats. The hope was widely expressed that we would be successful in preventing enemy supplies from getting through and so defeat the Americans' operations.

German Steamer Torpedoed in the Baltic
Sunday 22 November 1942, Stockholm
Svenska Dagbladet reported:
A Soviet submarine has torpedoed a German steamer of eight thousand tons in the Skerries of Abo. Apparently the submarine commander thought that the steamer was carrying German troops; in fact, there were one thousand Russian prisoners of war on board who, with the exception of approximately fifty men, were rescued.

German Troops in Toulon
Friday 27 November 1942, Vichy.
The *Havas Agency* reported:
The naval base at Toulon was today occupied upon orders issued by Hitler. This measure was adopted to prevent treacherous actions on the part of certain Gaullist sympathisers, acts of sabotage which, despite assurances given, had been prepared and were about to be implemented.

Daily Memorandum of the Reich Press Secretary
27 November 1942
The scuttling of the French fleet in Toulon should only be mentioned within the framework of the High Command reports. In our propaganda, we could point out that the word of honor of a French general or admiral can have no validity for us, as can be evidenced by the course of events with Darlan, Giraud and Nogues.

Tuesday 1 December 1942
The *German High Command* issued the following communiqué:
As already announced in a special report, German naval and air units sank a total of 166 ships aggregating 1,035,200 gross tons in November. An-

other 102 ships were heavily damaged, a considerable number of which must be considered total losses.

The Position in Toulon
1 December 1942, Toulon
The *Havas Agency* reported:
The thick clouds of smoke from burning oil tanks still hang over the city of Toulon. The ships *Algérie*, *Dupleix* and *Colbert* are still in flames. The *Strasbourg* has been run aground.

Daily Memorandum of the Reich Press Secretary
1 December 1942
The successes achieved in the U-boat war and the pessimistic voices heard on the other side should be advanced more strongly in order to brighten up the mood in Germany a bit. The population is worrying rather more on the situation in the East than is at present called for, and so the U-boat successes could be more strongly emphasised.

Swiss Radio Beromünster

Friday 4 December 1942
A number of various accounts of the course of events in Toulon early on 27 November have, in the meantime, been published. Two facts have generally been admitted and recognised: 1) the sudden—and, according to the German version,

11/10/1942, Casablanca, the French battleship *Jean Bart* after an attack by US dive bombers.

"lightning fast" — entry of German troops into the naval base; 2) the orders given by the French flag officer in Toulon, Adm. Delaborde, to scuttle all ships lying in Toulon — an order duly carried out by the crews. Scuttling is, however, the last defence left to a fleet when threatened with the danger of falling into the hands of the enemy. The best known example of this course of action from the history of the war at sea was the scuttling of the German High Seas Fleet in Scapa Flow after their handing over to the British in June 1919.

Operation Habbakuk: Artificial Icebergs in the Atlantic as Air Bases
W. Churchill to General Ismay
Monday 7 December 1942

I attach the greatest importance to the prompt examination of these ideas, and every facility should be given to the Chief of Combined Operations for developing them. He will report to me weekly on the setting up of the organization and the preliminary work. I do not of course know anything about the physical properties of a lozenge of ice 5,000 feet by 2,000 feet by 100 feet, or how it resists particular stresses or what would happen to an iceberg of this size in rough Atlantic weather, or how soon it would melt in different waters at different periods of the year.

The advantages of a floating island or islands, even if only used as refuelling depots for aircraft, are so dazzling that they do not at the moment need to be discussed. There would be no difficulty in finding a place to put such a "stepping stone" in any of the plans of war now under consideration. The scheme is only possible if we make nature do nearly all the work for us and use as our materials sea water and low temperature. The scheme will be destroyed if it involves the movement of very large numbers of men and a heavy tonnage of steel or concrete to the remote recesses of the Arctic night.

Something like the following procedure suggests itself to me. Go to an icefield in the far north, which is six or seven feet thick but capable of being approached by ice-breakers; cut out the pattern of the ice-ship on the surface; bring the right number of pumping appliances to the different sides of the ice-deck; spray on salt water continually to increase the thickness and to smooth the surface. As this process goes on, the berg will sink lower in the water. There is no reason why, at the intermediate stages, a trellis-work of steel cables should not be laid to increase the rate of sinking and give stability. The increasing weight and depth of the berg will help to detach the structure from the surrounding ice-deck. The necessary provision for oil fuel storage and motive power can be left at the proper stages. At the same time, somewhere on land the outlet of huts, workshops and so forth

will be made. When the berg begins to move southward, so that it is clear of the ice floes, vessels can come alongside and put all the equipment, including ample Flak, on board.

Strategy and Tactics

JULY TO DECEMBER 1942

On Wednesday 1 July 1942, the German 11th Army (Col.-Gen. von Manstein) completed the conquest of Sevastopol. The fall of Sevastopol also had political effects. Turkey now permitted ships of the Axis powers access through the Bosporus into the Black Sea.

On the early morning of 1 July 1942, Cpl. E. Reper of the 3/KFlGr 906 (coastal wing), flying a reconnaissance seaplane type Bv 138 C, sighted Convoy PQ-17 near Jan Mayen Island. Even before the convoy passed into the sea area kept under surveillance by German aircraft, four cruisers and six destroyers, under the command of Rear Adm. Hamilton, took up close cover positions. Adm. Tovey built up the outer cover group with the greater part of the Home Fleet, the battleship *Duke of York*, the carrier *Victorious*, the cruisers *Cumberland* and *Nigeria* as well as fourteen destroyers, together with the US battleship *Washington*.

When Convoy PQ-17 reached the area north of Bear Island during the evening of 4 July 1942, the Admiralty received a report that the battleship *Tirpitz* had been transferred to the Altafjord — nearly two hundred miles north of Narvik — where the heavy cruisers *Admiral Scheer* and *Admiral Hipper* were already lying. At this, the First Sea Lord, Admiral of the Fleet Sir Dudley Pound, sent a radio message at 8:11 P.M., "Immediate. Cruiser Force withdraw to the westward at high speed." As Rear Admiral Hamilton had received orders not to risk his cruisers, it seemed pointless to him to expose the even weaker six destroyers to the gunfire of the German capital ships. Cruisers and destroyers now set off at maximum speed from the presumed danger. At 9:23 P.M. the Admiralty radioed the order, "Immediate. Owing to threat from surface ships, convoy is to disperse and proceed to Russian ports." This was in direct contradiction of the experience gained that a convoy has a chance of escaping the attacker only if it stays close together. Adm. Tovey stated, "Scattering the convoy was nothing more than sheer bloody murder." The defenceless freighters were now only protected by a few armed fishing trawlers and corvettes. And now began the war's biggest convoy battle to date. German torpedo bombers, dive bombers and U-boats attacked the convoy, which the escorting cruisers and destroyers had left halfway between Iceland and Archangel for days on end.

It was not until Sunday 5 July 1942 at 11:00 A.M. — in other words, twelve hours after Convoy PQ-17 had scattered — that the *Tirpitz* left the Altafjord with its escorts, Operation Rösselsprung (knight's move). Adm. Kusnezov stated, "The German ships that put to sea with the object of intercepting Convoy PQ-17 were sighted on 5 July by the submarine K-21 commanded by Capt. 2d Grade Lunin. Lunin attacked the *Tirpitz*, firing four torpedoes. The German staff, uneasy because their formation was being threatened by British aircraft and Soviet submarines, gave orders to return to base. Capt. Lunin was awarded the Order of the Red Banner for his action." This Soviet torpedo attack is, however, entered neither in the log of the battleship *Tirpitz* nor in the archives of the Naval High Command.

The ships belonging to Convoy PQ-17, including American and Dutch vessels, were scattered across the Barents Sea and became easy prey for German

11/27/1942, Hitler marches in: German troops occupy the naval base at Toulon, the French Navy scuttles its own ships.

aircraft and submarines. Between 5 and 10 July 1942, 130 Ju 88 dive bombers, 43 He 111 bombers and 29 He 115 floatplanes belonging to Air Fleet 5 (Col.-Gen. Stumpff) sank eight ships; the nine U-boats forming Group Eisteufel (ice devil) sank nine ships; and, in addition, U-boats sank, administering the coup de grâce, seven more ships that had been damaged by air attacks. The total losses sustained by Convoy PQ-17 were twenty-four ships (143,977 gross tons). The cargoes lost with the freighters comprised 3,350 lorries and jeeps; 430 tanks; 210 aircraft; and 99,316 tons of spare parts, foodstuffs, armor-plating, ammunition, etc. The Luftwaffe lost five aircraft. Of the thirty-six ships making up Convoy PQ-17, only twelve reached Murmansk.

From that date on, the Arctic route was regarded by Allied seamen as a death route. Churchill wrote, "This was one of the most melancholy naval episodes in the whole of the war. The gloomy fate of each ship was the stuff of a true Odyssey." Adm. Kusnezov stated, "I immediately informed Stalin of the tragedy of the convoy. He was very angry at the British Admiralty's reaction. How could the warships possibly have left the convoy alone? The forces employed by the British were considerably superior in this case. Did it really seem necessary to disperse the convoy? Stalin asked me. I replied that so far as I was aware, there were no compelling reasons to do this."

Adm. Tovey suggested to Churchill that the Arctic convoys be terminated immediately, ". . . until either such time as the airfields in Norway are eliminated or until the onset of the Arctic winter, which will again provide some protection." Stalin protested most strongly, "The Red Army needs the weapons, ammunition and the equipment more than ever, having regard to the German summer offensive which has just begun."

At this time, there were again 108 fully laden freighters in Iceland ready to put to sea. Despite the strong reinforcements provided by heavy units of the US Navy, the British Admiralty did not have sufficient escort vessels at its disposal to secure the convoys effectively. Convoys on the northern route were held back until the commencement of the Arctic nights. Some of the supplies were directed over the Persian route. Stalin replied, "The Persian route cannot be a substitute for the northern convoys, and one cannot conduct war without risk or losses."

On Thursday 9 July 1942, Hitler warned the C-in-C West, Field Marshal von Rundstedt, by telex, "It is highly probable that enemy landings will shortly take place in the area of Command West." In Hitler's opinion, this supposition was sufficiently backed up by "an increasing number of statements made by agents and other results of intelligence activities, strong concentrations in transit ports in South England, and the recent holding-back of the Royal Air Force. Those areas which are to be seen as the most endangered are, above all, the Channel coast, and the area Dieppe–Le Havre in Normandy."

Upon being informed of the British Dieppe plans (Operation Jubilee), Hitler was so convinced of the accuracy of his sources of information that he immediately transferred from the Eastern Front to France the Waffen-SS divisions "Leibstandarte Adolf Hitler" and "Das Reich," the infantry division "Grossdeutschland" and the "Hermann Göring" brigade.

On Sunday 19 July 1942, the last five U-boats remaining in American coastal waters received orders from Dönitz to transfer their operational areas further eastward, as there would be no further opportunities of attacking the strongly escorted convoys proceeding along the North American coast. The North Atlantic convoy route was again to be the main operational area for the U-boats. Churchill stated that the main battle would again be fought along the North Atlantic shipping lanes.

In July 1942 the fourth phase of the Battle of the Atlantic came to an end. This phase had commenced in the middle of January 1942 with Operation Paukenschlag. The phase was characterised by the individual operations carried out by German U-boats off the north and central American seaboards. There was an average of fifty-four at sea.

Left: North Sea, German mine-sweepers in action

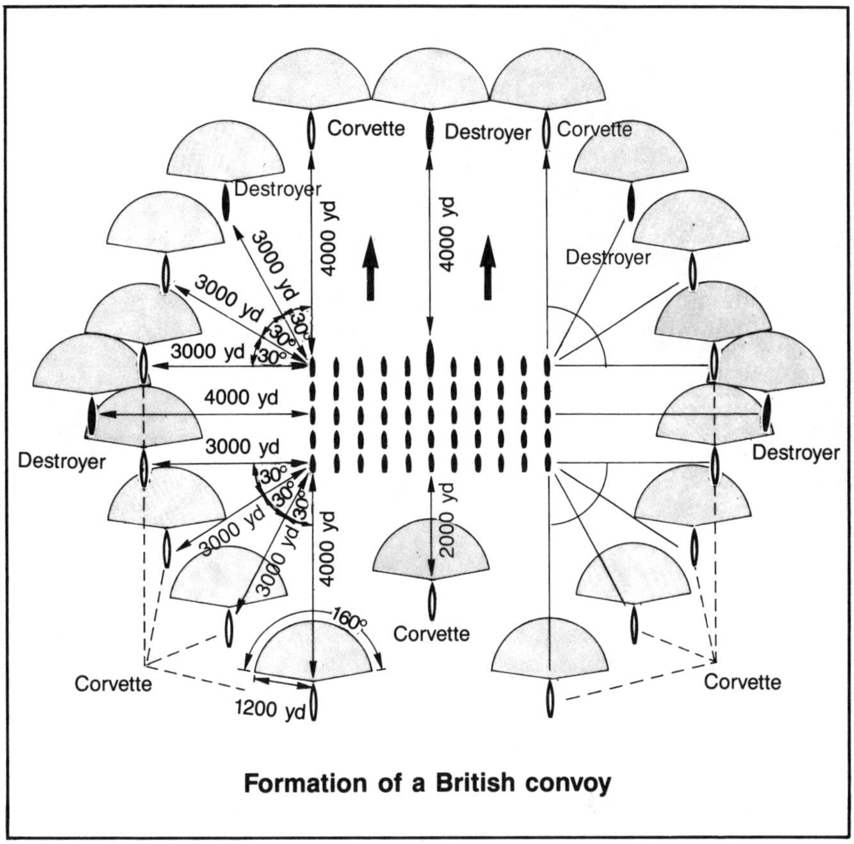

Corvette
Destroyer
Corvette
Destroyer
4000 yd
4000 yd
Destroyer
3000 yd
3000 yd
30°
30°
3000 yd
30°
4000 yd
Destroyer
3000 yd
30°
30°
30°
3000 yd
3000 yd
4000 yd
2000 yd
Destroyer
160°
Corvette
Corvette
Corvette
1200 yd
Formation of a British convoy

Right: The fanlike segments in front of the escort vessels describe the area scanned by Asdic (segment 160°). At a speed of 24 knots, a U-boat could be detected under normal conditions at a distance of 1,100 to 1,500 yards.

On Sunday 2 August 1942, the movement of US troops to Northern Ireland and the British mainland commenced within the framework of Operation Bolero. These troop movements were to be made using the largest passenger liners available to the Allies at that time, such as the *Queen Elizabeth* (83,673 gross tons), *Queen Mary* (81,235 gross tons) and the Dutch *Nieuw Amsterdam* (36,287 gross tons), although their deployment caused tactical problems. Their considerable speed (up to twenty-eight knots) made it impossible to give escort cover along the whole route. And so these ocean giants were committed to travelling alone under the control of the British Admiralty. During one voyage, they carried up to fifteen thousand soldiers—almost an entire division—across the Atlantic. Thanks to the Enigma secrets, the Admiralty could in each case choose the safest route, a route not threatened by U-boats. Consequently, over two million soldiers were transported to Europe within a few months.

On Wednesday 5 August 1942, the Japanese transport submarine *I-30* (Comdr. Endo) put into Lorient. This submarine had taken part in operations in the Indian Ocean on 20 April 1940 from its base in Penang and also took part with its aircraft in the Japanese midget-submarine operations off Diégo-Suarez.

On Friday 7 August 1942, under Operation Watchtower, eleven thousand men of the US Marine Corps made a surprise landing on Guadalcanal, the largest of the Solomon Islands, which was occupied by the Japanese in May 1942. This was the start of the successful policy of "island hopping." Using this strategy, the Americans started to reconquer the Pacific isles that had been occupied by the Japanese. Island hopping was based on a firm belief in the aircraft carrier. The Japanese underestimated the strength of their opponents and, first of all, attacked with insufficient forces. The fate of Guadalcanal depended on possession of the almost completed airfield, which the Americans promptly occupied the next day and named Henderson Field after an air force officer who had been killed at Midway. The bridgehead that arose around the runway remained endangered, as Japanese infantry kept breaking through the jungle. Victory was certain to be achieved on Guadalcanal by the side that could first establish air supremacy so that their combatant troops on the islands could be provisioned.

On Saturday 8 August 1942, twenty-six Japanese carrier aircraft attacked US ships bringing in supplies and reinforcements for Guadalcanal. Seventeen aircraft were shot down by antiaircraft guns and fighters. The pilots of two dive bombers type Aichi D3A "Val," which were hit, dived with their bo.nb loads onto the US transporter *G.F. Elliott*, later abandoned. This was the first intentional suicide mission (kamikaze) by Japanese airmen.

The most important task of the British Admiralty in the Mediterranean was to maintain the fighting ability of the island of Malta. Because of the failure of the double convoy operation, Harpoon and Vigorous (12–16 June 1942), the Admiralty was forced to carry out a new operation code-named Pedestal.

On Monday 10 August 1942 a convoy of fourteen merchantmen and tankers, bound for Malta, put to sea from Gibraltar, escorted by the aircraft carriers *Victorious*, *Indomitable* and *Eagle*, the battleships *Rodney* and *Nelson*, four cruisers and fourteen destroyers (Vice-Adm. Syfret).

At the same time, a diversionary convoy commanded by Rear Adm. Vian left Alexandria. By midday, a German reconnaissance had already spotted the westward convoy.

The next day, *U 73* (Lt. Comdr. Rosenbaum) sank the aircraft carrier *Eagle* (Capt. Mackintosh). The convoy suffered further losses caused by Italian submarines and German bombers. And so the Royal Navy lost five of the original fourteen merchantmen of the convoy transporting supplies to Malta, plus a carrier, two cruisers and a destroyer. The Admiralty now increasingly deployed converted submarines for bringing in supplies to Malta.

On Saturday 15 August 1942, three American fast transports succeeded for the first time, and without loss, in bringing in supplies for the troops fighting on Guadalcanal.

On Sunday 16 August 1942, the heavy cruiser *Admiral Scheer* (Capt. Meendsen-Bohlken) put to sea from Narvik, escorted by three destroyers. The task of these units was to disrupt the Siberian sea route to the Far East, in an operation code-named Wunderland (wonderland). The submarines *U 251* (Lt. Comdr. Timm) and *U 601* (Lt. Comdr. Grau) supported the operation by carrying out a reconnaissance of the limits of the ice floes.

On Monday 17 August 1942, the last preparations were being undertaken in southern England for the six thousand British and Canadian soldiers who were to land near Dieppe under the command of Lord Mountbatten, C-in-C Combined Operations.

At the same time, in occupied France, in Angers, sand table exercises were being carried out at the headquarters of the German Air Fleet 3 (Field Marshal Sperrle). These exercises had been ordered by Field Marshal von Rundstedt. The theme of the exercise was the British landing near Dieppe. Gen. Fröhlich acted as umpire: "We would have thrown out of France any Allied troops that had landed in less than five days." Lt. Gen. Kessler, head of Operations Department at OB West, said to his officers, "We know that the city of Dieppe is the sole objective of the main attack and that on both sides of the city, two support attacks will be put into operation to cut off the city from the flank and rear." This advance knowledge, for which the British and Canadians had to pay a heavy price forty-eight hours later, was attributable to the German B-Dienst (radio intelligence service), which had succeeded in decrypting some of the Royal Navy keys and had continually intercepted radio transmissions in the Portsmouth and Newhaven areas, the ports of embarkation for this operation.

On Wednesday 19 August 1942, 6,086 troops of the 4th and 6th brigades of the Canadian 2nd Division, together with thirty tanks, and Commandos 3 and 4 with nine infantry landing craft, were landed in Dieppe, a seaside resort on the French coast. They were escorted by eight destroyers, a number of motor torpedo boats and gunboats as well as light units — a total of 252 warships — with strong air cover (74 Allied bomber and fighter squadrons). The landing parties met unexpectedly

Right: 8/19/1942, Dieppe, British commandos taken prisoner; at the front, Lt. G. Brett; behind him, Lt. T. Watson; Sgt. R. Bradly last in the row.

Left: August 1942, Nevada (USA), this accurate mock-up of a Japanese Nagato-class battleship looks like a ghost in the middle of the desert. It was used by American bomber crews for target practice.

stiff resistance. The British Intelligence Service had estimated that the German garrison consisted merely of one battalion of older personnel.

After three hours, the remainder of the landing parties withdrew. They suffered heavy losses and had to abandon their armor. Anglo-Canadian losses amounted to sixty-eight percent of the troops deployed (4,359 men, of which 2,190 were taken prisoner and 1,179 were killed), 33 landing craft and small vessels, one destroyer damaged and 106 aircraft lost. During the fighting for a German radio station near Berneval/Dieppe, US Lt. E. Loustalot was killed. He was the first American soldier to be killed in France during World War II. German losses amounted to 591 men, 48 aircraft, a submarine hunter and a motor vessel.

The National Socialist propaganda machine now presented the Anglo-Canadian "armed reconnaissance" as a "futile invasion."

On Monday 24 August 1942, the Japanese transport submarine *I-30* (Comdr. Endo) put to sea from the U-boat base at Lorient, where it had arrived on 5 August 1942 as the first Japanese submarine in that port.

On the same day in the Pacific, the first carrier battle took place since the fateful air and sea battle at Midway. Around 4:00 P.M., aircraft from the *Saratoga* attacked the Japanese carrier *Ryuju*, scoring ten hits with bombs and one hit with a torpedo, causing the ship to sink rapidly. At the same time, Adm. Nagumo had sent up dive bombers, with fighter escorts from the *Zuikaku* and *Shokaku*, which dived on the carrier *Enterprise* from a height of fifteen thousand feet. The *Enterprise* withdrew in flames and had to be replaced by the *Wasp*. The Japanese then broke off the engagement without seeking a conclusion, and the Americans evaluated this maritime engage-

ment as their victory. The US Navy frustrated the Japanese attempt to land fifteen hundred soldiers on Guadalcanal.

Also on 24 August 1942, the "Knospe" meteorological detachment (deployed from 25 September 1941 in Signehamma on Spitsbergen) was taken off by *U 435* (Lt. Comdr. Strelow). This detachment had, among other things radioed detailed weather reports for the decisive forty-eight hours of the Channel breakthrough on 12/13 February (Operation Cerberus).

As the increasing surveillance of the Atlantic by Allied long-range reconnaissance aircraft had made the deployment of weather ships almost impossible, the German Navy established meteorological stations on the edge of the polar region (Spitsbergen and East Greenland) to gather the weather reports essential for their operations. The meteorological detachments, equipped with the latest instruments, radioed back their weather reports under the protection of the polar night.

In addition, German U-boats set up automatic weather stations (weather-reporting radio equipment) in the Arctic and Atlantic. These instruments could work for up to two months without any maintenance. Every twelve hours they surfaced and broadcast data on atmospheric temperature, atmospheric humidity, atmospheric pressure and wind direction and wind strength. These high-precision automata — the Allies had nothing like them at that time — were prized trophies for British fishermen to whom the Admiralty paid a bounty of £1,000 for every one handed in.

On Tuesday 25 August 1942, the heavy cruiser *Admiral Scheer* (Capt. Meendsen-Bohlken) put into the Kara Sea north of Novaya Zemlya and sighted the Soviet ice-breaker *Sibiryakov* (Capt.

Kazarev). As the ice-breaker did not comply with the order to heave to, the *Admiral Scheer* opened up with its heavy guns. Even while sinking, the *Sibiryakov* returned fire from its three old 7.6-cm guns.

On Thursday 27 August 1942, the *Admiral Scheer* reached the Dickson roads, one of the most important harbors along the northern sea lane, and opened fire on three Soviet merchantmen, the *Dieshniev, Revolutionary* and *Kara*. After that, the *Admiral Scheer* opened fire on the radio station on the island and the town of Dickson. The energetic resistance by a Soviet coastal battery caused Capt. Krancke to refrain from the planned landing on the island.

On Friday 28 August 1942 after an unsuccessful deployment, the *Admiral Scheer* received orders to break off Operation Wunderland.

On Monday 31 August 1942, the Italo-German armored divisions in Africa (Field Marshal Rommel) attempted to regain the initiative in North Africa. The offensive commenced on the southern sector of the El Alamein front with the objective of defeating Gen. Montgomery's 8th Army, occupying Alexandria and advancing to the Suez Canal.

Grand Adm. Raeder stated, "Rommel's offensive was at first so successful that the real objective of all operations in North Africa, the occupation of Suez, seemed to be within our grasp, and Field Marshal Rommel was authorised to continue this offensive until that point was reached. In so doing, the original plan was given up, in which first Malta was to be taken and then the advance to Suez was to begin—this was a mistake that soon proved to be fatal."

In August 1942 the fifth phase (until May 1943) of the Battle of the Atlantic began. Increased sea and air surveillance undertaken off the American coasts forced the U-boats to transfer their operations back to the open seas against shipping between America and Britain. This phase was characterised by U-boat pack operations against North Atlantic convoys and individual operations in the central and southern areas of the Atlantic. On average, there were 102 U-boats at sea.

In August 1942 German U-boats operating in the Atlantic and Mediterranean sank 105 merchant ships totalling 517,295 gross tons. German losses amounted to nine U-boats.

On Wednesday 2 September 1942, Rommel had to break off his offensive as the promised supplies—above all, fuel, oil and petrol—did not arrive. Rommel stated, "The failure of this offensive meant that our last chance to reach the Suez Canal had been lost. We could now only wait until the considerable British industrial output and, even more importantly, the enormous industrial potential of America would finally lead to a turning point against us."

At the beginning of September 1942, after the military situation of the Soviet Union had given rise for concern because of the German advance on Stalingrad and the Caucasus, Churchill and Roosevelt decided that despite all the risks, supply convoys would again be sent to Murmansk.

On Monday 7 September 1942, Convoy PQ-18 put to sea from Iceland.

By the next day, Tuesday 8 September 1942, a Bv 138 seaplane from KF1Gr 706 located Convoy PQ-18 (39 merchantmen and one tanker) in the area of Jan Mayen Island. The covering force comprised two destroyers, two Flak ships, two submarines, four corvettes, three motorboats, four trawlers and—for the first time on the northern route—the escort carrier *Avenger* with twelve old Hurricanes from the first production run before the war, and several submarine-chaser aircraft on board, escorted by two destroyers. The C-in-C Home Fleet, Adm. Tovey, stated, "It's a joke, transporters full of modern Hurricanes for the Soviet Union being protected by such antiquated fighters." The close escort group comprised one light cruiser, sixteen destroyers; the cover group, three heavy cruisers; the outer escort group, two battleships, one light cruiser and five destroyers. Nevertheless, through bombing attacks Convoy PQ-18 lost ten ships totalling 55,915 gross tons and, through U-boats, three ships totalling 19,742 gross tons. German losses amounted to twenty aircraft and three U-boats.

After this latest failure, Churchill again stopped convoy traffic along the Arctic route. Until December 1942, only individual ships sailed to Murmansk and Archangel. In addition to the shortest route around North Cape, which, owing to its being within the operational range of the Luftwaffe and Kriegsmarine, was also the most dangerous, Allied supplies were conveyed to the USSR by two other routes. Merchantmen sailed from the USA across the Pacific to Vladivostok, but because of political considerations—the Soviet Union had signed a neutrality pact with Japan on 13 April 1941—the ships had to sail under the Soviet flag exclusively. For these purposes, the USA provided some one hundred freighters totalling more than five hundred thousand tons. A number of ships sailing under the Soviet flag were sunk by American submarines that were conducting unrestricted submarine warfare in the Pacific at that time. The disadvantages of this route were the insufficient capacity of Soviet Pacific ports, and the limited efficiency and capacity of the Trans-Siberian Railway.

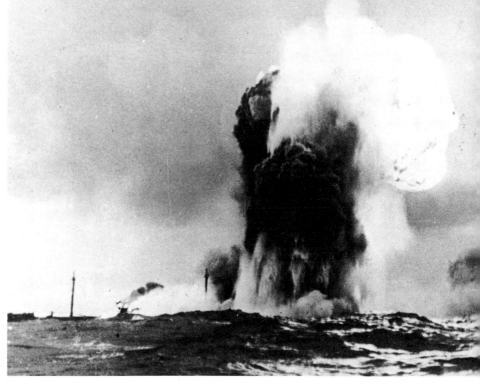

The fifth phase of the Battle of the Atlantic began in August 1942 with U-boat packs attacking convoys: A tanker blows up.

The third supply route to the USSR led from US ports on the Atlantic Coast, around Africa, and then through the Persian Gulf and Iran to South Russia. This route was flawed by the fact that it exceeded fifteen thousand nautical miles, and also by the enormous transport costs involved in the voyage, which lasted for approximately seventy-five days.

At daybreak on 9 September 1942, a Japanese Yokosuka E14Y1 floatplane (piloted by a naval officer, N. Fujita) took off from the deck of the submarine *I-25* (Comdr. Tagani). The pilot flew over the extensive woodlands on the coast of Oregon, fifty miles west of Cape Blanco, where he dropped incendiary bombs.

Early 10 September 1942, fighting on Madagascar again flared up. The transports *Dilwara*, *Dunera* and *Empire Pride* disembarked the British 29th Brigade near Majunga. After occupying Majunga, which was defended by a few French battalions, the 22nd East African Brigade (Brig. Dimoline) was disembarked. Supported by armored units, the formation pushed forward in the direction of Tananarive. French troops tried to hold up the advance in the rough country of the interior by blowing up bridges.

On the evening of 12 September 1942, *U 156* (Comdr. Hartenstein) sank the British troopship *Laconia* (19,695 gross tons), commanded by Capt. Shark, in the South Atlantic northeast of Ascension Isle. The troopship was carrying 3,000 men, including 1,800 Italian POWs guarded by 103 Polish troops. Surprisingly, the strongly armed *Laconia* (2 ships guns, a number of heavy Flak guns,

pom-pom Flak guns, as well as rocket and depth-charge launchers) was also carrying a large number of women and children. Comdr. Hartenstein used radio transmission in clear to appeal to all ships in the area to support him in the rescue operation. The C-in-C U-boats ordered *U 506* (Comdr. Würdemann), *U 507* (Comdr. Schacht) and the Italian submarine *Cappellini* (Comdr. Revedin) to proceed to the scene of the sinking. At the same time, he requested the French Navy in West Africa to take part in the rescue of survivors as well. The British Admiralty sent the auxiliary cruiser *Corinthian* and the freighter *Empire Haven* to the scene. The U-boats took survivors on board to the limit of the submarines' carrying capacity; in addition, they took the lifeboats in tow. Shortly afterward, a Liberator belonging to the USAAF (343 Bombardment Squadron, 2d Lt. Harden) made five bombing attacks on the U-boat, although its gun was draped with a Red Cross flag and its crew notified the pilot, using the international code, of the emergency situation existing. Some of the lifeboats were destroyed by bombs and a large number of survivors killed. *U-506*, with 142 survivors on board, was also attacked by an aircraft. Dönitz gave order — known as the "Laconia order" — that in such a situation, U-boats must leave the survivors so as not to endanger the U-boats. Dönitz stated, "After the sinking of the *Laconia*, I risked my U-boats in picking up survivors, while, for their part, the enemy risked the lives of British survivors in order to destroy U-boats even while they were engaged in rescue operations. I therefore had to issue orders exclud-

ing such activity in the future, and took away from U-boat commanders their freedom to exercise their own discretion on whether the danger of an air attack allowed rescue operations or not." Three French warships — the heavy cruiser *Gloire*, the gunboat *Dumont d'Urville* and the minesweeper *Annamite* — took 1,083 survivors off the U-boats.

In the middle of September 1942 there were, for the first time, twenty U-boats concentrated simultaneously on operations in the North Atlantic. The tactics employed by the C-in-C U-boats were now based on first ascertaining the convoy position and then concentrating the U-boats along the route before the convoy crossed the "gap" in the middle of the Atlantic. This gap lay outside the operational radius of Allied long-range aircraft. Churchill wrote, "It was now that we felt most acutely the lack of sufficient numbers of very long-range (VLR) aircraft in the Coastal Command." When the convoy reached the gap, the U-boats commenced concentrated operations and did not withdraw until the convoy had again reached the area covered by aircraft operating from the other side of the Atlantic. These tactics were made possible by the B-Dienst, which in the autumn of 1942 frequently succeeded in decrypting instructions given to convoys on the course to be taken. Support groups, organised specifically as U-boat hunters, were now deployed for the first time. Churchill stated, "The first of these support groups, which later became a most potent factor in the U-boat war, consisted of two sloops, four of the new frigates now coming out of the builders' yards, and four destroyers."

The night of 13/14 September 1942, the British raid on Tobruk (Operation Agreement) was carried out to relieve the British 8th Army, engaged in heavy fighting with the Italo-German armored divisions. The British destroyers *Sikh* and *Zulu*, with 350 Royal Marines on board, together with twenty-one fast motorboats carrying 150 men, attempted a landing operation in the harbor of Tobruk. The frontal assault carried out by these weak forces failed under the fire of the coastal batteries. Out of twenty-one fast motorboats, only two succeeded in putting ashore troops, who were, however, annihilated. The destroyer *Sikh* attempted to penetrate the harbor, despite strong defensive fire, to support the motorboats. The *Sikh* was, however, sunk. The Flak cruiser *Coventry* and the *Zulu* were destroyed by bombs. In addition, five boats were lost and MTB 314 was captured by German minesweepers. The survivors capitulated at daybreak; 576 soldiers and seamen were taken prisoner.

During September 1942 the Japanese succeeded in landing almost an entire division on Guadalcanal by means of destroyer operations dubbed the "Tokyo Express" because of their regularity. As a result, the Americans reinforced their units on the island. To prevent troop transports reaching Guadalcanal, twelve Japanese submarines were concentrated on the approaches to Guadalcanal where they acted as patrol vessels.

On Tuesday 15 September 1942, the Japanese submarine *I-19* (Comdr. Narahara) penetrated the US escort vessels off Guadalcanal and fired a salvo of six Long Lance torpedoes at the American task force. The first torpedo hit the battleship *North Carolina*; the second hit the destroyer *O'Brien*; three more torpedoes hit the aircraft carrier *Wasp*; and the last torpedo narrowly missed the aircraft carrier *Hornet*. This torpedo salvo was the most successful in the history of maritime warfare. The *Wasp* had to be abandoned, the *O'Brien* sank, and the *North Carolina* had to spend a long period in

Right: 9/15/1942, in the Pacific, another victim of the notorious Long-Lance torpedoes goes down in flames—the US carrier *Wasp.*

Left: 9/13/1942, in the South Atlantic, U-boats rescuing survivors from the *Laconia*

Below: Transporting six U-boats overland—a journey of more than 1,500 miles to the Black Sea

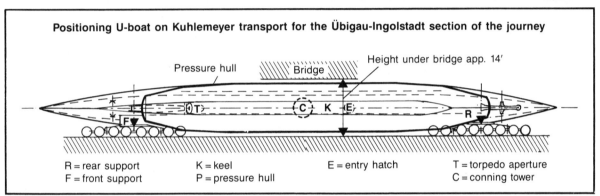

Positioning U-boat on Kuhlemeyer transport for the Übigau-Ingolstadt section of the journey

Pressure hull   Bridge   Height under bridge app. 14′

R = rear support   K = keel   E = entry hatch   T = torpedo aperture
F = front support   P = pressure hull   C = conning tower

the repair yards.

The night of 15/16 September, Italian frogmen set off from the *Oltera* (4,595 gross tons) lying in Algeciras harbor. The *Oltera* had been converted into a secret base for frogmen and manned torpedoes. The frogmen's target on this operation was British shipping lying in the Gibraltar roads, where they succeeded in sinking the freighter *Ravens Point* (1,787 gross tons).

On Sunday 27 September 1942, the German commerce raider ship no. 23 *Stier* (Capt. Gerlach) was lost. In conditions of poor visibility, the *Stier* had been surprised by the armed American freighter *Stephen Hopkins* (7,181 gross tons), commanded by Capt. Buck. Although the German commerce raider had succeeded in sinking the American ship, it had been so badly damaged that it was scuttled by its own crew. Successes achieved by ship no. 23 *Stier* amounted to four merchantmen totalling 29,400 gross tons. The crew of the *Stier* were picked up by the commerce raider *Tannenfels.*

The night of 28/29 September 1942, the Japanese floatplane piloted by N. Fujita took off from the *I-25* (Comdr. Tagami) to bomb the wooded area on the Oregon coast near Cape Blanco for the second time. This attack was the last ever carried out on the American mainland.

On orders from Grand Admiral Raeder, suitable ships were to be transferred overland to the Black Sea from the North and Baltic seas. In August 1942 the U-boats *U 9* (Lt. Comdr. Petersen), *U 18* (Lt. Arendt), *U 20* (Lt. Grafen), *U 23* (Lt. Arendt) and *U 24* (Lt. Lenzmann), previously stationed in Gdynia, put to sea for Kiel, where the submarines' diesel motors, electric motors and batteries were dismantled and their towers removed by oxyacetylene cutters. This was the first stage of a 1,500-mile journey overland. According to a plan conceived by a Mr. Baumgarten, an engineer and departmental manager in the shipbuilding offices of the Deutsche Werke Kiel AG, the empty hulls of the six U-boats, weighing 112–138 tons each, were to be tilted by an angle of ninety degrees so that they could be transported under the bridges along the autobahn, firmly secured on the heaviest transport lorries available, the Kuhlemeyer trucks. The most powerful traction machines available in Germany,

Right: Captain Grossi — two false reports, the Knight's Cross of the Iron Cross

Kälble tractors and Faun machines, were provided by the Luftwaffe. The U-boats — tilted and packed in floatable pontoon crates — were pulled by tugs through the Kaiser Wilhelm Canal and along the Elbe as far as Übigau near Dresden. From this point onward, at a speed of five miles per hour, the journey proceeded three hundred miles along the German autobahn, with its 150 bridges, numerous gradients, bends and several hilly stretches, as far as Ingolstadt.

Then the U-boats were again packed in their pontoon crates and transported on the non-navigable Danube as far as Regensburg. In Linz, the U-boats were again straightened up, and refitting the engines and all dismantled parts began. The operational U-boats were positioned between two large river barges, to disguise the nature of the transport, and towed to Galatz. From here the U-boats made for Constantsa under their own power. After this operation, unique in the annals of the German Navy, the Black Sea Flotilla was formed under the command of Lt. Comdr. Rosenbaum, who, as the commander of *U 73*, had sunk the British aircraft carrier *Eagle* in the Mediterranean.

Thirty more S-boats, twenty-three evacuation craft, fifty naval lighters, twenty-six submarine hunters, eighty-four launches, thirty tugs, eighteen motorboats, four dredgers, two paddle steamers, two ice-breakers and 153 coastal craft were transported on the route over the autobahn and the Danube by summer 1944.

In September 1942, German U-boats operating in the Atlantic, Arctic and Mediterranean sank ninety-seven merchant ships totalling 472,653 gross tons. German losses amounted to eleven U-boats.

On Tuesday 6 October 1942, the Italian submarine *Barbarigo* (Capt. Grossi) attacked, southwest of Freetown, the British corvette *Petunia* (925 tons), which Capt. Grossi thought was an American battleship of the Mississippi class: 33,500 tons! He judged the explosions of the depth charges dropped to be the sounds of his own torpedoes striking home on the American battleship, and reported it sunk. The next day Capt. Grossi was awarded the Knight's Cross of the Iron Cross by Hitler. But already on 20 May 1942, upon sighting a US battle group at night, Grossi had fired two torpedoes and claimed that he had sunk a battleship of the Maryland class. In fact, his torpedoes had just missed the destroyer *Moffet*. This was the first Knight's Cross awarded to a U-boat commander for a false report.

On Thursday 14 October 1942, the British motor torpedo boat *MTB 236* (Sub-Lt. Drayson) sank the German commerce raider ship no. 45 *Komet* (Capt. Brocksien) with the entire crew. The *Komet* was attempting to pass from Le Havre through the English Channel into the Atlantic. The Admiralty had heard of the planned breakthrough by means of Enigma decrypts and sent off eight MTBs as well as five destroyers with orders to intercept the *Komet*.

On Friday 15 October 1942, the "Nussbaum" meteorological detachment was put ashore in Signehamma on Spitsbergen from the *U 377* (Lt. Comdr. Köhler). The detachment (six men), led by the meteorologist Dr. F. Nusser, took over the station set up by the "Knospe" meteorological detachment (25 September 1941–24 August 1942), where they were to remain until 1943.

On Saturday 24 October 1942, the US fleet formation (Adm. Halsey) received orders to form a

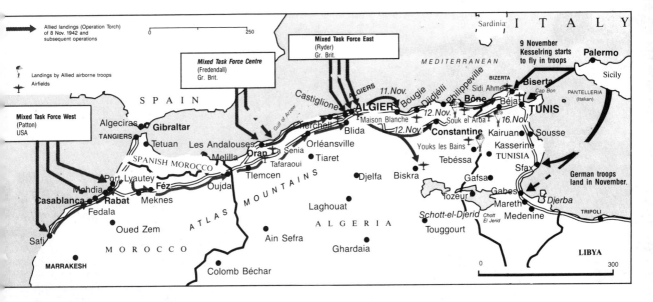

Above: Operation Torch, November 1942, Allied landings in North Africa

Map labels: Mixed Task Force West (Patton) USA; Mixed Task Force Centre (Fredendall) Gr. Brit.; Mixed Task Force East (Ryder) Gr. Brit.; Allied landings (Operation Torch) of 8 Nov. 1942 and subsequent operations; Landings by Allied airborne troops; Airfields; SPAIN; Gibraltar; Algeciras; TANGIERS; Tetuan; Les Andalouses; Oran; La Senia; Tafaraoui; Melilla; SPANISH MOROCCO; Port Lyautey; Mehdia; Casablanca; Rabat; Fedala; Safi; Féz; Meknes; Oued Zem; MARRAKESH; Colomb Béchar; ATLAS MOUNTAINS; MOROCCO; Ain Sefra; Tlemcen; Oujda; Tiaret; Orléansville; Djelfa; Laghouat; Ghardaia; Touggourt; Biskra; ALGERIA; Castiglione; Cherchell; Blida; Maison Blanche; ALGIERS; Gulf of Arzew; 11. Nov.; Bougie; Djidjelli; Philippeville; Sidi Ahmed; Bizerta; Bône; Béja; Souk el Arba; 12. Nov.; 12. Nov.; Constantine; 16. Nov.; Youks les Bains; Tebéssa; Kairouan; Kasserine; TUNISIA; Sfax; Gafsa; Tozeur; Schott-el-Djerid; Chott El Jerid; Gabes; Mareth; Medenine; Djerba; TRIPOLI; LIBYA; German troops land in November.; MEDITERRANEAN; Sardinia; ITALY; Cap Bon; PANTELLERIA (Italian); Sousse; 9 November Kesselring starts to fly in troops; Palermo; Sicily; TUNIS; German troops land in November.

ring around the Santa Cruz islands with Task Force 16 (the carrier *Enterprise*, one battleship, two cruisers and eight destroyers) and Task Force 17 (the carrier *Hornet*, four cruisers and six destroyers) to prevent Japanese units from gaining access to Guadalcanal. At midday the following day, an American Catalina flying boat sighted two Japanese aircraft carriers, but the American group was unable to locate them.

Subsequently, on 25 and 26 October 1942 in the area around Santa Cruz, east of the Solomons, a carrier battle took place with the Japanese advance group of Vice-Adm. Kondo and the main group of Vice-Adm. Nagumo. The carrier *Hornet* was sunk, a battleship and another carrier damaged. A number of hits were scored on the two Japanese carriers.

On Saturday 31 October 1942, sixty nautical miles to the northeast of Port Said, the *U 559* (Lt. Comdr. Heidtmann) was sunk by the British destroyers *Dulverton* and *Hurworth*, together with an aircraft from 47 Squadron RAF. The Admiralty's Intelligence Division succeeded in salvaging a new Enigma-M 4 enciphering machine from the U-boat. British cryptanalysts were now able to conclude their efforts, which had been going on since 1 February 1942, to decipher the Triton code.

By the end of October 1942, the total of U-boats deployed in the Atlantic rose to forty. The U-boat arm was now in a position to form groups in the West and East Atlantic.

Churchill stated, "In September and October the Germans reverted to the earlier practice of submerged attack by day. With the larger numbers now working in the 'wolf packs', and with our limited resources, serious losses in convoy could not be prevented."

In October 1942 U-boats operating in the Atlantic, off South Africa and in the Indian Ocean sank ninety-one merchantmen totalling 585,360 gross tons. German losses amounted to fifteen U-boats.

On Thursday 5 November 1942, the French governor of Madagascar accepted the conditions proposed by the British and surrendered with the rest of his forces.

The night of 7/8 November 1942, Operation Torch commenced. This operation comprised the Allied landings with five hundred ships, protected by the Royal Navy, at various points in Morocco and Algiers (Supreme Commander General Eisenhower – headquarters in Gibraltar). The Allies met with stiff resistance at practically all points from French naval units loyal to the Vichy government, who could not forget the Royal Navy's malicious attacks on Mers el–Kébir and Dakar in 1940, the fighting off the Syrian coast in 1941 and the British invasion of Madagascar.

The mighty Allied invasion fleet, appearing off the North African coast, was a complete surprise for the German war direction. Grand Admiral Raeder said, "The German naval staff, upon receiving the first news of the sighting of the transporters, at first reckoned with an attack taking place farther eastward. Accordingly, countermeasures were realised too late . . . The favorable opportunity had been lost. The propitious situa-

tion in the Mediterranean had been reversed."

At around 7:51 A.M. on Monday 9 November 1942, fighting flared up in Casablanca with intensive aerial engagements between French fighters and aircraft from the carrier *Ranger* (Lt. Comdr. Durgin). The still unfinished French battleship *Jean Bart* (Capt. Barthes) opened fire on Allied warships with its one operational turret until US bombers silenced it. The light cruiser *Primauguet* (Capt. Mercier) and six destroyers under the command of Adm. de Lafond carried out an attack on the Western Task Force. The US battleship *Massachusetts* (Comdr. Whiting), together with the cruisers *Augusta* (Lt. Comdr. Hutchins), *Brooklyn* (Rear Adm. Denebrink), *Tuscaloosa* (Comdr. Gillette) and *Wichita* (Rear Adm. Low), sank or damaged ships belonging to Adm. de Lafond's force.

At the same time, the British destroyers *Malcolm* and *Broke* attempted to break through the barriers into the harbor of Algiers and land US commandos. The coastal battery and French bombers sank the *Broke*, and the *Malcolm* had to withdraw under heavy fire. Two hundred American commandos were taken prisoner by the French.

In Oran, Allied warships sank five French destroyers, six submarines, a minesweeper and several smaller vessels. The French gunboat *Surprise* put to sea and, armed only with one old 10-cm gun, joined battle at first light with several British destroyers with, according to British reports, "a bravura worthy of a better cause." It went down with fifty-five men. In all, eight hundred French personnel lost their lives in the fighting against Allied landings in North Africa. Most of these losses were suffered by the French Navy.

Also on 9 November 1942, German troops arrived in Tunisia, where they had been directed by the C-in-C South, Field Marshal Kesselring, to forestall occupation by the Allies and to cover Rommel's retreat. Standby units of the newly appointed air commander for Tunis (Col. M. Harlinghausen), comprising 284 soldiers, landed on the airfield at El Aouina near Tunis. Supported by elements of 5 and 11 Parachute battalions, they now advanced to create a defensive line; some 25,000 men of the French Tunisian divisions pulled back. As there were no surface vessels available, the Naval High Command ordered the C-in-C U-boats to make submarines available to engage the Allied landing fleet.

In carrying out their attacks against the Allied landing fleet, German U-boats used the new-style FAT torpedoes (homing torpedoes) for the first time. Thanks to a supplementary installation, which was activated before the torpedo was fired, the torpedo began to turn after a preliminary straight run. The FAT torpedo could follow an escort vessel practically unaimed in this swinging movement, even when the escort was carrying out evasion maneuvers.

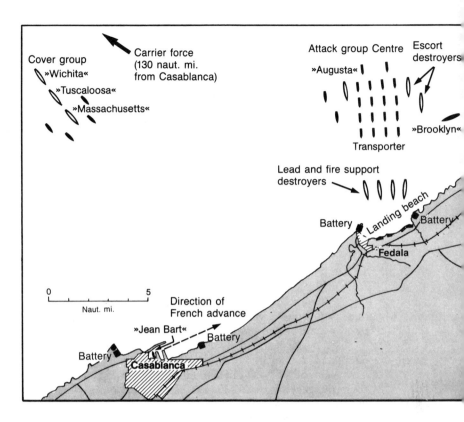

Left: 11/8/1947, Operation Torch, US battleship in an artillery duel with French naval units off the North African coast

Right: Landing in Casablanca under Operation Torch on 8 November 1942

Map labels:
Cover group »Wichita« »Tuscaloosa« »Massachusetts«
Carrier force (130 naut. mi. from Casablanca)
Attack group Centre »Augusta«
Escort destroyers
»Brooklyn«
Transporter
Lead and fire support destroyers
Battery — Landing beach — Battery
Fedala
0 — 5 Naut. mi.
Direction of French advance
»Jean Bart« — Battery
Battery
Casablanca

On Wednesday 11 November 1942 at 7:00 A.M., the 1st Army (Col.-Gen. Blaskowitz) with the Army Group Felber (Gen. Felber) crossed the demarcation line into unoccupied France (Operation Anton).

In the meantime, British forces had landed at Bougie, 130 miles east of Algiers, while the following day, 12 November 1942, airborne troops occupied Bône and, in so doing, forestalled the German paratroops. The Allies now advanced along the road to Tunis. On 15 November 1942, American airborne forces landed in Youks les Bains in support, and British units landed in Souk–el Arba on 16 November 1942. Despite that, the Axis powers won the race to Tunisia. The Germans flew in reinforcements and even withdrew some four hundred aircraft from the Eastern Front to Tunis. The weather came to their rescue. Heavy rainfall transformed the airfields of North Africa into seas of mud, while the Axis powers had firm runways at their disposal on Sardinia. They were therefore able to bomb Algiers, Oran, Bougie and Bône almost daily.

On the same day, in the Indian Ocean the Indian minesweeper *Bengal* (Lt. Comdr. Wilson), which was escorting the Dutch tanker *Ondina* (6,341 gross tons), sighted two suspicious silhouettes on the horizon and made toward them. They were the Japanese commerce raiders *Hokoku Maru* (10,438 gross tons) and *Aikoku Maru* (10,500 gross tons).

These two heavily armed ships doubled as supply ships for Japanese submarines. Both commerce raiders opened fire with their six 15.2-cm guns, the *Bengal* replied with its sole 7.5-inch gun. *Bengal* immediately scored several hits on the *Hokoku Maru*, which thereupon exploded. The minesweeper, which had already received two hits, put up a smokescreen. At the same time the *Aikoku Maru* opened fire on the tanker *Ondina*, which started to sink after a number of hits. The crew took to the lifeboats. *Aikoku Maru* now ceased firing in order to go to the assistance of the crew of the *Hokoku Maru*. During this operation, the crew of the tanker returned to their burning ship, extinguished the flames and managed to reach their port of destination, Fremantle.

On Thursday 19 November 1942, Churchill appointed the then C-in-C Submarines, Adm. Horton, as C-in-C Western Approaches. This distinguished World War I submarine commander, a competent organiser, was charged with bringing about a turning point in the Battle of the Atlantic. Dönitz stated, "Under the command of Adm. Horton, British defence against the U-boat made great strides in material and technical improvement but, above all, in tactical direction and increased fighting spirit."

On Friday 27 November 1942, Operation Lilo took place. At 4:25 A.M. the first German Panzers headed toward Fort Lamalgue in the French naval base at Toulon. The tanks belonged to an advanced detachment of the II SS Armored Corps (SS-Obergruppenführer and General of the Waffen-SS, Paul Hausser), which was to take Toulon and the French fleet on Hitler's orders. Adm. Marquis was taken by surprise while asleep, but his deputy succeeded in advising the fleet commander, Adm. de Laborde, on his flagship *Strasbourg*, who immediately issued orders to scuttle all vessels. The greater part of the French High Seas Fleet — three battleships, one aircraft tender, seven cruisers, twenty-eight destroyers, three torpedo boats and sixteen submarines (sixty-one ships totalling 225,000 tons) — was scuttled by its French crews. Four French submarines escaped. The submarine *Le Glorieux* left harbor under fire; the commander, Lt. Comdr. Meynier, returned fire from his conning tower with a pistol in his hand.

Adm. de Laborde told the German officer commanding that he would only leave his flagship upon the orders of his government superior. At the request of the Germans, a radio message was sent from Vichy: "I have just heard that your ship is sinking. I command you to abandon it immediately. Philippe Pétain." It was only when they heard this radio message that the Allies in North Africa learned of the events in Toulon.

On Monday 30 November 1942, the German commerce raider ship no. 10 *Thor* (Capt. Gumprich), lying in Yokohama harbor, fell victim to an explosion, unexplained to this day, that took place on board the German freighter *Uckermark* (Comdr. von Zatorski) lying alongside. The success achieved by the commerce raider *Thor* on its second voyage amounted to ten merchantmen totalling 56,036 gross tons sunk or taken prize.

In November 1942 German U-boats operating in the Atlantic, Mediterranean, Arctic, off South Africa and in the Indian Ocean sank a total of 118 merchantmen totalling 743,320 gross tons. German losses amounted to thirteen U-boats.

Churchill stated, "In November the Allied losses at sea were the heaviest of the whole war, including 117 ships of over 700,000 tons, by U-boats alone."

Dönitz stated, "One of the causes of the high success rate for November was the reduction of escort vessels allocated to merchant convoys in favor of landing operations in North Africa."

At the beginning of December 1942 the Naval Intelligence Division of the Admiralty succeeded in cracking the Triton code, which was used by the C-in-C boats for radio traffic with submarines operating in the Atlantic. On the other hand, just as the Allies learned of the positions of the U-boats maintaining contact by decrypting their radio messages, so the German U-boats could determine the positions of the convoys from the radio messages they received from the Allies — thanks to the

B-Dienst cryptanalysts commanded by Capt. Bonatz. In 1942 the B-Dienst located almost fifty percent of the Allied North Atlantic convoys.

The night of 6/7 December 1942, commando Operation Frankton began. The British submarine *Tuna* (Lt. Comdr. Cavenagh-Mainwaring) transported six canoes of the Royal Marine Boom Patrol Detachment (RMBPD), commanded by Maj. E. G. Hasler, to the Gironde estuary. The objective was to sink blockade-runners lying in the port of Bordeaux by means of limpet mines. A canoe was badly damaged when it alighted on the water, and three more were lost because of heavy seas. Only two folding canoes with their crews, totalling four men (Maj. Hasler and Marine Sparks, Cpl. Laver and Marine Mills), succeeded in reaching the harbor by travelling upstream at nights. They carried out their attack the night of 10/11 December. Four large freighters, the *Alabama, Dresden, Portland* and one more, were damaged. Only Maj. Hasler and his crewman, Marine W. E. Sparks, managed to get back to England after several months trekking across France and Spain. The rest of the men were either drowned or shot upon being taken prisoner in accordance with Hitler's "Order on Commandos."

It was not known until after the war that one of the resistance groups had planned a series of limpet mine attacks against shipping lying in the port of Bordeaux. These attacks were to start the night of 12 and 13 December 1942. Those dockworkers in Bordeaux who knew about the plan were not a little surprised when, on the morning of 12 December, a number of mysterious explosions shook the harbor, and the ships in the harbor basin, one after the other, went down twenty-four hours before the planned attack.

Late the evening of 8 December 1942, during an action with the escort vessels of Convoy HX-217 proceeding from Halifax to England in the Atlantic south of Cape Farvell, *U 221* (Lt. Trojer) collided with *U 254* (Lt. Comdr. Gilardone). Only four men from the *U 254*, who happened to be on the tower, were rescued by *U 221*. This was the first time during the war that a German U-boat had rammed and sunk another U-boat. Dönitz stated, "The danger of collision between U-boats when deployed as a pack was always present. It was a cause of worry to us even in peacetime; but we had to accept the risk in the interests of the military advantages to be gained by the use of the wolf-pack tactics."

In the middle of December 1942 Soviet submarines had to terminate operations in the Gulf of Finland because of ice. According to Soviet sources, submarines of the Red fleet sank in the Baltic in 1942 twenty-nine ships totalling 78,962 gross tons. Despite their limited success rate, these subs at least made certain that the German naval staff had to introduce a convoy system.

In the Black Sea the Red fleet was greatly hampered in its operations by the Luftwaffe. Only individual Soviet submarine attacks had any effect on the German and Rumanian supply routes.

On Friday 18 December 1942, Tito's partisans fighting on the Adriatic coast in the Italian-occupied zone of Yugoslavia formed the first partisan naval unit, comprising 150 men in Podgara, Tucepi and Igrane. Their first ships were the small motor vessel *Partizan* and the motor yacht *Pionier*, which were deployed against Italian coastal shipping. Along the coast, "points" were organised for the purposes of keeping surveillance on Italian coastal traffic.

On Thursday 24 December 1942, the French admiral Darlan was assassinated in Algiers. When the admiral entered his offices at 3:00 P.M., a young man in civilian clothes was waiting in the antechamber. At pointblank range he fired two

shots at the admiral, who fell, wounded, and died shortly afterward in a hospital. The assassin, 21-year-old Fernand Bonnier de la Chapelle, a member of a highly respected family, was immediately shot on the orders of Gen. Giraud, who took Darlan's place the very next day.

Also on 24 December, a German reconnaissance patrol in the Arctic sighted British Convoy JW-51 B south of Bear Island.

On Wednesday 30 December 1942, the German battle group (Adm. Kummetz) comprising the heavy cruisers *Admiral Hipper* (Capt. Hartmann) and *Lützow* (Capt. Stange) and six destroyers of 5 Z Flotilla (Capt. Schemmel) put to sea from the Altafjord to intercept Convoy JW-51 B (Operation Regenbogen = rainbow). The convoy, made up of fourteen merchantmen, had only a weak escort of six destroyers, two corvettes, one minesweeper and two trawlers, as the Soviet Arctic Fleet (Adm. Golovko) did not, as planned, send off their units to meet the convoy. Thanks to the British destroyer group under Capt. Sherbrooke, which carried out an utterly ingenious defence despite the loss of the destroyer *Achates* and the minesweeper *Bramble*, the close cover group under Adm. Burnett was able to launch an attack with two light cruisers. In

11/27/1942, Toulon, the end of the proud French fleet; warships totalling 225,000 tons scuttled by their own crews

December 1942. Hard fighting beyond the Arctic Circle: the heavy cruiser *Admiral Hipper* shortly before putting to sea for further operations against the Murmansk convoys

the resultant action, the *Admiral Hipper* received a number of hits and broke off on 31 December 1942 in accordance with instructions, ". . . we do not wish the cruisers to be put unduly at risk." The destroyer *Friedrich Eckoldt* (Capt. Schemmel) went down with all hands. The heavy cruiser *Lützow* sailed past the British convoy and missed it. And so the fourteen freighters arrived safely in Murmansk without having come into contact with the German battle group.

The night of 30/31 December 1942, the two vessels belonging to Tito's naval partisans scored, in the coastal area of Makarska, their greatest success. They captured six Italian coastal vessels in this one night.

In December 1942 German U-boats operating in the Atlantic, off South Africa and in the Mediterranean sank fifty-nine merchantmen totalling 315,670 gross tons. German losses amounted to six U-boats.

At this time the British Admiralty recognised that it would have to avail itself of new tactics if it were to counter the strategic maneuverability of the centralised German U-boat direction.

Since the German attack on the Soviet Union in June 1941 until the end of 1942, a total of 219

Allied ships reached Soviet Arctic ports. They transported 3,276 tanks; 2,665 aircraft; 24,400 vehicles; 615,000 tons of ammunition and war material, as well as 69,000 tons of oil. During this period a total of sixty-four ships were lost, together with a quarter of the supplies intended for the Soviet Union.

Although during the second half of 1942 the tonnage lost by the Allies on the convoy routes were reduced by some sixty-five percent because of decrypted Enigma radio traffic, which allowed the convoys to take evasive action, the Allies nonetheless lost a total of 7,706,000 gross tons of shipping capacity during 1942. Of this total, 6,250,000 gross tons were sunk by U-boats; 1,056,000 gross tons by the Luftwaffe, surface units and mines.

The securing of the coastal areas of Fortress Europe remained one of the most difficult and complex problems for the German Naval High Command.

One of the greatest threats for the C-in-C U-boats was the dramatically increased losses of U-boats on their way to and from their bases in the Bay of Biscay, which were now being kept under surveillance day and night by Allied long-range aircraft.

Between September 1939 and the end of 1941, only six U-boats had been sunk by aircraft, while in 1942 the RAF sank twenty-seven U-boats and the USAAF sank eleven. By the end of 1942, despite the increasing success rate achieved by the U-boat arm, the first signs of an imminent change in the Atlantic situation—in favor of the Allies—were already present.

1943

January–June

Sea Battle in the Arctic

Friday 1 January 1943, London
The *Reuters* News Agency reported:

Early yesterday, British warships came into contact with enemy naval units in the Arctic. During the engagement, an enemy cruiser was damaged and withdrew. An enemy destroyer was hit and, the last time it was seen, was listing heavily. The operation is continuing.

Sunday 10 January 1943
The *German High Command* issued the following communiqué:

As already announced in a special communiqué, the deployment of a German U-boat group against a convoy en route to Gibraltar from Trinidad has led to complete success. The strongly escorted formation consisted exclusively of large tankers carrying fuel to North Africa. During severe fighting, thirteen tankers totalling 124,000 gross tons were sunk and three tankers more torpedoed. The convoy was completely destroyed. The loss of 174,000 tons of fuel will deal a heavy blow to the Anglo-American war direction in North Africa.

Successes in the U-boat War

Tuesday 12 January 1943, Berlin
The German *DNB* News Agency reported:

The C-in-C Kriegsmarine has sent the following telegram to the C-in-C U-boats: The almost total destruction of the enemy tanker convoy in the area south of the Azores was a joint and brilliant success achieved by the operational planning of the C-in-C U-boats and the dashing attack carried out by the U-boat group. In addition to the tonnage sunk, there is also the destruction of enemy fuel supplies that will have the effect of relieving the pressure on our comrades on the Tunisian front.

Landings near Novorossisk

Saturday 6 February 1943, Moscow
Soviet Military High Command Headquarters *STAVKA* reported:

Friday night the Black Sea Fleet landed shock troops in the area around Novorossisk. A retreating German motorised column of approximately two thousand men was ambushed and completely annihilated. The port of Novorossisk has been cut off from all outside contact. The Soviet Black Sea Fleet is guarding the approaches, and the army is forming a strong defensive barrier some twenty miles from the town.

Sunday 7 February 1943
The *German High Command* issued the following communiqué:

As already announced in a special communiqué, during bitter fighting U-boats sank sixteen fully laden transports and tankers totalling 102,500 gross tons and four cargo sailing ships in convoys making for Britain with supplies intended for the African and Soviet fronts. Another three ships were damaged by torpedoes.

The Importance of the Azores

Most secret
Admiralty
C.O.S. (43) 73 (0)
22 February 1943

To the War Cabinet
Chiefs of Staff Committee

Ref: Use of the Portuguese Azores, note from the First Sea Lord and Chief of the Naval Staff

Experience has shown that U-boats cannot operate effectively as long as we can maintain one airplane in the air during the day and can thereby secure a convoy. The U-boats have to submerge and therefore cannot keep up with the convoys, which they then in general cannot relocate the following night. A large part of our shipping losses occur in those areas where we cannot give security from the air:

1. Air bases on the Portuguese Atlantic islands would place us in the position . . . of stopping the large and dangerous gaps over our main convoy routes. Air bases on the islands would therefore have a vital and possibly decisive effect on U-boat operations and would significantly increase the security of our supply lines to all overseas theaters of war.

2. The advantages offered by air bases on the Portuguese islands would be, in fact, extraordinarily high: a) they would offer us enhanced possibilities to secure all convoys that use the following routes: I. USA or West Indies and the Mediterranean, II. West Indies and the United Kingdom, III. South America and the United Kingdom, IV. United Kingdom and the Mediterranean, V. United Kingdom and West Africa, the Cape and eastward; b) because of the extended areas that would now lie under air cover, we would have a far greater area for evasive routes. If, for example, U-boats were to concentrate in northern waters, the North Atlantic convoys could be routed via the Azores instead of the Iceland route; c) we could increase the load capacity of our ships, as they would have the possibility of taking a more direct route across the mid-Atlantic; d) we would be able to carry out disruptive actions against U-boats not only when they are travelling to or from their bases

in the Bay of Biscay, but also during their rest period, in which they refuel or charge up their batteries in the Atlantic and during which they are, at present, practically immune from aircraft attacks. New direction-finding equipment and attack weapons that are due to come into service in the New Year should increase the effect of such actions; e) unlimited refuelling installations on the islands would put us in a position where we could make better use of our insufficient stock of escort vessels.

3. A further advantage of the utmost importance would be that the blockade-runners sailing between Germany and Japan would be so endangered that their voyages (and you are aware of the importance the enemy attaches to these) could not be resumed next winter. (We believe they will be temporarily terminated after April.) At present the blockade-runners can usually pass above or below the mid-Atlantic without danger, and we must mainly concentrate in detecting them during the short period in which they are within range of our aircraft operating from home bases, in other words, when they are crossing the Bay of Biscay.

4. German warships, commerce raiders and U-boat tankers putting out into the Atlantic would be impeded to the same extent, and they would be subjected to considerably increased risks by our subsequent hunting operations.

5. In addition, the islands would present the most favorable interim landing stations for air supplies from the USA to the Mediterranean war theaters.

6. Increasing Allied successes have now made the risk of a German invasion of the Iberian peninsula questionable and, probably, even impossible — a fact that Dr. Salazar [premier of Portugal] himself seems to acknowledge.

London (initialled) D. P. (Dudley Pound)

Sunday 28 February 1943
The *German High Command* issued the following communiqué:

During the night of 27 February, a formation of German S-boats attacked a strongly protected enemy convoy immediately off the English coast and sank two steamers and a tanker totalling 65,000 gross tons, as well as two escorts.

Friday 5 March 1943
The *German High Command* issued the following communiqué:

As already announced in a special communiqué, German U-boats again scored successes at the beginning of the month. Thirteen ships totalling 97,000 gross tons were sent to the bottom of the sea in heavy fighting. Another two ships were torpedoed.

Right: Red Army troops on their way to a mission. On 2/4/1943 the Soviet 165th Rifle Brigade landed south of Novorossisk, supported by the 83rd and 255th Naval Infantry Brigades, strongly secured by units of the Black Sea Fleet.

Left: U-boat successes always made the headlines in the National Socialist press.

W. Churchill to the First Lord
5 March 1943

I am shocked at the renewed disaster to the convoy off the Cape. I thought you had made arrangements for this area and that all had been carefully studied. We have now lost forty thousand tons of shipping. We simply cannot afford losses of this kind on this route. I understood that fifteen or sixteen corvettes and minesweeping trawlers had come from Canada. Where are the destroyers which belong to the Eastern Fleet? Are they all sharing the idleness of that fleet? This is a very serious disaster.

Massive U-boat Successes!

Wednesday 10 March 1943
The *German High Command* issued the following communiqué:

As already announced in a special communiqué, during the last five days in hard, bitter fighting, German U-boats, in North Atlantic snowstorms, in the blazing sun of the equator and in the autumn storms around the Cape of Good Hope, have sunk twenty-three ships totalling 134,000 gross tons. Six ships more were torpedoed.

Thursday 11 March 1943
The *German High Command* issued the following communiqué:

As already announced in a special communiqué, our U-boats have again been on the attack. For some days now they have been maintaining contact with a convoy making for Britain from North America. U-boat packs closed in and sank in a series of repeated attacks thirteen ships, totalling 73,000 gross tons, fully laden with war material.

Three more steamers were torpedoed. The U-boats thereby sank thirty-six ships totalling 207,000 gross tons within twenty-four hours. These ships included eight that carried ammunition which blew up when torpedoed.

Friday 12 March 1943
The *German High Command* issued the following communiqué:

As already announced in a special communiqué, during the last twenty-four hours our U-boats have reported magnificent successes in the Mediterranean, the Arctic and the Atlantic.

Eleven large ships totalling 75,000 gross tons, forming part of the supply convoys to North Africa, the Soviet Union and Great Britain, finished their voyages on the bottom of the sea. Four more ships were torpedoed. Successful sinkings by our U-boats, reported in three special communiqués released on three consecutive days, now total forty-seven ships aggregating 282,000 gross tons.

Secret report of the *SS Security Service* on the internal political situation:
No. 367, 15 March (Extract)

I. General: The three special communiqués relating to the sinking by U-boats of a total of 282,000 gross tons made a profound impression even on those members of the population who do not always judge the U-boat war to be of the utmost importance. In general the series of U-boat successes are regarded as the first effects of entrusting Grand Admiral Dönitz with the supreme command of the German Navy.

W. Churchill to General Ismay
Tuesday 16 March 1943

The sinkings in the South Atlantic bring the question of the Azores again to the fore. You know how keen the President is on establishing Allied control there. It seems hardly likely that at this moment such an event would bring the Germans down on Spain.

Saturday 20 March 1943
The *German High Command* issued the following communiqué:

As already announced in a special communiqué, the operations of our U-boats in the North Atlantic against a heavily laden enemy convoy on an easterly course, as reported in our communiqué dated 19 March, led to the largest and most successful action in the U-boat war to date. In several days of bitter fighting against the destroyers, corvettes and aircraft of the enemy covering force, our U-boats sank thirty-two ships (totalling 204,000 gross tons) of this convoy, and one destroyer.

Wednesday 31 March 1943
The *German High Command* issued the following communiqué:

As already announced in a special communiqué, our U-boat arm has dealt the enemy a number of severe blows against his lines of supply. In the North Atlantic, at times in extremely rough weather, in the mid-Atlantic and in the Mediterranean our U-boats sank seventeen heavily laden merchantmen totalling 103,500 gross tons. Most of these vessels were sailing in convoys.

Wednesday 7 April 1943
The *German High Command* issued the following communiqué:

As already announced in a special communiqué, our U-boats sank fourteen fully laden ships totalling 102,000 gross tons and a destroyer during heavy fighting against enemy supply lines in the Atlantic and Mediterranean. Another five ships were torpedoed. Because of immediate and heavy defensive measures, the actual sinking of these five ships cannot be confirmed. In the Bay of Biscay, one of our submarines shot down an attacking enemy bomber.

Swiss Radio Beromünster

Friday 9 April 1943

According to press reports from Berlin, opinion in the German capital has it that the fighting in Africa has now entered a decisive stage. The superiority of the enemy is emphasised, and the success of the 8th Army is admitted . . . . The transport situation continues to pose severe problems for the Allies. The total of Allied shipping capacity lost to U-boats during March exceeded the totals for January and February combined. In other words, the Axis powers are on the defensive with regard to the air war but, thanks to the effectiveness of their U-boats, are undoubtedly on the offensive in the sea war.

Warning to Fishing

Monday 19 April 1943, London
The *Reuters* News Agency reported:

The British government has already issued a warning, dated 20 July 1942, directed to all fishing vessels from enemy-occupied ports, that described as dangerous leaving coastal waters and entering specific zones. This warning is now renewed, as numerous fishing boats have been repeatedly sighted outside coastal waters. His Majesty's government again refers to the fact that the enemy often uses fishing boats for military purposes. Boats from enemy-occupied ports cannot be allowed to proceed through endangered areas. In future, any fishing boat found outside coastal waters in the zones described as dangerous will be treated as if participating in military operations.

Friday 30 April 1943
The *German High Command* issued the following communiqué:

U-boats operating in the North Atlantic and Mediterranean sank ten ships totalling 53,000 gross tons in strongly escorted convoys. Another

Right: A U-boat returns from an operational patrol. The pennants on the periscope show the successes.

Left: March 1943, climax of the Battle of the Atlantic: a special report practically every day on U-boat successes

Below: An almost peaceful picture—a large Allied convoy crossing the Atlantic

five ships, including one of the Winchester Castle class of 20,000 gross tons, were torpedoed. A U-boat shot down an enemy heavy bomber.

Convoys in the Atlantic
Saturday 1 May 1943, Ottawa
The *Associated Press* reported:

It has emerged from a statement made by Navy Minister MacDonald and Air Minister Power that the Allies are at present considering plans for a new-style convoy system in the Atlantic. The navies of Great Britain and Canada will be charged with securing the North Atlantic route between Canada and Britain with considerably reinforced air support.

Naval Battle in the North Pacific
Wednesday 5 May 1943, Washington
The *US Navy Department* issued the following communiqué:

Six weeks ago to the west of the Aleutians, a US formation of light units attacked two heavy Japanese cruisers, two light cruisers, six destroyers and two transporters. After an engagement that lasted for almost four hours and covered a wide area, three Japanese cruisers received direct hits and the enemy force retired. The attempt to reinforce Japanese outposts in the North Pacific was thereby frustrated.

The Fleets of the "Smaller" Allies
5 May 1943, London
The *Reuters* News Agency reported:

Vice-Adm. King, the British liaison officer with the Allied fleets in England, announced that the eighth independent fleet formation has just been created — a Danish fleet. Until now, with the exception of their considerable merchant marine sailing for the Allies, the Danes have only had harbor boats with their own crews. From now on, warships sailing under the Danish flag will take part in the war.

The other fleets of the Allies are the Free French, the Norwegian, Greek, Dutch, Yugoslav and Polish. The Belgian fleet is a section of the Royal Navy, as Belgium did not possess an independent fleet before the outbreak of war. In all, these fleets of our "smaller" Allies comprise 220 warships with 27,000 officers and men.

The strongest among these Allied fleets is the Dutch, which has 63 ships and 6,850 personnel. The second is the Norwegian with 53 warships and 5,100 men. The Free French fleet comprises 49

Early 1943: The Free French Navy fought on the Allied side with 49 units. General de Gaulle during an inspection.

Friday 21 May 1943, Tokyo
The *Japanese Imperial Headquarters* issued the following communiqué:

Adm. Isoroku Yamamoto, Commander-in-Chief of the Combined Forces, was killed on board an aircraft carrier last month during an engagement with the enemy. In Adm. Yamamoto, Japan has lost one of her greatest and most efficient fleet commanders. The Emperor has ordered a state funeral for Adm. Yamamoto and has posthumously promoted him the grand admiral. Adm. Koga has been nominated as his successor.

21 May 1943, Washington
The *United Press Agency* reported:

Radio Tokyo has announced that Adm. Yamamoto has been killed while leading fleet operations from an aircraft carrier.

Turn in the Battle of the Atlantic

21 May 1943, New York
The *Exchange* News Agency reported:

Brig. Gen. Larson, officer commanding anti-submarine operations, has made the following statement: "We are now over the worst of the sinkings by U-boats. With the support of the British Coastal Command, our reconnaissance patrols have driven most of the enemy U-boats out into the high seas. The activities of the U-boats will now be restricted to a small sector in the mid-Atlantic, where they will be a fine prey."

Superiority of Enemy Direction-finding Equipment
Annex I to the War Diary (Kriegstagebuch), 24 May 1943
From *C-in-C Kriegsmarine and U-boats*
To all U-boat commanders

Heavy U-boat losses sustained last month are, above all, caused by the current superiority of enemy direction-finding equipment and surprise air attacks thereby made possible. More than fifty percent of all losses are attributable to the element of surprise and, in fact, took place during the approach to and return from the operational area, as well as in the operational area in attack positions.

The losses sustained in the battle against the convoys themselves were, in contrast, slight except for one case where particularly unfavorable circumstances ruled. Here, too, some of these losses were attributable to air action.

The current situation vis-à-vis enemy air forces and direction-finding equipment must be overcome, while having to put up with other disadvantages, by special security precautions on the approach and in waiting positions. Orders have been

ships with 6,100 men; the Greek fleet, 33 ships and 5,450 men; the Polish, 12 ships and 2,600 men; the Belgian, 7 ships with 350 men; and the Yugoslav, 3 ships and 200 men. . . . Contact between the Allied fleets and the Royal Navy is maintained both by the staffs in London and by officers in the ports. On the 105 larger warships of the Allies, there are in addition special liaison officers. The crews are trained together with British cadets and sailors. Only the Free French and the Dutch have their own cadet-training facilities. The fleets of the "smaller" Allies operate jointly with the British and US forces under the same overall command and in all theaters of war.

New Secret Weapon?

Tuesday 11 May 1943, Washington
The *Reuters* News Agency reported:

Of the five German U-boats sunk in the Atlantic on 6 May while attacking an Allied Convoy, one was destroyed by a new secret weapon.

French Sink German Transport Submarine
Thursday 13 May 1943, New York
The *Associated Press* reported:

The French cruiser *George Leygues* has sunk a large German transport submarine and returned to Dakar with ninety prisoners of war on board. This action took place on 13 April near the equator.

General Alexander to W. Churchill
13 May 1943, 2:15 P.M.
Sir:

It is my duty to report that the Tunisian campaign is over. All enemy resistance has ceased. We are masters of the North African shores.

A highly dramatic photo: German submarine *(U 192?)* rammed and sunk by a British corvette on 5/5/1943. The U-boat was forced to the surface by a Hedgehog attack.

issued in this regard. In addition, I shall draw other conclusions from the choice of attack zones.

I shall devote all my energies to securing an improvement in our own direction finding, defence measures against enemy direction finding, and antiaircraft armament. All points will work on this task under maximum pressure. Practical results will be sent to the front in the shortest possible time. Until then, you must hold on with cunning and care on the approaches and in waiting positions and in battle itself with your usual stubborn toughness.

Secret report of the *SS Security Services* on the internal political situation:
No. 385, 24 May 1943 (Extract)

I. General: The absence in May of the special communiqués reporting U-boat successes, which have almost become a habit, is the subject of lively and anxious discussions, as it is precisely the long-term effect of the U-boat war that is given considerable, if not decisive, significance. It is frequently being assumed that the enemy is employing a new, highly effective defensive weapon.

Allied Successes in the Atlantic

Friday 28 May 1943, London
The *Reuters* News Agency reported:

In the Atlantic more U-boats were sunk in April, as well as May, than ever before, and shipping losses were substantially reduced — even though more ships crossed the Atlantic than previously. . . . This favorable development may be attributable to a number of reasons:

1. Improved securing of the convoys by new ships such as British frigates, US escort carriers and escort destroyers that have conclusively proved their worth.

2. The gradual closing of the "Atlantic gap" by a considerably increased deployment of long-range aircraft.

3. New weapons, still secret, used in the war against the U-boats.

4. Improved coastal and island defence on the western side of the Atlantic and on the west coast of Africa.

5. Evidence that the shortage of trained U-boat crews on the German side is making itself felt.

French Navy Now with the Allies
Monday 31 May 1943, Algiers
The *Reuters* News Agency reported:

As already reported here, the French fleet lying in Alexandria has gone over to the Allies. Details have not yet been received. The fleet consists of the battleship *Lorraine* (22,000 gross tons), four cruisers, three destroyers and a submarine.

Increasing U-boat Losses

Thursday 3 June 1943, London
The *Reuters* News Agency reported:

May was the most successful month of all for German U-boats destroyed. During the last twelve months more U-boats have been destroyed than in the entire war, and during the last six months the figures of sinkings were twenty-five percent higher than in the previous six months; in addition, many German U-boats have been severely damaged. It would seem that the figure of U-boats destroyed in May exceeds the number of newly commissioned submarines. There can be no doubt, in any event, that the number of U-boats at sea has been demonstrably reduced. . . . The enemy can be expected to do everything possible to improve this situation. We, however, shall do everything possible to frustrate his endeavors.

Extract from the War Diary of the Naval High Command
re U-boat War Direction
8 June 1943

The rapid increase in losses sustained this month

(from fourteen in April to thirty-eight) documents the crisis in which the U-boat war finds itself. . . . It is confirmed that the enemy has considerably increased surveillance over the entire Atlantic and, in addition to the direct securing of his convoys, has deployed additional surveillance along the entire convoy route by naval and aerial units. We have no counter to the superior direction-finding equipment developed by the enemy, which is particularly effective when used by aircraft and presents the utmost danger to our U-boats. . . .

Location of the convoys in May was favored by excellent back-up by air reconnaissance. It was again most apparent in this month that the enemy, as can be seen from his evaluation of the U-boat situation, has repeatedly recognised our positions and taken evading action. In a number of cases, it was only possible to track down the enemy on his amended course by continued good back-up by radio intelligence. In addition to radio intelligence, the combined rhythmic noises from the convoys provided a very good clue. . . .

The decrypting results achieved by the B-Dienst have shown that a new antisubmarine device, known as Hedgehog, is being used. Judging by this process, a new kind of heavy depth charge is being launched in a cluster or in a close ripple series. In addition to the large warhead, a new kind of detonator based on the magnetic or acoustic principle must be available. . . .

As the U-boats must in the future, even more than in the past, destroy the convoy securing force in order to get their principal targets, the value of the "destroyer busters"—the new torpedoes due to come into service at the end of the summer—is thereby very much enhanced. Equipping the submarines with four-barrelled antiaircraft guns will considerably reduce the danger from air attacks. . . . In the conviction that the U-boat will in future still be the main weapon of the war at sea, the Führer has ordered that U-boat building be increased to forty submarines per month.

Not a Single Merchant Ship Sunk
Monday 14 June 1943, New York
The *US Navy Department* issued the following communiqué:

Last week not one single Allied merchant vessel was sunk by U-boats, for the first time in seventeen weeks. From January 1943 in the West Atlantic, an average of four Allied and neutral ships were sunk each week. This represents a considerable improvement on the weekly average of ten merchantmen sunk each week in 1942.

Annex to the Lisbon Report No. 244
Most secret   British Embassy, Lisbon
                                          16 June 1943

His Excellency Dr. Antonio de Oliveira Salazar

Your Excellency, during our conversation on 8 June I explained to Your Excellency that the moment now seems right to consider the decisions taken during the Anglo-Portuguese staff discussions held in London some months ago. . . . The German U-boat offensive has now reached a point at which it is impeding the full deployment of the fighting ability of the United Nations' armed forces. His Majesty's government does not fear that this danger will prevent the final victory of the Allies, but it could well cause it to be seriously delayed.

His Majesty's government has examined the situation in the light of the above facts and from the point of view of the alliance with Portugal. The government has come to the conclusion that the establishment of facilities on the Portuguese Atlantic islands, in particular on the Azores, for the deployment of aircraft and surface vessels could be a decisive factor for a swift counter to the German U-boat offensive in the Atlantic and, as a consequence, present an important contribution to the speedy victory of the United Nations.

I list below the facilities upon which His Majesty's government places the utmost value: a) installations on São Miguel and Terceira for the deployment of long-range reconnaissance aircraft; b) unlimited refuelling facilities for naval escorts either in São Miguel or Fayal. The military advantages that, in the opinion of His Majesty's government, would accrue from these installations are summarised in Annex II to this letter.

His Majesty's government has therefore decided, in the name of the alliance that has existed between Portugal and Great Britain for the last six hundred years, to request the Portuguese government to extend its cooperation to the effect that it makes available the installations required in the Azores. His Majesty's government trusts that the Portuguese government is agreed in principle whereby detailed terms and conditions required for the provision of these installations shall be the subject of further discussions.

I would take this opportunity of again assuring Your Excellency of my deep respect.

(signed) *R. H. Campbell*

A Short Sunderland Mk I flying boat L 2163 bearing the code DA:G of 210 Squadron (Coastal Command) reconnoitering a convoy route.

Strategy and Tactics

JANUARY TO JUNE 1943

The night of 1 January 1943, Hitler learned in his headquarters of the report from the BBC in London on the failure of Operation Regenbogen. As communications between Norway and Germany had been disrupted, the reports had not yet reached the German Naval High Command. At 5:00 P.M., Hitler ordered Vice-Adm. Krancke to report to the Führer's headquarters. Hitler said, "I have decided the following and order you to inform the naval staff immediately of my irrevocable decision. Capital ships are an unnecessary waste of men and material. They are therefore to be taken out of service and broken up. Their guns are to be mounted on shore, where they will serve as coastal barriers." Krancke said, "That would be the cheapest naval victory that Britain had ever won." Hitler requested Krancke to get Grand Admiral Raeder to the Führer's headquarters as quickly as possible. Raeder said, "I received orders by telephone to re-

port immediately to the Führer's headquarters, but I requested that I could first gather together the necessary documentation."

The night of 2/3 January 1943, the British submarines *Thunderbolt* (Comdr. Crouch) and *Trooper* (Lt. Wraight) put to sea from Malta. Two manned torpedoes of the Chariot type, in pressurised containers, were fixed to the submarines' outer casing. These torpedoes were the same as the Italian Maiala torpedoes. The Chariots were sent off in the Palermo roads under the command of Capt. Sladen. The crews cut through the torpedo nets at the entrance to the harbor and fixed warheads to the modern Italian cruiser *Ulpio Traiano* (3,362 tons) and the transporter *Viminale* (8,657 tons). The explosions caused severe damage to both ships, and the cruiser *Ulpio Traiano* was no longer reparable. Two of the torpedo crewmen were killed and the others taken prisoner.

The evening of January 1943, Grand Admiral Raeder arrived in the Führer's headquarters to make his proposals. In the presence of the head of the OKW, Keitel, he had to listen to an uncontrolled monologue. After that, the grand admiral demanded to speak with Hitler in private. Raeder stated, "In the ensuing conversation, conducted between just the two of us, I first asked to be relieved of my command as C-in-C of the Kriegsmarine, as he had shown by his comments that he was dissatisfied with the manner in which I exercised my command and the results thereof. Without his confidence, I was unable to continue with my duties. Moreover, I was almost sixty-seven years of age, and my health was no longer what it was." It was agreed that the grand admiral would step down on 30 January, the tenth anniversary of Hitler's coming to power.

During January 1943 and the following three months, U-boat operations were made much more difficult by unusually strong storms.

On Saturday 9 January 1943, U-boat group Delphin (dolphin) commenced an attack south of the Azores against Convoy TM-1, which consisted of nine tankers and a weak escort group.

On Monday 11 January 1943, the operation conducted by the Delphin group against Convoy TM-1 terminated. Out of the nine tankers, only two reached their port of destination.

At the beginning of 1943 the new British radar equipment, which now worked on the 10-cm wavelength, was used by Coastal Command for the first time. The Metox search receiver fitted to German U-boats, which reacted to British radar equipment operating on a 1.5-m wavelength, was now useless. It was not until the middle of 1944 that a suitable search receiver was put into operation, giving the U-boats warning of location by centimetric radar equipment.

On Thursday January 1943, the Casablanca Conference took place between Roosevelt and Churchill and the operations staffs of the USA and Great Britain. They resolved that Anglo-American bomber formations would mount a combined bomber offensive against Germany. The absolute priority of combating U-boat bases and shipyards was not accidental: A victory in the Battle of the Atlantic was the prerequisite for any large-scale operation against the European mainland. Churchill stated, "Until the end of 1942, U-boats were sinking our ships quicker than we could build them." In addition, the disastrous concept of the "unconditional surrender" was announced.

On the same day the American submarine *Gudgeon* (Lt. Comdr. Stoval, Jr.) landed a team of five US secret agents, commanded by Maj. J. Villamor, on Negros Island in the central Philippines. This saw the beginning of a long series of special submarine missions that lasted for two years, until 23 January 1945. At the orders of MacArthur, this, the first team, was to organise military sabotage in the Japanese-occupied Philippines and establish contact with the guerrillas who had already been operating there for the previous year. In addition, the team was to establish a network of coastal surveillance posts, whose principal duty was to observe all the movements of the Japanese naval and air forces. The posts maintained radio contact with MacArthur's headquarters. Maj. Villamor also organised regular supplies to the guerrillas by means of American submarines.

British two-man torpedo "Chariot," a faithful replica of the Italian Maiala design, being tested before operational use

The night of 15/16 January 1943, RAF Bomber Command carried out its first pattern-bombing attack on Lorient. Although three hundred tons of bombs were dropped on the U-boat base, none of the bunkers was destroyed.

In the middle of January 1943 the Japanese resolved to give up Guadalcanal, and a large-scale evacuation operation was organised.

On Sunday 31 January 1943, Grand Admiral Raeder was formally given the title "Chief of Staff of the Kriegsmarine." Hitler appointed, at Raeder's suggestion, Adm. Dönitz to be his successor and promoted him to grand admiral. Dönitz succeeded in obtaining Hitler's agreement to "employ the capital ships as soon as a worthwhile target and the chance of success presented themselves."

One of the reasons why the large-scale convoy battles started from January 1943 was that the German B-Dienst, the German radio intelligence

Despite winter storms, the Liberty ships plough their way through the Atlantic

service, was in a position to decrypt constantly course instructions radioed by the British Admiralty to the convoys. Even the daily reports on the U-boat situation, radioed to all Allied units and service stations participating in the Battle of the Atlantic, were tapped by the B-Dienst. Dönitz stated, "These reports were extremely valuable for the U-boat direction. They showed what significance our own air reconnaissance would have had for our sea war; its main task would have been to establish position and course of the convoys and to transmit these details." On the other hand, thanks to the decrypting of German U-boat radio traffic by the British cryptanalysts, the average daily sinkings by a German U-boat in January 1943 fell to 51 tons (221 tons in December 1942).

On Sunday 31 January 1943, the German commerce raider ship no. 14 *Coronel* (Capt. Thienemann) set out from the Baltic on its first operational patrol disguised as the Dutch steamer *Utrecht*. This vessel was the motor vessel *Togo*, commissioned in 1938, with a complement of 350 men; the armament comprised six 15-cm guns, six 4-cm antiaircraft guns, four 2-cm twin antiaircraft guns, four torpedo tubes, one aircraft, a motorboat and ninety-three mines. Its scheduled operational area was to be the mid- and south-Atlantic waters.

At the end of January 1943 the strength of the U-boat arm reached its maximum. There were some four hundred German U-boats, so that for the first time three groups comprising seven, seventeen and eighteen submarines could operate simultaneously.

The storms that raged in the North Atlantic in January 1943 often prevented the deployment of U-boats so that Allied losses were reduced.

In January 1943 German U-boats operating in the Atlantic, Mediterranean and Arctic sank forty-two merchantmen totalling 218,449 gross tons. German losses amounted to six U-boats.

In the North Atlantic on Monday 1 February 1943, a concentrated attack was mounted by U-boats against fast Convoy HX-224 proceeding from Halifax to Great Britain. Quite by chance, this attack opened up a number of subsequent U-boat successes: *U 632* (Lt. Comdr. Karpf) picked up a survivor who stated that the next convoy, slow Convoy SC-118 from Halifax, would shortly pass along the same route.

On Tuesday 2 February 1943, as a result of the intelligence gleaned on board the *U 632*, a battle commenced between twenty U-boats comprising the Pfeil and Haudegen groups (= arrow and broadsword, resp.) and the securing units escorting Convoy SC-118. The U-boats sank thirteen ships for the loss of three of their own number. The severe defeat inflicted on Convoy SC-118, despite the strong cover provided by twelve escort vessels, sounded the alarm bells in the British Admiralty. An investigation revealed the necessity for offensive tactics and increased cooperation between escort groups and support groups. It was now to be their task — instead of the aircraft's — to attack U-boats converging on the convoy routes.

The night of 2/3 February 1943, a 10-cm radar was recovered from an RAF bomber shot down near Rotterdam. As a consequence, the C-in-C U-boats learned that aircraft deployed as submarine hunters were equipped with DF equipment operating on this wavelength.

The night of 3/4 February 1943, 19 Group, Coastal Command (Air Vice-Marshal Bromet) commenced the first Bay of Biscay offensive under the code-name Operation Gondola. A sea area lying across the approach route taken by German U-boats was now to be continuously kept under surveillance.

During the night of 4/5 February 1943, 120 aircraft from Bomber Command again attacked the U-boat base at Lorient.

One of the most unusual weapons used by the Admiralty in the Battle of the Atlantic was Atlantiksender (Radio Atlantic, a station headed by Sefton Delmer). On Friday 5 February 1943, the station, situated near London, began its first transmission with a shrill pipe melody. This shortwave station — based on the pattern of the forces networks in Belgrade and other cities — was used to undermine the morale of German U-boat crews by means of psychological warfare. The crews were certainly told by their officers that the station Atlantiksender, presumed German, was in fact situated in England. But the crews were influenced by the variety of programs offered and the fact that Atlantiksender knew everything that concerned U-boats, their crews and their families. British interrogating officers soon noticed that since the existence of the Atlantiksender, crews taken prisoner were much more ready to talk. The officers now heard more and more often, "The English know everything anyway."

As a rule the station directed itself to a specific U-boat that, according to details provided by the Admiralty, had just started off on its operational patrol. The radio operator of one U-boat later told an interrogator, "We were proceeding under the customary security and secrecy measures, observing absolute radio silence, but we were hardly two days at sea when the Atlantiksender broadcast to us direct and played a request concert for us. I can tell you, it's a most uncomfortable feeling to realise that you are being so closely watched! And in addition, to realise that the enemy knew exactly where we were." The station gleaned its information from a number of sources. Personal and family details, such as the dates of birth, marriage and the death notices of members of U-boat crews' families which appeared in German newspapers, were taken from the body of correspondence found on captured U-boat crews. By these means the station could send congratulations or messages of condolence and report on private matters. The most important information was given by the Ger-

man News Agency (DNB, or Deutsche Nachrichtenbureau) itself. When the war broke out, the London correspondent of the DNB left behind a telex machine on which the editors of Atlantiksender received all press and radio messages emanating from Germany at the same time as their German opposite numbers working for these media. And it was just such reports that were meant to convince the listener that he really was hearing a genuine German station. In addition, secret agents working for the British Naval Intelligence Division in German U-boat bases immediately radioed the order and even the results of football matches played between individual U-boat crews. It was therefore possible for the Atlantiksender to give precise details within hours of the matches ending. The station even had a German armed forces orchestra (conductor Harry Zeisel), which had been taken prisoner in North Africa with their entire equipment.

The night of 7/8 February 1943, Bomber Command carried out a saturation raid on Lorient, dropping 760 tons of bombs.

During the same night, eighteen Japanese destroyers evacuated the last troops from Guadalcanal to Rabaul. Six months of hard and bloody fighting were now over. Japanese propaganda gloated that the Americans would soon run out of breath if they had to waste as much time on every other island in the Solomons.

On Tuesday 9 February 1943, *U 180* (Comdr. Musenberg) left Kiel. Before leaving the harbor, a motorboat brought two civilians on board. The crew was informed that the two men, who had worked on the construction of U-boat bases in Norway, were to be landed there. The Indian nationalist leaders Subhas Chandra Bose and his ad-

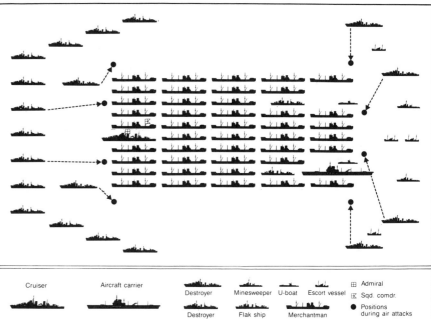

Left: Torpedo assembly at a German naval base

Right: Diagram showing the composition of a large convoy on the Murmansk route

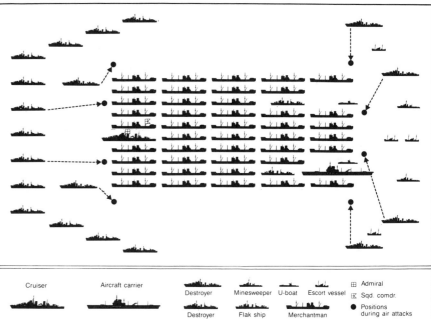

Cruiser	Aircraft carrier		⊞ Admiral
		Destroyer Minesweeper U-boat Escort vessel	⊠ Sqd. comdr.
			● Positions
Destroyer		Destroyer Flak ship Merchantman	during air attacks

jutant Habid Hasan, they were to be transferred at the end of this secret voyage to a waiting Japanese submarine. Bose and his supporters were then to conduct war against the British in India.

On Wednesday 10 February 1943, *U 519* (Lt. Comdr. Eppen) was sunk northeast of the Azores by a four-motored Liberator of 2 Squadron (USAAF) and was the first German U-boat to be sunk under Operation Gondola.

On Sunday 14 February 1943, the German commerce raider ship no. 14 *Coronel*, lying in Dunkirk, received orders to return to the Baltic. The ship had been attacked repeatedly by Allied aircraft during its voyage through the English Channel and had sustained damage from a number of direct hits. And so ended the last attempt by a German commerce raider to break out into the Atlantic. After conversion in the German Navy dockyards in Kiel, ship no. 14 was given back its original name of *Togo* and became the first night-fighter direction vessel deployed in the Store Belt north of Langeland. The *Togo* survived the war and was put back into service as one of the first freighters on 13 August 1945.

Already by the middle of February 1943 the situation in the Bay of Biscay had changed. U-boats returning from operations were increasingly being sunk by the enemy. The survivors reported that when they surfaced at nights in order to charge their batteries, they were suddenly illuminated from the air by dazzling searchlights and then immediately attacked with bombs.

On Thursday 18 February 1943, when the B-Dienst had deciphered the radio traffic from Convoy ON-166 making for Halifax from Great Britain, the C-in-C U-boats ordered the powerful U-boat groups Ritter and Knappen (= knight and squire) to proceed to the presumed convoy route. The attacks commenced shortly after ON-166 passed out of the operational range of Coastal Command aircraft and continued until 24 February. The U-boats sank fourteen ships.

The night of 28 February 1943, 409 British heavy bombers carried out an attack on the U-boat base at St. Nazaire, dropping 1,120 tons of bombs.

In February 1943 German U-boats operating in the Mediterranean and in the Atlantic, Arctic and Indian oceans sank sixty-eight merchantmen totalling 380,835 gross tons. German losses amounted to twenty U-boats.

During this month, for the first time, new tonnage built by the Allies exceeded the tonnage sunk by the U-boats. From now on, more than one million tons of shipping capacity were built monthly.

From March 1943 until the end of the year, convoys to Murmansk were terminated. Instead, Lend-Lease shipments were sent practically without loss through the Mediterranean, the Suez Canal to the Persian Gulf. The termination of convoys to Murmansk meant that the escort vessels thereby released could be allocated to the support groups.

The night of 4/5 March 1943, *U 333* (Lt. Schwaff) succeeded in bringing down a Wellington of 172 Squadron that was attacking the U-boat. When the aircraft switched on its Leigh Light, *U 333* opened up with its 2-cm antiaircraft guns and shot the bomber down.

During the next convoy battle, which commenced Sunday 7 March 1943, two U-boat groups attacked Convoy SC-121, a large convoy, proceeding from Halifax to Great Britain. A number of stragglers, which had been separated from the convoy because of heavy storms, fell victim to U-boat attacks. Overall, thirteen ships totalling 62,000 gross tons were lost with their crews. The U-boats suffered no losses.

After the battle with Convoy SC-121 was concluded, the next convoy battle commenced on Thursday 11 March 1943. The Neuland (new ground) Group, comprising thirteen U-boats, attacked Convoy HX-228 making for Great Britain from North America at a speed of ten knots. There were a number of troopships among the sixty freighters. The U-boats, however, achieved only a moderate success, sinking 24,175 gross tons for the loss of two U-boats.

On Monday 8 March 1943, the battlecruiser *Scharnhorst* (Capt. Hoffmann) put to sea from Gdynia. Under cover of the stormy weather, the ship succeeded in reaching Trondheim where it joined the battleship *Tirpitz* (Capt. Topp).

On Tuesday 16 March 1943, one of the bloodiest convoy battles of all took place. The U-boat groups Dränger, Stürmer and Raubgraf (= striker, forward and robber baron, resp.), totalling forty U-boats, crossed the paths of a forty-ship fast convoy, HX-229, proceeding from New York to Great Britain, and also the slow convoy SC-122, comprising sixty ships, travelling on the same route from Halifax to Great Britain. By evening both convoys had lost a total of twelve ships. *U 338* (Lt. Comdr. Kinzel) even succeeded in sinking four merchant ships with five torpedoes.

On the evening of 17 March 1943, Convoy HX-229 overtook Convoy SC-122, which was travelling even slower than expected. Both convoys now formed a giant conglomeration of ships, completely disordered, difficult to maneuver and to secure. In the following three days, the U-boats sank another nine ships. Overall, Allied losses from both convoys amounted to twenty-one ships totalling 141,000 gross tons, compared to the loss of only one U-boat, the *U 384* (Lt. von Rosenberg-Gruszczynski). The fact that almost seventy percent of losses occurred in strongly escorted convoys caused the British Admiralty to have some doubts on the advantages of the convoy system.

The Admiralty commented, "Never did the Germans come so near to disrupting communications between the New World and the Old as in the first twenty days of March 1943."

At this time the war against the U-boats in the Atlantic entered a decisive phase. The first escort carriers since the sinking of the *Audacity* on 22 December 1941 were now brought into service. In addition, five Atlantic support groups were now being deployed, and the number of long-range reconnaissance aircraft was doubled.

The first twenty days in March 1943 represented the climax of the Battle of the Atlantic. After this, the period of the greatest successes achieved by the U-boat service and the largest convoy battles of World War II, there was a sudden reversal. Although the position and course of the convoys continued to be regularly ascertained, thanks to the good work of the B-Dienst, the U-boats succeeded less and less in penetrating the convoy escort groups.

On Saturday 27 March 1943, near Kamchatka a US battle group (Rear Adm. McMorris), comprising two cruisers and four destroyers, attacked a Japanese convoy bound for Attu in the Aleutians. An engagement of three and a half hours took place between the American ships and the Japanese formation (Vice-Adm. Hosogaya), which consisted of four cruisers and five destroyers. The battle took place not far from the Commander Islands and was the last Pacific maritime engagement fought in accordance with old tactics: without the participation of aircraft, only artillery and torpedoes being used. Some ships were hit by shells. But even with this battle, aircraft contributed toward a decisive outcome although not directly. Vice-Adm. Hosogaya broke off the engagement because he feared the intervention of US aircraft and ordered his superior force to withdraw.

In the first three months of 1943 seventy-five percent of German front-line U-boats took part in convoy battles.

In March 1943 German U-boats operating in the Mediterranean and the Atlantic, Arctic and Indian oceans sank 105 merchantmen totalling 590,234 gross tons. German losses amounted to sixteen U-boats.

Dönitz stated, "The success achieved this month was, however, to be the last decisive German victory in the convoy war."

From April 1943 aircraft carriers, long-range Liberators and flying boats closed the gap, the only area remaining in the Atlantic without air cover.

On Wednesday 7 April 1943, the Japanese air offensive (Operation I) against the Solomons commenced. Adm. Yamamoto, deeply worried about the situation on the islands, resolved to lead the operation personally. After the four Japanese carriers had brought approximately 160 fighters and dive bombers to Rabaul and Buka to reinforce the 11th Air Fleet, the carrier-borne aircraft attacked US ships in the Tulagi and Lunga roads (Guadalcanal) the same day.

On Tuesday 13 April 1943, at 5:55 P.M. the commander of the 8th Fleet, Vice-Adm. T. Sameijima,

Admiral Yamamoto, C-in-C of the Imperial Japanese Navy, was the most important victim of cryptanalysts in WWII.

radioed details relating to an inspection flight to be undertaken by Adm. Yamamoto. Because of its importance, the message was coded absolute top secret. It stated that Adm. Yamamoto would take off from Rabaul at 6:00 the morning of 18 April in a bomber, escorted by six fighters, to carry out an inspection of the Japanese bases on Ballale and Shortland, near the southeastern spur of Bougainville Island. This secret message was picked up simultaneously by a number of US Navy monitoring stations and, within fourteen hours, was on the desk of Yamamoto's opposite number in Pearl Harbor, in clear. The C-in-C of the Pacific fleet, Adm. Nimitz, immediately recognised the unique chance of getting rid of his dangerous opponent forever. On the evening of 17 April 1943, four Liberators landed on Henderson Field (Guadalcanal) with special supplementary fuel tanks for the Lightning fighters. Operation Vengeance, the hunt for Adm. Yamamoto, was on.

On Sunday 18 April 1943, by 6:00 A.M. Yamamoto was flying from Rabaul to Bougainville in a Mitsubishi G4M Betty bomber accompanied by a second Betty and six Zero fighters. Adm. Yamamoto's habitual punctuality was fatal. At 7:25 A.M. sixteen Lightning P 38 fighters of 399 Squadron, led by Maj. J. W. Mitchell, took off from Henderson Field to intercept the Japanese admiral shortly before he landed on Ballale Isle near Bougainville, four hundred miles away.

When the Japanese bomber saw the twin-boom Lightnings, the pilot made one mistake. He dived toward the jungle around Bougainville and thereby lost the advantage of height. After an air battle lasting some thirty seconds, Yamamoto's bomber blew up forty miles north of Ballale in the middle of the jungle. Capt. T. G. Lamphier stated, "I fired a long burst into the bomber's side, almost exactly at right angles. The right engine caught fire and then the right wing. As I got within range of Yamamoto's aircraft guns, the bomber's wing broke away."

Adm. Isoroku Yamamoto, the 59-year-old C-in-C of the Imperial Navy, a former Harvard undergraduate and the brilliant strategist behind the attack on Pearl Harbor, was the most important victim of cryptanalysts in World War II. "There is only one Yamamoto and he cannot be replaced," said his successor, Adm. Koga, "His loss for us is a terrible blow." Japanese headquarters did not announce the death until one month later. The Americans finally reported, feigning ignorance of the facts of the matter, that Adm.

Yamamoto had been killed "on one of the aircraft carriers."

On Monday 26 April 1943, south of Mauritius the *U 180* (Comdr. Musenberg) rendezvoused with the Japanese submarine *I 29* (Comdr. Izu), which was to take on board the Indian nationalist leader Chandra Bose and his adjutant. Musenberg stated, "Wearing life jackets, Bose and his adjutant got into a Japanese dinghy. First Bose gave heartfelt thanks for the weeks spent on *U 180*. With flag signals sending greetings and wishes for a safe voyage home for both sides, the two boats made toward their home countries."

The night of 27/28 April 1943, in the climax of minelaying operations off the German coast by the RAF, aircraft of Bomber Command dropped 459 mines off the German and Dutch North Sea coast, as well as in the Bay of Biscay.

During the last night of April 1943, *U 515* (Lt. Condr. Henke), in the area of Freetown, carried out two attacks, sinking eight freighters of Convoy TS-37 proceeding from Trinidad and comprising eighteen ships. This astonishing feat, the most successful U-boat operation was accomplished by Lt. Comdr. Henke with only nine individually fired torpedoes equipped with the new improved magnetic firing pistol.

At the end of April 1943, Grand Admiral Dönitz made a decision with grave consequences, as a result of the successful attacks in the Bay of Biscay by Coastal Command aircraft fitted with 10-cm radar. He now ordered U-boats to proceed through the Bay submerged by night and surfaced by day.

He hoped that the lookouts would be more reliable than the Metox radar-detection equipment. Four U-boats were lost through these tactics. To provide a defence against aircraft attacks, the antiaircraft guns on the U-boats were increased, and some U-boats were converted to so-called aircraft traps. It was their job to secure the U-boat approach routes through the Bay of Biscay. This tactical mistake now made it possible for RAF Coastal Command to achieve extraordinary successes in the fight against the U-boat.

At the end of April 1943, more equipment and weapons were brought into service to help the Allies in their antisubmarine activities: among other things, the magnetic aircraft direction-finding equipment "MAD" [magnetic anomaly detection] that was able to locate the magnetic field of a submerged U-boat up to three hundred feet; and, as back-up weapon, the retro-bombs fitted with a rocket, making it possible to send the bombs down at right angles to the direction of flight onto the U-boat located by MAD. Another device employed was the sonobuoy, a small floating radio transmitter under which was suspended a highly sensitive listening apparatus that transmitted the noise from a U-boat's motors to an aircraft cruising in the area.

In April 1943 German U-boats operating in the Atlantic and Mediterranean sank forty-eight merchantmen totalling 276,517 gross tons. German losses amounted to fifteen U-boats.

The evening of 4 May 1943, the slow convoy ONS-5, proceeding from Great Britain to Halifax, came in contact with the fifty-one U-boats of Group Fink (finch). In the ensuing convoy battle, thirty percent (thirteen ships) of the convoy was lost, and seven U-boats were sunk.

On one day alone, 7 May 1943, six German U-boats were sunk in the Atlantic and four damaged.

In the next convoy battle, on 10 May 1943, U-boats attacking Convoy HX-237 sank three ships and lost three of their own number.

On Wednesday 12 May 1943, the Allies used successfully for the first time an acoustic homing torpedo (known as Mark 24 Mine and, sometimes, Fido). This air-launched torpedo with an acoustic homing head followed a submerged U-boat, drawn to it by the sound of the U-boat's propellors. A long-range Liberator (Flt. Lt. Wright) of 423 Squadron RAF damaged U 456 (Lt. Comdr. Teichert) with a homing torpedo; the next day the U-boat was sunk by the British destroyer *Pathfinder*.

On Thursday 13 May 1943, the remainder of the army group Africa (Col. Gen. von Arnim) in Tunisia capitulated. The Italian 1st Army (Gen. Messe) capitulated the following morning. The Allies had taken more than six months to conquer French North Africa, whereas their operational plans had allowed for six weeks; but hostilities in Africa were over. The Allies now proceeded to draw up plans and preparations for the invasion of Sicily.

There were now some sixty U-boats in the North Atlantic ranged against twelve escort groups, six support groups with three escort carriers and a total of forty long-range B-24 Liberators. The time was ripe for decisive action in the Atlantic.

On Tuesday 18 May 1943, the B-Dienst located Convoy SC-130, comprising thirty-eight ships. Dönitz ordered the U-boat group Donau (Danube) onto the assumed position. The convoy was secured by Escort Group B7, led by one of the best of the former submarine commanders, Comdr. Gretton (on the destroyer *Duncan*). Air cover was provided by long-range B-24 Liberators from 120 Squadron stationed on Iceland.

On the next day, 19 May 1943, U 954 (Lt. Loewe) was hit by two homing torpedoes dropped from a Liberator (Flt. Sgt. Stowes) in the battle of Convoy SC-130. During this action, Sub-Lt. Peter Dönitz, the 20-year-old son of Grand Admiral Dönitz, was killed.

Also on Wednesday 19 May 1943, the U-boat pack Mosel attacked the fast convoy, located by B-Dienst, thereby losing U 752 (Lt. Comdr. Schroeter) without achieving any positive result. This convoy, comprising forty-two ships, was en route from Halifax to Great Britain.

Now, at a time when the services provided by B-Dienst had reached their zenith with scarcely a convoy evading detection, the U-boats were no longer in a position to exploit this success. The age of the wolf-pack tactics was over.

In the decisive six weeks of the Battle of the Atlantic between 6 April 1943 and 19 May 1943, twenty-two convoys comprising 912 ships crossed the Atlantic gap in both directions. Fourteen convoys reached their destinations without loss; eight convoys reported lost twenty-four ships totalling 129,750 gross tons, of which fourteen were freighters in convoy and six were freighters sunk after they had left a convoy; and one ship was lost in a collision. The losses amounted to 2.6 percent of total tonnage.

Equipped with a search receiver that was now scarcely able to do its job, the U-boats could not — despite the self-sacrifice of the crews — cope with the offensive-defensive tactics adopted by escort and support groups, reinforced by escort carrier and long-range aircraft.

On Saturday 22 May 1943, the first "aircraft trap" U-boat, U 441 (Lt. Comdr. von Hartmann), put to sea from Brest on its first mission. The

The front page of a National Socialist publication: U-boat crew watching one of their victims going down

submarine was equipped with a 3.7-cm quick-firing gun, two 2-cm four-barrelled antiaircraft guns, a number of Type 42 machine guns and a rocket launcher.

Between 1 and 22 May 1943, thirty-one German U-boats were sunk, of which twenty-three (seventy-five percent) were destroyed by aircraft and eight by surface vessels. Dönitz stated, "We had already lost thirty-one U-boats by 22 May 1943, a terrifyingly high number, which we had not expected, as — despite the strongly increased defences deployed by the enemy in the fourth year of war — there had been until that time no corresponding increase in U-boat losses."

On Sunday 23 May 1943, rockets were used for the first time in antisubmarine activities. They were said to be able to hit the pressure hull of a U-boat at up to 150 feet underwater, and so to prevent the dive continuing; the U-boat then was to be attacked with conventional weapons. On this day, a Swordfish took off from the escort carrier *Archer* on a reconnaissance in the North Atlantic.

The Swordfish (Sub-Lt. Horrocks) was the first to fly operationally carrying the three-inch rockets that had just been brought into service. Horrocks sighted *U 752* (Lt. Comdr. Schroeter) 750 nautical miles west of Ireland and released a salvo of eight rockets, which pierced the hull of the U-boat. A carrier-borne Wildcat, which accompanied the Swordfish, sank the submarine, no longer capable of submerging.

On the same day Dönitz decided, after the latest failures and the loss of thirty-three U-boats in the first three weeks of May, to discontinue U-boat operations in the North Atlantic. They would not be resumed until new tactics had been worked out and the U-boats fitted with modern, improved equipment.

On Monday 24 May 1943, the war diary of the C-in-C U-boats contained the entry, "Losses have recently been sustained which make the U-boat crisis particularly apparent and demand positive measures. In May, each ten thousand tons sunk in the Atlantic had to be paid for with one U-boat." Dönitz stated, "I drew the necessary conclusions and cleared the Atlantic of U-boats. On 24 May 1943, I ordered the U-boats, under observance of all security precautions, to proceed to the area southwest of the Azores." And so the fifth phase of the Battle of the Atlantic, which had begun in August 1942, ended.

As U-boat operations in the North Atlantic held out no promise of further success, the C-in-C U-boats presumed that there would remain a gap in the mid-Atlantic without air cover. There were certainly no Allied airfields between the Bermudas and North Africa. The three U-boats that remained in the North Atlantic were given instructions to simulate powerful U-boat concentrations by means of radio traffic.

And while these U-boats kept up their deceptive radio traffic, Dönitz formed Group Trutz (defiance) out of the seventeen U-boats withdrawn from the North Atlantic and assigned them to the area southwest of the Azores, where they were to attack a convoy proceeding from Gibraltar westward. Thanks to Ultra, the Admiralty had deciphered radio instructions from the C-in-C U-boats to Group Trutz and deployed a powerful covering force — including the escort carrier *Bogue* — in the threatened area.

At the end of May 1943 the first auxiliary escort carrier or merchant aircraft carrier, the *Empire MacAlpine* (8,000 gross tons) was brought into service to give cover to the convoy. This fast merchant ship was equipped with a flight deck, some 390 feet long and 60 feet wide, that could take up to four Swordfish aircraft. In addition, it could carry up to eighty percent of its normal freight load.

On Monday 31 May 1943, Grand Admiral Dönitz transferred the entire marine armaments to the armaments minister, Albert Speer.

On the same day aircraft of Coastal Command sank *U 440* (Lt. Schwaff) and *U 563* (Lt. Borchardt). Following the orders of Grand Admiral Dönitz, the two U-boats had engaged the aircraft with their antiaircraft guns.

From January to the end of May 1943, a total of 3,568 Allied aircraft dropped 5,429 tons high-explosive bombs and 3,704 incendiary bombs on the U-boat bases for a loss of 98 aircraft. None of the bombs caused, however, serious damage to the roofs of the U-boat bunkers.

During the same period 3,414 Allied aircraft dropped 5,572 tons of high-explosive bombs and 4,173 incendiary bombs on German U-boat shipyards. Their losses amounted to 168 aircraft. None of the shipyards was put out of action, and none of the U-boats under construction was destroyed.

According to British sources, Allied shipping from January to the end of May 1943 lost 365 merchantmen totalling 2,001,918 gross tons. During the same period the U-boats sank 314 merchantment totalling 1,782,625 gross tons, which included 264 ships totalling 1,546,658 gross tons in the Atlantic and the waters around the British Isles.

From 3 September 1939 to the end of May 1943,

German yards built 608 U-boats. Despite all losses, the C-in-C U-boats had more than four hundred submarines at his disposal. Approximately a third of these were in their operational areas; a third were on the approach or return from the operational area; and a third were in the docks being overhauled or serving as training submarines. The U-boat arm finally had the numbers that Dönitz had demanded before the war.

In May 1943 German U-boats operating in the North Atlantic, mid-Atlantic, off South Africa and in the Mediterranean sank forty-four merchantmen totalling 225,772 gross tons. German losses amounted to forty-one U-boats.

The British Admiralty stated, "For the first time, U-boats have been unable to carry out their attacks, even when conditions have been in their favor. There are now reasons for assuming that the enemy's endeavors have passed their zenith." Dönitz: "We have now failed on a technical question regarding weapons, against which a countermeasure will be available." The loss of two thousand submariners, who were even more difficult to replace than the U-boats themselves, was simply too high a price to pay for the sinking of 225,000 gross tons.

There were now only 5,500 tons of enemy shipping capacity destroyed to show for each U-boat lost, forty times less than the monthly average in the first half of 1942. Dönitz stated, "The events of May 1943 showed unequivocally that the defence measures employed by the two large sea powers exceeded the fighting power of our U-boats."

On Friday 4 June 1943, Convoy HX-240 put into Liverpool, the seventh convoy that had crossed the North Atlantic in recent weeks without loss.

On the same day the German commerce raider ship no. 28 *Michel* (Capt. Gumprich, the ex-commander of *Thor*) put to sea from Batavia on what was to be the last operation carried out by a German commerce raider.

On Saturday 5 June 1943, a battle took place between the U-boat group Trutz and Convoy GUS-7A six hundred nautical miles west of the Azores. Aircraft from the escort carrier *Bogue* attacked the U-boats and sank *U 217* (Lt. Comdr. Reichenbach-Klinke). The convoy succeeded in getting away without loss.

From Monday 7 June 1943, the C-in-C U-boats deployed eight submarines in the North Atlantic. They were to cruise in this area and, by radio traffic and short signals, give the impression of a stronger U-boat concentration.

Between 27 January and 10 June 1943, the US 8th Army Air Force had mounted a series of heavy air raids against German U-boat bases along the Atlantic coast. Brest was bombed three times,

A British sailor gives a German U-boat man a helping hand.

Lorient four times, St. Nazaire five times and La Pallice twice. At the same time RAF bomber formations concentrated on raids at night, deploying between three hundred and five hundred aircraft against the same targets. In only one month Lorient was bombed nine times and St. Nazaire eleven. Of the attacks mounted, sixty-three percent of all American attacks and thirty percent of British were directed against U-boat bases, shipyards and subcontractors.

The C-in-C U-boats, who regarded the current situation as a temporary, technical superiority on the part of the Allies, hoped to be able to go over to the offensive again in late summer, with acoustic torpedoes, new search receiver equipment and antiaircraft weapons.

Dönitz said, "In June 1943 I had to make the hardest decision of the entire war. The simple question was whether I should withdraw U-boats from all areas and terminate the U-boat war, or whether I should let them fight on — despite enemy superiority — using some method of attack adapted to the circumstances. . . . I came to the decision that we had to fight on for reasons of sheer necessity."

On Thursday 17 June 1943, a four-engined Dornier Do 26 V6 flying boat from 1/KF1Gr 506 landed at Sabine Island (East Greenland). The aircraft took off the surviving members of the Holzauge meteorological detachment (led by Dr. G. Weiss). The detachment had had to fight fierce engagements with a Danish ski patrol during its stay on the island (from 22 August 1942), and the weather ship *Sachsen*, which had put the detachment ashore, had been bombed and sunk by American bombers while it was stuck fast in the ice. The Do 26 took the survivors to Banak (Norway); their sledge-dogs were also taken back, where they were used in a secret naval training center for meteorological detachments in Goldhöne (Riesengebirge, Silesia).

On Tuesday 22 June 1943, Dönitz signed the order to build U-boat types XXI and XXIII, which were to bring about a turn in the Battle of the Atlantic. Only one of type XXI and two of type XXIII were completed and commissioned before the capitulation.

On Monday 28 June 1943, the German meteorological detachment Nussbaum (nut tree), led by Dr. F. Nusser, was repatriated by U-boat from the operational area in northwest Spitsbergen, where they had been since 7 October 1942.

In June 1943 German U-boats operating in the Mediterranean and the Indian Ocean sank twenty merchantmen totalling 86,807 gross tons. German losses amounted to seventeen U-boats.

At the end of June 1943 there were already more than eleven hundred aircraft of all types permanently deployed as submarine hunters in the Atlantic area. Now that the convoys could cross the North Atlantic route without danger and the support groups and numerous fighters used on antisubmarine duties were released, the Admiralty decided to launch a new offensive against the approach routes of the U-boats in the Bay of Biscay.

To give each other mutual support during air attacks by means of their antiaircraft weapons, U-boats from the beginning of June had adopted new tactics. When crossing the Bay of Biscay, they now proceeded in groups of up to five submarines. They were also given fighter protection, albeit relatively weak, by aircraft of No. 1 Wing of Zerstörergeschwader 1 (a long-range and escort fighter group). To counter, Coastal Command now deployed a formation of seven aircraft three times daily to fly on parallel courses northwest of Cape Finisterre (Operation Musketry and Sea Slug). The area to be patrolled was the equivalent of the distance that a U-boat could cross carrying out its normal routine of four hours on the surface and twenty hours underwater.

At the end of June 1943 the C-in-C U-boats decided to deploy operational U-boats in distant waters in the hope that Allied countermeasures would not be quite so strong. The main points were to be the Caribbean, Brazilian coastal waters, the west and southeast coasts of Africa and the Indian Ocean. During their operational patrol the U-boats were to be provisioned and fuelled by transport submarines.

In June 1943 eleven U-boats, including two transport submarines, put to sea from Kiel. Their objective was to carry out patrols in the Indian Ocean.

In the Pacific, American submarines now adopted German wolf-pack tactics. The groups, which normally consisted of three subs, ran little risk. They were able to follow their targets with radar without being located. Japanese escort vessels were not equipped with radar sets.

Hitler, who had little time for the German Navy, had hoped for too long that the successes achieved by the German Army and the Luftwaffe would be decisive in winning the war. Now that he recognised the full significance of the Battle of the Atlantic, he regarded the U-boats as his last trump card. Hitler said, "The Atlantic is the advance battlefield in the west, and even if I have to fight a defensive war there, that is better than having to fight a defensive war along the coasts of Europe." But he never understood how to deploy the German U-boat arm within the framework of a comprehensive marine strategy. U-boats had to operate independently of surface units and, because of the

The end of a U-boat south of Ireland: The US Coast
Guard cutter *Spencer* attacks *U 175* (Lt. Comdr. Burns) with
depth charges.

lack of tactical support by surface units and the
lack of aerial reconnaissance, were forced to rely
on their own devices.

The Battle of the Atlantic was decided by – in
addition to particularly well-trained support and
escort groups using the new HF/DF location
equipment – long-range aircraft equipped with
centimetric radar; carrier-borne aircraft; new antisubmarine weapons; new heavy depth charges; improved installation for launching these weapons;
and the success achieved by radio intelligence
(Ultra decrypts). Dönitz said, "All this rendered
further action against the convoys impossible."

During the first half of 1943 Allied shipping lost
eight ships totalling 14,413 gross tons through
Luftwaffe attacks and the mining of British
waters. During this period German S-boats sank
two ships totalling 6,580 gross tons.

1943

July–December

Battle of the Atlantic

Saturday 10 July 1943, London
The *Reuters* News Agency reported:

Yesterday evening in London and Washington a joint declaration was given relating to the future reporting of the U-boat war. The president of the USA and the prime minister of Great Britain have been disquieted by the large number of bulletins issued by various persons on the subject of the U-boat scene. Through these statements, the enemy could gather more information on the facts of the matter than is considered desirable. It has therefore been resolved that from this moment on a report approved by the president and the prime minister will be published on the tenth of each month. With the exception of special communiqués, this monthly statement issued by the governments of the USA and Great Britain will from now on be the only information released on this theme. The following is the first of these monthly statements, for July 1943:

1. In June losses sustained by Allied and neutral merchant ships through U-boat attacks were the lowest since the entry of the USA in the war, as were losses through other enemy activities.

2. Opportunities for deploying Allied ships and aircraft in antisubmarine activities were fewer in June than previously; nonetheless, the number of Axis U-boats sunk is considered satisfactory.

3. The heavy losses sustained by German U-boats in May have had their effect in June to such an extent that the most important convoys in the Atlantic were left virtually in peace. No opportunity was neglected to attack German U-boats while proceeding to or from their bases on the French western seaboard.

Refugees from Norway

Wednesday 28 July 1943, London
The *Reuters* News Agency reported:

Crown Prince Olaf of Norway has stated that during the last two years thousands of Norwegians have arrived along the coasts of Great Britain in small fishing boats.

Attack on Allied Convoy

Sunday 15 August 1943, Berlin
The German *DNB* News Agency reported:

A strong formation of German bombers located east of Gibraltar a large convoy, secured by a large number of warships and escorts, heading toward the Mediterranean. The attack, launched by a strong formation of German torpedo bombers against the convoy's seventy fully laden merchantmen, took place on Friday evening. According to the latest reports, the attack has been extraordinarily successful. Despite intensive antiaircraft defence, thirty-two ships totalling approximately 170,000 gross tons were sunk or destroyed.

90 German U-boats Sunk!

15 August 1943, London
The *Reuters* News Agency reported:

A joint statement for July made by W. Churchill and F. D. Roosevelt on the U-boat war situation: During the last three months ninety enemy U-boats have been sunk, and Allied shipping capacity has increased since the beginning of the year by three million tons. . . . During July U-boats achieved only minimal success in all their widespread operational areas against Allied shipping. . . . It would seem that July was, in fact, our most successful month.

The Fighting on Sicily
Wednesday 18 August 1943, Berlin
The *DNB* Agency reported:

The Kriegsmarine has transported to and from Sicily some 65,000 troops, 16,000 vehicles, 350 guns, 78 tanks, and 39,000 tons of ammunition, building materials, rations and other supplies. These figures do not show the important transport contribution made by the Italian Navy, the German and Italian air forces, as well as the transports carried out before fighting on Sicily commenced.

Danish Warships in Sweden
Sunday 29 August 1943, Stockholm
The Swedish newspaper *Svenska Dagbladet* reported:

A part of the Danish fleet has succeeded in escaping to Sweden. Early this morning nine Danish ships, including a destroyer, a coastal protection boat as well as three sailing ships, arrived in Landskrona, while a minesweeper and several other ships carrying refugees arrived in Malmö. All the vessels were full of seamen, officers, police officials and civilians. In all some four hundred persons arrived in Sweden on these ships. . . . Another part of the fleet, which could not get through to Sweden, is said to have scuttled itself. German warships and aircraft are now keeping The Sound under surveillance.

Brazilians Sink U-boat
29 August 1943, Rio de Janeiro
The *Reuters* News Agency reported:

Brazilian air units sank an Axis submarine off Rio de Janeiro on 31 July. Two crew members were saved.

18,428,800 GRT Sunk by U-boats
Wednesday 1 September 1943, Berlin
The *DNB* Agency reported:

With the sinking of 142,500 gross tons in August 1943, the total tonnage sunk by the German U-boat arm in the last eight months has risen to 6,054,800 tons of enemy merchant and transport shipping capacity. In four years of war the German U-boats have sunk a total of 18,428,800 gross tons. These figures do not include shipping capacity damaged and warships sunk and damaged. Merchant tonnage sunk by the Axis sea and air forces during this period amount to approximately 33.4 million gross tons, of which 18.4 million (fifty-five percent) were sunk by German U-boats.

German Bombs on Italian Ships
Friday 10 September 1943, Berlin
The *DNB* Agency reported:

An Italian battleship and a cruiser were sunk by German bombers between Sardinia and Corsica on Thursday. The units belonged to an Italian formation that had fled La Spezia and, acting on instructions from the Allied Supreme Command, attempted to neutralise German shipping between Sardinia and Corsica.

Italian Warships in Malta
Sunday 12 September 1943
From Allied Headquarters:

Until now at least twenty-two Italian warships, including five battleships, seven cruisers and ten destroyers, have reached the port of LaValetta. Adm. Cunningham stated that other Italian ships, especially submarines, should make for Allied ports in the Mediterranean.

Italian S-boats Attack German Convoy
14 September 1943
From *Admiral Cunningham's Headquarters:*

According to reports, the first engagement has taken place between Italian S-boats and a strongly escorted German convoy between the Italian mainland and Elba. The S-boat formation sank a heavily laden transporter and scored hits on two escort vessels, causing them to burst into flames.

Heavy Allied Losses at Salerno
Thursday 16 September 1943, Berlin
The *DNB* Agency reported:

Allied shipping losses in the Gulf of Salerno have now reached such a scale that a positive weakening of the Anglo-American invasion fleet has been caused. During the period 8–15 September alone, four cruisers, two destroyers and other warships, plus ten merchantmen — totalling together 59,000 gross tons — and fifteen landing craft of various sizes have all been sunk by direct hits. Also believed destroyed are one cruiser, two destroyers as well as seven transporters, totalling 35,000 gross tons and a large landing boat.

Swiss Radio Beromünster
Friday 17 September 1943

The landings near Salerno, where the Allies have established five bridgeheads, are a textbook example of the risk taken by an amphibious operation without sufficient fighter protection. . . . The crisis that arose during the landing operations, which over three days had assumed really ominous proportions, has been overcome the more so, as the

Coastal patrol cruiser *Ingham* WPG 35 of the US Support Group (Iceland), commanded by Capt. Short

advance of units of Montgomery's 8th Army have joined up with the Americans near Salerno.

Soviets Harass British Seamen

W. Churchill to J. W. Stalin
Friday 1 October 1943

I must also ask your help in remedying the conditions under which our service personnel and seaman at present find themselves in North Russia. These men are of course engaged in operations against the enemy in our joint interest, and chiefly to bring Allied supplies to your country. They are, I am sure you will admit, in a wholly different position from ordinary individuals proceeding to Russian territory. Yet they are subjected by your authorities to the following restrictions, which seem to me inappropriate for men sent by an Ally to carry out operations of the greatest interest to the Soviet Union:

a) No one may land from one of H.M. ships or from a British merchant ship except by a Soviet boat in the presence of a Soviet official and after examination of documents on each occasion.

b) No one from a British warship is allowed to proceed alongside a British merchantman without the Soviet authorities being informed beforehand. This even applies to the British admiral in charge.

c) British officers and enlisted are required to obtain special passes before they can go from ship to shore or between two British shore stations. These passes are often much delayed, with consequent dislocation of the work in hand.

d) No stores, luggage, or mail for this operational force may be landed except in the presence of a Soviet official, and numerous formalities are required for the shipment of all stores and mail.

e) Private service mail is subjected to censorship, although for an operational force of this kind censorship should, in our view, be left in the hands of British Service authorities. . . .

The cumulative effect of these formalities has been most hampering to the efficient performance of the men's duties, and on more than one occasion to urgent and important operations. No such restrictions are placed upon Soviet personnel here.

Heavy Fighting on Kos

Monday 4 October 1943, Berlin
The *DNB* Agency reported:

The island of Kos, one of the Dodecanese group situated northwest of Rhodes, was occupied some time ago by British troops who have apparently been supplied by Badoglio's forces. Since its occupation, the island has primarily become a base for British aircraft that have carried out attacks against Rhodes. Yesterday morning resolute action by a number of German landing parties—who were able to approach the coast unnoticed in landing craft—took possession of all important military installations. The enemy, taken by surprise, put up a determined resistance only at certain points, during which he sustained severe casualties. More than two hundred British soldiers were taken prisoner. A number of British troops fled into the difficult hilly country in the island's interior. Among the booty taken were four British bombers.

Sardinia and Corsica Evacuated

Tuesday 5 October 1943, Berlin
The *DNB* Agency reported:

The evacuation of Sardinia and Corsica by German troops was carried out with only negligible losses. Small vessels from the Kriegsmarine and transport aircraft from the Luftwaffe evacuated between twenty-five thousand and thirty thousand men within a period of eighteen days. In addition, more than six thousand tons of army equipment, almost six thousand motor vehicles, guns and tanks were transported off the island onto the mainland. During this operation, 250 men were reported killed or missing, and twenty-five transport aircraft as well as a number of small transport ships were lost.

U-boat War Livens Up Again

Sunday 10 October 1943, London
The *Reuters* News Agency reported:

The joint statement for September made by W. Churchill and F. D. Roosevelt on the U-boat war situation: From the middle of May until 3 September, not a single Allied ship was sunk in the Atlantic by German U-boats. This four-month lull was broken on 19 September. A convoy sailing on a westerly course was attacked by a group of at least fifteen U-boats. This shows that the enemy has once again taken up operations with strong U-boat forces and intends, with all the means at his disposal, to force a turning point to his own advantage.

Midget-submarines against the Tirpitz
Monday 11 October 1943, London
The *Reuters* News Agency reported:

British midget-submarines caused damage to the *Tirpitz* below the waterline during an attack on German warships lying at their anchorage, presumed safe, in the Altafjord in Norway. Three of the midget-submarines failed to return from this operation.

British Bases on the Azores
Tuesday 12 October 1943, London
The *Reuters* News Agency reported:

Amid extraordinary tension, Prime Minister Churchill announced in Parliament today that Portugal had granted Great Britain military bases on the Azores.

"Contribution to the shortening of the war"
Wednesday 13 October 1943, London
The *United Press Agency* reported:

Foreign Secretary Eden sent Portuguese Premier Salazar a message of thanks in which he stated, "The use of naval and air bases on the Azores will make it possible for our forces to afford even more effective security for our Atlantic shipping. Portugal's decision will make a considerable contribution to the shortening of the war."

Kos Occupied by German Forces
13 October 1943
From General Wilson's Headquarters:

The last radio message from British troops on

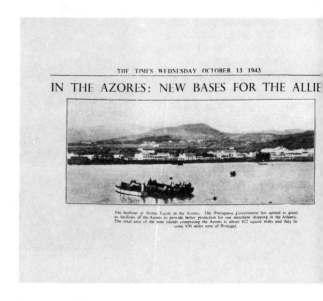

THE TIMES WEDNESDAY OCTOBER 13 1943

IN THE AZORES: NEW BASES FOR THE ALLIE

The harbour at Horta, Fayal, in the Azores. The Portuguese Government has agreed to grant us facilities in the Azores to provide better protection for our merchant shipping in the Atlantic. The total area of the nine islands comprising the Azores is about 922 square miles and they lie some 800 miles west of Portugal.

Kos read, "Do not expect to hear any more from us. We are at the end of our strength." With this, fighting on the island was terminated.

German-Japanese Protest in Lisbon
Friday 15 October 1943, Berlin
The *DNB* Agency reported:

The German government today delivered through its ambassador in Lisbon a formal note to the Portuguese government, protesting in the strongest possible terms Portugal's giving way to British pressure for the granting of military bases on the Azores, and thereby being guilty of a flagrant breach of Portuguese neutrality. The German government has reserved the right to undertake any measures that may be required, owing to the changed situation on the Azores.

Swiss Radio Beromünster

15 October 1943
The Royal Navy has also undertaken fresh operations in the Atlantic. British midget-submarines carried out a daring attack on the *Tirpitz* while it was lying at anchor in the Altafjord in North Norway. An important change affecting the safety of shipping in the South Atlantic, and the outcome of the U-boat war, has taken place in that Portugal has granted the Royal Navy the use of bases on the Azores for the duration of the war. This concession, made by Portugal to Great Britain, obviously also has a political significance, as the overall political situation in Europe has undergone characteristic changes as a consequence of the course of the war.

Right: An Allied convoy ploughs laboriously through heavy Arctic seas, nearest to the camera, a British escort vessel.

Left: 10/13/1943, the first picture and report in the British press on bases on the Azores

New Japanese U-boat Tactics

Saturday 23 October 1943, Los Angeles
The *United Press Agency* reported:

The Japanese submarine service has adopted the German U-boat wolf-pack tactics. By these means the Japanese intend to disrupt US shipping between Hawaii and the United States. The crews of American ships that have just put into Los Angeles report fierce submarine attacks, although these did not appear to lead to any sinkings of great significance. A tanker was twice torpedoed and set ablaze. The tanker's crew is missing. Another American tanker was able to ward off several attacks and escape. The local naval information office has permitted publication of this communiqué but will neither confirm nor deny it.

Germans in the Dodecanese

Friday 29 October 1943, Berlin
The *International Information Office* reported:

The isle of Levita in the Dodecanese is again in German hands. Several of the off-lying islands in the Dodecanese have again fallen into German hands after garrisons fighting on the side of Badoglio were driven out.

A U-boat Is Sunk

RAF leaflet *Luftpost*, 2 November 1943

"Look out!" yells the radio telegraphist petty officer, and in the same moment all we can hear is the thundering, roaring and crashing of depth charges. The depth charge battle has begun; depth charges are now dropped unceasingly, one after the other. We cannot even think clearly. The ship's lights go out. Some of the crew stampede into the control room — but what is the point of that? We are already nearly six hundred feet down. "Both hydroplanes out of action!" yells the No. 1. From astern the report comes in, "Port E-motors out of action." And still the depth charges keep coming. I look over at the captain in the tower, incapable of giving even one order. Suddenly there's an inhuman cry of "She's taking in water!" The first watch-keeping officer yells, "Oh God, I've had it!" and collapses. The captain has lost his nerve.

At this moment a cry, a mad cry echoes through the ship, "Chlorine gas — chlorine gas!" The new crewman bellow out, "Chlorine gas!" The seawater that leaked in has gotten into the batteries and is giving off chlorine gas that spreads quickly from compartment to compartment. The crew cough and gasp. An engine room petty officer suddenly stands beside me, his face is dark red, beads of sweat cover his forehead. His eyes, I think to myself, these eyes — bulging out of their sockets, staring at me; and suddenly he bursts into a mad, animal laugh. Two others are standing close to me. My heart thumps right up to my throat. I cough, and go quite lightheaded. I've no idea how I got into the control room. The chief engineer groans and collapses. Suddenly a shudder goes through the entire boat. It suddenly takes up an almost vertical position and slowly rises. We fall about all over the place. A few don't get up but stay where they are, rolling about the deck in convulsions of coughing. Nobody bothers to ask who gave the command to blow the tanks.

Now the sub breaks out onto the surface. A hissing noise goes through the boat, the captain has opened up the hatch. "Make the dinghy ready!" he growls. Suddenly a panic breaks out in the boat; out, I think to myself, let's just get out of it. For a moment I think my heart will jump through my chest. And now, now they're firing shells at us.

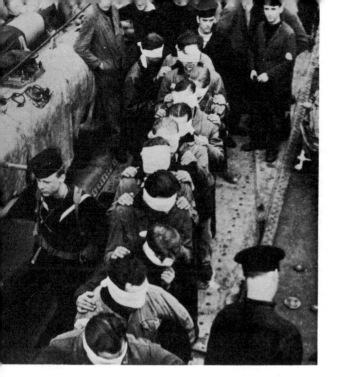

Members of a rescued U-boat crew, now POWs of the British, going ashore

Battle of the Atlantic

Air and Sea Battle off the Solomons
10 November 1943, Tokyo
The *DNB* Agency reported:

A spokesman for the Imperial government has made the following statement on the battle near Bougainville. An enemy battleship reported yesterday as badly damaged has now sunk. In addition, three more heavy cruisers, as well as a light cruiser or destroyer, were damaged and another three aircraft shot down. Japanese losses have been increased by five more aircraft.

Official Denial by the US Navy
10 November 1943, Washington
The *Reuters* News Agency reported:

Navy Secretary Knox stated at a press conference that not one word was true of the Japanese reports on the sinking of numerous US warships in the South Pacific. He added that this related to a false report, issued with the intention of gaining information.

New Type of German U-boat
Thursday 11 November 1943, Washington
The *Reuters* News Agency reported:

The commander of an American aircraft carrier, who recently took part in a battle between a convoy and U-boats, has stated that the Germans are now deploying considerably larger U-boats than has been hitherto the case. These are real submarine-cruisers.

Fighting on the Dodecanese

Saturday 13 November 1943
The *German High Command* issued the following communiqué:

During continued attacks against enemy naval forces in the eastern Mediterranean, the Luftwaffe scored a number of hits on a total of five units, which were badly damaged. After these successes and after continuous attacks on bases situated on Leros had created the right conditions for an assault on the island, a number of units, including paratroops, landed early the morning of 12 November. They acted in cooperation with naval and Luftwaffe warships and transports. Still in progress is fighting with the British troops and troops loyal to Badoglio.

Thursday 18 November 1943
The *German High Command* issued the following communiqué:

As already announced in a special communiqué, German Army and Luftwaffe troops, led by Lt. Gen. Müller, took the British naval base at Leros

Blow after blow thuds into the boat. Nobody's giving orders any more. . . . Another salvo of shells hits the boat like a giant fist—the boat breaks in half and goes down into the depths with more than a half of the crew.

Only two out of the three dinghies managed to get away from the sinking U-boat at the last moment. And one of these was sucked down into the depths with the submarine as it went under. The other boat, carrying the captain, the first watchkeeping officer, an engine room petty officer and two leading-seamen, managed to stay on the surface. They were picked up by a British destroyer and taken on board. I struck out with a few strokes, but everything went dark before my eyes, well, not exactly dark, but grey. My lungs must be burning, I thought to myself, they must be absolutely ablaze. Well, it was the gas, of course, it was the gas. I lost consciousness. When I awoke, I was on board a British corvette. They fished me and three of my mates out of the water, but two of them died as a result of gas poisoning before we reached port in England.

Saturday 6 November 1943
The *German High Command* issued the following communiqué:

S-boats again attacked the convoy on the east coast of England during the night of 5 November, and torpedoed three ships totalling nine thousand gross tons. Because of the strong defensive fire, it cannot be confirmed that they sank, but it is probable.

on 16 November, after four days of tough and changeable fighting against an enemy superior in both numbers and armaments.

Air attack on a U-boat: Two of the crew seek shelter near the twin Flak guns.

The Dodecanese in German Hands
18 November 1943, Berlin
The *DNB* Agency reported:

With the capitulation of Leros, practically the whole of the Dodecanese is in German hands. Only Castelrosso is still held by the enemy.

W. Churchill to Foreign Secretary Eden
Sunday 21 November 1943

Leros is a bitter blow to me. Should it be raised in Parliament, I recommend the following line:

One may ask should such operations ever have been undertaken without the assurance of air superiority? Have we not failed to learn the lessons of Crete, etc?. . . No attempts should be made to minimise the poignancy of the loss of the Dodecanese, which we had a chance of getting so easily and at so little cost and which we have now lost after heavy expenditure.

Monday 22 November 1943
The *German High Command* issued the following communiqué:

In bad weather in the Atlantic a bomber formation is attacking an enemy convoy and has damaged two merchantmen (totalling eighteen thousand gross tons) so badly that their destruction can be presumed.

Operations against the Gilbert Islands
Tuesday 23 November 1943, Pearl Harbor
The *United Press Agency* reported:

US naval circles stress that for the assault on the Gilbert Islands Adm. Nimitz has deployed one of the largest naval formation that has ever been in action, to ward off a counterattack by Japanese naval forces. Some of the most modern aircraft carriers, battleships and cruisers are taking part in the operation.

Saturday 27 November 1943
The *German High Command* issued the following communiqué:

German torpedo bombers successfully attacked off the Algerian coast a strongly defended convoy of large troopships. The bombers sank two destroyers and three troopships, totalling 38,000 gross tons. Two destroyers more, a large transporter and an escort vessel were heavily damaged.

Fierce Fighting for the Gilbert Islands
Monday 29 November 1943, Pearl Harbor
The *Associated Press* reported:

Fighting for the islet of Betio and the Tarawa atoll in the Gilbert Islands saw the bloodiest fighting ever engaged in by the US Marine Corps. The officer leading the attack, Col. Meritta, reports that two battalions of US Marines were almost completely wiped out in the first assaults. The marines had to wade through shallow water for seven hundred yards under heavy Japanese machine-gun fire, dragging their ammunition with them, as the coral reefs made it impossible for landing craft to approach the shore.

More U-boats Sunk than Merchantmen
Friday 10 December 1943, London
The *United Press Agency* reported:

A joint statement for November made by W. Churchill and F. D. Roosevelt on the U-boat war situation: In the U-boat war, the month of November was notable for the scant success achieved by U-boats despite their strong deployment. The number of merchantmen sunk by U-boats in November was the lowest since May 1940. Because of our air bases on the Azores, it was possible to reinforce the covering of Allied convoys and narrow the zone in which German U-boats could still operate undisturbed. The caution with which U-boats now operate has reduced the opportunity for Allied forces to attack them. Despite that, the number of U-boats sunk in November again exceeded the number of merchantmen sunk by the U-boats.

Left: The battleship *Duke of York* during the engagement with the battlecruiser *Scharnhorst*, cutting off the German ship's line of retreat (12/25/1943)

Right: 7/10/1943, Operation Husky, the invasion of Sicily, British soldiers unloading ammunition

First Report of Success from the Azores
Sunday 12 December 1943, London
The New York Times reported:

Only two weeks after British aircraft commenced operations from the Azores with the object of closing the Atlantic gap, a B-17 Flying Fortress of Coastal Command has sunk a German U-boat.

Sunday 26 December 1943
The *German High Command* issued the following communiqué:

U-boats operating in the Atlantic and in the Mediterranean have recently sunk five ships totalling 34,500 gross tons and torpedoed another ship. Nine enemy destroyers and escort vessels belonging to convoy covering forces and U-boat—hunting groups were sunk. Antiaircraft fire from the Kriegsmarine shot down a Sunderland flying boat over the Bay of Biscay.

Scharnhorst Sunk

Monday 27 December 1943
The *German High Command* issued the following communiqué:

Toward 11:00 A.M. on 26 December, the battlecruiser *Scharnhorst*, with Adm. Bey, flag officer of destroyers, on board, came into action with enemy convoy escorts made up of destroyers and cruisers. Shortly after the engagement commenced, a major naval unit of the enemy joined in the fighting.

During the battle, the enemy succeeded in bringing up more heavy units that were not at first

sighted because of the visibility conditions at the time. After a number of hours of bitter fighting, the *Scharnhorst*, commanded by Capt. Hintze, was overcome by the enemy naval units and sank toward 7:30 P.M. with its colors flying, having caused the enemy severe damage and having fought to its last shell. No losses were suffered by other German vessels taking part in the engagement.

Next of kin will be informed of the fate of the *Scharnhorst*'s crew as soon as news has been received.

Strategy and Tactics

JULY TO DECEMBER 1943

The morning of 1 July 1943, during the monsoons, troops of US Task Force 31 (Rear Adm. Turner) landed on the beaches of New Georgia (Central Solomons). Surprisingly, they encountered no Japanese resistance. For the first time the Americans deployed a landing force equipped with the most modern weapons and trained in the latest operational techniques. The little-known Coastwatching Organisation was allocated a special role during the fighting for the Solomons. This civilian group had been organised by the Royal Australian Navy at the end of World War I and, having been reactivated immediately upon the outbreak of World War II under Comdr. E. A. Field (RAN), was now to act on behalf of the intelligence service by reporting foreign ship movements. The

coastwatchers numbered over one hundred, spread around the three thousand–mile coastline of the islands, and from 1941/42 gave radio warning of Japanese air raids and carried out coastal watching duties. In addition to this intelligence gathering, they helped escaped prisoners of war, saved hundreds of flyers who had been shot down, rescued shipwrecked seamen, and also fought as guerrillas.

The headquarters of the organisation in Townsville (Queensland) maintained radio contact with the coastwatchers and was itself in contact with the Head of Naval Intelligence in Melbourne. From the middle of 1942, the coastwatching organisation was placed under the direct control of the Allied Intelligence Bureau (US Gen. Willoughby). Accordingly, its reports on Japanese ship movements could be radioed across the entire Pacific.

As a rule these groups combined four Australians and a dozen Solomon Islanders. Armaments were brought in by aircraft and submarines, food was provided by cooperative local inhabitants.

If the radio traffic of the coastwatchers was located by enemy radio intelligence, natives acting as observers warned of Japanese search parties. Adm. Halsey, Jr., C-in-C South Pacific, stated, "The coastwatchers saved Guadalcanal, and Guadalcanal saved the Pacific."

On Thursday 8 July 1943, a U-boat was sunk for the first time by an American acoustic homing torpedo, Fido (British description, Mark 24 Mine). It was the *U 514* (Lt. Comdr. Auffermann) and was hit by a Liberator (Flying Officer Campbell, 224 Squadron), the boat went down with its entire crew.

On Saturday 10 July 1943, Allied units commanded by Gen. Eisenhower landed on the southeast coast of Sicily (Operation Husky). A force of 200 Allied warships, 320 troop transporters, 900 large and 1,225 small landing craft took part in the operation. Axis troops offered determined resistance at various points, in particular the German paratroop division Hermann Göring. But after two days Syracuse and Augusta were occupied by the Allies.

To combat the U-boats and, in particular, the U-boat tankers, the US Navy formed special hunter-killer groups that, not used as convoy escorts, operated independently. As a rule these groups consisted of an escort carrier and five or more destroyers. Within three months, the hunter-killer groups sank fifteen U-boats, eight of which were U-boat tankers. Allied losses amounted to only three carrier-borne aircraft.

When the Grand Fascist Council met in Rome on Sunday 25 July 1943, it held Mussolini responsible for the defeats suffered by the country. King Victor Emmanuel III appointed Marshal Badoglio to head a new government. The Fascist party was dissolved, and the Fascist government in Italy collapsed. Marshal Badoglio gave his assurance that he certainly wished to continue the war on the side of the Germans but nonetheless immediately carried out secret negotiations with the Allies to end the war for Italy "as quickly as possible and by all possible means."

The British Naval Intelligence Division established a new radio station, Radio Livorno, in addition to the Atlantiksender. The task of the new station was to win over the Italian Navy for the Allied cause. This, the most successful psychologi-

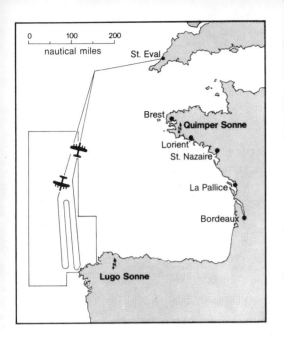

cal operation of the war, was arranged in the most cold-blooded manner. The station was situated on Malta, and the announcers were British subjects of Italian extraction. The task of Radio Livorno was, at the right moment, to persuade the Italian fleet to put into Allied ports. Sefton Delmer said, "The station pretended to be coming from an Italian warship in the naval base at Livorno, operating in the name of the Italian resistance."

Additionally, the British Admiralty's Naval Intelligence Division was responsible for the content of the broadcasts. During the evening broadcasts, the announcer of Radio Livorno would appeal to his comrades in the Italian Navy not to let themselves be taken unaware by the Germans who would possibly try to seize Italian ships by force. Radio Livorno entreated Italian crews not to move their ships without its express orders. The station implied that it was already conducting negotiations with the Allies to remove the Italian fleet from the Germans' grasp. Astonishingly, there was no German reaction to these broadcasts.

At this time the sixth phase of the Battle of the Atlantic commenced, lasting until the end of August 1943.

The Allied air offensive in the Bay of Biscay caused the U-boats more losses. On Wednesday 28 July 1943, Liberators sank the *U 404* (Lt. Schönberg).

On the following day, 29 July 1943, a Wellington attacked *U 614* (Lt. Comdr. Sträter).

Also on 29 July 1943, German military intelligence intercepted a radio conversation between Churchill and Roosevelt, in which they discussed a proclamation to be made by Gen. Eisenhower and the imminent armistice with Italy. Two days later, on 31 July 1943, Hitler issued his first instructions on action to be adopted should Italy drop out as an ally.

On Saturday 31 July 1943, an aircraft of the Brazilian Air Force sank the German U-boat *U 199* (Comdr. Kraus). The commander and eleven of his crew were saved.

In July 1943 the number of ships sunk by German U-boats in the Indian Ocean increased to seventeen. The Allies did not have a sufficient number of escort vessels at their disposal in this area; and so, when making up the convoys, they took into account only the most important routes between South Africa, the Arabian peninsula and India. On other routes, ships had to travel without escort. In addition, there were insufficient aircraft to carry out a comprehensive aerial reconnaissance on the convoy routes.

In July 1943 German U-boats operating in the Mediterranean and in the Atlantic and Indian oceans sank forty-six merchantmen totalling 245,178 gross tons. German losses amounted to thirty-seven U-boats, most of which were lost to aircraft, and of these, one-half went down in the Bay of Biscay.

The offensive in mid- and south-Atlantic waters brought the U-boats only modest success. July 1943 was the last month in which Allied shipping losses in the Atlantic exceeded two hundred thousand gross tons.

After several months of preparations, the Allies commenced their offensives in the Pacific. The first objective was to break through the Japanese defensive ring in the Bismark Archipelago. The center was based on Rabaul, between the western part of the Solomons and New Guinea.

From 27 July until the beginning of August 1943, ten U-boats were lost in the Bay of Biscay. Dönitz said, "The endeavors of the enemy to block our exit routes seems to have reached their zenith."

Left: Survivors on an emergency raft cross the path of a U-boat

Far left: Surveillance patrol by a Liberator off the Bay of Biscay—13 hours and 15 minutes

Right: Operation Wunderland II on Novaya Zemliya, the crew of *U 225* try in vain to save a Bv 138 flying boat from sinking.

On Sunday 1 August 1943, British Sunderlands sank *U 383* (Lt. Comdr. Kremser) and *U 454* (Lt. Comdr. Hackländer). The next day, 2 August 1943, *U 106* (Lt. Damerow) and *U 706* (Lt. Comdr. von Zitzewitz) were lost through air attacks.

On the same day the *U 255* (Lt. Harms) put into the quiet, remote bay near Sporyi Navolok, on the northern coast of Novaya Zemlya. The crew built a blockhouse out of large quantities of driftwood. Fuel, ammunition and provisions were put ashore. From this base, a Bv 138 flying boat from Sea Reconnaissance Wing 130 (SaGr 130) was to carry out reconnaissance patrols over Dickson, White Island, the Vilkitski Strait northeast of the Urals, as preparation for an operation against the Siberian sea lane (Operation Wunderland II). The U-boat group Viking (three U-boats) and the heavy cruiser *Lützow*, lying in the Altafjord and ready to put to sea, were to carry out this operation, supported by *U 255* (Lt. Harms) and *U 601* (Lt. Comdr. Grau). After the loss of the Bv 138 flying boat, which sank, the *Lützow* remained in the Altafjord, and the operation was cancelled.

On Monday 2 August 1943, Dönitz gave a provisional order stopping U-boats putting to sea from bases in the Bay of Biscay. Returning U-boats were instructed to stay close to the Spanish coast.

The night of 2/3 August 1943, Operation Gomorrha, a series of the heaviest air raids on Hamburg, came to an end. In addition to considerable civilian casualties, new U-boats in the shipyards of Blohm & Voss, *U 996, U 1011, U 1012*, were destroyed, and ships totalling 170,000 gross tons were destroyed in the harbor.

During the night of 3/4 August 1943, three teams of Italian torpedo men, led by Comdr. Notari, left their secret base on the freighter *Olterra*, lying at Algeciras in Spain, and launched another attack on shipping in the Gibraltar roads. The Italians sank the American freighter *Harrison Gray Otis* (7,176 gross tons) as well as a Norwegian tanker, *Thorshövdi* (9,944 gross tons) and damaged the freighter *Stanridge* (5,975 gross tons).

The British authorities in Gibraltar now turned their attention to the *Olterra*. With the agreement of the Spanish authorities, the ship was taken prize and brought to Gibraltar. The crew was able to make off before the action was carried out. On board the *Olterra* were compartments for assembling manned torpedoes and an exit for the torpedoes below the water line.

On Tuesday 17 August 1943, the Axis powers carried out an orderly evacuation of Sicily, Operation Lehrgang (neutral), and the Allied invasion of Sicily was thereby completed. Allied losses amounted to 7,800 dead and 1,400 wounded (five percent).

On Wednesday 25 August 1943, a new German secret weapon was deployed for the first time: The Henschel Hs 293 was a rocket-boosted glide bomb (Walter transmission) steered by radio links. The missile had a one thousand-pound warhead, the Trialen 106. The Germans hoped that this weapon would neutralise the pressure exerted by Coastal Command and the Royal Navy on the U-boats in their transit area, the Bay of Biscay.

Aircraft of II Wing (Capt. Molinus) KG 100 equipped with the Hs 293 missile—a total of twelve Do 217s, escorted by seven Ju 88 Cs—were ordered to hunt out British warships northwest of the Spanish coast. The first operation was, however, not very successful. Only four of the guided missiles got anywhere near their target, and the British sloop *Landguard* suffered only insignificant damage from these four near-misses.

Two days later, on Friday 27 August 1943, eighteen Do 217s of II/KG 100 deploying Hs 293 missiles again attacked British submarine hunters off Cape Finisterre. The frigate *Egret* (1,200 tons) exploded after two direct hits, and the Canadian destroyer *Athabaskan*, heavily damaged, had to be towed into Devonport. This successful attack brought the result the U-boats had been hoping for: The British Admiralty immediately ordered all units in the Bay of Biscay to station themselves at least two hundred miles off the French coast, until some defensive measure against the Hs 293 had been found. German U-boats could once again pass through the Bay of Biscay without having to anticipate attacks from surface craft.

On Saturday 28 August 1943, the weather ship *Coburg* left the port of Narvik with eight men of the meteorological detachment Bassgeiger, or double bass (Dr. H. Schatz). The detachment was to be stationed on the coast of East Greenland. The *Coburg* stuck fast in pack-ice off Shannon Island and was then used as a floating weather station.

In Denmark at the end of August 1943, relations steadily worsened between the German authorities and the Danish government, which was not prepared to give way to German pressure and declare a state of emergency in reply to the constant sabotage and assassinations by the Danish resistance movement.

On Saturday 28 August 1943, the Danish government resigned. German Panzers and artillery surrounded the exits from Copenhagen, and the Kriegsmarine blocked The Ore Sound to cut off the Danish Navy's (Vice-Adm. Vedel) escape route to Sweden.

On Sunday 29 August 1943, at 4:00 A.M. Vice-Adm. Vedel gave orders to scuttle the fleet when Germans under a flag of truce appeared at the gates of the naval harbor. The ships, which had merely settled on the bottom because of an insufficient water depth, were set ablaze, leading to a tragic accident. The ships' guns, armed with live ammunition, exploded, giving German troops advancing along the quay the impression that the Danes were shooting at them. At this moment, German patrol boats were putting into the harbor basin. Danish seamen marching to give themselves up were now fired on from all directions; a large number of casualties occurred. In Copenhagen, the coastal warship *Peder Skram*, seven submarines and four minelayers were scuttled by their own crews. In the Isefjord the German Luftwaffe attacked the coastal warship *Niels Juel* with bombs and machine guns. Finally the vessel was scuttled by its own crew, and the patrol boat *Havörnen* was blown up. In the ports of Nyborg, Korsor and Kalundborg, the minesweepers and auxiliary vessels were forcibly seized; in the process a number

of Danish seamen were killed and some severely wounded. Four more units and nine auxiliary vessels, which were carrying out patrol duties in The Sound at that time, were able to get to Sweden.

In August 1943 Allied shipping suffered only insignificant losses. German U-boats operating in the Mediterranean and in the Atlantic, Arctic and Indian oceans sank seventeen merchantmen totalling 88,957 gross tons. German losses amounted to twenty-five U-boats. For the first time, more U-boats than enemy ships were sunk.

After a large number of U-boats acting as supply vessels had been lost, the Naval High Command ordered a regrouping and withdrew U-boats from the West Atlantic. This ended the sixth phase of the Battle of the Atlantic – a transitional period which saw evasive action to the far reaches of the Atlantic.

On Wednesday 1 September 1943, the German fishing steamer *Kehdingen*, accompanied by a U-boat, put the German meteorological detachment Schatzgräber (treasure seeker), ten men led by Dr. W. Drees, ashore on the western side of Franz Josef Land in the Soviet Arctic. The detachment was to remain there until July 1944.

From 1 May until 2 September, Allied aircraft sank twenty-eight U-boats and severely damaged another twenty-two in the Bay of Biscay. Allied losses amounted to fifty-seven aircraft.

At the beginning of September 1943 the C-in-C U-boats was hoping for a speedy resumption of the convoy battles in the North Atlantic. The first wave of twenty U-boats, fitted with the new type T 5 – Zaunkönig (wren) – torpedo was ready to go into action. This torpedo had an acoustic homing device that was attracted by the noise of ships' propellors, a magnetic firing pistol and a speed of 24.5 knots. The new search receiver Wanze, or bug, was to give the U-boats early warning of the centimetric radar carried by Allied aircraft. Also, a new tactic promised success: If the U-boat group saw a convoy, they were to surface at an opportune moment and combat Allied air cover with their new, heavier antiaircraft weapons. The seventh phase of the Battle of the Atlantic began, and it lasted until May 1944. The fight against the convoys in the North Atlantic was now resumed with new weapons.

During the first days of September, thirteen U-boats put to sea from French bases and six more set sail from German as well as from Norwegian ports. They were to make up the Leuthen group. Apart from *U 669* (Lt. Köhl), sunk by an aircraft in the Bay of Biscay, they all reached the North Atlantic. The Leuthen group now took up position 840 nautical miles east of Cape Farvel near the southern tip of Greenland. The U-boats were some

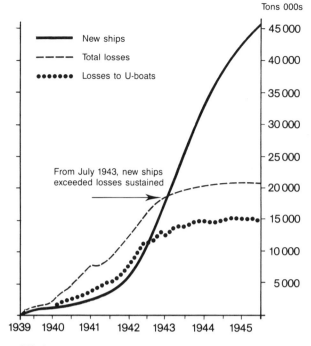

Tons 000s
45 000
40 000
35 000
30 000
25 000
20 000
15 000
10 000
5 000

New ships
Total losses
Losses to U-boats

From July 1943, new ships exceeded losses sustained

1939 1940 1941 1942 1943 1944 1945

Allied merchant shipping 1939–45

seventeen nautical miles from each other and lay in wait for convoys ON-202 and ONS-18, comprising eighty-four ships in all.

The evening of 6 September 1943, the German battle group (Adm. Kummetz) comprising the battleship *Tirpitz* (Capt. Meyer), the battlecruiser *Scharnhorst* (Capt. Hüffmeier) and nine destroyers put to sea from the Altafjord. Its task was to liquidate the Allied bases on Spitsbergen (Operation Sizilien, or Sicily).

On Wednesday 8 September 1943, toward 7:00 A.M. the battlecruiser *Scharnhorst* with its destroyer escort reached the Grönfjord and Advent Bay (Spitsbergen). A battalion from the 349th Grenadier regiment went ashore. The troops blew up the radio and meteorological station, mines, and set fire to the pithead stocks. In addition, the *Tirpitz* and the other destroyers in Barentsborg Bay took the mining settlement under fire. At 11:00 Operation Sizilien, the *Tirpitz*'s last, was over.

The same day at 6:30 P.M., Eisenhower, as previously agreed, officially announced from Algeria that Italy had capitulated. The German High Command immediately put Operation Achse, or Axis, into effect. These countermeasures involved occupying Rome and disarming Italian troops in Italy, the south of France, Yugoslavia, Albania and Greece, who were then to be either taken prisoner or demobilised. The American 5th Army celebrated, believing the war to be over.

On Thursday 9 September 1943, at 4:25 A.M. four divisions of the US 5th Army (Lt. Gen. Clark) and the British X Corps (Lt. Gen. McCreery) landed on a twenty-mile front at Salerno

(Operation Avalanche).

On the same day, the British 8th Army (Gen. Montgomery) went ashore in Taranto. Its first operational objective was Naples, where the harbor would be used in the provisioning of the army in its advance on Rome, scheduled to be occupied by Christmas 1943.

Also on 9 September 1943, Radio Livorno gave its instructions to the Italian fleet to put to seas and make for Malta. Sefton Delmer stated, "Everything ran so smoothly and successfully that I was convinced the commanders of the Italian Navy must have known that Radio Livorno was Admiral Cunningham's mouthpiece, and were fully aware of what they were doing when they followed his instructions."

Early the morning of 9 September, German troops pushed into La Spezia just as Adm. C. Bergamini was leaving with the battleships *Roma, Italia,* the *Vittorio Veneto,* three cruisers and eight destroyers. Three cruisers and two destroyers from Genoa joined this formation. The flagship of Adm. Bergamini, the *Roma* (46,215 tons), the most modern battleship and the pride of the Italian Navy, had been in service for less than one year. This formation was ostensibly out to attack the Allies' invasion fleet on its way to Salerno. In reality, the objective was Malta and surrender to the British.

The III Wing (Maj. Jope) of KG 100, stationed in Istres near Marseilles, received orders to intercept the Italian fleet. Shortly after 2:00 P.M. twelve Do 217 K 2 bombers took off, armed with a guided armor-piercing bomb, type Fritz X (FX 1400 X). This new secret weapon, constructed by Dr. M. Kramer (Ruhrstahl AG), was now to be used for the first time. It was a normal freefall 3,300-lb. bomb with a high penetration capacity but without individual projection. The bomb's fall could, however, be controlled by radio-controlled guidance spoilers built into the tail.

The Italian fleet formation reached Maddalena and sailed through the Strait of Bonifacio between Corsica and Sardina close to Asinara Island, when at 3:30 P.M. the lookout reported a number of aircraft. The Italians believed they were Allied aircraft, thinking they had come from Sicily to provide air cover. Not until they saw the bombs falling did the Italians recognize their mistake and make attempts, in vain, to take evasive action. The first bombs missed their target, but the *Roma* was hit by an FX 1400, which penetrated the deck and exploded in the ship's interior. The speed of the battleship was reduced by sixteen knots. Five minutes later a second FX 1400 hit the foredeck, causing an explosion in the ammunition chamber. The *Roma* was torn apart. Adm. Bergamini and 1,254 of the crew went down with the ship. Another FX 1400 hit the battleship *Italia*, penetrating deeply. The resultant leak caused it to take on some eight hundred tons of water; it nevertheless managed to make Malta under its own steam.

On Saturday 11 September 1943, six British midget-submarines, each one towed by a full-sized submarine, put to sea from their base in northern Scotland and made for the Norwegian coast. Their objective was to attack the German battle group consisting of the *Tirpitz, Scharnhorst* and *Lützow,* lying in the Altafjord (Operation Source).

On the same day, II/KG 100 (Capt. Molinus) and III/KG 100 (Maj. Jope) carried out with their radio-controlled missiles a number of attacks against the invasion fleet off Salerno. They scored a near-miss against the US cruiser *Philadelphia*. An FX 1400 penetrated the forward turret on the light cruiser *Savannah*. The explosion ripped open a hole in the deck, killed a number of men and caused considerable damage.

On Monday 13 September 1943, III/KG 100 again appeared over Salerno. This time the British light cruiser *Uganda* was badly damaged. The FX 1400 only narrowly missed the US cruiser *Philadelphia* and two British destroyers. The hospital ship *Newfoundland*, despite its clearly visible Red Cross markings, was sunk.

In the middle of September 1943 the head of the Deutsche Arbeitsfront, (German Labor Front) suggested to the head of the army research unit in Peenemünde, Gen. Dornberger, that the A-4 (V 2) being developed should be fired from floating containers at land-based targets along the US Atlantic coast in a surprise attack. Lafferentz — a distant relation of Richard Wagner and chief executive of the Volkswagenwerk — funded with Deutsche Arbeitsfront money a company engaged in research and development, the Gesellschaft für Forschung und Entwicklung. The most interesting project was the underwater long-range rocket that was not, however, used operationally until December 1944.

On Thursday 16 September 1943, III/KG 100 reported a significant success at Salerno. They scored direct hits on the battleship *Warspite* (Capt. Crutchley) with two FX 1400s. The first bomb penetrated the mess deck and exploded in no. 4 boiler room. A second FX 1400 went down close to the side and tore open a hole below the waterline. Two tugs succeeded only with great difficulty in towing the battleship to Malta. The battleship was out of action for almost a year.

On Saturday 18 September 1943, KG 100 carried out its last attack with FX 1400s in the Salerno area. This attack was also directed against the US cruiser *Philadelphia*. Once again the *Philadelphia* was narrowly missed, and it escaped with slight damage.

On Monday 20 September 1943, a convoy battle erupted in the North Atlantic in a violent storm. Thanks to the use of the new acoustic homing torpedoes T 5 Zaunkönig, U-boats sank six ships and three escort vessels from convoys ON-202 and ONS-18.

On Wednesday 22 September 1943, the midget-submarines *X 6* (Lt. Cameron) and *X 7* (Lt. Place) succeeded in penetrating the torpedo nets around the *Tirpitz* in the Altafjord. Three of the midget-submarines taking part in this mission were lost, and one had to turn back because of technical faults. *X 6* and *X 7* laid their mines under the hull of the *Tirpitz*. Approximately twenty minutes later the mines exploded and damaged the battleship, cracking its hull, distorting the propeller shafts and loosening the turbine housing. Five hundred tons of water poured into the ship, and some of the ship's ribs were broken. The *Tirpitz* was rendered unseaworthy by the attack, and its speed was reduced by two-thirds. Lieutenants Cameron and Place with four of their crewmen were taken prisoner.

Dönitz stated, "The loss of the *Tirpitz* for such a long time was a great military disadvantage."

At the end of September 1943 new U-boats equipped with acoustic T 5 torpedoes put out into the Atlantic with a supply submarine. The task of the U-boats was to put the escort vessels out of action with the new torpedoes and then attack the ships in convoy with traditional torpedoes. Notwithstanding the valuable support supplied by the B-Dienst, the C-in-C U-boats remarked that his hopes for success in the North Atlantic were noticeably dwindling. The Allies swiftly found a countermeasure to neutralise the dangerous T 5 torpedoes: Escort vessels towed the Foxer, a device that made sufficient noise to drown the sound of ships' propellers. In addition, the new U-boat Flak guns proved to be too weak against attacking aircraft.

During this month U-boats from the Monsun (monsoon) group patrolled off Mombasa, Colombo and Bombay. When their fuel began to run out, they made for Japanese-occupied Penang.

At the end of September 1943 five more German U-boats reached the Cape of Good Hope in order to relieve U-boats operating in the Indian Ocean.

In September 1943 German U-boats operating in the Mediterranean and in the Atlantic and Indian oceans sank nineteen merchantmen totalling 106,820 gross tons. German losses amounted to ten U-boats.

In September 1943 German and Japanese submarines operating in the Indian Ocean sank twelve merchantmen totalling 65,304 gross tons.

Success by the German Fritz X armor-piercing bomb 9/11/1943, direct hit on the US cruiser *Savannah* (above); 9/16/1943, direct hit on the British battleship *Warspite* (right).

The tension that existed between the British and the Soviets in the Soviet Arctic ports reached a new high this month. The city of Archangel, for example, ordered that the British military hospital be closed.

Attacks on two westbound convoys, ON-204 and ONS-19, were prevented by Allied air cover. Convoy HX-258, on an easterly course and accompanied by a strong cover group, also managed to cross the Atlantic without loss. During this action, aircraft based on Iceland sank *U 279* (Lt. Comdr. Finke) and *U 336* (Lt. Comdr. Hunger) on 4 October 1943.

On Monday 4 October 1943, the German fishing boat *Carl J. Busch*, accompanied by a U-boat, put into the Liefdelfjord (North Spitsbergen) and disembarked the meteorological detachment Kreuzritter (crusader), led by Dr. H. R. Knöspel and comprising twelve men. The detachment was to remain here until July 1944, provisioned by the Luftwaffe.

On Tuesday 5 October 1943, aircraft forming part of the cover group for Convoy HX-258, sank the *U 389* (Lt. Comdr. Heilmann).

On Friday 8 October 1943, British troopships, tankers and freighters — escorted by a group comprising the escort carrier *Fencer*, nine destroyers, four corvettes and sloops — appeared off Fayal and Terceira in the Azores. This marked the beginning of Operation Alacrity, the installation of naval and air bases on the Azores, which belonged to neutral Portugal. Situated at the halfway mark between Europe and America, the Azores are an archipelago comprising nine volcanic islands inhabited by some 280,000 people. The islands were discovered by Portuguese mariners in 1427 and were subsequently populated by Flemings and Portuguese. Toward the end of the sixteenth century, the Azores became the starting point for voyages of discovery, and they were also a port of call for shipping homeward-bound from the East Indies.

The establishment of these strategically vital bases meant that the remaining "Atlantic gap" could now be closed — this was of inestimable value for the Allies. The mere shortening of air transport routes meant that one million tons of

9/10/1943, in its base, a British midget-submarine that took part in the action against the *Tirpitz* on 9/22/1943

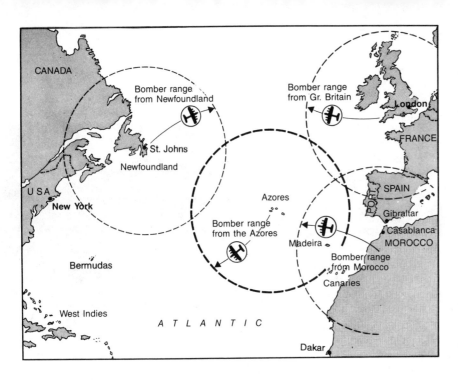

Left: The Azores played a decisive role in the Battle of the Atlantic.

Right: 10/8/1943, Operation Alacrity, occupying bases on the Azores. British destroyers of 8 Support Group off Fayal.

shipping capacity and more than 450,000 tons of aviation spirit could be saved. This was the equivalent of two months' fuel for Allied aircraft operating from Great Britain. These bases were established after two years of hard bargaining with the Portuguese president, Dr. Salazar, who feared that such a violation of neutrality would bring about an immediate reaction by Hitler and the occupation of the Iberian peninsula by the German armed forces.

In fact, the USA wanted to forceably erect bases on the Azores, but at Churchill's insistence it was agreed to seek amicable cooperation with Portugal, especially as Salazar stated in autumn 1943 that there was now little threat from the Germans. If he had not spun out negotiations over a period of more than two years, in order to win time, the collapse of the German U-boat offensive in the Atlantic would have happened much sooner.

In order to find some pretext for establishing military bases on the territory of neutral Portugal, Churchill hit upon the idea of invoking the treaty signed between England and Portugal. That this treaty had been signed in London 16 June 1373 by King Edward III, and King Ferdinand and Queen Eleanor of Portugal (fifty-four years before the Azores were discovered) did not trouble Churchill at all. Indeed, Churchill forced the inclusion of the USA as a co-user of the bases, as article I of the treaty of 1373 expressly mentioned that the contracting parties "shall henceforth, reciprocally, be friends to friends and enemies to enemies." Salazar only reluctantly accepted such interpretation of the 500-year-old treaty that had been concluded seventy-eight years before Columbus discovered America. As Pres. Salazar obstinately refused to

exceed the bilateral treaty with Great Britain, it was agreed that for a specific period, US warships would enter British bases on the Azores only while flying the British flag.

As Portugal took no notice of the nationality of the RAF aircrews, the markings on American aircraft were simply overpainted with RAF roundels. If this procedure proved to be impossible from time to time because of technical reasons, the Portuguese declared themselves satisfied if at least one member of the crews of American long-range aircraft was British. It was certainly feared that Hitler, possibly as a precedent, might demand concessions from Spain regarding the Balearics. The only action taken, however, was that the Germans filed a note of protest containing the words, "The German government has reserved the right to undertake any measures that may be required owing to the changed situation in the Azores."

On Friday 8 October 1943, acting on a report received from B-Dienst, the Rossbach group (eighteen U-boats) launched an attack against the thirty-nine ships making up Convoy SC-143, bound from Halifax to Great Britain. During the day, Allied aircraft sank *U 419* (Lt. Giersberg,) *U 610* (Lt. Comdr. Freiherr von Freyberg) and *U 643* (Lt. Comdr. Speidel), all belonging to the Rossbach group. The convoy lost only one ship (5,612 gross tons). Operations against Convoy SC-143 were terminated by the C-in-C U-boats after this failure. During the next convoy battle in the North Atlantic, with convoys ONS-20 and ON-206, the Schlieffen group lost six U-boats for the sinking of a ship of 6,625 gross tons. Nonetheless, the Battle of the Atlantic went on. On 11 October 1943, the newly arrived U-boats set up an intercep-

tion barrier some five hundred nautical miles off Newfoundland. Convoys ON-207, ONS-21, HX-263 and ON-208 suffered no losses, while three U-boats, the *U 274* (Lt. Jordan), *U 282* (Lt. Müller) and *U 420* (Lt. Reese), were lost.

On Tuesday 12 October 1943, Churchill made a statement to the House of Commons on the facilities to be constructed on the Azores. Churchill subsequently wrote his account as follows: "'I have an announcement,' I said, 'to make to the House, arising out of the treaty signed between this country and Portugal in the year 1373 between His Majesty King Edward III, and King Ferdinand and Queen Eleanor of Portugal.' I spoke in a level voice, and made a pause to allow the House to take in the date, 1373. As this soaked in, there was something like a gasp."

On Saturday 16 October 1943, the *U 533* (Lt. Comdr. Henning) was sunk in the Persian Gulf by two aircraft of 244 Squadron RAF.

On Sunday 17 October 1943, the American submarine *Tarpon* (Comdr. Wogan) sank with three torpedo hits the last German commerce raider, ship no. 28 *Michel* (Capt. Gumprich), ninety nautical miles to the east of Yokohama. This event marked the end of the deployment of commerce raiders. The success achieved during this second operation amounted to three ships totalling 27,632 gross tons. Of the 300 crew, 116 survivors took to the lifeboats and succeeded in reaching Japan.

On Monday 18 October 1943, in Hvar Marshal Tito founded the naval division of the National Liberation Army (MNBA) under Comdr. J. Cerni. Operationally and administratively the force was subordinate to the VIII Partisan Army Corps operating in Dalmatia. The Yugoslav coast was divided into six sectors, two of which, the Trieste sector and the Bokel sector, were still in German hands.

Tito's navy had at its disposal a few light units of the former Italian Navy, which the force had confiscated after the Italian capitulation. In addition, they had a former Yugoslav floatplane. The Operational Staff for Island Defence was formed from the staff of the MNBA and the staff of the 26th Partisan Division. Individual partisan units landed with coastal vessels and fishing boats on the islands, in order to offer resistance to German forces. Both sides emphasised in their operations guarding supply lines between the innumerable islands. The partisans successfully took prize a total of thirty German supply vessels sailing mainly with Italian crews.

In October 1943, German U-boats operating in the Mediterranean and in the Atlantic, Arctic and Indian oceans sank twenty-four merchantmen totalling 82,199 gross tons. German losses amounted to twenty-six U-boats.

In this same month, carrier-borne aircraft from US escort carriers operating off the Azores sank six U-boats. In two months, September and October, only nine freighters were sunk out of a total of 2,468 ships representing sixty-four different convoys. Most of the nine ships sunk were travelling independently. After this, Grand Admiral Dönitz transferred the main operational area of the U-boats to the area off Gibraltar.

Early the morning of 2 November 1943, the German patrol boat *V 1606*, in the Skagerrak between Skav and the Swedish coast, detected engine noises. Toward 5:00, a dark shadow was sighted that was first thought to be another German patrol boat. But the unidentified ship gave the wrong reply to the German recognition signal and made a plain-language signal with its searchlight, asking for a pilot to be sent across. Shortly afterward, the vessel attempted to make off at full steam on a westerly course. The *V 1606* immediately opened fire, scoring several hits on the bridge and the radio operator's cabin. The captain, two of the crew and both radio operators were wounded. The crew of the *V 1606* boarded the mysterious ship, the crew of which—as the German report noted—capitulated after some hesitation. The ship was taken to Frederikshavn in Denmark, where the wounded were taken to a naval hospital.

That was the end of the voyage of the *Master Standfast* (Capt. Holdsworth), carrying out Operation Bridford, one of the most daring operations undertaken by the British Admiralty's Operations Intelligence Center. This operation aimed to transport machine tools, machinery and other equipment from Sweden to Britain for the construction of a high-capacity ball bearings factory. The shortage of ball bearings had already led to bottlenecks in the armaments program, which could not be covered by the standing courier flight between Britain and Sweden with Mosquito aircraft. Operation Bridford was the brain child of Comdr. Sir George Binney, an agent of the British intelligence service, who was the naval attaché in Stockholm. Churchill supported the operation. Five fast motorboats, which had been built in Britain for the Turkish Navy but had not been delivered at the outbreak of war, were to carry out this operation. The shallow draught of the motorboats allowed them to cross the German minefields, and, thanks to their powerful motors, they could easily shake off any pursuer. The boats could reach a speed of thirty-eight knots with the 3,000 horsepower diesel motors. They were armed with two twin Oerlikon antiaircraft guns, two twin Vickers 303 MGs, a four-barrelled MG, as well as ASV radar. The motorboats, *Nonsuch* (Capt. Jackson), *Hopwell* (Capt. Stokes), *Master Standfast* (Capt. Holdsworth), *Gay Corsair* (Capt. Tanton) and *Gay Viking* (Capt. Whitfield), had an astonishing loading capacity of forty-five tons. By means of cloak-and-dagger operations, carried out during winter 1943–44 when the danger from the German Luftwaffe and Kriegsmarine was no longer so great, they were to shuttle the necessary parts for the ball bearing factory from Lysekil, a port on the Kattegat, to Immingham, a port on the Humber. In each instance, the crew consisted of eighteen specially trained men with an average age of twenty-five years. The shipping company, Ellermann & Wilson Ltd., Hull, was used as a cover for the boats. The five motorboats were the first Brit-

ish merchant ships to put into Swedish ports since the outbreak of war. Sir George Binney stated, "The success of the entire operation depended particularly upon an exact weather forecast and absolutely reliable information on the position of German patrol boats and convoys passing through the Skagerrak." Decrypted Enigma reports made it possible for the OIC to supply the necessary data in good time. Even after the mishap with the *Master Standfast*, the operation continued successfully. The German interrogating officers, who questioned the captured crew of the *Master Standfast* on 2 November 1943, confirmed the correct attitude of the British. The sailors gave no information on the purpose of their voyage and denied all knowledge of the freight. They all stated that the hatches had been battened down before they took over the ship. They were taken to the naval POW camp. Capt. Holdsworth succumbed to his wounds on 10 November 1943, two days before his 36th birthday. After the capitulation the *Master Standfast* was found in prime condition in Kiel as the barge *RA 11*.

On Tuesday 9 November 1943, RAF Coastal Command units operating from the base at Lajes in the Azores reported their first success: A B-17 Flying Fortress "J-for-Johnny" (22 Squadron) sank the badly damaged *U 707* (Lt. Gretschel) east of the Azores as it was returning to base—it went down with all hands.

On Sunday 14 November 1943, the first Walter experimental U-boat, type Wa 202, the *U 794*, was commissioned in Kiel. Since the beginning of the war, experiments had been carried out with the

Right: Bari, the coastal steamer *Morava*, part of Tito's navy (The third man from the left is agent Thompson of the US Intelligence Service OSS.)

Left: King Edward III of England (1312–77), who signed a treaty with Portugal on 6/16/1373

Walter U-boat drive which promised to revolutionise submarine warfare. The new ship was said to be a real "underwater ship" and not just a submersible torpedo carrier. The drive system worked on the principle of a steam turbine with an enclosed cycle. The hydrogen peroxide thereby displaced was burned with the diesel oil to a mixture of gas and steam. The theoretical submerged speed was twenty-five knots. Dönitz knew that on one hand, the currently available type of submarine had had its day, while on the other hand, it was now too late for the Walter U-boat to be developed. As an emergency solution, Professor Walter now offered Dönitz a bewilderingly simple device—a tube with an automatic valve (Schnorchel), which brought in the necessary fresh air for the diesels, took care of the ventilation of the submerged U-boat and made it possible, to a large extent, to forego use of the electric motors. This long established and long forgotten principle (the American submarine *Argonaut* had used this device in 1897) could turn the current U-boats into real underwater craft.

However, several months elapsed before the first U-boats fitted with the Schnorchel came into front-line service, in the spring of 1944.

The German Naval High Command resolved that an electro-submarine (type XXI) would close the gap between the first submarines employing the Walter drive (type XVII) and the old diesel-electro-boats fitted with the Schnorchel. Two types of electro–U-boats were built: the type XXI, a 1,600-ton ocean-going boat with a streamlined hull, adapted from the Walter U-boat, and more

powerful batteries; and a smaller boat, type XXIII (three hundred tons), designed for operations in coastal waters. But these types did not finally come into operational service until the autumn of 1944.

Between 15 and 22 November 1943, another large-scale convoy battle took place. On 15 November 1943, a long-range reconnaissance aircraft, a four-engined Ju 290 of FAGr 5 (Maj. Fischer), sighted the double convoy SL-139 and MKS-30 some one hundred nautical miles south of Cape São Vicente (Portugal). The convoys comprised sixty-six ships making toward Great Britain. The C-in-C U-boats concentrated first twenty-six, then eight more U-boats on this convoy route. The Allies increased their escort groups from seven units to a total of nineteen destroyers, frigates and corvettes. All the U-boat attacks were successfully warded off, and three of the U-boats, *U 211* (Lt. Comdr. Hause), *U 536* (Lt. Comdr. Schauenburg) and *U 538* (Lt. Comdr. Gossler), were sunk. Only one of the freighters, the *Marsa* (4,405 gross tons), was lost, to an attack from a German He 177 long-range bomber using a Hs 293 rocket-boosted glide bomb.

In the middle of November 1943 the Americans concentrated their main thrust on the Gilbert Islands (Operation Galvanic). Air reconnaissance and intelligence services established that the small island of Betio in the Tarawa atoll was the most strongly defended, and the off-lying island of Makin, to the north, was more weakly defended. For this operation, Adm. Spruance gathered together two powerful fleets, Task Force 52 (Rear Adm.

Turner) and Task Force 53 (Rear Adm. Hill). In addition to the troopships, there were seven battleships, eight escort carriers and eight cruisers. Escort was provided by Task Force 50 (Rear Adm. Pownall), made up of eleven aircraft carriers, six battleships, six cruisers and twenty-one destroyers.

On Friday 19 November 1943, units of Task Force 52 landed on Makin. The island was defended by only three hundred soldiers and some five hundred civilian workers, the highest-ranking Japanese officer was a lieutenant, and the Americans had a thirtyfold superiority; nevertheless, it took five days before this weakly defended island was overcome.

In the early hours of 20 November 1943, Task Force 53 appeared in the lagoon off Betio. Twelve troopships carried 18,600 men of the US Marines 2nd Division; three battleships, four cruisers and nine destroyers opened fire. The Japanese had built the three square miles of this island into one of the most powerful fortresses in the Pacific. A number of 20.3-cm guns had even been brought from Singapore. Five thousand soldiers made up the garrison, and there was an airfield for fighters and bombers in the middle of the island. Betio was surrounded by a broad coral reef that protruded from the water at low tide.

The Japanese had constructed powerful obstacles from cement and iron bars and coral stones and had distributed them so cleverly that landing craft were forced to make for only certain sections of the beach. These lay within the direct fire of the coastal batteries. Along the beach the Japanese had made a man-high wall from coconut palm trunks, which could only be destroyed by heavy artillery fire. Beyond this wall were fire positions covered by a labyrinth of communication trenches covered with sandbags and palm trunks — connected to or protected by reinforced concrete bunkers. From these positions, the beach and the sea could be fired upon through slits in the walls. At various points were bunkers with coastal artillery, field guns and antiaircraft guns. Near the airfield and directly behind the wall along the beach, bombproof shelters had been made in the earth with nine-foot-thick roofs constructed from layers of coconut trunks reinforced with iron bars. The commandant on the island, Rear Adm. Shibasaki, said, "Betio cannot be conquered, not even by a million men in a hundred years."

US air reconnaissance did not discover these extremely well camouflaged defensive installations, and so the US General Staff, when drawing up their landing plans, had no idea of the extent of the fortifications and the strength of the defending forces. After the final massive bombing attacks on Betio, the island gave the appearance of being completely deserted.

At dawn on 20 November, the ships ceased firing. Now the carrier-borne aircraft were to execute the planned attacks on the island. But there was not an aircraft to be seen. The radio installations

Left: Operation Bridford, Skagerrak, Capt. D. Stokes on the bridge of *Hopewell* with *Nonsuch* in the background

Above far right: 11/24/1943, London, a British leaflet

Top right: Operation Bridford, route taken by the motorboats

Below right: Copied from a Dutch patent taken as booty, Schnorchel head with radar-deflecting protective layer

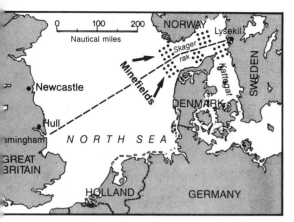

Luftpost
Extrablatt
London, 24. November 1943

Dönitz' Herbstoffensive gescheitert
Neue U-Boot-Katastrophe

Mehr U-Boote als Handelsschiffe versenkt
Churchill: Den U-Booten ist das Rückgrat gebrochen

on Rear Adm. Hill's flagship had been put out of action by the shaking it received from the ship's guns. Consequently, there were no means of informing the carrier group. The carrier-borne aircraft finally appeared at sunrise over Betio and bombed the island for seven minutes. In two and a half hours Task Force 53 had fired off almost 300,000 tons of ammunition, and the island appeared to be ablaze. Rear Adm. Hill believed that all resistance on Betio had certainly been crushed.

The landing boats suddenly ran against coral reefs that had not previously been detected. When the boats could not get free, the troops jumped into the water and swam ashore. Competely unprotected, they ran into the murderous fire of the Japanese and suffered heavy casualties. This fire also destroyed most of the landing boats. When the marines finally got onto the beach, they had to dig the Japanese out of their bunkers and foxholes in hand-to-hand fighting.

Late the afternoon of 23 November 1943, the last resistance on Betio was overcome. Of the Japanese troops, only one officer and sixteen enlisted men surrendered. In addition, 129 Korean workers were taken prisoner. The American losses amounted to 1,009 dead and 2,101 wounded.

The fighting for Betio taught the Americans the tactics necessary for a successful amphibious operation: armored amphibious landing craft were shown to be indispensable, and the defenders had to be pinned down by ships' artillery until the moment the landing took place. The experience gained during Operation Galvanic proved to be decisive in winning the strongly defended island coasts in the central Pacific.

Frogmen and small-ship formations were organised for underwater reconnaissance in enemy coastal waters. The US learned that the Japanese staff had not yet decided to deploy their fleet for defensive purposes—even for the defence of key positions on Japanese soil.

On 26 November 1943, twenty-one Heinkel He 177s of II/KG 40 (Maj. Mons) again carried out operations with the Hs 293 guided missile. This time their objective was the Allied convoy KMF-26, which had just passed by Cape Bougie (Algeria). Just after take-off, a bomber with engine trouble crashed. After a long flight, the formation certainly sighted the convoy but ran into strong air cover. During the skirmishing, Allied fighters shot down six He 177s. On the return flight, one of the He 177s managed to sink the British troopship *Rohna* (8,602 gross tons) with a direct hit. Approaching darkness impeded rescue operations and more than one thousand American soldiers were drowned.

Operations against the next convoy, the joint convoys KMS-30/OS-59 from Great Britain, did not take place. The sixteen U-boats making up the Weddingen and Schill groups could not locate the

convoys. Instead, they ran into the destroyers of the British escort group, which sank two U-boats, *U 648* (Lt. Stahl) and *U 600* (Lt. Comdr. Zurmühlen). During attacks on convoys SL-140 and MKS-31, two U-boats, *U 542* (Lt. Coester) and *U 86* (Lt. Comdr. Schug), were sunk. Apart from damage sustained by the corvette *Dahlia*, the Allies suffered no losses.

The night of 27/28 November 1943, *U 764* (Lt. von Bremen) put up a fine performance in the North Atlantic — the submarine shot down a B-17 Flying Fortress of 220 Squadron (Coastal Command).

In November 1943 German U-boats operating in the Atlantic sank fourteen merchantmen totalling 66,585 gross tons. German losses amounted to twenty-one U-boats.

Transferring attacks from freighters to escort vessels had achieved no success; it merely increased U-boat losses. Hunting out solitary vessels also brought little chance of success, as out of the thousand ships that daily crossed the oceans, only seventeen travelled without a protective escort.

After the daylight operation by the He 177s and the heavy losses sustained, II/KG 40 attempted, at the beginning of December 1943, night operations using the Hs 293 against Atlantic and Mediterranean convoys. New tactics were employed; some of the aircraft dropped flares over the convoy while the remaining He 177s fired their stand-off missiles. But these operations proved that a high degree of coordination between the aircrews was necessary — something that could not be achieved without protracted practice flights. The unsuccessful night attacks using Hs 293 missiles were then cancelled.

On Saturday 25 December 1943, the motor vessel *Osorno* (Capt. Hellmann), the German blockade-runner, put into the harbor at Bordeaux. This was the last German blockade-runner from Japan (it left Kobe on 14 October 1943) to reach Europe. From December 1940 to December 1943, the German Naval High Command succeeded in importing by means of blockade-runners the following goods: 44,495 tons of rubber; 15,158 tons of fats and oils; 6,666 tons of metals and ores; 86 tons of quinine; 611 tons of oil; 10,789 tons of various materials — a total of 103,509 tons. The loss rate on the shipping lanes from Japan to Europe amounted to sixty-five percent. The *Osorno* and the Italian blockade-runner *Pietro Orseolo* achieved something extraordinary: Both ships managed to complete two voyages from Japan to Europe and one voyage from Europe to Japan. The significance of the blockade-runners can be demonstrated by the fact that Captain Hellmann, of the *Osorno*, was the only civilian to be awarded

the Knight's Cross of the Iron Cross in all of World War II.

Increasing Allied aerial reconnaissance over the Atlantic forced the German naval staff to discontinue voyages by surface units. Attempts were now made to beat the blockade by using submarines. The Kriegsmarine did not, however, have a sufficient number of U-boats converted for the transport of goods. Those front-line U-boats that were deployed for these purposes were ordered to Japanese-occupied Indochina after some months spent in long-range operations. After undergoing thorough overhaul, these U-boats loaded up with goods essential for the war effort and set off on the journey home.

On Christmas Day 1943, the German Naval High Command decided to deploy the only operational battlecruiser, the *Scharnhorst* (Capt. Hinze), with Rear Adm. Bey on board, escorted by five destroyers from the 4 Z Flotilla (Capt. Johannesson) against the Murmansk convoys JW-55B and RA-55A. The "Admiral Arctic" had to give all orders to the battle group by radio, as other means of communication were out of order; and the Admiralty — thanks to Ultra — knew everything.

As soon as the Ultra reports had been deciphered, the Murmansk convoys were diverted northward, and the British cruiser squadron received orders to make for the assumed position of the German battlecruiser.

The morning of 26 December 1943, Rear Adm.

Bey sent off his five destroyers to seek out the convoys. During ferocious storms the *Scharnhorst* ran into the cruiser squadron belonging to the escort group. Two British cruisers were able to maintain radar contact with the *Scharnhorst* until other British units could join them. As the German destroyers had wandered off course seeking the convoy, they were unable to relocate the *Scharnhorst*. At the same time, the British units cut off the *Scharnhorst*'s retreat to the Norwegian coast. The German battlecruiser, on its own, was subjected to heavy fire and, after being hit ten or eleven times by torpedoes, sank at 7:45 P.M. on 26 December 1943 off North Cape. Of its complement of eighteen hundred, only thirty-six survivors were picked up by British vessels from the ice-cold water.

The sinking of the *Scharnhorst* meant the end of the German High Seas Fleet. At the same time, it showed the importance of decrypting the Ultra secret reports. Dönitz stated, "The loss of the *Scharnhorst* had far-reaching consequences for our strategic situation in North Norway."

In December 1943 German U-boats operating in the Mediterranean and in the Atlantic and Indian oceans sank nine merchantmen totalling 63,038 gross tons. German losses amounted to eight U-boats.

In the Baltic in 1943, according to Soviet reports, the Baltic Fleet (Adm. Tribuc) sank thirty-two German ships totalling 77,261 gross tons, with the cooperation of the Red Air Fleet.

At the end of December 1943 the German Kriegsmarine started to build up a small-ships formation which initially consisted of thirty volunteers. The staff undertook special assignments from the C-in-C Navy, Adm. Weichold. In the ensuing months, the small-vessels formation won respect through its spectacular operations.

In the second half of 1943, the German U-boat arm was unequivocally weakened by the success of the British HF/DF system of locating U-boats. Accordingly, Dönitz had to discontinue operations deploying larger packs and could only operate with small packs of two or three U-boats. The short-wave direction-finding equipment installed in Allied escort vessels proved to be the most reliable secret weapon during the Battle of the Atlantic. Neither Dönitz nor the Naval High Command nor the intelligence service of the Kriegsmarine attributed to HF/DF any significance. U-boats betrayed their position by their own radio traffic and were sunk, one after the other, because of this. The Allies' technical advantage in this respect robbed the U-boats of their most important advantage: invisibility.

In the Pacific, the Imperial Japanese Navy, despite its excellent torpedoes, never deployed the submarine weapon in a planned tonnage war. On the other hand, even at the end of 1943, neither Japanese troopships nor merchant ships were assembled in convoys. American submarines could therefore deal Japanese shipping some very heavy blows. The losses in merchant shipping made the provisioning of the island bases problematical and upset Japanese strategic planning. Japan now tried to provision by submarine these remote bases and cut-off garrisons. The army, whose supplies were insufficient, started to build its own supply submarines.

Likewise, the U-boats of the German Navy were frequently diverted from their proper purpose and converted into supply vehicles.

Above left: November 1943, Lajes airfield on the Azores, Flying Fortress "J for Johnny" of 220 Squadron (Coastal Command), operating from the new Azores base, sinks the first U-boat.

Above right: The New York Times, 12/13/1943, the first U-boat is sunk two weeks after the Azores bases became operational.

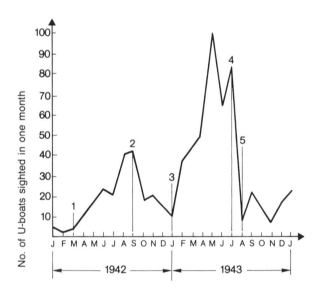

1 Start of night operations with 50-cm radar
2 U-boats equipped with 50-cm search receivers
3 Aircraft fitted with 10-cm radar bomb-aiming equipment
4 U-boats surface less often
5 U-boats equipped with 10-cm search receivers

1944

January–June

Battle of the Atlantic

Tuesday 11 January 1944, Washington
The *United Press Agency* reported:

A joint statement for December 1943 made by W. Churchill and F. D. Roosevelt on the U-boat war situation: Although German U-boats have extended their operations, Allied shipping losses for December were again negligible. Allied air and sea units sank fewer U-boats in December than in the previous month, attributable to a number of causes including the greater caution shown by the enemy.

German Attack on Bari

Thursday 20 January 1944, Naples
The *Reuters* News Agency reported:

The destruction of seventeen Allied ships in the harbor of Bari, which was attacked the evening of 2 December 1943 by thirty German aircraft, was the result of a coincidence. A report on the action has now been released by the Allied censor. The Germans themselves had no idea of the extent of damage. They claimed having sunk three ships. In reality, two ammunition ships were hit by bombs and exploded. Because of this incident, fifteen other ships were sunk. More than one thousand people lost their lives, and houses in the vicinity of the harbor were badly damaged.

Nine Hundred Jewish Refugees Cross the Mediterranean

Wednesday 2 February 1944, Jerusalem
The *Reuters* News Agency reported:

The Portuguese steamer *Ryassa* has put into Haifa with nine hundred Jewish refugees on board. The steamer (9,000 gross tons) left Lisbon 23 January; it is the first neutral ship that has crossed the Mediterranean without escort since the outbreak of war. The belligerent powers allowed the vessel free passage.

Hitler's Nephew in the US Navy

Wednesday 9 February 1944, Washington
The *Exchange* News Agency reported:

The 33-year-old nephew of Adolf Hitler, William Patrick Hitler, has been accepted for service in the US Navy. He is already on active service. By birth, he is a British subject and comes from Liverpool. His father, Alois Hitler, a stepbrother of Adolf Hitler, comes from Vienna, while his mother was born in Dublin. Alois Hitler lives in Berlin and opened a restaurant in the western part of the city some years ago.

Secret report of the *SS Security Service* on the internal political situation:
No. 506, Thursday 10 February 1944 (Extract)

Reports received on the changes in public opinion: The report on the figures of ships sunk for January, even though they do not bear comparison with earlier figures, has been received with satisfaction, in particular the sinking of twenty-eight destroyers. Also, the report on ships sunk in the Arctic and on the African coast was well appreciated. Conversations frequently expressed the hope that our U-boats will again take up their full operational activities.

Minimal Tonnage Losses

10 February 1944, London
The *Reuters* News Agency reported:

A joint statement for January made by W. Churchill and F. D. Roosevelt on the U-boat war situation: The tonnage lost in January 1944 from Allied ships sunk was the lowest figure of the entire war. As usual, German claims are a gross exaggeration and are simply intended for propaganda purposes.

A New U-boat Arm

Naval High Command
Secret/Most secret/Officers only
Address by the *C-in-C of the Kriegsmarine* given
before other C-in-Cs on 15 February 1944

The current U-boat arm is, by and large, no
longer able to give battle, as enemy air superiority
and location methods have overtaken the current
U-boat. We are, of course, in a position to minimise this superiority, a consequence of enemy aircraft carrying out location activities, by providing
improved Flak armament and our own location
methods. But this would simply be a reduction of
enemy superiority and not a change in the basic
situation. In modern marine warfare, we must increasingly take the development and use of high-
frequency techniques into account. Everything
travelling on the water is located. These are matters that just cannot be dismissed out of hand. In
addition, we must reckon with permanent and increasing enemy air superiority in the Atlantic, and
our current U-boat is unable to do anything about
it. We shall therefore need to create a new U-boat
arm that is able to outmaneuver these factors. As
this new weapon promises the greatest success, all
other objectives must be subordinated to this main
one.

Deployment of the Italian Navy by the Allies
Wednesday 16 February 1944, London
The *Reuters* News Agency reported:

The First Lord of the Admiralty stated on
Wednesday in the House of Commons that all
those Italian warships surrendered to the Allies
were now being deployed in suitable war zones. He
added that he was unable to make further com-
ment on the expression "suitable war zones" in

Left: In the English Channel—on the bridge of a German
patrol boat: in action day and night

Right: On the other side, patrol boats of the Royal Navy
patrolling along the English Channel coast

order not to give the enemy any information. The
ships were being manned by Italian crews.

Evacuation of the South Coast of France
Tuesday 22 February 1944, London
The *Reuters* News Agency reported:

The evacuation of the south coast of France
commenced today. The government has undertaken this precautionary measure, as it believes
that the Allies will start the invasion of France in
the Mediterranean area.

Operations from the Azores
Saturday 26 February 1944, London
The *Reuters* News Agency reported:

A Wellington bomber operating from a base on
the Azores after making three attacks in bright
moonlight, destroyed a surfaced U-boat in the
vicinity of an Allied convoy.

Transfer of Italian Warships to the USSR?
Friday 3 March 1944, Washington
The *United Press Agency* reported:

Pres. Roosevelt announced during a press conference that plans had been prepared whereby a
third of the Italian naval units surrendered to the
Allies, or an equivalent number of ships of other
nationalities, were to be handed over to the Soviet
fleet.

German Coastal Reconnaissance
Wednesday 8 March 1944, London
The *Reuters* News Agency reported:
   The thrust by British light naval units toward the Dutch coast is considerably more important than the sparsely worded official communiqué would suggest. The operation may well have been designed to test the German coastal patrol service in order to gather valuable intelligence. In any event, the German coastal batteries were forced into action for the first time.

February Losses the Lowest Ever

Friday 10 March 1944, London
The *Reuters* News Agency reported:
   A joint statement for February made by W. Churchill and F. D. Roosevelt on the U-boat war situation: Losses suffered by the Allied merchant fleet in February 1944 as a result of U-boat action were the lowest since the USA entered the war. This was despite the fact that a record number of American merchantmen crossed the Atlantic in February.

Naval Battle in the Channel
Friday 17 March 1944, London
The *British Admiralty* issued the following communiqué:
   Light naval units patrolling in the Strait of Dover Thursday night encountered a superior enemy formation of six heavily armed fishing boats and six S-boats. The British formation immediately attacked. During a fierce exchange of fire, one of our motor torpedo boats was hit by concentrated enemy fire and must be considered lost.

Ships for the "Free Danish Navy"
Friday 31 March 1944, London
The *Reuters* News Agency reported:
   Yesterday, in the presence of the Danish ambassador, two British minesweepers were handed over to the "Free Danish Navy" in a Scottish port. The ships will sail under the Danish flag and will be manned exclusively by Danish seamen.

Successes by US Submarines
Wednesday 5 April 1944, Washington
The *United Press Agency* reported:
   American submarines operating in the Pacific and Far East report the sinking of fourteen enemy ships, which includes two medium-sized tankers, eleven medium-sized freighters and a small freighter.

U-boat Arm Still a Threat

Monday 10 April 1944, London
The *Reuters* News Agency reported:
   A joint statement for March made by W. Churchill and F. D. Roosevelt on the U-boat war situation: In March 1944 action taken against enemy U-boats operating in the vast area from the Barents Sea to the Indian Ocean has been intensively carried out. The enemy made unsuccessful attempts to disrupt the supply routes to Russia. Our merchant shipping losses mainly occurred in distant waters. They were certainly somewhat higher than in February but still relatively low. In any event, the strength of the enemy U-boat arm remains considerable and continues to demand joint efforts by our air and sea forces.

Swiss Radio Beromünster

Friday 14 April 1944
   It can scarcely be denied that the mood in Europe is not unlike the mood prevailing in early 1940. The signs are that large-scale fighting is imminent, which will determine the military predominance on the European mainland. . . . The British Isles have become a powerful Anglo-American army camp whose potential strength is a permanent threat to the Atlantic coast. For some considerable time now, transports of men and material, essential for the Allied war direction, have been crossing the Atlantic and the Mediterranean without hindrance by German U-boats. . . . Reports emanating from Great Britain give numerous and unmistakeable signs that the time is approaching when the Anglo-American armies massed along the south coast of the British Isles will carry out that maneuver that will lead them to the heaviest and most bitter fighting they have yet to encounter.

. . .If the enormous concentration of men and material and the preparations being made along the south coast of England are a fact, the significance of these events cannot be misunderstood. But the situation in the Mediterranean is completely impenetrable: Nobody who is not a party to the secrets of the general staff can say whether invasion operations are planned for the coasts of the south of France, Italy or the Balkan peninsula.

Mining the Danube

Wednesday 19 April 1944
The *Headquarters of the Allied Mediterranean Fleet* issued the following communiqué:

Allied forces in the Mediterranean commenced mining operations against the Danube some time ago. Liberator and Wellington bombers of the RAF have been dropping mines for several nights.

Mutiny on Greek Warships
Sunday 23 April 1944, Cairo
The *United Press Agency* reported:

The crews of the three Greek warships *Apostolis, Ierix* and *Sachtouris* (Alexandria) have for three weeks refused to carry out the orders of the C-in-C. A number of Greek officers and soldiers acting under orders issued by the Greek fleet commander, Vice-Adm. Boulgaris, seized the three ships. After a short action between the mutineers and loyal troops equipped with machine guns and machine pistols, the mutiny was suppressed. Crews loyal to the government took over the three warships. There were a number of casualties.

Before the Invasion

Paragraph 27 of the operational order "Channel 1 for U-boats in Channel, C-in-C U-boats West No. gkdos (confidential) 1037 A 1," 26 April 1944

Every enemy vessel engaged in landing operations, even if it is carrying only fifty soldiers or a tank, is a target demanding the full deployment of the U-boat. This vessel must be attacked, even at the risk of the loss of the U-boat. If approach to the enemy landing fleet is possible, there must be no regard paid to danger through shallow water or mines or any other cause.

Every enemy soldier and every enemy weapon destroyed before landing will reduce the enemy's prospects of victory.

But the U-boat that has caused the enemy losses on landing has fulfilled its highest obligation and justified its existence.

Attack on a British Convoy
Friday 28 April 1944, Berlin
The German *DNB* News Agency reported:

Last night German S-boats operating along the south coast of England to the west of the Isle of Wight attacked a convoy escorted by destroyers and a number of smaller warships. Despite strong defensive fire, the German vessels sank three ships totalling approximately 6,400 gross tons and torpedoed another ship of 200 gross tons that is presumed to have gone down. During the fierce exchange of fire, an enemy destroyer was so badly damaged by torpedoes that it can be presumed sunk. The sinking could not, however, actually be observed, owing to the strong defensive activity of the enemy and the necessarily swift evacuation of the battle area.

The Sea War in the Pacific
28 April 1944, Tokyo
The *DNB* Agency reported:

The Imperial Headquarters have announced that a Japanese submarine has torpedoed a large American aircraft carrier in the waters east of the Marshall Islands. Details are not yet available.

Secret Battle School in the Atlantic
Monday 1 May 1944, London
The *Exchange* News Agency reported:

We can now reveal that for four years an Allied naval base has been used as a battle school in the middle of the Atlantic. Approximately 150,000

6/2/1944, Great Britain, US troops prepare for the invasion.

men have been trained there on hundreds of vessels for the war against the U-boats. By means of practical exercises, the crews learn the use of defensive weapons against U-boats and aircraft, dropping depth charges, detecting the approach of U-boats by means of special instruments, as well as rapid repairs to damaged ships. The school is commanded by Com. Sir Gilbert Stephenson, who was himself formerly a commodore in charge of convoys crossing the Atlantic. The training base is an old Dutch horse transporter, now named the *Western Isles*. The ship has been converted and modernised; for example, it has a cinema on board. Bases similar to the *Western Isles* were recently established elsewhere.

W. Churchill to First Lord and First Sea Lord
Monday 28 May 1944
Do not hesitate to be blunt with these Russians when they become unduly truculent. This is better done by manner and attitude than by actual words, which can be reported, and also by neglect of certain civilities to the superior people when they have been intolerably offensive. They should certainly be given a feeling that we are not afraid of them.

German Warships through the Dardanelles?
Monday 5 June 1944, London
The *Reuters* News Agency reported:
  The British government has energetically protested to the Turkish government against the passage of German warships, disguised as merchantmen, from the Black Sea into the Aegean. Some half dozen of these ships have already passed through the straits with the permission of the Turkish authorities.

Normandy Invasion
Tuesday 6 June 1944, London
The *British War Office* issued the following communiqué:
  Under the command of Gen. Eisenhower, Allied naval units, supported by strong air force units, have commenced landing Allied troops on the coast of France. The landings were preceded by intensive air bombardment.

Naval Battle with Soviet Fast Motorboats
Thursday 8 June 1944, Berlin
The *DNB* Agency reported:
  German naval units deployed in patrolling Narva Bay in the Gulf of Finland last night sank two Russian fast motorboats that were escorting a minesweeper. Three other motorboats were set ablaze, one of which probably sank.

Turkey Interns German Ships
Friday 9 June 1944, Constantinople
The *Exchange* News Agency reported:
  Six German auxiliary warships trying to break out of the Black Sea were interned by Turkey. It seems that the Germans were transferring these ships to the Aegean to be used for evacuation purposes in the event of an attack on the Dodecanese and the Aegean islands.

New U-boat Offensive?
Saturday 10 June 1944, London
The *Reuters* News Agency reported:
  A joint statement for May made by W. Churchill and F. D. Roosevelt on the U-boat war situation: Last month, for every Allied merchant ship sunk, several German U-boats were destroyed. Figures of ships lost in May 1944 were the lowest since the outbreak of war. . . . German U-boat activity has become appreciably weaker, and it is presumed that this is a respite during which preparations will be undertaken for a new offensive.

U-boats Again in the North Atlantic
Thursday 15 June 1944, Boston
The *United Press Agency* reported:
  A German U-boat was sighted off the North Atlantic coast for the first time in two years. The district command of the US fleet stated that a German U-boat had attacked an American fishing boat and damaged it by gunfire. The crew of the fishing boat suffered no losses. No date was given for the attack, it was simply stated that the incident happened only "recently."

Bitter Fighting for the Marianas
18 June 1944, Washington
The *Associated Press* reported:

The US troops that landed Wednesday on Saipan had to withdraw, owing to intense Japanese artillery and mortar fire. Intensive bombardment by the fleet enabled troops to push forward again on Thursday. The bitterly resisting Japanese occupation force numbers some thirty thousand men.

Naval Engagement in the Pacific

Tuesday 20 June 1944, Pearl Harbor
Admiral Nimitz issued the following communiqué:

A powerful Japanese fleet formation has gathered between the Marianas and the Philippines. This may possibly be the entire Japanese fleet. A decisive naval battle between the American and Japanese fleets either is imminent, or has possibly already begun.

Japanese Radio Report
Wednesday 21 June 1944, London
The *Reuters* News Agency reported:

The Japanese radio today announced that there is currently a massive naval battle in progress in the area of the Marianas. The outcome of this engagement will be of decisive significance for the situation in the Pacific.

Warships for Tito
21 June 1944, London
The *Reuters* News Agency reported:

Foreign Secretary Eden informed the House that Marshal Tito had requested the Allies to release to him those units of the Royal Yugoslav Navy currently held under Allied protection. The ships were required for use against the common enemy. Eden stated that the matter was the object of discussions between the Yugoslav prime minister and Tito.

Swiss Radio Beromünster

Friday 23 June 1944

Events during the week were dominated by the fighting in Normandy, central Italy and on the Karelian Isthmus and by the trials inflicted upon southern England by the flying bombs — the long-announced German secret weapon. During the last eight days in Normandy, the Allies have concentrated their efforts mainly on the conquest of the Cotentin Peninsula, at whose northern tip the port of Cherbourg is situated.

Allied Cruisers Sunk off Cherbourg
Tuesday 27 June 1944, Berlin
The *DNB* Agency reported:

According to definitive reports, the mixed Anglo-American fleet formation under the command of the American Rear Adm. Deyo suffered the loss of two cruisers and a light cruiser during the bombardment of Cherbourg on 25 June.

Damage in the Port of Cherbourg
Friday 30 June 1944
From General Eisenhower's Headquarters:

According to the latest reports from Cherbourg, damage to the harbor is not so bad as at first assumed. The ships sunk can be easily raised, and the extensive destruction of the quay installations has not seriously hindered troop disembarkation. The harbor in Cherbourg is predicted to be again operational within some ten days. The garrisons of the four fortresses guarding the harbor approaches have now surrendered.

Strategy and Tactics

JANUARY TO DECEMBER 1944

On Tuesday 4 January 1944, the last German blockade-runner, *Rio Grande* (6,062 gross tons), was on course to East Asia under the command of Capt. von Allwörden when it was sighted by a floatplane from the US cruiser *Omaha*. The cruiser and the destroyer *Jouett* opened fire. The *Rio Grande* went down with the entire crew, except for one man who was rescued.

The following day, 5 January 1944, a US Catalina flying boat sighted off the African coast near Natal the last blockade-runner from East Asia. It was the *Burgenland* (7,320 gross tons), carrying a cargo of rubber and other important raw materials. Capt. Schültz gave the command to scuttle the ship when the US cruiser *Omaha* and the destroyer *Jouett* approached.

On Saturday 22 January 1944, Operation Shingle commenced, the landing of the VI US Corps (Maj. Gen. Lucas) of the 5th US Army (Lt. Gen. M. Clark) by means of 9 transporters, 226 landing craft, a tanker and 4 hospital ships in the area between Anzio and Nettuno, south of Rome. In an attempt to prevent the landing, He 177 bombers from II/KG 40 and Do 217s from KG 100 attacked with FX 1400 and Hs 293 missiles. To neutralise the remote control system on these missiles, the US destroyers *Woolsey, Frederick C. Davis* and *Her-*

bert C. Jones used radio-jamming equipment, and only a few of them reached the targets.

The following day, 23 January 1944, the British destroyer *Jervis* became the first ship off Anzio to be hit by a rocket-boosted Hs 293 glide bomb. Despite heavy damage, the destroyer reached Naples under its own steam.

On Saturday 29 January 1944, II Wing of KG 100 attacked the British antiaircraft cruiser *Spartan*, lying at anchor off the coast and acting in an antiaircraft role, and freighter *Samuel Huntington* (7,818 gross tons). At 7:05 P.M. an Hs 293 hit the *Spartan*, which shortly afterward capsized and sank. Almost simultaneously an Hs 293 set fire to the *Samuel Huntington*. Toward 3:00 the next morning, the freighter blew up when the flames reached its cargo of ammunition and fuel.

The night of 11/12 February 1944, fifteen Soviet Petlyakov Pe-8 heavy bombers attacked the battleship *Tirpitz* with two thousand-lb. bombs while it was lying in the Altafjord. Only four aircraft found the target, they caused slight damaged with near misses.

The night of 18/19 February 1944, the first U-boat equipped with the Schnorchel, *U 264* (Lt. Comdr. Looks), was sunk, southwest of Ireland while on its first voyage, by the sloops *Woodpecker* and *Starling* of the Second Escort Group (Capt. Walker).

When the second U-boat with a Schnorchel was lost, front-line U-boat commanders refused this additional equipment. The first Schnorchel attachments comprised a pair of retractable tubes hand-operated by means of a cable. Later on Schnorchels were operated by hydraulic equipment. The head of the Schnorchel mast was covered with a rubberlike, grained coating that partially absorbed radar emissions. The older type of U-boat was subsequently equipped with the new Schnorchel, and the new type of submarine, with its greater capacity, was similarly equipped during building.

On Monday 13 March 1944, at 7:30 P.M. *U 852* (Lt. Comdr. Eck) sank the Greek merchant ship *Peleus* (4,695 gross tons) between Freetown and Ascension. The old ship went down quickly, and only two or three rafts bearing a few survivors were to be seen among the wreckage. Lt. Comdr. Eck ordered that a machine gun MG 15 be mounted and a case of hand grenades be brought up on deck. The submarine's doctor, Dr. Weisspfennig, was given the order to open fire on the survivors. The U-boat commander wanted to destroy all traces of the torpedoeing for fear of Allied air reconnaissance. Twenty-five days after the sinking of the *Peleus*, a raft with three survivors was sighted by the Portuguese steamer *Alexandre*, which picked up the men and so heard about the incident. The "*Peleus* affair" is the only recorded incident of survivors being fired upon by a German U-boat. On 2 May 1944, Lt. Comdr. Eck, Dr. Weisspfennig and Lt. Hoffman were taken prisoner. They subsequently appeared before a British military court—the trial began on 17 October 1945 in Hamburg—and were sentenced to be executed by firing squad.

On Saturday 18 March 1944, Operation Bridport, which had started in October 1943, ended when the nights began to get shorter. This opera-

Above: February 1944, Altafjord, the majestic shape of the *Tirpitz* emerging from the early morning mist

Below: 6/6/1944, Allied invasion of Normandy, the *Ramillies* opens fire on German coastal fortifications.

tion, "the most adventurous shipping line in the world," was conducted by the British Admiralty's Operations Intelligence Centre. MGBs brought in supplies for the British armaments industry on the Hull-Lysekil, Sweden route.

In a number of night voyages carried out during the winter months, 347 tons of valuable precision machinery and tools for a planned ball bearing works were transported, including finished ball bearings, tungsten wire, replacement parts and seventy-six "passengers," most of them British secret agents. Lord Leathers: "I believe I do not need to underline the importance of this operation."

On Monday 3 April 1944, a British task force under Vice-Adm. H. R. Moore, which included three cruisers and five destroyers in addition to the carriers *Furious* and *Victorious*, carried out Operation Tungsten—an attack by forty-two Barracuda torpedo bombers on the *Tirpitz*, lying in the Altafjord in Norway.

The first wave (Lt. Baker-Faulkner) took off at 4:38 A.M. flying the Barracuda, a new carrier aircraft stressed to operate as a level-flight bomber, dive bomber and torpedo bomber. The Barracudas were escorted by twenty-one Corsairs, twenty Hellcats and ten Wildcats, which were to fire at the antiaircraft guns on the *Tirpitz*.

Not a German fighter was to be seen in the skies. At 5:25, the first wave had just left the Altafjord, and the second wave under Lt. Rance took off. One of the Barracudas stopped dead with engine trouble on the flight deck of the *Victorious* and was straightaway rolled off into the sea. A second Barracuda crashed after taking off and went down with its crew.

The battleship *Tirpitz* received fourteen direct hits and was no longer seaworthy. Of its crew, 122 were killed and 316 wounded, some seriously. Apart from the two Barracudas mentioned, British losses amounted to only one fighter, which, on its return, could not land. The pilot was, however, rescued.

Operation Tungsten caused Grand Admiral Dönitz to make a decision that had grave consequences. The *Tirpitz* was certainly to be repaired but would never again take part in any attack on a convoy, as the superiority of the RAF and the Royal Navy presented the risk of total loss. Dönitz said, "Keeping the *Tirpitz* in North Norway was justified in that its presence tied down enemy capital ships that could have been used in some other theater of war."

On Thursday 6 April 1944, mutiny broke out on some of the Greek naval units (Vice-Adm. Voularis) in Alexandria. The crews of the destroyer *Terax* and the corvettes *Sachtouris* (former *HMS Peony*), *Apostolis* (former *HMS Hyacinth*), stirred up by Communist agitators, joined the rebellion mounted by the 4,500 men of the Greek 1st Mountain Brigade. This brigade was scheduled to be transferred to Italy on the Monte Cassino front as a special unit supporting the planned Allied offensive. Led by Private Andriottis, who proclaimed himself brigade commander, the soldiers barricaded themselves in their camp near Alexandria and brought fifty guns into position. The mutineers intended to force the entire Greek cabinet to be made up of members of the Greek Liberation Front (EAM), which was loyal to Moscow. The rebellion spread to other units in Egyptian ports, and before long the crews of forty-three warships and merchantmen had mutinied.

On Friday 7 April 1944, British X-craft, the midget-submarine *X 24* (Lt. Shean), was towed by the submarine *Sceptre* across the North Sea. The X-craft entered the harbor at Narvik, where its crew fixed explosive charges to the German merchant ship *Bärenfels* (7,569 gross tons) and another ship of 1,923 gross tons. Damage was also caused to the floating dock of the Laksevag Shipyards.

On Friday 14 April 1944, an explosion took place in Bombay, one of the most important Allied supply bases for the planned invasion of Japan. This mysterious explosion, never explained to this day, was the largest in the history of sea warfare. At 1:30 P.M., a fire was spotted on board the British freighter *Fort Stikine* (7,142 gross tons), laden with ammunition, explosives and gold bullion. Despite all attempts to extinguish the fire—the *Fort Stikine* neither showed the prescribed red flag warning that it had explosives on board nor sounded a warning with the ship's siren—the ship exploded toward 3:00 with such a force that the resultant tidal wave flung the 350-foot-long steamer *Japalanda* (5,500 gross tons) on land, where it crushed under its hull part of the harbor buildings. One of the gold bars from the *Fort Stikine's* cargo was later found on the verandah of a house fifteen hundred yards away. Burning cotton whirled in the air, then fell on the dock area and ships.

While this was going on, Allied soldiers carried away 39,398 ammunition boxes—each weighing more than one hundred pounds—from the Alexandria dock. Sixteen ships, of which seven carried explosives, were saved just in time by being taken out to the open sea. The second explosion flung red-hot metal, beams and balls of cotton over three thousand feet into the air. Almost 100,000 tons of Allied shipping capacity were destroyed or damaged; and there were 336 fatalities (the unofficial figure was 1,500) and more than 1,000 wounded (the unofficial figure was 3,000). In all, the damage caused amounted to more than half a billion US dollars.

The first operational deployment of the German

In the early hours of 4/21/1944, Anzio (Italy), German one-man torpedo "Neger" (Negro) washed ashore near the 5th US Army bridgehead

small vessels formation (Vice-Adm. Heye) took place on Hitler's birthday, 20 April 1944. Thirty one-man torpedoes of the "Neger" (Negro) type, carrying a G7E torpedo under their hulls, arrived by rail in the Anzio-Nettuno area. They were accompanied by their crews who had crash courses at the torpedo research institute in Eckernförde, and Langenargen on Lake Constance. At a suitable section of the coast near Torre Vaianica, five hundred army personnel had to drag the Negers into the water by hand. Only seventeen of the one-man torpedoes succeeded in getting under way to the Anzio-Nettuno roads, some eighteen nautical miles away. The remainder had to be blown up at sunrise. Because of Ultra decrypts, the Allies had known about this operation for some days, and, with the exception of a few small coastal vessels, their ships all put out to sea. The Negers reported two ships sunk, but this report was not confirmed by the Allies. Three Negers were lost, possibly because the crewmen succumbed to carbon dioxide poisoning. The Allies recovered one of the Negers, and consequently the tactically important surprise element of the weapon was lost. Experts established that, astonishingly, the perspex dome over the crewman's head — this dome protruded from the water — only had to be smashed in and the crewman would be killed.

Also on 20 April 1944, the Kriegsmarine gave Hitler a magnificent present to celebrate his 55th birthday: the launching of the first new type XXI U-boat. Building the *U 3501* on the Danzig Schichau yards took only thirty-one days from laying down (20 March 1944) to launching. The speed of this operation resulted from the planning carried out by O. Merker, who was appointed by Albert Speer to be the chairman of the shipbuilding committee in June 1943. The Kriegsmarine ordered 290 type XXI U-boats. The boats were made up from eight prefabricated parts built by sixty independent assembly plants, widely spread across Germany because of the threat of air raids. The eight prefabricated parts, complete with all internal fittings, were transported via the German canal network to the three final assembly points — Blohm & Voss (Hamburg), AG Weser (Bremen) and Schichau (Danzig) on Hellingen — where they were assembled and launched.

The night of 22/23 April 1944, heavily armed officers and sailors loyal to the Greek king carried out a coup against those Greek naval crews and merchant seamen who had mutined since 6 April. After a series of bloody encounters, the ships were captured; fifty of the mutineers were executed. The British cruiser *Ajax* (which had taken part in the battle against the *Admiral Graf Spee* in December 1939) dropped anchor and held the mutineers in check, its guns ready to fire. This mutiny, the largest during the war, gave some indication of the future problems of Western fleet commanders.

The next day, 24 April 1944, when the British positioned heavy artillery on the hills surrounding the Greek camp and threatened to open fire, the rebellious Greek 1st Mountain Brigade also surrendered. The Greeks, suffering from both thirst and hunger, put up only weak resistance; only one British officer was killed. The brigade was led away to captivity.

The night of 28/29 April 1944, 101 aircraft from IX Air Corps appeared over Plymouth. Do 217 Ks from III Wing of KG 100 launched an unsuccessful attack against warships with FX 1400 armor-piercing missiles. Two Do 217 Ks were shot down by British Flak.

On Sunday 7 May 1944, a German long-range aircraft type Arado Ar 232 VB (B-06) picked up the Schatzgräber meteorological detachment (led by W. Drees) from Franz Joseph Land in the Soviet Arctic. The ten men of this detachment had to break off their period of service prematurely, as they were all suffering from trichinosis caused by eating polar bear meat.

On Saturday 13 May 1944, the US escort destroyer *Francis M. Robertson* sank the Japanese submarine *RO 501* (Lt. Comdr. Norita) northwest of the Azores. This was the former German U-boat *U 1224*, which had been presented to the Japanese Navy by the Germans.

On Sunday 14 May 1944, the German 5 S-boat Flotilla made an attack against Allied landing craft lying off the Isle of Wight. During the action, the French destroyer *La Combattante* (former HMS *Haldon*) sank the *S 141*. Grand Admiral Dönitz's second son, Lt. Klaus Dönitz, went down with the S-boat.

On Friday 19 May 1944, *U 453* (Lt. Lührs) sank a merchantman of 7,147 gross tons, part of Convoy HA-34 escorted by Italian torpedo boats and British corvettes. This was the last success achieved by a German submarine in the Mediterranean.

In May 1944 the seventh phase of the Battle of the Atlantic ended. This particular phase had commenced in September 1943. The resumption in the North Atlantic of convoy battles deploying new weapons proved to be a failure, as escort carriers now provided convoys with air cover for the entire voyage across the Atlantic. As a consequence, U-boats not equipped with a Schnorchel were withdrawn from Atlantic operations effective 1 June 1944.

On Wednesday 31 May 1944, the US destroyer *England* (Lt. Comdr. Pendleton) sank the Japanese submarine *RO 105* northwest of New Ireland (Papua New Guinea). This was the sixth Japanese submarine sunk by Lt. Comdr. Pendleton within a period of twelve days—the most successful submarine-killer operation by a single ship of the entire war.

On Saturday 3 June 1944, a four-engined Ju 290 of the former FAGr 5 (long-range reconnaissance wing) and now I/KG 200 (Maj. Koch) landed on the frozen surface of Nordenskjöld Bay (East Greenland) and took off the eight men of the Bassgeiger meteorological detachment, led by Dr. H. Schatz, as well as the crew of the weather ship *Coburg*. The party, numbering twenty-six men, was flown back to Dröbak in Norway.

On Sunday 4 June 1944, Task Group 22.3 (Capt.

Gallery) with the carrier *Guadalcanal* and five destroyers followed a submarine located by HF/DF, the *U 505* (Lt. Lange) in transit to its home base. While the first carrier-borne aircraft from the *Guadalcanal* were taking off at around 11:20 A.M., the American destroyer *Chatelein* carried out a depth-charge attack on the *U 505* approximately one hundred nautical miles west of Cape Blanco on the African coast. The damaged submarine was forced to the surface. The crew opened the hatch and left the sinking submarine under heavy fire from the three American destroyers, *Chatelein*, *Jenks* and *Pillsbury*. One man was killed, and several, including the commander, were badly wounded.

The U-boat crew had no idea that the Americans were firing only with light machine guns in order not to penetrate *U 505*'s pressure hull. Capt. Gallery immediately sent off a boat from the *Pillsbury* with a prize crew (Lt. David), comprising eight men, ordered to keep the boat afloat. When the prize crew went aboard, the stern was already underwater up to the tower, and the bow rising. At the last moment the prize crew managed to stop the water flooding in and make the submarine watertight. Five "Zaunkönig" acoustic torpedoes, practically all the documents and secret books, as well as the cipher codes were found on board. *U 505* was towed by the carrier to the Bermudas (one thousand nautical miles away) and from there taken to the mainland. The submarine was later used for experimental and training purposes. The U-boat crew were held until the end of the war in a

Right: Normandy, 6/6/1944, Operation Overload, Canadian troops going ashore

Left: 6/4/1944, south of Madeira, the US prize crew on *U 505*. An American aircraft patrols overhead.

segregated POW camp so that the secret of the submarine's capture would be preserved. As far as the C-in-C U-boats was concerned, *U 505* was classified as "probably sunk after 4 June."

The *U 505* has been on display in the Museum of Science and Industry in Chicago since 1955.

On Thursday 6 June 1944, after days of intensive air raids and the deployment of airborne troops and paratroops on the flanks of the invasion area, the Allied invasion, code-named Operation Overlord, commenced. Powerful naval forces from the US Western Naval Task Force (Rear Adm. Kirk) took part, including the battleships *Arkansas, Nevada, Texas;* the heavy cruisers *Augusta, Quincy, Tuscaloosa*; five British light cruisers and the monitor *Erebus*; the French light cruisers *Montcalm* and *Georges Leygues*; the Dutch gunboat *Soemba*; 35 destroyers; 12 frigates; 118 minesweepers; 4 corvettes; 140 light warships; and 1,700 landing craft and boats. The British Eastern Naval Task Force (Rear Adm. Vian) also participated, with the battleships *Ramillies* and *Warspite*; 11 light cruisers; the monitor *Roberts*; the Polish destroyer *Dragon*; the Dutch cruiser *Sumatra* and gunboat *Flores*; plus 34 destroyers, 4 sloops, 19 frigates, 17 corvettes, 129 minesweepers, 116 light naval units and 2,426 landing craft and boats.

The 4th US Division landed on the east coast of the Cotentin Peninsula (Utah Beach), the 1st US Division at Vierville (Omaha Beach), the British 50th Division at Arromanches (Gold Beach), the Canadian 3rd Division at Courseulles (Juno Beach) and the British 3rd Division at Lyon-sur-Mer (Sword Beach).

Dönitz stated, "When the Allies landed the night of 5/6 June 1944 in the Seine Bay, they encountered no effective minefields and there were no patrol boats at sea."

The German Naval Group Staff West (Vice-Adm. Krancke) had merely 5 torpedo boats, 34 S-boats, 163 minesweepers, 57 patrol boats and 42 gunships at its disposal in the Channel area. In addition, the command had 9 U-boats fitted with Schnorchel. They were opposed by some 800 Allied warships, including 6 battleships, 2 monitors, 22 cruisers, 93 destroyers, 26 escort destroyers, 113 frigates and corvettes, as well as MTBs and MGBs and other warships.

The success of Operation Overlord was guaranteed by the erection of the artificial Mulberry harbors and anchorage facilities in the next few days. Landing boats and coastal boats ran straight up onto the beach where, at low tide, they stuck fast, making swift disembarkation that much easier.

In June 1944 the eighth and final phase of the Battle of the Atlantic began. U-boats equipped with Schnorchel carried out lone operations in British and North American coastal waters. On average there were forty-eight U-boats at sea. This phase lasted until May 1945.

On Sunday 11 June 1944, three destroyers from Task Group 22.5 (Capt. Vest) sank the last submarine-tanker, *U 490* (Lt. Gerlach), northwest of the Azores after it had been located by HF/DF.

On Thursday 15 June 1944, after preparatory air attacks, the American V Corps (Lt. Gen. H. M.

Smith) landed on the island of Saipan in the Marianas. At this, the Japanese fleet (Vice-Adm. Ozawa) left their anchorage at Tawitawi and made for the Marianas to prevent any invasion of these strategically important islands. The American C-in-C resolved not to reveal the landing fleet off Saipan and waited until Adm. Ozawa opened his attack.

On Monday 19 June 1944, a fierce air-sea battle took place in the Philippines Sea between the Japanese fleet under Vice-Adm. Ozawa, including nine aircraft carriers and land-based naval aircraft, and US Task Force 58 under Vice-Adm. Mitsher, which included fifteen aircraft carriers.

The Japanese attempted to prevent an occupation of the Marianas by US forces, who would then have had naval and air bases only fifteen hundred miles from the Japanese mainland. With bases on the Marianas, the Americans would have been in a position to attack Japanese industrial centers and disrupt communications with the Philippines and the East Asian mainland. From this point Tokyo, too, would have been within range of the B-29 Superfortresses.

Early 19 June 1944, Vice-Adm. Ozawa's fleet was southwest of Guam. It was a glorious day with blue skies and unrestricted visibility.

Whereas Japanese reconnaissance had meanwhile located Task Force 58, the Americans had not yet established the position of the Japanese fleet. The Japanese had another advantage at this point: Their aircraft, lighter because they were not armored, had an extra one hundred miles range compared with the Americans. The US fleet was therefore within range of Vice-Adm. Ozawa's fleet, which was, however, out of range of US carrier-borne aircraft.

At 8:30 A.M., the first sixty-four machines took off from the aircraft carriers making up the Japanese vanguard, the *Chiyoda, Shitose* and *Zuiho*. At 8:56, twenty-eight aircraft took off from Vice-Adm. Ozawa's main formation carriers, *Taiho, Shokaku* and *Zuikaku*. The pilot of one of these aircraft, Petty Officer Kamatsu, was gaining height when he spotted a torpedo, fired by the US submarine *Albacore*, heading straight toward the flagship, the carrier *Taiho*. He dived his aircraft onto the torpedo to save the carrier.

Japanese formation II (light carriers *Hiyo, Junyo* and *Ryuho*) ordered up another forty-seven aircraft at 10:00. At 11:00 Ozawa ordered up 114 aircraft from carrier formations I and III. By then, eighty percent of the Japanese carrier aircraft were approaching Task Force 58, thus only a dozen fighters remained to protect the Japanese fleet: a grave error on the part of Vice-Adm. Ozawa that he would soon bitterly regret.

For the next eight hours, Japanese pilots attacked the US carriers. Radar had already located most of the Japanese aircraft at a distance of 155 nautical miles. The American fighters took off when the Japanese aircraft approached, and a fierce battle ensued during which the attackers suffered heavy losses.

The American pilots were absolutely superior to their less experienced Japanese counterparts. The Japanese lost 218 aircraft, compared to only 29 American aircraft shot down.

Of the 375 Japanese carrier aircraft, only 40 succeeded in getting close to the American task force. By the late afternoon of 19 June 1944, 402 Japanese land-based and carrier-borne aircraft had been shot down, at a distance of up to sixty nautical miles before reaching the American warships. A sole Japanese aircraft managed to hit the battleship *South Dakota*; although the ship suffered only slight damage, twenty-seven sailors were killed. The battleship *Indiana* and the heavy cruiser *Indianapolis* also suffered slight damage.

The flagship of Vice-Adm. Ozawa, the carrier *Taiho*, was hit by a second torpedo fired from the submarine *Albacore*. Some six hours later, after a massive explosion in the fuel tanks, the carrier had to be abandoned with a number of aircraft on board. The carrier *Shokaku*, torpedoed by the submarine *Cavalla*, burst into flames. Around midnight, both carriers sank. Ozawa, who still had no idea of the catastrophe suffered by his aircraft, refused to give up. His fleet made off on a northwesterly course during the night simply to refuel.

On Tuesday 20 June 1944, at 3:00 P.M. Vice-Adm. Ozawa's fleet was again located by US reconnaissance aircraft. Vice-Adm. Mitscher ordered off all his dive bombers and torpedo-strike aircraft, although it was already late in the afternoon and they would not be able to get back before dark. Lighting up the carriers after dark would increase the risk of attack by submarines.

While Ozawa's fleet was still being refuelled, 216 American aircraft approached, encountering only 35 fighters over the Japanese fleet. Despite intense antiaircraft fire, the Japanese lost the carrier *Hiyo* and two tankers. The carriers *Zuikaku* and *Chiyoda*, the battleship *Haruna* and the heavy cruiser *Maya* were damaged. Twenty American aircraft were lost.

Those Japanese carriers still afloat reported heavy damage on their flight decks, and Ozawa had to withdraw during the night of 21 June 1944 on orders given by the C-in-C of the Imperial Fleet (Adm. Toyoda). By this time, the battle had cost the Japanese three-quarters of all aircraft deployed: a total of 480 machines lost.

The US carriers, despite lighting up the flight decks, reported 72 aircraft lost in landing accidents or emergency ditchings in the sea. Out of 209

June 1944, mid-Pacific, a formation of Dauntless dive bombers of the US Navy overflying a US fleet formation. Below to the left, an aircraft carrier and on the horizon, other heavy units.

pilots, 49 were lost.

The most important result of the battle in the Philippines Sea, also officially known as the Great Marianas Turkey Shoot, was the almost complete destruction of the Japanese fleet air arm. The way to the Philippines was now open. Landings on the Marianas could be continued unhampered, and Japan's outer defensive ring was lost.

On Wednesday 21 June 1944, an Anglo-Italian group of frogmen and manned torpedoes was set off by the Italian destroyer *Grecale* and the MGB *MS 74* off La Spezia. The group in the harbor sank two Italian heavy cruisers sailing under the German flag, the *Bolzano* (13,885 tons) and the *Gorizia* (14,600 tons).

On Thursday 22 June 1944, a detachment of German frogmen from naval Commando 60 arrived in Caen. The following night they were to blow up two of the most important bridges over the Orne and the Orne Canal in the vicinity of

Bénouville. The bridges had been taken during the first hours of the invasion in an attack launched by the British 6th Airborne Division (Maj. Gen. Gale). Supplies and provisions were now being transported over the Orne to British troops in the bridgehead north of Caen. As an air raid by the Luftwaffe was shown to be impracticable because of the massed antiaircraft guns, frogmen would now have to blow the bridges up with explosive devices. In two groups of five men to a group, they started off at 10:30 P.M., and after a difficult ten miles along the river and canal bed, they — undiscovered by numerous patrols — reached their target. The explosive devices were fixed, in each instance, to the center pier and detonated on both bridges at 5:30 the next morning.

When the frogmen returned to their point of departure, it was discovered that through faulty reconnaissance along the Orne Canal, the wrong bridges had been blown up.

On Saturday 24 June 1944, west of the Azores the last Japanese submarine attempting to reach the French Atlantic coast, *I-52* (Comdr. Uno), was sunk by two Avengers from the US carrier *Bogue*.

The night of 24/25 June 1944, a new German weapon was deployed against the invasion fleet in

Synchronising watches before the operation begins: German frogmen of marine Commando 60. Frogmen were equipped with diving gear and flippers. They wore a protective suit made from sailcloth that was designed to protect the actual diving suit from damage.

the Seine Bay. The weapon was the Mistel (official code-name "Beethoven") — a pilotless version of the Ju 88 — carrying 3.5 tons of explosives. There were two basic types of Mistel, known also as Father-and-Son or Piggyback aircraft. The S1 was mounted below an Me 109 and the S2 below an Fw 190. The Mistel composite aircraft had been tested at the beginning of 1944 in Nordhausen and Peenemünde and was delivered in May 1944 to the special operations squadron of IV/KG 101, which was to operate these aircraft from Denmark against the Royal Navy's base at Scapa Flow. Because of the Allied invasion, the special operations squadron was rushed by night to Saint-Dizier (Pas de Calais). The night of 24/25 June 1944, five Mistel S1 aircraft, accompanied by Me 109 G fighters, took off from their base at Saint-Dizier on their first operation — a real death or glory mission, as the French skies at that time were alive with Mosquito nightfighters. During the flight, one of the Ju 88s had to be dropped. The four other aircraft reached the Seine Bay and, dropping flares, attacked the ships lying at anchor without, however, having any idea that these were discarded vessels serving merely as blockships and breakwaters. As the bay was covered in fog, the results of the attack were

not visible. The five piloted aircraft returned to their base in safety. The following day it was established that one of the blockships had been sunk. And so ended the first and last Mistel operation in northern France.

The invasion of Normandy was proof of the Allied supremacy on the seven seas. And this supremacy was decisive in bringing troops from America across the Atlantic to Great Britain. It spared the Allies the need of fighting for maritime superiority in the English Channel. The Germans' primary handicap was the 3,500-mile-long coastline that they had to defend. In June 1944 the world experienced the greatest display of military and naval power in the history of maritime warfare — the invasion of Normandy and, nine days later, the US landings on the Marianas in the Pacific.

From June 1944, German submarines changed their tactics. In order to outweigh the principal disadvantage suffered by Schnorchel-equipped U-boats, i.e., their much reduced speed underwater, they could only operate successfully in the areas close to ports where the largest concentration of shipping was to be found. As a consequence, they were deployed mainly off British and American coastal waters. But U-boat defence measures were particularly strong in these areas, and the success hoped for did not materialise.

During this half-year, the German U-boats destroyed an average of only 80,000 gross tons per month, but the C-in-C nonetheless hoped that he could tie down the entire Allied antisubmarine defence force of some 350,000 men, until the new large U-boats were ready for operations, ready to open the offensive planned for the end of the year.

1944

July–December

Saturday 1 July 1944
The *German High Command* issued the following communiqué:

During attacks on the enemy invasion fleet and seaborne supplies, the Luftwaffe, Kriegsmarine, army and coastal batteries during June destroyed fifty-one freighters and transporters totalling 312,000 gross tons. Another fifty-six ships totalling 328,000 gross tons, including numerous transport vessels and landing craft, were damaged, some seriously. Of the enemy's warships, two heavy and three light cruisers, twenty-two destroyers, fifteen MTBs and MGBs, one submarine, three landing craft and one patrol vessel were sunk. Several battleships including a ship of the Nelson class, twenty-one cruisers, twenty-two destroyers, twenty-six special landing craft and twelve MTBs were heavily damaged by bombs, torpedoes and artillery; some of these ships are assumed to have been destroyed. Enemy shipping losses were also increased by mines.

Hitler's U-boat Arm Has Failed

Monday 10 July 1944, London
The *Reuters* News Agency reported:

A joint statement for June made by W. Churchill and F. D. Roosevelt on the U-boat war situation: Hitler's U-boat arm in June 1944 has failed in all regards. Enemy U-boats were unable either to prevent the invasion of the European mainland by the Allies or prevent the supplies reaching our ever-increasing armies in Europe. The U-boats kept to the west of the invasion zone or were spread out across the Atlantic. The number of merchant ships sunk by U-boats during June was almost the lowest figure recorded since the outbreak of war. German U-boat losses, in comparison, were greater than Allied merchant shipping losses.

After the Greek Mutiny
Wednesday 12 July 1944, Cairo
The *Reuters* News Agency reported:

The naval court sitting in Alexandria on Friday sentenced three Greek sailors to death. They were found not guilty of high treason but guilty of mutiny with violence. Three sailors found guilty of the same crime were sentenced to a term of twenty years penal servitude and six to a term of twenty years in prison. Four sailors were acquitted.

Secret report of the *SS Security Service* on the internal political situation:
No. 638, Thursday 13 July 1944 (Extract)

Reports on the trends of public opinion. The heavy fighting taking place on all fronts is a matter of increasing concern for the entire population. . . . The deployment of the "V 2" is awaited with great anticipation, and this weapon is said to have something to do with our U-boat arm. In mentioning this, some people refer to the remarks said to have been made by Grand Admiral Dönitz to the Gauleiters, "I'll show the enemy U-boats that will put everything that has gone before in the shade. I'm only waiting for the command to put to sea. The enemy has been able to destroy up to fifty percent of our U-boats through his inventions. With things as they are now, he won't be able to find us."

Landing on Guam

Friday 21 July 1944, Pearl Harbor
The *United Press Agency* reported:

American troops have landed on Guam in the Marianas.

Loss of American Submarines
Saturday 22 July 1944, Washington
The *US Navy Department* issued the following communiqué:

Left: The launching of a new electro–U-boat type XXI. With more powerful E-motors and increased battery capacity, plus improved aerodynamic hull, it was no longer the traditional submersible. Speed, submerged, at eighteen knots was almost twice that of many convoys.

Right: Leading Seaman Walther Gerhold, mentioned in the OKW report dated 7/18/1944, in his Neger

The submarines *Trout* and *Tullibee* were sunk during naval operations in the Pacific. At the beginning of the war, the *Trout* was successful in breaking through the Japanese blockade in Manila Bay and bringing the Philippine gold from Corregidor to safety. Since the outbreak of war, the US Navy has lost twenty-seven submarines.

Fighting on the Marianas
Wednesday 26 July 1944, Tokyo
The *Japanese Imperial Headquarters* issued the following communiqué:

Since the morning of 23 July, the enemy has attempted landing operations in the harbor of Tinian Island and on the northwest coast. Japanese troops immediately offered resistance. They thereby caused the enemy heavy casualties in Tinian harbor, forcing the enemy to retreat. In the northwest of the island, the Japanese undertook intensive counterattacks; nevertheless, the enemy succeeded in landing at midday. In the meantime, his troops have been reinforced, but the Japanese forces are resisting the landing parties with all the force at their disposal.

US Successes in the Pacific War
Thursday 27 July 1944, Pearl Harbor
Admiral Nimitz issued the following communiqué:

The American invasion troops have occupied the northern part of Tinian (Marianas), where one of the most important airfields on the Marianas is situated. Our troops are now in control of the west coast of Guam.

Swiss Radio Beromünster

Friday 28 July 1944
It had been announced that the Germans would either stop the invasion in front of the Atlantic Wall or deal the invasion army a decisive blow, throwing it back into the sea. After this the German forces would turn again to the East with their full strength in order to crush the Russians. What we have seen in the last five weeks has been the complete failure of this plan. There has been no victory on the invasion front, but a relative defensive success by Rommel's army.

Friday 4 August 1944
The *German High Command* issued the following communiqué:

Units of the Kriegsmarine, including submarines, have sunk in the sea area of the invasion front one cruiser, three destroyers, two corvettes, as well as five transports and one special ship totalling thirty-six thousand gross tons. Numerous ships totalling more than fifty-six thousand gross tons have been torpedoed; the greater part of these ships can be assumed destroyed. The night of 3 August in the eastern part of the Seine Bay, S-boats sank a British MGB.

Loss of a Refugee Ship
Monday 7 August 1944, Sofia
The *DNB* Agency reported:

It has been reported from Ankara that a Turkish ship with 250 Jewish refugees on board, proceed-

ing from Constantsa to Turkey, was sunk in the Black Sea early this morning.

Sunday 12 August 1944
The *German High Command* issued the following communiqué:

U-boats sank four freighters totalling twenty-two thousand gross tons, two minesweepers, three other ships and torpedoed one destroyer off the invasion coast and in other sea areas. Three enemy aircraft were shot down.

Allied Landing in the South of France

Tuesday 15 August 1944
General Eisenhower's Headquarters issued the following special communiqué:

Today American, British and French forces, supported by the Allied air forces and the American, British and French navies, landed on the south coast of France.

Wednesday 16 August 1944
The *German High Command* issued the following communiqué:

The enemy attempted a number of landings between Toulon and Cannes on the south coast of France, which were beaten back. The enemy succeeded nonetheless in gaining a foothold at several points along the coast. Bitter fighting is taking place in these areas. Enemy airborne forces that landed in the rear of our defensive positions have

been attacked by our reserve forces. In air battles, antiaircraft units of the Luftwaffe and the Kriegsmarine and also a number of our naval units accounted for twenty-three enemy aircraft over the western and southern French coasts.

Naval Operations off the Riviera
Friday 18 August 1944
From *General Wilson's Headquarters:*

The French battleship *Lorraine* and the cruiser *Emile Bertin* today opened fire on the island of Porquerolles. An American cruiser and the French cruiser *Gloire* opened fire on the mainland east of Toulon. In another sector, a US cruiser, together with the cruisers *Ajax* and *Gloire*, supported the advance of army units. A US cruiser and a destroyer entered the Bay of Rapoule and opened fire on enemy coastal batteries. Other US destroyers attacked enemy artillery positions at Cannes. Practically no enemy aircraft activity was reported over the southern French bridgehead. According to a report from the marine commandos, support given by Allied aircraft operating from the carriers was highly effective.

Swiss Radio Beromünster

18 August 1944
It was with the greatest surprise that the landing forces invading the South of France noted the widespread lack of German resistance. Not one German U-boat, not one bomber, scarcely a coastal battery was said to be in action while, in the meantime, landing craft put ashore troops, ammunition, war equipment and the numerous articles of provisioning and supply necessary for this kind of operation. The only demolitions carried out by the Germans were in precisely those large ports—Cannes, Nice and others—avoided by the Allies.

Thursday 24 August 1944
The *German High Command* issued the following communiqué:

Submarine hunters sank a Soviet MGB in the Black Sea east of Constantsa.

Saturday 26 August 1944
The *German High Command* issued the following communiqué:

During a large-scale operation against guerrilla shipping in the Aegean, the Communists suffered bloody losses, and 142 of their coast boats and sailing boats were destroyed or taken prize.

Left: On board a French warship off the coast of France, heavy Flak-MG

Right: U-boat bunker in Brest, one of the few where a direct hit with the heaviest type of bomb penetrated nearly 40 ft. of reinforced concrete

Naval Battle in the Channel
Saturday 2 September 1944, London
In a joint communiqué issued by the *British Royal Navy* and the *Royal Dutch Navy*, the following was announced yesterday evening:

Intercepted by light coastal units of the British, Canadian and Dutch navies were a number of enemy formations, which last night and early Saturday morning attempted to break out of French Channel ports threatened by the Allied advance.

Large Convoy Reaches England

Thursday 7 September 1944, Ottawa
The *Reuters* News Agency reported:

As announced by the navy minister, Mr. Mac-Donald, the largest convoy ever to cross the ocean recently reached Great Britain. It comprised 150 merchant ships carrying more than one million tons of freight.

Fate of the German Black Sea Fleet
Saturday 9 September 1944, Moscow
The *TASS* News Agency reported:

The remainder of the German Black Sea Fleet — a total of 112 units — has had to put into the ports of Varna, Burgas and into smaller Bulgarian ports after the loss of their last bases in Bessarabia and Rumania. After the coup d'état in Bulgaria, the Germans scuttled seventy-four ships, including seven U-boats, without being stopped by the Bulgarians. The Bulgarian government declined to intern the crews of the scuttled ships, returning them to Germany. After an energetic Soviet protest, the remainder of the ships have been seized by the Bulgarians and their crews interned.

Atlantic Bases Neutralised

Sunday 10 September 1944, London
The *Reuters* News Agency reported:

A joint statement for August made by W. Churchill and F. D. Roosevelt on the U-boat situation: Last month the most important U-boat bases on the Atlantic seaboard were neutralised by Allied operations in France. As a result of this, the Germans have been forced to operate U-boats from Norwegian and Baltic bases, thereby making their transit routes appreciably longer.

Return of the French Fleet to Toulon
Friday 15 September 1944, Toulon
The French *Havas* News Agency reported:

Tens of thousands of enthusiastic French men and women stood on the quay when the French fleet put into Toulon. The joy was indescribable when the flagship of the French squadron, the cruiser *Georges Leygues*, with Adm. André de Monnier on board, put into the harbor. Despite pouring rain, officers and crew of the Allied warships paraded on deck and saluted. The French units lowered their colors in greeting. Up to now, the old battleship *Lorraine*, the cruisers *Emile Bertin, Montcalm, Gloire* and the destroyers *Le Malin, Le Fortune, Forbin* and *Basque* have arrived. A number of submarines and several smaller units will arrive later.

Swiss Radio Beromünster

Friday 6 October 1944

A large-scale British invasion of Greece has followed on the landings on the Adriatic islands and coast of Dalmatia and Albania. Allied units have been brought ashore on the northwest coast of the Peloponnese by air and by sea. Naval units entered the Gulf of Patras, and Tuesday and Wednesday nights Allied troops entered the town of Patras. Allied troops made contact with Greek partisan formations at various points. A number of Greek islands both in the Ionian Sea and in the Aegean were occupied by the Allies before the landings on the Greek mainland.

New German U-boats?

Tuesday 10 October 1944, London
The *Reuters* News Agency reported:

A joint statement for September made by W. Churchill and F. D. Roosevelt on the U-boat war situation: There was a lull in the fighting in September 1944; shipping losses sustained by the Allies were practically as low as in May 1944, a month that recorded the lowest figures for shipping sunk. It is probable that the German Naval High Command will again take up U-boat operations in the autumn, deploying new and improved types of submarine. Accordingly, ever greater vigilance is called for.

Attack on Leyte

Thursday 19 October 1944, Tokyo
The *Headquarters of the Imperial Navy* issued the following communiqué:

An enemy fleet formation accompanied by a large number of transports appeared in the Bay of Leyte on 17 October. Since the afternoon of 18 October, the force has been bombarding the coast with naval and air units. Japanese units in this area have taken up counterattacks.

New Naval Battle in the Pacific
Wednesday 25 October 1944, Tokyo
The *DNB* Agency reported:

Since early Wednesday morning, a fierce battle has been raging east of Samar. Sixteen warships and six aircraft carriers have been sunk or damaged in these waters.

American Submarines Supporting Guerrillas
25 October 1944, New York
From *General MacArthur's Headquarters*:

The secret radio transmitter that was set up on Panay Island and heard for the first time in August 1942 has made a substantial contribution to the anti-Japanese movement in the Philippines. American submarines have been supplying the Philippine guerrillas with war material. We have been supported by an extensive network of radio stations and also by the fact that on each of the larger islands, there is one or more meteorological stations that several times a day furnish headquarters with precise weather reports. A well-developed system of alarms means that we are aware of any movements by the enemy air force. In addition, a number of enemy documents, including secret defence plans and instructions from the Japanese staff, have been captured.

Naval Battle off Leyte
25 October 1944, Pearl Harbor
The *United Press Agency* reported:

A new naval battle has broken out near the Philippines. As stated by Adm. Nimitz, strong Japanese naval forces, including battleships and cruisers, are said to be making toward the island of Leyte, north and southwest of the American operational zone. American squadrons taking off

from a formation of carriers have attacked the Japanese warships. No details have as yet been released.

Friday 27 October 1944, Leyte
The *Reuters* News Agency reported:
Vice-Adm. Kincaid, whose Seventh Fleet attacked a Japanese naval squadron, today ended the action with a signficant victory.

Swiss Radio Beromünster

27 October 1944
In the South Seas, far from Europe, a remarkable change in the war situation has come about as a result of the American landing operations on the Philippine islands of Leyte and Samar. For those of us who are not sailors, it is difficult to get a firm grasp of the conduct of the war in the Pacific and the organisational and military services carried out. We need only remind ourselves that just one year ago, the American army and navy formations were 3,500 miles away from the Philippines, where they are now fighting: a distance equal to that from Gibraltar to Trondheim in Norway. There are the land forces under MacArthur's overall command fighting against the Japanese forces occupying Leyte, the central island in the Philippines; the fleet has won a battle against the Japanese, which is reported by Washington as an important victory; and the legal government of the Philippines has already returned home in the wake of the Americans.

W. Churchill to J. Stalin
Sunday 5 November 1944
Congratulations on your advance on Budapest. We now have effective control over the approaches to Antwerp and I hope to have the port open to coastal shipping within ten days and ocean shipping within three to four weeks. That should solve the problem of the northern flank of the advance into Germany.

Lowest Figure of Ships Sunk Since Outbreak of War

Friday 10 November 1944, London
The *Reuters* News Agency reported:
A joint statement for October made by W. Churchill and F. D. Roosevelt on the U-boat war situation: The extent of U-boat activity in October 1944 was considerably less than in any other month of the entire war. As a result, the number of freighters sunk during this month by U-boats was the lowest since the outbreak of war.

Tirpitz Sunk!

Tuesday 14 November 1944, London
The *British Air Ministry* issued the following communiqué:
On Sunday morning, twenty-nine Lancasters from Bomber Command, led by Wing Comdr. J. B. Tait and Squadron Leader A. G. Williams, attacked the battleship *Tirpitz* with twelve thousand-pound bombs. A number of direct hits was scored. Within a few minutes the ship turned over on its side and sank. One of our aircraft is missing.

German U-boats off the Canadian Coast
Sunday 19 November 1944, Montreal
The *Exchange* News Agency reported:
A large number of German U-boats are currently operating along the Canadian Atlantic coast. This has been described as a "serious threat to coastal shipping." Canadian and US destroyers have taken up hunting operations.

Thirteen Japanese Admirals Killed
Saturday 9 December 1944, New York
The *Reuters* News Agency reported:
We have heard from the Japanese news agency that in the southwest Pacific thirteen Japanese admirals have been killed on active service.

Right: 9/1/1944, the coast of East Greenland, the crew of the US Coastguard vessel *Northland* take prisoner the German meteorological detachment Edelweiss I.

Left: 10/30/1944, off Leyte (Philippines), the US carrier *Belleau Wood* after kamikaze attack. To the rear, the blazing carrier *Franklin*, which was again set ablaze two weeks later during another kamikaze attack.

Below: The race between building and losses — German U-boats 1939–45

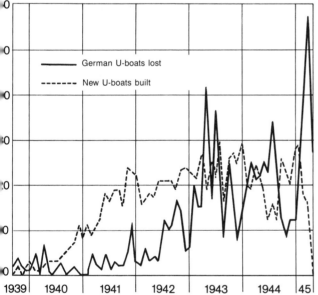

German U-boats lost
---- New U-boats built

1939 | 1940 | 1941 | 1942 | 1943 | 1944 | 45

Japan Faces the "Hardest Phase"

9 December 1944, Tokyo
Prime Minister Koiso stated in a speech:

"Using all the force and weapons at his disposal, the enemy is advancing ruthlessly and determinedly on all fronts. Every day bitter fighting takes place on the Philippines and in the waters bordering Japan. The further course of the war will be decided in these battles."

U-boats Will Not Give Up

Sunday 10 December 1944, London
The *Reuters* News Agency reported:

A joint statement for November made by W. Churchill and F. D. Roosevelt on the U-boat war situation: Shipping losses caused by U-boat activities were very low in November 1944, and the figures for U-boats sunk relatively satisfactory. But the enemy has by no means given up the U-boat war; on the contrary, new types are coming into operation that enable fresh air supplies to be taken in over a long period and the U-boat can thereby stay submerged longer. By these means the U-boats can enter areas that they have been unable to reach during the last three years. Reports that U-boat building has been terminated are probably of German origin and do not express the factual situation.

Secret German Meteorological Detachment Taken Prisoner
Friday 15 December 1944
The *Reuters* News Agency reported:

During a weeks-long journey through the Arctic, four American coastal vessels frustrated an attempt by the Germans to establish bases on the north coast of Greenland. The Americans finally attacked the Germans during the polar night. One of the German freighters was hit and scuttled by its own crew; the freighter *Externsteine* was captured by the Americans; the third ship was found abandoned. Sixty Germans have been taken prisoner. Near the coast of Greenland, the Americans discovered an abandoned radio station and meteorological station; these German outposts had been provided with a year's supply of foodstuffs, fuel and weapons. Both these installations were destroyed. A twin-engined German bomber attempted without success to attack the coastal vessels. Three of the cutters were damaged by ice.

Strategy and Tactics

On Saturday 1 July 1944, the Kreuzritter meteorological detachment (twelve men), which had been operational in the Liefdelfjord (Spitsbergen) since 4 October 1943, was taken off by U-boat. While the station was being evacuated, a mine laid by the detachment went up and killed the leader, Dr. Knöspel.

The night of 5/6 July 1944, thirty manned torpedoes of the Neger type set out from Villers-sur-Mer, a seaside resort in Normandy, on their first operation. The vessels were a part of Flotilla 363 (Capt. Böhme) of the small vessels formation, and their target was Allied shipping in the Orne estuary. Leading Seaman Gerhold certainly sank the small minesweeper *Cato*, and Able Seaman Berger the minesweeper *Magic*; but of the thirty one-man Neger torpedoes that set out, only fourteen returned.

Late the evening of 7 July 1944, twenty-one one-man torpedoes again set out from Villers-sur-Mer. In the area of Houlgate, Midshipman K. Potthast scored a hit on the cruiser *Dragon* (Lt. Comdr. Dzienisiewicz), of the Polish Navy in exile. The crew suffered thirty-seven fatalities and over one hundred wounded. Potthast stated, "I forgot to stop when I fired. Nothing happened for what seemed an eternity. Disappointed, I bowed my head. But suddenly there was a tremendous underwater blast; the Neger nearly jumped out of the water. A sheet of flame shot up from the target ship. Seconds later the fire had quite blinded me; the smoke drove toward me and completely covered me. For some minutes I couldn't get my bearings.

Not until the smoke had lifted could I again see the ship. It was burning intensely and listing. Its silhouette was much shorter than it had been, and I suddenly realised that the stern had been torn away."

Petty Officer Kurkowski from the cruiser *Dragon* stated, "The night of 7/8 July 1944 is memorable for the extraordinarily heavy strikes by the Luftwaffe and S-boats. There was a ghostly beauty about the starry night. The coast was illuminated by the reddish reflections of the fires on the horizon.

"Innumerable searchlights cut through the darkness over the sea. Flares crisscrossed like millions of glass beads. We had already taken up battle stations by 5:00 A.M., as we were to bombard the German coastal defence installations twenty minutes later. The morning quiet was suddenly shattered by an ear-splitting explosion, and at the same time massive columns of fire and water shot up into the sky. The effects of the explosion were terrifying: Five men manning the Oerlikon-Flak guns were flung off their gun platform into the sea. Four were picked up dead, and one had simply disappeared. Seven seamen died in the ammunition chamber. All engine room personnel were also killed." The badly hit *Dragon* was towed into the nearest Mulberry artificial harbor and sent to the bottom as a breakwater.

The torpedo man, Midshipman Potthast, was attacked by a British corvette. Decidedly unlucky, he was taken prisoner; this success, achieved by one-man torpedoes, was credited to Leading Seaman Gerhold, who upon his return reported the torpedoeing of a large warship, at least a destroyer. Gerhold, mentioned in the OKW report on 18 July 1944, was awarded the Knight's Cross of the Iron Cross and made a hero by the Nazi propaganda machine.

To rid themselves of this troublesome one-man torpedo menace, the Allies deployed a simple but reliable method. One night they poured oil around their ships gathered off the Normandy coast. The oil smeared all over the torpedo's perspex dome, robbing the crewman of all visibility. At dawn the next day, Allied MGBs cut off the retreat of the half-blinded Negers and carried out a thoroughgoing slaughter of the one-man torpedoes, which could make barely four knots. Either rammed or with smashed perspex domes, the torpedoes immediately sank.

The night of 19/20 July 1944, a disguised one-man torpedo operating from its base in Villers-sur-Mer sank the British destroyer *Isis* in the Orne estuary.

On Sunday 30 July 1944, the Soviet submarine hunters *MO 103* (Lt. Kolenka) and *DS 910* dropped depth charges on the German U-boat *U 250* (Lt. Comdr. W. K. Schmidt) in the narrows of the Gulf of Finland. This submarine went down with its entire crew but was later raised by Soviet ships from the shallow waters where it lay and taken to Kronstadt. The submarine contained, in addition to a complete set of secret documents, an Enigma-

M 4 enciphering machine and one of the latest German acoustic torpedoes, the homing torpedo "Zaunkönig."

When authorities of the British Admiralty heard about this find, they turned to Stalin with a request that a British team be allowed to inspect the U-boat and the torpedoes. Adm. Kusnezov stated, "Stalin called me and asked what I thought of this. I answered that I could see no reason why we should not grant our allies this request. This was advised to Churchill. For my part, I gave the C-in-C of the Baltic Fleet, Admiral Tribuz, instructions to allow British specialists on board the salvaged U-boat. The British made a thorough investigation and evaluation of the U-boat and the torpedo, and afterward gave Stalin their warmest thanks. This made Stalin uneasy, and he asked me, 'Do you think we might have given the British access to far too valuable a secret?' Just like Tribuz, I was really nervous about this incident. Stalin has always warned us that our allies only reluctantly gave us their military secrets. But everything went off all right this time."

In July 1944 U-boats operating in the Atlantic and Indian oceans sank sixteen merchant ships totalling 76,199 gross tons. German losses amounted to thirty-one U-boats.

The night of 1/2 August 1944, twenty of the new Linsen assault boats and twelve control boats of KFl 211 (small vessels flotilla, Lt. Comdr. Bastian) put to sea from Houlgate to attack Allied shipping in the English Channel. The Linsen was nineteen feet long, carried six hundred pounds of explosives and was radio controlled by the control boat, which guided it to the target. The Linsen had a petrol engine of ninety-five horsepower and was capable of thirty-three knots. These weapons sank the destroyer *Quorn*, a landing boat and the trawler *Gairsay*, and they damaged the freighters *Fort Lac La Ronge* (7,131 gross tons) and *Samlong* (7,219 gross tons). Only ten of the control boats returned. The most successful of the helmsmen, Lt. Vetter, was mentioned in the OKW report of 15 September 1944.

After intensive, preliminary bombing strikes, Operation Dragoon commenced on 15 August 1944. This was the landing of the 7th US Army (Lt. Gen. Patch) with the VI US Corps (Maj. Gen. Truscott) and the French 1st Army (Gen. de Lattre de Tassigny) on the French Mediterranean coast between Toulon and Cannes. Approximately 14,000 landing troops were flown from Corsica. Under the command of Vice-Adm. Hewitt, Task Forces 84, 85, 86, 87—with 32 troopships, 466 landing craft, 111 destroyers, frigates, corvettes and other escort vessels, as well as 100 minesweepers—took part in the operation. The four escort groups comprised 5 battleships, 23 cruisers and 29 destroyers. Air cover was provided by aircraft from 9 escort carriers of Task Force 88 (Rear Adm. Troubridge). Approximately 200 German aircraft were available to oppose the 5,000 Allied carrier-borne aircraft and land-based aircraft. The invasion force pushed northward without meeting any serious resistance, and the first wave lost no more than 183 men. Fighter bombers from the escort carriers were deployed to give air support. For the first time in the European war theater, carrier-borne aircraft provided tactical air support for landing troops—a tactic regularly employed in the Pacific.

In the middle of August 1944, Allied troops drew close to the Atlantic ports of Brest, Lorient and St. Nazaire.

On Friday 18 August 1944, the *U 123* (Lt. von Schroeter) and *U 129* (Lt. von Harpe) in Lorient

7/8/1944, on the deck of the cruiser *Dragon* (4,850 tons) of the Polish Navy in exile: ". . . was suddenly shattered by an earsplitting explosion . . ."; 37 dead and more than 100 wounded—the result of a one-man torpedo strike

and *U 78* (Lt. Comdr. Spahr) and *U 188* (Lt. Comdr. Lüdden) in Bordeaux were scuttled by their crews, in compliance with orders given because the boats were not ready to put to sea. Toward the end of August 1944, seventeen U-boats left the bases along the Biscay coast. They reached the Norwegian bases at Bergen, Trondheim, Kristiansund and Narvik after a difficult voyage around the north of Scotland, mainly submerged in order to avoid the strong formations of Coastal Command aircraft. During this voyage, only *U 445* (Lt. Count von Treuberg) was lost in the Bay of Biscay.

On Sunday 20 August 1944, the heavy cruiser *Prinz Eugen*, as well as four destroyers and two torpedo-boats, used guns in support of units of the Army Group North, which had been cut off by Soviet forces along the Gulf of Riga near Tukum. From this date, heavy German surface units were increasingly used to support threatened army units along the Baltic seaboard.

On Tuesday 22 August 1944, the Naval Group Command South issued orders for the evacuation of the port of Constantsa.

On Friday 25 August 1944, Marshal Antonescu's government collapsed and Rumania declared war on Germany. Dönitz stated, "The sea war in the Black Sea was now over. Our naval units scuttled themselves."

On this day German warships evacuated the port of Constantsa. The head of the Black Sea docks staff, Rear Adm. (Eng.) Zieb, ordered all vessels carrying units from the evacuated areas of Galatz and Macin to assemble at Braila on the Danube. They were then to proceed westward, forcing their way upstream along the Danube. The convoy,

known as the Zieb Group, was joined by ever more Danube barges, tugs, repair ships; stragglers from the army, including a punishment battalion; a detachment of eighteen hundred engineers; the 1 Coastal Protection Flotilla; and a number of refugees. Without pilots and travelling at a speed of 5–6 miles per hour, the convoy dragged itself along the Danube like a fifteen-mile-long snake. At almost every town more women and children and badly wounded personnel found refuge on the ships. Before long refugees numbered more than eight thousand persons.

The convoy route led across Rumania, now at war with Germany. Rumanian soldiers, no longer kindly disposed towards the Germans, took up positions along both banks of the Danube. Although the ships belonging to Zieb Group had more than one hundred guns with calibers up to 7.5 cm, they would not – even if they had used the guns – have had much chance of success. In the vicinity of Cernavoda the ships were caught in the crossfire of Rumanian batteries. Until the batteries were silenced, Zieb Group lost 11 boats and 480 persons. The next action with the Rumanians cost more than 20 ships. When Rear Adm. Zieb received the news that the Soviets had already occupied the Iron Gate and were now blocking the group's path to the west, the 160 remaining units were scuttled near Prahova. Five weeks later the survivors of Zieb Group finally reached Belgrade, having marched across territory held by partisans and under constant attack by low-flying Soviet aircraft.

In August 1944 Soviet submarines succeeded in breaking out of the Bay of Kronstadt. For the first time, there were twelve Soviet front-line sub-

marines in action in the Baltic.

The night of 29/30 August 1944, midget-sub-marines of the Biber (beaver) class, KF1 261 (Comdr. Bartels), set off from their base in Fécamp (Normandy) on their first operation. These vessels were equipped with petrol/electric motors of twenty-three horsepower and armed with two torpedoes. The Biber was a surface weapon for torpedo strikes that could, in an emergency, submerge. Despite the heavy seas, eighteen of the Bibers attacked Allied shipping. Only two of them were able to fire off torpedoes. According to German reports, Lt. Dohse sank a landing craft and Petty Officer Bösch a freighter. The Bibers all returned safely to base.

In August 1944 German U-boats operating in the Atlantic and Indian oceans sank eighteen merchant ships totalling 98,876 gross tons. German losses amounted to thirty-one U-boats.

On Friday 1 September 1944, the German weather ship *Kehdingen* was surprised and captured by the US Coast Guard ship *Northland* in the Arctic off eastern Greenland. At the time of the incident, the German ship was putting ashore the eleven-man Edelweiss I meteorological detachment (leader Dr. G. Weiss). The escort submarine *U 703* (Lt. Brünner) fired off torpedoes that, however, detonated prematurely in the ice.

On Tuesday 5 September 1944, the last operational U-boat, *U 155* (Lt. von Friedeburg), left the base at Lorient. Servicing the *U 155* was the last job undertaken by the Kriegsmarine dockyards in Lorient.

On Friday 8 September 1944, Bulgaria declared war on Germany.

At the beginning of September 1944, the next

meteorological detachment prepared for operations. Because the Edelweiss I meteorological detachment, together with its leader Dr. G. Weiss, had been taken prisoner by the US Navy off eastern Greenland, the Haudegen meteorological detachment under the famous meteorologist Dr. Wilhelm Dege was to be deployed in the Arctic. Showing prudent foresight, Dr. Dege equipped his detachment for two winters, with eighty tons of material, three thousand different articles of equipment in eighteen hundred packing cases stowed on board the weather ship, the former fishing steamer *Carl J. Busch*, and the escort U-boat. Dr. Dege said, "I had decided upon Nordaustlandet Island at Spitsbergen as an operational area. The area was some ten thousand square miles in size and was classed as one of the most difficult of territories in the Arctic." The detachment reached Hammerfest by way of Sassnitz and Narvik.

On Saturday 9 September 1944, the fishing steamer *Carl J. Busch* and the escort U-boat *U 307* (Lt. Herlle) left Hammerfest. Dr. Dege said, "The escort U-boat under Lt. Herlle had found out that six or seven British destroyers were waiting for us off the west coast of Spitsbergen. We then changed our plans and decided to make our way around the difficult east coast of Spitsbergen. In the area of Bear Island, we ran into a powerful Allied convoy and managed, despite all the difficulties, to escape this convoy.

"We arrived at Nordaustlandet on 13 September and found an unusual situation regarding the ice, something not seen for a hundred years: The area was completely free of ice. We now built up our station with the assistance of the crews of the *Carl J. Busch* and the U-boat. In addition to the station hut, we later built a hut for the manufacture of hydrogen for our weather balloons and then, finally, a sauna. This work claimed our entire time, but I managed to take time off with two of my colleagues, as the U-boat, a 500-ton operational submarine, was at my disposal for fourteen days for my private scientific research in the area. I was able to put this time to good use and was the first scientist to circumnavigate the island. When I returned, both ships made their way back to Germany — and we were alone."

On Tuesday 12 September 1944, German troops in the Mediterranean began to evacuate the Aegean and Ionian islands.

The night of 15/16 September 1944, German frogmen from MEK 60 (Naval Special Commando under Lt. Prinzhorn) carried out an attack on the main floodgate at Antwerp harbor, which had fallen undamaged into Allied hands on 4 September 1944 when the port was hastily evacuated. The floodgate was essential in maintaining a constant water level, regardless of tides, in what was the most efficient port in West Europe at that time.

Two Linsen control boats, each with a helmsman and three frogmen (Sgt. Schmidt, Petty Officers Greten and Ohrdorf), arrived separately at the outer gates, thanks to good soundproofing and thick mist. Three men swimming with a torpedo mine in tow covered the remaining distance of some one thousand yards to the hundred-foot-wide gate. After crossing the protective nets, they placed the mine in position at the bottom of the floodgate, forty-five feet down, set the detonators and swam back to their boat. The second group missed their target in the thick fog and had to turn back. At 5:00 A.M. the mine exploded and destroyed the floodgate. The port of Antwerp was unusable for ocean shipping for six weeks.

On Friday 15 September 1944, the British midget-submarine *XE 24* (Lt. Westmacott), towed to the Norwegian coast by the submarine *Sceptre* (Lt. Comdr. McIntosh), attacked the repair yards in the Lakesvag Shipyards, the only facility in Norway suitable for larger ships. After the floating dock was sunk, all ships requiring repairs had to be transferred to Germany and were then liable to be attacked on the way by Coastal Command aircraft and Allied submarines.

On Tuesday 19 September 1944, the last German Schnorchel-equipped U-boat in the Mediterranean, *U 407* (Lt. Kolbus), was proceeding at a depth of ninety feet off the isle of Milos north of Crete on operational patrol. That afternoon, the captain gave the order to use the Schnorchel, and the boat rose to thirty feet. Records exist about the sinking of the last German U-boat in the Mediterranean, drawn up both by the pursuer and the pursued.

The log of the Polish destroyer *Garland* states, "19.20 hours, ship approached, exhaust emissions sighted, force 4–5 wind, swell 5. A thin tube giving off fumes was sighted at a distance of 400 yards. When the distance was reduced to 200 yards, burning oil could be smelled, and it was established that this was the exhaust pipe from the diesel motor of a U-boat charging its batteries at periscope depth. Simultaneously, the periscope was sighted three feet behind the exhaust. Action stations was sounded."

K. Hopp (*U 407*): "I was off watch and lying in my hammock when, toward 19.30 hours, the alarm bells sounded through the ship. I sprang out of the hammock and dashed off to my battle station at the forward tubes. Everything proceeded very quickly and the boat reached a depth of 600 feet without difficulty. After holding this position for a while, the captain gave orders to make for attack periscope depth."

Garland's log: "19.43 hours. After Asdic contact, attack commenced with forward Hedgehog. No hit scored. 20.28 hours attack carried out with depth charges; ten depth charges dropped. No results."

K. Hopp: "When our boat reached 200 feet, the silence was shattered by deafening explosions from a number of depth charges. The lights went out throughout the ship. . . .The destroyer continued to drop depth charges at short intervals. Our ship had now dropped further and apparently the safety limit of 720 feet had been exceeded. The depth gauge had broken."

Garland's log: "20.40 hours, four destroyers from the 24th Flotilla have arrived. Because of darkness, attack discontinued until morning. Overnight Asdic contact with U-boat."

K. Hopp: "Everybody who did not need to be on his feet lay down on the deck, or in the bunks, to ease air consumption. Because of the extreme water pressure, the stuffing boxes along the boat's hull began to leak. . . .To spread out the water to some extent, we had to pump it into the control room, using auxiliary and trimming pumps. We relieved tension by telling a number of jokes, such as 'See you in Cairo' or 'Off to do a bit of wood-chopping in Canada' [destination for many a POW— Trans.].

"Nothing special had happened by 04.00, except that the air had gotten a bit thin and stuffy. The E-motors had deteriorated, and we couldn't stay underwater for much longer. . . .Toward 04.50 hours the captain gave the order 'Make ready to surface, make ready escape gear and life jackets!' . . . A number of attempts showed that the sub didn't want to go any higher. It had become far too heavy because of the water shipped. . . .Everybody started to make all manner of guesses. Fresh efforts. Then a sudden cry, 'Hatch open, everyone out!'"

Garland's log: "06.30 hours. One of the destroyers opened fire on the surfaced U-boat sighted at 600 yards."

K. Hopp: "An explosion shattered the silence. They'd just fired off their first artillery greeting. We stood in a queue and waited our turn to abandon ship."

Garland's log: "Garland opened fire with No. 1 gun and the Oerlikon. Six hits with 5-inch guns and numerous strikes with the Oerlikon observed on the U-boats tower."

K. Hopp: "Although there were a number of strikes, I managed to make my way to my shipmates who were pulling a rubber dinghy in which our non-swimmer, Paul Albrecht, was lying."

Garland's log: "06.47 hours. Six depth charges dropped. Explosions under the U-boat's hull and in immediate vicinity."

K. Hopp: "When firing ceased, the Polish de-

Effects on an intense RAF air raid on the German inland canal system. Prefabricated parts of the revolutionary U-boat type XXI, which could not be transported by other methods because of their size, awaiting "breaking up" operations.

stroyer made toward our submarine and rammed it. It went down stern first. We gave three cheers as a final salute to our submarine and our dead comrades who went down with it. After another half-hour we were picked up by a British destroyer."

On Tuesday 19 September 1944, an armistice was signed in Moscow between the USSR and Finland. All German troops had to be evacuated from Finland within fifteen days. Dönitz said, "Our blockades shutting off the Gulf of Finland were thereby made ineffective."

Also on 19 September 1944, the US VII Corps occupied the Atlantic port of Brest.

The night of 22/23 September 1944, RAF bombers carried out the first attack on the Dortmund-Ems canal over which prefabricated U-boat parts were transported to the assembly yards. The destruction of the aqueduct over the river Glan near Münster brought inland shipping to a standstill over a seven-mile stretch. According to the calculations of the committee on shipbuilding chaired by O. Merker, more than one-half of the 290 type XXI U-boats, due to be delivered by the end of February 1945, were not assembled.

On Wednesday 27 September 1944, Sweden closed its Baltic ports to all German ships.

In September 1944 German U-boats operating in the Atlantic and Indian oceans sank seven merchant ships totalling 43,368 gross tons. German losses amounted to twenty-eight U-boats.

On Tuesday 3 October 1944, Hitler gave orders to evacuate the rest of Greece, southern Albania and southern Macedonia.

The night of 3/4 October 1944, approximately two hundred American Coast Guard soldiers landed on Koldeway (East Greenland) with the ice-breaker *East Wind*. Their objective was to take prisoner the eleven-man Edelweiss II meteorological detachment (leader Dr. K. Schmidt). The team had just commenced operations. The weather ship *Externsteine*, which had transported the team, was at the same time located by US reconnaissance, captured and taken back to Boston.

On Sunday 15 October 1944, the battleship *Tirpitz* put into Tromsö Sound after having left the Altafjord. The same day Egie Lindberg, an agent of the Norwegian section of SOE, radioed London that the *Tirpitz* was now lying at anchor in Tromsö. In accordance with Grand Admiral Dönitz's orders, the ship was now to be converted into a floating fortress.

Dönitz stated, "In order to neutralise the most disadvantageous possibility (the *Tirpitz* could be capsized through bombing strikes), it had to be sighted on the tactically most favorable point in as shallow water as possible. Following this directive, the C-in-C of the Battle Fleet, Capt. Peters, found an anchorage in a fjord close to Tromsö.

"The irregular course and steep drop to the sea bed along the banks of the fjord meant that the desired shallows under the *Tirpitz's* hull were not everywhere available. The officer commanding attempted to fill the gap by means of sand. The probability that the ship could even capsize on an anchorage prepared to this extent was now reduced to an absolute minimum."

In Tromsö, an area surrounded by low hills, the *Tirpitz* did not lie close to a protective mountain slope as it had done in the Altafjord. A number of antiaircraft batteries along the bank and an old Norwegian coastal protection vessel with a few Flak guns made up the defence against air attack.

On Tuesday 17 October 1944, the Greek fleet (Vice-Adm. Voulgaris) returned after an absence of three and a half years. The fleet was led by the cruiser *Georgios Averoff*, built in 1907. With a light breeze and cloudless skies, the ships put into Salamis Bay. The same day the blue-and-white flag of Greece flew over the Acropolis.

On Wednesday 18 October 1944, the radio transmission of 15 October 1944 from the Norwegian, Egie Lindberg, was confirmed. An aircraft from the carrier *Implacable* sighted the battleship *Tirpitz* at its new anchorage three miles west of Tromsö. The AOC-in-C Bomber Command, Air Marshal Harris, stated, "That made our job a lot easier. Tromsö is one hundred miles nearer than the Altafjord."

On Friday 20 October 1944, the landing by US forces (Gen. MacArthur) on Leyte signalled the reconquest of the Philippines. The Seventh Fleet (Vice-Adm. Kinkaid)—secured by Task Force 38 (Adm. Halsey) acting as the escort group and air cover provided by thirty-two carrier-borne aircraft with aircraft of the 5th USAAF—brought landing troops of the 6th US Army (Lt. Gen. Krueger) into the Gulf of Leyte.

The American troops gained a foothold only after strenuous efforts. The Japanese on the neighboring islands brought up reinforcements with destroyers and light cruisers and used all the means at their disposal to prevent the American invasion.

During the fighting, a Japanese pilot crashed his aircraft onto the *Australia*, severely damaging the Australian cruiser. This kamikaze attack, the first, hit the bridge of the cruiser, killing the captain, E. F. Dechaineux, and eighteen men. In addition, fifty-four were wounded.

From Sunday 22 October 1944, the Japanese fleet (nine battleships, four aircraft carriers, thirteen heavy cruisers, six light cruisers and thirty-four destroyers) launched a three-day large-scale attack on the American landing forces off Leyte. But the Americans deployed thirty-two aircraft carriers, twelve battleships, twenty-three cruisers, ninety-four destroyers and almost a thousand landing craft.

On Monday 23 October 1944, Adm. Onishi, C-in-C of the Japanese Naval Air Fleet on the Philippines, formed the kamikaze (divine wind) corps. The first kamikaze pilots were recruited from volunteers from the Navy's 201 Air Wing, stationed on Clark Field some fifty miles north of Manila.

On Tuesday 24 October 1944, Japanese aircraft from Luzon attacked the US Task Force 38.1 (Vice-Adm. McCain). The Japanese aircraft were intercepted by American fighters. Receivers on the US warships had, in fact, intercepted radio transmission from the Japanese torpedo bombers thirty minutes before the Japanese themselves.

Only one aircraft got through, hitting the light carrier *Princeton* with a five hundred-pound bomb. The bomb penetrated the flight deck and exploded in the ship's interior. The aircraft waiting on the hangar deck, already fuelled up, were set ablaze. The fire caused the aircraft torpedoes to explode, which set off a chain reaction. Despite fire-fighting attempts by other units, the ship burned out and had to be abandoned.

Further in the course of the fighting around Leyte, two kamikaze squadrons led by Lt. Yuhiho Seki carried out an attack on 25 October 1944. They damaged the escort carriers *Santee, Suwannee* and *Sangamon, Kitkun Bay, White Plains* and *Kilinin Bay*. Lt. Seki then dived his Zero onto the deck of the carrier *Saint Lo*. Seven massive explosions tore the ship apart, and the entire crew was lost in the flames. This was the first US escort carrier to be sunk by a kamikaze attack. In heavy fighting with the Seventh US Fleet (Vice-Adm. Mitscher) the Japanese aircraft carriers *Zuikaku*,

Zuiho, Chitose and *Chiyoda*, as well as three battleships, six heavy cruisers, three light cruisers and nine destroyers totalling 306,000 tons were sunk by air attacks and submarines. The US fleet lost the aircraft carrier *Princeton*, two escort carriers, two destroyers, one escort destroyer and one submarine.

The largest maritime battle in history was now over. On the Allied side, 216 American and 4 Australian ships participated in the fighting; on the Japanese side there were 64 units. The Japanese Navy suffered the most serious defeat since the outbreak of the war, losing four aircraft carriers. After this battle, the Japanese fleet ceased to exist as a battleworthy fighting force.

In October 1944, German U-boats sank one merchant ship of 6,131 gross tons. This was the lowest figure of tonnage sunk for the entire war. At this time, there were 141 front-line U-boats in the Atlantic, Arctic and Indian oceans and in the Baltic Sea. German losses amounted to 14 U-boats.

On Wednesday 1 November 1944, troops of the British No. 4 Commando (Lt. Col. Dawson) with a Dutch section from No. 10 Interallied Commando, 4 Special Service Brigade (Brig. Leicester) and 152 Brigade of the 52nd Infantry division (Maj. Gen. Hakewell-Smith) landed on Walcheren Island, situated in the Scheldt estuary (Operation Infatuate). The German 70th Infantry division (Lt. Gen. Daser) bitterly defended the island, whose coastal batteries—equipped with a number of captured British and French heavy artillery pieces—blocked access to the port of Antwerp. The battleships *Warspite* and the *Erebus* and *Roberts* supported the operation with their guns.

On Wednesday 8 November 1944, German forces on Walcheren capitulated.

On Sunday 12 November 1944, eighteen Lancasters of 617 Squadron and twenty Lancasters of 9 Squadron, under the overall command of Wing Commander Tait, stood ready to take off for an attack on the *Tirpitz* in Tromsö. In addition, there was a Lancaster piloted by Pilot Officer Gavin, whose crew filmed and photographed the attack. At 2:39 A.M. the engines were started up. Seven of 9 Squadron's aircraft failed to get away because of frost and icing problems.

At 9:30 the Lancasters approached their target from a height of fourteen thousand feet. At 9:40 turrets A and B on the *Tirpitz* opened fire on the approaching formation with their main fifteen-inch guns. The Lancasters attacked from the beam in formations of three.

At 9:42 the twelve thousand-pound Tallboy bombs went down toward the ship, mostly falling inside the protecting netting. Two bombs hit the *Tirpitz* on the port side. The first destroyed the aircraft catapult, penetrated the armored deck and

10/24/1944, off Leyte, a kamikaze Zero shortly before crashing *(left)*. The US carrier *Saint Lo* went down with all hands after Lt. Seki had made his kamikaze strike *(right)*.

exploded. The second bomb went straight through C turret, while the remaining Tallboys were near-misses. The battleship began to list. Only some of the crew were able to carry out the captain's last command—"Abandon ship!"

At 9:55 the *Tirpitz* capsized. The dark under-part of the ship protruded from the waters, and the entire port side was submerged. Of the crew, 28 officers and 874 crew were killed and 880 rescued. After working day and night with oxyacetylene cutters, personnel from the repair ship *Neumark* were able to rescue another 28 men, trapped in the ship's hull.

Dönitz stated, "With the loss of the *Tirpitz*, naval activities with surface units came to an end."

After the sinking of the last German heavy ship, the Kriegsmarine lost all significance in the further conduct of the war. A number of factors contributed to the collapse of this once-mighty war arm. Above all, there was Hitler's inability to think in global terms and therefore in terms of marine strategy, leading to the wrong employment priority for the shipyard capacity available. This could be seen particularly in the planning and preparation of fictitious operations such as Sea Lion (Hitler had never really intended putting this move into effect) and in his failure to create a U-boat arm along the lines put forward by Dönitz: Hitler did not want to see the war-winning significance of such a weapon. There was Göring's failure to appreciate cooperation between Luftwaffe and Kriegsmarine—which led to a total neglect of air cover for U-boats and aerial reconnaissance over the sea. There was also Göring's failure to develop high-frequency direction-locating techniques, which also lay within his jurisdiction. Moreover, there were the contradictory orders given by Hitler for operational U-boats that were frittered away instead of being concentrated against British supply lines across the Atlantic.

On Saturday 18 November 1944, a day with clear skies and perfect visibility, two RAF Bostons sank the hospital ship *Tübingen* (3,509 gross tons) in the Adriatic south of Cape Promontore near Pola. Acknowledged by HM Government as an accepted hospital ship, it was on passage to Trieste.

The Bostons came down to two hundred feet, opened fire with their guns and dropped bombs. Capt. Hermichen said, "After both aircraft had overflown the ship, they turned and approached individually, one machine from the port and the other from the starboard, again flew over the ship and again attacked it."

At 7:45 A.M. the hospital ship *Tübingen* went down. With the sinking of this ship and the seizing of other German hospital ships (*Bonn, Freiburg* and *Konstanz*), the Allies created an additional burden for the railway lines needed to provision troops fighting in Italy.

On Monday 20 November 1944, Japanese Kaiten

manned torpedoes (Kikusui Group) carried out their first operation. The target was the US anchorage at the Ulithi atoll. The Kaiten was some forty-five feet long, had a three thousand-pound warhead, a range of approximately fifteen nautical miles and could make thirty knots. Manned and destined for kamikaze operations, this torpedo was the guided version of the well-known Long Lance type 93 torpedo. The Kaiten KM 1 (Lt. Nishina) sank the US fleet tanker *Mississinewa* (11,316 gross tons). One of the Kaiten was rammed and sunk by the US destroyer *Cuse*; the others were destroyed by depth charges.

On Tuesday 28 November 1944, an Allied convoy, totalling eighteen ships, put into the port of Antwerp, the first since the floodgates had been blown up by German frogmen on 16 September 1944. It had taken that long to carry out repairs.

In November 1944 German U-boats operating in the Atlantic and Indian oceans sank four merchant ships totalling 18,026 gross tons. German losses amounted to seven U-boats.

On Monday 11 December 1944, discussions were held in the army research institute at Peenemünde regarding project "Test Stand XII" — the codename for the top secret work on underwater launching facilities for the A-4 (V 2) rocket. Taking part in the discussions were Maj. Gen. Rossmann, Dr. Dickmann (manager of the Vulkan Shipworks, Stettin), a Mr. Riedel, manager of the development works, code-named Elektromechanische Werke Karlshagen/Pommerania, and a team of specialists. Their agenda included the construction of containers, with a displacement of five hundred tons, to be used in launching the V 2 rockets. Three of these floating containers were to be towed underwater, in a horizontal position, by a U-boat. Each container was designed to be a fuelstore, a control mechanism and a test bed and to carry replacement parts, all at the same time. The design intended that containers be used both as a launching pad for the V 2 and as a fuel reservoir for the U-boats. Some 180 nautical miles off the east coast of the USA, the container's ballast tanks were to be flooded, setting it in an upright position. The bow protruded from the water, through which the servicing team, comprising three men, gained access into the body of the container. The team would make the V 2 ready to operate, leave the container and operate the rocket's mechanism from the U-boat. The electro-batteries of the U-boat were to supply the current necessary for launching. Once the rocket had been launched, the U-boat would return to base with the empty container, which could then be used again.

The project team concerned with Test Stand XII could be reached through the accommodation address of Volkswagenwerk Wolfsburg. The Vulkan

Shipping Losses 1939–44

U-boats
Mines
Surface vessels
Aircraft
Other and unknown causes

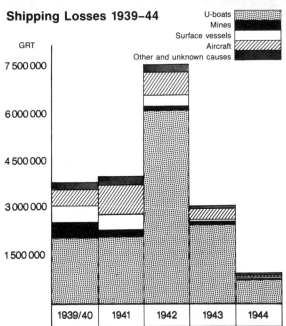

Shipyards in Stettin was contracted for the first three floating containers, and delivery date was fixed for 25 March 1945.

On Tuesday 19 December 1944, the French submarine *Rubis* (Lt. Comdr. Rousselot) laid a minefield off the Norwegian coast. This was the last such operation undertaken by the *Rubis*, the most successful French submarine of the war. These mines caused the loss of fifteen ships (25,770 gross tons) and eight small vessels of the Kriegsmarine.

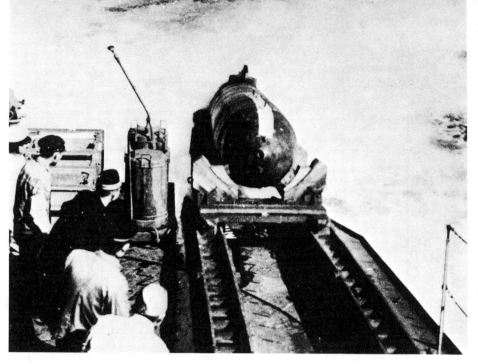

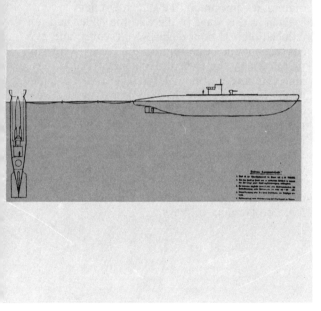

Above left: Altafjord, the vast hull of the *Tirpitz*

Left: Allied shipping losses 1939–44 and their causes

Above right: November 1944, Pacific, tests on a Japanese manned Kaiten torpedo for kamikaze attacks

Above: Confidential orders "Test Stand XII," diagram showing U-boat with floating container and A-4 (V 2) rocket

At the end of 1944 the U-boats returned to the tactics used during the first phase of the Battle of the Atlantic (1939–40). They now operated close to the British coast, because Allied U-boat killers were not always able to be deployed successfully in these shallow waters. The U-boats attacked in the submerged position and only seldom in groups.

On Sunday 24 December 1944, the *U 862* (Lt. Comdr. Timm), operating from the base in Djakarta, sank a freighter of 7,180 gross tons in Sydney harbor.

On Tuesday 26 December 1944, the Japanese fleet formation in the southwest Pacific under Rear Adm. Kimura carried out the last attack in Philippine waters. Two cruisers and six destroyers opened fire on the US bridgehead on Mindoro.

The evening of 31 December 1944, eighteen two-man U-boats of the Seehund (seal) class put out from Ymuiden in Holland to take part in operations off the Scheldt estuary. The Seehund was a midget-submarine with a fifteen-ton displacement (surfaced), equipped with a sixteen-horsepower motor that enabled the craft to make six knots submerged. It carried two torpedoes, one each side of its keel, and could remain on patrol for two days. Locating the craft was practically impossible, and because of its small measurements, depth charges had little effect. In addition, the Seehund had almost all the features of a full-size U-boat, with the exception of radio and radio-location equipment.

Of the eighteen crews that left from Ymuiden, only two returned.

In December 1944 German U-boats operating in the Atlantic, Arctic and Indian oceans sank twelve merchant ships totalling 72,051 gross tons. Ger-

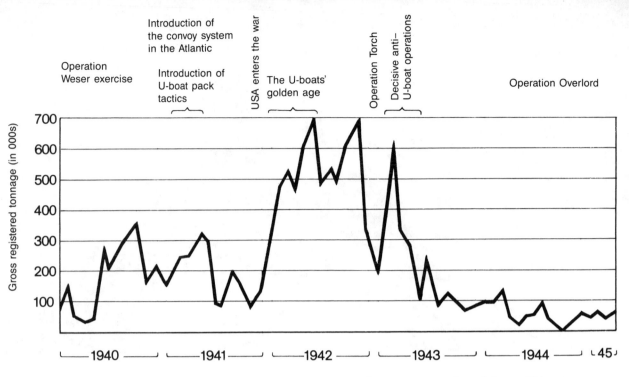

Operation
Weser exercise

Introduction of
the convoy system
in the Atlantic

Introduction of
U-boat pack
tactics

USA enters the war

The U-boats'
golden age

Operation Torch

Decisive anti-
U-boat operations

Operation Overlord

Gross registered tonnage (in 000s)

700
600
500
400
300
200
100

1940   1941   1942   1943   1944   45

Above: Allied shipping capacity destroyed by U-boats
between January 1940 and April 1945

Below: December 1944, off the Dutch coast, a one-man
submarine of the Biber class used in attacking Allied supplies
(shown here without torpedoes)

man losses amounted to eighteen U-boats.

Even at this stage in the war, the Allies had not
reduced their U-boat defensive measures, and as a
consequence a large number of forces were still
tied down by the U-boat arm. In the Baltic, German shipping continued large-scale activities practically unhindered by the Red fleet. Out of a total
of 1,279 ships aggregating 2,700,000 gross tons,
accompanied by weak escort vessels, only one fishing steamer was lost during the last two months of
1944. Astonishingly enough, no larger Soviet warships appeared in the Baltic in the second half of
1944, despite the favorable opportunities for successful attacks against the slow and insufficiently
escorted German convoys.

1945

January–August

Battle for the Philippines

Tuesday 9 January 1945
The United Press Agency reported from Allied Headquarters on Leyte:

Whereas the Japanese broadcasting services continue to speak of the imminent invasion of the Philippines, Gen. MacArthur's headquarters speak only of intensified American activities against Luzon.

V 2 against the United States?

9 January 1945
The *Exchange* News Agency reported:

The C-in-C of the US Armed Forces in the Atlantic, Adm. Ingram, stated on Monday that possibly during February or March, the German U-boat offensive would enter a new phase "for propaganda reasons." The enemy has reportedly gathered together in Atlantic waters at least three hundred U-boats, possibly with orders to fire on targets along the American seaboard using V-weapons in a series of revenge attacks. The admiral added that all necessary defence measures had been taken.

Memorandum from the Deputy Chief of the General Staff

Friday 19 January 1945
. . .
3. Kriegsmarine:
a) All mobile land units (artillery!) of the German Navy on the North Sea and Baltic coasts, to be made available at short notice as ordered, are to be deployed immediately in reinforcing the defensive units of Army Group North (previously Center) on the Eastern Front.
b) Intensification of the U-boat war must be accelerated with all possible means in order to increase Anglo-American difficulties regarding capacity or fuel supplies (tankers) and, in so doing, delay the enemy's offensive plans in the western theater of war.
c) With the same considerations in mind, the small vessels formation of the Kriegsmarine is to be deployed, as previously, as the main force in attacks off the Scheldt estuary.
d) The Atlantic fortresses are required to engage in as much activity as possible with a view to tying down enemy forces during the next eight weeks, the most decisive phase of the war.

Monday 22 January 1945
The *German High Command* issued the following communiqué:

During attacks on Anglo-American supplies, our U-boats operating in the Atlantic sank six ships totalling thirty-one thousand gross tons and three corvettes belonging to strongly escorted convoys.

Friday 26 January 1945
The *German High Command* issued the following communiqué:

Despite intense defensive measures, our U-boats sank three tankers and three freighters totalling 43,900 gross tons, as well as two large destroyers forming a part of the enemy supply lines to Britain and France.

New German U-boats

Tuesday 30 January 1945, Washington
The *Exchange* News Agency reported:

Dr. Fránk B. Jewett, president of the US Academy of Science, stated that the Germans were now deploying U-boats that could not be detected with current radio-location equipment. This would lead to a considerable hindering of defence measures undertaken against U-boats.

Dr. Hans Hass Helps the Frogmen
Münchner Neueste Nachrichten, 2/7/1945

The equipment of the frogmen is imperative for their success. A three-piece protective suit, the woolen cap with the camouflage netting, breathing apparatus and, above all, the rubber flippers. The last item was suggested by Dr. Hans Hass, who is well known as a diver and underwater photographer. His scientific experiments with these items have been used in the military sphere.

Friday 9 February 1945
The *German High Command* issued the following communiqué:

On 8 February the heavy cruiser *Lützow* and torpedo boats *T 33, T 28,* and *T 8* supported the brave defenders of Elbing with effective fire. In addition, this formation put up a powerful bombardment of the Soviet positions and approach routes to the Frisches Haff.

Wednesday 14 February 1945
The *German High Command* issued the following communiqué:

Our U-boats, equipped for some time with breathing apparatus, have — thanks to this new equipment — been able to sink during untiring operational patrols eight ships totalling fifty-one thousand gross tons in the waters around Great Britain and the vastness of the ocean.

Heavy Fighting on Corregidor
Saturday 17 February 1945, Tokyo
The German *DNB* Agency reported:

US troops commenced landing operations on the island fortress of Corregidor this morning. In the southern part of the island, reports from the front state that heavy fighting is in progress in which many enemy airborne units have also taken part.

Ship Carrying POWs Sunk

17 February 1945, Appleton (Wisconsin)
The *Exchange* News Agency reported:

An American sergeant, liberated from Japanese captivity, has stated that last October an Allied submarine sank a Japanese ship with prisoners of war on board, whereby eighteen hundred Allied POWs, mostly Americans, were killed. The ship was on passage in a Japanese convoy, together with Japanese troopships and war-equipment transporters, so that it could not have been identified by the submarine. Only five Allied prisoners escaped the catastrophe. They reported that for the majority of their comrades, death came as a release because of the terrible suffering they had endured

Above: Soviet submarine takes a torpedo on board, a considerable menace to German evacuation ships in the Baltic.

Right: 2/9/1945, Baltic, on the deck of the *Admiral Scheer* during fighting for Elbing, ". . . supported the defenders with effective fire . . ."

in Japanese captivity. They were, for example, crammed together so tightly in POW camps on the Philippines and in the transporters that many died of exhaustion or lost their reason.

Sunday 18 February 1945
The *German High Command* issued the following communiqué:

Midget-submarines sank a supply freighter of three thousand gross tons and torpedoed another, the loss of which is probable; both were part of an enemy convoy between the Thames and Scheldt estuaries.

Americans on Iwo Jima?

Sunday 18 February 1945, Guam
The *United Press Agency* reported:

Japanese reports on US landing attempts on Iwo Jima island have not yet been confirmed by American sources. On the other hand, it has been stated here that the fleet has continued the bombardment of this important Japanese base. This bombardment has now lasted three days.

Wednesday 21 February 1945
The *German High Command* issued the following communiqué:

As announced on 20 February, torpedo-strike

aircraft formations led by Lt. Col. Stemmler made a surprise attack from the clouds on a convoy passing from Murmansk to England, during bad weather conditions with heavy seas. Two light cruisers, one of them of the Leander class, two destroyers and eight merchantmen totalling fifty-seven thousand gross tons were sunk.

Friday 23 February 1945
The *German High Command* issued the following communiqué:

The night of 22 February, S-boats attacked a strongly escorted convoy off the east coast of England, sinking seven ships totalling 21,500 gross tons. Another four ships totalling 11,000 gross tons were torpedoed.

Monday 26 February 1945
The *German High Command* issued the following communiqué:

Midget-submarines sank an enemy troopship of five thousand gross tons and a large destroyer and two escort vessels off the English coast. The ships were on the Thames-Scheldt route.

Wednesday 28 February 1945
The *German High Command* issued the following communiqué:

Units of the Kriegsmarine sank a steamer of five thousand gross tons on the Thames-Scheldt route and two sailing vessels totalling around fourteen hundred gross tons in the Adriatic.

Allied Landing on an Island near Rhodes
Sunday 4 March 1945, Cairo
The *Reuters* News Agency reported:

The night of 28 February/1 March, Allied troops landed on Piscopi Island northwest of Rhodes. Twenty of the German garrison were killed and 144 taken prisoner.

Friday 9 March 1945
The *German High Command* issued the following communiqué:

German naval units effectively supported the fierce defensive fighting of the army around the Bay of Stettin.

Saturday 10 March 1945
The *German High Command* issued the following communiqué:

Assault troops from the Channel Island occupation forces, transported by escort vessels of the Kriegsmarine led by Lt. Comdr. Mohr, carried out a surprise attack the night of 8/9 March against the supply harbor of Granville on the Gulf of Saint-Malo. They destroyed the floodgates, set fire to the town and harbor and took a number of

Left: The final sacrifice — a troop of Hitler Youth conscripted into the Kriegsmarine to help defend the Baltic seaboard

Right: No escape for the U-boat attacked from the air. The submarine zigzags in a vain attempt to escape an RAF Sunderland flying boat.

prisoners, including a lieutenant colonel and four other officers. In addition, fifty-five German soldiers were released from captivity. An American patrol vessel was sunk, five supply ships totalling 4,800 gross tons destroyed and a supply steamer seized.

Thursday 15 March 1945
The *German High Command* issued the following communiqué:

During the last few days, numerous "Sturmwikinge" and midget-submarines attacked targets in the area of the Scheldt estuary. According to reports received, four ships totalling twelve thousand gross tons have been sunk. Further successes achieved by Sturmwikinge that have not returned may be safely assumed.

German Refugees from the East

Thursday 15 March 1945, Berlin
The *DNB* Agency reported:

Since the Russians began their advance into East and West Prussia, ships of the German Navy and Merchant Navy have, with the participation of a number of shore-based units, evacuated by sea to Germany some 590,000 refugees — mainly women and children — from the eastern regions. The crews of German warships and escort vessels, former passenger ships, freighters and any other available ships have performed outstanding services — often with their ships fully iced up — in the face of enemy bombing attacks, minefields and submarines.

British Submarine Successes in the Pacific
15 March 1945, London
The *Reuters* News Agency reported:

The British Admiralty has stated that British submarines operating in Far Eastern waters have sunk or damaged approximately one hundred ships belonging to the Axis powers. The ships destroyed include small tankers, minelayers, armed cutters, U-boat hunters and auxiliary vessels, landing craft and motor ships.

Tuesday 27 March 1945
The *German High Command* issued the following communiqué:

In the West Prussian battle areas near the coast and along the Frisches Haff our navy took part in the fighting with continuous heavy artillery bombardment. . . .

Units of the Kriegsmarine sank two fully laden ships totalling fifteen thousand gross tons and torpedoed two more totalling nine thousand gross tons, including a tank transporter, in the Scheldt and off the English coast.

Saturday 21 April 1945
The *German High Command* issued the following communiqué:

The Gironde South coastal fortress was stormed yesterday by the enemy after its ammunition had run out, and after continuous destruction of the harbor installations.

Thursday 26 April 1945
The *German High Command* issued the following communiqué:

During fighting with enemy supply vessels, our U-boats sank five fully laden ships totalling thirty-two gross tons and one patrol boat off the English coast. In addition, one strongly protected aircraft carrier of the *Illustrious* class was torpedoed and badly damaged by one of our U-boats operating in the Atlantic.

The Kriegsmarine Mentioned for the Last Time in an OKW Report

Wednesday 2 May 1945
The *German High Command* issued the following communiqué:

The Führer has fallen while at the head of the heroic defenders of the German capital, Berlin. . . . The remainder of the courageous defenders of Berlin, mainly in individual fighting groups located around the government buildings, are continuing their bitter resistance. . . . In southern French coastal waters, assault boats of the Kriegsmarine sank an enemy cruiser and a patrol boat.

Thursday 3 May 1945
The *German High Command* issued an additional communiqué:

The German High Command has declared the naval bases at Kiel and Flensburg to be open cities and has given orders that they are not to be defended.

Wednesday 9 May 1945
The *German High Command* issued the following communiqué:

Since midnight, fighting on all fronts has ceased. Upon orders issued by the Grand Admiral, the German armed forces have ceased the hopeless struggle. Six years of heroic fighting are now over. During this time we achieved splendid victories but also suffered serious defeats. The German armed forces finally submitted, with honor, to overwhelming superiority.

Last Radio Message from U 1023 (Lt. Comdr. Schroeteler)
Thursday 10 May 1945, 3:55 P.M.
To the Grand Admiral

On our last operation, a 46-day Schnorchel patrol, we sank one steamer of eight thousand gross tons and one destroyer in convoy. In addition, a large freighter of ten thousand gross tons and a steamer of eight thousand gross tons were torpedoed. Three failures. Ammunition used up. With firm trust in you, Grand Admiral, we now carry out the most onerous order of all [surrender of U-boats to the Allies].

German U-boat Interned in the Argentine
Wednesday 11 July 1945, Buenos Aires
La Prensa reported:

The news that a German U-boat has put into an Argentine port strengthens the view that the explosion on board the Brazilian cruiser *Bahia* can be attributed to its being torpedoed. The Argentine naval secretary has stated in a communiqué that the German U-boat was, however, not responsible for this explosion.

Invasion Preparations against Japan

Tuesday 17 July 1945
Admiral Nimitz's Headquarters issued the following communiqué:

The strongest fleet formation that has ever been seen in the Pacific is cruising off Japan. . . . As already reported, British aircraft and warships are operating against the Japanese mainland for the first time.

Further German U-boats in the Argentine?
Wednesday 18 July 1945, Buenos Aires
The *Exchange* News Agency reported:

In an official statement, the Argentine government has given its assurance that there was no confirmation of the reports that two more German U-boats had surrendered in Argentine waters. The government wishes to make absolutely clear that if this were true, the two U-boats would have been handed over exactly as was the *U 530*.

The Argentine government has resolved, after considerable pressure from Washington and London, to hand over to the USA not just the U-boat itself but also the crew. American sources have publicly stated that the crew of the U-boat must give a convincing explanation as to why the ship stayed at sea so long after the German capitulation without making a radio report and surrendering as required. For the time being, the captain and crew will formally be regarded as pirates, and there is the distinct possibility that because of deliberate infringement of the surrender terms, the death penalty may be inflicted. In addition, the crew will be interrogated at some length as to the U-boat's position when the Brazilian *Bahia* went down with the loss of three hundred lives.

The U-boat indeed remained at sea until all its fuel was consumed. It put into port in a fully rusted condition. The entire armaments, all the ship's papers and nautical instruments had been previously destroyed. The seven hundred-ton boat put in with fifty-four men instead of the usual twenty-eight. The captain has stated that there were no passengers on board. This statement has been treated with the utmost suspicion.

Explosive with a Thousand-fold Effect?

Monday 6 August 1945
President Truman stated:

US bombers today dropped a new kind of bomb, known as the atomic bomb, on the Japanese naval base of Hiroshima. We spent two billion dollars on the production of these bombs, but we have solved one of the most difficult scientific procedures.

A Japanese Hospital Ship

Wednesday 8 August 1945, in a South Pacific port:
The *Reuters* News Agency reported:

Special correspondent Robert Reuben, who was on board the Japanese hospital ship *Tachibana Maru*, reports, "This ship, which had transported over fifteen-hundred completely healthy Japanese 'patients' and approximately thirty tons of arms and munitions, put in here on Wednesday, escorted by two US destroyers. The warships had taken it prize in the Banda Sea four days ago.

The Last Report

Thursday 16 August 1945
The *Reuters* News Agency reported:

At 1:00 P.M. Japanese time (6:00 A.M. Central European summer time) Tokyo radio station broadcast to all "Japanese fronts," giving orders to lay down their arms.

Strategy and Tactics

JANUARY TO SEPTEMBER 1945

On New Year's Day 1945, the activities of the Special Mission Unit in support of the guerrillas—mainly on the Philippines—were concluded with the last mission of the American submarine *Stingray* (Comdr. Stoner). Since activities began on 4 January 1943, nineteen submarines carried out forty-one missions: *Narwhal* nine, *Nautilus* six, *Stingray* five and the other submarines one or two

A rare photo—7/10/1945, Mar del Plata (Argentine):
U 530 (Lt. Wehrmuth), rusted and covered with seaweed just after reaching the Argentine coast

missions each. Only one submarine, the *Seawolf*, was lost, having been sunk in error on 3 October 1944 by the American destroyer *Rowell*. The ships landed 331 guerrilla instructors and agents, took off 472 persons and also brought in 1,325 tons of supplies, weapons, ammunition and other equipment for the guerrillas.

The Allies had already learned by the beginning of January 1945 of increased German attempts to construct underwater containers for rockets with which to attack the North American east coast. The competent authorities of the US Navy received orders to deal with this menace.

On Saturday 6 January 1945, there were again determined kamikaze attacks on the US landing fleet approaching the Philippines. Ten ships suffered serious damage. The increasing success of the suicide flyers caused the Americans to hold back the aircraft carriers that were due to attack Formosa on the following day, 7 January 1945.

On Tuesday 9 January 1945, the landing craft of US Task Forces 78 and 79 put troops of the 6th Army (Lt. Gen. Krueger) ashore in Lingayen Gulf on the west coast of Luzon (Philippines) and, in fact, at the same point where three years earlier, on 21 December 1941, the Japanese themselves landed. Even while the American landing fleet was approaching Lingayen Gulf, kamikaze pilots took off and over a period of eight hours carried out surprise attacks. They knew well how to make use of the surrounding hills on their approach run and, in addition, interrupted radar equipment with strips of aluminum foil. A number of ships were hit by the kamikaze pilots; the cruiser *Australia*, for example, was hit five times. Its captain nevertheless declined Adm. Oldendorf's offer to be allowed to withdraw from the fighting.

The danger of these self-sacrificing pilots was best shown by the fact that ordinary Japanese bombers only succeeded in sinking a ship after 6,000 operational sorties, whereas 722 kamikaze pilots sank six ships. Between 6 and 9 January — their most successful period of operations during the entire war — the kamikazes sank almost as many US units as the entire Japanese fleet during this period.

On Saturday 13 January 1945, the 3rd White Russian Front (Gen. Tchernyakhovsky) opened its offensive in the area of Pillkallen in East Prussia. The objective was to destroy the German 3rd Panzer Army (Col.-Gen. Raus) and push forward in the direction of the Kurisches Haff (Kurski Zaliv) on the Baltic coast. This was the first stage of the

Soviet offensive between the Baltic and the Carpathians, which would reach the Oder within three weeks.

This meant mammoth undertakings for the German Kriegsmarine in the Baltic. The navy had to support the army from the sea, secure convoys of troopships and supply transports against Soviet submarines, S-boats, aircraft and mines. After the treatment by the Russian soldiers of the German civil population, a spontaneous flight across land took place which was, in the beginning, brutally suppressed by the Nazi authorities.

Dönitz stated, "The U-boat war was no longer the main objective of the Kriegsmarine. I deployed a large number of units to give support on the Eastern Front and to save the German population." The Kriegsmarine had to put into effect the largest evacuation operation of all time. The overall command of this massive operation was undertaken by the Naval Staff East (Adm. Kummetz), and making merchant shipping available to the army was undertaken by Rear Adm. Engelhardt. 9 Escort Division of the navy (Comdr. von Blanc) and 10 Escort Division (Rear Adm. Butow) undertook the securing and organisation of the convoys on a local basis with 17 flotillas and some 350 smaller warships. They had special staff and branches in all the larger ports.

That this mass breakout by millions of refugees did not lead to immediate chaos was because of the parties carrying out the operation and also the discipline of the refugees themselves. The branches of

the OC Sea transport and the Kriegsmarine administrative departments (KMD), Danzig and Stettin—mainly run by experienced merchant marine captains—were responsible for the preparation of convoys in individual Baltic ports. Everyday they advised the National-Socialist (NS) administrative department of the shipping capacity and number of places available or gave this information direct to the refugees. If refugees, having reached the evacuation ports, were billetted in private houses, schools or other accommodation, they were within the competency of the appropriate administrative department, which allocated places on board the ships. If the refugees were quartered by the army, they received their allocation direct from the navy. The suffering endured by the refugees was indescribable—predominantly women, children, the sick and the elderly, the refugees shared mass accommodation under conditions of extreme cold, or even sleeping rough, with insufficient food and frequently under artillery and air bombardment for days on end. The Red Air Force, against which only ground or ships' antiaircraft guns were available as defence, presented a very real danger. The merchant vessels had to put into the narrow harbors under the worst weather conditions, frequently under artillery fire. Despite constant air raids, they had to lie in the roads until, carrying twenty times their normal load, they could again put out to sea in a westerly direction.

Because of the danger of mines, shipping had to keep to specific deep-water lanes that were checked when possible. On the other hand, the increasing deployment of Soviet submarines and MTBs meant that the vessels often had to keep to the shallows immediately off the coast, which were frequently mined. But there they were also within range of the Soviet artillery. Winter weather conditions, rough seas and the increasing shortage of

fuel made a purposeful deployment of the ships, predominantly small, extremely difficult. Off the harbors of Pillau, Danzig, Gdynia and Kolberg the large passenger liners, until now used as accommodation, began operations. Warships of every kind and size, auxiliary and escort vessels were also deployed in this evacuation.

On Friday 19 January 1945, Maj. Gen. Rossmann, who was in charge of the preparations for the underwater launching of the V 2, stated in a secret report that the Peenemünde army research institute would definitely conclude the preliminary trials for Test Stand XII before the end of March 1945. Plans were drawn up for the construction of the first towing vehicle.

On Sunday 21 January 1945, eight kamikaze pilots (Niitaka Group) of the 1 Air Fleet carried out attacks on the US carrier *Ticonderoga* (Task Group 38.3), causing severe damage.

On Thursday 25 January 1945, the first ships put to sea from Pillau, the *Robert Ley* (27,288 gross tons), *Pretoria* (16,662 gross tons) and *Ubena* (9,554 gross tons), carrying a total of 7,100 refugees. This was the first large-scale evacuation of a German city, and it went off perfectly, without enemy action intervening. Nevertheless, the infamous Gauleiter E. Koch (Nazi district chief) threatened to court-martial the naval officer responsible for the operation.

At 7:10 P.M. (Moscow time) 30 January 1945, with heavy seas, strong winds and a temperature of eighteen degrees below zero, the watchkeeping petty officer on the Soviet submarine *S 13* (Capt. Marinesko), lying off the Stolper Sands, sighted the silhouette of a large ship. It was the *Wilhelm Gustloff* (25,484 gross tons), the former "Strength through Joy" passenger liner of the German Labor Front, carrying 6,500 passengers including refugees, Kriegsmarine dependents and major casual-

Right: Capt. 3rd Grade Marinesko, ". . . an entire division wiped out!"

Left: The former "Strength through Joy" ship, the liner *Wilhelm Gustloff*

ties.

Marinesko stated, "I had a good position between the land and the target. The coast protected us from discovery and attack by securing vessels. *Wilhelm Gustloff* was making sixteen knots. I gave orders to proceed full ahead, which meant that I could make twenty knots and overtake the ship. Thereafter, I altered course onto the target, and when it came into sight, I fired off three torpedoes, still submerged."

The *Wilhelm Gustloff* was hit; its radio was out of action, as the accumulators had not been brought on board in Gdynia and the only course left was to send off an SOS on the shortwave transmitter. Warships turning up at the scene of the sinking managed to rescue only 904 people from the icy water.

By the end of January 1945, advance units of the Red Army had reached a number of points along the Oder. The remainder of the German troops in East Prussia was concentrated in the area around Samland, Königsberg and Elbing. Those heavy units of the Kriegsmarine that were still operational joined in the fighting, using their ship's guns.

On Wednesday 31 January 1945, the heavy cruiser *Prinz Eugen* supported land operation with its ship's guns off Cranz (Samland).

At the end of January 1945 the first type XXIII light U-boats operated from Norwegian bases against British east coast shipping. They scored a number of successes and, thanks to their high underwater speed, were able to elude their pursuers.

In January 1945 German U-boats operating in the Atlantic sank fifteen merchant ships totalling 80,844 gross tons. German losses amounted to thirteen U-boats.

On Friday 2 February 1945, the *Prinz Eugen,* lying off Cranz, and the *Admiral Scheer,* lying off Fischhausen (near Pillau), again supported defensive fighting near the coast.

On Friday 9 February 1945, the British submarine *Venturer* (Lt. Launders) — equipped with Asdic type 147 B Sonar — sank the German U-boat *U 864* (Comdr. Wolfram) in the Fedjefjord to the west of Bergen. Both submarines were operating while submerged, and this was the first instance of one submarine destroying another submarine in an underwater attack.

Shortly after midnight on 10 February 1945, the Soviet submarine *S 13* (Capt. Marinesko) sank the passenger liner *General von Steuben* (14,660 gross tons), which had put to sea from Pillau the day before. Some 300 were saved, but 2,700 refugees and wounded went down with the ship.

Adm. Kusnezov stated, "This success meant that the crew of the submarine commanded by Capt. 3rd Grade Marinesko in one operational patrol had destroyed almost eight thousand Hitlerite soldiers. An entire division! And what a division! The elite of the officers, specialists of the U-boat arm, SS men and party officials."

In the middle of February 1945, the Red Army launched heavy attacks via Stargard to Stettiner Haff, Köslin and Kolberg.

On Monday 19 February 1945, after almost three days of continuous air raids and a bombardment by the warships of Task Force 51 (Vice-Adm. Turner), the V Amphibian Corps (Maj. Gen. Schmidt) landed on Iwo Jima, an island lying midway between the Marianas and Tokyo. The fighting for the island was among the bitterest of the entire Pacific war.

On Wednesday 21 February 1945, Japanese airmen sank the US carrier *Bismarck Sea* and damaged the carrier *Saratoga* during the landing operations on Iwo Jima.

On Friday 9 March 1945 — two days after the US 9th Armored Division under Maj. Gen. Leonard succeeded in taking the partially damaged Ludendorff Bridge at Remagen and forming a bridgehead on the other side of the Rhine — the Kriegsmarine mounted their last offensive some four hundred miles to the west. From the German-occupied Channel Islands, on which there were some thirty thousand German troops in a decidedly perilous supply situation, the C-in-C Channel Islands, Vice-Adm. Hüffmeier, resolved to carry out an operation against the picturesque harbor town of Granville, now an American supply base, some thirty-five nautical miles away. Taking part in the surprise attack were four type 40 minesweepers of 24 M-Flotilla (Lt. Comdr. Mohr) carrying German commando troops, three ferry barges equipped with 8.8-cm Flak guns, two fishing steamers converted into patrol boats, as well as three harbor protection boats.

Shortly after midnight, at approximately 1:20, the German minesweeper put the commando troops ashore. The weakly armed American soldiers offered scant resistance. Welcome support was provided by German prisoners of war who had just unloaded a supply freighter. The commandos blew up the harbor installations, sank four steamers totalling 3,612 gross tons, and took prize the British freighter *Exwood,* which was carrying coal. Vice-Adm. Hüffmeier said, "The British crew, including the captain who had just left a bistro, were so surprised and finally so taken by the sporting manner in which the operation was carried out that they willingly took part." In the meantime, the artillery ferries — making a diversion — shot up the American patrol boat *PC 564.* The raiding party surprised a number of American staff officers asleep in the Hotel des Bains. They went into German captivity wearing their pajamas and slippers.

Toward 3:30 the operation was over. The commandos took the collier back with thirty Allied prisoners and sixty-seven liberated German prisoners. The minesweeper *M 412* remained behind in Granville as a dumb witness; it had run aground in low water in the harbor and had to be blown up. Those taking part in the attack were awarded the Iron Cross, cigarettes and a glass of liqueur each. Vice-Adm. Hüffmeier said, "The soldiers . . . brought new heart to their units which had become lackluster because of the enforced inactivity and poor food."

On Saturday 10 March 1945, the "heavies," *Prinz Eugen, Admiral Scheer, Lützow* and *Schlesien,* commenced firing on land-based targets. This bombardment continued for the next four weeks, until 8 April 1945.

In the meantime, the Haudegen meteorological detachment continued to send its weather reports from the Arctic Circle.

Spitsbergen, 10 March 1945, the leader of the meteorological detachment, Dr. Dege: "Our meteorological activities went off extremely well, and we were the first detachment that succeeded in maintaining radio contact, every day, with our nearest radio station in Tromsö. Above all, this was due to the efforts of our leading radio operator, Staff Sgt. Heinrich Ehrich, a splendid technician, and also Cpl. Gustav Scheidweiler, another technical genius. And so the Arctic night passed; but at the end of it, toward the last of March, Allied radio stations made their presence known, cursed us and said they would soon be paying us a visit. We had not the slightest intention of undertaking any military actions whatsoever, although we did not, on the other hand, wish to be taken by surprise. And so we fortified our station, but there was no further talk of the Allies paying us a visit, and, in fact, it didn't happen."

Early the morning of 17 March 1945, ships' boats from the destroyers *Z 34* (Comdr. Hetz), *Z 43* (Capt. Wenninger) and the torpedo boat *T 33* went ashore and picked up the last defenders of Kolberg, together with their commanding officer, Col. Fullriede. The garrison had been besieged for two weeks, and only a small section of beach measuring about a half a mile square remained free for the landing boats. During the last few days, a total of 77,500 soldiers and refugees had been evacuated by sea from the burning city.

While Pomerania was gradually being lost to the enemy, there were still a number of German bridgeheads along the Baltic coast of Kurland (Lithuania), East Prussia and Poland, such as Libau, Heiligenbeil, Pillau, the estuary of the Vistula, Danzig, Gdynia and the Hela peninsula.

On Friday 23 March 1945, the tanks of the Soviet 70th Army (Col.-Gen. Popov) broke through to the sea near Zoppot between Danzig and Gdynia, thereby dividing the estuary of the Vistula at Danzig from Oxhöft-Hela. Showing great courage, Comdr. Hetz took his destroyer *Z 34* to the famous landing stage near the casino at Zoppot and, one thousand yards from the beach, turned his front turrets on the Russian tanks, destroying them one after the other. By these means, lines of communication between Danzig and Gdynia were kept open for twelve hours.

On Sunday 25 March 1945, the last German ship, the passenger liner *Ubena* (9,523 gross tons), left Danzig-Neufahrwasser with four thousand people on board.

On Wednesday 28 March 1945, the Soviet 70th Army occupied Gdynia. North of the city, on the hills of the Oxhöfter Kämpe, close to the coastline of the Gulf of Danzig, the remainder of the VII Armored Corps, comprising eight thousand soldiers, still held out.

In March 1945 German U-boats operating in the Atlantic sank sixteen merchant ships totalling 67,386 gross tons. German losses amounted to thirty-five U-boats.

On Sunday 1 April 1945, the American 10th Army (Lt. Gen. Buckner) landed on Okinawa, one of the Ryukyu islands, together with the III Amphibian Corps (Maj. Gen. Geiger) and the XXIV Corps (Maj. Gen. Hodges). Okinawa, seventy miles long and five miles across, was large enough

The Japanese super-battleship *Yamato* was sacrificed to make the kamikaze attacks easier.

to take a number of airfields for medium bombers. The invasion fleet comprised 318 units and 1,139 auxiliary units. Almost 600,000 men took part in this operation, code-named Iceberg. This was the largest landing operation of the war in the Pacific.

The night of 4/5 April, Operation Walpurgisnacht (Walpurgis night) – the highly detailed plan to evacuate the eight thousand men of the German VII Armored Corps together with thirty thousand refugees from the Oxhöfter Kämpe – was carried out. The operation was led by 9 Escort Division (Comdr. von Blanc). The ferries, coastal steamers and other auxiliary vessels took five hours during the night to transport almost forty thousand people and a part of their equipment to the Hela peninsula. The Hela peninsula, twenty miles long and a half-mile wide, now became the reembarkation point for refugees and troops evacuated from the bridgeheads in East Prussia. Some ten thousand arrived every day and were transported to the west.

On Friday 6 April 1945, 335 kamikaze pilots commenced Operation Kikusui I, another large-scale attack against the landing fleet, off Okinawa. In addition, 344 Japanese dive bombers and torpedo bombers took part in this operation. Although many of the aircraft were intercepted, some two hundred reached the target area. The US warships opened up such a strong defensive fire that thirty-eight of their own seamen were killed by falling shell fragments. The Japanese aircraft succeeded only in sinking the minesweeper *Emmons* and one landing craft, as well as the ammunition transports *Hobbs Victory* and *Logan Victory* (7,607 gross tons each). The destroyers *Bush* and

Colhoun were also victims; they were some way off on radar patrol and ran into the full fury of the kamikaze pilots. Out of 699 Japanese aircraft deployed, only three returned.

On the same day at 3:30 P.M., the 72,800-ton super-battleship *Yamato*, commanded by Rear Adm. Ariaga and accompanied by the light cruiser *Yahagi* and eight destroyers, left the naval base at Tokuyama, southeast of Hiroshima. This gigantic battleship had nine 18-inch (46 cm) guns in three turrets, three guns to a turret, the heaviest guns ever carried on board a ship. The shells fired weighed over 3,200 pounds.

In certainly one of the most bizarre operations of the entire sea war, the most powerful battleship in the world was carrying ammunition for every weapon available, up to maximum capacity, but only sufficient fuel for the one-way journey to Okinawa. The *Yamato* was to serve off the island as gigantic bait for the superior US air forces, luring them away from the kamikaze aircraft. While this was happening, the kamikazes would dive onto the US landing fleet lying off Okinawa. Midshipman Yoshida, second radar officer on the *Yamato*, stated, "My task on the bridge was to pass on messages from the lookouts to the commandant and staff. On my left was Vice-Adm. Ito, flag officer of the formation, while his chief of staff, Rear Adm. Morishita, was to the right of me. I felt happy and very proud. Everybody was ordered to the fo'c'sle for 18.00 hours. As the commander could not leave the bridge, the first officer read the message that the fleet commander had sent us. 'May this operation be the turning point of the war.' We followed the singing of Kimigayo, the national anthem, with warlike songs and then three bonzais for His Imperial Majesty."

The Task Force (Vice-Adm. Ito) made for the Bungo Strait, which joined Japanese inland waters

to the Pacific. By 5:00 P.M. the American sub-marine *Threadfin* had already sighted the Task Force and radioed details relating to its course.

On Saturday 7 April 1945, at 12:35 P.M. 150 enemy aircraft were located some thirty-five nautical miles from the *Yamato*, which was making twenty-six knots. The alarm was sounded. Barely ten minutes later, the first US Helldivers attacked and scored the first hits on the battleship close to the stern. Yoshida stated, "We zigzagged through the water at a speed of twenty-six knots. The rolling and the vibration were terrible. And then bombs dropped, and bullets from the aircrafts' guns began to hail down onto the bridge." The planned long-range bombardment of the aircraft, approaching in tight formation, with eighteen-inch schrapnel shells—the most devastating effect had been promised—could not be carried out because of the American attacking tactics and the poor weather conditions.

Yoshida stated, "One after the other, the gun turrets were put out of action by direct hits. . . . Numerous casualties meant that it was soon impossible to carry out normal operations to secure the leaks." The first wave of the attacking aircraft had already scored four torpedo hits, all of them on the port side, causing a vast amount of water to be shipped. Yoshida stated, "We were now listing at an angle of thirty-five degrees. It seemed as if the enemy had just been waiting for this moment to dive on us from the clouds to deliver the coup de grâce. . . . There was no escaping the bombs. All of them struck home. Lying flat on the deck, I could only look after myself, just to resist these blows. I heard the commander calling out in vain, 'Hold out men! Hold out!'

"At 2:23 P.M. the *Yamato* turned over onto the badly damaged port side and now lay 'flat' on the surface with a ninety-degree list. Shells for the large guns slipped and dropped over the deck of the magazines, crashed against the bulkheads—then came a series of explosions. The ship turned right over and went down with its thousands of unfired armor-penetrating shells. As the massive hull went down, the sounds of objects rumbling and crashing around inside it, cracking bulkheads and explosions from magazines could be heard. Giant fingers of flame stabbed up into the sky, flashing like lightning, like rockets into the dark clouds above us as the capsized ship went under. . . . Coughing and gasping for air, I was dragged down. Half choked, I fought my way toward the only light to be seen, a grey-green glimmer in this strange, watery world. And then I was suddenly spat out into the daylight. The whirling waters again dragged me under the surface. A few seconds later a gigantic explosion threw me upward. A great number of the crew was sucked down by the terrifying suction of the ship's funnel. Nine feet closer and I too would have been a victim. Oil from the burst tanks burned my eyes when I swam on the surface. I wiped my face clear and gasped for air. All around me there were little groups of swimmers, bodies floating and, here and there, shattered wreckage and charred debris. These were the last remains of the mightiest battleship in the world after only two hours fighting against a superior air power."

Right: RAF Beaufighters attacking German North Sea shipping with rockets

Left: 4/7/1945, 1:23 P.M., the *Yamato* turns onto its severely damaged port side and blows up.

The last, and at the same time the largest, major surface unit sunk at sea during World War II took 2,498 men, almost the entire crew, down with it into the depths. The attempted breakout by the Japanese force cost 3,665 lives. The four surviving destroyers, heavily damaged, made for Sasebo. The American losses amounted to four Helldivers, three Avengers and three Hellcats out of the 386 carrier-borne aircraft deployed. Sixteen airmen lost their lives.

Astonishingly, only ten torpedoes and five bombs were required to sink this giant. By way of comparison, the much smaller German battleship, the *Bismarck*, needed eighteen torpedoes and over three hundred shells before it went down.

On Saturday 14 April 1945, the Seewolf U-boat pack was formed. The pack's objective was the east coast of North America. The six submarines making up this group were located while on passage by US reconnaissance. Task Group 22.2 (Capt. Ruhsenberger) and Task Group 22.5 (Capt. Craig) were immediately sent off to intercept the U-boats northeast of the Azores. The US intelligence service suspected that the Seewolf pack had underwater containers for V 2 weapons in tow, to launch rocket attacks against cities along the eastern seaboard of America.

On Sunday 15 April 1945, the last German U-boat — U 234 (Lt. Comdr. Fehler), a former minelaying submarine type XB (1,800 tons) converted into a U-boat transport — put to sea from Christiansund in Norway and set course for Japan. In addition to a complement of sixty-two, it carried members of the Luftwaffe staff led by Gen. Kessler, and also two senior Japanese officers. The U-boat had been made available specially by the German Naval High Command at the request of the Japanese government to take German air defence specialists to Japan where they would help iron out problems with defence of the mainland. Gen. Kessler had been appointed Luftwaffe attaché and, together with his staff, was to organise the air defence of Tokyo.

Commencing in the early hours of 16 April 1945, waves of Soviet bombers attacked ships lying off the tip of the Hela peninsula — "the Dunkirk of the Baltic." The motor vessel *Goya* (5,230 gross tons) was hit a number of times, the antimine defence measures as well as the latest submarine locating equipment were destroyed and Capt. Plünnecke badly wounded.

The attacks affected, above all, the thousands of refugees waiting on the quayside, hoping to be picked up by one of the ships. At 7:00 P.M. a convoy was finally made up off Hela. The *Goya*, the steamer *Kronenfels* and the ocean-going tug *Ägier*, together with the escort vessels *M 256* and *M 328*, made up the convoy. All the ships were fully laden with refugees and wounded.

At 11:50 P.M. the *Goya* was twelve nautical miles off Stolpmünde, the point where Soviet submarine *S 13* (Capt. 3rd Grade Marinesko) had sunk the *Wilhelm Gustloff* on 30 January 1945 and the steamer *General Steuben* on 10 February 1945. Eight thousand people lost their lives.

Five minutes before midnight, the commander of the Soviet submarine *L 3* (Capt. 3rd Grade Konovalov) gave orders to fire. Seconds afterward, two torpedoes ripped open the *Goya*'s hull. All the lights were put out on board the motor ship. Any attempt at rescue was hampered by the strong list, and hardly a boat was launched. The darkness shrouded the terrible end of thousands of helpless people.

At 11:59, four minutes after the torpedoeing, the *Goya* lay on its side and sank. Of the 6,385 people on board the steamer, 165 were rescued. The loss of the *Goya* was the greatest maritime catastrophe of all time.

On Wednesday 25 April 1945, the German High Command was toying with the idea of refusing, under any circumstances, to lay down their arms—even if Germany was swamped by the Allies—but carrying on fighting in Norway with the hope of some change in fortune. The meteorological detachment in the Arctic was also included in these prospects. Dr. Dege stated, "At the end of April 1945 I was asked by Oslo if we would remain on Spitsbergen until the autumn of 1946 instead of 1945. If this should be the case, we were to be provisioned by two aircraft.

"From the point of view of the history of the war, it is very interesting to hear that there was some intention of continuing the struggle from Norway. But nothing came of provisioning by these two aircraft. Instead of this, we heard over our radio about the collapse on all fronts and the capitulation of Germany. And so we became the forgotten men of the Second World War. Any secret documents relating to us and, as a consequence, the details of our position had now been destroyed. We also heard nothing more from our home radio base. What we did hear, however, interested us from a scientific point of view. The Soviet Union was the first to recommence broadcasting weather reports, uncoded, over the air. And so we said to ourselves, what the Soviets can do we can do. And we continued once again to broadcast our weather reports."

The evening of 30 April 1945, two years after drawing up the plans, *U 2511* (Comdr. Schnee), the first type XXI U-boat, (1,621 tons), left its base in Bergen on its first, and last, operational patrol of a submarine of this class. The *U 2511* had all the qualities of a real underwater ship. Also named the Electro–U-boat because of vastly extended batteries and more powerful E-motors, the sub, with improved hydrodynamic form, could attain an underwater speed of eighteen knots. At an underwater speed of 5.5 knots, it was absolutely silent while moving. It also had an extended operating radius—as far as Cape Town without necessity of topping-up its fuel. Its capability for "blind" torpedo attacks from greater depths also distinguished the type XXI from previous U-boats.

Contracts had been given for 752 type XXI U-boats by September 1944. The commander of the U-boat, Comdr. Schnee, had been until recently a staff officer responsible for large-scale convoy operations, their evaluation and the ensuing tactics.

In addition to Comdr. Schnee, there was another senior officer on board the *U 2511*, Comdr. Suhren of the engineering branch who, like Schnee, had worked on the development of this class of U-boat since its inception. Both officers were to give Grand Admiral Dönitz their assessment of the new submarine after its maiden voyage. Submerged, *U 2511* set course for the Atlantic.

The sub made contact with the enemy the very next day in the North Sea, much to the astonishment of the Allied submarine hunters, who well knew that any U-boat they located did not get away. Comdr. Schnee stated, "I increased speed from five knots to sixteen knots, changed course by approximately thirty degrees in order to follow the same course as the surface vessels were taking against the waves and the wind. . . . We heard them searching with their equipment for quite some time, but they were certainly unable to detect our new vessel. We experienced several more similar situations once into the Atlantic. But not one of the enemy ships came to drop even a single depth charge."

In April 1945 the staff of the C-in-C U-boats transferred headquarters to Flensburg/Mürwik in the face of the advancing British troops.

On 30 April 1945, toward 6:00 P.M. Dönitz received a coded telegram from Berlin, "Grand Admiral Dönitz. The Führer appoints you, Grand Admiral, as his deputy in place of the former Reichsmarschall Göring. Written authority to follow. You should immediately take all measures demanded by the current situation. Bormann."

Dönitz stated, "This appointment took me completely by surprise. . . . It was obvious that the blackest hour that a soldier could experience, unconditional surrender, was imminent. . . . My governmental policy was clear: to save as many human lives as possible."

By the end of April 1945 German midget-submarines of the Seehund class (Comdr. Brandi) had sunk 120,000 tons of shipping capacity. Even the French destroyer *La Combattante* fell victim to a Seehund. These two-man U-boats proved to be the most successful small vessel of the German Kriegsmarine.

In April 1945 German U-boats operating in the Atlantic sank nineteen merchant ships totalling 103,489 gross tons. German losses amounted to sixty-one U-boats.

On Wednesday 2 May 1945, *U 977* (Lt. Schäffer) put to sea from its base at Christiansund South. Its orders were to maintain position off Southampton

End of April 1945, Bergen, eleven type XXI U-boats, ready to put to sea, lying on their base in Norway. Only one, the *U 2511* (center), had been on an operational patrol.

and, if possible, penetrate into the harbor. The message sent from the flotilla commander on its departure finished with the obligatory, "Fight to the last, we shall never capitulate!"

On Thursday 3 May 1945, the code word "Regenbogen" (rainbow) – for the order to scuttle all units of the Kriegsmarine in the case of defeat – was confirmed by the Naval High Command. The following day Grand Admiral Dönitz nevertheless gave orders that "Regenbogen" should not be put into force.

Also on 3 May 1945, twenty fighter bombers of 8 Group stationed in Huntingdon sighted the German passenger liners *Cap Arkona* (27,562 gross tons) and *Thielbek* (3,000 gross tons). Both ships were carrying concentration camp victims who were being moved from Neuengamme camp on Himmler's orders because of the approach of the British army. Orders issued by the Reichsführer SS did not say what was to become of these people. Attacking continuously, RAF aircraft sank the *Cap Arkona* and *Thielbek*. More than seven thousand detainees from twenty-four different countries were killed. Only two hundred were able to save themselves. Thousands of corpses were washed ashore in Lübeck Bay, where that same afternoon British troops entered, at Neustadt. In order to prevent the spread of an epidemic, they buried the dead in mass graves in the dunes. The graves were not marked.

Early the morning of 4 May 1945, orders to cease fighting reached the new Electro–U-boat

U 2511, on its maiden voyage. Shortly afterward its receivers picked up engine noises at some strength, coming from a northerly direction. Comdr. Schnee said, "We went to periscope depth and I saw a British cruiser of the Suffolk class escorted by a number of destroyers. I had not seen such a prize during the entire war, and it had to happen then, just after we had received orders to cease hostilities. I made a dummy attack as one used to do, training in the Baltic, and continued on the same course as the cruiser. Our boat dived under the destroyer escort and went back to periscope depth between escort and cruiser. I then called my senior officers and let them see the unusual sight of a cruiser in the periscope. At that point, we were some six hundred yards abeam of the cruiser, a distance that would have led to certain success in the event of an attack. Then I went down to a lower depth and passed under the cruiser. We set course for home."

On the same day *U 234* (Lt. Comdr. Fehler), now in the Atlantic on passage to Japan, also received Grand Admiral Dönitz's orders that U-boats should make to the nearest enemy port. Col. von Sandrart, an antiaircraft artillery officer on the staff of Gen. Kessler, said, "What were we to do then? We had two senior Japanese officers on board and Japan was continuing the struggle. At first we decided we would inform the Japanese of the position and then make them prisoner. They weren't at all surprised. They even received the news of being taken prisoner with impassive, smiling politeness. But to carry our decision out was certainly difficult. I proposed that I should speak openly to the Japanese, with whom I had been on the best of terms for some time. The commander and Gen. Kessler were in agreement. I explained

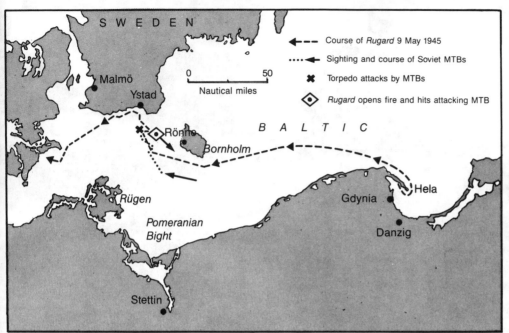

Left: 5/9/1945, 6:00 P.M., the last engagement seen by the Kriegsmarine in WWII

Right: The former pleasure steamer *Rugard* used a French gun dating from WWI in the last engagement of WWII.

our fears to the Japanese. They openly admitted that their first thoughts were to destroy the submarine—this would not have been at all difficult for them, as one of their number, Lt. Col. Tomonaga, was a submarine specialist. But because of the friendship existing between us, they couldn't find it in their hearts to do such a thing. Their honor as officers forbade them to surrender, alive, to the enemy. They gave me their word that the submarine and crew would have nothing to fear from them. Under these circumstances, the commander said there would be no further need to guard them. They threw their secret documents over the side, lay down on the bunks above me and took a lethal dose of poison. They died slowly, seemingly without end. . . . We surfaced and radioed our position. An American destroyer picked up our message. . . . A few hours later, we sighted the smoke trails of the American destroyer *Sutton* on the horizon. The long and difficult road into captivity now began."

Also on 4 May 1945, *U 977* (Lt. Schäffer) received the message from Grand Admiral Dönitz. But the U-boat commander thought this was a ploy by the Allies, as the message did not bear a signature. The next message received seemed even more ominous. "German submarines should surface immediately, report their position, destroy their weapons and hoist a blue flag." The order was signed off "Allied committee."

Lt. Schäffer now resolved to make for the Argentine. He had sufficient fuel and provisions on board, and the crew hoped that a new future could be found in a country friendly to Germany. They held a referendum. Of the forty-eight men, thirty opted for the Argentine, two would have preferred Spain and sixteen petty officers—most of them married and with children—wanted to go home.

The following night the 16 were put ashore near Bergen in Norway. They reported themselves as the sole survivors of the *U 977*, which they reported as having struck a mine and gone down; consequently, the U-boat was registered as lost.

Now that the older, more experienced petty officers were no longer on board, every emergency dive was a hazardous maneuver for the lower-ranking sailors remaining. Subsequently when an emergency dive was made, the first watchkeeping officer forgot to retract the periscope. The guide wires were unable to withstand the water pressure at a depth of three hundred feet and the periscope collapsed onto the deck, damaging the prisms. The second periscope, used exclusively for attacks during darkness, was too short when the Schnorchel was being used.

A second German U-boat made for the Argentine: This was *U 530* (Lt. Wehrmuth).

On Saturday 5 May 1945, the Electro–U-boat *U 2511* put into Bergen after its maiden voyage. The British cruiser with its escort, sighted by *U 2511* the previous day, was also in the harbor. Comdr. Schnee said, "I was immediately taken on board the British cruiser and taken to the admiral. Not surprisingly, I was really quite cagey and said practically nothing during this first encounter with the enemy. But when the British admiral asked me about contacts with the enemy during my last patrol, I said that the last contact I had had with the enemy had, in fact, been this very cruiser, where we

were at this moment. Things now got very lively; I was told it was quite out of the question. The commander of the cruiser and the destroyer commanders were interrogated, and finally proof was established only when all the log books were gathered together and compared, thereby confirming the position at the time of the dummy attack."

Eisenhower, as supreme commander of the Allied forces in Europe, demanded a simultaneous total capitulation on all fronts, meaning that each soldier would lay down his arms precisely where he was at the given time. The time that the capitulation order was to come into effect was postponed — twice by twenty-four hours to 9 May 1945 at midnight — which allowed the Kriegsmarine a limited opportunity to continue rescue operations in the Baltic.

By Sunday 6 May 1945, a record forty-three thousand refugees had been saved.

On Monday 7 May 1945, at 2:41 A.M. Gen. Jodl in Reims signed — authorised by Grand Admiral Dönitz — the order to cease hostilities on all fronts. On the same day RAF Coastal Command made its last attack on a German U-boat. A Catalina flying boat from 210 Squadron (Flt. Lt. Murray) located a U-boat between the Shetlands and Norway. The U-boat, submerged, had hove to, and the noises picked up showed that it must be in difficulty. The Catalina dropped a series of depth charges. This submarine was the *U 320* (Lt. Emmerich), and it later signalled that it was badly damaged. On Wednesday 9 May 1945, the *U 320* went down off Bergen with its entire crew.

Also on 7 May 1945, a German type XXIII U-boat, *U 2336* (Lt. Klusmeyer) sank the freighter *Sneland I* (1,791 gross tons) and the *Avondale Park* (2,878 gross tons) sailing in a convoy off the Firth of Forth. The submarine escaped undetected. This

was the last success achieved by a German U-boat in World War II.

From 1 to 7 May 1945, German U-boats operating in the Atlantic sank four merchant ships totalling 10,370 gross tons. German losses amounted to forty U-boats.

The afternoon of 8 May 1945, the former pleasure steamer *Rugard* left Hela — followed by evacuation craft and units of 9 Escort Division (Comdr. von Blanc) — with six hundred German soldiers who had managed to reach Hela from the Lithuanian front. In a few hours the capitulation was to come into force. The "last convoy of WWII" was to attempt to reach Kiel Bay by sailing through Swedish territorial waters. If the *Rugard* were to be attacked by Soviet warships, its sole hope of survival would be defence by an obsolescent 7.5-cm gun of French origin. Petty Officer Pittler stated, "We took a last look at Danzig Bay. . . . With good visibility and a pair of binoculars, Russian troop movement could be clearly made out. . . . Standing along the edge of the peninsula were those who had to stay behind because there was no room for them on the ship. I shall never forget the last salute of despair fired off by the 8.8-cm guns on Hela when we reached the open sea. . . . Every corner of the ship, every cabin was filled to overflowing with those of our people who had been fortunate enough to get on board at the last minute." The first few hours passed without incident, and the mood on board the old *Rugard*, which formerly plied between Stettin and Rügen island, was optimistic.

The evening of 8 May 1945, three torpedo boats, *Karl Galster, T 23* and *T 28*, put into the Hela roads. They picked up soldiers from the 61 Grenadier Regiment and Assault Brigade 232. *T 28* was the last boat to leave Hela. From midnight 8/9 May 1945, the guns fell silent. By the afternoon of 9 May 1945 the last German warships had put into Kiel and Glücksburg. They disembarked twenty-one thousand soldiers and refugees.

Petty Officer Pittler of the *Rugard* stated, "Toward 18:00 hours on 9 May 1945, we had long since put Bornholm behind us when the stern lookout on the *Rugard* suddenly sighted four bow waves approaching rapidly. . . . The approaching boats turned out to be Soviet MTBs. They dashed past, only two hundred yards away from us, and tried to block the passage of the leading boat of 9 Escort Division."

One of the Soviet MTBs came alongside the *Rugard*. The Soviet commander called to the bridge, "Ship go back at once, or everything finished!" — and in so saying, pointed at the torpedo tubes, which were ready to fire. At that, the MTB put off and waited astern on the assumption that the steamer would follow the course indicated.

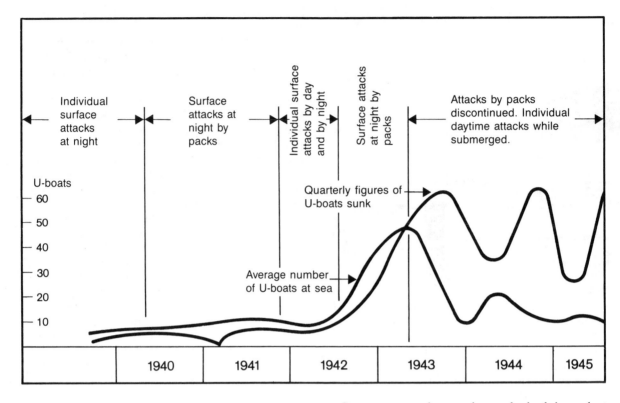

Individual surface attacks at night

Surface attacks at night by packs

Individual surface attacks by day and by night

Surface attacks at night by packs

Attacks by packs discontinued. Individual daytime attacks while submerged.

U-boats
— 60
— 50
— 40
— 30
— 20
— 10

Quarterly figures of U-boats sunk

Average number of U-boats at sea

| 1940 | 1941 | 1942 | 1943 | 1944 | 1945 |

The effect of the convoy system 1939–45

Pittler said, "The captain of the *Rugard* ordered "Full ahead!" The ship lurched forward as the screws, driven by full power, turned wildly. The three-mile limit was very close, and we could already see the lights of a Swedish port shining in the distance." It was hoped, in vain, that the MTBs could be shaken off. Soon the *Rugard* was on its own, as the companion vessels had dashed off at top speed to avoid their pursuers.

The bridge officer on the steamer reported first one and then a second torpedo, both of which missed the *Rugard* by a hair's breadth. The MTBs now opened fire with machine guns, and permission was given to fire the deck gun. Pittler said, "A column of water shot up close to the Russian boat at the head of the column. The second or possibly the third shot hit the target square on. The Soviet MTB disappeared from view in a pall of smoke, and a little later we saw only three MTBs, which now, impressed by the salvo from the last gun to be fired in WWII by a German warship, withdrew — still firing. . . . Under the cover of darkness that now descended upon the water, we sailed a few miles along the Swedish coast, lighted up just as in peacetime, only a few nautical miles from us."

On Thursday 10 May 1945, the *Rugard* put into Strander Bay near Kiel during the early morning hours.

Some twenty thousand people had been lost along this sea route — a cruel tribute to the evacuation operation that had no parallel in the annals of sea war. The final calculations showed that 2,204,477 people, including 1,420,000 refugees, succeeded in escaping across the sea, thanks to the German Navy. Losses amounted to scarcely one percent, whereas for those travelling across land; losses were said to be sixteen percent.

The German Navy retained supremacy in the Baltic and, thanks to this, was able to support German troops along the seaboard in their defensive actions.

Of the last defenders remaining in the bridgeheads, there were some sixty thousand men left behind on Hela, twenty thousand at the mouth of the Vistual, ten thousand in East Prussia and two hundred thousand in Kurland in Lithuania. Their fate was to take the long journey into Siberian prison camps.

From 1 September 1939 to 8 May 1945, 1,113 U-boats were commissioned, in addition to the 57 already at sea when the war broke out. Out of 863 German U-boats in front-line service, 630 were sunk on operations. Out of approximately 41,300 submarines who saw action, 25,870 lost their lives, according to the statistics supplied by the Wehrmacht Information Center in Berlin. On a comparative basis, the U-boat crews suffered heavier losses than any other branch of the armed forces.

In addition, 81 U-boats were lost in their bases

5/7/1945, Hamburg, shipyards building submarines:
Officers of the Royal Navy contemplate their most dangerous
opponents.

and in German ports through air raids and mines, and another 42 through various accidents. At the end of the war and before evacuating the bases, 215 U-boats were scuttled by their own crews. After the cessation of hostilities, 153 U-boats were handed over in Allied ports.

The Royal Air Force achieved a remarkable success in that they sank more German U-boats than the Royal Navy, although the aircraft, in contrast to naval vessels, were not equipped with under-water-location equipment.

The defeat of the German Kriegsmarine could not, despite the self-sacrificing fight put up by the service, be avoided. Up until the end of 1942, Hitler was still convinced that successes achieved on land would bring about the final victory. He was incapable of developing a rational joint strategy for the Kriegsmarine and Luftwaffe. The new types of U-boat, which would have revolutionised the war at sea, came far too late to have any influence on the Battle of the Atlantic. Only the Allies profited from their existence; after the capitulation, they were used as models for building the most modern submarines.

During the war 5,150 Allied merchant ships of all classes, totalling 21,570,720 gross tons were sunk. These losses can be contrasted with the 38,900,000 gross tons new shipping capacity built.

German U-boats sank 2,779 ships totalling 14,119,413 tons. The German merchant marine lost 1,563 ships totalling 3,000,000 gross tons. At the outbreak of war the Germans had 4,500,000 gross tons shipping capacity available.

Despite all their endeavors and spectacular successes, the Kriegsmarine and Luftwaffe succeeded in destroying only a small percentage of the 2,660 shiploads of equipment delivered to the USSR under the Lend-Lease agreement concluded between the USA and Great Britain. On the Murmansk route, 77 Allied ships were lost. Although it would certainly not be admitted in Moscow today, there is no doubt that these supplies helped the Soviets to recover from the enormous losses sustained in the first months following Hitler's invasion. The supplies included, among other things, 17,246 aircraft; 15,000 tanks; 427,284 trucks; and 345,735 tons of ammunition. The Soviet Union still owes the USA 12 billion US dollars. Indirectly the navies of the Western Allies thereby had a decisive participation in the land operations in Eastern Europe.

Shortly after the German capitulation, a strange column of jeeps and trucks rumbled along the quiet Thüringen country roads. The vehicles were transporting a special detachment of the Royal Marines, troops that had been deployed on difficult amphibious operations during the war and were now carrying out one of their last special

Left: July 1945, Spitsbergen, Haudegen meteorological detachment, ". . . well into summer we were covering distances up to 650 miles on homemade sleds and skis, exploring the country."

Right: Losses sustained by the Japanese Imperial Navy from December 1941 to August 1945

operations on the continent of Europe, now in a state of chaos.

This group, led by one of the principal officers of the IOC, Comdr. Jan Fleming (the creator of James Bond — 007), was out to seize the entire archives of the German Navy, dating from its inception in 1871 up to 1945, before the Americans and the Russians got them. The British Admiralty believed that these documents would not only reveal various secrets of the German Naval High Command but would also give important pointers on how Great Britain could protect her supply lines from danger in the event of another war. Fleming, one of the best men in the IOC, had found out some months previously that the German naval archives had been moved, because of the danger from air raids, from Berlin to an estate near Tambach (Thüringen) in the autumn of 1944. A moat had been dug around the large house and filled with wood logs. At the time of an enemy approach, the logs were to be soaked with petrol and set on fire to destroy the mountain of archives stored in the house. But during the severe winter of 1944/45, the inhabitants of Tambach unknowingly played a trick on the OKM: Thinking the logs were just lying around fulfilling no useful purpose, they picked them up and took them home to burn in their own fireplaces.

When the American troops marched into Thüringen at the beginning of May 1945, they confiscated this magnificent country seat as accommodation for American officers. But nobody paid any attention to the files of documents stored on the upper floor and attic of this spacious mansion. Unexpected, the British group led by Comdr. Fleming, who was now disguised as an American

MP, drove up to the house and started work. The US made no objections. The British loaded up the entire archives onto their trucks in double-quick time and disappeared as quickly as they had arrived.

The Red Army occupied Thüringen some time later, thanks to the Yalta Agreement. However, the German naval archives finished up intact in London, where they were later handed over to the Naval Historical Branch of the Admiralty whose Foreign Documents Section (Comdr. M. G. Saunders) was set up to administer the captured documents. And there, ever since, the greater part of the archives of the German Kriegsmarine — or at any rate that part applicable to the U-boats — has remained. Many records are still on the secret list.

On Monday 14 May 1945, one of the most successful U-boat commanders (225,712 gross tons shipping capacity sunk and the longest operational patrol of the war — 205 days) fell victim to a tragic accident. Capt. Wolfgang Lüth was walking in the dark through the grounds of the Naval Academy Flensburg-Mürwik, where he was the officer commanding, when he failed to hear the challenge of the German sentry who had orders to fire immediately should his challenge be disregarded. Lüth fell to the ground, killed by the first shot.

On Tuesday 5 June 1945, units of the Fifth US Fleet were hit by a typhoon in Philippine waters. Numerous warships, including four battleships as well as four aircraft carriers, were seriously damaged. A total of 36 ships had to go into the repair yards, and 150 aircraft were lost.

By Sunday 17 June 1945, the *U 977* (Lt. Schäfer) had already been seven weeks in passage, underwater, without sun, without sufficient fresh air,

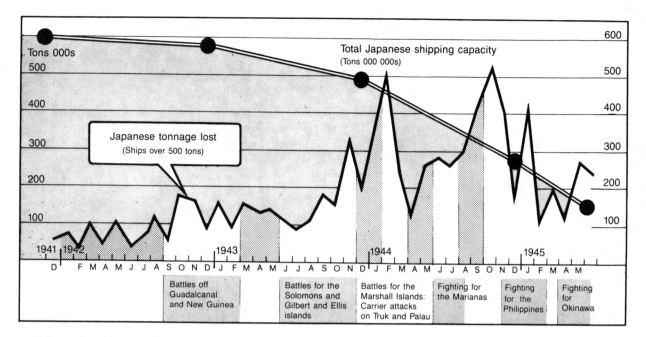

Tons 000s

Total Japanese shipping capacity
(Tons 000 000s)

Japanese tonnage lost
(Ships over 500 tons)

1941 1942 1943 1944 1945

D F M A M J J A S O N D J F M A M J J A S O N D J F M A M J J A S O N D J F M A M J J A S O N D J F M A

Battles off Guadalcanal and New Guinea

Battles for the Solomons and Gilbert and Ellis islands

Battles for the Marshall Islands: Carrier attacks on Truk and Palau

Fighting for the Marianas

Fighting for the Philippines

Fighting for Okinawa

without diversion — and always the same old faces. While *U 977* was travelling southward, a number of U-boat hunters crossed its path, and each time the crew expected to hear exploding depth charges. With the increasing temperature, the submarine developed the oppressive atmosphere of a hot-house. The sides of the ship were covered with thick mold, the metal parts with rust. The crew's clothes stuck to their bodies, and washing with salt water caused painful irritation and boils. The engine room personnel suffered particularly badly; hands, faces and upper bodies were covered with a crust of grime that was impossible to remove.

By Sunday 1 July 1945, the *U 977* had been two months in passage to Argentina. Lt. Schäffer recorded, "Sixty days underwater. Now we, too, are beginning to go moldy. All color has drained from our faces. Our eyes have lost their shine, dark beards frame our sunken, pale faces. We no longer have any appetite, fits of coughing are spreading. We seldom indulge in conversation, and duties are carried out in a mechanical fashion. You'd think you were looking at walking corpses."

On Monday 2 July 1945, underwater missiles fired from a submarine were first deployed. The American submarine *Barb* (Comdr. Fluckey) fired at Kaihyo, one of the Kurile Islands, on which a Japanese garrison was stationed. The rockets used had a two-and-a-half-inch rocket drive and a high-explosive five-inch warhead with contact detonator armed by a wind-driven rotor.

The night of 6/7 July 1945, the *U 977* surfaced somewhere to the north of the Azores. It had been underwater for sixty-six days, one of the first of the underwater marathon voyages in naval history. Lt. Schäffer said, "I opened the hatch and stood

on the bridge; behind me came the first watch-keeping officer. A thorough look around showed that there were no vessels in sight. The unending skies opened up above me, the stars shone like diamonds."

While life in Germany began to get back to normal after the turmoil of war — in München on Sunday 8 July 1945, the philharmonic under Eugen Jochum gave its first concert, playing works by Mozart and Tchaikovsky before a capacity audience in the Prince Regent Theater — the Haudegen meteorological detachment was still hanging on in the Arctic. Dr. Dege said, "Well into summer we were covering distances up to 650 miles on home-made dogsleds and skis, exploring the country. But we became more and more unhappy about the situation at home. We ourselves were in the best physical condition but were unhappy as to how things would be back in Germany. When the first ice floes came again into the fjord, we asked our radio contacts if we would be picked up this year."

On Tuesday 10 July 1945, *U 530* (Lt. Wehrmuth) reached the Mar del Plata. The radio report on this event had a considerable effect on the crew of *U 977*. The Argentine authorities handed over the crew and the submarine to the USA, several days later.

On Wednesday 11 July 1945, while the first meeting of the Allied Kommandatura took place in the bombed-out German capital, the last German U-boats in running order, taken by British troops in Wilhelmshaven and other German naval bases, were transferred to Great Britain. Nobody had any idea of the existence of *U 977* in the mid-Atlantic or of the last unit of the German Navy, the meteorological detachment on the edge

8/17/1945, Mar del Plata, the *U 977* reaches its objective after 108 days. On the right, the Argentine submarine tender.

of the Arctic in Spitsbergen, still carrying out their duties.

After the end of the war in Europe, the Japanese government decided to ask the Soviets to mediate with the Americans with regard to ceasefire terms. They approached J. Malik, the Soviet ambassador in Japan, but the Soviet Union made no reply.

Not until Thursday 12 July 1945 was the Japanese ambassador in Moscow advised by radio from Tokyo to take up direct contact with the Soviet government. The Americans, who had known the Japanese code for some time, learned of the content of the radio message.

In the tropical warmth of the mid-Atlantic, *U 977* now proceeded submerged during the day and on the surface at nights, displaying navigation lights. It met a number of ships; a passenger liner overtook the submarine. The crew of the U-boat looked with great longing at the luxury liner, which seemed like a mountain of light majestically proceeding on its course; the strains of dance music wafted across to the *U 977*.

There was no longer any apparent need to submerge during the day. Canvas shapes were made to disguise the appearance of the *U 977*, so that from the distance it resembled the outline of a small collier. A smoke-stack was constructed from tin cans, and oil-soaked rags gave off the necessary smoke. The crew enjoyed the freedom gained by this deception, and the men spent their time swimming, fishing or simply lying on the deck dozing.

On Tuesday 24 July 1945, the last Japanese on Okinawa ceased their resistance. The fighting had lasted for eighty-two days (from 1 April 1945) and was the hardest in the Pacific war. The Americans lost 12,000 dead and 36 wounded; the Japanese lost 110,000 men.

Late the evening of 29 July 1945, the Japanese submarine *I-58* (Comdr. Hashimoto) fired off six torpedoes at the US heavy cruiser *Indianapolis* (Capt. McVay) east of Luzon. The warship, travelling alone, had just transported parts of the atom bombs from San Francisco to Tinian and was now returning to Leyte. Two of the six torpedoes hit the 9,950-ton cruiser, which went down with 883 men in less than two minutes. American flying boats and destroyers picked up 316 survivors. This was at once the biggest and last success achieved by Japanese submarines during the war.

On Monday 30 July 1945, at 10:30 A.M. the British midget-submarines *XE-1* (Lt. Smart) and *XE-3* (Lt. Fraser) pushed forward to the torpedo nets, guarded by minesweepers, at the entrance to Singapore harbor (Operation Hard Job). Their objective was to destroy the Japanese heavy cruiser *Takao* (13,400 tons), which was being repaired and refitted. The crews of the midget-submarines cut through one of the nets and by 1:40 P.M. had reached the cruiser. It took forty minutes for the *XE-3* to find a suitable position in the shallow water where it could dive under the *Takao*. A frogman fixed six limpet mines to the ship's hull. *XE-1* and *XE-3* succeeded in regaining the open sea, undetected, where they met their submarine tugs *Stygian* and *Spark* and returned to their bases at Labuan (Borneo).

The next day at 9:30 P.M. the limpets went up. The cruiser *Takao* settled on the bottom, totally destroyed. Operation Hard Job was the last operation by midget-submarines in World War II.

On Monday 6 August 1945, the Superfortress B-29 "Enola Gay" (Col. Tibbets) of the 20 USAAF dropped the first atom bomb on Hiroshima, Japan's most important naval base. A total of 92,167 people were killed, and 37,425 suffered severe injuries.

On the same day a Japanese aircraft surprised the surfaced American submarine *Bullhead* (Lt. Comdr. Holt) off the coast of Bali. The aircraft immediately launched an attack and with two direct hits sank the submarine together with its entire crew. This was the last submarine sunk by the Japanese.

On Wednesday 8 August 1945, the USSR declared war on Japan. The Soviet Pacific Fleet (Adm. Yumasev) commenced operations against shipping lanes that connected Japan with its forces in China.

On Thursday 9 August 1945, the Superfortress B-29 (Maj. Sweeney) dropped the second atom bomb, this time on Nagasaki. There were approximately forty thousand dead and sixty thousand injured.

On Sunday 12 August 1945, Soviet formations landed along the northeast coast of Korea. This operation was to support the advance of the Soviet 25th Army of the first Far Eastern Front (Marshal Merezkov). The weak Japanese forces offered only patchy resistance.

On the same day Japanese manned Kaiten torpedoes carried out the last attack of the war. One of the Kaiten, put off by the submarine *I-58* (Comdr. Hashimoto), grazed the dock landing craft LSD 7 *Oakhill*.

From Thursday 16 August 1945, the Soviet North Pacific Fleet (Vice-Adm. Andrev) carried out landings at various points along the coast of south Sakhalin.

Early the morning of 17 August 1945, after 108 days *U 977* reached its objective — the Argentine coast was visible on the horizon and the submarine made towards the Mar del Plata lighthouse. The entire off-watch crew pressed onto the bridge. While still outside the three-mile zone, the submarine signalled with its lamp, "German submarine." After a while, a motor barge came alongside *U 977*, and Argentinian officers, wearing white uniforms, went on board. Their task was to bring the submarine into the port and, above all, make sure it was neither scuttled nor damaged by its own crew. Lt. Schäffer said, "I suggested that we should bring the ship into port, as my crew did not speak any language other than German, and, in addition, the complicated machinery could only be operated with difficulty by non-specialised personnel. My word of honor was accepted, and I gave orders for the last time to my crew."

The crew now had to face wearying interrogation, during which they were accused of having put Hitler, Eva Braun and their closest followers ashore, secretly, somewhere in South America. This story, having been put out by the Soviets (although Stalin had complete proof of Hitler's suicide), weighed upon the U-boat crew for a long time. They were even accused of having torpedoed the Brazilian cruiser *Bahia* (3,150 tons), which had gone down after a mysterious explosion close to the island of Penedo de São Paulo on 9 July 1945. Finally Argentina handed over the crew to the USA. *U 977* was sunk on 2 February 1946 by US Navy torpedoes.

On Saturday 18 August 1945, the Soviet Pacific Fleet (Adm. Yumasev) commenced operations on the Japanese-occupied Kurile Islands. There was bitter fighting on Shumshu that caused both sides to suffer heavy losses.

On Tuesday 21 August 1945 — the day on which Japanese forces in Manchuria surrendered to the Red Army — the responsible authority in Oslo, still active and cooperating with the British, remembered the Haudegen meteorological detachment. Dr. Dege said, "To our surprise, we received news that a Norwegian ship would come and pick us up. It had some difficulty in reaching us, as we had been living in the remotest possible area on the edge of where it is possible for humans to survive."

On Wednesday 22 August 1945, the first Japanese garrison in the Pacific, a 150-man force occupying the small Mili atoll (Marshall Islands), capitulated. The highest-ranking officer signed the surrender agreement on board the US escort carrier *Levy*.

On Monday 27 August 1945, Task Force 38 (Vice-Adm. McCain), a part of the Third US Fleet (Adm. Halsey), put into Sagami Sea off Tokyo.

On Thursday 30 August 1945, a special aircraft carrying Gen. MacArthur landed in Yokohama. Gen. MacArthur set up his headquarters in the Grand Hotel in the American-occupied city. Enemy troops were on Japanese soil for the first time in the country's 2,500-year history.

On Sunday 2 September 1945, at 10:30 A.M. (local time) the Japanese foreign minister, Shigemitsu, and chief of the General Staff, Gen. Umezu, as well as Gen. MacArthur and the representatives of the Allied states, signed the unconditional surrender of Japan on the US battleship *Missouri*, lying at anchor in Tokyo Bay.

Exactly six years and one day had passed since the first salvo was fired from the old battleship *Schleswig-Holstein* on 1 September 1939, heralding the outbreak of World War II.

Japan's capitulation had no parallel in history. For the first time a country had capitulated with-

9/2/1945, Tokyo Bay, the sun sets behind Fujiyama; all is now finally at peace.

out any enemy forces having landed on her shores. The US Navy had made a decisive contribution to this victory by cutting Japan's lines of communication, thereby preventing the import of raw materials vital for Japanese industry.

Before the war the Japanese Merchant Navy comprised 2,337 ships—after the capitulation the total was only 231. The Imperial Navy lost 10 battleships, 16 aircraft carriers, 37 cruisers, 137 destroyers and 127 submarines.

Two days after the Japanese had capitulated, signalling the end of the war, the time had come for the Haudegen detachment to do the same. Dr. Dege said, "On 4 September 1945, I had to sign my own surrender with the captain of the Norwegian sealer. This was the surrender of the last German unit of the Second World War."

The Smaller Fleets of the Second World War

Organisation — Structure — Strength

The index is in order by country, and data on the fate of individual ships covers 9/1/1939 to 9/2/1945. The warships listed are units from 200 t (standard) upward, auxiliary vessels are only mentioned in specific instances. Ships' dimensions are given in the standard formula of length x beam x draught, and dimensions, weapons, etc. are shown in metric measure.

AUSTRALIA

Operationally, the Royal Australian Navy (RAN) was under the control of the Royal Navy 1939–45. The RAN in 1939 comprised 2 heavy and 4 light cruisers, 5 destroyers and torpedo boats, as well as a number of smaller units; there were 5,230 regular personnel. By 1945 the RAN had been expanded to 100,000 t and 40,000 men.

BELGIUM

The navy was dissolved in 1927, and since that date Belgium maintained only a number of smaller vessels for fishery protection. Obsolete former Ger. torpedo boats served these purposes. Units available were under the control of the director général de la marine. From May 1940, the Belg. crews in GB received a number of smaller auxiliary vessels and one frigate. The Belgian Navy in exile was thereby created as a Belg. division of the Royal Navy.
Operational: North Sea and Atlantic.

Fishery protection vessels
Zinnia (ex GB → 1920 Belgium) blt. 1915 GB; 1,200 t; dim: 82m x 10m x 3.6m; 17 kt; wpns: 1 Flak 1.3 cm; seized by Ger. 5/1940 → tng. ship. **Barbara** → 1945 Belg. • **Artevelde** blt. 1940; 1,600 t; dim: 98.5m x 10.5m x 3.3m; 22 kt; wpns: 4 Flak 10.2 cm, 2 Flak 2 cm, depth charges, mines; seized by Ger. 5/1940 → **K4** → 1945 Belg.

BRAZIL

Naval forces were under the control of the naval secretary. In 1940 the navy comprised 14,847 men, 11,172 with the fleet and 1,229 the naval air arm and 2,446 marines.
Operational: Battle of the Atlantic (South).

Battleships
São Paulo (Minas Gerais class) blt. 1910 GB; 19,200 t; dim: 162.4m x 25.3m x 7.6m; 21 kt; wpns: 12 x 30.5 cm, 12 x 12 cm, 2 Flak 7.6 cm • **Minas Gerais** as above; modernised 1937; 22 kt; wpns: 12 x 30.5 cm, 14 x 12 cm, 4 Flak 10.2 cm, 4 Flak 4 cm.

Cruisers
Bahia (class → 1926 Brazil) blt. 1910 GB; 3,150 t; dim: 122.4m x 11.9m x 4.2m; 27 kt; wpns: 10 x 12 cm, 4 Flak 7.6 cm, 4 torp. tbs. 53.3 cm. Rio Grande do Sul.

Destroyers
Maranhao (GB class K → 1920 Brazil) blt. 1913 GB; 934 t; dim: 80.8m x 8.1m x 3m; 28 kt; wpns: 3 x 10.2 cm, 1 Flak 7.6 cm, 4 torp. tbs. 53.3 cm.
Marilio Dias (class) • **Greenhalg** • **Mariz e Barros**
blt. 1943/1944; 1,500 t; dim: 109.7m x 10.7m x 3.1m; 36.5 kt; wpns: 4 x 12.7 cm, 4 Flak 4 cm, 4 Flak 2 cm, 4 torp. tbs. 53.3 cm.

Amazonas (class) • **Acre** • **Ajuricaba** • **Apa** • **Araguaia** • **Arguari**
blt. 1943/46; 1,450 t; dim: 98.4m x 10.7m x 2.6m; 34 kt; wpns: 4 x 12.7 cm, 2 Flak 4 cm, 4 Flak 2 cm, 8 torp. tbs. 53.3 cm.

Torpedo Boats
Mato Grosso (class) • **Paraiba** • **Piaui** • **Rio Grande do Norte** • **Santa Catarina** • **Sergipe**
blt. 1908/10 GB; 560 t; dim: 73.2m x 7.2m x 2.1m; 27 kt; wpns: 2 x 10.2 cm, 4 x 4.7 cm, 2 torp. tbs. 45.7 cm.

Submarines
Humaita blt. 1929 Ital.; 1,380/1,884 t; dim: 86.7m x 7.8m x 4.3m; 18.5/10 kt; range: 4,700 naut. miles at 8 kt; submerged: 72 naut. miles at 4 kt; wpns: 1 x 12 cm, 6 torp. tbs. 53.3 cm, 16 mines.
Tamoio (Ital. Perla class) • **Timbira** • **Tupi**
blt. 1938 Ital.; 615/853 t; dim: 60.2m x 6.4m x 3.7m; 14/7.7 kt; range: 4,000 naut. miles at 9 kt; submerged: 74 naut. miles at 4 kt; wpns: 1 x 10 cm, 6 torp. tbs. 53.3 cm.

Escort vessels
Babitonga (US Cannon class → 1944/45 Brazil) ex US Alger/DE 101 • **Baependi** — ex US Cannon/DE 99 • **Bauru** — ex US Reybold/DE 177 • **Beberibe** — ex US Herzog/DE 178 • **Benevente** — ex US Christopher/DE 100 • **Bertioga** — ex US Pennewill/DE 175 • **Bocaina** — ex US Marts/DE 179 • **Bracui** — ex US McAnn/DE 176
blt. 1943 USA; 1,240 t; dim: 93.3m x 11.1m x 2.7m; 21 kt; wpns: 3 x 7.6 cm, 2 Flak 4 cm, 4 Flak 2 cm, 3 torps. tbs. 58.3 cm, depth charges.

Patrol boats
Barreto Menezes (ex **Paru**) Matias de Albuquerque class • **Felipe Camarao** (ex **Papaterra**) • **Fernandes Vieira** (ex **Parati**) • **Henrique Dias** (ex **Pargo**) • **Matias de Albuquerque** (ex **Pampano**) • **Vidal de Negreiros** (ex **Pelegrime**)
blt. 1942/46; 650 t; dim: 53.6m x 8.2m x 4.3m; 12.5 kt; wpns: 1 x 7.6 cm, 4 Flak 2 cm, depth charges.

Submarine hunters
Goiana (US PC 461 class, ex US **PC 554** → 1942/43 Brazil) • **Grajau** (ex US **PC 1236**) • **Grauna** (ex US **PC 561**) • **Guaiba** (ex US **PC 604**) • **Guajara** (ex US **PC 607** • **Guapore** (ex US **PC 544**) • **Gurupa** (ex US **PC 605**) • **Gurupi** (ex US **PC 547**)
blt. 1942/43 USA; 280 t; dim: 53.3m x 7m x 2.3cm; 20 kt; wpns: 1 x 7.6 cm, 1 Flak 4 cm, 5 Flak 2 cm, depth charges.

Minesweepers
Carioca (class) • **Cabedelo** • **Camaqua** — 7/23/44 (lost in storm off Pernambuco) • **Camocim** • **Cananea** • **Caravelas**
blt. 1939/40; 522 t; dim: 57.7m x 7.8m x 2.4m; 14 kt; wpns: 2 x 10.2 cm, 4 Flak 2 cm, 50 mines.

BULGARIA

1939, the navy had only coastal protection duties.

Torpedo boats
Derski blt. 1907/8 Fr.; 98 t; 18 kt; 2 Flak 4.7 cm, 2 torp. tbs. 45 cm • **Hrabri** • **Smely** • **Strogi**

Patrol boats
Belomorets (ex. Fr. submarine hunter) blt. 1920 USA; 80 t; 16 kt; wpns: 1 Flak 4.7 cm, 2 MG • **Tschernomorets** 1939 two Ger. S-boats type S 1, 1941 two Dutch S-boats (Ger. booty) S 201, S 202. The Danube flotilla actively supported the Red Army against the Germans from 9/1944.

CANADA

Operationally, the Royal Canadian Navy (RCN) was under the control of the Royal Navy 1939–45. The RCN in 1939 comprised 6 destroyers, 4 minesweepers and a number of smaller units. Strength comprised 514 regulars, 500 on the reserve and 1,000 in the Volunteer Reserve. By 3/31/1941, the RCN comprised 87,080 men and 5,739 women, 373 warships and 556 auxiliary units.
Operational: Battle of the Atlantic, the Normandy invasion.

CHINA (KUOMINTANG)

At war with Japan from 1937, and also civil war activities. Accordingly, more precise details are not available.

Reconnaissance cruisers
Ning Hai blt. 1931/32 Jap.; 2,500 t; 20 kt; wpns: 6 x 14 cm, 6 Flak 7.6 cm. • **Ping Hai** • **Yatsen**
blt 1930 Jap.; 1,650 t; 20 kt; wpns: 1 x 15.2 cm, 1 x 14 cm, 4 Flak 7.6 cm.
6 torpedo boats (blt. 1895, 1914/8) 90 t-400 t • 12 MTBs (blt. 1934/6 GB) • 35 patrol boats, approx. 300 t, 10 kt • some gunboats (blt. 1895, 1914/8) 600 t-950 t, 11 kt • 2 aircraft tenders (blt. 1922), 950 t, 15 kt, each with 2 aircraft • several survey ships • 10 river gunboats, 60 t-225 t; wpns: max 1 x 10.2 cm or 1 x 8.7 cm and light Flak.

COLUMBIA

Destroyers
Antioquia (class) • **Caldas**
blt. 1934 Port.; 1,239 t; dim: 98.1m x 9.4m x 3.2m; 36 kt; wpns: 4 x 12 cm, 3 Flak 4 cm, 8 torp. tbs. 53.3 cm, 2 depth-charge launchers.

Patrol boats
Bogota (ex Ger. M-boat **M 139**) • **Cordova** (ex. Ger. M-boat **M-158**)
blt. 1919 Ger.; 690 t; dim: 59.3m x 7.4m x 2.23m; wpns: 1 x 8.8 cm, 2 x 7.6 cm.

CUBA

Gunboats

Cuba blt. 1911 USA; 2,055 t; dim: 79.2m x 11.9m x 4.3m; 18 kt; wpns: 2 x 10.2 cm, 6 x 7.6 cm • **Patria** blt. 1911 USA; 1,200 t; dim: 61m x 11m x 4m; 16 kt; wpns: 2. 7.6 cm, 4 x 5.7 cm.

Patrol boats

Baire blt. 1906 Ger.; 500 t; dim: 59.7m x 7m x 2.7m; 14 kt; wpns: 4 x 7.6 cm.

Diez de Octubre • Veinte y Cuatro de Febrero blt. 1911 GB; 218 t; dim: 33.5m x 6.1m x 2.4m; 12 kt; wpns: 3 x 4.7 cm.

DENMARK

The C-in-C of the navy, who was subordinate to the Navy Department, was the king. Strength amounted to 1,500 men. During the Ger. occupation, the navy did not see action. In accordance with the agreement made with Ger., the Dan. crews remained on board ship. After the disturbances of 8/29/1943, most of the units were scuttled by their own crews, some escaped to Sweden and the remainder were taken over by the Kriegsmarine.

Coastal warships

Peder Skram blt. 1908; 3,500 t; dim: 83.8m x 15.5m x 5m; 16 kt; wpns: 2 x 24 cm, 4 x 14.9 cm, 8 x 7.5 cm, 2 Flak 3.7 cm, 4 Flak 2 cm, 4 torp. tbs. 45.7 cm; scuttled 8/29/43; raised by Ger. → tng. ship **Adler • Neils Juel** blt. 1918; mod. 1936; 3,800 t; dim: 90m x 16.3m x 4.9m; 16 kt; wpns: 10 x 14.9 cm, 2 x 5.7 cm, 10 Flak 2 cm, 4 torp. tbs. 45.7 cm; scuttled 8/29/43, raised by Ger. → tng. ship **Nordland.**

Torpedo boats

Dragen (Dragen 31 class), 1942 → Kriegsmarine **TFA 3**, sunk 5/14/45 (mine off Flensburg) • **Hvalen**, 1942 → Kriegsmarine **TFA 5 • Laxen**, 1942 → Kriegsmarine **TFA 6** blt. 1931; 290 t; dim: 60.6m x 5.9m x 2.4m; 27.5 kt; wpns: 2 x 7.5 cm, 2 Flak 2 cm, 8 torp. tbs. 45.7 cm • **Glenten** (Dragen 34 class), 1942 → Kriegsmarine **TFA 4 • Hogen**, 1942 → Kriegsmarine **TFA 1 • Ornen**, 1942 → Kriegsmarine **TFA 2** blt. 1939; 290 t; dim: 60.6m x 5.9m x 2.4m; 27.5 kt; wpns: 2 x 8.7 cm, 2 Flak 2 cm, 6 torp. tbs. 45.7 cm, depth charges.

Najaden (class) • **Nymphen** blt. 1942/43; 710 t; dim: 86.3m x 8.3m x 3.1m; 35 kt; wpns: 2 x 8.7 cm, 2 Flak 4 cm, 4 Flak 2 cm, 6 torp. tbs. 53.3 cm, depth charges.

Submarines

Rota (class) • **Bellona** scuttled 8/29/1940 (Copenhagen) • **Flora** blt. 1919/21; 290/369 t; dim: 47.5m x 4.4m 2.9m; 14.5/8 kt; wpns: 1 x 5.7 cm, 3 torp. tbs. 45.7 cm • **Daphne** (class) scuttled 8/29/1943 (Copenhagen) • **Dryaden** blt. 1926/27; 300/380 t; dim: 49m x 4.9m x 2.5m; 13.4/6.8 kt; wpns: 1 x 7.5 cm, 1 Flak 2 cm, 6 torp. tbs. 45.7 cm • **Havmanden** (class) scuttled 8/29/1943 (Copenhagen) • **Havfruen** scuttled 8/29/1943 (Copenhagen) • **Havhesten** scuttled 8/29/1943 (Copenhagen) • **Havkalen** scuttled 8/29/1943 (Copenhagen) blt. 1938/40; 320/402 t; dim: 47.5m x 4.4m x 2.8m; 15/8 kt; wpns: 2 Flak 4 cm, 5 torp. tbs. 45.7.

Fishery protection vessels

Beskytteren blt. 1900; mod. 1920; 415 t; dim: 43.4m x 7.5m x 3.8m; 11 kt; wpns: 1 x 5.7 cm,

1943 → Kreigsmarine • **Islands Falk** blt. 1906; mod. 1921; 730 t; dim: 55.9m x 8.9m x 5.1m; 11.7 kt; wpns: 2 x 7.5 cm, 2 x 4.7 cm • **Hvidbjornen** blt. 1929; 1,050 t; dim: 60m x 9.8m x 4m; 4.5 kt; wpns: 2 x 8.7 cm, 2 Flak 1.3 cm, 1 aircraft, 1943 → Kriegsmarine • **Hejmdal** blt. 1935; 705 t; dim: 53.3m x 9.1m x 3.7m; 12.5 kt; wpns: 2 x 7.5 cm, 4 Flak 2 cm, 1943 → Kriegsmarine • **Freja** blt. 1939; 322 t; dim: 40.8m x 7.7m x 2.2m; 10.5 kt; wpns: 2 x 7.5 cm, 2 Flak 2 cm, 1943 → Kriegsmarine.

Minelayers

Lossen blt. 1910; 640 t; dim: 45.5m x 8.5m x 3m; 12 kt; wpns: 2 x 7.5 cm, 175 mines, 1943 → Kriegsmarine • **Lindormen** blt. 1940; 614 t; dim: 51m x 8.8m x 2.4m; 14 kt; wpns: 2 x 7.5 cm, 3 Flak 2 cm, mines, 1943 → Kriegsmarine **VS 1401 • Laaland** blt. 1940; 260 t; dim: 30.9m x 6m x 2m; 11 kt; scuttled 8/29/1943 • **Laugen** blt. 1940; 260 t; dim: 30.9m x 6m x 2m; 11 kt; scuttled 8/29/1943.

Minesweepers

Soloven (class) seized 8/29/1943 in Korsor by Ger. → **MA 1 • Sobjornen** scuttled 8/29/1943 (Holmen); raised by Ger. → **MA 2 • Soulven** scuttled 8/29/1943 (Holmen) • **Sohesten** seized 8/29/1943 in Kalundborg by Ger. → **MA 5 • Sohunden** scuttled 8/29/1943 (Holmen); raised by Ger. → **MA 6 • Soridden** seized 8/29/1943 in Korsor by Ger. → **MA 4** blt. 1939/42; 274 t; dim: 53.8m x 6.3m x 2m; 19 kt; wpns: 2 x 7.5 cm, 2 Flak 2 cm, depth charges, mines if required.

FINLAND

The president of Finland was also C-in-C of the navy. Strength in 1939 was approximately 4,000 men. Used operationally to support the army in the Winter War 1939/40. 1941–44 cooperated with the Kriegsmarine in the Baltic and Gulf of Finland against the Soviet Baltic Fleet.

Coastal warships

Väinämöinen (class) • **Ilmarinen** blt. 1932/33; 3,900 t; dim: 93m x 16.9m x 4.5m; 15 kt; wpns: 4 x 25.4 cm, 8 Flak 10.5 cm, 4 Flak 4 cm, 2 Flak 2 cm; sunk 9/13/1941 (mine off Utö Island).

Submarines

Vetehinen (class) • **Iku-Turso • Vesihiisi** blt. 1930/31; 493/715 t; dim: 63.5m x 6.2m x 3.3m; 15/9 kt; range: 1,500 naut. miles at 10 kt; submerged: 75 naut. miles at 4 kt; wpns: 1 x 7.6 cm, 1 Flak 2 cm, 4 torp. tbs., 53.3 cm, 20 mines.

Experimental submarines

Saukko blt. 1930; 99/136 t; dim: 32.5m x 4.1m x 3.2m; 9/5 kt; range: 375 naut. miles at 8 kt; submerged: 45 naut. miles at 4 kt; wpns: 1 Flak 2 cm, 2 torp. tbs. 45.7 cm, 9 mines • **Vesikko** blt. 1936; 250/300 t; dim: 40.9m x 4m x 3.8m; 13/7 kt; range: 1,500 naut. miles at 10 kt; submerged: 50 naut. miles at 4 kt; wpns: 1 Flak 2 cm, 3 torp. tbs. 53.3 cm.

Patrol boats

Hämeenma • Uusimaa ex Russ. → 1918 Finland 400 t; dim: 42m x 7.5m x 3.4m; 15 kt; wpns: 2 x 10 cm, 1 x 4 cm, 2 Flak 2 cm, 40 mines. • **Karjala • Turunmaa** ex Russ. → 1918 Finland 342 t; dim: 50m x 6.9m x 2.9m; 15 kt; wpns: 2 x 7.5 cm, 1 Flak 4 cm, 2 Flak 2 cm, 30 mines • **Tursas • Visko** blt. 1940/41; 360 t; dim: 40m x 7m x 4.4m; 12 kt; wpns: 1 x 7.5 cm, 1 Flak 4 cm, 2 Flak 2 cm; sunk 9/16/1943 (by Sovt. aircraft Gulf of Finland).

Minelayers

Louhi ex Russ. → 1918 Finland blt. 1916; 640 t; dim: 50m x 8m x 2.6m; 11 kt; wpns: 1 x 7.5 cm, 1 Flak 4 cm, 2 Flak 2 cm, 140 mines; sunk 1/12/1945 (mine off Hanko).

Minelayers/minesweepers

Riilahti (class) sunk 8/23/1943 (Sovt. torpedo boat in Gulf of Finland) • **Rautu • Ruotsinsalmi • Vilppula** sunk 7/25/1944 (Sovt. aircraft in Gulf of Finland) blt. 1940; 290 t; dim: 50.1m x 7.9m x 1.8m; 15 kt; wpns: 1 Flak 4 cm, 2 Flak 2 cm, 100 mines.

GREECE

The Navy Department was the highest command authority. The fleet had, above all, been created with escort and coastal protection in mind. Strength amounted to some 8,000 men and reserves of 11,000. After the 1941 defeat, the remainder of the Greek Navy succeeded in reaching Egypt, where they joined the Royal Navy as the Greek Navy in exile.

Operational: Mediterranean, Indian Ocean, Normandy invasion.

Cruisers

Georgios Averoff blt. 1911 Ital. → 1927 Greece; 9,450 t; dim: 140.8m x 21m x 5m; 22 kt; wpns: 4 x 23.4 cm, 8 x 19 cm, 4 x 7.6 cm, 2 Flak 4 cm, 5 Flak 4 cm, 3 torp. tbs. 45.7 cm • **Elli** blt. 1914 USA → 1928 Greece; 2,115 t; dim: 98.1m x 11.9m x 4m; 21 kt; wpns: 3 x 15.2 cm, 2 Flak 4 cm, 2 torp. tbs. 45.7 cm, 100 mines; sunk 8/15/1940 (Ital. submarine Delfino off Tenos).

Destroyers

Aetos (class) • **Ierax • Leon** sunk 4/22/1941 (Luftwaffe off Piraeus • **Panthir** blt. 1912 GB → 1927 Greece; 1,013 t; dim: 89.3m x 8.5m x 2.6m; 32 kt; wpns: 4 x 10.2 cm, 2 Flak 4 cm, 6 torp. tbs. 53.3 cm • **Indra** (class) sunk 4/22/1941 (Luftwaffe off Piraeus) • **Kountouriotis • Psara** sunk 4/20/1941 (Luftwaffe off Piraeus) • **Spetsai** blt. 1932/33 Ital.; 1,329 t; dim: 92.4m x 9.8m x 2.5m; 39.5/41.8 kt; wpns: 4 x 12 cm, 3 Flak 4 cm, 6 torp. tbs. 53.3 cm, 40 mines if required • **Vasilefs Georgios** (class) sunk 4/20/1941 (Luftwaffe off Salamina); raised by Ger. → ZG 3 • **Vasilissa Olga** sunk 9/26/1943 (Luftwaffe off Leros) blt. 1939 GB; 1,414 t; dim: 97.6m x 10.1m x 2.6m; 36 kt; wpns: 4 x 12.7 cm, 4 Flak 3.7 cm, 8 torp. tbs. 53.3 cm.

Salamis (ex GB **Boreas** → 4/1944 Greece) blt. 1931 GB; 1,360 t; dim: 98.1m x 9.8m x 2.6m; 35 kt; wpns: 3 x 12 cm, 1 Flak 7.6 cm, 2 Flak 4 cm, 2 Flak 2 cm, 4 torp. tbs. 53.3 cm, depth charges • **Navarinon** (ex GB **Echo** → 4/1944 Greece) blt. 1934 GB; 1,405 t; dim: 100.3m x 10.1m x 2.6m; 35.5 kt; wpns: 4 x 12 cm, 1 Flak 7.6 cm • **Aigaion** (Hunt II class, GB ex GB **Avon Vale** – 3/1944 Greece → 5/1944 GB) • **Kriti** (ex GB **Hursley** → 12/1943 Greece) • **Themistoklis** (ex GB **Braham** → 3/1941 Greece) blt. 1941/42; 1,050 t; dim: 85.3m x 9.6m x 2.4m; 27 kt; wpns: 6 x 10.2 cm, 4 Flak 4 cm, 2 Flak 2 cm, depth charges.

Adrias (Hunt III class GB) (ex GB **Border** → 5/1942 Greece) sunk 10/22/1943 (mine off Kalimnos) • **Kanaris** (ex GB **Hatherleigh** → 7/1942 Greece) • **Miaoulis** (ex GB **Modbury** → 11/1942 Greece) • **Pindos** (ex GB **Bolingbroke** → 5/1942 Greece) blt. 1942 GB; 1,087 t; dim: 85.3m x 9.6m x 2.4m; 27 kt; wpns: 4 x 10.2 cm, 4 Flak 4 cm, 2–3 Flak 2 cm, 2 torp. tbs. 53.3 cm, depth charges.

Torpedo boats

Aspis · **Niki**

blt. 1907 Ger.; 275 t; dim: 67.1m x 6.3m x 2m; 24 kt; wpns: 2 x 8.8 cm, 1 Flak 4 cm, 2 torp. tbs. 45.7 cm.

Sphendoni · **Thyella** sunk 4/22/1941 (Luftwaffe Piraeus area)

blt. 1905 GB; 305 t; dim: 67.1m x 6.3m x 2.1m; 24 kt; wpns: 2 x 8.8 cm, 1 Flak 4 cm, 2 torp. tbs. 45.7 cm.

Kios sunk 4/22/1941 (Luftwaffe Piraeus area) · **Kyzikos** sunk 4/25/1941 (Luftwaffe off Salamina) · **Kyzikos** sunk 4/25/1941 (Luftwaffe off Salamina) · **Kidonia** (ex war booty) sunk 4/26/1941 (Luftwaffe north of Peloponnese)

blt. 1915; 241 t; dim: 60m x 6.5m x 1.8m; 24 kt; wpns: 2 Flak 4 cm, 2 torp. tbs. 45.7 cm.

Pergamos (ex war booty) · **Proussa** sunk 4/4/1941 (Luftwaffe off Crete)

blt. 1915; 241 t; dim: 57.4m x 5.7m x 1.9m; 24 kt; wpns: 2 Flak 4 cm, 2 torp. tbs. 45.7 cm; sunk 4/25/1941 (Luftwaffe, Salamina).

Submarines

Katsonis (class) sunk 9/14/1943 (Kriegsmarine, Aegean) · **Papanikolis**

blt. 1927 Fr.; 576/775 t; dim: 62.3m x 5.3m x 3.4m; 14/9.5 kt; range: 3,500 naut. miles at 10 kt; submerged: 100 naut. miles at 5 kt; wpns: 1 x 10 cm, 1 Flak 4 cm, 6 torp. tbs. 53.3 cm ·

Glafkos (class) sunk 4/4/1942 (Luftwaffe off Malta) · **Nereus** · **Proteus** sunk 12/12/1940 (Ital. Navy, south Adriatic) · **Triton** sunk 11/16/1942 (Kriegsmarine west of Eubei)

blt. 1928 Fr.; 730/960 t; dim: 66.8m x 5.7m x 4m; 14/9.5 kt; range: 4,000 naut. miles at 10 kt; submerged: 100 naut. miles at 5 kt; wpns: 1 x 10 cm, 1 Flak 4 cm, 6 torp. tbs. 53.3 cm.

Xifias (ex GB Untiring → 7/1945 Greece) · **Amfitriti** (ex GB Upstart → 8/1943 Greece)

blt. 1943 GB; 545/735 t; dim: 60m x 4.9m x 3.9m; 11.7/9 kt; range: 4,500 naut. miles at 10 kt; submerged: 30 naut. miles at 9 kt; wpns: 1 Flak 7.6 cm, 4 torp. tbs. 53.3 cm.

Pipinos (ex GB Veldt – 1945 Greece) · **Delfin** (ex GB Vengeful – 1944 Greece)

blt. 1943 GB; 545/740 t; dim: 62.3m x 4.9m x 3.9m; 12.7/9 kt; range: 4,700 naut. miles at 10 kt; submerged: 30 naut. miles at 9 kt; wpns: 1 Flak 7.6 cm, 4 torp. tbs. 53.3 cm.

Matrozos (ex GB P 712, ex Ital. Perla) blt. 1936 Ital.; 618/855 t; dim: 60.2m x 6.4m x 4.7m; 14/7.5 kt; range: 5,200 naut. miles at 8 kt; submerged: 74 naut. miles at 4 kt; wpns: 1 x 10.2 cm, 2 Flak 1.3 cm, 6 torp. tbs. 53.3 cm.

Corvettes

Apostolis (ex GB Hyacinth → 1943 Greece) · **Kriezis** (ex GB Goreopsis → 1943 Greece) · **Sachtouris** (ex GB Peony → 1943 Greece) · **Tompazis** (ex GB Tamarisk → 1943 Greece)

blt. 1940/41 GB (Flower class); 925 t; dim: 62.5m x 10.1m x 4.4m; 16 kt; wpns: 1 x 10.2 cm, 1 Flak 4 cm, 4 Flak 2 cm, 6 depth-charge launchers.

MTBs/MGBs

Vasilefs Georgios (ex US PC 622 → 1943 Greece) blt. 1942 USA; 280 t; dim: 53.3m x 7m x 2.3m; 20 kt; wpns: 1 Flak 7.6 cm, 1 Flak 4 cm, 5 Flak 2 cm, 4 depth-charge launchers.

Minelayers/trawlers

Tenedos blt. 1906 GB; 460 t; dim: 43.3m x 7.3m x 3m, 13 kt; 40 mines; seized by Ger. 1941 → **UJ 2106** · **Korgialenios** blt. 1916 Holl.; 380 t; dim: 45.7m x 6.7m x 3m; 13.5 kt; 50 mines; seized by

Ger. 1941 → **UJ 2110** · **Paralos** blt. 1925 Holl.; 395 t; dim: 45.7m x 6.7m x 3m; 52 mines; seized by Ger. 1941 → **UJ 2101** · **Pleias** blt. 1926 Ital.; 520 t; dim: 49.4m x 8.2m x 3.7m; 14 kt; 50 mines; seized (?) 4/1941.

Minesweeping/trawlers

Aliakmon sunk (?) 4/1941 · **Axios** sunk (?) 4/1941 · **Nestos** sunk (?) 4/1941 · **Strymon** seized by Ger. 1941 → **UJ 2101**

blt. 1926 GB; 500 t; dim: 42.3m x 7.2m x 4.1m; 11 kt; wpns: 1 x 3.7 cm; 40 mines.

Coastal minesweepers

Kassos (ex GB Byms 2074 → 12/15/1943 Greece) sunk 10/15/1944 (mine off Piraeus) · **Paralos** (ex GB Byms 2066 → 8/12/1944 Greece) · **Karteria** (ex GB Byms 2065 → 8/12/1944 Greece) · **Salaminia** (ex GB Byms 2067 → 12/8/1944 Greece)

blt. 1943 USA; 207 t; dim: 41.5m x 7.5m x 1.8m; 12 kt; wpns: 1 Flak 7.6 cm, 2 Flak 2 cm.

Afroessa (ex GB Byms 2185 → 8/12/1944 Greece) · **Kos** (ex GB Byms 2190 → 12/15/1943 Greece) · **Leros** (ex GB Byms 2186 → 12/15/1943 Greece) · **Patmos** (ex GB Byms 2229 → 12/15/1943 Greece)

blt. 1943 USA; 215 t; dim: 41.5m x 7.5m x 1.8m; 12 kt; wpns: 1 Flak 7.6 cm, 2 Flak 2 cm.

INDIA

Operationally, the Royal Indian Navy was under the control of the Royal Navy from 1939. The RIN comprised 5 coastal protection vessels, 1 patrol boat, 1 survey ship and several smaller units. Strength comprised approximately 2,300 men. 1940–45 the navy was expanded by 6 coastal protection vessels, 1 corvette, 16 minesweepers and several smaller units.

Operational: Mediterranean, mainly Indian Ocean.

IRAN

Gunboats

Babr (class) sunk 8/1941 (GB warship off Khorramshahr) · **Palang** sunk 8/1941 (GB warship off Abadan)

blt. 1932 Ital.; 950 t; dim: 62.4m x 9m x 3.1m; 15 kt; wpns: 4 x 10.2 cm.

Patrol boats

Chahbaaz (class) seized by India 8/1941 → Hira – 1946 Iran · **Charokh** seized by India 8/1941 → Nilam – 1946 Iran · **Karkas** seized by India 8/1941 → Moti – 1946 Iran · **Simorgh** seized by India 8/1941 → Lal – 1946 Iran

blt. 1932 Ital.; 331 t; dim: 51.8m x 6.7m x 1.8m; 15 kt; wpns: 2 x 7.6 cm, 2 x 3.7 cm.

MANCHUKUO

Founded 1934, empire under Japanese protection.

River gunboats

1 x blt. 1903, former Ger. **Risui**; 220 t; 9 larger, 6 smaller, 3 medium (blt. 1895) 360 t; 2 Jap. class Junten blt. 1940; 270 t; 13 kt; 2 Flak 12 cm; 2 Jap. Teihen class, blt. 1940; 290 t; 13 kt; 3 Flak 1.2 cm; 30 patrol boats, 30 t-190 t; 1 destroyer (Jap. Momo class) blt. 1917 Jap.; 755 t; dim: 75.8m x 7.7m x 2.4m; 31.5 kt; wpns: 3 x 12 cm, 6 torp. tbs. 45.7 cm.

MEXICO

Gunboats

Nicolas Bravo blt. 1903 Ital.; 1,227 t; dim: 73.8m x 10.4m x 3m; 12.2 kt; wpns: 2 x 10.2 cm, 4 x 5.7 cm.

Potosi (class) · **Guanajuato** · **Queretaro**

blt. 1935 Span.; 1,300 t; dim: 79.2m x 11.4m x 3m; 20 kt; wpns: 3 x 10.2 cm, 4 Flak 2.5 cm, 4 Flak 1.3 cm.

Durango (class) blt. 1936 Span.; 1,600 t; dim: 86m x 12.3m x 3m; 20 kt; wpns: 2 x 10.2 cm, 4 Flak 2.5 cm, 4 Flak 1.3 cm.

Patrol boats

Acapulco (class) · **Mazatlan** · **Veracruz**

blt. 1920 Can.; 486 t; dim: 40.5m x 7.3m x 4.1m; 8 kt; wpns: 1 x 5.7 cm.

NETHERLANDS

The navy was under the control of the Defence Ministry. In 1939 the navy was divided into the Home Fleet, the colonies of the Dutch East Indies and the Dutch West Indies. In 1939 the navy's strength amounted to some 11,750 men, including 4,000 marines. The navy hardly saw any action when the Germans invaded in May 1940 but suffered heavy losses. Only 1 light cruiser, 1 destroyer and 4 small torpedo boats succeeded in making their way to Great Britain where they became the basis for a Royal Netherlands Navy in exile under the Royal Navy, equipped further with ships from Great Britain and the USA.

Operational: Pacific and Indian oceans, Battle of the Atlantic, the Normandy invasion.

Coastal warships

Soerabaja (tng. ship) blt. 1910, mod. 1936; 5,664 t; dim: 103.5m x 17.1m x 6.2m; 16 kt; wpns: 2 x 28 cm, 2 x 7.5 cm, 6 Flak 4 cm, 6 Flak 1.3 cm; sunk 2/12/1942 (Jap. air force Surabaja).

Cruisers

Gelderland (tng. ship – blt. 1900; 3,512 t; dim: 95m x 14.8m x 5.4m; 18 kt; wpns: 8 x 12 cm, 4 x 7.6 cm, 2 Flak 3.7 cm, 1 Flak 4 cm, 4 Flak 1.3 cm; seized by Ger. 1940 → Flak ship Niobe.

Sumatra sunk 6/9/1944 (part of artificial harbor/Normandy coast) · **Java** sunk 2/27/1945 (Jap. warships Java Sea)

blt. 1925/26; 6,670 t; dim: 155.3m x 16m x 5m; 31 kt; wpns: 10 x 15 cm, 8 Flak 4 cm, 4 Flak 1.3 cm, 12 mines, 2 aircraft.

De Ruyter blt. 1936; 6,450 t; dim: 170.9m x 15.7m x 5m; 32 kt; wpns: 7 x 15 cm, 10 Flak 4 cm, 8 Flak 1.3 cm, 2 aircraft; sunk 2/27/1942 (Jap. warships Java Sea) · **Tromp** blt. 1938; 3,450 t; dim: 132m x 12.4m x 3.2m; 33.5 kt; wpns: 6 x 15 cm, 4 Flak 7.6 cm, 8 Flak 4 cm, 6 Flak 2 cm, 6 torp. tbs. 53.3 cm, 1 aircraft · **Jacob van Heemskerck** blt. 1940; 3,450 t; dim: 132m x 12.4m x 3.2m; 33.5 kt; wpns: 6 x 15 cm, 10 Flak 10.2 cm, 8 Flak 4 cm, 8 Flak 2 cm.

Destroyers

Van Ghent (class) scuttled 2/15/1942 (Bangka Island/Pacific) · **Eversten** sunk 3/1/1942 (Jap. warships, Sunda Strait)

Kortenaer sunk 2/27/1942 (Jap. warships Java Sea) · **Piet Hein** sunk 2/19/1942 (Jap. warships southwest of Bali)

blt. 1928; 1,310 t; dim: 98m x 9.5m x 3m; 36 kt; wpns: 4 x 12 cm, 2 Flak 7.5 cm, 4 Flak 1.3 cm, 6 torp. tbs. 53.3 cm, 24 mines.

Banckert (van Ghent class, mod.) badly damaged 2/28/1942 (Jap. air force); scuttled 3/2/1942; raised by Jap. → **No. 106** · **Van Galen** sunk 5/10/1940 (Luftwaffe Rotterdam) · **Van Nes** sunk 2/17/1942 (Jap. air force south of Bangka/Pacific) · **Witte de With** badly damaged 3/1/1942 (Jap. air force); scuttled 3/2/1942 (Surabaja) blt. 1929/31; 1,316 t; dim: 98m x 9.5m x 3m; 36 kt; wpns: 4 x 12 cm, 1 Flak 7.5 cm, 4 Flak 4 cm, 4 Flak 1.3 cm, 6 torp. tbs. 53.3 cm.

Isaac Sweers (class) sunk 11/13/1942 (**U 431** off Algiers) · **Gerard Callenburgh** scuttled 4/15/1940 (Rotterdam), raised by Ger. → **ZH1** · **Philips van Almonde** scuttled 5/17/1940 (Vlissingen Shipyards) · **Tjerk Hiddes** scuttled 5/15/1940 (Rotterdam)

blt. 1940 (finished in GB); 1,628 t; dim: 106.3m x 10.3m x 3.2m; 37.5 kt; wpns: 6 Flak 10.2 cm, 4 Flak 4 cm, 8 Flak 2 cm, 8 torp. tbs. 53.3 cm, depth charges.

Tjerk Hiddes (GB "N" class, ex GB **Nonpareil** → 5/27/1942 Neth.) · **Van Galen** (ex GB **Noble** → 2/11/1942 Neth.)

blt. 1942; 1,773 t; dim: 108.7m x 10.9m x 2.7m; 36 kt; wpns: 6 x 12 cm, 1 Flak 10.2 cm, 4 Flak 4 cm, 6 Flak 2 cm, 8 torp. tbs. 53.3 cm, 3 depth-charge launchers.

Torpedo boats

Z 6 scrapped in GB 2/1943 · **Z 7** · **Z 8** scrapped in GB 8/1944

blt. 1916/17; 263 t; dim: 58m x 6m x 1.7m; 27 kt; wpns: 2 x 7.5 cm, 2 Flak 1.3 cm, 4 torp. tbs. 45 cm.

Z 3 mod. 1932; 22 kt; without torp. tbs. 1940 → GB **Blade** sunk 5/19/1940 (Enkhuizen)

blt. 1920; 277 t; dim: 61m x 6.2m x 1.9m; 27 kt; wpns: 2 x 7.5 cm, 2 Flak 1.3 cm, 4 torp. tbs. 45 cm.

Submarines

O 8 (GB H class) blt. 1915 Can. → Neth.; 388/440 t; dim: 46.2m x 4.6m x 3.9m; 11.5/8 kt; range: 1,350 naut. miles at 11 kt; wpns: 1 Flak 3.7 cm, 4 torp. tbs. 45.7 cm; seized 5/14/1940 by Ger. → **VD 1**, destroyed 5/3/1945 Kiel · **K V** (class) · **K VII** sunk 2/18/1942 (Jap. air force Surabaja)

blt. 1922; 499/640 t; dim: 57.3m x 5.1m x 3.8m; 13.5/8 kt; range: 3,500 naut. miles at 12 kt; submerged: 13 naut. miles at 8 kt; wpns: 1 x 7.6 cm, 1 Flak 1.3 cm, 6 torp. tbs. 45 cm.

K VIII (class) taken out of service 8/27/1942 (Australia) · **K IX** taken out of service 8/27/1942 (Australia) · **K X** sunk 3/1/1942 (Jap. warship south of Java)

blt. 1922/23, 513/715 t; dim: 64.2m x 5.5m x 3.6m; 15/9.5 kt; range: 3,500 naut. miles at 11 kt; submerged: 12 naut. miles at 8.5 kt; wpns: 1 x 8.8 cm, 1 Flak 1.3 cm, 4 torp. tbs. 45 cm.

K XI (class) taken out of service 4/5/1945 (Australia) · **K XII** taken out of service 10/8/1944 (Australia) · **K XIII** badly damaged 12/24/1941 (Singapore); scuttled 3/2/1942 (Surabaja)

blt. 1925/26; 601/820 t; dim: 69.7m x 5.7m x 3.7m; 15/8 kt; range: 3,500 naut. miles at 12 kt; submerged: 13 naut. miles at 8 kt; wpns: 1 x 8.8 cm, 1 Flak 1.3 cm, 2 torp. tbs. 53.3 cm, 4 torp. tbs. 45 cm.

O 9 (class) taken out of service 12/20/1944 (GB) · **O 10** taken out of service 10/12/1944 (GB) · **O 11** seized 5/14/1940 by Ger. (Den Helder), destroyed 9/1944

blt. 1926; 474/645 t; dim: 54.9m x 5.5m x 3.5m; 12/8 kt; range: 3,500 naut. miles at 8 kt; submerged: 11 naut. miles at 7.5 kt; wpns: 1 x 8.8 cm, 1 Flak 1.3 cm, 2 torp. tbs. 45 cm, 3 torp. tbs. 45 cm.

O 12 (class) seized 5/14/1940 by Ger. (Den Helder) → **UD 2** destroyed 5/3/1945 Kiel · **O 13** sunk 6/13/1940 (mine North Sea) · **O 14** taken out of service 9/5/1943 (GB) · **O 15**

blt. 1931/3; 537/700 t; dim: 60.4m x 5.6m x

3.6m; 15/8 kt; range: 3,500 naut. miles at 10 kt; submerged: 12 naut. miles at 8 kt; wpns: 2 Flak 4 cm, 5 torp. tbs. 53.3 cm.

K XIV (class) · **K XV** · **K XVI** sunk 12/24/1941 (Jap. warships near Kushingu Sarawak) · **K XVII** missing 12/19/1941 (?) east of Malacca Straits) · **K XVIII** scuttled 3/2/1942 (Surabaja) blt. 1934/5; 759/1 020 t; dim: 73.9m x 7.6m x 3.9m; 17/9 kt; range: 3,500 naut. miles at 11 kt; submerged: 26 naut. miles at 8.5 kt.

O 16 (class) blt. 1936; 882/1 170 t; dim: 77.5m x 6.6m x 4m; 18/9 kt; wpns: 1 x 8.8 cm, 2 Flak 4 cm, 8 torp. tbs. 53.3 cm; sunk 12/15/1941 (mine east of Malaysian peninsula).

O 19 (minelaying-submarine class) ran aground 7/8/1945 (China Sea); scuttled 7/10/1945 · **O 20** scuttled 12/19/1941 (Bay of Siam)

blt. 1939; 967/1 468 t; dim: 80.7m x 7.4m x 3.9m; 19.2/9 kt; range: 6,150 naut. miles at 12 kt; wpns: 1 x 8.8 cm, 2 Flak 4 cm, 1 Flak 1.3 cm, 8 torp. tbs. 53.3 cm, 40 mines.

O 21 (class) · **O 22** sunk 11/8/1940 (Ger. warship near Lindesnes, south Norway) · **O 23** · **O 24** · **O 25** scuttled 5/1940 (Rotterdam); raised by Ger. → **VD 3**, destroyed 5/3/1945 (Kiel) · **O 26** seized by Ger. 5/1940 (Rotterdam shipyards) → **VD 4** destroyed 5/3/1945 (Kiel) · **O 27** seized by Ger. 5/1940 (Rotterdam shipyards) → **VD 5** − 5/1945 Neth.

blt. 1940; 888/ (?) t; dim: 77.7m x 6.6m x 4m; 19.5/9 kt; range: 6,515 naut. miles at 12 kt; wpns: 1 x 8.8 cm, 2 Flak 4 cm, 1 Flak 1.3 cm, 8 torp. tbs. 53.3 cm.

Zeehond (GB Sturgeon class → 10/11/1943 Neth.) blt. 1932/(?) GB; 640/935 t; dim: 61.2m x 7.2m x 3.2m; 13.7/10 kt; range: 3,690 naut. miles at 10 kt; wpns: 1 x 7.6 cm, 1 Flak 2 cm, 6 torp. tbs. 53.3 cm · **Dolfijn** (ex GB **P 47** → 1942 Neth.) blt. 1942 GB; 545/735 t; dim: 60m x 4.9m x 3.9m; 11.7/9 kt; range: 4,500 naut. miles at 10 kt; wpns: 1 Flak 7.6 cm, 1 Flak 2 cm, 4 torp. tbs. 53.3 cm.

Tijgerhaai (GB T class ex **Tarn** → 1945 Neth.) · **Zwaaardvis** (GB T class, ex GB **Talent** → 12/6/1943 Neth.)

blt. 1943/45 GB; 1,090/1,570 t; dim: 83.4m x 8.1m x 4.5m; 15/8.5 kt; range: 9,000 naut. miles at 10 kt; wpns: 1 x 10.2 cm, 1 Flak 2 cm, 11 torp. tbs. 53.3 cm.

Escort vessels

Van Kinsbergen blt. 1939; 1,700 t; dim: 103m x 11.6m x 3.1m; 25.5 kt; wpns: 4 x 12 cm, 4 Flak 4 cm · **Van Nassau** (GB River class, ex GB **Ribble** → 6/25/1943 Neth.) blt. 1943 GB; 1,370 t; dim: 91.8m x 11.1m x 2.7m; 20 kt; wpns: 2 x 10.2 cm, 4 Flak 2 cm, depth-charge launchers · **Friso** (GB Flower class, ex GB **Carnation** → 1943 Neth. → 2/18/1945 → GB) blt. 1941; 925 t; dim: 62.5m x 10.1m x 3.5m; 16 kt; wpns: 1 x 10.2 cm, 1 Flak 4 cm, depth charges.

Gunboats

Brinio (class) damaged 5/14/1940 (Luftwaffe); scuttled (Ijsselmeer) · **Friso** damaged 5/12/1940 (Luftwaffe); scuttled (Ijsselmeer) · **Gruno** blt. 1914/15; 542 t; dim: 52.5m x 8.5m x 2.8m; 14 kt; wpns: 4 x 10.5 cm, 1 Flak 1.3 cm.

Flores (class) · **Soemba**

blt. 1926; 1,457 t; dim: 76m x 11.5m x 3.6m; 15 kt; wpns: 3 x 15 cm, 1 Flak 7.6 cm, 4 Flak 1.3 cm, 1 aircraft.

J. M. van Nassau blt. 1933; 1,520 t; dim: 79m x 11.5m x 3.7m; 15 kt; wpns: 3 x 15 cm, 2 Flak 4 cm, 4 Flak 1.3 cm, 1 aircraft; sunk 5/14/1940 (Luftwaffe off Callantsoog Island).

Coastal protection vessels (former customs or police launches)

Albatros blt. 1911; 807 t; dim: 50m x 9.4m x 3.3m; 12.2 kt; wpns: 2 x 7.5 cm, scuttled 3/2/1942 (Surabaja); raised by Jap. → **Abatoe Maru** → 1945 Neth.

Aldebaran blt. 1913; 725 t; dim: 53.3m x 8.2m x 3.5m; 12.2 kt; scuttled 3/2/1942 (Surabaja).

Bellatrix (class) scuttled 3/1/1942 (Tanjong Priok/Java); raised by Jap. → 1945 Neth. · **Canopus** sunk 3/5/1942 (Jap. air force, south of Java); raised by Jap. → **Ariake Maru** → 1945 Neth. · **Deneb** sunk 2/4/1942 (Jap. air force Riau Archipelago)

blt. 1914/15; 763/773 t; dim: 53.3m x 9m x 3m; 12.2 kt; wpns: 2 x 7.5 cm.

Gemma blt. 1918; 795 t; dim: 53.3m x 9m x 3.2m; 12.2 kt; wpns: 2 x 7.5 cm; scuttled 3/2/1942 (Surabaja); raised by Jap. → **Kita Maru** → 1945 Neth. · **Eridamus** blt. 1918; 926 t; dim: 56.5m x 9m x 3.5m; 12 kt; wpns: 2 x 7.5 cm; scuttled 3/2/1942 (Surabaja); raised by Jap. → **Enoshima Maru** → 1945 Neth.

Sirius (class) scuttled 2/28/1942 (west of Java) · **Wega** sunk 1/26/1942 (Jap. air force)

blt. 1922; 936 t; dim: 55.6m x 9.5m x 3.3m; 12.2 kt; wpns: 2 x 7.5 cm

Fomalhout blt. 1923; 800 t; dim: 56.7m x 9.4m x 3.4m; 13.5 kt; wpns: 2 x 7.5 cm; scuttled 3/2/1942 (Surabaja) · **Merel** blt. 1928; 592 t; dim: 46.5m x 8.4m x 2.8m; 12 kt; wpns: 1 x 7.5 cm; scuttled 3/2/1942 (Tanjong Priok/Java).

Arend (class) scuttled 3/1/1942 (Tanjong Priok/Java); raised by Jap. → **No. 108** · **Valk** scuttled 3/2/1942 (Tjilatjap/Jap.); raised by Jap. → **No. 104** blt. 1929; 1,011 t; dim: 70m x 9m x 2.8m; 12 kt; wpns: 2 x 7.5 cm, 2 Flak 1.3 cm, 1 aircraft. **Fazant** (class) scuttled 3/1/1942 (Tanjong Priok/Java); raised by Jap. → **No. 109** → 1945 Neth. · **Reiger** ran aground 2/28/1942 (northwest Java) blt. 1930; 592 t; dim: 47.8m x 8.4m x 2.8m; 12 kt; wpns: 1 x 7.5 cm.

MTBs/MGBs (new class)

Queen Wilhelmina (US class PC, ex **PC 468** → 8/1942 Neth.) blt. 1942 USA; 280 t; dim: 53.3m x 7m x 2.3m; 20 kt; wpns: 1 Flak 7.6 cm, 1 Flak 4 cm, 5 Flak 2 cm, depth-charge launchers.

Minelayers

Hydra (class) sunk 5/15/1940 (Ger. forces Duiveland) · **Medusa** blt. 1911/2; 593 t; dim: 50m x 9m x 2.8m; 12 kt; wpns: 3 Flak 7.6 cm, 2 Flak 1.3 cm, 70 mines.

Douwe Aukes (class) · **Van Meerlant** sunk 6/4/1941 (mines Thames estuary)

blt. 1922; 687 t; dim: 55m x 8.7m x 3.2m; 13 kt; wpns: 3 Flak 7.6 cm, 2 Flak 1.3 cm, 60 mines.

Pro Patria blt. 1923; 537 t; dim: 47m x 8.6m x 2.3m; 10 kt; wpns: 1 Flak 7.6 cm, 2 Flak 1.3 cm, 80 mines; scuttled 2/15/1942 (River Musi/Sumatra) · **Krakatau** blt. 1924; 982 t; dim: 65m x 10m x 3.2m; 15.5 kt; wpns: 2 Flak 7.6 cm, 4 Flak 1.3 cm, 150 mines; scuttled 3/8/1942 (Madury coast) · **Nautilus** (class) blt. 1930; 800 t; dim: 58.7m x 9.5m x 3.5m; 15 kt; wpns: 2 x 7.6 cm, 1 Flak 3.7 cm, 2 Flak 4 cm, 1 Flak 1.3 cm, 40 mines; sank 5/22/1941 after collision (GB, Humber) · **Jan van Brakel** blt. 1936; 740 t; dim: 59m x 10m x 3m; 15 kt; wpns: 2 x 7.6 cm, 1 Flak 3.7 cm, 4 Flak 1.3 cm, 80 mines.

Gouden Leeuw (class) scuttled 3/7/1942 (Surabaja) · **Prins van Oranje** sunk 1/12/1942 (Jap. warships east of Borneo)

blt. 1932; 1,261 t; dim: 70m x 11m x 3.3m; 15 kt;

wpns: 2 x 7.6 cm, 2 Flak 4 cm, 2 Flak 1.3 cm, 150 mines.

Willem van der Zaan blt. 1939; 1,390 t; dim: 75.2m x 11.2m x 3.3m; 15 kt; wpns: 2 x 12 cm, 4 Flak 4 cm, 4 Flak 1.3 cm, 120 mines, 1 aircraft **Ram** (class) scuttled 3/3/1942 (Tjilatjap/Java), raised by Jap. → **Nanshin** → Neth. · **Regulus** destroyed by crew 3/2/1942 (Surabaja shipyards); repaired by Jap. → **Nankai**, sunk 7/16/1945 (west of Surabaya)
blt. 1941; 2,220 t; dim: 84.9m x 13m x 3.5m; 18 kt; wpns: not fitted.

Minesweepers
Jan van Amstel (class) sunk 3//8/1942 (Jap. warships, Madury/Java area) · **Abraham Crijnssen** · **Abraham van der Hulst** scuttled 5/14/1940 (Enkhuizen), 8/1940; raised by Ger. → **M 552** → 1945 Neth. · **Eland Dubois** scuttled 3/8/1942 (Madury/Java area) · **Jan van Gelder** · **Pieter de Bitter** scuttled 3/6/1942 (Surabaja) · **Pieter Florisz** scuttled 5/14/1940; 8/1940 raised by Ger. → **M 551** → 1945 Neth. · **Willem van Ewijck** sunk 9/8/1939 (mines Terschelling area) · **Willem van Ewijck** (blt. 1940) seized 5/14/1940 by Ger. (Rotterdam) → **M 553** → 1945 Neth.
blt. 1937; 460 t; dim: 56.6m x 7.8m x 2.2m; 15 kt; wpns: 1 x 7.6 cm, 4 Flak 1.3 cm.

Duiveland (ex GB MMS 1004) · **Ijsselmonde** (ex GB MMS 1026 · **Overflakkee** (ex GB MMS 1046) · **Schockland** (ex GB MMS 1082) · **Tholen** (ex GB MMS 1014) · **Voorne** (ex GB MMS 1043) · **Walcheeren** (ex GB MMS 1042) · **Wieringen** (ex GB MMS 1025)
blt. 1943 GB; 255 t; dim: 42.6m x 7.9m x 3.2m; 10 kt; wpns: 2 Flak 2 cm.

NEW ZEALAND

Operationally, the Royal New Zealand Navy (RNZN) was under the control of the Royal Navy 1939–45. The RNZN in 1939 comprised 2 light cruisers and several smaller units.
Operational: Pacific.

NORWAY

The navy was under the control of the Defence Ministry and was divided into the Naval Staff and Naval district commands (1–5): Horten, Kristiansund, Bergen, Trondheim and Ramsund. In 1939 strength was approximately 2,400 men (including 900 regulars).
Operational April 1940: Despite a spirited resistance, the greater part of the units were sunk or seized by the Germans. Only 5 torpedo boats succeeded in reaching Great Britain. Thereafter, the Norwegian Navy in exile was built up with units from GB and the USA and was operationally under the control of the Royal Navy.
Operational: Battle of the Atlantic, Normandy invasion.

Coastal patrol vessels
Harald Haarfagre seized 4/1940 by Ger. (Horten) → Flak ship **Thetis** · **Tordenskjold** seized 4/1940 by Ger. (Horten) → Flak ship **Nymphe**
blt. 1898 GB; 3,380 t; dim: 92.7m x 14.8m x 5m; 16.9 kt; wpns: 2 x 21 cm, 6 x 12 cm, 6 x 7.6 cm, 2 Flak 7.6 cm, 2 x 3.7 cm · **Eidsvold** sunk 4/9/1940 (Kriegsmarine Narvik) · **Norge** sunk 4/9/1940 (Kriegsmarine Narvik). blt. 1901/2 GB; 3,645 t; dim: 91.8m x 15.4m x 5m; 16.5 kt; wpns: 2 x 21 cm, 6 x 15.2 cm, 8 x 7.6 cm, 2 Flak 4.7 cm.

Destroyers
Bath (US Flush-Decker class, ex US **Hopewell** → 1/1/1941 Norw.) sunk 8/19/1941 (U 201, south-

west of Ireland) · **Lincoln** (ex US **Yarnall** → 2/1942 Norw. → 1942 GB) · **Mansfield** (ex US **Evans** → 12/1940 Norw. → 3/20/1942 GB) · **Newport** (ex US **Sigourney** → 3/1941 Norw. → 6/1942 GB) · **St. Alban** (ex US **Thomas** → 4/18/1941 Norw. → 1942 GB)
blt. 1918/9 USA; 1,060 t; dim: 95.8m x 9.7m x 2.6m; 35 kt; wpns: 3 x 10.2 cm, 1 Flak 7.6 cm, 2 Flak 3.6 cm, 2 Flak 1.3 cm, 6 torp. tbs. 53.3 cm.
Stord (GB S class, ex GB **Success** → 8/1943 Norw.) · **Svenner** (ex GB **Shark** → 3/8/1944 Norw.) 6/6/1944 sunk (Kriegsmarine off Normandy coast)
blt. 1943 GB; 1,710 t; dim: 110.6m x 10.9m x 3m; 36 kt; wpns: 4 x 12 cm, 2 Flak 4 cm, 8 Flak 2 cm, 8 torp. tbs. 53.3 cm, 6 depth-charge launchers.
Arendal (GB Hunt II class, ex GB **Badsworth** → 11/16/1944 Norw.) blt. 1941; 1,050 t; dim: 85.3m x 9.6m x 2.4m; 27 kt; wpns: 6 x 10.2 cm, 4 Flak 4 cm, 2 Flak 2 cm, 5 depth-charge launchers.
Eskdale (GB Hunt III class – 1942 Norw.) sunk 4/14/1943 (Kriegsmarine, English Channel) · **Narvik** (ex GB **Glaisdale** – 6/1/1942 Norw.)
blt. 1942 GB; 1,087 t; dim: 85.3m x 9.6m x 2.4m; 27 kt; wpns: 4 x 10.2 cm, 4 Flak 4 cm, 6 Flak 2 cm, 2 torp. tbs. 53.3 cm, 4 depth-charge launchers.

Torpedo boats
Draug · **Garm** sunk 4/26/1940 (Luftwaffe, Björdal) · **Troll** seized 5/4/1940 Ger.
blt. 1910/4; 468 t; dim: 69.2m x 7.2m x 2.7m; 27 kt; wpns: 6 x 7.6 cm, 3 torp. tbs. 45.7 cm.
Snögg seized 5/4/1940 by Ger. → **Zack (V 5504)** · **Stegg** sunk 4/20/1940 (Kriegsmarine Hardangerfjord) · **Trygg** seized 4/25/1940 by Ger. → **Zick (V 5503)**
blt. 1919/21; 220 t; dim: 53m x 5.5m x 1.6m; 25 kt; wpns: 2 x 7.6 cm, 4 torp. tbs. 45.7 cm.
Sleipner (class) seized 4/1940 by Ger. → **Tiger** 1945 Norw. · **Aeger** sunk 4/9/1940 (Luftwaffe, Stavanger area) · **Balder** seized 4/1940 by Ger. → **Leopard** → 1945 Norw. · **Gyller** seized 4/1940 by Ger. → **Löwe** → 1945 Norw. · **Odin** seized 4/1940 by Ger. → **Panther** → 1945 Norw.
blt. 1937/40; 590 t; dim: 74.1m x 7.7m x 2.1m; 30 kt; wpns: 3 x 10 cm, 3 Flak 4 cm, 2 Flak 1.3 cm, 2 torp. tbs. 53.3 cm.

Submarines
A 2 (A class) seized 4/1940 by Ger.; scrapped · **A 3** scuttled 4/16/1940 (Tönsberg, south Norw.) · **A 4** scuttled 4/16/1940 (Tönsberg, south Norw.)
blt. 1914 Ger.; 250/335 t; dim: 46.5m x 5m x 2.9m; 14/9 kt; range: 900 naut. miles at 10 kt; submerged 75 naut. miles at 3 kt; wpns: 3 torp. tbs. 45.7 cm.
B 1 (B class) scrapped 1944 · **B 2** seized 4/1940 by Ger. (Kristiansund) scrapped · **B 3** scuttled 6/9/1940 (Gavlfjord) · **B 4** seized 4/1940 by Ger. (Horten) scrapped · **B 5** seized 4/1940 by Ger. (Horten) → **UC 1** → scrapped 1942 · **B 6** seized 4/1940 by Ger. (Horten) → **UC 2** → 1945 Norw.
blt. 1923/30; 420/545 t; dim: 51m x 5.3m x 3.5m; 14.5/10.5 kt; wpns: 1 x 7.6 cm, 4 torp. tbs. 45.7 cm.
Ula (GB U/V class, ex GB **Varne** – 3/28/1943 Norw.) blt. 1941/3 GB; 545/735 t; dim: 60m x 4.9m x 3.9m; 11.7/9 kt; range: 4,500 naut. miles at 10 kt; wpns: 1 x 7.6 cm, 4 torp. tbs. 45.7 cm.
Ured (ex GB P 41 → 12/1941 Norw.) sunk 2/24/1943 (mines Bodö) · **Utsira** (ex GB **Variance**) blt. 1944 GB; 545/740 t; dim: 62.3m x 4.9m x 3.9m; 12.7/9 kt; range: 4,700 naut. miles at 10 kt; sub-

merged: 30 naut. miles at 9 kt; wpns: 1 x 7.6 cm, 4 torp. tbs. 53.3 cm.

Escort vessels · Corvettes
Andenes (GB Flower class, ex GB **Acanthus** → 10/1941 Norw.) · **Montbretia** (ex GB → 9/16/1941 Norw.) sunk 11/18/1942 (U 624, North Atlantic) · **Nordkyn** (ex GB **Buttercup** → 4/24/1942 Norw.) · **Potentilla** (ex GB → 1/16/1942 Norw.) · **Rose** (ex GB → 10/23/1941 Norw.) 10/26/1944 lost after collision (North Atlantic) · **Soröy** (ex GB **Eglantine** → 8/29/1941 Norw.)
blt. 1941 GB; 925 t; dim: 62.5m x 10.1m x 4.4m; 16 kt; wpns: 1 x 10.2 cm, 1 Flak 4 cm, 2 Flak 2 cm.
Tönsberg Castle (GB Castle class, ex GB **Shrewsbury Castle** → 7/17/1944 Norw.) blt. 1944 GB; 1,010 t; dim: 76.8m x 11.2m x 3m; 16.5 kt; wpns: 1 x 10.2 cm, 6 Flak 2 cm, depth-charges; sunk 12/12/1944 (mine Arctic).

Fishery protection vessels
Heimdal blt. 1893; 640 t; dim: 55.2m x 8.8m x 4m; 12 kt; wpns: 4 x 7.6 cm · **Michael Sars** blt. 1900; 300 t; dim: 38.4m x 7m x 3.4m; 10 kt; wpns: 2 x 7.6 cm · **Fritjof Nansen** blt. 1932; 1,275 t; dim: 72.9m x 10.5m x 5.1m; 15 kt; wpns: 2 x 10.2 cm, 2 Flak 4.7 cm, 1 aircraft; ran aground 11/8/1940 (Jan Mayen) · **Nordkapp** (class) · **Senja** seized 4/1940 by Ger. → **Löwe (V 6735)**
blt. 1937; 243 t; dim: 39.8m x 6.6m x 2.3m; 13.7 kt; wpns: 1 x 4.7 cm.

Patrol boats
Jelöy (GB Isles class, ex GB **Shiant** → 1944 Norw.) · **Karmöy** (ex GB **Inchmarnock** → 1944 Norw.) · **Oksöy** (ex GB **Kerrera** → 1944 Norw.) · **Tromsöy** (ex GB **Eday** → 8/1944 Norw. → 10/19/1944 GB)
blt. 1941 GB; 545 t; dim: 50m x 8.4m x 3.2m; 12 kt; wpns: 1 x 10.2 cm, 3 Flak 2 cm, depth charges.

MTBs/MGBs
Kong Haakon (US PC class ex US **PC 467**) blt. 1942 USA; 280 t; dim: 53.3m x 7m x 2.3m; 20 kt; wpns: 1 Flak 7.6 cm, 1 Flak 4 cm, 5 Flak 2 cm, 4 depth-charge launchers.

Minelayers
Glommen (class) seized 4/1940 by Ger. → **SMNK 101** · **Laugen** seized 4/1940 by Ger. → **SMNN 05** blt. 1916; 350 t; dim: 42m x 8.5m x 1.9m; 9.5 kt; wpns: 2 x 7.6 cm, 50 mines · **Fröya** blt. 1917; 595 t; dim: 75.8m x 8.2m x 2.5m; 22 kt; wpns: 4 x 10.2 cm, 1 Flak 7.6 cm, 2 Flak 3.7 cm, 2 torp. tbs. 45.7 cm, 160–200 mines; scuttled 4/13/1940 (Trondheim) · **Olaf Tryggvason** blt. 1934; 1,596 t; dim: 97.3m x 11.4m x 3.7m; 23 kt; wpns: 4 x 12 cm, 1 Flak 7.6 cm, 2 Flak 4.7 cm, 250–280 mines; seized 4/1940 by Ger. → **Brummer**.

Minesweepers
Otra (class) seized 4/1940 by Ger. → **Togo (V 6512)** · **Rauma** seized 4/1940 by Ger. → **Kamerun (N 001)**
blt. 1939; 320 t; dim: 50.9m x 7m x 1.8m
Orkla (GB MMS 1001 class, ex GB **MMS 1085** → 1944 Norw.) · **Vefsna** (ex GB **MMS 1086** → 1944 Norw.)
blt. 1944 GB; 225 t; dim: 42.6m x 7.9m x 1.9m; 10 kt; wpns: 2 Flak 2 cm.
Vinstra (US YMS class, ex US **YMS 247** → 5/18/1945 Norw.) · **Gaula** (ex US **YMS 305** → 5/18/1945 Norw.) · **Driva** (ex US **YMS 377** → 5/18/1945 Norw.) · **Alta** (ex US **YMS 379** → 3/22/1945 Norw.) · **Vorma** (ex US **YMS 380** →

3/22/1945 Norw.) • **Begna** (ex US **YMS 381** → 3/22/1945 Norw.) • **Rana** (ex US **YMS 406** → 5/18/1945 Norw.)

blt. 1943 USA: 215 t; dim: 41.5m x 7.5m x 1.8m; 12 kt; wpns: 1 Flak 7.6 cm, 2 Flak 2 cm.

POLAND

C-in-C and officer commanding the coastal fortifications Rear Adm. J. Unrug. Strength 4,500 men (without reserve). The weak Polish Navy had little chance of success in battle against the superior Kriegsmarine. Even prior to 9/1/1939, 3 destroyers had been dispatched to GB. The Polish Navy in exile was formed in GB and placed under the operational control of the Royal Navy.

Operational: Baltic and North seas, Battle of the Atlantic, Norway 1940, Mediterranean, Normandy invasion.

Cruisers

Dragon (GB D class, ex GB **Dragoon** → 1/15/1943 Pol.) blt. 1918 GB; 4,850 t; dim: 143.6m x 14.2m x 4.4m; 29 kt; wpns: 5 x 15.2 cm, 2 Flak 10.2 cm, 8 Flak 4 cm, 8 Flak 2 cm; sunk 7/8/1944 (Ger. one-man torpedo Normandy) • **Conrad** (GB D class, ex GB **Danae** → 10/4/1944 Pol.) blt. 1918 GB; 4,850 t; dim: 143.6m x 14.2m x 4.4m; 29 kt; wpns: 5 x 15.2 cm, 2 Flak 10.2 cm, 10 Flak 4 cm, 12 Flak 2 cm.

Destroyers

Wicher (class) sunk 9/3/1939 (Luftwaffe Hela) • **Burza** blt. 1930/2 Fr.; 1,540 t; dim: 107.2m x 10.5m x 3m; 33 kt; wpns: 4 x 13 cm, 2 Flak 4 cm, 4 Flak 1.3 cm, 6 torp. tbs. 55 cm • **Grom** (class) sunk 5/4/1940 (Luftwaffe Narvik) • **Błyskawica** blt. 1937 GB; 2,144 t; dim: 114m x 11.3m x 3.1m; 39 kt; wpns: 7 x 12 cm, 4 Flak 4 cm, 8 Flak 1.3 cm, 6 torp. tbs. 55 cm, 2 depth-charge launchers, 60 mines • **Garland** (GB class, ex GB – 5/3/1940 Pol.) blt. 1936 GB; 1,350 t; dim: 98.1m x 10.1m x 2.6m; 35.5 kt; wpns: 4 x 12 cm, 1 Flak 7.6 cm, 2 Flak 2 cm, 8 Flak 1.3 cm, 4 torp. tbs. 53.3 cm, 3 depth-charge launchers • **Piorun** GB N class, ex GB **Nerissa** → 11/5/1940 Pol.) blt. 1940 GB; 1,773 t; dim: 108.7m x 10.9m x 2.7m; 36 kt; wpns: 6 x 12 cm, 1 Flak 10.2 cm, 4 Flak 4 cm, 4 Flak 2 cm, 4 Flak 1.3 cm, 4 torp. tbs. 53.3 cm, 3 depth-charge launchers • **Orkan** (GB M class, ex GB **Myrmidon** → 11/1942 Pol.) blt. 1942 GB; 1,920 t; dim: 110.3m x 11.3m x 3m; 36 kt; wpns: 6 x 12 cm, 1 Flak 10.2 cm, 4 Flak 4 cm, 6 Flak 2 cm, 4 torp. tbs. 53.3 cm, 4 depth-charge launchers; sunk 10/8/1943 (U 378 North Atlantic) • **Krakowiak** (GB Hunt II class, ex GB **Silverton** → 5/1941 Pol.) blt. 1941 GB; 1,050 t; dim: 85.3m x 9.6m x 2.4m; 27 kt; wpns: 6 x 10.2 cm; 4 Flak 4 cm, 2 Flak 2 cm, 5 depth-charge launchers • **Kujawiak** (ex GB **Oakley** → 6/1941 Pol.) sunk 6/16/1942 (mine off Malta) • **Slazak** (ex GB **Bedele** → 4/1942 Pol.) • **Krakowaiak** (ex Ger. **A 64** → 9/30/1920 Pol.) blt. 1918 Ger.; 381 t; dim: 61.1m x 6.41m x 2.21m; 28 kt; auxiliary from 1939; sunk 9/4/1939 (Luftwaffe Bay of Danzig). **Kujawiak** (ex Ger. **A 68** – 9/30/1920 Pol.) blt. 1917 Ger.; 392 t; dim: 60m x 6.42m x 2.34m; 26.5 kt; auxiliary from 1939; sunk 9/4/1939 (Luftwaffe Bay of Danzig) • **Slazak** (ex Ger. **A 59** → 9/30/1920 Pol.) blt. 1917 Ger.; 381 t; dim: 61.1m x 6.41m x 2.21m; 28 kt; auxiliary from 1939 • **Podhalanin** (ex Ger. **A 80** → 9/30/1920 Pol.) blt. 1917 Ger.; 381 t; dim: 60.37m x 6.41m x 2.11m; 26.6 kt; auxiliary from 1939 • **Mazur** (ex Ger. **V 105** → 1919 Pol.) blt. 1914 Ger.; 360 t; dim: 62.6m x 6.2m x 2.4m; 20 kt; wpns: 3 x 7.5 cm, 1 Flak 4 cm, 2 Flak 1.3 cm; sunk 9/1/1939 (Luftwaffe Gdynia).

Submarines

Wilk (class) taken out of service 1942 GB • **Rys** interned in Sweden 9/17/1939 → 1945 Pol. • **Zbik** interned in Sweden 9/27/1939 → 1945 Pol. blt. 1931/32 Fr., 980/1,250 t; dim: 78.5m x 5.9m x 4.2m; 14/9 kt; range: 2,500 naut. miles at 10 kt; submerged: 100 naut. miles at 5 kt; wpns: 1 x 10 cm, 2 Flak 1.3 cm, 6 torp. tbs. 55 cm, 38 mines. **Orzel** (class) missing 6/8/1940 – unexplained (North Sea) • **Sep** interned in Sweden 9/16/1939 → 1945 Pol.

blt. 1939 Neth.; 1,100/1,473 t; dim: 84m x 6.7m x 4.2m; 20/9 kt; range: 7,000 naut. miles at 10 kt; submerged: 100 naut. miles at 5 kt; wpns: 1 x 10.5 cm, 2 Flak 4 cm, 12 torp. tbs. 55 cm.

Sokol (GB U class, ex GB **Urchin** → 1/11/1941 Pol.) • **Dzik** (ex GB **P 52** → 10/11/1942 Pol.) blt. 1941 GB; 540/730 t; dim: 58.7m x 4.9m x 3.9m; 11.7/9 kt; range: 4,500 naut. miles at 10 kt; submerged: 30 naut. miles at 9 kt; wpns: 1 x 7.6 cm, 4 torp. tbs. 53.3 cm.

Jastrzab (US S 1 class, ex GB **P 551** → 11/4/1941 Pol.) blt. 1923 USA; 800/1,062 t; dim: 66.8m x 6.3m x 4.6m; 14.5/10.5 kt; range: 5,000 naut. miles at 10.5 kt; submerged: 20 naut. miles at 8 kt; wpns: 1 x 10.2 cm, 4 torp. tbs. 53.3 cm; sunk 5/2/1942 (by Allied warships in error, North Sea).

Gunboats

General Haller (Russ. class ex Fin. → 1921 Pol.) blt. 1919 Fin.; 342 t; dim: 50m x 7.2m x 2.9m; 14 kt; wpns: 2 x 7.5 cm, 2 Flak 1.3 cm, 30 mines; sunk 9/6/1939 (Luftwaffe Hela) • **Komendant Pilsudski**, seized 10/2/1939 by Ger. → **Heisternest (M 3109)** sunk 9/16/1944 (Allied aircraft Nantes).

Minesweepers

Jaskolka (class) sunk 9/14/1939 (Luftwaffe Jastarnia) • **Czajka** seized 10/2/1939 by Ger. (Hela) → **Westerplatte (TFA 11)** • **Mewa** sunk 9/3/1939 (Luftwaffe Hela); raised by Ger. → **Putzig (TFA 7)** • **Rybitwa** sunk 9/14/1939 (Luftwaffe near Jastarnia); raised by Ger. → **Rixhöft (TFA 8)** blt. 1935/6; 165 t; dim: 45m x 5.5m x 1.6m; 16 kt; wpns: 1 x 7.5cm, 20 mines. **Czapla** sunk 9/14/1939 (Luftwaffe near Jastarnia) • **Zuraw** seized 10/2/1939 by Ger. (Hela) → **Oxhöft**

blt. 1939; 185 t; dim: 45m x 5.5m x 1.7m; 16 kt; wpns: 1 x 7.5 cm, 2 Flak 1.3 cm, 20 mines.

RUMANIA

The navy was under the control of the Air and Naval Department and was divided into the High Seas Fleet (Black Sea) and the Danube Flotilla. The main task was coastal defence. Strength amounted to approximately 5,000 men.

Operational: Black Sea, Danube.

Destroyers

Marasti (class) • **Marasesti**

blt. 1920 Ital.; 1,391 t; dim: 94.3m x 9.4m x 3.5m; 34 kt; wpns: 4 x 12 cm, 2 Flak 7.6 cm, 2 Flak 3.7 cm, 4 Flak 2 cm, 4 torp. tbs. 45 cm.

Regele Ferdinand (class) • **Regina Maria**

blt. 1930 GB; 1,700 t; dim: 101.9m x 9.6m x 3.5m; 35 kt; wpns: 4 x 12 cm, 4 Flak 4 cm, 8 Flak 2 cm, 6 torp. tbs. 53.3 cm, mines.

Torpedo boats

Naluca (ex war booty → 1920 Rum.) sunk 8/20/1944 (Sovt. aircraft, Constantsa) • **Smeul** blt. 1915 Aust.; 262 t; dim: 57.4m x 5.7m x 1.5m; 28 kt; wpns: 2 x 6.6 cm, 2 Flak 2 cm, depth charges • **Sborul** (ex war booty → 1920 Rum.) blt. 1916 Aust.; 262 t; dim: 57.4m x 5.7m x 1.5m; 28 kt; wpns: 2 x 6.6 cm, 2 Flak 2 cm, 2 torp. tbs. 45 cm.

Submarines

Delfinul blt. 1936 Ital.; 650/900 t; dim: 68.6m x 5.9m x 3.6m; 14/9 kt; range: 5,200 naut. miles at 8 kt; submerged: 74 naut. miles at 4 kt; wpns: 1 x 10.2 cm, 8 torp. tbs. 53.3 cm • **Marsuinul** blt. 1942; 620 (?) t; dim: 58m x 5.6m x (draught unknown); 16/9 kt; wpns: 1 x 10.5 cm, 1 Flak 1.3 cm, 6 torp. tbs. 53.3 cm • **Requinul** blt. 1942; 585/(?) t; dim: 66m x 5.1m x (draught unknown); 17/9 kt; wpns: 1 Flak 2 cm, 4 torp. tbs. 53.3 cm, 40 mines.

Patrol boats

Capitan Dumitrescu (Fr. class → 1920 Rum.) • **Locotenent-Commandor Stihi Eugen** • **Locotenent Lepri Remus** sunk 1/11/1940 (Danube estuary) • **Sublocotenent Ghiculescu**

blt. 1916/17 Fr.; 310 t; dim: 60.9m x 2.3m x 2.3m; 15 kt; wpns: 2 x 10 cm, 4 Flak 2 cm.

Minelayers

Admiral Murgescu blt. 1941 Rum.; 812 t; dim: 76.9m x 9.1m x 2.5m; 16 kt; wpns: 2 x 10.5 cm, 2 Flak 3.7 cm, 4 Flak 2 cm, 135 mines.

SIAM/THAILAND

The navy was an independent armed force. In 1939 it was still in the course of being built up. In 1940 and 1941 the navy fought against the French Navy; 1941–44 the navy cooperated closely with the Japanese Navy.

Cruisers

Naresuan (class) seized by Ital. 1942 (shipyards) → **Etna** • **Taksin** seized by Ital. 1942 (shipyards) → **Vesuvio**

blt. 1941 Ital.; 4,300 t; dim: 153.8m x 14.5m x 5.2m; 30 kt; wpns: 6 x 15.2 cm, 6 Flak 7.6 cm, 4 Flak 2 cm, 4 Flak 1.3 cm, 6 torp. tbs. 53.3 cm, 1 aircraft.

Gunboats (armored)

Ratanakosinra (class) • **Sukothai**

blt. 1925 GB; 880 t; dim: 52.7m x 11.3m x 3.3m; 12 kt; wpns: 2 x 15.2 cm, 4 Flak 7.6 cm, 2 Flak 4 cm, 2 Flak 2 cm.

Sri Ayuthaia (class) • **Thonburi** sunk 1/17/1941 (Fr. navy Gulf of Siam)

blt. 1938 Jap.; 2,015 t; dim: 77m x 14.4m x 3.9m; 16.5 kt; wpns: 4 x 20.3 cm, 4 Flak 8 cm, 4 Flak 4 cm, 6 Flak 2 cm.

Destroyers

Phra Ruang (GB R class) blt. 1917 GB; 730 t; dim: 83.5m x 8.3m x 3.8m; 35 kt; wpns: 3 x 10.2 cm, 1 Flak 7.6 cm, 2 Flak 2 cm, 4 torp. tbs. 53.3 cm.

Torpedo boats

Trad (Ital. class) • **Chandaburi** • **Cholburi** sunk 4/17/1941 (Fr. navy Gulf of Siam) • **Chumporn** • **Pattani** • **Phuket** • **Rayong** • **Songhkla** sunk 1/17/1941 (Fr. navy Gulf of Siam) • **Surasdra** blt. 1936/37; 318 t; dim: 68m x 6.4m x 2.1m; 31 kt; wpns: 3 x 7.6 cm, 2 Flak 2 cm, 6 torp. tbs. 45.7 cm.

Submarines

Mujchanu (class) • **Plai Chumpol** • **Sinsamut** • **Wirun** blt. 1937/38 Jap.; 370 (?) t; dim: 51m x 4.1m x 3.6m; 14.5/8 kt; range: 3,000 naut. miles at 10 kt; wpns: 5 torp. tbs.

Gunboats

Maeklong (class) • **Tacin** sunk 6/1/1945 (Allied aircraft Gulf of Siam) blt. 1937 Jap.; 1,400 t; dim: 82m x 10.5m x 3.1m; 14 kt; wpns: 4 x 12 cm, 2 Flak 4 cm, 2 Flak 2 cm, 4 torp. tbs. 45.7 cm.

Minelayers

Bang Rachan (class) • **Nhong Narhai**

blt. 1936/37 Ital.; 368 t; dim: 49m x 7.9m x 2.2m; 13 kt; wpns: 2 x 7.6 cm, 2 Flak 2 cm, 150 mines.

SOUTH AFRICA

The South African Navy (SAN) was under the operational control of the Royal Navy. In 1939 the SAN comprised 2 minesweepers and a number of smaller auxiliary vessels. 1939–45 the SAN was considerably expanded with the assistance of GB and the USA.
Operational: South Atlantic, Indian Ocean.

YUGOSLAVIA (KINGDOM)

In 1939/41 Vice-Adm. M. L. Polic was the C-in-C of the Yugoslav Navy. Strength amounted to 6,250 men, with a reserve of some 1,000. During the Ger. invasion of 1941 the Yugoslav Navy saw scarcely any action. The greater part of the vessels was seized by Ital. Only 1 submarine and 2 MTBs succeeded in reaching Egypt.

Destroyers
Dubrovnik (class) blt. 1932 GB; 1,800 t; dim: 113.2m x 10.7m x 3.6m; 37 kt; wpns: 4 x 14 cm, 2 Flak 8.4 cm, 6 Flak 4 cm, 2 Flak 1.5 cm, 6 torp. tbs. 53.3 cm; seized by Ital. 4/17/1941 (Cattaro) → **Premuda** seized by Ger. 9/9/1943 → **TA 32** · **Beograd** (class) seized by Ital. 4/17/1941 (Cattaro) → **Sebenico**, seized by Ger. 9/11/1943 → **TA 43** · **Ljubljana** seized by Ital. 4/17/1941 (Cattaro) → **Lubiana**, run aground 4/1/1943 · **Zagreb** scuttled 4/17/1941 (Cattaro) blt. 1939 Fr.; 1,210 t; dim: 98m x 9.5m x 2.9m; 38 kt; wpns: 4 x 12 cm, 4 Flak 4 cm, 2 Flak 1.5 cm, 6 torp. tbs. 55 cm, seized by Ital. 4/17/1941 (Cattaro) → **Sebenico** → Ger. 9/11/1943 – **TA 43**

Split (class) blt. 1940 – not completed; 2,400 t; dim: 114.7m x 11.1m x 3.2m; 37 kt; wpns: 5 x 14 cm, 10 Flak 4 cm, 8 Flak 1.3 cm, 6 torp. tbs. 53.3 cm; seized by Ital. 4/17/1941 (Split) → **Spalato** → 1945 Yug.

Torpedo boats
T 1 (class ex war booty) seized by Ital. 4/17/1941 (Split) → **T 1** → 12/7/1943 Yug. · **T 3** seized by Ital. 4/17/1941 (Split) → **T 3** · **T 5** seized by Ital. 4/17/1941 (Split) → **T 5** 12/7/1943 Yug. · **T 6** seized by Ital. 4/17/1941 (Split) → **T 6** · **T 7** seized by Ital. 4/17/1941 (Split) → **T 7** · **T 8** seized by Ital. 4/17/1941 (Cattaro) → **T 8** blt. 1914 Aust. → 1920 Yug.; 240 t; dim: 57.5m x-5.7m x 3m; 21 kt; wpns: 1 x 6.6 cm, 1 Flak 6.6 cm, 4 torp. tbs. 45 cm.

Submarines
Hrabri (class) seized by Ital. 4/17/1941 (Cattaro); scrapped · **Nebojsa** blt. 1928 GB; 975/1,164 t; dim: 72m x 7.3m x 4m; 15/10 kt; range: 5,000 naut. miles at 9 kt; wpns: 2 x 10.2 cm, 6 torp. tbs. 53.3 cm · **Smeli** (class) seized by Ital. 4/17/1941 → **Antonio Bajamonti**, scuttled 9/9/1943 (La Spezia) · **Osvetnik** seized by Ital. 4/17/1941 → **Francesco Rismondo** seized by Ger. 9/14/1943 (Bonifacio/Corsica); scuttled 9/18/1943 blt. 1929 Fr.; 630/809 t; dim: 66.5 x 5.5m x 3.8m; 14.5/9.2 kt; range: 5,000 naut. miles at 14.5 kt; submerged: 100 naut. miles at 9 kt; wpns: 1 x 10 cm, 1 Flak 4 cm, 6 torp. tbs. 55 cm.

Escort vessels, etc · Training ships
Dalmacija (ex Ger. lt. cruiser **Niobe**) blt. 1899 Ger.; 2,360 t; dim: 105m x 12.2m x 4.84m; 21 kt; wpns: 6 x 8.4 cm; seized by Ital. 4/17/1941 (Cattaro) → **Cattaro** seized by Ger. 9/11/1943 →

Niobe sunk 12/12/1943 (GB warship **Zara**).

Corvettes
Nada (GB Flower class, ex **Mallow** → 1/11/1944 Yug.) blt. 1940 GB; 925 t; dim: 62.5m x 10.1m x 4.4m; 16 kt; wpns: 1 x 10.2 cm, 1 Flak 4 cm, 6 Flak 2 cm · **Bieli Orao** blt. 1939 Ital.; 567 t; dim: 65m x 8.1m x 2.9m; 18 kt; wpns: 2 Flak 4 cm, 2 Flak 1.3 cm; seized Ital. 4/17/1941 (Cattaro) → **Zagabria** → 12/7/1943 Yug.
Minelayers (ex Ger. M-Boats)
Galeb seized by Ital. 4/17/1941 (Split) → **Selve** sunk 11/6/1942 (RAF Benghazi) · **Jastreb** seized by Ital. 4/17/1941 (Cattaro) → **Zirona** sunk 11/25/1941 (RAF Benghazi) · **Kobac** seized by Ital. 4/17/1941 (Cattaro) → **Unie** sunk 1/30/1943 (RAF Bizerta) · **Labud** seized by Ital. 4/17/1941 (Split) → **Oriolo** scuttled 5/10/1943 (Augusta) · **Orao** seized by Ital. 4/17/1941 (Split) → **Vergada** → 12/7/1943 Yug. · **Sokol** seized by Ital. 4/17/1941 (Split) → **Eso** sunk 1/19/1943 (RAF Djerba) blt. 1918/19 Ger. → 1921 purchase; 330 t; dim: 59.3m x 7.4m x 2m; 15 kt; wpns: 2 Flak 8.4 cm.

YUGOSLAVIA (Liberation Navy)

The new Yug. Navy came into being in autumn 1942 after the first partisan operations on the Adriatic coast. The first partisan naval division was formed on 9/10/1942. After the Ital. capitulation on 10/18/1943, the C-in-C Navy was created on Vis Island. By 1944 more than 100 smaller units were available. Their task was to disrupt supply lines and carry out landing operations, and also to transport wounded, evacuees and their own supplies.
Operational: Adriatic and numerous smaller islands.

Index

Abbreviations

AC	Aircraft-carrier
ACr	Auxiliary cruiser
BC	Battlecruiser
BR	Blockade-runner
BS	Battleship
Co	Corvette
Cr	Cruiser
D	Destroyer
EC	Escort carrier
F	Flakship
GTS	Gunnery training ship
HCr	Heavy cruiser
HS	Hospital ship
LAC	Light aircraft-carrier
LCr	Light cruiser
MV	Merchant vessel
PBS	Pocket battleship
PL	Passenger liner
SS	Supply ship
ST	Supply tanker
Sub	Submarine
T	Tanker
WS	Weather ship

Numbers in italics refer to illustrations.

Achilles (Brit. LCr) 25, 47, 49f.
Adelaide (Brit. Cr) 90
Admiral Graff Spee (Ger. PBS) 16, *26*, 29, 32, 33, 38, 39, 40, 44, 46, 47f., 52, 64, 297
Admiral Hipper (Ger. HCr) 47, 71f., 80, 83, 102, 106, 107, 123, 124, 145, 228, 243, *244*
Admiral Scheer (Ger. PBS) 24, 25, 31, 33, 47, 103, 104, 108, 125, 130, 132, 145, 168, 228, 232, 233, *320*, 329, 330
Ahrens, A. (Ger. Comdr.) see *Bremen*
Ajax (Brit. LCr) 24, 25, 47, 49, 50, 143, 297

Akagi (Jap. AC) 172, 214
Alexander, A.V. (Brit. First Sea Lord) 78, 92
Allwörden v. (Ger. Capt.) see *Rio Grande*
Alster (Ger. MV) 69
Altmark (Ger. SS) 32, 33, 47, 48, 52, 53f., *54*, 55, 63f., 143
Altnbacher (Ger. Lt. Comdr.) 100
Anton Schmitt (Ger. D) 75
Arbutus (Brit. Cr) 128
Archer (Brit. EC) 261
Arendt (Ger. Lt.) see *U 18*
Arendt (Ger. Lt.) see *U 23*
Arethusa (Brit. Cr) 70, 182
Arizona (US-BS) *169*, 177
Arkansas (US-BS) 299
Ark Royal (Brit. AC) 34, 50, 95, 101, 111, 123, 129, 141, *141*, 142, 156, 156, 170, 172, 173
Athabaskan (Can. D) 276
Athenia (Brit. PL) 19, *21*, 31, 137
Atlantis, Ship 16 (Ger. ACr) 77, 78, 174, 175, *175*
Aubrietia (Brit. Co) 137, *137*
Audacity (Brit. EC) 170, 179, 181, 258
Auffermann (Ger. Lt. Comdr.) see *U 514*
Augusta (US-Cr) 163, 240, 299
Auricula (Brit. Co) 210
Aurora (Brit. Cr) 122, 143, 164
Australia (Austral. Cr) 316, 327
Avenger (Brit. EC) 234

Bahia (Brazil Cr) 326, 343
Bärenfels (Ger. MV) 69, 296
Bargsten (Ger. Lt.) see *U 563*
Barham (Brit. BS) 52, 101, 131, 132, 142, 174
Bartels (Ger. Comdr.) 313
Bartolomeo Colleoni (Ital. Cr) 89, *91*, 96
Bastian (Ger. Lt. Comdr.) 311
Baumbach (Ger. Mil. Att) 32, 42, 44, 47, 63
Baumann (Ger. Comdr.) see *U 131*
Bauer (Ger. Lt. Comdr.) see *U 126*
Belchen (Ger. ST) 143

Belfast (Brit. LCr) 44
Belleau Wood (US-AC) 308
Bergamini (Ital. Adm.) 277f.
Bey (Ger. Rear Adm.) 286f.
Bigalk (Ger. Lt. Comdr.) see also *U 751* 160, 181
Birmingham (Brit. Cr) 122, 136
Birnbacher (Ger. Lt. Comdr.) 100
Bismarck (Ger. BS) 97, 117f., *119*, 120, 128, 136, 138f., *141*, 142f., 170, 173, 206
Bismarck Sea (US-AC) 329
Blagrove (Brit. Rear Adm.) 40f.
Blanc, v. (Ger. Comdr.) 327, 331
Bleichrodt (Ger. Lt. Comdr.) see *U 109*
Blücher (Ger. HCr) 73
Bogue (Brit. EC) 261, 262, 301
Böhme (Ger. Capt.) 70
Bolzano (Ital. HCr) 301
Bonte (Ger. Comdr.) 65
Borchardt (Ger. Lt.) see *U 563*
Bougainville (Fr. HCr) 210
Bremen (Ger. PL) 29, 32, 50, 129, *129*
Bremen, v. (Ger. Lt.) see *U 764*
Bremse (Ger. GTS) 74
Bretagne (Fr. BS) *89*, *93*, 94
Brinkmann (Ger. Capt.) see *Prinz Eugen*
Brooklyn (US-Cr) 240
Brünner (Ger. Lt.) see *U 703*
Bulldog (Brit. D) 137, 138
Burgenland (Ger. BR) 294
Burrough (Brit. Rear Adm.) 182
Butow (Ger. Rear Adm.) 327

Caio Duilio (Ital. BS) 105
California (US-BS) 177
California (Ital. HS) 163
Calypso (Brit. Cr) 60, 82
Camelia (Brit. Cr) 128
Campbeltown (Brit. D) 206, *207*
Campioni (Ital. Adm.) 95
Cap Arkona (Ger. PL) 335
Cape Matapan *130*, 134f.
Capetown (Brit. Cr) 124

Carl J. Busch (Ger. WS) 279, *312*, 313
Caribbean 202f.
Ceres (Brit. Cr) 124
Charlotte Schliemann (Ger. T) 127
Chicago (US-Cr) 212
Chikuma (Jap. HCr) 177
Chitose (Jap. AC) 316
Chiyoda (Jap. AC) 300, 316
Churchill, W.S. 23, 30, 36, 43, 46, 52, 56f., 56, 63, 68, 74, 78, 79, 82, 84, 87, 90, 92, 93, 94, 97, 102, 105, 108, 114, 116, 126, 128, 149, 150, 155f., 156f., 157, 159, 161, 162, 163, 171, 178, 179, 180, 185, 190, 193, 204, 205, 216, 218, 228, 229f., 230, 234f., 236, 239, 241, 247, 254, 263f., 265, 267, 268, 271, 274, 280, 281, 282, 289, 291, 293, 303, 306, 307, 308, 311
Ciliax (Ger. Vice-Adm.) 168, 202, 205
Clausen (Ger. Lt. Comdr.) see *U 37*, *U 129*
Coburg (Ger. WS) 276, 298
Coester (Lt.) see *U 542*
Cohausz (Ger. Lt. Comdr.) see *UA*
Collings, E. (Brit. Vice-Adm.) 70
Columbus (Ger. PL) 26, *51*, 52
Conte di Cavour (Ital. BS) 105
Cornwall (Brit. HCr) 129, 137, 208
Coronel, Ship 14 (Ger. BR) 255, 257
Cossack (Brit. D) 63, 141, 142, 156, 170, 173
Courageous (Brit. AC) 21, *22*, 35
Courbet (Fr. BS) 93
Coventry (Brit. F) 134, 143, 144, 236
Cruiser "L" see also Petropavlovsk 44, 52, 63, 77, 78, 144
Cumberland (Brit. HCr) 47, 50, 106, 228
Cunningham (Brit. Vice-Adm.) 70, 95, 104, 106, 121, 128, 131, 132

Dähne, W. (Ger. Capt.) see *Columbus*
Damerow (Ger. Lt.) see *U 106*
Darlan (Fr. Adm.) 96, 199f., *199*, 225, 243f.
Dau (Ger. Capt.) see *Altmark*
Deecke (Ger. Lt. Comdr.) see *U 584*
de Gaulle (Fr. Gen.) see FNFL
Dege, Dr. W. (Ger. meterologist) 313
De Ruyter (Dutch Cr) 204
Detmers (Ger. Lt. Comdr.) see *Kormoran*
Deutschland (Ger. PBS) – later *Lützow* (HCr) 16, 18, 29, 39, *39*, 43, 44, 45, 46
Devonshire (Brit. HCr) 174
Dietl, E. (Ger. Maj. Gen.) *62*, 70, 75
Dönitz, K. (Ger. Capt./Grand Adm.) 13, 16, 18, 30, 40, 42, 65, 81, 85, 98, 99, 103, 106, 108, *108*, 111, 121, 123, 125, 162, 167, 178, 182, 199, 216, 230, 235, 241, 242, 247, 254, 258, 259, 261f., 263, 264, 274, 278, 281, 283, 287, 296, 299, 315, 317, 327, 334, 335, 336
Dorsetshire (Brit. HCr) 142, 176, 208
Dragon (Pol. D) 299, 310, *311*
Dresky, v. (Ger. Lt. Comdr.) see *U 33*
Duke of York (Brit. BS) 179, 228, *272*
Dunedin (Brit. Cr) 144
Dunkerque (Fr. BS) 40, 94, 95

Eagle (Brit. AC) 134, 218, *219*, 232, 238
Echo (Brit. D) 122
Eck (Ger. Lt. Comdr.) see *U 852*
Eckermann (Ger. Comdr.) see *UA*
Edinburgh (Brit. LCr) 42, 122, 127, 136
Electra (Brit. D) 30, 121, 140, 204
Emden (Ger. LCr) 73

Emile Bertin (Fr. Cr) 305, 306
Emmerich (Ger. Lt.) *see U 320*
Express of Britain (Brit. PL) 103
Endrass (Ger. Lt. Comdr.) 103, 155
Engelhardt (Ger. Rear Adm.) 327
England (US-D) 298
Enterprise (US-AC) 106, 211, 213f.
Eppen (Ger. Lt. Comdr.) *see U 519*
Erich Giese (Ger. D) 48
Erich Koellner (Ger. D) 65
Ermland (Ger. BR) 133
Eyssen (Ger. Rear Adm.) *see Komet*
Exeter (Brit. HCr) 25, 27, 47, 49f., 204
Externsteine (Ger. WS) 315

Falkenhorst, N. v. (Ger. Gen.) 64f.
Feige (Ger. Rear Adm.) 145
Fein (Ger. Capt.) *see Gneisenau* 201f.
Fiji (Brit. Cr) 138
Finke (Ger. Lt. Cdr.) *see U 279*
Fiume (Ital. Cr) 132
Fletcher (US Rear Adm.) 211
Folkers (Ger. Lt. Comdr.) *see U 125*
Forbes (Brit. Adm.) 47, 70, 74
Formidable (Brit. AC) 131, 142
Franklin (US-AC) *308*
Franz (Ger. Lt. Comdr.) *see U 27*
Freyberg (Brit. Lt. Gen.) 135, 142
Freyberg, Frhr. v. (Ger. Lt. Comdr.) *see U 610*
Friedeburg, v. (Ger. Lt.) *see U 155*
Friedrich Breme (Ger. SS) 144
Friedrich Eckoldt (Ger. D) 244
Friedrich Ihn (Ger. D) 28
Furious (Brit. AC) 296

Galathea (Brit. Cr) 70
Genda (Jap. Comdr.) 122, *122*, 169f.
General von Steuben (Ger. PL) 329, 333
Gensoul (Fr. Vice-Adm.) 94
Georges Leygues (Fr. LCr) 90, 250, 299, 306
Georgios Averoff (Gr. Cr) 315
Georgius (Gr. Cr) 135
Gerlach (Ger. Comdr., Capt.) *see Stier*
Gerlach (Ger. Lt.) *see U 490*
Giersberg (Ger. Lt.) *see U 419*
Gilardone (Ger. Lt. Comdr.) *see U 254*
Giovanni della Bande Nere (Ital. LCr) 89
Guilio Cesare (Ital. BS) 95
Glasgow (Brit. LCr) 74, 125
Glattes (Ger. Lt. Comdr.) *see U 39*
Gloire (Fr. LCr) 236, 305, 306
Glorious (Brit. AC) 81
Gloucester (Brit. Cr) 138f.
Glowworm (Brit. D) 71, *72*
Gneisenau (Ger. BC) 39, 44f., 60, 64, 70, 73, 80f., 83, 121, 123, 125, 128, 129, 130, 132, 134, 144, 150, 186, *200*, 201f.
Godfroy (Fr. Vice Adm.) 95f.
Goebbels, Dr. J. (Ger. Propaganda Min.) 30, 226
Göring, H. (Ger. Col. Gen./Reichsmarsch.) 16, 121, 123, 318, 334
Gorizia (Ital. HCr) 301
Gossler v. (Ger. Lt. Comdr.) *see U 49, U 538*
Goya (Ger. Motor vessel) 333f.
Grafen (Ger. Lt.) *see U 20*
Grau (Ger. Lt. Comdr.) *see U 601*
Graziani, R. (Ital. Marshal) 100
Grecale (Ital. D) 301
Greer (US-D) 151f., 166f., 170
Greger (Ger. Lt.) *see U 58*
Gretscher (Ger. Lt.) *see U 707*
Greyhound (Brit. D) 138f.
Griffin (Brit. D) 138
Grom (Pol. D) 18, 43
Grossi (Ital. Capt.) 238, *238*
Guadalcanal (US-AC) 298f.
Guggenberger (Ger. Lt. Comdr.) *see U 81*
Gumprich (Ger. Capt.) *see Michel*

Hackländer (Ger. Lt. Comdr.) *see U 454*
Halsey (US Adm.) 238, 273, 315, 343
Hamilton, L.K.H. (Brit. Rear Adm.) 182
Hans Lody (Ger. D) *48*
Hardegen (Ger. Lt. Comdr.) *see U 123*
Harms (Ger. Lt.) *see U 225*
Harpe, v. (Ger. Lt.) 311f.
Hartenstein (Ger. Comdr.) *see U 156*
Hartmann (Ger. Capt.) *see Admiral Hipper*
Hartmann (Ger. Comdr.) *see U 37*
Hartmann, v. (Ger. Lt. Comdr.) *see U 441*
Haruna (Jap. BS) 300
Hass, Dr. Hans 322
Hause (Ger. Lt. Comdr.) *see U 211*
Heidtmann (Ger. Lt. Comdr.) *see U 559*
Heilmann (Ger. Lt. Comdr.) *see U 389*
Henke (Ger. Lt. Comdr.) *see U 515*
Henning (Ger. Lt. Comdr.) *see U 533*
Herrle (Ger. Lt.) *see U 307*
Hermes (Brit. AC) 95, 124, 134, 208f., *208*
Hermione (Brit. Cr) 209f., 215
Hetz (Ger. Comdr.) 330
Heye (Ger. Vice-Adm.) 297
Hill (US Rear Adm.) 284, 285
Hintze (Ger. Capt.) 272
Hiryu (Jap. AC) 172, 214
Hitler, A. 12, 13, 15, 16, 17, 18, 22, 32, 38, 42, 43, 44, 46, 50f., 65, 75, 79, 80f., 83, 88, 93, 96, 100f., 103, 108, 110f., 121, 123, 127, 138, 144, 161, 167, 178, 179, 199, 201, 227, 230, 253, 254, 263, 280, 289, 297, 317, 334
Hiyo (Jap. LAC) 300
Hoffmann (Ger. Capt.) *see Scharnhorst*
Hoffmann (Ger. Lt. Comdr.) *see U 451*
Hood (Brit. BC) *94*, 117f., *118*, 119f., 138, *138*, 140
Hoover, H.C. (US President) 11
Hornet (US-AC) 209, 211, 213, 236, 239
Horton (Brit. Adm.) 241
Hosogaya (Jap. Vice-Adm.) 258
Hüffmeier (Ger. Capt.) 277
Hüffmeier (Ger. Vice-Adm.) 329
Hunger (Ger. Lt. Comdr.) *see U 336*
Hunter (Brit. D) 56, 75, 207
Hurworth (Brit. D) 239
Hyperion (Brit. D) 52

Iachino (Ital. Adm.) 106, 130f.
Illustrious (Brit. AC) 104f., 105, 109, 121, 122, 209f.
Ilmarinen (Finn. Cr) 46, 167
Implacable (Brit. AC) 315
Indiana (US-BS) 300
Indianapolis (US-HCr) 300, 342
Indomitable (Brit. AC) 209f., 211, *219*, 232
Ingram (US Rear Adm.) 222
Italia (Ital. BS) 277

Jan Wellem (Ger. SS) 46, 65, *67*, 70, 74, 75
Java (Dutch Cr) 204
Jean Bart (Fr. BS) 224f., *226*, 240
Jenisch (Ger. Lt.) *see U 32*
Jervis Bay (Brit. HCr) 104
Johannesson (Ger. Capt.) 287
Jordan (Ger. Lt.) *see U 274*
Junack, G. (Gen. Comdr.) 142
Junyo (Jap. LAC) 300

Kaga (Jap. AC) 122, 214
Kähler (Ger. Comdr.) *see Thor*
Kals (Ger. Capt.) *see U 130*
Karlsruhe (Ger. LCr) 74
Karpf (Ger. Lt. Comdr.) *see U 632*
Kearny (US-D) 170, *171*
Kehdingen (Ger. WS) 313
Kenya (Brit. Cr) 143, 182
Keyes, Sir. R. (Brit. Adm.) 171
Kilinin Bay (US-EC) 316
Kimmel (US Adm.) 123, 174, 206
Kimura (Jap. Rear Adm.) 319
King (Brit. Rear Adm.) 139, 143, 178
King (US Adm.) 123, 206
King George V (Brit. BS) 115, 141
Kinzel (Ger. Lt. Comdr.) *see U 338*
Kirk (US Rear Adm.) 299
Kirov (Sovt. HCr) 154
Kitkun Bay (US-EC) 316
Kleikamp (Ger. Capt.) *see Schleswig-Holstein*
Klusmeyer (Ger. Lt.) *see U 2336*
Köhl (Ger. Lt.) *see U 669*
Köhler (Ger. Lt. Comdr.) *see U 377*
Kolbus (Ger. Lt.) *see U 407*
Köln (Ger. LCr) 18, 39, 74, 145
Komet, Ship 45 (Ger. ACr) 63, 100, 164, 175, 238f.
Kondo (Jap. Vice-Adm.) 239
Königsberg (Ger. LCr) 74, 75
Kormoran, Ship 41 (Ger. ACr) 68, 174
Kortenaer (Dutch D) 204
Krancke (Ger. Capt./Vice-Adm.) 103, 125, 132, 253, 299
Kraus (Ger. Comdr.) *see U 199*
Kremser (Ger. Lt. Comdr.) *see U 383*
Kretschmer (Ger. Lt. Comdr.) *see U 99*
Kronenfels (Ger. PL) 333
Krüder (Ger. Capt.) *see Pinguin*
Kummetz (Ger. Adm.) 327
Kusnezov (Sovt. Fleet Comdr.) 144f., *145*, 229, 329

Laconia (Brit. troopship) 235f., *236*
Lancastria (Brit. troopship) 82, 84
Lange (Ger. Lt.) *see U 505*
Langsdorff (Ger. Capt.) *see Admiral Graf Spee*
Lauenburg (Ger. WS) 134, 147
Leander (Brit. LC) 126, 144
Leatham (Brit. Vice-Adm.) 124, 125
Leberecht Maass (Ger. D) 65
Lehmann-Willenbrock (Ger. Lt. Comdr.) *see U 96*
Leipzig (Ger. LCr) 18
Lemp (Ger. Lt. Comdr.) *see U 30, U 110 136*
Lenzmann (Ger. Lt.) *see U 24*
Lexington (US-AC) 158, 211
Lindemann (Ger. Capt.) *see Bismarck*
Littorio (Ital. BS) 105, 215
Loewe (Ger. Lt.) *see U 954*
Lohmeyer (Ger. Lt. Comdr.) *see U 651*
Looks (Ger. Lt. Comdr.) *see U 264*
Lorraine (Fr. BS) 83, 251, 305, 306
Lothringen (Ger. SS) 144
Lüdden (Ger. Lt. Comdr.) *see U 188*
Lueders (Ger. Lt. Comdr.) *see Python*
Lührs (Ger. Lt.) *see U 453*
Lüth, W. (Ger. Capt.) 346
Lütjens, G. (Ger. Vice-Adm./Adm.) 70, 117f., 138f., *141*
Lützow (Ger. HCr, ex *Deutschland*) 44, 46, 73, 75, 145, 243, 275, 278, 322, 330
Lützow (new) *see* Cruiser "L"
Lynx (Fr. D) 94

MacArthur, D. (US Gen.) 178, 198, *198*, 203f., 315, 343
Malaya (Brit. BS) 111f., *113*, 123
Manchester (Brit. Cr) 46, 136
Marat (Sovt. BS) 167f., 169
Marschall (Ger. Adm.) 44, 60, 81
Maryland (US-BS) *169*, 177
Massachusetts (US BS) 240
Matsunaga (Jap. Rear Adm) 178
Matz (Ger. Lt. Comdr.) *see U 70*
Max Schultz (Ger. D) 65
Maxim Gorki (Sov. Cr) 167, 208
Maya (Jap. HCr) 300
McCain (US Vice-Adm.) 316, 343
McMorris (US Rear Adm.) 258
Meendsen-Bohlken (Ger. Capt.) *see Admiral Scheer*
Meisel (Ger. Capt.) *see Admiral Hipper*
Merten (Ger. Comdr.) *see U 68*
Meteorological detachments:
"Bassgeiger" 276, 298
"Edelweiss I and II" 313, 315
"Haudegen" *312*, 313, *313*, 330, 334, 341f., 342, 344
"Holzauge" 263
"Knospe" 233, 238
"Kreuzritter" 280, 310
"Nussbaum" 238, 264
"Schatzgräber" 276, 298
Metzler (Ger. Lt. Comdr.) *see U 69*
Meyer (Ger. Capt.) 277
Michel, Ship 28 (Ger. ACr) 205, 262, 281
Mikawa (Jap. Vice-Adm.) 172
Mikoyan (Sovt. People's Comm.) 42, 61
Mikuma (Jap. Cr) *215*
Mitscher (US Vice-Adm.) 300, 316
Mohr (Ger. Lt. Comdr.) 323, 330
Mohuczy (Pol. Comdr.) 18
Molotov (Sovt. For. Sec.) 32, 36, 46, 61
Molotov (Sovt. HCr.) 198
Montcalm (Fr. LCr) 90, 299, 306
Moore, H.R. (Brit. Vice-Adm.) 296
Mountbatten, Lord L. (Brit. Capt./Adm.) 119, 171
Müller, R. (Ger. Lt.) *see U 282*
Müller-Stöckheim (Ger. Lt. Comdr.) *see U 67*
München (Ger. WS) 134, 136, 137, 143
Muselier (Fr. Vice-Adm.) *86*, 87
Musenberg (Ger. Comdr.) *see U 180*

Nagumo (Jap. Adm.) 162, 172, 206, 208, 214, 239
Naiad (Brit. Cr) 122, 138
Nelson (Brit. BS) 47, 134, 143, 154, 232
Neptune (Brit. Cr) 143
Netzbandt (Ger. Capt.) *see Gneisenau*
Nevada (US-BS) *169*, 177, 299
Newcastle (Brit. Cr) 45
Newfoundland (Brit. LCr) 278
Niels Juel (Dan. Coastal warship) 276
Nieuw Amsterdam (Dutch PL) 231
Nigeria (Brit. LCr) 127, 147, 164, 228
Nimitz (US Adm.) 194, 211, 213, 259, 307f.
Norfolk (Brit. Cr) 139, 142
Normandie (Fr. BS) 116, 201, 206
North Carolina (US-BS) 236
Nürnberg (Ger. LCr) 18, 145

Odenwald (Ger. BR) 172
Oehrn (Ger. Lt. Comdr.) *see U 37*
Oesten (Ger. Lt. Comdr.) *see U 106*
Oklahoma (US-BS) *169*, 177
October Revolution (Sovt. BS) 154, 169, 208
Omaha (US-Cr) 172, 294
Onishi (Jap. Adm.) 122
Opitz (Ger. Lt. Comdr.) *see U 206*
Ordzhonikidze (Sovt. HCr.) 163
Orion, Ship 36 (Ger. ACr) 70, 164, 175
Orzel (Pol. Sub) 18, 21, 27, 32, 34f., *35*, 40, 42, 72
Oscar (*Bismarck's* cat) 142, 170, 173, *173*
Oshima (Jap. Amb. in Ger.) 179
Oster (Ger. Col., Intelligence) 70
Oxley (Brit. Sub) 33
Ozawa (Jap. Vice-Adm.) 206, 300

Paris (Fr. BS) 93
Parishskaya Kommuna (Sovt. BS) 158
Peder Skram (Dan. Coastal warship) 276
Pennsylvania (US-BS) 177
Pétain, P. (Fr. Marshal) 82, 96, 225
Peters (Ger. Capt.) 315
Petersen (Ger. Lt. Comdr.) *see U 9*
Petropavlovsk (Sovt. KCr, ex Ger. Cruiser "L") 145, 167f., 208
Philadelphia (US-Cr) 278
Phoebe (Brit. Cr) 143
Piening (Ger. Lt. Comdr.) *see U 155*
Pillsbury (US-D) 298
Pinguin, Ship 33 (Ger. ACr) 84, 121, 137, 175
Pola (Ital. HCr) 132
Poser (Ger. Lt. Comdr.) *see U 202*
Pownall (US Rear Adm.) 284
Primauguet (Fr. LCr) 240
Preuss (Ger. Lt. Comdr.) *see U 568*
Prien, G. (Ger. Lt. Comdr.) *see U 47*, 42f., 115, *115*, 117, 128, 129
Prince of Wales (Brit. BS) 115, 138, 150, 156f., *156*, 157f., 159, *161*, 178
Princeton (US-LAC) 316
Prinz Eugen (Ger. HCr) 136, 138, 140, 144, 161, 186, 201, 312, 329, 330
Privall (Ger. Chile sailing ship) 120
Provence (Fr. BS) *89*, 94
Python (Ger. SS) 174, 176

Queen Elizabeth (Brit. BS) 174, 179, 180
Queen Elizabeth (Brit. PL) 66, *68*, 231
Queen Mary (Brit. PL) 231
Quincy (US-HCr) 299
Quisling, V. 50, 112

Raeder, E. (Ger. Adm./Grand Adm.) 11, 12, 15, 16, 19, 40, 42, 43, 50, 52, 65, 79, 82, 102, 103, 106f., 116, 142, 178, 199, *199f.*, 234, *238*, *254*
Rahmlow (Ger. Lt.) *see U 570*
Ramillies (Brit. BS) 209f., 212, *295*, 299
Ramsay (Brit. Adm.) 79
Ranger (US-AC) 240
Rauenfels (Ger. MV) 69, 75
Rawalpindi (Brit. ACr) 24, 45
Rawlings (Brit. Adm.) 138
Reese (Ger. Lt.) 281
Reichenbach-Klinke (Ger. Lt. Comdr.) *see U 217*
Rejewski, M. (Pol. mathem.) 121
Renown (Brit. BC) 46, 50, 73, 74, 111f., 123, 129, 142
Repulse (Brit. BC) 22, 70f., 150, 158, 178, *179*
Reschke (Ger. Lt. Comdr.) *see U 205*
Resolution (Brit. BS) 101, 102
Reuben James (US-D) 171f.
Riccardi (Ital. Adm.) 130, 131
Richelieu (Fr. BS) 95, 101f.
Ringelmann (Ger. Lt. Comdr.) *see U 75*
Rio de Janeiro (Ger. troopship) 72f., *73*
Rio Grande (Ger. BR) 177, 294
Robert Ley (Ger. PL) 328
Rodney (Brit. BS) 70f., 74, 128, 142, 232
Rogge (Ger. Capt.) *see Atlantis*
Roma (Ital. BS) 277f.
Roosevelt, Franklin D. (US Pres.) 79, 97, 109, 112, 114, 116, 139, 149, 153, 158, 162, 167, 174, 178, 179, 203, 206, 234, 248, 266, 268, 274, 289, 291, 293, 303, 306, 307
Rosenbaum (Ger. Lt. Comdr.) *see U 73*
Rosenberg-Gruszczynski v. (Ger. Lt.) *see U 384*
Rosenstiel v. (Ger. Lt. Comdr.) *see U 502*
Rossmann (Ger. Maj. Gen.) 328
Royal Oak (Brit. BS) 22, 41f., *41*
Różycki, J (Pol. mathem.) 121
Ruckteschell, v. (Ger. Comdr.) *see Widder, Michel*
Rugard (Ger. ex pleasure boat) 337
Ryuho (Jap. LAC) 300
Ryuhu (Jap. AC) 233

Sachsen (Ger. WS) 263

Saint Lo (US-EC) 316, *317*
Salazar, Dr. A. D'Oliveira 252, 280f.
Sangamon (US-EC) 316
Santee (US-EC) 316
Sachsenwald (Ger. WS) 46, 142
Saratoga (US-AC) 233, 329
Savannah (US-Cr) 278, *279*
Schacht (Ger. Comdr.) *see U 507*
Schäffer (Ger. Lt.) *see U 977*
Scharnhorst (Ger. BS) 44f., 60, 64, 70, *71*, 73, 80f., 113, 121f., 123, 125, 128, 129, 130, 132, 144, 150, 162, 186, *200*, 201, 258, 272, *272*, 277, 278, 286f., *287*
Schauenburg (Ger. Lt. Comdr.) *see U 536*
Schemmel (Ger. Capt.) 244
Schendel (Ger. Lt. Comdr.) *see U 134*
Schepke (Ger. Lt. Comdr.) *see U 100*
Schewe (Ger. Lt. Comdr.) *see U 105*
Schlesien (Ger. BS) 36, 330
Schleswig-Holstein (Ger. BS) 17f., 19, *20*, 27f., *28*, 30f., 32, 36, 343
Schmidt, W.K. (Ger. Lt. Comdr.) *see U 250*
Schnee (Ger. Comdr.) *see U 2511*
Schönberg (Ger. Lt.) *see U 404*
Schroeter (Ger. Lt. Comdr.) *see U 752*
Schroeter, v. (Ger. Lt.) *see U 123*
Schug (Ger. Lt. Comdr.) *see U 86*
Schuhart (Ger. Lt. Comdr.) *see U 29*
Schulenburg, von der (Ger. Amb. in Moscow) 32, 43, 46, 74
Schultze (Ger. Lt. Comdr.) *see U 48*
Schulz (Ger. Lt. Comdr.) *see U 124*
Schwaff (Ger. Lt.) *see U 333, U 440*
Shark (Brit. Sub) 78, *79*
Sheffield (Brit. Cr) 111f., 123, 129, 142, 144
Shibasaki (Jap. Rear Adm.) 284
Shitose (Jap. AC) 300
Shoho (Jap. AC) 210
Shokaku (Jap. AC) 172, 211, 233, 300
Shropshire (Brit. Cr) 124
Sikh (Brit. D) 236f.
Somali (Brit. D) 121, 127, 136, 137
Somerville, Sir. J. (Brit. Vice-Adm.) 93f., 101, 111, 123, 129, 135, 140, 206, *206*
Soryu (Jap. AC) 172, 214
South Dakota (US-BS) 300
Southampton (Brit. Cr) 42, 74, 109, 121
Sovetskaya Ukraina (Sovt. BS) 163
Spahr (Ger. Lt. Comdr.) *see U 78*
Spartan (Brit. Cr) 295
Speer, A. (Ger. Armaments Min.) 262, 297
Speidel (Ger. Lt. Comdr.) *see U 643*
Stalin, J. 14, 47, 52, 65, 117, 149, 162, 193, 218, 267, 308, 311

Stahl (Ger. Lt.) *see U 648*
Stange (Ger. Capt.) *see Lützow*
Stier (Ger. Lt. Comdr.) (Ger. ACr) 212, 237f.
Stonegate (Brit. SS) 39
Strasbourg (Fr. BS) 94, 227, 242
Sträter (Ger. Lt. Comdr.) *see U 614*
Strelow (Ger. Lt. Comdr.) *see U 435*
Stuart (Australian D) 102
Suffolk (Brit. Cr) 139
Sumatra (Dutch Cr) 299
Surcouf (Fr. Sub-Cr) 87, 93, 203, *203*
Suwannee (US-EC) 316
Sydney (Austral. LCr) 91, 96, 174f., *175*
Syfret (Brit. Rear Adm.) 209

Taiho (Jap. AC) 300
Takagi (Jap. Vice-Adm.) 210
Takao (Jap. HCr) 342
Tennessee (US-BS) *169*, 177
Texas (US-BS) 299
Thielbek (Ger. PL) 335
Thienemann (Ger. Capt.) *see Coronel*
Thor, Ship 10 (Ger. ACr) 81, 106, 108, 133, 135, 175
Ticonderoga (US-AC) 328
Tiesenhausen Frhr. v. (Ger. Lt.) *see U 331*
Timm (Ger. Lt. Comdr.) *see U 251*, (Ger. Comdr.) *see U 862*
Tirpitz (Ger. BS) 101, 144, 150, 168, 193, 199, 204f., 206, 217, 229, 258, 268, 277, 278, 295, 296, 308, 315f., *318*, *319*
Tone (Jap. HCr) 177
Topp (Ger. Capt.) *see Tirpitz*
Topp (Ger. Lt. Comdr.) *see U 552*
Tovey (Brit. Adm.) 139, 140, 142, 230, 234
Toyoda (Jap. Adm.) 300
Trento (Ital. Cr) 215
Treuberg, Count v. (Ger. Lt.) *see U 445*
Triton (Brit. Sub) 33
Trojer (Ger. Lt.) *see U 221*
Tübingen (Ger. HS) 317
Turkey 116
Turner (US Rear Adm./ Vice-Adm.) 272, 284, 329
Tuscaloosa (US-HCr) 240, 299

U *A* (Lt. Comdr. Cohausz) 97, 205 (Comdr. Eckermann) 176
U 9 (Lt. Comdr. Petersen) 237f.
U 18 (Lt. Arendt) 237f.
U 20 (Lt. Grafen) 237f.
U 22 (Lt. Comdr. Winter) 32
U 23 (Lt. Arendt) 237f.
U 24 (Lt. Lenzmann) 237f.
U 27 (Lt. Comdr. Franz) 36
U 29 (Lt. Comdr. Schuhart) 35
U 30 (Lt. Comdr. Lemp) 30, 34, 52, 95
U 32 (Lt. Jenisch) 103
U 33 (Lt. Comdr. v. Dresky) 63
U 37 (Comdr. Hartmann) 40 (Lt. Comdr. Oehrn) 78, 81 (Lt. Comdr. Clausen) 124, 128

U 39 (Lt. Comdr. Glattes) 34
U 40 43
U 47 (Lt. Comdr. Prien) 31, 39, 40, 41, 42f., 75, 101, 116, 117, 125, 126, 128, 129, 139
U 48 (Lt. Comdr. Schultze) 31, 103, 146
U 49 (Lt. Comdr. v. Gossler) 75
U 58 (Lt. Greger) 209
U 66 (Comdr. Zapp) 182
U 67 (Lt. Comdr. Müller-Stöckheim) 202
U 68 (Comdr. Merten) 176
U 69 (Lt. Comdr. Metzler) 138
U 70 (Lt. Comdr. Matz) 128
U 73 (Lt. Comdr. Rosenbaum) 232, 238
U 75 (Lt. Comdr. Ringelmann) 142
U 78 (Lt. Comdr. Spahr) 312
U 81 (Lt. Comdr. Guggenberger) 172
U 86 (Lt. Comdr. Schug) 286
U 96 (Lt. Comdr. Lehmann-Willenbrock) 125
U 99 (Lt. Comdr. Kretschmer) 77, 92, 103, 115, 116, 128, 129
U 100 (Lt. Comdr. Schepke) 90, 93, 103, 110, 115, 116, 128, 129
U 105 (Lt. Comdr. Schewe) 127
U 106 (Lt. Comdr. Oesten) 127 (Lt. Damerow) 275
U 109 (Lt. Comdr. Bleichrodt) 182
U 110 (Lt. Comdr. Lemp) 128, 137, *137*, 138
U 123 (Lt. Comdr. Hardegen) 183, 193 (Lt. v. Schroeter) 311
U 124 (Lt. Comdr. Schulz) 127
U 125 (Lt. Comdr. Folkers) 184
U 126 (Lt. Comdr. Bauer) 174
U 129 (Lt. Comdr. Clausen) 177 (Lt. v. Harpe) 311
U 130 (Comdr. Kals) 183
U 131 (Comdr. Baumann) 179
U 134 (Lt. Comdr. Schendel) 198
U 155 (Lt. Comdr. Piening) 204 (Lt. v. Friedeburg) 313
U 156 (Comdr. Hartenstein) 202, 235
U 180 (Comdr. Musenberg) 257, 259
U 188 (Lt. Comdr. Lüdden) 312
U 199 (Comdr. Kraus) 274
U 202 (Lt. Comdr. Poser) 216
U 205 (Lt. Comdr. Reschke) 215
U 206 (Lt. Comdr. Opitz) 175
U 211 (Lt. Comdr. Hause) 283
U 217 (Lt. Comdr. Reichenbach-Klinke) 262
U 221 (Lt. Trojer) 242
U 234 (Lt. Comdr. Fehler) 333, 335
U 250 (Lt. Comdr. Schmidt) 310
U 251 (Lt. Comdr. Timm) 232
U 254 (Lt. Comdr. Gilardone) 242
U 255 (Lt. Harms) 275
U 264 (Lt. Comdr. Looks) 295
U 274 (Lt. Jordan) 281
U 279 (Lt. Comdr. Finke) 279
U 282 (Lt. Müller, R.) 281
U 307 (Lt. Herrle) 313
U 320 (Lt. Emmerich) 337
U 331 (Lt. Frhr. v. Tiesenhausen) 174

U 333 (Lt. Schwaff) 257
U 336 (Lt. Comdr. Hunger) 279
U 338 (Lt. Comdr. Kinzel) 258
U 377 (Lt. Comdr. Köhler) 238
U 383 (Lt. Comdr. Kremser) 275
U 384 (Lt. v. Rosenberg-Gruszczynski) 258
U 389 (Lt. Comdr. Heilmann) 279
U 404 (Lt. Comdr. Schönberg) 274
U 407 (Lt. Kolbus) 314
U 419 (Lt. Giersberg) 280
U 420 (Lt. Reese) 281
U 435 (Lt. Comdr. Strelow) 233
U 440 (Lt. Comdr. Schwaff) 262
U 441 (Lt. Comdr. v. Hartmann) 260
U 445 (Lt. v. Treuberg) 312
U 451 (Lt. Comdr. Hoffmann) 179
U 453 (Lt. Lührs) 298
U 454 (Lt. Comdr. Hackländer) 199, 275
U 490 (Lt. Gerlach) 299
U 502 (Lt. Comdr. v. Rosenstiel) 202
U 505 (Lt. Comdr. Lange) 298f., *298*
U 506 (Lt. Comdr. Würdeman) 235
U 507 (Comdr. Schacht) 235
U 514 (Lt. Comdr. Auffermann) 273
U 515 (Lt. Comdr. Henke) 259
U 519 (Lt. Comdr. Eppen) 257
U 530 (Lt. Wermuth) 325f., *326*, 336, 341
U 533 (Lt. Comdr. Henning) 281
U 536 (Lt. Comdr. Schauenburg) 283
U 538 (Lt. Comdr. Gossler) 283
U 542 (Lt. Loester) 286
U 552 (Lt. Comdr. Topp) 171
U 556 (Lt. Comdr. Wolfarth) 103, 147
U 559 (Lt. Comdr. Heidtmann) 239
U 563 (Lt. Bargsten) 170, (Lt. Borchardt) 262
U 568 (Lt. Comdr. Preuss) 170
U 570 (Lt. Comdr. Rahmlow) 159f., 165, *166*
U 584 (Lt. Comdr. Deecke) 216
U 600 (Lt. Comdr. Zurmühlen) 286
U 601 (Lt. Comdr. Grau) 232, 275
U 610 (Lt. Comdr. Frhr. v. Freyberg) 280
U 614 (Lt. Comdr. Stäter) 274
U 632 (Lt. Comdr. Karpf) 255f.
U 643 (Lt. Comdr. Speidel) 280
U 648 (Lt. Stahl) 286
U 651 (Lt. Comdr. Lohmeyer) 147
U 652 (Lt. Fraatz) 167
U 669 (Lt. Köhl) 276
U 703 (Lt. Brünner) 313
U 706 (Lt. v. Zitzewitz) 275, 313
U 707 (Lt. Gretschel) 282
U 751 (Comdr. Bigalk) 181
U 752 (Lt. Comdr. Schroeter) 260
U 764 (Lt. v. Bremen) 286
U 794 (Walter experimental U-Boat) 282
U 852 (Lt. Comdr. Eck) 295
U 862 (Comdr. Timm) 319
U 864 (Comdr. Wolfram) 329

U 954 (Lt. Loewe) 260
U 977 (Lt. Schäffer) 334, 336, 340f., 341f., *342*, 343
U 2336 (Lt. Klusmeyer) 337
U 2511 (Comdr. Schnee) 334, *335*, 336
Ubena (Ger. PL) 328, 330
Uganda (Brit. LCr) 278
Ulpio Traiano (Ital. Cr) 253
Unrug, J. (Pol. Rear Adm.) 18, 22

Väinämöinen (Finn. Cr) 46
Valiant (Brit. BS) 70, 106, 131, 174, 179, 180
Valorous (Brit. D) 42, 207
Valmy (Fr. D) 143, *143*, 144, 161
Vedel (Dan. Vice-Adm.) 276
Vian (Brit. Rear Adm.) 63, 134, 164, 174, 299
Victorious (Brit. ACr) 163, 228, 232, 296
Ville d'Alger (Fr. HCr) 76
Vittorio Veneto (Ital. BS) 130, 131, 132, 277
Voularis (Gr. Vice-Adm.) 296

Warspite (Brit. BS) 57f., 75, 95, 106, 131, 132, 138, 142, 278, *279*, 299, 316
Warburton-Lee (Brit. Capt.) 75
Washington (US-BS) 228
Wasp (US-AC) 233, 236, *237*
Wenninger (Ger. Capt.) 330
Wermuth (Ger. Lt.) *see U 530*
West Virginia (US-BS) *169*, 177
Weyer (Ger. Comdr.) *see Orion*
White Plains (US-EC) 316
Wicher (Pol. D) 18, 19, 29f.
Wichita (US-Cr) 240
Widder, Ship 21 (Ger. ACr) 78, 103, 175
Wilhelm Gustloff (Ger. PL) 328f., 328, 333
Wilhelm Heidkamp (Ger. D) 75
Wilk (Pol. Sub) 18, 28, 34, 36
Winter (Lt. Comdr.) *see U 22*
Winterbotham (Brit. Wing Comdr.) 130
Wolfarth (Ger. Lt. Comdr.) *see U 556*, 103
Wolfram (Ger. Comdr.) 329
Würdemann (Ger. Lt. Comdr.) *see U 506*

Yahagi (Jap. LCr) 331
Yamamoto (Jap. Adm.) 106, 122, 174, 178, 212, 213, 250, 258f., *259*
Yamato (Jap. BS) 331, *331*, 332, *332*
York (Brit. HCr) 119, 130
Yorktown (US-AC) 211, 213

Zara (Ital. Cr) 132
Zapp (Ger. Comdr.) *see U 66*
Zitzewitz, v. (Ger. Lt. Comdr.) *see U 706*
Zuiho (Jap. AC) 300, 316
Zuikaku (Jap. AC) 172, 211, 233, 300, 316
Zurmühlen (Ger. Lt. Comdr.) *see U 600*
Zygalski, H. (Pol. mathem.) 121

Front endpaper:
German minesweepers set out on North Sea operations

Page 2:
8/4/1940, Operation "Weser exercise" — German invasion of Norway: German Task Force on its way to operational objective

Page 4/5:
US aircraft-carrier in the Pacific after an attack by a Japanese kamikaze pilot

Rear endpaper:
Winter 1939/40, the Schillig roads off Wilhelmshaven: On the deck of the battlecruiser *Gneisenau*; in the background the battlecruiser *Scharnhorst*